THE TITANS

Books by André Maurois

ARIEL

BYRON

CAPTAINS AND KINGS

DISRAELI

MAPE

LYAUTEY

THE SILENCE OF COLONEL BRAMBLE

GENERAL BRAMBLE

DICKENS

PROPHETS AND POETS

THE THOUGHT READING MACHINE

RICOCHETS

THE MIRACLE OF ENGLAND

CHATEAUBRIAND

THE ART OF LIVING

TRAGEDY IN FRANCE

I REMEMBER, I REMEMBER

THE MIRACLE OF AMERICA

WOMAN WITHOUT LOVE

FROM MY JOURNAL

THE MIRACLE OF FRANCE

PROUST: *Portrait of a Genius*

LÉLIA: *The Life of George Sand*

OLYMPIO: *The Life of Victor Hugo*

THE ART OF BEING HAPPILY MARRIED

THE TITANS: *A Three-Generation Biography of the Dumas*

ANDRÉ MAUROIS

THE TITANS

A THREE-GENERATION BIOGRAPHY
OF THE DUMAS

Translated from the French by
GERARD HOPKINS

ILLUSTRATED

HARPER & BROTHERS PUBLISHERS
NEW YORK

This book is published in England
under the title of THREE MUSKETEERS

Library of Congress catalog card number: 57-8173

Contents

CONTENTS

CONTENTS

Illustrations

The following will be found in a separate section after page 128:

Thomas-Alexandre, General Dumas (1762-1806)

Waldor (Mélanie Villenave, wife of François-Joseph) (1796-1871) [Bibliothèque Nationale]

Ida Ferrier (Marguerite Ferrand) (1811-59)
Wife of Alexandre Dumas *père*

Marie Duplessis (Alphonsine Plessis) (1824-47)
[From a portrait by Viénot]

The Château de Monte-Cristo, built by Alexandre Dumas *père*
[Photograph: *Match*]

Alexandre Dumas *père* (1803-70)

Alexandre Dumas *fils* (1824-95) at the time of his marriage to Princess Naryschkine in 1864

Nadejda Knorring (1826-95), widow of Prince Alexander Naryschkine

Two photographs by Liebert of Dumas *père* and Adah Menken, the circus horsewoman (1835?-68), taken in Paris in 1867

Henriette Regnier de la Brière (1851-1934), divorced wife of Félix Escalier, second wife of Alexandre Dumas *fils*
[Collection of Madame Alexandre Sienkiewicz]

Aimée Desclée (1836-75), the famous actress

Alexandre Dumas *fils* in his old age. A photograph taken in the apartment at Nº 11 rue Ampère after his separation from his first wife. The room shown in this picture was his last study
[Collection of Madame Alexandre Sienkiewicz]

Preface

FEW names are better known throughout the world than that of Dumas *père*. In every country people have read his books, and read them still. There is no need for me to justify my choice of subject. After making a study of the lives of George Sand and Victor Hugo, I ought, it seemed to me, since the chances of research had put me on the track of new documents, to add to my romantic comedy a portrait of Alexander Dumas. The critics of the generation of Doumic and Brunetière, though recognizing the man as something of a 'force of nature', had denied the importance of the writer. The excellent book by Monsieur Henri Clouard has restored to him his proper place in the history of French literature.

'He has been blamed for being entertaining, prolific and prodigal. Would his value have been greater had he been boring, sterile and miserly?' The dividing line, drawn in our own day, between writing which is difficult — the only kind to which any value is nowadays attached — and that which is commonly described as 'vulgar', did not exist in the great periods. 'Molière was a natural product of the barnstorming tradition', says Roger Caillos, 'and made an easy transition from popular farce to the Court. Balzac normally published his novels serially in the daily papers, as did Dickens and Dostoievsky. Hugo, throughout his working life, knew how to conquer and to keep a popular audience.' Homer was the poet of everyman.

It is right to rank Balzac, Dickens and Tolstoy higher than Dumas, and I, for my part, prefer them. But that does not keep me from feeling admiration and affection for a writer who was the delight of my boyhood, or from still loving his strength, his zest and his generosity of mind. Hugo set him on the level with the greatest writers of his day. 'You leave us in the wake of Dumas, Lamartine and Musset', he wrote in his *Tombeau de Théophile Gautier*. The author of *Les Misérables* saw no reason why a writer should be ashamed of having more than five hundred readers: nor should it be forgotten that Dumas managed to pack as much action into his own life as into his novels. He is the darling of the biographers.

Some people may think it strange that I should devote so much space in this book to Dumas *fils*. 'Which Dumas?' said Henri Clouard.

'Why, the only one', meaning Dumas *père*. I hope that I may succeed in persuading so fair-minded a critic to amend that view. Little is known of the life of Dumas *fils*. I have here utilized a great deal of hitherto unpublished material. His letters, greatly superior to those of Dumas *père*, will help the reader to know him better, who will be able, I trust, to realize that the work of the younger Dumas in the theatre, though it astonished and, sometimes, shocked contemporary audiences, responded to what in him was a deeply felt need.

In point of fact, and in spite of appearances, father and son were very close to one another. They both of them had the 'family sinews' which they inherited from General Dumas. Both had had, early in life, to fight against painful injustices. Dumas *père* suffered from racial prejudice; Dumas *fils* from the stigma of illegitimacy. Both had to prove to their own satisfaction that they were worth as much as, and more than, other men. Their favourite heroes were 'Righters of Wrongs'; musketeers, with Dumas *père*; moralists, with Dumas *fils*.

In the case of the father, the 'purging of passions' was achieved by a refusal to bear the burden of reality. He was looked upon as a braggart, whereas the truth would seem to be that, like Balzac, he was incapable of seeing the boundary which separates the real from the imaginary. For the son, the paternal example was a constant lesson. The prodigal father engendered a prudent son; the libertine, a strict mentor. Dumas *fils*, after a wild youth, forced himself to take his life in hand, and so to shape it that it would coincide with his moral principles. That he failed to do so is his own particular drama. Dumas *fils*, in real life, was for ever acting in a play by Dumas *fils*. I have done my best to paint a true picture of that tormented face.

My debts of gratitude are numerous. Many people, personally unknown to me, hearing that I was engaged on a book about the Dumas, were kind enough to entrust to me precious and unpublished letters. Alexandre Lippmann, grandson and great-grandson of the two Alexanders, let me see his father's diary. Madame Balachowsky-Petit, who has given to the Bibliothèque Nationale the papers of Dumas *fils*, was introduced to me by my old friend and colleague, Émile Henriot, with the result that she most generously gave me free access to her private collection. A similar kindness was shown me by Madame Alexandre Sienkiewicz, Madame Théodore Rousseau, Madame H. Dumesnil, Francis Ambrière, Monsieur Alphandéry, Monsieur Alfred Dupont, Madame Georges Privat, Monsieur Daniel Thirault, Monsieur Raoul

Simonson, Monsieur José Camby, and ten others. Lucienne Julien-Cain was so kind as to translate for me certain texts published in Russia. At the Bibliothèque Nationale and the Bibliothèque de l'Arsenal, I was hospitably received and greatly helped, as also was I by the Curator of the Spœlberch de Lovenjoul Collection. The Archives of Soissons, Laon and Villers-Cotterets have thrown much light on the military career of General Dumas. Finally, my wife, as always, has been my second self.

Translator's Note

I have retained, throughout, the name Alexandre instead of transposing it into Alexander (except once, in the Preface). Also, in order to avoid clumsiness, I have used 'Dumas' for the plural, as in the French.

Such translations of verse as I have provided in the notes claim no more than 'crib' value, and, even so, are confined to the more important quotations.

G. H.

PART ONE

*

VILLERS - COTTERETS

Take my advice; marry a West Indian negress. They make excellent wives.
BERNARD SHAW

MY purpose is to study, through three generations, the successive manifestations of a temperament so fantastic as to have become legendary, originating in the union of a Frenchman of gentle birth and a black slave-girl of San-Domingo. The men whose lives I am about to narrate had, in different degrees and diverse forms, the same qualities of physical strength, courage, chivalrous devotion and a lively horror of ill-natured persons — and one fault, the longing to astonish, bred of a desire for vengeance. But temperament alone is not enough to account for a man's destiny: it is never more than the basic material on which is woven a pattern made by events and a determined will.

Here, then, is my monument to the three Dumas.

CHAPTER I

*In which a Soldier of the Queen's Regiment of Dragoons
becomes, in the space of three years, a General
of the Republic*

IN the year 1789, after the taking of the Bastille, the small town of
Villers-Cotterets, standing to the north of Paris, on the Laon-
Soissons road, was alarmed by rumours of peasant risings and wide-
spread looting. It had a very fine Renaissance château, formerly royal,
which had been given by Louis XIII to his brother, along with the
Duchy of Valois, and had remained an apanage of the Orléans family,
in other words, of the younger Bourbon branch. It was there that
Louis XIV had paid court to his charming sister-in-law, Henrietta of
England, whom her husband, Philippe d'Orléans, 'Monsieur', consistently neglected as the result of a passionate devotion to his favourite,
the Chevalier de Lorraine. At a later date, the King took Louise de la
Vallière to the château, where he presented her to 'Madame Henriette',
thus placing her in the awkward position of having to play hostess to
her former lady-in-waiting.

On September 1st, 1715, Philippe d'Orléans, son of the Philippe
just mentioned, became Regent of France. For eight years, Villers-
Cotterets was the country resort of all the rakes and libertines who
formed his court. 'The château', says Saint-Simon, 'was the scene of
indescribable orgies, of suppers at which the guests, men and women
alike, appeared stark naked.' A letter written by Madame de Tencin
tells us that these gatherings went by the name of 'The Adam and Eve
nights'. The duc de Richelieu provides us with the following additional
information:

Madame de Tencin, who presided on these occasions, gave
instructions that, after the champagne had been served, the lights
should be extinguished, and the unclothed company proceed to
indulge in the exercise of mutual flagellation, seeking their
partners as the fortune of the dark dictated, and with a thorough-
ness which mightily diverted His Highness ... The officials of

the château were included in pleasures of every description, and even the inhabitants of the town of Villers-Cotterets, whose sense of decency became thereby much relaxed. It was no rare thing for the Regent to invite to his suppers and his pastimes the notables of the said town, who could not refuse to be present, as, too, on more than one occasion, were various members of the domestic staff, and even those employed in the gardens.[1]

It is necessary to recall these scandals, because, even fifty years later, the effect of them on men's minds was still noticeable, and, to some extent, explains the cynical, and, at the same time, somewhat artless tolerance of moral laxity shown by Dumas *père* all through his life. During the intervening years, however, the presence of a court in its midst had brought prosperity to the little town. The magistrates, registrars and other high officials of the House of Orléans, built themselves many charming houses. The lovely forest in which Louis XIV had hunted, and dined in the open air, attracted saunterers, and so great was the number of visitors that thirty inns and hostelries were able to do a thriving trade. One of these — 'À l'Enseigne de l'Écu' — belonged to a certain Claude Labouret, a former butler in the service of His Royal Highness the Duke of Orléans.

Labouret was, consequently, something of a personage, and, when the Revolution broke out, he became the local Commandant of the National Guard. The rich and peaceful town had good reason to fear the 'pillagers' who were said to be operating in the neighbouring countryside. The officers of the civil militia asked the Government of Louis XVI to provide an armed force for their protection. The Regiment of the Queen's Dragoons, stationed at Soissons, detailed for the purpose twenty horsemen who arrived at Villers-Cotterets on August 15th, 1789. People flocked in from all around to admire the splendid-looking cavalrymen drawn up in front of the château. One of them, in particular, drew all eyes, a superb mulatto, whose deeply bronzed complexion, powerful frame and delicate wrists, gave him a vaguely aristocratic appearance. When the townspeople were called upon to billet the newly arrived troops, Marie-Louise-Elisabeth Labouret asked her father, who as Commandant of the National Guard had first pick, to choose the handsome mulatto.

Marie-Louise Labouret to her friend Julie Fortin: The long-awaited dragoons arrived two days ago . . . Everywhere they have received a warm welcome. My father applied for a coloured man who is one of the detachment. He is very nice, and is called Dumas. He is the son of a large landowner at San-Domingo. He is as tall as cousin Prévost, but by much his superior in manners. I would have you know, dear Julie, that he is a fine figure of a man.[2]

His hosts soon came to adore Dumas, who was as good-hearted as he was strong. Labouret was informed by the dragoon's superior officers that the soldier living under his roof was the son of a marquis, and that his real name was Dumas Davy de la Pailleterie. This was true. His father, a one-time colonel, and Commissaire-Général of artillery, came of a noble Norman family, and held the courtesy-title of marquis. In 1760 he had decided to leave France for the West Indies, with the idea of trying his fortunes in San-Domingo. He bought a plantation at the eastern extremity of the island, close to Cap Rose. There, on March 27th, 1762, a son, to whom he gave the names of Thomas-Alexandre, was born to him by a black slave-girl, Cessette Dumas. Whether the mother was subsequently promoted to the position of wife, we do not know for certain. Her grandson maintained that she was. The manners of the time, however, make such a marriage improbable. There are no documents in existence to prove that it ever took place, though there are none to prove that it did not. The young woman looked after the marquis's house, while he acknowledged the child and became deeply attached to the lively and intelligent mulatto boy.

In 1772 the black mother died and the youngster was brought up, at first in San-Domingo, by his father. Somewhat later, in 1780, the marquis de la Pailleterie, seized by a longing for the life of a capital city and of a court, returned to Paris. It was the custom at that time for planters of noble blood to take their half-caste sons back with them to France, leaving their daughters behind them. The young man was now eighteen years old. His colouring gave him an exotic appearance, but his features were well formed, and his eyes magnificent. He had beautifully moulded limbs, and his hands and feet were as delicately shaped as those of a woman. He was treated as the son of the family and, while still scarcely more than a boy, had many successes as a lover. His physical strength was astonishing. One evening at the opera, a musketeer entered the box where he was sitting, and insulted him. The young Dumas de la Pailleterie lifted the man off his feet and pitched him over the front of the box on to the spectators beneath. A duel followed, in the course of which he ran his adversary through the body, being an expert swordsman and trained in all bodily exercises.

The young visitor from the West Indies, however, found little to amuse him in Paris, where the marquis left him short of money. At the age of sixty-eight, the father, who kept a careful hold on his purse, married his housekeeper, Françoise Retou, and his son, acting on an impulse bred of boredom, decided to enlist in the king's army.

'As what?' asked his father.

'As a simple private.'

'Splendid!' exclaimed the old man. 'But I am marquis de la Pailleterie; I have held the rank of colonel, and I do not intend that you should drag my name through the lowest ranks of the army. If you enlist, you must do so under an assumed name.'

'As you will. I shall enlist under the name of Dumas.'

It was as Dumas, therefore, that he became a trooper in the Queen's regiment of Dragoons.

It was not long before his herculean achievements made him famous in the regiment. He was the only dragoon who, by taking hold of one of the beams of the stable roof, could hoist himself and his horse off the ground, and none of his comrades-in-arms could equal his feat of thrusting four fingers into the barrels of four muskets, and then raising all four weapons at the full extent of his arm. This athlete was fond of reading Caesar and Plutarch: but he had joined the colours with the name of a commoner, and nothing short of a revolution could turn him into an officer.

In August 1789 when the Labourets were welcoming him to the 'Écu', the required revolution had just broken out, though no one at that time could foresee that it would go so far as to sweep aside the rules of promotion then obtaining. Marie-Louise Labouret, a serious-minded young woman with many solid virtues, was much attracted by the magnificent and generous-hearted young man who enjoyed the triple prestige of physical strength, a soldier's uniform, and a birth wrapped in mystery. When the two young people confessed their mutual love to the former butler and expressed their intention of getting married, Claude Labouret made only one stipulation — and that a very modest one. The marriage should take place as soon as Dumas had reached the rank of corporal.

At the end of the year, he left for the wars. There was fighting on all the frontiers. He was given his corporal's stripe on February 16th, 1792, in the course of a campaign in the Tyrol. Like most of the mulattoes of noble blood — and they were fairly numerous in France — Dumas had enthusiastically espoused the cause of the Revolution. In it lay the only hope he could have of equality. Regiments of volunteers were being recruited up and down the country. The famous Chevalier de Saint-Georges, a man prominent in the world of fashion at the end of the eighteenth century, like Dumas, of mixed blood, a musketeer, a composer, and acknowledged by the Prince of Wales to be the 'most attractive gentleman of colour now living', had, too, been conquered by the new ideas. He had raised a *Légion Franche des Américains* with himself as its commander. He offered Dumas the rank of second lieutenant. Another colonel, Boyer, who had been told of the young dragoon's gallantry, promised to make him a lieutenant. Saint-Georges outbid this offer with one of a captaincy. Dumas at once added to his exploits by capturing, single-handed, three enemy cavalrymen. To cut a long story short, he was gazetted lieutenant-colonel on October 10th, 1792.

The Minister of War to Citizen Dumas: This, sir, is to inform you that you have been appointed to fill a vacancy as Lieutenant-Colonel of Cavalry in the Légion Franche des Américains... You are to report for duty in one month at the latest from the date of this letter, otherwise you will be deemed to have refused this employment, and another officer will be appointed in your stead.

Signed
LEBRUN
Acting Minister of War[3]

And so it was that at the age of thirty, the dragoon who had set off for the wars with the intention of being promoted corporal, had become a lieutenant-colonel. He had done more than he had undertaken to win his lovely young bride. The marriage was celebrated on November 28th, 1792, before the Mayor of Villers-Cotterets. It was the marriage, at short notice, of an officer, and a man marked out for success. *Witnesses*: Lieutenant-Colonel Espagne and Lieutenant de Bèze, both of the 7th Hussars, stationed at Cambrai; Jean-Michel Deviolaine, Inspecteur des Eaux et Forêts, all-powerful in the domains of the duc d'Orléans, and Françoise Retou, widow of Davy de la Pailleterie, stepmother of the groom. *Honeymoon*: seventeen days at the 'Écu', after which the husband set off to join his regiment in Flanders, leaving his young wife with child.

The Campaign of Holland. On July 30th, 1793, Dumas was promoted general and, on September 3rd of the same year, the 'man of colour' became General of Division. Seven days later, Marie-Louise Dumas was brought to bed of a daughter, Aimée-Alexandrine. Those were epic days, when the army made generals more quickly than women produced children.

But the Revolution treated a general like a 'shuttlecock on a battledore'. Appointed Commander-in-Chief of the Army of the Pyrenees, the fond husband could snatch no more than four days at Villers-Cotterets.

Claude Labouret to his friend Danré de Faverolles, September 20th, 1793: The General arrived here on the 15th, and left again yesterday, the 19th, by stage-coach. In a few days' time he will be in the Pyrenees. The little girl is well, as, too, is Marie-Louise. She behaved with great courage in the presence of her husband, and shed tears only after he had gone. Today she is once more mistress of herself. She finds consolation in the thought that all these sacrifices must be for the good of the Nation. Please bring me, on Thursday, six brace of chickens . . . I have to offer entertainment to certain officers of the district who are coming to carry out an examination of the *ci-devant* château.[4]

For the château and the forest, so dear to the dukes of Orléans, had become, like the aristocrats, *ci-devant*.

It would be possible to follow, in a variety of military documents, all the bounds and rebounds of the shuttlecock: but to do so would be both wearisome and pointless. The Commissioners of the Republic with the armies had little liking for generals. They might end their letters with the words '*Salut et fraternité*', but there was little enough of fraternity in their greetings, and less than usual when the general was, like this one, indulgent to the civil population. They nicknamed Dumas, who burned the wooden frames of the guillotines in order to keep warm, '*Monsieur de l'Humanité*'. Those of Bayonne received in a mood of bitterness the newcomer sent to them by the *Commission de l'Organisation et du Mouvement des Armées*, and demanded that he should be replaced. The Commission, which enjoyed little authority, agreed to this request, and set Dumas dancing off from his command of the Army of the Pyrenees to La Vendée and, later, to the Alps, where he gained distinction, as always, by his epic deeds. At the head of a handful of men, he stormed the Mont-Cenis where the Austrians had taken up an entrenched position, by scaling a sheer rock with the aid of climbing irons. On reaching the top, his men found themselves confronted by a palisade which they had considerable difficulty in surmounting. 'Leave it to me!' cried General Dumas and, taking hold of them, one after the other, by the seats of their trousers, threw them over the obstacle on to the heads of the terrified enemy — a tactical measure worthy of Gargantua.

In Thermidor of Year II (1794) the Committee of Public Safety appointed him Commandant of the *École de Mars* at the *Camp des Sablons* (Neuilly-sur-Seine). This, in appearance, at least, was a great honour. It was the business of the school to turn the sons of sansculottes into Republican officers. But it had recently taken an active part in the 'days of Thermidor', and, although it had made its contribution to the overthrow of Robespierre, Tallien thought it unwise to leave such hot-headed young men at the very gates of Paris. Three days after Dumas's appointment the school was broken up, and the general sent to the Army of the Sambre-et-Meuse. At the end of two months: 'Citizen, you have been appointed Commander-in-Chief of the Army des Côtes de Brest, with headquarters at Rennes. *Salut et fraternité.*' This employment was as ephemeral as the others had been.

He was tired of so much pointless moving about, of commands without substance. What this courageous man really liked was to fight battles and to win them. Being himself of a frank and open nature, he detested quarrels and suspicions. He sent in his papers, and went to live in retirement with his wife's family at Villers-Cotterets. There he spent the first eight months of 1795. He was enjoying a quiet and happy existence when, on the 14th Vendémiaire, Year IV, the Convention, feeling itself threatened by the gilded youth of the capital, called for its protection on a leader whom it knew to be both honest and reliable. Dumas started off at once, but arrived one day too late. The safety of the Convention had been secured by other Jacobin generals, among whom was a young man with a Roman profile who went by the name of Napoléon Buonaparte.

CHAPTER II

General Bonaparte and General Dumas

THE Directory now assumed power. It was not popular. The country was in a ruined condition. Only the war could endow with a certain degree of prestige such a make-believe government. Consequently, the Directors let their thoughts turn back to an old dream of the French kings: the conquest of Italy. Buonaparte was appointed Commander-in-Chief of the army designated to carry out this task. 'General Vendémiaire' had some claim on the gratitude of the Director, Barras, who, for other reasons, felt confidence in the thin-faced soldier, since it was he who had introduced his former mistress, the creole Joséphine de Beauharnais, into the Corsican's bed.

After some months spent with the Army of the Alps, Dumas found himself directly under the orders of Bonaparte, who had given a French form to his name by suppressing the 'u'. He and his comrades looked upon themselves, at thirty-two, as hardened veterans, and disliked the thought of having to serve under a callow youth of twenty-six. But Bonaparte, since his arrival in Italy, by sheer intelligence, and because he had the gift of imposing his will on others, had succeeded in dominating these flamboyant soldiers of fortune. As men, they aroused only his contempt, and he regarded them all more as 'things than equals'. A born despot, he wished to have yes-men round him, and would 'ration out glory only to those of his generals who were incapable of turning it to their own account'.

The decent, good-natured Dumas, he thought, would cause him no anxiety. When the latter reached Milan in October 1796 he was well received by the Commander-in-Chief, and, in particular, by Joséphine, who, having been born in Martinique, had a weakness for anything and anyone who reminded her of her 'dear islands'. Furthermore, Bonaparte had need of men like him. In spite of his rich harvest of victories, he was far from easy in mind. The Directory was grudging of men and money. The Army of Italy showed signs of exhaustion. A Dumas was, in his own person, worth a squadron to him.

The man's legendary exploits were scarcely credible; but they were true. Letters written by Bonaparte are proof that General Dumas had captured, single-handed, six standards from a detachment considerably stronger than his own; that by shrewd questioning of a spy he had revealed the Austrian plans; that he had pinned down Wurmser's army in Mantua, and had had two horses killed under him. Like the heroes of Homer, those of the Italian campaign indulged in mutual jealousies. From time to time, some new Achilles, wearing the tricolour sash, withdrew to sulk in his tent. Dumas, after, as he thought, being unfairly treated, threatened to send in his papers, but Bonaparte knew that he could always win him back by entrusting him with a dangerous mission. It was the giant's strange pleasure to find himself alone in a world of enemies and, by daring and skill, to make himself master of the field. Provided the battle was in a good cause, *Monsieur de l'Humanité* was prepared to kill without scruple. There was something of defiance in his bravery. True, he had coloured blood in his veins, and was proud of it, but he wanted to prove himself the better man.

General Thibault, who served with him, has left this portrait. 'There was another general of division under Masséna's orders, named Dumas. He was a mulatto, not without ability, and quite the bravest, strongest and most active man whom I have ever known. His reputation in the army was extraordinary. His many deeds of chivalrous daring and athletic skill were quoted far and wide. Nevertheless, in spite of his great personal courage, and no matter how important the duties laid upon him, and even of his being known as one of the foremost soldiers of the day, Destiny never intended Dumas to be a general.' Indeed, he was famous more as a fine swordsman than a strategist, and what Bonaparte wanted was fine swordsmen. He was prepared to take on the strategy.

First-hand accounts left by witnesses make it clear that the famous incident of Clausen, when the general, brought to a halt at one end of the Bridge of Brixen, held it alone against a whole squadron, is true. Since the bridge was narrow, he could be attacked by only two or three men abreast, and these he cut down as they reached him. He was thrice wounded, and there were seven bullet-holes in his cloak. But he checked the enemy's charge. After such proof of prowess, the soldiers would have followed him to the end of the world. The Austrians called him 'the black devil'. General Joubert, his commanding officer and his friend, looked upon him as a modern Bayard. But Berthier, of the General Staff, who was Bonaparte's right-hand man and disliked front-line generals, played down the black devil's reputation to the Commander-in-Chief, who long refused to give the hero any praise. Once again the anger of Achilles rose. So many, however, were his exploits that a day came when Bonaparte said to Joubert: 'Send Dumas to me.'

Dumas was sulking and refused to obey the summons. The French Revolution had given the armies a peculiar stamp. In generals of republican sympathies, such as Hoche, Marceau and Dumas, discipline was tempered with independence. Dumas, too, in whom, as is often the case with men of the West Indies, impetuosity alternated with periods of indolence, had occasional moods of profound disgust. If he found himself crossed, his mind turned to Villers-Cotterets, and he sent in his resignation. Fortunately, his aide-de-camp kept a watchful eye on him, and was careful to see that the resignation was carefully locked away in a drawer. When, at long last, the general appeared at headquarters, Bonaparte received him with open arms.

'Welcome!' said the Commander-in-Chief. 'Welcome to the Horatius Cocles of the Tyrol!'

Faced by so flattering a reception, the decent Dumas could scarcely remain bogged down in his grudge. He, too, flung his arms wide, and the two men embraced fraternally. Bonaparte appointed Dumas Governor of the Province of Treviso, a post in which he made himself so deeply loved that, when he left it, he received the thanks of Mestre, Castelfranco and other places for the mildness and wisdom with which he had carried out his duties. It should have been said of him, as it was later said of another French general: 'He came to us as an enemy: he leaves us as a good friend.' By the time that happened, Bonaparte was making a triumphal entry into Paris.

When the Italian peace was signed, General Dumas got some leave. On December 20th, 1797, he returned to his family at Villers-Cotterets. The little town which, ten years before, had been so prosperous, was wasting away. The petty court of the duc d'Orléans had provided its livelihood. But no longer did distinguished visitors go there with great trains of attendants. Rich travellers were things of the past, and there was no more hunting in the forest. The 'Écu' was in a bad way. Labouret, who had never failed to provide shelter for his daughter and granddaughter, decided to close his hotel in which 'nothing but money was eaten', and to live simply on the savings which he had amassed during the years of plenty.

The arrival of his son-in-law, the general, who was a considerable personage in the armies of the Republic, enabled him to make plans for the future. He disposed of the furniture, which represented the working-capital of the 'Écu', for thirteen hundred and forty francs, five centimes. General Dumas, for his part, sold five of the six horses belonging to his personal stables. For these he received nine hundred and eighty livres and ten sous. On the 12th Germinal, 1798, Labouret leased a modest but roomy house in the rue de Lormalet for the sum of three hundred livres a year. From thenceforward this was to be the family home.

Meanwhile, Bonaparte, in Paris, was becoming the hope of all Frenchmen. In order to soothe any fears which the Directory might have of him, he declared that he had but one ambition — to drive the English from Egypt, and, perhaps, from India. Only the East, he said, could provide territory vast enough to allow for the founding of an Empire worthy of the ancients. But for Bonaparte the Directory would never have conceived so grandiose a plan. At the same time, the Directors, who regarded the conqueror with considerable uneasiness, saw in this programme the great merit of enabling them to keep him at a distance. On April 12th, 1798, Bonaparte became Commander-in-Chief of the Army of the East.

He lost no time in sending for Dumas. He thought him too honest to be really intelligent, but had it in mind to entrust his cavalry for the Egyptian campaign to this superb leader of men. Dumas once again bade farewell to his family and reported to his chief at Toulon. Bonaparte received him in bed in the room which he shared with Joséphine. She, naked under the sheets, was in tears.

'She wants to go to Egypt with us,' said Bonaparte. 'Are you proposing to take your wife along, Dumas?'

'Gracious no! She would be a great embarrassment to me!'

'If we have to stay there for several years,' said Bonaparte, 'we will send for our wives. Dumas, who produces only daughters,[1] and I who have failed to do even that, will each of us try to get a son. He shall stand godfather to mine, and I to his.'

With these words he gave a friendly smack to the well-fleshed backside under the sheet.

Joséphine was consoled. She had the habit of being consoled quickly — a little too quickly.

On his way from the Presence, Dumas ran into his friend, Kléber. 'Have you any idea what we're going to do over there?' he asked.

'We're going to establish a colony,' said Kléber.

'That's where you're wrong: we're going to establish a royal dynasty.'

'Oh! oh!' replied Kléber. 'That remains to be seen.'

'You'll see it soon enough!'

Dear, decent Dumas was right. This vast, this wanton adventure could serve only to build the prestige of one man. In Egypt, Bonaparte, the absolute master of events, and freed from all control, 'played the part of a sultan'.[2] Between the new master and the republican general things went wrong from the very first. Dumas displayed all his customary courage. His cavalry, with him at its head, threw back the Mamelukes into the Nile. When he made his horse rear and whirled his sabre, even the bravest Arabs cried in terror: 'the avenging Angel!' — and fled before the glorious Exterminator. But soon a mood of discouragement made itself felt in the ranks of the victorious army.

The generals did not understand the purpose of this war, and feared that Bonaparte intended to use them as the instruments of his selfish ambition. Over melons in Dumas's tent, questions were asked: 'Why have we left France, with its great forests and its fertile soil, to change its climate for this burning sky, this shelterless desert? Is Bonaparte bent on carving for himself an Empire from the East? . . . Is it right that the soldiers of the nation, the patriots of 1792, should become the satellites of an individual?'

Every ambitious man has his secret police, and these words were at once reported to the master by one of those who had heard them. For some considerable while, the 'Horatius Cocles of the Tyrol' had become the 'man of colour'. It was in the following terms that Bonaparte narrated what had happened, to Desgenettes, senior medical officer in the Army of Egypt:

On my arrival at Gizeh, I was informed that there were discontented elements in the army, and that several generals had gone so far as to declare that they would stop me from proceeding farther. I knew that Dumas was a prominent member of this faction, and that Murat and Lannes also belonged to it. I sent for Dumas, and said to him: 'I know what is being said. If I believed that you, or other men like you, were looking for an opportunity to transform into action the lunatic thoughts on which you have been brooding, I would at once order my guards to shoot you before my eyes. That done, I would summon the grenadiers of the army to pass judgment on you, and would see to it that your memory should be covered in shame.' He started to cry, and I realized that he was a decent enough fellow who had got too big for his shoes. Intelligence was not his strong point. In any case, I long ago forgot the whole incident.[3]

The general's son, in his *Mémoires*, gave a different account of the incident. According to him, what Bonaparte said to Dumas was this: 'General, you are trying to demoralize the army. You have been indulging in seditious talk. Take care that I do not do my duty. You may be tall, but your inches would not save you from being shot in two hours from now!'

Alexandre Dumas adds that his father replied with no little courage: 'Yes, I did say that for the honour and glory of my country I would march round the world, but that if it were merely a question of your personal whim, I should not budge.'

'You are willing, then, to be separated from me?'

'Certainly, once I have convinced myself that you have separated yourself from France.'

'You are wrong, Dumas.'

This conversation is not improbable. Dumas was a brave man, and Bonaparte, in his better moments, could be tolerant.

Thereafter, General Dumas continued to conduct himself as a hero. He put down a rising in Cairo, was the first to enter the Great Mosque, and sent much treasure to Bonaparte.

Dumas to Bonaparte: Citizen general: the leopard cannot change his spots, nor can the honest man change his conscience. I am sending you a treasure which I have just discovered. Its value is estimated at close on two million. Should I be killed, or should I die here from melancholy, remember that I am a poor man, and have left behind me in France a wife and child. *Salut et fraternité*.[4]

But his heart was no longer in the business. The superb mulatto appeared to be afflicted by the nostalgia to which those of creole blood are so frequently exposed. He asked for leave to return to France. But that was easier said than done. The English fleet was in complete control of the Mediterranean. Bonaparte — only too glad to be rid of a censorious grumbler — consented to Dumas's departure, but could not, even had he wished to, provide him with a sure means of transport. After prolonged delay, Dumas managed to charter a small ship, *La Belle Maltaise*, and put to sea with some of his comrades. The captain had promised to land them in France. But *La Belle Maltaise* turned out to be unseaworthy. Caught in a storm, she had to run for safety to the nearest harbour, which happened to belong to the Kingdom of Naples.

The plain, blunt soldier had, while in Egypt, been entirely without news from Europe and believed, in his innocence, that the Parthenopoean Republic, founded by Neapolitan patriots after the outbreak of the French Revolution, was still in existence, and would extend him a great welcome. But one result of the disaster of Aboukir was that the English and Austrians had undertaken to restore the Bourbons of Naples. At Tarento the republican general fell into the hands of a government of adventurers whose policy it was to wage against the French a war of poisoning and assassination. He was taken to Brindisi, and quickly realized that his life was in danger:

On the day following my arrival at the castle of Brindisi, while I was resting on my bed with the window open, a packet of some considerable size was passed through the bars, and fell on to the floor of my room . . . It contained two volumes entitled, *The Country Doctor*, by Tissot. On a slip of paper, inserted between the first and second pages, these words were written: 'From the patriots of Calabria: see the word POISON.' I did as I was told, and noticed that the word was doubly underlined. I understood that my life was threatened. . . .

A few days later, the doctor [of the prison] prescribed for me a diet of biscuit soaked in wine, promising, at the same time, to send me a supply of biscuit. Ten minutes later this arrived. I immediately followed his advice, and about two in the afternoon was seized with violent intestinal pains accompanied with vomitings, which made it impossible for me to eat any dinner and, redoubling in intensity, brought me to within measurable distance of death . . . The pain and the sickness showed all the symptoms of arsenical poisoning. . . .

As a result of having been poisoned, I found myself afflicted with deafness. One of my eyes had completely lost its sight, and I was in an advanced stage of paralysis . . . What proved the presence of a virulent agent was that these symptoms of senile decay came upon me at the age of thirty-three years and nine months.[5]

At last, on April 5th, 1801, as the result of an armistice, General Dumas was set at liberty, being exchanged for the famous Austrian general, Mack. He left prison a lame, half-paralysed man with a duodenal ulcer. Ill-treatment had changed the athlete of former days into a cripple. During his captivity many things had happened. Bonaparte had driven out the Councils, overturned the Directory, won a great victory at Marengo, in Italy, and entrusted Murat with the task of freeing Rome and Naples. It was in Florence that Dumas once more made contact with Murat, his faithful friend and comrade-in-arms. The two great cavalry leaders had fought shoulder to shoulder in Italy and, later, in Egypt. Murat, a man with a warm heart, who was no less chivalrous than Dumas, was a tower of strength to the hero who had been vanquished by destiny. Though he was now the brother-in-law of the First Consul, whose youngest sister, Caroline, had been carried away by his courage, passion and good looks, he forgot the spiteful prejudices of Bonaparte, and did what he could for his friend. Thanks to his good offices, Dumas was enabled to send a courier from Florence to Villers-Cotterets.

General of Division Alexandre Dumas to the citoyenne Dumas. Florence, the 8th Floréal, Year IX of the Republic: It is but an hour since I was reunited with my worthy friend Murat. His behaviour to you has made him but the more dear to me, and never, while life remains, shall I cease to show him my gratitude. I am sending from this place, as I have already told you was my intention, a statement addressed to the Consul, in which I have related the horrors inflicted upon me by the contemptible neapolitan government. I do not intend to speak of them in detail to you because it is no part of my duty to add grief to a heart which has already been sufficiently embittered as the result of prolonged privations. I hope within a month to bring the balm

of consolation to your rare and lovely spirit. I have read all your
letters to General Murat and to Beaumont, and the little one in
which my divine Aimée has spoken of her beautiful little mamma.
I gave it a thousand kisses as I did too to the lines you had added
to it in your own hand. I realize with a lively sense of gratitude
that she means as much to you as she does to me, since it is you
who have so carefully overseen her education. Such conduct,
conduct so worthy of you, makes you dearer even than before in
my eyes, and I am impatient to give you a proof of my feelings.
Adieu, beloved: henceforth you will ever count for much in
my heart, if only because unhappiness cannot but draw tighter
the bonds which hold us fast to one another. Embrace for me my
child, our dear parents, and also all our friends. Yours, without
reserve

AL. DUMAS
General of Division

The General has been so very good as to instruct his wife to
remit to you the sum of 50 louis. These you can send for to her
house as soon as you receive this letter.

The wife in question was Caroline Bonaparte. The wretched Dumas
had, as yet, no idea of the extent of his disgrace, nor of the great gulf
which would separate a family, already sovereign, from those who,
five years earlier, had been its equals. The style of the letter may be
open to question, the punctuation is distressing, but the charming tone
recalls that of General Hugo. These soldiers, so long separated from
their homes, grew to love them with a truly touching passion. Their
wives, their children became for them as precious as they were inacces-
sible. To Dumas, in particular, who had suffered much in Egypt, and
still more in prison, the quiet house at Villers-Cotterets with all its
load of affection must have seemed like paradise. Madame Hugo, of
Breton birth, romantic by temperament and married against her wishes,
showed little taste for the conjugal state. The wife of General Dumas,
a wise and gentle daughter of the Valois, had chosen her husband for
herself and adored him.

On May 1st, 1801, the general turned up at the Labourets' door. He
found waiting for him his young wife, an eight-year-old daughter, and
parents-in-law who were approaching old age. The crippled athlete was
without a penny. The gaolers had taken all his money from him and

for two years he had received no pay. But what of that? Was he not General Dumas, the paragon of bravery? Had he not his rank with all the rights pertaining to it? Could he not still claim to have faithful friends in the army, men like Murat, and, above all, men like Brune in whom the republican flame still burned bright? He bombarded the authorities with letters, but in vain. Bonaparte — though, maybe, he was not a cruel man — never forgave a lack of devotion to his person. To the Senior Medical Officer, Desgenettes, who after examining Dumas had pronounced him to be a very sick man and had put in a plea for him, the First Consul wrote: 'Since you tell me that his health will never again permit him to sleep for six weeks on desert sand, or wrapped in a bearskin, he is no longer any use to me as a cavalry commander. Any corporal would be as good.'[6]

The exile of Villers-Cotterets actually dared to send a letter direct to the Master:

General Dumas to General Bonaparte, 7th Vendémiaire, Year X: General consul, you are aware of the misfortunes which have come upon me! You know the state of my purse! You remember the treasure of Cairo! ... The successive doses of poison which were administered to me in the prisons of Naples have so wrecked my health that at thirty-six I am already subject to the infirmities which ought not to have afflicted me until a much more advanced age ... But I have another cause for grief General consul which I confess is still more terrible than those of which I have just complained. The Minister of War has informed me, in a letter of the 29th Fructidor last, that I have been placed with other generals on the unemployed list. Am I at my age and with my name to be exposed to a sort of cashiering! I am the senior general officer in my rank ... and now I have to see my juniors given commands while I am condemned to inactivity! I appeal to your feelings General consul: permit me to lay my grievances before you, and to place in your hands my defence against such enemies as I may have.[7]

To this there was no reply. He tried to win the support of Berthier, Chief of the General Staff and his former enemy in Italy, by asking him to a shoot in the lovely forest of Villers-Cotterets. Berthier accepted, carried off his share of the game and thanked his host. But he set his career above the obligations of friendship and was not the man to run counter to a decision made by the First Consul.

On July 24th, 1802, Marie-Louise Dumas was brought to bed of a son who was entered in the official Register as Alexandre Dumas. Some years later (1813) this name was corrected by the addition of the words — Davy de la Pailleterie. The general asked his old army friend, Brune, to stand godfather:

Dumas to Brune, 6th Thermidor, Year X: My dear Brune — I announce to you with joy the news that my wife was brought to bed yesterday morning of a strapping boy who weighs nine pounds and is eighteen inches in length. So you see if he continues to grow in the outer world as he has done in the inner he looks like reaching a respectable height. But there is something I want you to know and that is that I count on you to be godfather. My little daughter who sends you many messages of affection from the tips of her little black fingers will be your fellow sponsor. Come quickly, though the newcomer to this world seems to have no wish to leave it again soon. Come quickly all the same, for I have not seen you these many years and have a strong wish to do so.

Your friend —
ALEX. DUMAS

P.S. I open this again to inform you that the little ruffian has just peed higher than his head. A good sign, eh?[8]

Brune to Dumas, 10th Thermidor, Year X: I have a prejudice which keeps me from doing as you wish. I have been a godfather on five separate occasions, and all my godsons have died. When the last of them went, I registered a vow never again to stand sponsor . . . I am sending a few boxes of goodies for the little godmother and her mamma.[9]

The fact of the matter was that Brune, though deploring the fall of his old comrade into disfavour, was afraid of the Master's possible reactions. But Dumas was insistent, and a compromise was arrived at: Brune should be godfather, but would be represented at the ceremony by a proxy, old Labouret, who would thus hold his own grandson at the font.

The general had placed his daughter Aimée at a boarding-school in

Paris. He now developed a passionate attachment to the pretty little boy, whose skin was so white, whose eyes were so blue, whose dose of black blood showed only in his crinkly hair. The child, on his side, as soon as he was of an age to form opinions of his own, adored his good, kind father. He was full of admiration for his physical strength — which, in spite of his ailments, remained prodigious — for his handsome, gold-embroidered uniform, and his silver-mounted fowling-piece with its little green leather pad on the butt. The family was now living in a small château, not far from Villers-Cotterets, in the village of Haramont. It went by the name of 'Les Fosses'. Their standard of living was still fairly luxurious. The general employed a gardener, a kitchen-maid, a game-keeper and a personal body-servant who was a negro called Hippolyte.

In 1805, feeling that his health was still further deteriorating, he decided to go to Paris there to consult the great Corvisart. He took with him his wife and his son, both of whom he wished to introduce to his friends. He was convinced that he had not long to live, and wanted to make sure that the boy should have protectors on whom he could rely. Murat and Brune were brave enough to accept an invitation to luncheon. Brune's attitude was cordial, Murat's distant. The Empire had come into being only a year earlier. Between the new dignitaries — marshals, princes, too, and kings in the not very distant future — and the lame dogs of the Revolution, there was now no common bond but unwelcome memories. The boy never forgot that he had pranced round the table astride on Brune's sabre, with Murat's hat on his head.

General Dumas had asked to see the Emperor, but the desired audience was not granted. Corvisart having been unable to relieve his ailments, he left Paris 'with death in his heart and in his body'. Perhaps from lack of money, perhaps to be within easier distance of doctors, the family returned to Villers-Cotterets, where it settled down at the 'Hôtel de l'Épée', which stood on the main road to Soissons. There, grandfather Labouret was living, too, having left his own house.

The little Alexandre did at least retain a pleasing memory of his father's last months. He had a vivid picture of a boudoir with cashmere hangings, and of a young and beautiful woman reclining on a sofa. This was Pauline Bonaparte, Princess Borghese, who, at that time, was separated from her husband.

She did not rise [writes Dumas] when my father entered the

room, but held out one hand, and raised her eyes: that was all. My father made as though to sit down beside her on a chair, but she made him sit at her feet, which she rested on his knees, playing with the buttons on his coat with the point of her slipper. That foot, that hand, that delicious little lady, so white of skin, so plump, in close proximity to the herculean mulatto, who, in spite of his sufferings, was still a fine figure of a man, made the most charming group imaginable.

Suddenly the sound of a horn came from the park.

'That's the hunt drawing near,' said my father. 'The animal will run up the avenue. Come and look, Princess.'

'Gracious me, no, General!' said she, 'I am very comfortable where I am, and have no intention of moving. Walking tires me — though, if you like, you may carry me.'

My father lifted her between his two hands, as a nurse might have lifted a child, and carried her to the window. He held her there for close on ten minutes ... Then he took her back to the sofa, and sat down again near to her. What happened behind my back I do not know. My attention was wholly given to the stag which had just broken cover and was crossing the avenue, to the hounds and to the huntsmen. For I much was more interested in what was going on outside than I was in the princess.[10]

In 1806 Jean-Michel Deviolaine, a cousin of the Labourets, who was still Chief Ranger of the forest and administered it in the interests of the Imperial domain, as he had once done for the duc d'Orléans (who had died on the scaffold), came to tell General Dumas that Berthier had managed to procure for him a permit to hunt. Such is ever the way of important personages, who, by means of small favours, rid themselves of a sense of guilt for great injustices.

Once again the general tried to mount his horse to go riding in the forest of Villers-Cotterets, but pain conquered the conqueror. On his return from this last equestrian outing, he had to take to his bed. For a moment he was a prey to delirium and despair.

'Oh!' he cried. 'Must a general who, when he was no more than thirty-five, had already been commander-in-chief of three armies, die at forty, like a coward, in his bed. Oh! my God, my God, what have I done that you should condemn me so young to leave my wife and children?'

He saw a priest, made his confession, and then, turning to his wife, died in her arms on the stroke of midnight.

A few days earlier, the little Alexandre had been removed from the house and sent to stay with a female cousin. He was already asleep when, at midnight, they were both of them roused by a loud knocking at the door. The boy, without the slightest sign of fear, ran to open it.

'Where are you going, Alexandre?' called his hostess.

'You can see for yourself . . . I am going to let in Papa who has come to say goodbye to us.'

She put him back in his bed, where he fell fast asleep. Next day, he was told the sad news.

'My poor child, your father, whom you loved so well, is dead.'

'Papa dead? . . . what does that mean?'

'It means that you will never see him again.'

'And why shall I never see him again?'

'Because the good God has taken him to Himself.'

'Where does the good God live?'

'In the sky.'

The little Alexandre said no more, but, as soon as he could make his escape, ran to his mother. He entered unobserved, went straight to where his father's gun was hanging, took it down and marched up the stairs. On the landing he met his mother who was just leaving the death-chamber, bathed in tears.

'Where are you going?' she asked.

'I am going to the sky.'

'And what are you going to do in the sky, my poor boy?'

'I am going to kill the good God who has killed Papa.'

She took him in her arms and hugged him. 'You must not say things like that, my pet,' she said, 'we are already wretched enough as it is.'

CHAPTER III

A Childhood of Laziness, Freedom and Forest-roaming

THEY were, indeed, in the depths of wretchedness. The general had left nothing, and from the Emperor, who consistently refused to grant an audience to the wife of a 'rebel', they could expect nothing. A few of Dumas's old comrades, Brune, Augereau, Lannes, made mention of the dead man's exploits. Napoleon's rejoinder was swift and harsh. 'I forbid you,' he said, 'ever to mention his name in my hearing.' It was impossible even to procure for the young Alexandre a *bourse* to either a *lycée* or to one of the military schools. Napoleon's clemency was not that of Augustus.

Jean-Michel Deviolaine, the Inspector of Forests, the cousin and protector of the Dumas family, wrote a letter to General Pille, a Count of the Empire, who was related to him and had, formerly, as Commissioner-General of the armies under the Revolution, known of the hero's exploits. In it he announced the death of the brave but unfortunate General Dumas:

> He ended his career yesterday, at eleven o'clock at night, at Villers-Cotterets, whither he had returned to follow the instructions of his doctors. The ailment of which he died was a result of the ill-treatment which he received at Naples, on his return from Egypt. Ever since being placed on the retired list, and during the whole course of his malady, he never ceased to wish well to French arms. It was a deeply moving experience to hear him express, only a few hours before his death, a wish to be buried on the field of Austerlitz.[1]

Deviolaine requested that a pension should be granted to the widow and the orphaned children whom the general had left entirely unprovided for, his long illness having eaten up such resources as had remained to him. Pille's reply was sorrowful, official and negative.

Every approach to authority was vain, and the Labouret grandparents had, themselves, to maintain their daughter and their grandchildren.

The young Alexandre showed himself to be intelligent, but an unsatisfactory worker. His mother and his sister taught him to read and write. In arithmetic he could never get further than the multiplication-table. His handwriting, however, even in his early years, was that of a sergeant-major, neat, legible and florid. A graphologist would have deduced from it a plentiful supply of vanity, and it was true to say that the boy showed a marked tendency to boast. He had read the Bible, Buffon and a treatise on mythology by his compatriot, Demoustier, and thought that he knew all there was to be known. He was not afraid to intervene with complete self-assurance in grown-up conversations, and this habit, much to his surprise, brought him more kicks on the backside than praise. His mother, who was anxious about his future, tried to give him music lessons, but no one could well have had a worse singing voice. To set against this, he did learn how to dance, fence and, somewhat later, to shoot. In each of these accomplishments he attained a high standard.

At ten he showed much enthusiasm for bodily exercises, and dreamed of sabres, swords, pistols and guns. The real centre of his life was not his family, but the forest. The forest of Villers-Cotterets is of vast extent. All the young scamps of the little town went there to shoot, to set snares and to play at savages. They made friends with poachers. Dumas was ten years old when one of his cousins, the abbé Conseil, died and left money for his maintenance at the seminary, on condition that he should consent to take Holy Orders. His poor mother, who was at her wits' end to know what to do with him, saw a hope in this conditional legacy, and begged him at least to try. At first he agreed, and was given twelve sous with which to buy a seminarist's ink-stand. He used them, however, to purchase bread and sausage, furnished with which he spent three nights in the forest, shooting birds. He returned home on the fourth day.

Prodigal children ever get the warmest welcome. His mother, who had been badly frightened, embraced him, promised that there should be no further question of the seminary, and sent him to the school over which the abbé Grégoire presided at Villers-Cotterets. This saintly man soon perceived that, if the young Dumas had a good heart and more than his fair share of self-satisfaction, he did not make the best of these good qualities. He was vain and often insolent. He did not learn much — a little Latin, a little grammar — but did perfect his hand-writing by complicating it with flourishes, hearts and rosettes. It was both superb and hideous. In the matter of prayers he was as backward as he was at arithmetic. He knew only three: the *Pater*, the *Ave Maria* and the *Credo*. His natural bent turned him into a child of the forest, undisciplined, wild, and 'sensitive to all the sounds of nature which awake in the woods as soon as darkness falls'.

His mother, an excellent woman, a hard worker, but timid, saw a replica of the husband whom she had adored in this great hulking boy who looked thirteen or fourteen when he was ten, and, with his broad back and well-developed muscles, had something of an African appear-ance. She was completely under his influence and let him do as he liked. But she was not left to bring up, unaided, this high-spirited and attractive young savage. Friends rallied round her in her time of troubles. Specialists in no matter what employment are seldom affected by political changes and chances. Deviolaine, under the Bourbons, despite the fact that he had faithfully served the Empire, was retained in his office of Chief Ranger, a post which gave him, in the eyes of the young Alexandre, an immense prestige. Surly in manner and sharp-tempered, he was, at bottom, the best and kindest of men. To the growing boy he seemed 'king of the trees and emperor of the rides'.[2]

Another neighbour, Jacques Collard,[3] a lovable fellow, always prone to laughter, had been appointed by the general to act as his son's tutor. His wife was the natural daughter of Madame de Genlis by the duc d'Orléans. Madame Collard's stories plunged the young Dumas into the atmosphere of the *ancien régime*, and those of his mother into that of the Empire.

He was living in a great and romantic age. Villers-Cotterets was on the direct route taken by the invaders, and, during the Campaign of France, the boy saw the Czar of Russia ride by at the head of his Cossacks. At the sound of the galloping horses, the women took refuge in the cellars, but young Alexandre clung to the window-catch, eager not to miss the fighting. In spite of the Emperor's harsh treatment of them, mother and son were generally thought of as Bonapartists. Villers-Cotterets, on the other hand, was staunchly monarchist. After the Restoration, gangs of urchins shouted 'Vive le Roi!' under the widow's windows. But the Dumas family remained faithful to the general's uniform. Deep within its members burned the republican fire.

In 1815, while the Emperor, on the island of Elba, was waiting for his hour to strike, two generals, the brothers Lallemand, who had conspired against Louis XVIII and been arrested by the police of Villers-Cotterets, were hooted by the populace of that small town. Madame Dumas was deeply outraged by this insult to the epaulettes once worn by her husband.⁴

'We are going to do something,' she told her son, 'which may cruelly compromise us; but we owe it to the memory of your father.'

She took him to Soissons, where François and Henri were imprisoned, and charged the twelve-year-old boy with the task of supplying them with money and pistols. This mission he carried through with great courage. The two generals, aware that the Emperor had just landed, refused both money and weapons; but the young Dumas, as a result of this exploit, was strengthened in his self-reliance, in his passion for the romantic, in the love, which he had inherited from his father, of playing the part of Righter of Wrongs.

In the course of the Hundred Days, Napoleon twice passed through Villers-Cotterets, once when he was moving north to join his troops, once after Waterloo, when he was a sick and silent man with a drooping head. After him came the remnants of the Grande Armée. The spectacle was terrible yet magnificent; its very horror gave it something of sublimity. The wretched hordes of wounded men, piled into farm-carts and only roughly bandaged, waved scraps of bloodstained rag, with cries of 'Vive l'Empereur!' Shortly after this occurrence, terrible news reached the family. The most faithful of all Dumas's friends, Marshal Brune, had been assassinated at Avignon.

The old and gouty Louis XVIII returned from Ghent 'in the baggage-waggons of the invader'. The change of regime presented a problem. Would it not be well, suggested the widow, for the young Dumas to resume the name to which he was legally entitled — Davy de la Pailleterie? The title of marquis would, under the Restoration, open many doors to him.

'Dumas is my name,' the boy proudly declared, 'and none other ... What would my father have said had he known that I should deny him, and call myself after a grandfather I had never known?'

His mother's face beamed: 'Is that really how you feel?'

'Well, it is how you feel, too, isn't it, Mother?'

'Alas, yes! But what is to become of us?'

The general's widow, having obtained a licence to sell tobacco, had leased, for the purpose of carrying on her trade, the shop belonging to an ironmonger named Lafarge. The man's son came one day to see his father. Auguste Lafarge was a handsome, fair-complexioned young fellow. His calling was that of articled clerk to a Paris notary. He sported a box-coat with thirty-six capes, a watch-chain with many dangling ornaments, skin-tight pantaloons and Wellington boots. Young Dumas was dazzled. He made advances to the articled clerk which were well received. It pleased Lafarge to talk to this intelligent youth about Paris, the literary world, the theatres, and to show him a number of epigrams in verse of his own composition. Dumas had his first glimpse of glory. He was being treated to the vision of a way of getting himself talked about, the existence of which he had never, till then, even suspected. He begged the abbé Grégoire to teach him how to write French poetry.

'I ask nothing better,' said the abbé, 'but by the end of a week you will be as sick of that as you are of everything else.'

The old man had a thorough knowledge of his pupil. By the end of a week Alexandre had had enough. Corneille and Racine bored him to death. General Dumas's son, like all the young men of his generation, had heard too many thrilling stories to be content with the analysis of human emotions. What he wanted was action, no matter how mad.

But no adolescent can live on a diet of shooting-parties. It was time for him to find some kind of a situation. Madame Dumas went to see the notary of Villers-Cotterets, a certain Maître Menneson, a republican like herself. She asked him to employ Alexandre as a junior clerk. The young savage greatly disliked the idea of saying goodbye to his independence, but remembered the brilliant articled clerk with the thirty-six capes and the gold chains. If working in a notary's office meant a fine future, an income, and times off for shooting, then to the notary's office he would go. At first he was not unhappy there. He was sent on numerous errands, among them the taking round to peasants in the neighbourhood of legal documents requiring signature. These provided a splendid excuse for riding and, now and again, for taking a few pot-shots in the forest.

CHAPTER IV

Growing-pains, Sensuality and Drama

His life remains the most entertaining of his works, nor did he ever write a stranger novel
than the story of his adventures.   BRUNETIÈRE

SPRING 1818 — Alexandre Dumas was now sixteen. That is the
age at which the cravings of the flesh become conscious, the age at
which growing boys, till then scornful of girls, begin to look for
them, the age at which the adolescent begins to learn about delicious
and forbidden matters from books previously withheld from him.
Our young man had recently come upon certain volumes inherited
from his grandfather; among them *The Adventures of the Chevalier de
Faublas*, the hero of which, disguised as a woman, moves from conquest to conquest. 'I', thought the vainglorious Dumas, 'will be a
second Faublas.'   .

But Lafarge had told him that if a man wants to charm the opposite
sex, he must be elegant. An opportunity to show his prowess soon
came his way — the Whitsuntide ball, which was always a great occasion at Villers-Cotterets. Young women would be present whom he
had not yet seen: Laurence, one of the abbé Grégoire's nieces, and a
Spanish friend of hers called Vittoria — both of them twenty years old
and, by common report, remarkably pretty. He rummaged through
the wardrobe of his now deceased Labouret grandfather. There, carefully preserved in camphor and sweet-smelling herbs, he found gar-
ments dating from the days of the *ancien régime*: brocaded satin coats;
red, gold-embroidered waistcoats; nankeen trousers. He jumped for
joy, chose a bottle-green dress-coat and thought himself irresistible.
In point of fact this get-up was out of date and ridiculous; but how
should the poor youth have known that?

Proud as a peacock, he offered his arm to Laurence. She was a
Parisienne, fair-haired and intelligent. Her friend Vittoria, with a
provocative bust and a small waist, was the very image of the stage
conception of what an Andalusian maiden should be. He noticed that
when the two girls looked at him, they exchanged smiles. He blushed
a fiery red. But when the dancing began he enjoyed his revenge. The

two friends were surprised to find that he acquitted himself remarkably well. Vittoria went so far as to find him not altogether lacking in intelligence. The orchestra struck up a waltz.

'But you waltz beautifully!' she said, overcome with amazement.

'That you should think so is the more pleasing to me seeing that I have never till now waltzed except with chairs.'

'How d'you mean, with chairs?'

'You see, the abbé Grégoire would never let me dance with women ... so my dancing master had to make do with chairs.'

She burst out laughing. This was the first time he had ever felt the touch of a woman's hair against his cheek; the first time that his eyes had ever explored the secrets of a low-necked dress; the first time that he could look with wonder at the spectacle of a pair of naked shoulders. He heaved a tremulous and happy sigh.

'What is the matter with you?' she asked.

'Only that I find it much nicer to waltz with you than with a chair.'

For the moment, all she could do was to sit down.

'What a very strange young man he is!' she said to Laurence. 'I find him quite charming!'

He emerged from this adventure humiliated to think that he had been treated as a plaything by two pretty girls, and madly in love — not with any particular person, but with love, or, rather, with pleasure. If the two young women from Paris had to some extent made fun of him, they had been prodigal of those lessons which only women can give. They had taught him that he was a handsome, well-made young fellow, but also that he must turn these natural gifts to advantage by being neat and elegant. In short, they had made him cross the line which separates childhood from youth.

He now proceeded to exercise his new-found prowess on the maidens of Villers-Cotterets. They were well endowed to play the part of temptress. In each of the three classes into which local society was divided — aristocracy, bourgeoisie and people — the rising generation was indeed ravishing. What a delight to see them on Sundays in their spring frocks, with pink and blue sashes and little bonnets trimmed by their own hands, playing, running, linking and unlinking the long chain of their bare and rounded arms!

Soon he was leading a very pleasant life. From nine each morning until four in the afternoon he copied legal instruments 'in chambers'. Then he dined with his mother and, round about eight in summer or six in winter, there was a gathering of young people, sometimes in the open air, sometimes at the home of one of the girls. Hands were clasped, couples paired off, lips offered. At ten o'clock each of the young men escorted the girl of his choice back to her home. There she granted him one more hour of dalliance on the bench by the front door, while from time to time a scolding voice would call to her by name and she reply ten times over before obeying: 'Here I am, Mamma . . .' O shades of Marguerite and Goethe!

Alexandre Dumas's first love went neither to the Collard girls who made smart marriages with neighbouring squires, nor to those of the Deviolaine family, but to somebody in that intermediate class between bourgeoisie and people, from which were drawn the dressmakers, laundresses and purveyors of trifles for the toilet. He discovered two adorable young women, one fair, the other dark, who were always to be seen together, as though each was intent on being a foil to the other. The fair one, Adèle Dalvin, whom he called *Aglaé* in the first edition of his *Mémoires* so as not to compromise her, was gay rather than melancholy, short rather than tall, plump rather than slim. 'It was easy and it was sweet to love her, though far from easy to be loved in return. Her mother and father were good old land-workers, of decent but common stock, and it was matter for no little surprise that they should have produced so fresh and fragrant a flower. . . .'[1]

All these young women enjoyed a delightful degree of freedom. 'There was, at Villers-Cotterets', says Dumas, 'a custom, more English than French, of permitting a free and easy relationship between young people of both sexes, such as I have never found in any other town in France. This was the more remarkable in that the girls' parents were decent, honest folk who, in their hearts, believed that these boats launched on the waters of Sentiment were rigged with white sails and crowned with orange-blossom. . . .'[2]

Unfortunately the local parents had a very imperfect knowledge of human nature, and their optimism went to dangerous extremes. After a year of the sweet sparring in which 'young love is always asking, and takes no refusal as final; after the successive winning of petty favours, each one of which, at the moment of granting, fills the male heart with joy', Adèle was given permission by her mother to sleep in a little garden-house. One night, the inexorable door which for the last twelve months had been shut at eleven o'clock behind the young Dumas whom Adèle had pushed out of the house, opened again quietly half an hour later. Behind it he found two caressing arms, felt a heart beating against his heart, heard ardent sighs and a sound of prolonged weeping. On that night, Alexandre took possession of the first of his mistresses. This idyll was to last for two years of perfect happiness.

On Sundays, groups of young people went to village merrymakings. It was during one of these that Dumas, having left his companions to call on a farmer, saw coming towards him round a bend in the road someone whom he knew well — Caroline Collard, for some years now the Baroness Cappelle. She had with her a strange man with the look of a German student. He was tall, dark-complexioned, rather gaunt, with cropped hair, fine eyes, a strongly modelled nose, and an easy, aristocratic carriage. His name, it turned out, was the vicomte Adolphe Ribbing de Leuven. He was the son of that comte Adolphe-Louis Ribbing de Leuven, a Swedish nobleman, who had achieved fame by the part he had played in the murder of Gustavus III, King of Sweden.

The comte, who was known as 'the handsome regicide', had been obliged to go into exile. He had lived first in Switzerland, then in France, where he had struck up a close friendship with the Collards. Dumas had seen but little of his former tutor's family, since love had taken him into quite different social circles. Madame Cappelle greeted him in the warmest possible fashion, saying that Adolphe de Leuven, who was about his own age, would be a friend to him. He was invited for a visit of three days to the château of Villers-Hellon, where the Collards were living. There he discovered not only that Adolphe de Leuven wrote poetry, but that he sent to young women elegies of his own composition — news which filled the young Dumas with admiration. Already Lafarge, the articled clerk, had revealed to him the fact that there was much prestige to be gained by the making of verses. This theory now seemed to be confirmed and he was deeply struck.

Leuven returned to Paris, but another friend took his place, a hussar officer, Amédée de la Ponce, who had been drawn to Villers-Cotterets, no doubt by love, since he married there. He was a man of culture and took an interest in Dumas, to whom he said:

'Believe me, dear boy, there are other things in life besides love and shooting! There is work, for instance. Learn to work and you will learn the secret of happiness!'

Work? That, for the young Dumas, was a new idea. Amédée de la

Ponce, who knew German and Italian, offered to teach him these two languages. Together they translated a fine novel by Ugo Foscolo, and the officer revealed to the young clerk Goethe's *Werther* and Burger's *Lenore*.

At this point it is important that the reader should know something of the character which had been formed by heredity and upbringing. To his father, Alexandre owed great physical strength, generosity of mind, imagination and bodily appetites above the normal. Like all the young men whose mental development had been shaped by the soldiers of the Empire, he had been nourished on tales of adventure marked by both splendour and the shedding of blood. Drama was his natural element. He believed in the power of chance, and in the influence wielded by seemingly trivial occurrences. 'All these soldiers had been saved by a portrait, killed by a stray bullet, condemned to disgrace by a decision taken by the master in a moment of ill-humour.' What Dumas was to love in history was all that led the mind to dwell on the mysterious operations of fortune. How should he not have had a feeling for the theatre? The very age was theatrical. He was better fitted than most to express the dramatic aspects of life, for which everybody at that time was hungry, because he himself was a 'force of nature'.

A force of nature, primarily as a result of the primitive blood which his father had brought from San-Domingo. 'He was', it has been said, 'a sort of a Diderot, an aristocrat on his father's side, of the people on his mother's.' That, no doubt, is true, though he had, in addition, the prodigious exuberance and the gift of myth-making of the African Negro. A force of nature, too, by reason of his refusal to accept any form of discipline. Because of the lack of a man in the family to keep him to heel, he had run freely in the woods. He had been neither formed nor deformed by school influences. He had grown up in such a way as to make him incapable of enduring any constraint. Women? He loved them en bloc, had found them an easy prey from the beginning. That he should swear fidelity to any one of them was an idea beyond his understanding. He was not so much immoral as unable to adhere to conventional conceptions of morality. The only tales of love he had heard were those of the Regent and his suppers at Villers-Cotterets, which were not entirely suited to a child's ears; those of the more than life-size figures of the Empire, who had conquered hearts as they had conquered provinces, and were indulgent in their attitude to the women left high and dry as the result of their weakness. In his

47

youth he had been a great sportsman, a great braggart, in love with every girl who would listen to him, filled with the desire to have all that a man *could* have. At eighteen he found temptation in everything, especially in the impossible. Had he not the gift of magnetism which would enable him to triumph where others would fail?

Of that he was convinced. He felt that his zest was inexhaustible. He did not know much, but for that very reason everything seemed new to him. One day, a troup of actors had come to Soissons and had played Ducis's *Hamlet.*[3] In this way he discovered Shakespeare, of whose works he had been, till then, entirely ignorant. *Hamlet*, as adapted by Ducis, had very little of Shakespeare in it. Nevertheless, for the young Dumas, the play was a revelation. 'Imagine', he said, 'a blind man whose sight has been suddenly restored: imagine Adam waking up after the creation.' In point of fact, what Dumas found in Shakespeare was himself. He, too, possessed the physical energy of the men of the Renaissance. He felt closer to them than to the bourgeois of the Restoration. What he looked for in Shakespeare was not thought, not the metaphysical monologues, nor yet the painting of human passions. It was freedom in the construction of drama, and reliance on the concrete — the handkerchief in *Othello*, Hamlet's rat, Shylock's pound of flesh in the *Merchant of Venice*: in short, the melodramatic element. He was overwhelmed and, since he never doubted anything, least of all himself, he decided that he would be a dramatic author.

He succeeded in communicating this fever of excitement to a few of his friends at Villers-Cotterets, among them a certain Paillet, a fellow-clerk in the chambers of Maître Mennesson, who thirty years later, as a magistrate of long standing, recorded his memories of this company of amateurs. Adolphe de Leuven, who had returned from Paris, where he had been living with one of his father's friends, the dramatist Arnault, and had become familiar with back-stage life and with a number of actresses, guided the 'prentice steps of the young Dumas:

> The presence of certain young and attractive women awoke in us a desire to appear upon the stage with them. A barn was the setting for our sublime or comic efforts. It belonged to a fairly large house standing at the far end of a yard which adjoined the Hôtel de l'Épée. The ground-floor was occupied by a timber-merchant who lent us the planks from which our friend Arpin fashioned the benches for the spectators. The décor presented no

difficulties. The neighbouring forest, with its clumps of ever-greens, the various family wardrobes, and a few boxes of flowers, soon transformed the barn into a decked and decent auditorium. The scenic side of our performances was a triumph, but the presentation of the plays, whether drama or comedy, demanded far greater efforts. It was there that Dumas turned out to be indispensable. He was everywhere and everything — actor, pro-ducer, instructor in all matters of movement and diction. It was he who chose the works to be performed, when, that is, he did not impose his own upon us: *Artaxerxes, l'Abencérage,* etc. It was he who taught the actors the proper intonations, who arranged the entrances, and planned the necessary movements. He decided what words were to be stressed, what the expression of the performers' faces should be, how long a smile should be 'held' — in short, imparted to each member of the company, a full understanding of the character he had to personify. Applause was the breath of life to him . . . If it was not sufficiently en-thusiastic he grew angry: it was not his fault but the fault of the actors.'

In 1820 and 1821, he sketched, together with Adolphe de Leuven, several pieces for the theatre, including an extravaganza in rhymed couplets, *Le Major de Strasbourg,* which Alexandre considered to be a near-masterpiece. But Leuven went off again, carrying his wit with him, and Adèle Dalvin got married, thereby breaking the young author's heart. He wanted to get away, to follow Leuven to Paris. He saw himself in imagination already crowned with laurels and loaded with gold. Meanwhile he had to go on copying marriage con-tracts and drawing up wills for a notary of Crépy-en-Valois who, in return, gave him free board and lodging. One day his friend Paillet came to see him and suggested that the pair of them should spend two days in the capital.

How was he to defray the costs of such a trip? The young poacher refused to let such considerations bother him for a moment. He would take a gun with him, do some shooting on the road, sell the game thus acquired, and so have to spend nothing. This plan was duly carried out. By the time he reached Paris, he still had four hares, two par-tridges, and two quails, in exchange for which the 'Hôtel des Grands-Augustins' agreed to lodge him for two days. So far so good. All he now needed were theatre tickets. The Comédie-Française was to play *Sylla* on the following day, with the famous Talma in the leading part. Dumas registered a silent oath that he would be present, and hastened off to see Adolphe de Leuven who agreed to introduce him to Talma. They found the great man dressing. Adolphe explained that his friend was the son of General Dumas. Talma remembered the heroic giant, and signed a card of admission.

Talma at this time was the dominant personality at the Théâtre-Français, where he alone could still successfully impose classical tragedy upon the public. In a period of violence, that particular form of drama had suffered from its apparent coldness. Tradition had been so dinned into actors and actresses that they thought of nothing but imparting excessive nobility to both voice and gesture. It is to Talma's credit that he tried to establish his acting on the emotional level of the ordinary members of the audience. Napoleon, himself an enlightened lover of the great tragic dramas, had once said to him: 'Look at me now. I am beyond all doubt the greatest tragic figure of the age, but you don't see *me* waving my arms, studying my gestures, assuming attitudes, or affecting grandiose airs, do you? Have you ever heard me shouting and shrieking? Of course you haven't! I talk naturally . . . you should ponder these things. . . .'⁵

And ponder them he did. He tried to break free from the monotonous and rhythmic delivery of spoken verse, and to express shades of meaning by employing varieties of silent 'business'. When, in *Britannicus*, during the great scene with Agrippina, he conveyed Nero's boredom by making him play with his cloak and study the pattern of the material, this was an innovation of incredible daring! To the characters of the classic repertory he gave a quality which could, already, have been styled 'romantic'. The heroes, as played by him, had an air of the star-crossed, the sombre, the inspired. Not for nothing had Chateaubriand written *René*! At the same time he studied history, tended to break away from the 'universal man' of the classics, and to give to the figures on the stage the manners proper to their country and their age. He was a constant visitor to museums and libraries. In short, his mind was moving in the direction later taken by Hugo, Vigny and Dumas. In order to please the younger generation, of which he was the idol, he transformed tragedy into drama. Whether he was right or wrong in so doing is another question. He had a nose for his period: he both understood and gratified it.

Next day, Alexandre saw Talma in action, and was carried away by his mingling of simplicity, strength and poetry. When the curtain fell to a storm of applause, the young spectator was stunned, ravished, fascinated. Adolphe proposed a visit to the actor's dressing-room. He entered it blushing, and with a beating heart. He felt humbled.

'Talma,' said Leuven, 'we have come to thank you.'

'So, your young poet is satisfied, is he?' said Talma. 'He must come back tomorrow and see me in *Regulus*.'

'Unfortunately,' sighed Dumas, 'I have to leave Paris tomorrow. I am a lawyer's clerk in a country town.'

'Bah!' exclaimed Talma, 'Corneille was an attorney's clerk ... Gentlemen, allow me to present to you a Corneille of the future!'

Dumas went pale. 'Touch my forehead,' he said to Talma, 'that will bring me luck.'

'So be it! I baptize you poet in the name of Shakespeare, of Corneille and of Schiller,' said Talma, and added: 'This young man has got enthusiasm. We shall make something of him.'[6]

The young man did, indeed, have enthusiasm, and a solid appetite for glory. 'Don't worry,' he said to Adolphe de Leuven, 'I shall come back to Paris, that I promise you.' On returning to the hotel, he found Paillet, the articled clerk, who had been to the Opera to hear *La Lampe Merveilleuse*, waiting for him. They decided to leave Paris at dawn next day. But Alexandre, walking through the city streets still wrapped in slumber, felt convinced that there, in Paris, was to be the scene of his future triumphs.

PART TWO

*

THE CONQUEST OF PARIS

CHAPTER I

Discovery of the Palais-Royal, Charles Nodier, and Paternity

He cast upon that buzzing hive a look which seemed already to be extracting the honey, and spoke these mighty words: 'Now it's between you and me: the fight is on!' BALZAC

WHEN he got back to Villers-Cotterets, drunk with joy and ambition, the young Dumas told his mother that his mind was made up: he would settle in Paris. Only there would he find a theatre worthy of his talents, a stage over which he would one day, he felt, reign as king. But how was he to get the money for his initial expenses? The poor widow of General Dumas, having lost her parents, had been compelled to realize such assets as she had inherited, in order to pay her outstanding debts. The total sum remaining to her was two hundred and fifty-three francs. She was prepared to give fifty to her son. He, for his part, had sold his dog, Pyrame, for a hundred. But all this amounted to no more than a drop in the ocean. How was he going to live in the capital?

'I will go to see some of my father's old friends: Marshal Victor, duc de Bellune, who is now Minister of War; General Sebastiani, and Marshal Jourdan . . . They will find me a job as clerk in one of the departments of the Civil Service, at a starting salary of twelve hundred francs a year. Later on, I shall get a rise, and when I am earning fifteen hundred, I will send for you to join me.'

For Alexandre, to want a thing badly enough was to have it. His mother, whose head was less in the clouds, raised objections. How would those military men, now royalists, and the more ardent for being only recently converted, receive the son of a republican general? That presented no problem to Alexandre. He would furnish himself with a letter of introduction to General Foy, a Deputy, and Leader of the Opposition. As to the price of his fare, he would win that at billiards with old Cartier, who was agent for the sale of diligence tickets. And this, in fact, was what he did.

At five o'clock one morning, the diligence dropped the young Dumas at N° 9 rue de Bouloi, in the very heart of Paris. He was twenty years old, without any experience of life, but with enough and to spare of hope. He took up his quarters at the 'Hôtel des Grands-Augustins', where he was remembered as the hare and partridge boy. He slept for four hours, then hastened to Adolphe de Leuven for the addresses of Marshal Jourdan, General Sebastiani, and the duc de Bellune. Leuven, not a little surprised, consulted the directory, provided the required information, and warned his visitor that his plans would probably come to nothing. He was right. Two of the generals saw the applicant, but one seemed to entertain doubts of the young man's identity, while the other quite simply showed him the door. The Minister of War refused to see him. The Opposition was now his only hope, in other words, General Foy. His reception there was very different.

'Are you the son of the General Dumas who commanded the Army of the Alps?'

'Yes, sir.'

'He was a brave fellow, and I shall be glad to do anything in my power to help you.'

Alexandre explained what he needed. He was looking for work, and the matter was of some urgency.

'Well now, let us see. How much do you know? A little mathematics, I suppose, a few odds and ends of algebra, geometry and physics?'

'No, sir.'

'Have you read any law?'

'No, sir.'

'Damnation! ... I might, perhaps, get the banker Laffitte to give you a chance ... Do you know anything of book-keeping?'

'Nothing at all, sir.'

The general was more and more at a loss. Dumas admitted that his education had been neglected, but undertook to repair the gaps.

'But meanwhile, young man, have you got enough to live on?'

'No, sir.'

'Hell and brimstone! ... You'd better give me your address. I must think matters over.'

The young man wrote down his address. The general watched him doing so, and suddenly clapped his hands.

'We are saved!' he exclaimed. 'You write a good hand!'

That, indeed, was his only recommendation, except his genius, which had not yet been revealed. But the general seemed to think that it was sufficient.

'I am dining today with the duc d'Orléans,' said he. 'I will speak to him about you as a possible member of his secretariat.'

The duc d'Orléans (later to reign as Louis-Philippe) was on better terms with the Opposition deputies, in whose plotting he played something of a part, than with the Government of his cousin, Charles X. Next day, when Dumas, who, in spite of his self-assurance, was beginning to feel uneasy, called again on General Foy, the latter said to him with a smile:

'It's all fixed up. You are to enter the secretariat of the duc d'Orléans at a salary of twelve hundred francs a year. That's not much I'm afraid, but it is up to you now to work well and better yourself.'[1]

Not much! For Dumas it was untold wealth. He lost no time in writing to his mother, telling her to sell what possessions she still had and to join him. She had sufficient common sense to insist on delay. Meanwhile, she sent him a few pieces of furniture, and he took a small room at N° 1 Place des Italiens.[2] He would be working at the Palais-Royal, which was the headquarters of the Orléans family. The Prince had installed there his personal secretariat, and the office charged with the administration of his private estates, which were immense. A whole staff of officials was employed, and one of these was Dumas's cousin, Deviolaine, now Director-General of all forest lands. When Dumas reported to his chief, Monsieur Oudard, he was kindly received, and given an office. It was there that, from now on, he would work each day, from ten in the morning until five in the afternoon, returning again in the evening from seven till ten. How was he going to find the time in which to become a Great Man?

He had promised General Foy that he would go on with his studies, and in this undertaking he was helped by the second-in-command of his department, Lassagne, a man of remarkably wide and deep literary culture. Lassagne showed astonishment at the young man's ignorance, but also at his intelligence. He drew up for him an excellent programme of reading, which extended from Aeschylus to Schiller, taking in Plautus and Molière on the way. He lent him the French and foreign classics, as well as memoirs and volumes of literary criticism. Dumas devoured everything with the appetite of a virgin mind. When one reads the masters at too early an age, one does not understand them, and develops a loathing for their works. When one comes upon them at twenty, one is beginning to be conscious of the feelings they describe, and grows attached to them. So it was with Alexandre Dumas. When he arrived in Paris in 1823, a new literature was emerging from its birth-pangs. Lamartine had published his *Méditations*; Victor Hugo his *Odes et Ballades*; Alfred de Vigny, a number of poems. The junior assistant in the secretariat of the duc d'Orléans did not know even the names of these writers, but without being aware of it he shared their longing for some sort of renewal.

His first contact with the literary school which soon took Paris by storm was brought about by the most efficient of all guides — chance. From the moment of his arrival he had been filled with a longing to go to the theatre that he might learn his *true* trade — since meeting Leuven and Talma he had felt sure that he would one day be a dramatist. At a performance of *Le Vampire*, a ridiculous melodrama, he found himself sitting next to a charming, erudite and white-haired man with whom the young provincial, in his bold, rough and ready way, started a conversation. This agreeable neighbour, amused by the simple-minded frankness exhibited by Dumas, gave him a lesson in the love of books, followed by a lecture on taste, and then, at the end of the third act, was thrown out for indulging in cat-calls. Next day, Dumas read in the papers that the name of the disturber of the peace was Charles Nodier, a celebrated author. Lassagne informed him that Nodier was a brilliant critic and a writer of novels and strange tales, and that to be accepted by him as a friend would be a great honour. But, he added, before one could hope to be received by a man of Nodier's stamp, one must be successful.

But how? Leuven, with whom he remained in close contact, encouraged him to try his wings in one of the easier forms of dramatic writing. In collaboration they produced a verse comedy, *La Chasse et l'Amour*. Apart from a few fairly funny caricatures of the Villers-Cotterets sportsmen, it was a vulgar and mediocre affair, though when it was produced at the Ambigu, it put three hundred francs in Dumas's pocket — the equivalent of three months' salary! This, to be sure, was encouraging, and the fifteen gold louis arrived just in the nick of time, for the young author, having already forgotten his rustic love affair, had embarked on the seduction of a sentimental dressmaker who was eight years his senior.

Catherine Labay lived on the same landing as he did in the Place des Italiens. She had established a small work-room, employing a few work-girls, which she ran very competently. Fair and rather plump, with a very white skin and a serious temperament, she was a native of Rouen, where she claimed to have married, and then left, a 'half-mad' husband. In point of fact, this union was wholly fictitious, the madman entirely imaginary. Later, when Catherine Labay acknowledged Alexandre Dumas *fils* as her child, she had, in order to make the declaration legally valid, to confess that she was unmarried.[3]

On Sundays, Alexandre Dumas took his fair neighbour for walks in the woods of Meudon. There they would rest, first upon the grass, then in a dark grotto. There is nothing more dangerous for the virtue of young dressmakers than a grotto. The blue-eyed quadroon was ardent, persuasive, terrifyingly virile, and quite unusually handsome. Before long, Catherine realized that she was with child by him. She induced her lover, on the score of economy, to share her lodgings, and there, on July 27th, 1824, gave birth to a fine boy who was given the name of Alexandre, third of the name.

So here was the young assistant-secretary a father at twenty-two, filled with the highest regard for the mother of his son, but by no means disposed to take her as his companion for life. He had quite other ideas. His reading had led him to imagine great ladies throwing themselves at his feet, beautiful actresses mad with love for him, and rake-helly suppers. The little dressmaker had many good qualities — common sense, a love of hard work, loyalty and even charm. But she was entirely uneducated and had no presentable relations. Dumas was determined to keep himself available for adventures of a more intoxicating kind.

Then, too, there was the general's widow, his mother, to whom he had not dared to mention either his liaison or his paternity. She had found her separation from him over-long and, fearing that she had not many years to live, now suggested that she should join him. He at once acquiesced and took an apartment for her — 53 Faubourg-Saint-Denis — at a rental of three hundred and fifty francs a year. His salary had been raised and he was now in receipt of fifteen hundred, instead of twelve hundred, francs. His beautiful handwriting had made such an impression that Oudard, his chief, had recommended him to the duc d'Orléans as the best copyist in the office, and a man capable of working fast and well.

'You are, are you not, the son of a brave man whom Bonaparte left to die of hunger? . . . You write a good hand, your addressing of envelopes is admirable. Come into this room, sit down at the table, and I will give you a document to copy.'⁴

A fortnight after this memorable interview, Dumas was 'established', that is to say, he was confirmed in his employment and guaranteed against dying of hunger. His work had only one disadvantage; it took up so much of his time that he had very few opportunities of going to the theatre. Every other week, he was responsible for 'making up the pouch', that is to say for sending after dinner, to Neuilly, for the duc d'Orléans to see, the evening papers and the whole of the day's mail. This done, he had to stay at the office until such time as Monseigneur's instructions should reach him. On those evenings it was impossible for him to see a play, except at the Comédie-Française, which was under the same roof as the Palais-Royal offices. This was fine when Talma was playing, or Mademoiselle Mars. When they were not, Dumas settled down to read translations of Walter Scott and Byron, while awaiting the arrival of the messenger from Neuilly.

'Those are the authors with whom the future lies!' his brilliant sub-director, Lassagne, would say to him. 'The neo-classical tragedies of our day will be soon forgotten. More venturesome writers will emerge. See that you are one of them!'

He knew that if only he had time for his own work, he could produce masterpieces. Somehow or other he must get rid of the 'pouch', which ate away his evenings. How could he observe human passions unless he moved freely in the world of real men and women? How could he do that, when he never left the office until ten p.m. and then in a state of exhaustion?

CHAPTER II

Discovery of the Drama: of 'Christine' and of Mademoiselle Mars

IN 1827 a company of English players visited Paris and gave a number of performances, first at the Odéon, then at the Théâtre Favart. Earlier still, in 1822, another company had tried the experiment of giving Shakespeare in English at the Porte-Saint-Martin. But the time had not been ripe. France was too close to Waterloo and Wellington. The English were the friends of Louis XVIII, and that was enough to put them out of favour with the pit. The wretched actors had been pelted with apples and oranges — a somewhat strange form of patriotism.

Five years after this first, unfortunate attempt, the intellectual climate had completely changed. Great actors, Frédérick Lemaître, and Marie Dorval, had raised melodrama to the level of true art. But the victory was not yet complete. Drama, exiled to the boulevard, had still to be granted the freedom of the Comédie-Française. Even in times of revolution, France has certain consecrated fanes in which it insists that all glory shall be duly anointed. Napoleon had insisted on being crowned in Notre-Dame: and now the young iconoclasts of the stage were intent on invading the Théâtre-Français. Consequently a comparison between Shakespeare — who was only very little known in France through the medium of appallingly bad translations — and the great classical tragedies was much looked forward to.

The success of the English actors was staggering. The violence of their pantomime produced first astonishment, then enthusiasm. The death-scenes, in which Kean writhed and twisted, stunned a public accustomed to the decent deceases of the Théâtre-Français. Kemble died as 'people really do die'. His satanic and sardonic laughter was to infect the French stage for a long time to come. Miss Harriet Smithson, in her scenes of madness and starvation, was no less realistic than her companions. When Mademoiselle Mars went again and again to see the English company, the 'romantics' were triumphant. 'Our actors have gone back to school', they said, 'and stare their eyes out.'[1]

The English influence led the performers of the boulevard to exaggerate their effects, and to demand more and more scenes of madness, delirium and death. Bocage and Dorval longed for plays which would give them the chance of rivalling the all-conquering visitors. Dumas swore to himself that he would provide them. He was present at every one of the English performances, and took notes.

I have seen *Othello* played by Talma, Kean, Kemble, Macready, and Joanny. Talma made of him a Moor with a thin veneer of Venetian culture: Kean, a wild and ferocious beast, half tiger, half man: Kemble, a man in his ripe maturity, swept beyond the point where he could exercise self-control, and turned violent. With Macready, he was an Arab of the time of the Abencérages, elegant and chivalrous. With Joanny, he was — Joanny.[2]

He wildly applauded Macready and Kean, Kemble and the lovely Harriet Smithson. The scenes of frantic jealousy, assassination and suicide, Othello's torment, Desdemona's death, completely bowled him over. 'For the first time', he wrote, 'I saw in the theatre real passions felt by women and men of real flesh and blood.'[3] He knew no English, but the actors' movements and the inflexions of their voices were sufficient to arouse his enthusiasm.

It was while witnessing Shakespeare's tragedies that he realized what it was that he wanted to do: to paint with a free brush; to bring upon the stage that physical violence which the classic writers had left in the wings; to work upon the public through the medium of sensational dramatic contrivances. He was far from having any profound experience of the passions; but what he did have was an inborn sense of drama. What subjects should he choose? The themes of antiquity had been annexed by the classic authors. The history of his own day was too ticklish. Chance brought it about that, while paying a visit to the annual Salon of painting and sculpture, he found himself attracted by a bas-relief representing the murder of Giovanni Monaldeschi, who had been killed by order of Queen Christina of Sweden, in 1657, in the *galérie des cerfs* at Fontainebleau. Monaldeschi? Christina? Who, precisely, had they been? The young Dumas had no knowledge of that grim incident. He borrowed a *Universal Biography* from a friend, Frédéric Soulié, a man of culture and substance, who had inherited a thriving carpentry business. He read the articles on Monaldeschi and Christina.

He learned that Monaldeschi, who was the lover of the Queen of Sweden and jealous of the rising star of another Italian, Sentinelli, had written a number of abusive and imprudent letters, and had been put to death by his rival in the Palace of Fontainebleau at the behest of the furious queen. There to his hand was the raw material of a drama.

'Let's do it together,' he said to Soulié, with whom he had already tried to adapt for the stage one of Walter Scott's novels.

'But it's not a drama,' objected Soulié, 'it's a tragedy.'

They decided that they should each produce a *Christine*. The one who finished first should try his luck. Dumas was still no more than a minor clerk in the secretariat of the duc d'Orléans, with little spare time. At all costs, he must have his evenings to himself. Plucking up courage, he sought another interview with Monsieur Oudard.

'The only way in which I can give you what you want,' said that gentleman, not unkindly, 'is by getting you moved from the personal secretariat to one of the departments where you would not have to work at night, say Forestry Inspection ... but the whole of your future would be compromised by such a change.'

Dumas was convinced that there was no future for him in office work and accepted the change. He was duly moved to the Forestry Department ruled over by the rough-tongued, soft-hearted Deviolaine. He at once caused a scandal by demanding a room to himself where he could work in solitude. Thanks to his protector, Oudard, he obtained this further favour. Freed now from all detailed supervision, separated from his chief and from his fellow-clerks, he found it possible, thanks to the rapidity with which he could write in his admirable hand, to get through his work at high speed, and filch several hours each day in the interests of the theatre. Soon *Christine*, a verse-drama in five acts, was ready.

'I felt as much embarrassment', said Dumas, 'as a poor girl who has just given birth to a child out of wedlock.'⁴ What was he to do with the bastard — smother it, as he had smothered the tragedies which he had written in former years? That seemed to him a cruel expedient. The child gave every sign of being strong and of wanting only to be allowed to live. All that was needed was a theatre which would take the foundling in, and a public ready to adopt it. But how to find either of these? If only Talma had been still alive, Dumas would have reminded him of their meeting. But Talma had died in 1826, and Dumas knew nobody at the Théâtre-Français.

The prompter of that illustrious playhouse used to go each month to the office in the Palais-Royal with the tickets to which the duc d'Orléans was entitled. Dumas stopped the man with the bushy eyebrows as he was on his way to carry out this monthly duty, and asked what he should do in order to be granted the honour of being allowed to read a play to the Committee. He was told that the manuscript must be deposited with the 'Examiner', that there was already an accumulation of several thousand, that he might have to wait for years.

'Is it not possible to shorten the formalities?'

'Certainly there is, if you know Baron Taylor.'

Baron Taylor, an Englishman born in Brussels, naturalized a Frenchman, and holding a commission in the French army, the friend of Victor Hugo and of Alfred de Vigny, had become in 1825 at the age of thirty-six, through the patronage of Charles X by whom he had been ennobled, *Commissaire du Roi auprès de la Comédie-Française.* The appointment was by no means a bad one. Taylor was, among other things, a painter, and had designed stage-settings and costumes. He had produced a number of comedies and, in collaboration with Nodier, had translated an English play. He had served in the army with Vigny; Hugo had been introduced to him by Chateaubriand, and Adèle Hugo had invited him to an informal luncheon. He had been appointed to the Comédie-Française for the purpose of introducing a little order into that establishment. As was right and proper, he had big ideas, one of which consisted in putting on unactable plays, such as Chateaubriand's *Moïse.* His English name was an offence in the eyes of the classicists. 'This compatriot of Shakespeare', said one disgruntled actor, 'despises Corneille, Racine and Voltaire.' He was rudely criticized for his sumptuous settings, his lavish expenditure, and his literary tastes. In the opinion of impartial witnesses, his administration was honest and liberal-minded, and he did a great deal to establish the romantic school in France. In 1828 *Roméo et Juliette* by Vigny and Deschamps had, thanks to him, been accepted for production by the Comédie-Française. True, the play never reached the stage, but one can't have everything at once.

Dumas asked Lassagne, the erudite and friendly sub-director: 'Do you know Baron Taylor?'

'No,' replied Lassagne; 'but he is very intimate with Nodier ...
You've told me that you once exchanged words with Nodier when you
happened to be sitting next him at the theatre ... write and remind
him of the meeting.'

'He'll have forgotten all about me!'

'He never forgets anything: write.'

The risk was not great; Dumas wrote, mentioning *Le Vampire*,
their bookish talk, the cat-calls, Nodier's expulsion, and begging for a
letter of introduction to Taylor. The reply was not long delayed and
took the form of a note from Taylor himself, making an appointment
for seven o'clock in the morning. At the hour fixed, Dumas turned up
at the house of the *Commissaire du Roi*. An old woman opened the
door to him.

'Come along in, young man. I'm listening,' called Taylor, who was
in his bath.

'I propose to read one act only. If that bores you, you must stop
me.'

'Capital!' muttered Taylor. 'You have more compassion than most
of your kidney. Start away — it's a good sign. I am all ears.'

Dumas read the first act, and then, without looking up from his
manuscript, asked: 'Shall I go on, sir?'

'Yes, indeed,' said Taylor who was shivering. 'I'm going back to
bed ... It's really dam' good.'

It was the *Commissaire du Roi* himself who insisted on the third, the
fourth and, finally, the fifth, act. When the reading was finished, he
jumped out of bed, exclaiming: 'You're coming along with me to the
Théâtre-Français, now, at once!'

'What for?'

'To get put on the reading-list.'

'Does that mean that I'm going to read *Christine* to the Committee?'

'Next Saturday.'

Dumas did read *Christine* to the Committee, and made acquaintance
for the first time with the kings and queens of the theatre. The play was
accepted 'subject to alteration'. Because of its many audacities, it was
to be submitted to an author upon whom the authorities could rely.
But Dumas was too much excited to attach much importance to this
stipulation. His play had been taken by the Comédie-Française! He
was only twenty-six! What a miracle! His mother, seeing him come

home well before his usual time, was frightened. What had happened? Had Alexandre been given the sack from the Palais-Royal?

'Accepted, Mother!' he cried. 'Accepted with applause!'

He began to dance round the room. The general's widow thought he had gone mad. She pointed out to him that he would be late back at the office and might be dismissed.

'So much the better! That'll give me time to attend rehearsals!'

'And if your play is a failure, what are we going to live on?'

'I'll write another, which will be a success.'

In the course of the day, the famous actor Firmin called on Alexandre Dumas in his office, to inform him that Monsieur Picard, the author of a hundred comedies (*Le Collatéral, La Petite Ville, Les Provinciaux à Paris, Les Deux Philibert, Les Ricochets*) which had enjoyed a glittering, if ephemeral, success, had been chosen as the man to work over the manuscript of *Christine*.[5] The choice was ridiculous. This comic writer, devoid alike of talent and generosity of mind, could scarcely be expected to feel anything but horror at so violent and audacious a drama. When, a week later, Firmin and Dumas called to hear the verdict, the little hunchback with a pointed nose, after having politely inquired after his visitors' health, said to Dumas, with a charming smile:

'My dear sir, I sincerely hope that you have the means of earning your livelihood.'

'Monsieur,' replied Dumas, 'I am a junior clerk in the service of Monsieur le duc d'Orléans, at a salary of fifteen hundred francs a year.'

'Good. The best advice I can give you, my dear young man, is to go back to your office-stool.'[6]

Was the man sincere or merely jealous? Firmin asserts that he spoke in good faith. This Dumas could not believe. How could anyone read *Christine* without realizing that the author had 'something in him'? That, certainly, was the opinion of Baron Taylor, who insisted upon a second opinion — this time, that of the good Charles Nodier. Nodier wasted no time. On the very next day, Taylor was able to show Dumas a note in Nodier's own hand on the first page of *Christine*: 'It is my true and honest opinion that *Christine* is one of the most remarkable works which I have read for twenty years.'

Was this a sound judgment? The verse was nothing like so good as that of the young poets who were Dumas's contemporaries. Victor

Hugo, born in the same year, 1802, had a power, a gift of words and a virtuosity far superior to Dumas's mere animal high spirits. Nevertheless, the latter stood out as a born man of the theatre. He knew, as though by instinct, how to construct a play, and how to appeal to the feelings of an audience. The actors were present on the following Sunday (so as not to encroach on the hours which Dumas, alas! had to devote to the office) at a second reading. Once again *Christine* was accepted, on condition that the author should agree with Samson, the doyen, on certain changes. Dumas, says Samson, showed himself to be most accommodating.

As matters turned out, the play was not, after all, performed in the Théâtre-Français. Why? The home of Molière was not very hospitable. Since the death of Talma, Mademoiselle Mars had reigned there as queen. She was rounding the promontory of her fiftieth year with considerable wariness. She reserved the best parts, from courtesans to ingénues for herself — with a special partiality for ingénues. She had the reputation of being a 'bad trouper', and was fighting tooth and nail to hold her position. Her enemies, with feigned generosity, said that she did not look a day more than forty-eight. Sometimes she herself would announce the approaching end of her long reign, but it was put about, all the same, that she would give a 'farewell performance — till the next time'. The truth of the matter was that her miraculous appearance of youthfulness, her air of ripe tranquillity and her perfect diction were her sufficient guarantee of an authority which nothing could shake. Where casting was concerned, her word was law. She put the fear of God into authors. Mademoiselle Mars had made her reputation in classic roles and was ill-suited to romantic drama as understood by Hugo and Dumas. Marivaux, not Shakespeare, was her natural element. In the dramas of which Dumas was dreaming, the heroine would have to tear her hair, shriek and drag herself about the stage on her knees. Mademoiselle Mars lacked the bad taste which makes a good shrieker. Her voice, even when she raised it, still retained its pleasing quality. She was more like a young girl in a temper than a roaring lioness.

She went to see the young Dumas in his miserable little office at the Palais-Royal, surrounded by dusty files, and talked to him about *Christine*. Assuming her most gracious manner (and, God knows, she could be charming when she liked!) she criticized the way in which the parts had been allotted, the play, and, more especially, certain lines which she would have to speak and which she wanted him to delete. Dumas was dazzled by the sight of this Tragedy Queen among the quill-drivers, but stuck to his belief — quite wrongly — that the offending lines were the most beautiful ever written. He therefore defended them with fierce determination. The discussion lasted for a few minutes, at the end of which Mademoiselle Mars rose to her feet and, as tight-lipped on leaving as she had been ingratiating on arrival, said: 'Have it your own way, then: your verses shall be spoken, but I think you will be not a little surprised when you see the effect they produce.'

With these words she swept out. During rehearsals, however, whenever she came to the lines in question, she suppressed them.

'Cut!' she said to Garnier, the prompter. 'The author is going to delete the next few lines.'

'The author is going to do nothing of the sort!' said Dumas. 'I insist on your speaking them.'

'*Ah diable!*' sighed Garnier.

Dumas asked what precisely he meant by '*ah diable!*'

'I mean that if Mademoiselle does not wish to speak your lines then they will remain unspoken.'

'If the piece is going to be played, she's just *got* to speak them!'

'Yes, *if* — but it won't be!'

The prompter knew better than anyone of what diabolical tricks Mademoiselle was capable. *Christine* never did reach the stage of the Comédie-Française. Specious reasons were advanced. Another *Christine*, by a man called Brault, a dramatist and a former sub-prefect, had been accepted a week after Dumas's. Brault being at death's door, his play must be given priority. Furthermore, Frédéric Soulié, too, had finished *his* version, and had offered it to the Odéon. This procession of *Christine*s was becoming farcical. The only thing to be done was to withdraw the play. This decision was fortunate for Dumas, since it would give him time in which to revise and improve a text which badly needed attention.

But how was he to live without *Christine*? Alexandre Dumas's two establishments were dependent, for their existence, on the presentation of his drama. Garnier breathed a word of advice in his ear:

'Write another play and give the principal part to Mademoiselle Mars. Avoid lines of thirty-six feet. Be careful not to cross her *in anything*, and you'll be certain of a production.'

'But, my dear Garnier,' said Dumas, 'one writes only the sort of verse one is capable of writing . . . As a matter of fact, I'm planning to write a drama in prose.'

'So much the better.'

'I'll try to dig up a subject.'[7]

At precisely this moment, chance, his best friend, most fortunately supplied him with a new theme. Going one day into the office of one of his colleagues, he saw, lying open on a table, a large tome by the historian Anquetil, in which he read an anecdote having to do with the reign of Henri III. The duc de Guise, Henri le Balafré, aware that his wife, Catherine de Clèves, was deceiving him with one of the king's 'minions', Paul de Caussade, comte de Saint-Mégrin, had decided to give a lesson to his duchess, in spite of the fact that he cared very little about her infidelity.

One day, at dawn, he entered her room, holding a dagger in one hand and a potion in the other. 'Choose, madame,' he said, 'how you will die, by dagger or by poison.' She wept, implored, begged to be forgiven. 'No, madame, you must choose.' She drank the 'poison', fell on her knees, called upon God to pardon her, and waited for death. At the end of an hour, Guise reassured her. The 'poison' had been nothing but a bowl of excellent soup. Nevertheless, the lesson had been a cruel one.

What a marvellous scene! thought the young Dumas. I'd love to write it. But who was this duc de Guise? Who was Saint-Mégrin?

As always, he had recourse to his faithful and knowledgeable friend, the *Universal Biography*, which provided him with a certain number of details and referred him to the *Mémoires* of Estoile . . . Who was Estoile? . . . The invaluable *Universal Biography* informed him that Pierre Taisan de l'Estoile (1546-1611) had been the famous chronicler of the reigns of Henri III and Henri IV. Dumas borrowed the book and found it fascinating. From it he learned that Saint-Mégrin, first gentleman of the Royal Chamber, had been assassinated in the street in 1578, by order of Henri de Guise, nicknamed le Balafré, to teach him what happened to those who made love to princesses. A good scene, though somewhat commonplace. Farther on in the work of the same chronicler, he came upon an admirable motive which would give an added flavour to the drama. The fact that it concerned another personage of the same period, Bussy d'Amboise (1549-1579), made no odds. Dumas was writing a play, not a history-book.

This young Bussy, the lover of Françoise de Chambes, comtesse de

Montsoreau,* received a note in her hand, asking him to visit her on a specified night during her husband's absence. This she had written in obedience to the husband's orders, and, in order to save her life, had agreed to be caught 'in the act' by the jealous Charles de Montsoreau. Bussy was killed at midnight in his mistress's bedroom by her husband, who burst in, accompanied by several friends, all armed.

With the passage relating to Bussy ready to his hand, and memories of Schiller and Walter Scott in his head, Dumas decided that he now had the necessary materials for a play. He would have to work up a few period details, and provide some local colour, 'good Henri III stuff', but he was not the man to be put off by such minor considerations! He had at his service books, learned friends, and a richly equipped imagination. He wrote the whole of *Henri III et sa Cour* in two months.

CHAPTER III

How Success comes to Young Men

IT was by no means a bad play. Doubtless, the learned and the sophisticated had some reason to make fun of a young 'hoodlum' who had discovered the history of France in a book left open, by chance, on a table. Doubtless, too, it might be said that his analysis of feelings and character was lacking in depth; that there was no subtlety in his portrayal of the duc de Guise and the King; that he placed too much reliance on incidental 'business' (the duchess's arm gripped by an iron gauntlet — a lost handkerchief, as in *Othello*); that he had borrowed most of his ideas from Shakespeare and Schiller.

This is all perfectly true; all the same, Dumas did manage to construct a well-made play which was capable of appealing to an audience. He had ransacked every available source — memoirs, chronicles, contemporary prints. A whole period was recreated for the spectator as, through his reading, it had been for the young enthusiast. Could it be called history? No more and no less than what was to be found in Walter Scott. History is a confusion of mysteries. In Dumas's play, everything was made as clear as daylight. Catherine de Medicis controls the action. Henri III outwits the plots of the duc de Guise. Dumas was perfectly well aware that the real story had been much more complicated.

But why should he let that bother him? All he wanted was violent action. The age of Henri III, with its duels, its intrigues, its debauchery, and the bitterness of its political hatreds, reminded him of the Napoleonic period. History, rearranged by Dumas, was what the French people longed for; something lightly handled, highly coloured, with simple contrasts of white and black, the Good on one side, the Bad on the other. The public of 1829 which filled the pit was made up of those who had carried through the Great Revolution and fought in the wars of the Empire. They liked to see kings and queens placed in situations which were 'heroic, familiar and dramatic'.[1] Brutality was food and drink to old 'sweats'. They, too, had held white arms in too tight a grip, and threatened their rivals with drawn swords. Dramatic realism? Murders done in full view of the audience? Goethe had not been afraid of such things, nor had Shakespeare. Hugo and Vigny, when their time came, would not disdain them. Dumas was the first writer in France to introduce melodrama to the serious stage.

But, it will be asked, what about Hugo's *Cromwell*? Well, *Cromwell*, though read in public, had never been played. Hugo had had to be satisfied with a reading, with publication, and with a *Préface*. Dumas was quite determined to get *Henri III* staged at the Comédie-Française. He began by reading the play to a select gathering at the house of a romantic hostess, Mélanie Waldor, the wife of an army officer, and the daughter of a man of letters.[2] This was followed by a second reading at the house of Nestor Roqueplan, a journalist. Fifteen young men listened to it, crowded together on mattresses. Dumas's audacities were much to their taste. 'To hell with *Christine*!' they shouted. 'We want *Henri III*!' Firmin, the actor, was enthusiastic, and organized a third reading. Among those who heard it was Béranger, the song-writer, who was considered at that time to be the greatest poet of the day, a liberal, a scoffer, the friend of Laffitte, the banker. Mademoiselle Mars was present, and the widow of General Dumas. Mademoiselle Mars saw in the duchesse de Guise — and rightly — a part well within her capabilities. It would give her an opportunity to express that mingling of modesty and passion in which she excelled. She would be involved in scenes of violence only as a victim. She pressed for the play's acceptance.

The actors present decided to ask the Théâtre-Français to smile on the venture, and preparations were made for its production. On the next day, at the Palais-Royal, the baron de Broval, the Director-General of the Secretariat, sent for Dumas. He was a bit of a curmudgeon, arrogant in manner, and a glib talker. His attitude, when he received his young subordinate, held a threat of storm. He began the interview by telling the budding playwright that literature and the Civil Service were incompatible. He must choose between them.

'Sir,' replied Dumas, 'Monseigneur le duc d'Orléans is generally regarded as being a patron of letters. I shall take no steps until he informs me that I must leave his service. I shall *not* send in my resignation. As to my salary, if the hundred and twenty-five francs a month which I receive lays too heavy a burden on His Highness's budget, I am prepared to do without them.'

'What will you live on?'

'That, sir, is my business.'

Next day, the payment of his salary was suspended. But he had already planned to get an introduction to Laffitte, through the good offices of Béranger. A meeting was arranged, and Laffitte agreed to pay Dumas three thousand francs. The only security he demanded was that the manuscript of *Henri III* should be placed in his strongroom. The sum represented two years' salary! The young man hastened with the money to his mother. The general's widow was dumbfounded. Perhaps, after all, the theatre *was* a way of earning a living!

The rehearsals brought no very serious disagreements. The duc de Guise was played by Joanny, 'a former soldier, firm and vigorous',[3] who spoke the 'curtain lines' — on which Dumas always lavished great care — to perfection:

'Saint-Paul! Let me have the same men who killed Dugast!'

'Now shall this door open but once again — for him!'

'We have done with the servant: our business now is with the master!'

Christine had taught Dumas a lesson, and he was affable and accommodating in his dealings with the company.

'You understand these matters better than I,' he said. 'Whatever you do will, I am sure, be well done.'

The work was the more delightful to him, in that he was beginning to take a personal interest in Virginie Bourbier, a young actress who had been given a small part in his play. Alexandre was incapable of resisting the temptations of the body. He was still helping Catherine Labay and providing money for the upbringing of his son, but the idea of remaining loyal to one woman seemed to him sheer lunacy.

Naturally he still had to face difficulties with the divine Mademoiselle Mars. But he was gaining experience and, this time, succeeded in outwitting the tricks of Célimène, though not without much fury and grinding of teeth. 'Oh! this Théâtre-Français!' he wrote: 'it is certainly one of the circles of hell which Dante overlooked, where God has seen fit to confine dramatic authors who have had the curious idea of making a great deal less money in the theatre than they could have done in any other employment, and getting a decoration at the end of their lives, not for any success they may have had, but as some compensation for all the sufferings they have endured.' In this he was less than fair, for the actors and actresses of the Comédie served him well.

One major misfortune occurred during rehearsals. The general's widow had an apoplectic seizure which left her paralysed down one side. What was to be done? Postpone the production? That would have been of no use to his mother who was, unfortunately, beyond all help. He agreed that the first night should be fixed for February 11th, 1829. On the day before the crucial date, he went to the Palais-Royal and sought an audience with the duc d'Orléans. He was ushered into the Presence.

'Why, Monsieur Dumas,' said the duke, 'what good wind blows *you* here?'

'Monseigneur, I have come to ask a favour. *Henri III et sa Cour* is being played tomorrow for the first time. Will you do me the honour of being present? Your Royal Highness has passed sentence upon me rather too quickly. Tomorrow, the case is to receive a public trial. You would be doing me a great kindness by being in court when the verdict is given.'

The duke said that nothing would have given him greater pleasure, but that, as it happened, he was to entertain thirty princes and princesses at dinner on that evening.

'If you, sire, will advance the hour of your dinner, I will postpone the opening of my play, so that your august guests may have the opportunity of witnessing a very curious spectacle.'

'Damme! That's an idea! Tell Taylor that I wish to reserve the whole of the circle.'

The long-expected moment arrived. The house presented a wonderful appearance. Princes covered with decorations; princesses dripping with diamonds: the demi-monde in all its beauty. Béranger, Vigny and Hugo in a box. The stalls solid with friends. The play was a great success. The brutality of the third act, in which the jealous Guise forces his wife to write the fatal note to Saint-Mégrin, not only shocked nobody, but was greeted with applause. In the interval, Dumas rushed to the rue Saint-Denis to embrace his mother. At the end of the fourth act, pandemonium broke loose. When Firmin announced the name of the author, the whole house, including the duc d'Orléans, rose to its feet. Next morning, Dumas received a letter from the baron de Broval, who had so harshly dismissed him. 'I cannot go to bed, my dear young friend, without telling you how delighted I am at your success. Your colleagues and I rejoice in your triumph.'[4]

When success comes, one is always astonished at the number of those who suddenly discover that they are one's friends.

The play was performed thirty-eight times. The box-office receipts were splendid, in spite of the intrigues set on foot by the 'classic' authors and the 'experts'. The Battle of the Romantics was setting the Théâtre-Français by the ears. The classicists attributed the triumph of the new school to the 'formidable forces which had packed the pit and even sprinkled the boxes'.[5] Sympathy was extended to the talented actors who had to demean themselves to perform at the level of mere drama. 'If the public wants sobs', said the 'experts' contemptuously, 'let it look for them on the boulevards, but let the Théâtre-Français, at least, be preserved from this deplorable contagion.' The actors, whose bread and butter was provided by the public, were not of this opinion.

In the morning, Alexandre Dumas awoke to find himself famous. His poor mother's bedroom was filled with bouquets which the sick woman could not even see. A bookseller bought the right to publish *Henri III* for six thousand francs, more than the salary of a director of a Civil Service department. But the second night found the committee of the Comédie in a state of consternation. The play had been banned! The King, Charles X, had suddenly decided that Henri III and his cousin of Guise were intended to represent the reigning monarch and his Orléans relative! It was the duc d'Orléans himself who had the ban lifted.

'I have written to the King as follows,' said the duke: ' "Sire, you have been misled on three grounds. In the first place, I do not beat my wife. In the second place, the duchess does not cuckold me. In the third place, Your Majesty has no more loyal subject than myself. . . ." '[6]

And so it came about that, at twenty-seven, the young man who had so recently arrived from Villers-Cotterets, without any prospect of work, without influence, without academic distinctions of any kind, without money, and without even an adequate education, turned himself into a well-known, an almost illustrious, figure, acknowledged as an equal by the small and brilliant group which was about to bring new life to French poetry and the French theatre. What an astonishing sequence of coincidences it had needed to land him, in the end, on the dizzy pinnacle of success: his meeting with Leuven, who had been the means of directing his attention to the stage; his meeting with Nodier one evening when they had both gone to see *Le Vampire*; a bas-relief glimpsed in a gallery; a book left lying open by Destiny at precisely the right page; the presence at the Théâtre-Français of Taylor, with his sympathetic attitude to the new school. But chance helps only those who deserve help. Every man has ten chances offered to him every day which may alter the whole course of his life. Success comes to those who know how to take them. The young Alexandre Dumas enlisted in the service of an immense ambition a prodigious imagination, a passion for the heroic, an astonishing power of work, a culture which, though desultory, was ardent. He succeeded, not because circumstances had been kind to him, but because he was ready and able to turn every circumstance to his advantage.

PART THREE

★

ANTONY

What a good creature! He was like an overgrown child, so artless and so honest was his face!
MARCELINE DESBORDES-VALMORE

CHAPTER I

Mélanie Waldor

IN 1829 Dumas was twenty-seven, a colossus endowed with a strange and virile beauty. The author of a play which had won him esteem, the creator of a *manner*. Behold him admitted to the friendship of writers and artists. It is easy to understand that, to Victor Hugo, the head of a 'Holy Family', dressed always in haughty reserve and black broad-cloth, this exuberant and torrential giant must have seemed somewhat vulgar. But Dumas was so obviously, so artlessly, happy in his own good fortune that his boastings were quickly forgiven.

Charles Nodier, his first patron, had made him free of the Arsenal 'salon', the favourite meeting-place of the new school. There, the master of the house, who was a delightful talker, reigned over the library in which he held the post of Curator. His daughter, Marie, was growing into a beautiful woman. All the poets were her friends, and not a few were in love with her. On Sundays, the salon at the Arsenal was all lit up. Taylor was to be found there, the patron of the Comédie-Française, as were, also, Sophie and Delphine Gay, the former wonderfully fair; Hugo, Vigny, all the young poets; Boulanger, Devéria, all the young painters. From eight till ten, Nodier, with his back to the mantelpiece, told stories with infinite skill. At ten o'clock, Marie Nodier sat down at the piano and dancing began, while the more solemn of the menfolk, in a corner, went on with their literary and political discussions.

From the very first day on which Dumas put in an appearance at the Arsenal, Nodier found it sometimes possible to take a rest. The young Alexandre was blessed with a talent for story-telling which was equal to that of their host. Whatever it was he embarked upon — tales of his childhood, of his father the general, of Napoleon I, or of his differences of opinion with Mademoiselle Mars — was lively and amusing. Dumas loved the sound of his own voice. One evening when he had been dining out, somebody asked: 'How did the dinner go off, Dumas?'

'All I can say about that,' he replied, 'is that if I had not been there, I should have been terribly bored.'

This young, self-educated man, whose ignorance of many subjects was really staggering, felt a profound respect for Nodier, who knew everything 'and a great deal more'. Nodier did what he could to refine Dumas's taste. He even tried to modify his boasting, though without success. As soon as he began to make money with *Henri III*, the dramatist began to cover his person with jewellery, trinkets, rings and chains, and took to sporting multi-coloured waistcoats.

'You negroes are all the same,' said Nodier, affectionately. 'You love glass beads and toys.'

Alexandre did not in the least mind being reminded of his origins. He was proud of them and never took offence, provided the comments were made in a friendly tone, as they always were by Nodier. Others could hurt his feelings, but he felt himself to be in too strong a position to waste his time in hating them. All he needed was to feel self-confident, to know at every moment that he was as good as, and better than, them. This certainty produced an occasional note of conceit in his voice, as, also, a natural tendency to understand the rebellion of bastards, outlaws and foundlings against society. He felt himself to be the brother of all 'outsiders', no matter what the reason for their alienation from the social norm, whether colour, race, birth, illegitimacy or physical disability. In 1829, Byron was still the model on whom the young fashioned themselves. They copied his dandyism, his rages and, when they were in a position to do so, his courage and his genius. Hugo, Vigny and Lamartine, married men, all of them, and holding religious views, were at that time far removed from Byron's attitude of sensual licence. Dumas, a free man, with an ardent temperament, was only too glad to embrace it.

He had not been faithful to Catherine Labay, the gentle dressmaker, the mother of his son. He had never, it is true, failed to provide for her and her child, and even went quite often to spend a night with her. But what likelihood was there that her charming, but prosaic, virtues would long satisfy a man who lived his life in close communion with Christina of Sweden, the duchesse de Guise, and Mademoiselle Mars?

One day in 1827, a friend had taken him to hear a lecture at the Palais-Royal by a man of great learning, Monsieur de Villenave. When it was over, he was introduced to the lecturer's family and invited to take tea with them. The distance to the rue de Vaugirard was considerable, the journey was made on foot, and Dumas gave his arm to his host's daughter, Mélanie. The walk was long enough to provide time for mutual confidences and a conquest. Mélanie was older than Dumas by six years and had been married for seven to an officer in his forties who, born at Namur, had become a naturalized Frenchman.

François-Joseph Waldor, a captain in the quartermaster's stores of the 6th Regiment of Light Infantry, was stationed in a remote garrison town. We learn from the files relating to this 'very sturdy officer' that he had a private income of 2200 francs and 'expectations' which would eventually bring him in a similar amount. The report on him was admirable:

Behaviour: Excellent, and in strict accordance with regulations.
Morals: Irreproachable.
Capabilities: Considerable.
General Education: Varied and brilliant.
Military acquirements: Leave nothing to be desired.
Attitude to His Duties: Zealous and expert.[1]

It seems strange that Mélanie, a typical romantic heroine, 'athirst for the infinite' and 'curious about everything', should have fallen in love with this irreproachable Walloon. She complained that his courtship had been 'cold'. After presenting her husband with one child, a girl, and nearly dying in the process, Mélanie, who was thoroughly bored with provincial life, settled down in Paris with her parents. In their house she presided over a literary 'salon'. Her father, at one time editor of the *Quotidienne*, then manager of the *Journal des Curés* and founder of the *Mémorial Religieux*, had managed to amass in a small, old house a 'valuable collection of manuscripts, prints and, especially, autographs — a taste for which he was the first man to awaken in his countrymen'. This Professor of the History of Literature, this translator of Virgil and Ovid, was as suspicious as he was erudite. He never ceased to be jealous of his old wife, and watched over his daughter Mélanie with such care that he even intercepted her letters.

Every collector has an Achilles heel. The cunning Dumas had wormed himself into the favour of Villenave by giving him a number of letters written by Napoleon and by the Marshals of the Empire to the general, his father. As a result of this astute move he was invited to give a reading of *Henri III et sa Cour* in the museum-cum-salon of which Mélanie did the honours.

'The sister-soul' was fragile, pretty, with caressing eyes and a modest air which maddened Dumas. She preferred the preliminaries of love to its battles. Like Juliette Récamier, 'she would have liked love's year to stop dead at the Spring', so that the period of courtship might last the longer. This was not at all to the taste of the lusty Dumas. He took her one day by surprise, crushed her in his arms — the strength of which recalled those of the general — and stifled her protests under an interminable succession of passionate kisses. Gradually she surrendered to his ardour. He inundated her with daily letters which were violent, sensual and promised her pleasures more than human, and eternal love.

> May the words, 'I love you', sound ceaselessly in your ears . . .
> I send your lips a thousand burning kisses, and to every inch of
> your body yet other kisses to set you trembling and to fill you
> with the assurance of all delights . . . Farewell my life, my love: I
> could write you a volume, but a fatter envelope than this would,
> no doubt, be noticed.[2]

Mélanie's resistance lasted from June 3rd, the day on which she first made Dumas's acquaintance, until September 12th, 1827. Then she surrendered. How was it possible to stand out against this 'force of nature'? It did her no small honour to have undergone a siege of three and a half months. To 'shelter their happiness', he rented a small room which added to his responsibilities. He now had to provide for three establishments: one for Catherine Labay; one for his mother; and now one for his bachelor pleasures. Mélanie agreed to visit him there and became his mistress. Since the virtuous Captain Waldor had given her only the most elementary notions of physical love, she was at first as much dazzled as staggered.

> *Alexandre Dumas to Mélanie Waldor*: Oh!, one whole day
> together! What bliss! . . . I *devoured* you . . . and I feel sure that
> though you are far from me now, you must still be feeling the
> imprint of my kisses, kisses the like of which no one else has ever
> given you. Oh! what freshness you have in love, the freshness
> and, I might almost say, the ignorance of a child of fifteen!
> Forgive the blank at the bottom of the page, but my mother
> has been at me, calling out — 'your eggs are ready, Dumas! they'll
> be hard-boiled if you don't come!' — and how can I resist so

urgent a logic? Farewell, and again, farewell, my angel! All right, Mamma, if my eggs are hard, I'll eat them in oil.[3]

She soon began to complain of his voracious sensuality. He lacked delicacy, she said. He did not give her that ration of 'noble' sentiments which a sensitive woman has the right to demand. She reproached him for not knowing how to take his pleasure slowly, and, like every human being who has not yet discovered an appropriate carnal rhythm, suffered from palpitations, dizziness and 'vapours'. He hastened to plead in his defence:

> Mad, bad, good and excellent friend whom I love! Sick or well, gay or sad, grumbling or caressing, when you are on my knees and pressed to my heart, what do your words matter? In that voice of yours, you might, if you wanted to, and provided I held you tight, tell me that what you feel for me is hatred, detestation — but your touch would contradict it.[4]

Now that Dumas had money, he spent it. As soon as the success of *Henri III* gave him the necessary means, he leased a small house at Passy for Catherine Labay and her child, as well as an apartment for himself at N° 25 rue de l'Université. It had geraniums in the window and these became, for Alexandre and Mélanie, the symbols of their love.

There Mélanie reigned as queen, and thither came the small group of the faithful: Adolphe de Leuven, the Swede turned Frenchman; the lovely Muse, Delphine Gay; and, occasionally, Hugo, Balzac and Vigny. It was there that Dumas read aloud the new version of *Christine*. He had taken advantage of the delay imposed by the censor to revise the play from end to end, adding a Prologue in Stockholm, an Epilogue in Rome, building up a secondary intrigue, and introducing an additional character, Paula, Monaldeschi's mistress. The treachery, therefore, which dictated the Queen's vengeance, from being political, became sentimental.

Meanwhile, Soulié's *Christine* had fallen flat at the Odéon. The Director of that theatre, Félix Harel, wrote to Dumas offering to produce his. Dumas, feeling some scruple in the matter, consulted Soulié, who replied: 'Pick up the scraps of my *Christine* — I warn you that there are a good many of them — drop them in the basket of the first rag and bone man you meet — and go ahead.'[5]

Armed with this authority from his friend, Dumas accepted Harel's offer.

The Odéon, at that time, was regarded as lying 'beyond the bounds of any possible world'. In 1828 it had even been closed, but the mayors of the three districts lying around the Luxembourg had asked for it to be reopened. 'For them', wrote Dumas, 'it is a matter more of business than of art, of restoring life to one side of the Parisian body which has become paralysed . . .'[6] He was of the opinion that the competition offered by the Odéon would act as a stimulant to the Théâtre-Français, which more or less closed its doors against unknown authors. But the journalists showed no mercy to the remote playhouse on the Left Bank . . . 'The Odéon? Where is it? . . . The Odéon has gone up in smoke, though there has been no fire.' Then, in 1829, Harel had taken it over.

This astonishing man had been Auditor to the Conseil d'État, Inspector of Bridges, and, under the Empire, Prefect of Les Landes. Then, finding his career as an administrator stopped short by the Restoration, he had turned theatrical director for the best of all possible reasons: he was in love with Mademoiselle George. He was intelligent, witty, and always on the verge of bankruptcy. He deserved more confidence than he received; 'but', wrote Dumas, 'his company is a never-ending delight, because he talks so amusingly. If he had Mascarille and Figaro as body-servants, and didn't get the better of both of them, then my name's George Dandin. . . .'[7]

It was the fashion to pull Harel's leg about his Bonapartism and his lack of scruple. But he had a genius for publicity and was to become the herald of the romantic drama. His mistress, Mademoiselle George, had stood in the same relation to Napoleon, and was still the idol of the Bonapartists. Even at forty-three, her statuesque beauty was still a matter for astonishment. 'George,' said Dumas, 'who was a good girl if ever there was one, found room, beneath her airs of an Empress, for every variety of wit, and could laugh heartily, whereas the smile of Mademoiselle Mars was always confined to her lips. . . .'[8]

The Czar had once declared that George wore the crown better than Catherine II had ever done. In 1830 the gossip-writers, with guttersnipe cruelty, had made fun of her figure: 'Monsieur Harel says that the whole of the Odéon is in Mademoiselle George. That accounts for her size!' . . . 'The English horse which galloped round the Champ de Mars in four minutes, took no more than five, yesterday, to make the circuit of Mademoiselle George!'⁹ But Banville wrote: 'The savagery of *Le Temps* was powerless to distort this radiant Helen and to turn her into an old woman.'¹⁰ The Romantics made a special effort to provide her with suitable parts. 'How many fat queens and outsize empresses have we not disinterred from history for her sake!' wrote Théophile Gautier: 'we are left now only with princesses of moderate girth. What *is* to be done?'¹¹

Was Christina of Sweden on the plump side? Whether or no, she was a queen, and Mademoiselle George was eager to play the part. Soulié having failed, she was whole-heartedly for Dumas. Harel wished to make certain changes in the text, but the actors over-persuaded him. Not only was Mademoiselle George determined to appear as Christina, but Lockroy, young, poetical-looking and ready to take risks, had fallen in love with the part of Monaldeschi. The play was far from perfect, but it had plenty of action and, as always with Dumas, some fine curtain-lines. On the first night, March 30th, 1830, it was as though Paris were still caught up in the *Hernani* battle. Purveyors of cat-calls and professional trouble-makers had migrated from the Théâtre-Français to the Odéon. The noise was deafening. There were cries of 'Blackguards! Fools! Barbers! Cads!' When, in the Epilogue, Christina asked her doctor: 'How long will it be before I die?' somebody in the audience jumped up and shouted: 'If she's not dead by one o'clock, I'm off!' Lockroy played with such passion that Delphine exclaimed loudly: 'Bravo! Lockroy, bravo!'¹²

Strictly speaking, *Christine* was not a patch on *Henri III et sa Cour*. It was a bastard production, half drama, half tragedy. Dumas's verse — he was far less good as a poet than as a story-teller — was far below the level of his prose. Soulié, an honest colleague, realizing that there was a plot afoot to bring the play down, asked for fifty seats in the pit and offered Dumas all the workmen from his sawmill to back up the new *Christine*. In spite of these reinforcements, so great was the noise after the final curtain that no one could tell, said Dumas, whether the piece was a success or a failure. There was a supper in the rue de l'Université after the first night. Hugo, fresh from his triumph with *Hernani*, was present, and Vigny, whose *More de Venise* had been well received. With the generosity of true friends, they undertook, while the rest of the party was feasting, to revise, at Dumas's request, a hundred or so lines which the audience had been 'down on', though they were not especially bad. There had been much laughter, for instance, when Mademoiselle George, speaking of the reception of the Swedish ambassadors in audience, said: '*Ils s'avançaient vers moi comme de vieux sapins.*' Taken in hand, no doubt by Victor Hugo, the passage was changed to:

> Comme nos vieux cyprès que la tempête assiège,
> Les ouragans des cours les ont couverts de neige
> Et, sans cesse contre eux déchaînés et soufflants,
> Ont fait leur barbe grise et puis leurs cheveux blancs.

That was a great improvement, and since, in addition, the obliging pair had made some necessary cuts, the second performance was greeted with loud applause. Dumas, drunk with success, was crossing the Place de l'Odéon when a cab drew up beside him. A woman lowered the window, and called out: 'Dumas!' He recognized Marie Dorval. 'Ah! what a fine talent you have!' she said. This was the beginning of a friendship — and a liaison.[13]

Next day, he was offered twelve thousand francs for the book-rights. Money was walking arm-in-arm with fame.

CHAPTER II

Antony

T HE year 1830 was a crucial one for the romantic movement. A revolution in literature was to be doubled by a revolution in the streets. It was a red-hot period, with battle everywhere — in the theatres, on the barricades, even between husbands and wives. Great passions are necessary to the romantic. It was the year in which Sainte-Beuve paid court to Madame Victor Hugo; in which the future George Sand broke away from the Baron Dudevant; in which Alfred de Vigny became desperately attached to Marie Dorval; in which Balzac, growing tired of his *Dilecta*, caught fire anew at the flame of an elusive marquise de Castries. The light-hearted Dumas was not of a nature to indulge in self-torment, but had, all the same, to follow the fashion. In order to be like everybody else, he had to be jealous of somebody, and chose for the purpose Captain Waldor, his mistress's peace-loving husband.

When one day Mélanie, after a long conjugal holiday, received from the military gentleman a letter in which he announced his impending arrival in Paris on leave, Dumas rushed to the War Ministry where he asked an officer friend of his to get the leave cancelled. 'The thought of it well-nigh sent me mad!' he said. This madness was confined to words. The husband did not put in an appearance, but the comedy began again, more than once.

Alexandre Dumas to Mélanie Waldor: I devoutly hope that God was listening when you said it was possible that your husband would not come in January! Yes, I hope that He was listening and will send you back to me, gay and happy. You cannot conceive how complete the illusion is for me. I cannot bear to think that another man should possess you. I think of you as mine, all mine, and his return would destroy the illusion ... Oh! tell me again why you believe he may not come in January: let me know what precise sentence in his letter made you assume that ... I would rather you spent six months away from me at Jarrie[1] than that he should come for two days to Paris. At Jarrie I should not see you, but at least you would be there by yourself, whereas here![2]

Oh! my love, if your plan for your husband to take a room [at an hotel] should be realized, what happiness it would be for me . . . You cannot understand what tortures I should endure, alone, and far from you, knowing that *one bed* . . . Oh! torment! . . . that the two of you were side by side . . . My angel, my love, do arrange that.[3]

At the same time, Dumas was missing no opportunity of deceiving his languishing Mélanie. But he was bent on having his tremendous romantic passion. He spoke to Mélanie of their 'burning, grievous kisses': he threatened to mingle Love with Death, and even to kill her captain spouse, who certainly did not deserve such savage treatment. What, in fact, he did do was to multiply his pleas to the War Ministry, urging that Waldor should not be transferred to Paris, nor even to Courbevoie, which was too close to Paris. 'He must be given his Majority, my angel. That is the only way of getting this matter settled satisfactorily . . .' What a subject for a Balzac novel! — *What it Costs an Officer to get Promotion.*

Alexandre Dumas to Mélanie Waldor: At last you have understood me. You now know about love because you know about jealousy. Can you imagine anything comparable to it? And yet these idiotic religion-mongers can think of nothing worse to invent than a Hell of physical torment! One can feel only sorry for them. Hell, for me, would be to see you eternally in the arms of another! That cursed thought is enough to drive me to crime![4]

All literary posturings, no doubt, but from them a new drama, *Antony*, was born. It marks a very important stage in the history of the theatre, because it is no longer a drama on an historical subject, but a play of modern life in which, for the first time, the writer brings upon the stage that stock figure of the Adulterous Wife which for more than a hundred years was to haunt French playwrights, much to their detriment.

Alexandre Dumas to Mélanie Waldor: You will find many things in *Antony* which have been taken from our life together, my angel, but they are things which only you and I know. So, what does it matter? The public will make nothing of them, though in us they will wake eternal memories. Antony, himself, will, I am pretty sure, be recognized, for he is a madman with a remarkable resemblance to me.[5]

The conflict between the individual and society, between passion and duty, which the seventeenth century had resolved in favour of society, and the eighteenth had evaded by indulging in licence and frivolity, was now reaching the stage of violence. 'The passions of this modern age have been unloosed!'[6] Throughout the whole of the nineteenth century they were to dominate the theatre with a tumult of instincts, words, dagger-thrusts and pistol-shots. *Antony* scared the actors of the Comédie-Française. It was destined to convulse its audiences.

Antony, a social rebel and a bastard (like Didier in *Marion de Lorme*) is unable to marry Adèle, whom he loves, because he has neither family, position, calling nor fortune. The girl has been given in marriage to Colonel Baron d'Hervey (Captain Waldor, as represented on the stage, had been promoted). One day Antony reappears and stops the runaway horses of Adèle's carriage. He is injured, and taken to her house. The two young people mutually confess their love, but Adèle, a slave to the social conventions, tries to resist. With his fits of rage, his grievances, his feeling of resentment against an unjust world, Antony leads her to the 'very verge of downfall'. Adèle, as an honest woman, tries to flee to her husband, who is in garrison at Strasbourg. Antony, having led her into a trap, contrives to have a night of passion with her at the Inn of Ittenheim. The world condemns her. The colonel sets off in haste and surprises the guilty lovers.

ADÈLE Someone is coming upstairs ... he has rung the bell ... It is my husband ... Fly! ... fly!

ANTONY I will not ... You told me a while ago that you have no fear of death.

ADÈLE Nor have I! ... Oh! kill me, kill me for pity's sake!

ANTONY A death that may save your reputation and your daughter's?

ADÈLE I ask it of you on my knees!

A VOICE (*without*) Open! open I say! ... Break down the door!

ANTONY Say with your latest breath you do not hate your murderer!

ADÈLE Nay, I bless him! But hasten, hasten, the door. . . .

ANTONY Have no fear; death will be here before him . . . But think upon it . . . think on death!

ADÈLE I ask it of you — I want it — I beg for it (*throwing herself into his arms*) — I run to meet it!

ANTONY (*kissing her*) Then, die! (*stabs her*)

ADÈLE (*falling into an armchair*) Ah! . . .

At this moment the door (*off*) *is broken in, and* COLONEL D'HERVEY *rushes on to the stage.*

COLONEL D'HERVEY Villain! . . . what do I see? . . . Adèle, dead!

ANTONY Yes, dead . . . She resisted me . . . and so I killed her!

(*He throws his dagger at* COLONEL D'HERVEY'S *feet*)

CURTAIN⁷

The play is skilfully constructed. With praiseworthy economy of means the action moves swiftly through five acts until it reaches a denouement to which everything has been designed to lead. It was Dumas's theory that a dramatist should always think out his final 'curtain', and then build his play backwards. At a time when dramas were either historical or dissolute, the stage portrayal of the contemporary world and its passions must have seemed both new and courageous. In the course of *Antony*, Dumas puts the following words into the mouth of one of his characters, Eugène d'Hervilly:

History has left us with a legacy of facts. They belong to the poet. But if we, of this age and society, attempt to show a man's heart beneath a modern dress-coat, no one will recognize it. The resemblance between the hero and the spectators in the pit will be too great, the analogy too intimate. The man in the audience who follows the actor's presentation of passion wishes it to stop precisely at the point where it would have stopped in his own case. If it exceeds *his* powers of feeling or expression, he fails to understand. He says: 'That is false: I don't feel in that way. If the wife of my bosom deceives me, I suffer, of course . . . it is only natural that I should . . . for a while, but I don't stab her, and I don't die. The proof of that is that here I am, as large as life.' Such charges of exaggeration and melodrama drown the applause of those few who, more happily (or unhappily) organized than their neighbours, feel that there is no essential difference between human passions in the fifteenth century and in the nineteenth; that the heart's blood beats as strongly under a dress-coat as under a breastplate. . . .[8]

What Alexandre Dumas had tried to do was to give to a modern hero the violent reactions of a man of the Renaissance and, once again, what he had done seemed new: so new, indeed, that the censor would never have allowed the play to be produced had it not been for the revolution of 1830. After the Days of July it became possible to paint the morals of society frankly and without gloss. This recovered freedom gave us Balzac. But when Dumas wrote *Antony* (that is to say, before 1830) the censorship was still severe. Dumas could not remain content merely to point to the fact of adultery; he had to condemn and punish it. Balzac could allow himself a high degree of cynicism. Diane de Maufrigneuse, princesse de Cadignan, could pass with impunity through flames which burned Adèle d'Hervey alive. But Dumas had not then the right to say, in a public theatre, that a woman might be at once guilty and happy, however much he might think it — perhaps wrongly, for his own code of facile morals made more than one mistress in real life miserable.

CHAPTER III

Joseph! My Double-barrelled Gun!

FAITHFULNESS in love had never been his strong suit. Though Mélanie Waldor was still his 'angel', he was now surrounded by a regiment of lesser angels. He had not only Virginie Bourbier of the Comédie-Française, but, probably, little Louise Despréaux who, as a page in *Henri III*, had revealed a pair of perfect legs, and, certainly, the great Marie Dorval, who gave herself as freely in private life as on the stage. There was also another actress, Belle Krelsamer (Mélanie Serre in the theatre) who had played the duchesse de Guise on tour, and had been introduced to Dumas by Firmin at the end of May 1830. This lovely creature had 'jet-black hair, deep blue eyes, a nose as straight as that of the Venus de Milo, and pearls instead of teeth'.[1] She had asked for an engagement and been offered a liaison. She held out against him for three weeks — which was less than the first Mélanie had achieved, though still honourable. She settled into a lodging near Dumas in the rue de l'Université — she at N° 7, he at N° 25. In June 1830, Mélanie Waldor having gone with her mother to La Jarrie, Dumas spent all his spare time with Mélanie the Second. She was an intelligent woman and it was not long before she was exercising a strong influence over him.

In July, with *Antony* all but finished, he was on the point of starting for Algiers to see the city, which had just been captured. Belle Krelsamer was to go with him as far as Marseille. Very naturally she disapproved of the impending separation. Love, she thought, should be strong enough to overcome curiosity. On the morning of the 26th, Dumas told her that she could unpack her bags. The *Moniteur* had published the decrees of the Polignac Ministry against the freedom of the press. To Dumas, as to many others, this meant the end of the monarchy. He was at heart a republican and hoped sincerely that Paris would rise.

'What we're going to see here will be even more interesting than what I might have seen over there.' Then, summoning his servant:

'Joseph,' he said: 'go to the gunsmith and bring me back my double-barrelled gun, with two hundred cartridges, size 20.'

The instructions were in the true style of melodrama, but the courage that issued them was genuine. When *Les Trois Glorieuses* (the three glorious days of the revolution) turned into a Drama in the Great Manner, Dumas wished to be its laughing and heroic jeune premier, a part which he played with gallantry and not a little braggadocio.

For three days he ran about Paris, from the streets where fighting was going on to the places where public opinion was being shaped — the Hôtel de Ville, the Institut, the editorial offices of *Le National*. In his *Mémoires* he has painted a vivid picture of the battles and the meetings. Between two bursts of gunfire, he hurried to his bedridden mother, who knew nothing of what was happening, and to Belle, in the rue de l'Université. 'She was informed of everything. I gave her my word to be a mere spectator of events and to take no part in them. Having extracted this promise she let me go.'[2] But what he saw was so rousing that he could not keep himself from joining in. Wearing his shooting-jacket with the pockets stuffed with cartridges, and his gun slung over his shoulder, he mixed with the crowds. He was a familiar figure in the neighbourhood.

'What ought we to do?' somebody asked him.

'Build barricades!'

That was in the good old tradition. He visited his former office in the Palais-Royal and found his one-time protector, Oudard, keeping a close watch on events so as to be in a position to declare for the winning side. At sight of Dumas's warlike appearance, and at the sound of his bellicose talk, he was seized with a fit of trembling.

On his way to the Seine, Dumas stopped on the quays, overwhelmed with happiness at seeing the tricolour on the towers of Notre-Dame. His double-barrelled gun entitled him to the position of a leader. Students, young men from the École Polytechnique, and workmen were fraternizing in an atmosphere thick with the hatred of the Bourbons. The mob hoisted an elderly man of military bearing on to a horse, and addressed him as 'General'. Drama was developing a strain of musical-comedy. A captain, waving the King's commission, stopped Dumas and his followers:

'Where are you going?'

'To the Hôtel de Ville!'

'What are you going to do there?'

'Fight!'

'Really, Monsieur Dumas, I didn't think you were quite so mad as that!'

'Ah! so you know who I am?'

'I was on guard-duty at the Odéon when *Christine* was played for the first time . . . which reminds me, when are we going to see *Antony*?'

'As soon as we've finished with the revolution!'

The two men saluted one another and parted. Dumas went to see his friend Lethière, the painter. The booming of the bells of Notre-Dame drowned the rattle of musketry. Lethière's son was sent off to the rue de l'Université to reassure 'someone who is very dear to me' — in other words, Belle Krelsamer.

Next day, Dumas returned to the 'front'. He entered the Tuileries with 'The People', and there, in the duchesse de Berry's library, came upon a copy of *Christine*, bound in purple velvet and stamped with the princess's arms. This he took away and gave to young Félix Deviolaine. At the Hôtel de Ville the fall of the Bourbons had already been proclaimed. The cloth had been cut; now it had got to be sewn together. Who could ensure the unity of the country? La Fayette, as President of a Republic? No; he seemed to be as much averse to responsibility as he was in love with popularity. Thiers and Laffitte put forward the name of the duc d'Orléans. But what if Charles X should attack Paris with such troops as had remained loyal to him? Dumas heard La Fayette say: 'Four thousand rounds of small-arms ammunition is all we've got.'

So there was a lack of powder, was there? But hadn't Soissons got a powder-factory? Dumas, a native of the district, knew it well.

'General,' said he to La Fayette, 'would you like me to round up some powder?'

The idea of returning as a warrior to the scenes of his childhood enchanted him. He overcame all resistance, furnished himself with written orders, and started off in high spirits. At Villers-Cotterets an ovation awaited him. The sight of his gig, flying the tricolour flag, brought from their houses those who until then had been underground members of the opposition. Everyone wanted to ask him to dinner. He went to the house of Paillet, the one-time managing-clerk of the lawyer's office in which he had worked. There he told the epic story of the 'Three Days'. Those present loudly expressed their admiration, but he was advised not to proceed to Soissons. How could one man,

or several men for that matter, get the better of a royalist garrison?
Nevertheless, go he did, and all turned out well. In his *Mémoires* he
has dramatized the incident. According to him, he made his way,
pistol in hand, into the presence of the commandant, the vicomte
de Linières. Madame de Linières burst into the room:

'Yield, my dear, yield!' she cried. 'This is a second negro revolt! . . .
Remember my father and mother who were massacred in San-
Domingo! Give the necessary orders, I beg you! . . .'

Members of the Linières family have since stated that, well before
Dumas's arrival, the commandant had already promised to send the
powder to the National Guard of Soissons. But what do facts matter?
The author has so great an air of conviction, and describes so well an
exploit worthy of the Horatius Cocles of the Tyrol! Besides, what
exactly *was* the truth of the matter? Alexandre Dumas's report to
General La Fayette on the seizure of the supplies of powder, appeared
in the *Moniteur* on August 9th, 1830, and no one at that time contradicted it. One thing is certain that he did bring back to the Hôtel de
Ville more than three thousand five hundred pounds of powder, and
that the duc d'Orléans himself, the future King of the French, said to
him, perhaps with a smile: 'Monsieur Dumas, you have just written
your finest drama!'

From that moment he entertained high hopes of seeing himself a
minister. To Mélanie Waldor, whose return from La Vendée he
dreaded, he wrote:

> It's all over. As I predicted to you more than once, our
> revolution lasted only three days. I am in the happy position of
> having played a fairly active part, and was noticed by La Fayette
> and the duc d'Orléans. I was sent on a mission to Soissons where,
> single-handed, I took possession of a store of gunpowder, and
> made a military reputation for myself . . . It looks as though the
> duc d'Orléans will be made king. Your letters will have to be
> differently addressed in future. You should be grateful for my
> laziness . . . I feel sure you realize how difficult it is for me to
> leave Paris just now. All the same, so eager am I to see you, that I
> will take the coach at the first possible moment, if only just to clasp
> you in my arms. There may be a great change in my position. I
> cannot talk about it in a letter, but I think you are justified in
> having fine hopes for your Alexandre.[3]

And again, a few days later:

> Do not worry, my angel; all goes well. The duc d'Orléans
> was proclaimed king yesterday. I spent the evening at Court.
> The whole family is as simple and kindly as ever. I have written
> three letters to you, and sent them to three different addresses.
> Farewell, my love. It would be a mistake for you to come to Paris
> just now.[4]
> I shall set off, my love, the day after tomorrow. Just a
> short tour and then straight to you. I am delighted to be
> leaving Paris ... By the time you get my first letter, I shall be on
> the road.[5]

What had happened was that he had asked La Fayette to send him
to La Vendée for the purpose, so he said, of raising a National Guard
capable of dealing with any Chouan rising. His real reason was that
he wanted to rejoin, and pacify, his mistress. In the absence of
Villenave who, in times of trouble, insisted on standing guard over his
precious autographs, Madame Villenave, an accommodating mother,
had invited Dumas to spend a few weeks at La Jarrie. La Fayette,
who just then was complying with everybody's wishes, gave him a
letter of introduction to the Liberal leaders in La Vendée. Dumas
immediately ordered a quite staggering uniform — shako with red
feathers, silver epaulettes and belt, tunic and trousers of royal blue,
and a tricolour cockade. In La Vendée, where the elements of a National
Guard were non-existent, and the tricolour flag, in spite of orders
issued by the Prefecture, was nowhere to be seen, Dumas spent his
time in consuming copious meals, and in performing acts of contrition
for the benefit of Mélanie who, informed of her lover's 'gallantries',
and egged on by her mother, wrote a number of wild and foolish
letters to Marie Dorval and Belle Krelsamer. He started for home on
September 22nd, leaving Mélanie in a very bad state of health.

In Paris he found a heart-breaking condition of 'no change'. Dis-
content with the Ministry, and love of the King, were both increasing.
Dumas believed the love to be genuine, if for no better reason than
that he hoped to gain the support and gratitude of the Sovereign. He
drew up a report on his 'mission' — *Mémoire sur La Vendée* — in
which he noted the possible danger of further trouble with the Chouans,
gave some wise advice, and 'kneeled at the feet of the King'.

Alexandre Dumas to Mélanie Waldor, September 30th, 1930:
Dear love; just these few lines to embrace you, to calm your fears,
and to embrace you again . . . Your mother's letter caused me
considerable uneasiness. I received your note yesterday evening.
Let them apply as many leeches as they like. Don't worry about
anything, not even about the broken geranium. It was the tail-end
of *our* storm which committed that atrocity — for atrocity it is.

Nothing has changed in the entourage of the King. I have sent
him a report, but do not know whether he has even read it. He is
kept in a condition of unbroken blockade. Only those who have
nothing to say are allowed to approach him. He is becoming
more and more beloved every day, and is even being treated with
indecent familiarity. The other day, Monsieur Dupaty sent him
a card of membership of the National Guard, on the grounds that
he lived in the Palais-Royal district! A nonsensical thing to do.[6]

The broken geranium had been the symbol of a hoped-for pregnancy
which had ended in a miscarriage. 'Have no fears for the future; we
will have a geranium of our own.' One is reminded that Balzac, too,
wanted '*l'Étrangère*' to present him with a 'Victor Honoré'.

The King, Louis-Philippe, read the report on La Vendée and even
made marginal notes. Dumas had advised the removal of certain
legitimist priests. '*Écrit aux Cultes*' commented the King in his own
hand.[7] He let Dumas know, through Oudard, that he was to be
received in audience. The young man presented himself in National
Guard uniform. He was received with an affectionate smile, and
that appearance of good-fellowship which Ministers found so dis-
arming. The King told him that he was wrong about the Chouans.

I, too, let me tell you, have my finger on the pulse of La
Vendée . . . There is something of the doctor in me, as you
know . . . Politics are a melancholy trade. Leave it to kings and
their ministers . . . You are a poet, and should be writing
poetry. . . .[8]

All hopes of a portfolio vanished into thin air. Dumas's feelings
were hurt, and he asked to be transferred to the Artillery of the
National Guard which was known to hold republican views. Already,
the marks left by the bullets of July were being removed from the
walls and public monuments of Paris.

CHAPTER IV

Way for the Theatre!

AT once, the theatre engulfed him. The ending of the July Revolution had given Félix Harel what he believed to be an idea of genius. Since the Bonapartists had joined hands with the Orleanists in the setting up of the new regime, the Emperor could be freely referred to on the stage. Mademoiselle George, who, having been the god's mistress, still retained for Napoleon an ardent devotion, was in favour of putting on a play about him. Dumas, however, showed little enthusiasm for the project. General Dumas had suffered so much at the hands of Bonaparte that his son was far from willing to speak well of the dead master, though that did not mean that he wanted to speak ill. Besides, it seemed to him that the great events of the Empire were too near in time to be a fitting subject for dramatic treatment.

But one evening, after his return from La Jarrie, when he was supping after the theatre with the Harel-George menage, together with Lockroy and Janin, his host and hostess asked him to stay behind after the others had left. With an air of great mystery, he was led through Mademoiselle George's bedroom to a handsome room adjoining, and was told that he would not be allowed to leave it until the play for which he had been asked was written. The subject might not be to his taste, but the situation of his 'study' most certainly was. Though no longer in her first youth, and something of 'an out-size Melpomene', Mademoiselle George could still boast shoulders, arms and a bosom which would have done honour to a statue. She had a natural and unselfconscious way of taking a bath in full view of her male friends, and making a full display of breasts which would have become a Greek goddess, and were calculated to inflame men of a far less ardent temperament than Dumas. He wrote the whole of *Napoléon Bonaparte* in a week. Though he expended considerable ingenuity on the task, it never rises to the level of its subject. 'A bad play which he ought never to have written,' said Vigny. 'I blamed him for kicking the Bourbons when they were down.'

Harel launched a publicity campaign which, though noisy, was of bad quality. He announced that he had spent a hundred thousand francs on the production. At the first night, a band played regimental marches in the intervals. The members of the audience had been asked to wear National Guard uniform. The house was both military and militant. The part of the Emperor had been given to Frédérick Lemaître. This actor had achieved fame at the age of thirty as a result of his interpretation of Robert Macaire in *l'Auberge des Adrets*. He had played the part not as that of a low blackguard but of a comic and cynical hero, almost a righter of wrongs. In his hands, the melodrama became a Revolutionary and social comedy, a *Mariage de Figaro* of the July Revolution. There was something Shakespearian in his interpretation — bursts of sinister laughter, a derisive bitterness. The play was changed into a criticism of society by a gangster, a Manfred of the gutter. It was a triumph for the actors.

In order to build up his Napoleon, Frédérick consulted all those (and they were numerous) who had known the Emperor well. From fear (entirely unjustified) of being commonplace, he carefully avoided the most famous characteristics — the hand behind the back; the snuff-box in the waistcoat pocket. It was a brilliant and audacious piece of acting, but it was not Napoleon. Harel was disappointed, so was the public, and Dumas, thoroughly upset by his first failure, began to wonder whether his inspiration was 'drying up'. On reaching home, however, he found a note to the effect that, since the censorship had been suppressed (for a short while), *Antony* was to go into rehearsal at the Théâtre-Français.

Mademoiselle Mars had agreed to play the part of Adèle: Firmin, that of Antony. The choice was flattering but dangerous. Mademoiselle Mars, who possessed to a high degree the grace, wit and coquetry so necessary in the plays of Marivaux, was wholly unfitted to understand the 'essentially modern character of Adèle, with its alternations of passion and remorse'. Firmin was still what he had always been, a classic actor, with nothing about him of Antony's 'star-crossed' quality. One sign among many that these two were completely out of their depth was that neither of them would dare to show themselves on the stage with a pale make-up. Pallor was an indispensable accompaniment of Dumas's type of drama.

When, before the July Revolution, *Antony* had been read to the actors of the Comédie-Française, it had had a very cold reception. It was scarcely possible to 'turn it down', in view of the resounding success which the author had had with *Henri III*. But when rehearsals started, Mademoiselle Mars, with a determination and a cleverness of which only she was capable, decided to reduce the part of Adèle to the proportions of one in a play by Scribe. Firmin made matters worse by smoothing out all the asperities in the role of Antony. 'The result', said Dumas, 'was that, after three months of rehearsing, Adèle and Antony were just two charming young lovers, such as might be seen at the Gymnase. They might just as well have been called Monsieur Arthur and Mademoiselle Céleste.'[1] How came it that the author had allowed his play to be so disastrously expurgated? 'Ah! how do these things happen? How is it that rust eats away steel, that the breaking of the waves wears down the rocks?' The implacable sweetness of Mademoiselle Mars had had, in many other cases, no less destructive an effect. Those of Dumas's friends who came to the rehearsals, said: 'It's a pretty little piece, quite charming, in fact. Who'd ever have thought that you were capable of working in that medium?'

'I certainly shouldn't!' was his answer.

At last the bills were up — 'On Saturday next, the first performance of *Antony*'. Dumas, entering the Théâtre-Français for the dress-rehearsal, found Mademoiselle Mars all sugar and honey:

'Have you been told?'

'Told what?'

'That they're lighting us with gas.'

'So much the better.'

'They're having a new chandelier made for us.'

'Allow me to congratulate you.'

'But that's not what I wanted to say.'

'What is it you want to say, mademoiselle?'

'I have incurred expenses to the tune of twelve hundred francs for your play.'

'Bravo!'

'I have four different changes.'

'You will look superb.'

'So, you see . . .'

'No, I do not see.'

'But I want *them* to be seen.'

'Very right and proper.'

'And since we shall be having a new chandelier . . .'

'How soon?'

'In three months.'

'Well?'

'Well, we think it would be a good idea to inaugurate the new chandelier with *Antony*.'

'Do you, indeed!'

'Yes.'

'That is to say, in three months?'

'In three months.'

'In May?'

'In May: it is a very good month.'

'You mean, it is a very *beautiful* month?'

'A very good one, too.'

'So you're not having any holidays this year, in May?'

'No, they start on June 1st.'

'So, if we don't open until after the 20th, for instance, I shall have three performances?'

Mademoiselle made a short calculation:

'Four, there are thirty-one days in May.'

'Very nice, very nice indeed, four performances!'

'I shall continue with it when I get back.'

'Is that a bargain?'

'You have my word for it.'

'Thank you, mademoiselle: that is extremely kind.'

I turned my back on her [Dumas goes on] and found myself face to face with Firmin.

'Did you hear that?' I said.

'Yes, indeed . . . didn't I tell you she'd never play the part?'

'But *why* won't she play it?'

'Because it's a Dorval part. . . .'[2]

That was what Dumas had long been thinking. Small, dark, fragile, with a curly fringe, liquid eyes, quivering lips and a poetic face, Dorval was more than an actress. 'She was spirit incarnate . . . Her figure was like a flexible reed, responsive to every mysterious breeze . . .'[3] Marie Dorval was the natural child of two poor strolling players, and had been brought up among sordid and violent passions. When she was in a temper she could scream like a fishwife. Her private life had been eventful. Though twice married, she had had numerous lovers — among them, the young Alexandre Dumas. On the stage, this sublime creature seemed to vibrate with inspiration, to overflow with life — to have the devil in her.

Between the two of them, she and Frédérick Lemaître had 'created' *Trente ans ou la vie d'un joueur*, a play in which she played a wife compelled to watch the gradual degradation of her husband. There had been real genius in her delineation of the mother's agony, 'the wife's desolate grandeur'. 'There was nothing she could not turn to advantage,' wrote Banville, 'the ravaged face, the wildly passionate lips, the eyes burned dry with tears, the body quivering from head to heel, the thin, pale arms emaciated with fever.'⁴ And George Sand: 'With her, everything, every single thing, was resolved in terms of passion — motherhood, art, friendship, devotion, indignation, yearning. And, since she could never moderate or suppress anything, her whole existence was lived out in such violent superlatives, that one was terrified. One felt that no human being could go on living in such a constant state of excitement. . . .'⁵

Yes, Marie Dorval would most certainly play Adèle a great deal better than Mademoiselle Mars.

And the man opposite whom she usually acted, Pierre Bocage, would play Antony better than Firmin. A native of Rouen, where he had once worked as a teaseler, he had taken to the stage from a sense of vocation. There was warmth and feeling in his acting, though he had his faults. His arms were too long, and he spoke through his nose. It had been said of him that he was 'one of Frédérick Lemaître's colds in the head'. He had been fortunate to fall in with Dorval, and she had recognized in him a partner who would be the perfect foil for her. She was fully conscious of his absurdities. She thought him conceited and something of a fool, but she knew that he was just the man for Antony, far more so than Frédérick Lemaître, who would have 'stolen' the play. With a tall figure, regular features and bushy eyebrows, Bocage was the gloomy hero of whom the readers of Byron dreamed. Poetic, severe, passionate and sombre; amorous, savage and sublime by turns, he was, for Antony, as to the manner born. Dumas retrieved his manuscript from the Comédie-Française, and took it to Marie Dorval. She was not in the least like Mademoiselle Mars. There was nothing in her of the aristocratic Célimène. Very much 'of the people', deliciously natural, she received Dumas with that drawling, lazy voice which, in her mouth, was always so charming.

'This *is* nice of you, *mon bon chien* . . . It must be six months since I last saw you.'

'What would you have? Since then I have produced a child and made a revolution⁶ . . . Hey! what sort of a kiss d'you call that?'

'I can't really kiss you now . . . I have become discreet.'

'And who, may I ask, has made *that* revolution?'

'Alfred de Vigny. I am mad about him . . . Love is the only thing he makes naturally . . . but that compensates for everything else . . . He treats me like a duchess. He calls me his angel . . . He tells me that I have an inventive body.'

'Bravo! . . . I have a part for you here . . . I'll read it.'

'D'you mean you're going to read it just to me? . . . I really do believe you take me for a great artist!'

That evening he read *Antony* to Dorval. She wept; she was filled with admiration and gratitude.

'Just you wait and see how I'll say "*Mais elle ne ferme pas, cette porte!*" . . . No need for you to worry. It's easy to act in *your* plays, the only trouble is you grind one's heart to powder. Ah! *grand chien*, where did you learn about women? There's precious little you don't know!'⁷

She asked him to alter the fifth act which she found 'too flabby'. Mademoiselle had thought it too hard. Oh! these actresses! Dumas sat up all night in Marie Dorval's lodgings. When morning came, the act had been rewritten. At nine o'clock the actress clapped her hands for joy, and exclaimed:

'*How* I'll say —"*But I am lost, lost!*" —a pause and then—"*My child! Oh! I must kiss my child!*" . . . and then — "*Kill me*" . . . and then straight on to the curtain.'

'So, you're pleased?'

'I should think I am . . . Now, we must get Bocage round to lunch, after which he must hear the play.'

Bocage was no less enthusiastic than Dorval. Vigny attended some of the rehearsals and got Dumas to suppress the hero's declaration of atheism. By May 3rd, 1831, *Antony* was ready for production at the Porte-Saint-Martin. It is not generally realized today that the play made as great a sensation as *Hernani* on its first night. 'All the young men were there: writers, painters, craftsmen. Strange, fierce faces were to be seen by the score, walrus moustaches, pointed beards, long curly hair, extravagant doublets, dress-coats with velvet lapels . . . The ladies, a bit scared, stepped from their carriages dressed in the fashion of the day, with their hair done à la giraffe, their great tortoise-shell combs, their leg-of-mutton sleeves, their short skirts revealing feet shod in buskins.'[8] The success was immense. Dorval, giving an astounding display of emotion and naturalness, uttered cries which were genuinely terrifying. When, collapsing across an armchair, all adorable femininity and instinctive terror, she said: '*But I am lost, lost!*' the audience burst into tears.

At first the public had been surprised to find Marie Dorval playing the part of a woman of the world. Her rather hoarse voice seemed better suited to popular melodrama. But the play was so well constructed, the dramatic situations followed one another so rapidly, the interpretation was so realistic, that at the end of the fourth act the applause lasted until the curtain rose on the fifth. When Bocage, throwing his dagger at the feet of the furious colonel, said calmly, coldly: '*She resisted me — and so, I killed her!*' there were cries of terror from the audience. Actor and actress enjoyed a well-deserved triumph. 'Both', wrote Dumas, 'had reached the very highest level of art.'

Frédérick Lemaître, who knew what he was talking about, always maintained that the fourth act of *Antony*, as played by Dorval and Bocage, was the finest thing he had ever seen. Dumas, with his instinct for the theatre, realized how important it was not to let the enthusiasm of the audience have time in which to cool. He had trained the stagehands to achieve a remarkably rapid change of scene. The fifth act was Dorval's own. 'She cried as people do cry, with genuine tears; she shrieked as people do shriek, cursed as women do curse, tearing her hair, casting her flowers aside, rumpling up her dress to the knees, without any consideration for the standards of the Conservatoire.'[9]

The audience was hysterical. People were clapping, sobbing, weeping, shouting. The flaming passion of the play had set all hearts on fire. The young women were all hopelessly in love with

Antony; the young men were ready to blow their brains out for Adèle d'Hervey. 'Modern love', said Gautier [he meant, of course, love as it was understood in 1830], 'was admirably portrayed by this company of players. Bocage and Madame Dorval gave to their parts a quite extraordinary intensity of life; Bocage the man of destiny, and Madame Dorval the poor, weak woman, par excellence.' At that precise moment in time 'tenderness, passion, even beauty, were not enough to make an accomplished lover; there had also to be a something of disdainful pride, of the mysterious, in the manner of Lara and the Giaour, in a word a touch of the true Byronic climate. Behind the lover one had to feel the presence of the unknown hero, exposed to the injustice of Fate, and rising above it. . . .

As to Madame Dorval, she spoke with the true accents of nature; the cries torn from the depths of her heart overwhelmed the audience. In the way she loosened the ribbons of her hat, and threw it on to a chair, there was a power which produced in the spectators a shudder as intense as any caused by the most terrifying scene. What truth there was in her gestures, her poses, in the flashing of her eyes when, on the point of collapse, she leaned against some piece of furniture, writhed her arms, and raised to heaven those pale blue eyes of hers swimming in tears.[10]

It is not difficult to imagine the effect which this tempestuous play had upon a public worked to a white heat, and the volcanic youth of the period. Dumas was set upon by the crowd, dragged this way and that, embraced. Some of his fanatical admirers cut pieces from the tails of his dress-coat to serve as souvenirs of that memorable evening. The first-night audience, as a rule so reserved, so quietly elegant, completely lost its head. At twenty-eight, Dumas had become the most celebrated dramatist of the day. He was ranked with Victor Hugo. So frequently were they called 'the two rivals' that their happy friendship was, at times, almost spoiled as a result of the activities of not wholly unmalicious familiars, but never for long, because they both had the gift of generosity.

The success of Antony was solid and lasting. It was acted thirty times in Paris. Members of the intelligentsia went for the first time in their lives to the Porte-Saint-Martin. In the provinces, the play long remained Marie Dorval's triumph. She adored it, and served it well. At Rouen, an ignorant stage-manager rang down the curtain on Antony's dagger-thrust, without waiting for the final line. Bocage, in a fury, rushed to his dressing-room and locked himself in. The audience, deprived of the expected and already celebrated denouement, raised a hubbub of protests. Dorval, a good trouper if ever there was one, resumed her position on the chair. But Bocage refused to return to the stage. The public raised a cry of 'Dorval! Bocage!' and threatened to break up the benches. The stage-manager, terrified by this outbreak, sent the curtain up again, in the hope that Bocage would repent. The shouts went on. Marie Dorval felt that something must be done. The dead woman rose to her feet, and advanced to the footlights.

'Gentlemen,' she said, 'I resisted him, and so, he killed me.'

Then, with a deep curtsy, she made her exit, 'to an accompaniment of thunderous applause'. That is the kind of thing that happens in the theatre.

CHAPTER V

Mille e Tre

THE triumph of *Antony* restored all Dumas's exuberant self-confidence. As a man he was popular — thirty, slender, well set-up and dandified. His great thatch of hair, his blue eyes — 'two points of light' — and his little black moustache, gave him a curious charm. His successes with women surrounded him with an aura of prestige. Mélanie Waldor did not survive the success of his play. Once an author has transformed a woman into a 'character', she is dead for him. Besides, that particular woman, jealous, anaemic, eaten up with literary ambitions, entirely concerned with her own reputation, was becoming intolerable.

The Don Juan type has many varieties. There is the mocking and ferocious Don Juan, who takes his revenge on all women for the scorn shown him by one, or because of the accident of his birth, or his personal ugliness. There is the diabolical Don Juan who is less concerned to be loved than to defy all laws, divine and human. There is the disappointed Don Juan, for ever seeking love in its perfection, never finding it, but gloomily keeping up the search. Finally, there is the sensual Don Juan who, without evil intentions, collects women merely because he desires them, just in the same way as he would pick fruit when he is thirsty. This last is neither satanic nor vicious. He has no wish to cause pain to any of his mistresses, but tries to keep all of them, which, though showing a charitable feeling on his part, is apt to be exhausting, and, since they are jealous, compels him to lie to all of them, with the result that he finds himself in the special district of Hell reserved for liars — the Circle of Insecurity.

This was precisely what happened to Dumas. He had not, strictly speaking, broken with Mélanie Waldor, but all the symbolic geraniums standing in the windows of their hearts were faded. In October 1830, after his return from La Jarrie, he was still promising her a child: 'Yes, my love, I am always thinking of our little Antony', for the natural son was to bear the name of the child of his brain. He swore to give up Belle Krelsamer. 'I don't, if it comes to that, believe that she is capable of a deep love ... Besides, she knows that I shall always keep a watchful eye on her career in the theatre and that will console her for everything. ....'

Words! words! words! ... When Mélanie Waldor got back to Paris, she found that Dumas was far from being separated from Belle Krelsamer (known on the stage as *Mademoiselle Mélanie*); that, on the contrary, she was living close to him, and was in the habit of being visited by him every evening. She conceived the fatal idea of going there herself one day and creating a terrible scene in the presence of her rival. Dumas, thoroughly annoyed, made a vague attempt at rupture. Mélanie the First, in despair, played her last card:

> *Mélanie Waldor to Alexandre Dumas*: I am writing this while the night hours move on. I am feverish and cannot sleep ... I wish to remember only the sweet and noble Alex. who would rather know himself guilty of a wrong than suspect me of one. It was *that* Alex. who was my glory, my joy, my God, my idol. That I have broken him I know only too well, but I have done so because of the very violence of my love, as monkeys kill their young by hugging them too tightly. Oh! Alex., make it possible, I beg, for me to see in you the best and noblest of men. I do not want my love to be only shame and regret! I want to find in you the justification of my follies and my faults, of more than my faults. Be good and generous. *Away with that pride* which can endure no word of reproach ... and be more indulgent to me. In whom can I hope to find pity and kindness, if not in you? I do not know, but I believe, that were you to be with me when I draw my latest breath, your lips, instead of covering me with kisses, would set bitter words between myself and Death. Oh! mercy, a thousand times mercy! as you are a man.[1]

At this point, there appears upon the scene a third person who played, between Mélanie Waldor and Dumas, much the same part as did Dr Regnault between George Sand and Jules Sandeau — Dr Valerand. This doctor, who acted as confidant to the unhappy lovers, seems to have been one of the traditional go-betweens of romantic comedy.

Mélanie Waldor to Doctor Valerand [a letter containing her testamentary wishes]: *Monday* 22nd, eleven o'clock in the morning. I want, before he goes, to get from him:

My letters, that I may re-read them, and my portrait.
Our chain and our ring.
His watch — which I will buy.
His bronze medal.
La Prière, Le Lac, La Jalousie.
The rings made from poor Jacques's hair.
His seal *Ecce Labia.*

It is my wish that, should I die, all these objects (with the exception of the portrait) shall be buried with me in the Ivry cemetery, in a grave next to that of Jacques. I want to have only a white marble slab with, on it, the date of my death, my age, and, below, the words: *Sara di te o di morte.* At the four corners I would have these four dates inscribed:

September 12th, 1827. (The date of his avowal)
September 23rd, 1827. (The date of my fall)
September 18th, 1830. (The date of his departure from La Jarrie)
November 22nd, 1830. (The date of Mélanie's projected suicide)

These four, alone, determined my fate and the course taken by my life.

I also wish, for as long as my mother lives, to have geraniums upon my grave, and I beg my child, when she grows up, to take my mother's place in carrying out that duty. I want to be dressed not in a winding-sheet, but in my blue dress and yellow shawl. I want our black chain to be clasped about my neck . . . and his watch, and our ring laid upon my heart, with our broken geranium. I would have his poems and our letters placed at my feet.

I leave my portrait to my mother, and my hair to him, should he ever express a wish to have it, as well as the drawings by Boulanger and Johannot. To Laura I leave my chain and my bracelets: to Henriette, my rings: to my child, my cornelians . . . My album, to him, should he desire it. . . .[2]

Mélanie Waldor was destined to outlive by forty-one years her romantic will and this fatal rupture.

Belle Krelsamer was with child by Dumas. Mélanie knew it.

Write to her, my Alexandre, oh! write to her, and let me see the letter . . . Promise her money, consideration, influence, esteem, friendship — everything except your love and your caresses! Those are mine, mine only — or else, Mél[anie] Serre's, hers only. But in *that* case, then farewell Alex! Alive or dead we shall be separated for ever. . . .'

Mélanie the Second was brought to bed, on March 5th, 1831, of a child who was given the names Marie-Alexandrine. Because she was already burdened with a six-year-old son, born of an earlier, and ephemeral, liaison, the far-sighted mother insisted that Dumas should acknowledge their daughter, and gained her point. Forty-eight hours after the baby's birth, all was regularized. It would have been difficult for the author of *Antony*, the champion of natural children, to refuse to give his name to those who were his own. He was good-hearted but careless. For seven years he had forgotten to acknowledge his son, Alexandre. He wanted to be fair.

Alexandre Dumas to the notary, Jean-Baptiste Moreau: I want you to draft the necessary documents which will enable me to acknowledge as my own a child, registered at the Mairie in the Place des Italiens, under the name of Alexandre, on July 27th, 1824:

Mother: Madame Labaie [*sic*]: *Father*: unknown.

I wish the acknowledgment to be made without the mother's knowledge. This, I believe, is possible.

My names are: Alexandre Dumas Davy de la Pailleterie; rue de l'Université, 25.

The matter is urgent. I have reason to think that the child, of whom I am very fond, may be taken from me. Please instruct the person who delivers this letter, what steps had best be taken. You will, I think, require an extract from the Register of Births. If so, I will procure it for you.

I am, sir, yours faithfully

ALEX. DUMAS³

When *Antony* was produced in May 1831, Mélanie Waldor, who was the original of Adèle d'Hervey and knew it, was sent by the author a voucher for a front box, with this note: 'I send you, my friend, seven seats. I cannot bring them in person. I must attend a meeting which is deliberating about the cross. I shall try to visit you in your box—Your friend; A. D.'[4]

There was good reason to fear that *Antony* would pour oil upon the flames of the abandoned mistress. Everybody in Paris at once identified Adèle d'Hervey. The officer-husband, the only daughter, as well as certain details of dress and peculiarities of speech, made recognition easy. Mélanie, thus publicly compromised, accused Dumas of having 'put her into a play'. Soon, she said, her virtuous father, her growing daughter, would see in Mélanie Waldor only the heroine of *Antony*! When, instead of Mademoiselle Mars, Marie Dorval created the part, Mélanie found it difficult to endure the sight of herself being portrayed by a rival. There was a further aggravating circumstance. Belle Krelsamer, another rival, was cast in the small part of Madame de Camps, under her irritating stage-name of Mademoiselle Mélanie. The whole audience was soon speaking about the little Marie-Alexandrine as being the daughter of the author and the actress.

Mélanie Waldor stifled her wrath. The fact that she was a cast-off mistress did not alter the fact that she was a woman of letters. She presided over a 'salon', and Dumas, the triumphant author of *Antony*, would be an ornament not to be missed. 'You will come, will you not? Hugo will be there. The evening will be one of intimate conversation. Your presence would give me much pleasure . . .' She asked him to use his influence with a critic: 'It is important for me that my verses should be publicly talked about . . .' In accordance with the best traditions, she offered him her friendship:

> The love which I no longer have has been transformed into a *cult of the past*. To be the recipient of your praise gives you back to me. I feel, at such times, as though I had recaptured you, as though you were once more mine. Ah! all that is great and good in you will ever bind my soul to yours! No longer shall I live *for myself* alone, but in the knowledge that you are happy, loved and honoured; that you will still be making me a gift of the life you have constructed for yourself. Farewell my friend; brother, farewell.[5]

He now regarded the whole business as settled, and lived openly with Mélanie Serre, but he frequently met the first Mélanie at the houses of mutual friends. She was to be seen with the Nodiers, at the Arsenal, 'wearing a startlingly red dress, and dancing the gallop with her husband'. Once, when blind-man's-buff was being played, Dumas, watching her from a distance, found her ugly, and wondered how he could ever have been in love with her. Still, she had, to some extent, been responsible for *Antony*.

> Malheur, malheur à moi que le Ciel en ce monde
> A jeté comme un hôte à ses lois étranger . . .⁶

Such were the Byronic verses which at that time he was writing, though, under the cloak of *Antony*, as rebel-cum-good fellow he was gaily carrying a triple burden — as haunter of the great world, as male, and as a man burdened with a load of women. All he wanted was that the Furies should come to some sort of agreement among themselves. Mélanie Waldor had gracefully withdrawn, but Catherine Labay and Belle Krelsamer who, now that she was living in a state of domesticity with the father of her daughter, called herself *Madame Dumas*, were for ever quarrelling over the little Alexandre. It was the boy who suffered the greatest damage.

An admirable, sensual, and irresponsible man can do a great deal of harm without meaning to, and without even realizing the effect he is having. Dumas found it perfectly natural to run from mistress to mistress, and he would have liked to think that those whom he abandoned were happy. When his infidelities drove them to despair, he tried to make it up to them with presents. The son of Catherine Labay was to remember all his life the day when, because the youngster bawled at night, his father who was prevented by the noise from working, flung him carelessly on to the bed. His mother, frightened out of her life, had made a scene and, next day, Dumas had come home looking sheepish and bringing with him a melon as a peace-offering.⁷ How many propitiatory melons he must have offered in the course of his life, always serenely unaware of what he had done, always kindly in his moods of repentance!

Now that, in 1830, he had made some money, he installed Catherine and her son in a small apartment at Passy. Thither he sometimes went 'for a breath of country air', in his uniform of an artilleryman in the National Guard. It was from the Louvre, when he was on duty, that he was fetched at such times as the child was ill or had had an accident. One day, the doctor having ordered leeches, the boy violently resisted. His father gave him his word that they would not hurt.

'Put them on yourself, then!' said the small Alexandre.

Dumas at once applied two leeches to the palm of his left hand.[8]

He wanted only to be loved, but the child, not unnaturally, preferred the mother who had brought him up. Catherine Labay was a 'simple, upright and honest woman, a hard worker, a devout churchgoer, and *orderly* by temperament in all things'.[9] There can be little doubt that Dumas *fils* inherited from the Belgian needlewoman strong common sense, and a healthy, moderate, moral outlook which counterbalanced the vivid imagination, the passion, and conscious desire to astonish, which were the legacy of his father's family. He, later, charmingly described the modest apartment, always spotlessly clean, and the work-room where his mother distributed among her girls the tasks which she had cut out with her own hands.

The official act of acknowledgment of March 17th, 1831, which conferred parental authority on the author of *Antony*, marked the beginning of a painful struggle between Catherine Labay and her former lover.

Egged on by Belle Krelsamer, who accused Catherine of vulgarity and maintained that she was wholly unfitted to bring up Dumas's son, Alexandre the elder applied for custody of the child. The mother instituted proceedings against him, which she lost. Her case could have been better pleaded, had she taken the trouble to declare, when she was brought to bed, her intention of acknowledging maternity of the bastard according to French law. In the absence of any formal instructions, the doctor in attendance, and two neighbours as witnesses (one a tailor, the other a dentist) had gone to the Mairie where they had registered the birth of 'Alexandre, on the 27th of the current month, at six o'clock in the evening, at his mother's place of residence ... *natural son of Marie-Catherine Labay*', whereas they should have added '... and *formally acknowledged as such*'.[10] In 1831, Catherine, in her turn, had the child removed from his father's care, and legally acknowledged him on April 21st. But by then it was too late. The father's declaration had priority. Catherine carried on the fight, but all in vain; sometimes hiding her beloved son under her bed, sometimes getting him out of the room by the window. Finally, 'the Tribunal had the seven-year-old Alexandre taken in charge by the police commissioner, and placed at a boarding-school'.[11]

It is easy enough to see what a disturbing effect this long-drawn-out struggle between two persons, both of whom he would have liked to respect, must have had upon the young boy. He had to choose between them, and his heart went out to his mother. She called upon him to bear witness to his father's neglect of them. He could see for himself how quiet and well-ordered was the life she led, while his father, on the contrary, was cohabiting with a stranger. He felt confusedly that a grave fault had been committed against his irreproachable mother and that she was the victim of injustice. Children do not speak about their feelings, nor do they reveal their most secret griefs except by giving way to seemingly irrational fits of anger. Even when he was forty-two, the younger Dumas told a friend that he had 'never forgiven his father'.

When he was compelled to live under the roof of the great man's mistress, he grew rebellious. Madame Krelsamer, who tried to tame the spirit of her little girl's half-brother, found herself up against a fierce and determined resistance. She wrote to Dumas:

Dear friend: you know how truly I love your son, and that, consequently, I judge him with indulgence rather than severity. What I have to say to you now is this; that I believe it to be impossible for you to bring him up in your own home. The basis of his training has been vitiated, and the evil will have to be repaired as quickly as possible. I do not doubt but that he would be drawn more closely to you if you were in a position to take charge of him. But the most you can spare him is an occasional two hours. When you are absent he cares not a fig for anybody, and no one can control him. I have tried, with prayers and with threats, to get some sense into him, but all in vain. He will learn neither to read nor write, and goes his own way in so violent a manner that I am frequently compelled to give him a scolding. What makes matters far worse, what lies at the root of all the trouble, is my having to tell him that he can see his mother on Sundays and Thursdays. Each time he has been with her, he returns more completely unbiddable than ever, thoroughly cantankerous and surly with all of us. I am convinced that his mother instils into him a strong dislike of us, and even of you. He never asks for a toy, as he used to do. He has but one thought in his head — his mother! Nothing else matters to him at all. He came home on Tuesday, at three o'clock, and goes to see her again tomorrow! She comes in person to fetch him. He will probably sleep there, and will thus spend more time with, than without, her. There lies the trouble, and it will grow worse.

This morning, Adèle took him out walking. He did all he could to persuade her to lead him to his mother, and came back in tears, furious at not having been obeyed. The more he sees of her, the more he will want to see, and the more estranged from you he will become. Your earlier firmness has born no fruit. You have put between yourself and your child a woman whose whole purpose is to alienate his affections. A time will come when, filled with love for her, the boy will say to you: 'You have separated me from my mother, and you have dealt harshly with her.' That is the attitude he is being taught to adopt. . . .

What I am saying to you, my angel, I say with as much conviction as I should were I your wife, and this child ours. Your son has, in many ways, the intelligence of a ten-year-old, but he will always believe his mother rather than you. If this state of affairs is to be changed, there is no time to lose, and you may well congratulate yourself on having, at least momentarily, separated him from her. You would do well to write *to her* about all this. A thousand kisses, my angel, and tear this letter up.[12]

Dumas soon grew tired of this endless battling and decided to send his son back to boarding-school. The first choice made by the Tribunal de la Seine had been the *institution Vauthier*, in the rue de la Montagne Sainte-Geneviève. Dumas *fils* described in *l'Affaire Clemenceau* the last day he spent with his mother, of how the poor woman bought forks, spoons and a silver mug for him, and prepared his school outfit with her own hands. 'Each single article represented money earned in the sweat of her brow; long periods of sitting up late into the night, sometimes until nearly dawn. I wonder whether the man who reduced her to the position of a poor, unmarried mother, forced to provide unaided for the needs of his child, ever realized what he was doing? . . .'[13] To pass from a mother's tender care to the cruelty of a boys' school was a terrible ordeal for him.

CHAPTER VI

Paris in 1831

PARIS had not been consoled for the half-completed revolution.
Like Dumas, the capital was holding aloof from the regime.
Every evening, between the Gymnase and the Ambigu, street-
urchins threw stones at the police. The theatre-public remained
extremely nervous. The founders of the romantic school had lost much
of their earlier unity. Lamartine had taken to politics; Sainte-Beuve
and Hugo were no longer on speaking-terms. In 1830, Hugo, Vigny
and Dumas had formed a dramatic triumvirate. But no triumvirate
endures. One day, Hugo said indignantly to Dumas: 'Would you
believe it, here's a wretched scribbler who claims that Vigny invented
the historical drama!'

'The fool!' replied Dumas: 'as though everyone didn't know that
it was I!'

The outstanding success of *Antony* had 'caused a rift between the
young men who, until then, had followed one single flag, who,
together, had opened a breach with *Henri III*, and moved to the assault
with *Hernani*. They were now divided into two groups — the adherents
of Monsieur Victor Hugo, and those of Monsieur Alexandre Dumas.
They no longer presented a compact mass to the enemy, and even
sniped at one another'.[1] Dumas's relations with his fellow-writers, in
spite of his unfailing good-humour, were becoming less and less easy.
Many were jealous of his rapid rise to fame. More than one of them
declared that he did not deserve his success. His 'tilbury' and his
'tiger' caused more annoyance than amusement. Little red-haired
Sainte-Beuve, a critic of refined and exacting taste, said: 'Dumas?
His ideal is the eternal schoolboy's idea of a good tuck-in. *Christine?*
— a second-rate affair — as inferior to *Hernani* as hyssop is to the cedar.'
This judgment was all the harsher because Sainte-Beuve was not really
an admirer even of *Hernani*. But it was Dumas who had opened
the breach and, in any case, *Antony* owed nothing to *Hernani*. 'A
good tuck-in, eh?' growled Dumas. 'Let me do the cooking, and I'll
show 'em!'

Hugo remained friendly and courteous. He was now publicly recognized as the leader of the romantic school. For budding writers, a preface from his pen was as good as a mention in dispatches by an army commander. Hugo wanted to be a thinker: Dumas was content to be an entertainer. His enemies would have added 'and to make a lot of money'. It is true that he wanted money, but only because he loved giving it away, spending it lavishly, wasting it — not hoarding it. Hugo, a great poet, lived like a penny-wise bourgeois; Dumas, like a generous, thriftless bohemian. It was Hugo, not Dumas, who kept a watchful eye on the box-office. 'Really, it is quite terrible how concerned Victor is over the takings', wrote Fontaney in his Diary.[2] But then Hugo's receipts were on a princely scale.

When Dumas had heard Hugo give a reading of *Marion de Lorme*, he had said in a loud voice: 'He's got us licked to a frazzle!' and, to himself: 'No one knows better than I do how to construct a play: I only wish my verse was as good as his!' After re-reading *Marion*, he said: 'I'd give a year of my life for each one of those magnificent acts: but it only makes me feel more admiration and more of warm friendship for Victor — not a scrap of jealousy . . .' and in this he was perfectly sincere.

So sincere, indeed, that, having written a play in verse — *Charles VII chez ses grands vassaux* — he was tempted, after reading *Marion de Lorme*, to write it all over again, in prose. The actors, however, reassured him, and the statuesque Mademoiselle George 'created' the part of the heroine at the Odéon on October 20th, 1831. The subject, once again, was one he had come on in a book left open by accident. The theme was that of Racine's *Andromaque*. A woman in love with a man who does not respond has him killed by a man she does not love, but who loves her. King Charles VII and Agnès Sorel were introduced only for reasons of prestige. The three essential characters are the cruel wife, Bérengère; her husband, the comte de Savoisy, and the murderer, Yaqoub the Saracen, who has been brought back from the Crusade by Savoisy. Yaqoub's life has been saved by the crusading knight. But he loves Bérengère and, urged by her, kills his benefactor. The play is quite valueless, except for some rather fine declamatory passages, put into Yaqoub's mouth, on the subject of race-prejudice, a problem which touched Dumas to the quick, and about which, therefore, he wrote well.

It was not a resounding failure: far from it. But the first-night audience remained cold. The imposing Mademoiselle George played Bérengère, a woman of twenty-five, slim and pale. The part had obviously been written for Marie Dorval. The handsome Lockroy was the young Arab, Yaqoub, for whom Bocage had been originally intended. This accounted for the weak points in the interpretation. *From Fontaney's Diary*: 'Not up to Dumas's usual standard. The play is a sort of *Othello* turned inside out and encrusted with heaven knows how many classic and romantic imitations. Such originality as it has is that of marquetry. A production belonging to the composite Order.'[3]

Dumas had taken his little boy to see it in the hope that, by associating him with a great success, he might regain his affection. Later, when Alexandre Dumas *fils* was a famous dramatist, he still remembered that strange evening, and how he had said to himself: 'It is Papa who has done all this', and the gloomy walk home through the Paris night, with his own little hand in his father's larger one, which was trembling slightly. Papa is unhappy, thought the little fellow. He felt that it would be best not to talk about the play, perhaps, even, not to talk at all. All the same, the public crowded the Odéon.

It is always dangerous for an artist, unless he is very conscientious, to feel the need for a lot of money: for at such times he cannot resist tempting offers of remunerative work. *Antony* was regarded as a model of dramatic construction, and a number of half-completed plays were submitted to its author, with a request that he should collaborate with their writers.

It was in this way that Prosper Goubaux, the founder of a well-known boarding-school, and Jacques Beudin, a banker with a passion for literature, brought him the draft of a drama, *Richard Darlington*, over the last act of which they were at a standstill. Harel offered the services of Frédérick Lemaître as leading actor, and Dumas rewrote the piece with him in view. But 'a Frédérick' was not 'a Bocage'. In order that the actor's gifts should be seen to full advantage, the hero must be both cynical and strong. Dumas cut to his measure the passages of coarse dialogue and the trenchant sallies in which Frédérick excelled. It was already a matter of common talk that the authors were uncertain how to get rid of Jenny, Richard's wife. 'Chuck her out of the window!' said Dumas. This unpremeditated assassination became, in fact, the crucial incident of the play. A beam of green light, focused on the actor's face, gave it so frightful an appearance that Louise Noblet (in the role of Jenny) uttered cries of genuine terror.

Fontaney, who witnessed the final rehearsal, commented as follows:
'Well-made melodrama — The "Young France" gang present in force
— leather hats, overcoats with large lapels, thick bunches of curls,
cloaks of green American-cloth: lizards swimming in the rain. — Petrus
Borel and his poetry! Ah!'[4]

The audience had taken on the tone of the drama. At the end,
Dumas, seeing that Musset looked very pale, said: 'Hullo! What's the
matter?'

'I feel as though I were suffocating!' replied Musset.

The box-office returns were impressive. But already a new subject
had been suggested to Dumas. Bocage, who had the happiest memories
of *Antony* had submitted to him a draft by Anicet Bourgeois, who had
a number of fairly efficient melodramas to his credit. Out of this,
Dumas made a play, *Térésa*. He did not care much for it, except that
it contained the part of a young girl, of whom he said modestly:

'She is a flower from the same garden as Miranda in *The Tempest*
and Klärchen in *Egmont*.'

For this part, Bocage suggested a beginner who, according to him,
had a deal of talent.

'What's her name?' asked Dumas.

'Oh! you wouldn't know anything about her. She's called Ida — acts
at Montmartre and Belleville: but she's highly gifted, quite ravishing,
and the part would fit her like a glove.'

'Ravishing' would seem to have been an optimistic epithet when
applied to Ida Ferrier. Small, and with a not very good figure, she had
little in her favour beyond fine eyes, a good complexion, and thick
fair hair. She tried to imitate Dorval, 'to speak with her shoulders,
and make undulating motions with her neck, like a turtle-dove'. She
had nothing of Marie's inimitable naturalness.

Ida Ferrier's real name was Marguerite Ferrand. She dragged a
widowed mother at her heels wherever she went. Small though her
part was, she made a considerable success in *Térésa*, and flung herself,
in a highly emotional state, into the author's arms, saying that he had
'assured her future'. She did not then know how true those words
were. Dumas gave her supper, took her home, and made her his
mistress. He was never tired of wondering at the youth, beauty and
poetry of his new conquest. He even praised her chastity. 'She is a
statue in crystal!' he said. 'You think that lilies are white, that snow
is white, that alabaster is white. You are wrong. There is nothing

white in the whole world but the colour of Mademoiselle Ida Ferrier's hands.' This caused a deal of amusement.

In *Térésa*, Ida Ferrier had managed to create an illusion. But, once she had become Dumas's mistress, and knew that, for the future, there would always be a part for her in any new play by her lover, she neglected her craft and sank to a level 'well below that of mediocrity'. She was a 'minor Dorval, in the same sense that Mélingue was a minor Frédérick ... She waved her arms like a scythe and opened her big mouth to chew over a lot of words she didn't understand ...'⁵ She was a serious danger to Dumas. So long as the romantics wrote for performers of genius, they could get away with anything. A commonplace phrase, spoken by Dorval, could sweep an audience off its feet. When it was spoken by Ida Ferrier, it showed for the sad stuff it was. It is far better for a dramatist to struggle with a great actor than to dominate a poor one. Life may be made more difficult, but the play is safe.

It is clear from a reading of Fontaney's Diary, that Dumas's increasingly numerous collaborations were beginning to make the world of letters feel uneasy:

> *Monday, February 6th*: Went to see *Térésa* at the Opéra-Comique — It is a great success — still about adultery, but this time, in double-harness ... The play is announced as by Dumas. There is another author as well, but he has had to agree that his name shall not appear ... *Thursday, February 16th*: Lunched with Dumas, his lady-love and Goubaux ... Later, to Madame Gay. Dumas was there, solemnly talking Republic and Revolution. They want to make him pay for the powder he brought back from Soissons: a good joke! He had with him M. Anicet Bourgeois, who collaborated with him over *Térésa*. They are busy with four other plays, all written in the same way. *For shame!* Walked home at two o'clock with Dumas, in bright moonlight.⁶

At the moment of Ida Ferrier's irruption into Dumas's life, Belle Krelsamer was away on tour. When she returned, there were storms. Nothing was easier for women who were prepared to accept his quasi-oriental habits than to live with him. All he insisted upon was that his hours of work should be respected. In everything else, his good nature went almost to the extremes of weakness. Ever since he had begun to make money, he had been supporting his mistresses, his past mistresses, his friends, his collaborators, and his toadies. Together, they made a sizeable regiment of hangers-on. When people did not know where to get a dinner, they would say: 'Let's go along to Dumas.' They would find him at work. On the mantelpiece would be the latest of his golden earnings.

'Dumas, I'm in need of money: I'm going to take this.'

'All right.'

'Let you have it back next week.'

'Just as you like.'

He loved arranging and sharing the pleasures of others. The King, Louis-Philippe, had recently given a fancy-dress ball. As carnival-time drew near, Bocage and the rest of his friends urged Dumas, who, since his successes in the theatre, had become a nabob of letters and loved the part, to do likewise. 'Yours will be better in two ways,' they told him, 'you won't have the people who go to the royal parties, and you won't have the Académie.' The main difficulty was that Dumas's apartment consisted only of four rooms, and that he would have to invite at least four hundred people. Fortunately there was another apartment on the same floor. It was to let, and contained not a stick of furniture. The only decoration was the grey-blue lining-paper on the walls. Dumas asked his landlord for permission to use this empty suite of rooms and got it. All that remained was to make it presentable.

The most famous painters of the day, Eugène Delacroix, Célestin Nanteuil, Decamps, Barye, the brothers Johannot, the Boulanger cousins — all friends of Dumas — contributed to the task. Each was asked to take a subject from the works of the writers who had been invited. A theatrical scene-painter, Ciceri, had canvases stretched on the walls and, a few days before the day of the party, the artists arrived to work on the spot. The only absentee was Delacroix, who did not put in an appearance until the last day, and improvised a wonderful scene in the space of a few hours, composing and painting as he went along.

There remained the most important item of all, in the eyes of Dumas — the supper. He prided himself on being a good cook and on always providing good cheer for his guests. Naturally his first thought was to lay a sound, and not very costly, foundation of game killed by himself. This would be at once economical and attractive. From his cousin Deviolaine he obtained a permit to shoot in the State Forest. This done, he set off with a few companions and brought home with him nine deer and three hares.

Then, as on the occasion of his very first visit to Paris, he decided to get together the rest of the menu by employing a system of barter. He summoned the famous caterer, Chevet, who agreed to supply a salmon weighing thirty pounds, and a sturgeon of fifty, in return for three deer. A fourth deer was exchanged for a monumental galantine. Two deer were roasted and served whole. The detailed arrangements were entrusted to the mistress of the house, in other words, Belle Krelsamer.

She decreed that fancy dress should be obligatory, or, at least, the wearing of a Venetian domino. The most famous, the loveliest, actresses of the Paris stage had promised to be present, and many women of fashion begged for cards of invitation. At seven o'clock, Chevet set up a buffet worthy of Gargantua. Three hundred bottles of bordeaux were put to warm, and three hundred bottles of burgundy to cool. Five hundred bottles of champagne stood waiting for the ice to arrive. Two orchestras were engaged to play in the two flower-decked sets of rooms.

By midnight, the scene was one of extraordinary brilliance. The bearers of all the great names in Paris were there, not only artists, writers and actors, but serious-minded men like Lamartine, Odilon Barrot, François Buloz of the *Revue des Deux Mondes*, and Dr Véron of the *Revue de Paris*. Mademoiselle Mars, Joanny, Michelot and Firmin wore the costumes in which they had appeared in *Henri III et sa Cour*. The young actresses, radiant with the certainty that, if only for one evening, they were the favourites of La Fayette, found him as gallant and as stylish as he must have been, before the Revolution of 1789, at the court balls of Versailles. Rossini, disguised as Figaro, competed with him in popularity.

It is impossible to imagine what this Dumas ball must have been like. A writer in *l'Artiste*, said of it:

No matter who you are, prince, king or banker; no matter whether you have a civil list of twelve million, or a fortune of a milliard — I defy you to create anything like so brilliant, so gay, so novel an occasion. You may have, for all I know, rooms more vast, suppers better arranged, with uniformed attendants at the doors, but certainly you cannot have, no matter how much you are prepared to pay, such wall-paintings improvised and carried out by the hands of masters. You cannot have so youthful and gay an assemblage of artists and celebrities. Least of all can you have the unaffected and contagious cordiality of our leading dramatist — Alexandre Dumas.'

This was truly said. What millionaire could have provided rooms painted like the loggias of Raphael? Who else could have brought together so much fame and beauty? Belle Krelsamer, dressed as Hélène Fourment, wore her broad-brimmed hat with its white plumes, with grace and dignity. Alexandre Dumas appeared as Titian's brother, in a parti-coloured costume with wide, hanging sleeves, his great chest confined in a doublet; Célestin Nanteuil was got up as an 'old sweat', Delacroix as Dante, Barye as a Bengal tiger, Alfred de Musset as Paillasse,⁸ and Eugène Sue in a domino. The bibliophile, Jacob (Paul Lacroix), in spite of his ninety years, had donned a pointed cap and a velvet jerkin. It was noticed that Baron Taylor was there, and Bocage in his Didier dress from *Marion de Lorme*. Mademoiselle George, as an Italian peasant-girl, looked like an empress. In short, every world, every century, every country; history, geography, fantasy — all were represented. When, at three o'clock in the morning, the gigantic supper was served, 'it would be impossible to give any idea of the extraordinary spectacle presented by this jumble of beggars, men-at-arms, cowled monks, raised arms, plumed heads, chickens, hams, glasses and red faces. The wedding-feasts of Cana and Ganache can have been nothing to it. . . .'⁹

After supper the dancing was resumed. A noisy galop eddied and swirled. 'The floors shook under the impact of the dancing ring. It was as though one had been transported to the very heart of a witches' sabbath, whither young and lovely warlocks had flocked from the four corners of the globe to win souls for the Devil. Even the gravest heads were turned . . .' Odilon Barrot, a pompous, timorous politician was seen cavorting with a madcap. At nine o'clock in the morning, preceded by a band of music, the guests went into the street, where they indulged in a final processional galop, the head of which reached the boulevard while the tail was still wriggling about in the Square d'Orléans.

This frenzied galop seemed like a symbol. Scarcely ten years before, the host had left his native town, a young man with fifty francs in his pocket, determined to take Paris by storm. Ten years ... and now, here he was, the only living person capable of leading, in this enormous farandole, all that was most brilliant, most intelligent, most beautiful in Paris. Disraeli, when somebody once asked him what life should be, replied with great seriousness: 'A magnificent procession from Youth to the Tomb.' Dumas would have wanted it to be a gorgeous serpentine of friends moving to the rhythm of a galop. Already he had at his heels a whole retinue leaping to the music of his violins. We shall see him later gathering round him readers from all the world, who hung on his lips, eager for more and more of those tales which were as stirring as that same music, and leading them, disguised now as musketeers, now as cardinals, in an everlasting gallop which even now is still continuing.

PART FOUR

★

THE PRODIGAL FATHER

CHAPTER I

'La Tour de Nesle'

That melodrama, hail! where Margot weeps! ALFRED DE MUSSET

REVOLUTIONS are illnesses, in which the time of incubation is short, the convalescence interminable. The new king's reign had opened in an atmosphere of fever from which the theatre suffered. In Paris there was a succession of riots. In La Vendée, the duchesse de Berry was rallying the disaffected. Everywhere the cholera was rife, and fear dried up the flow of box-office receipts. No one has ever determined (microbes being, at that time, anonymous) the precise nature of this deadly epidemic, but all over the world multitudes were dying of it, perhaps as a result of fright and auto-suggestion. The doctors advised against the eating of raw fruit. Dumas, as always, was assailed by money troubles. One of his friends who was in the habit of criticizing his prodigal ways was surprised to find him sitting at a table in front of an enormous cantaloup.

'How unwise!' exclaimed the visitor, 'to be eating melon at such a time!'

'My dear fellow, they're dirt cheap!'

After saying which, he like everybody else got the cholera, but, unlike everybody else, cured himself by drinking a glassful of ether. While he was still in bed, though convalescent, he was called upon by the witty and dangerous Félix Harel, Manager of the Porte-Saint-Martin.

'Is that you, Harel?' exclaimed Dumas: 'what news of the cholera?'

'It's gone.'

'Are you sure?'

'It didn't cover its costs,' said Harel: 'a wonderful time, dear friend, for putting on a new production . . . The public, once they are reassured, will be all agog for pleasure. That will react very favourably on the theatres . . . I want a play from you, Dumas.'

'Come, come, old man: d'you really believe I'm in any sort of condition to think of such things?'

Harel explained that it was merely a question of *adapting*. A young man from Tonnerre (Yonne), named Frédéric Gaillardet, had offered the Porte-Saint-Martin a drama. He had got hold of an idea, but couldn't write. All the same, Harel had done a deal with him, and then given the manuscript to Jules Janin, the critic, who lived in the same building as the George-Harel couple. Janin had rewritten it.

'Well?'
'It's better written now, but not a bit more actable.'

What Harel wanted was that Dumas should reconstruct the whole play.

'But shan't I get into trouble with the young man from Tonnerre?'
'Just a sheep, dear boy.'
'I see . . . and you want me to shear him?'
'There's no doing anything with you!'

By the time Harel took his leave, Dumas had promised to remake the drama within a fortnight. 'See that there's a good part for George!' said the manager from the threshold.[1]

It is remarkable that Alexandre Dumas's most famous play, a play which has been performed thousands of times, has taken its place as the very type of French melodrama, and is still quoted (with laughter), should originally have been the work of Frédéric Gaillardet of Tonnerre (Yonne), and that nobody, or scarcely anybody, is aware of that fact. Was Gaillardet the victim of a grave injustice? Certainly not. It needed Dumas's zest, artlessness and generous philosophy of life to give to the ridiculous story the movement and the tone which turned it into a classic of over-acting.

The subject is as follows: The period is the beginning of the fourteenth century. Opposite the Louvre (at the precise spot where the Palais de l'Institut now stands) there is an ancient tower, a place of mystery over which there hangs a cloud of terror. It is part stronghold, part prison, and its foundations are lapped by the Seine. Each morning, at a point a little way down-stream, the watch find the dead bodies of three young men. Who has had them killed? The Queen, Marguerite de Bourgogne, and her two sisters, after indulging in a secret room of the tower, every night, in an orgy of adulterous pleasure. To be their partners, these royal princesses choose strong and handsome gentlemen

Thomas-Alexandre, General Dumas (1762-1806)

Waldor
(Mélanie Villenave,
wife of François-Joseph)

Ida Ferrier
(Marguerite Ferrand,
wife of Alexandre
Dumas *père*)

Château de
Monte-Cristo

Alexandre Dumas *père*

Marie Duplessis
(Alphonsine Plessis)

Alexandre Dumas *fils*
at the time of his marriage
to Princess Naryschkine
in 1864

Nadejda Knorring,
widow of
Prince Alexander Naryschkine

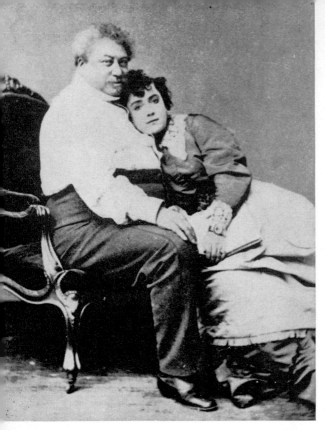

Two photographs by Liebert
of Dumas *père* and Adah Menken
in 1867

Henriette Regnier de la Brière,
second wife of Dumas *fils*

Aimée Desclée

Alexandre Dumas *fils*
in 1891, at his apartment in the Rue Ampère

newly arrived in Paris (knowing nobody), arrange with them, by trusted messengers, a triple rendezvous, have them brought into the tower blindfold, and, after one night of passion, arrange for them to be assassinated, since the King of France, Marguerite's husband,² must never know of the crimes committed by the grand-daughter of Saint-Louis.

It so happens that a day comes when one of these condemned lovers makes his escape and forces his way into the Queen's presence. He goes by the name of Captain Buridan, and formerly, when he was, under his real name, a page in the service of the duc de Bourgogne, was Marguerite's first 'fancy', and had had a son by her. She had given him a dagger and told him to kill her father, Robert II, duc de Bourgogne. Buridan is, therefore, in a position to bring blackmail to bear upon the Queen, for he knows the terrible secrets of her youth. She goes to see him in the cell where she has had him confined, being determined to have him made away with. At the very moment at which we believe him to be irrevocably doomed, he embarks, with calm indifference, upon a pleasant little passage of narrative: 'In 1293, twenty years ago, Burgundy was happy . . . Duke Robert had a young and lovely daughter . . . Duke Robert had an innocent and credulous page.'³

Buridan threatens Marguerite. He tells her that he will arrange for the King to see the letter in which (in 1293) she had revealed her intention of committing parricide. This letter is in a safe place. All this is said with such assurance that she promises him his freedom and has his fetters struck off. He next insists that she shall make him First Minister. The Queen has him at once appointed to this important post. 'We live in strange times', remarks one of the characters. They most certainly did! More crimes are committed, but now Marguerite and Buridan are accomplices. In the long run, the wicked are punished. Louis X has the guilty pair arrested.

'What!' exclaims Marguerite: 'arrest the Queen and the First Minister!'

'There is here,' replies the representative of public authority, 'neither queen nor first minister. There are only a corpse and two assassins.'

A wonderful curtain! The whole story delighted Dumas. He adored heroes who bounced up again after the most terrible disasters, who fought hammer and tongs, and always successfully, against a world of enemies, and 'reappeared at the window when they had just been flung out of the door'. It was in some such manner that General Dumas, and he himself, had conducted their own lives. His father had defended the bridge at Brixen, single-handed, against an army, and he himself had always entertained the illusion that he had taken the town of Soissons in 1830, waving a pistol. His father had held his ground against an emperor, he, against a king. His need to be triumphant, to 'brazen things out', had not always found satisfaction in real life, but on the stage he could give free rein to his fantasies.

La Tour de Nesle is a true picture neither of human passions nor of a period in history. It is not a tragedy, and it is not a drama; Dumas was neither Racine nor Shakespeare. The play is pure melodrama, the very type of melodrama. That is to say, its plot is dependent upon chance, in which the most unlikely coincidences serve to keep interest alive and to resolve all problems, just when the play appears to be at death's door.

But why, in spite of its excesses, should not melodrama be entitled to be regarded as a form of art, if only a minor one? The purpose of art is not to copy reality, but to transform, or *deform*, it in order to arouse certain emotions which the spectator wants to feel. Now, the spectator of 1832 was no longer the spectator of 1782. What had come to be known as the boulevard public, the working-class audiences which made the fortune of the Porte-Saint-Martin, consisted of people who took little interest in the analysis of feelings which is the product of leisure and life as it is lived in courts and salons. The success of men like Pixérécourt, of melodramas like *l'Auberge des Adrets*, gave writers something to think about. Romantic drama is nothing but melodrama ennobled by verse. Cultured authors, Hugo and Vigny, would not admit this. They had hesitated, though not for long, before permitting their plays to be performed at the Porte-Saint-Martin. Dumas, a self-educated man, had no such scruples. 'My sort of dramas', he had said from the very beginning, 'will be better played on the boulevard than in the Théatre-Français.'

And he was right — not only for the advancement of his own career, but for the salvation of the theatre. Mademoiselle Mars and her school had imposed on the Comédie-Française a convention even more inhuman than that of the boulevard. In time, it is true, the boulevard itself grew tired of the innovation. Rachel gave new life to the classic tragedies, polite society discovered a fresh vitality, and Racine returned to the boards — which was all as it should be. The swing of the pendulum is a dominant feature in the history of art. In 1832, melodrama was at its peak, and Dumas was the man of all others marked out for success in that particular form, because he shared the feelings of the man in the street — a desire for justice, a wish to tell a few home-truths to those who sat in the seats of the mighty, a tendency to divide humanity, somewhat crudely, into heroes on the one hand, and villains on the other.

As soon as Dumas had read the manuscript sent to him by Harel, he saw at once what could be made of it. The first thing to be done was to open the play by presenting and establishing the various characters, and then to follow quickly with a prison scene which, in Gaillardet's version, did not exist. But the really essential thing was to stress the central motif of the drama which, in Dumas's eyes (and, later, in those of the public) was 'the struggle between Buridan and Marguerite de Bourgogne, between an adventurer and a queen, the one armed with the full force of his genius, the other assured in her rank'. It went without saying that genius must triumph over power.

It was necessary, too, to introduce into the piece some of those passages of flamboyant dialogue which were the delight of Dumas, and of his audiences. For instance, at the end of the scene in which Orsini, the assassin, meets, in a tavern, with the three young men whose lives and happiness he is threatening, the curfew sounds.

ORSINI The curfew, gentlemen.
BURIDAN (*taking his cloak, and going out*) Good night. I am
    expected by the second tower of the Louvre.
PHILIPPE I, at the rue Froid-Mantel.
GAULTIER I, at the Palace.
    (*They go out,* ORSINI *shuts the door and whistles.* LANDRY *and
three men enter*)
ORSINI And we, my lads, at the Tour de Nesle.[4]

Vulgar, noisy music, but what a curtain! When the three young men, after their rapturous night of passion, have to pay for it with their lives, Philippe d'Aulnay falls bleeding to the ground, and cries:

PHILIPPE Help! help! help me, brother!
    (*The queen enters, carrying a torch*)

QUEEN 'Show me your face, then let me die' — that is what you
said, is it not? Your wish shall be granted! (*She tears off her
mask*) Look your fill, and die!
PHILIPPE Marguerite de Bourgogne, the Queen of France! (*Dies*)
(*The Voice of the Watchman* (*off*)) Three of the clock and all's
well. Sleep quietly, people of Paris.[5]

There are passages of superb grandiloquence:

Come, thou devil's landlord, thou may'st search my heart with
twenty daggers, and yet not find my secret! . . .

On thy arms are veins, and in those veins is blood! . . .

Dumas, completely conquered and won over, wrote to Harel that
he 'was his man' in the matter of *La Tour de Nesle*, and that the sooner
the financial details of the collaboration were settled, the better. It was
stipulated in Gaillardet's contract that he should receive an author's
royalty of forty francs for each performance, plus tickets to the value
of eighty francs (which he was at liberty to resell). One half of these
sums he had agreed to make over to Jules Janin at the time when the
latter (before Dumas had come into the picture) had undertaken to
revise the play. But Janin had abandoned the attempt, and generously
bowed himself out. Dumas did, however, retain one of Janin's passages
of declamation, which afterwards became famous: the tirade against
Great Ladies.

BURIDAN Have you never had suspicion of these ladies' rank?
Has it never occurred to you that they are highly placed? Have
you ever, in your garrison amours, seen many hands so white,
many smiles so cold? Have you noticed the richness of their
dresses, the soft tones of their voices, the falsity in their eyes?
Oh! great ladies they are, and no mistake! They had us sought
for in the darkness by a veiled and ancient crone who spoke
honeyed words to us. Oh! great ladies, surely. No sooner had
we come into this place of dazzling brightness, so perfumed, so
warm, that the senses reel, than they welcomed us with loving
words, gave themselves to us without timidity, without delay!
At once they fell into our arms, strangers though we were, and
wet from the storm. Not difficult to see how great these ladies
are! . . . At table . . . To all the transports of love and wine they

yielded unabashed, untarrying. They blasphemed, they made
strange talk, they uttered hateful words. They forgot all reticence, all shame: forgot the world and Heaven, too. I say again,
these are great ladies, very great ladies!⁶

This passage Dumas had relished on the palate of a connoisseur. It
was melodrama of a choice vintage. But, Jules Janin having abdicated,
Gaillardet was now once more the play's proprietor. Dumas offered
to let him have the terms as originally set down, on condition that he,
Dumas, should receive, say, 10 per cent of the takings. To this Harel
consented. In the event of success, Dumas would make a great deal
of money; otherwise, nothing. A struggle ensued when Dumas said
that he intended to remain incognito. This was not at all what Harel
had in mind, for he was reckoning on Dumas's name to fill his theatre.
But Alexandre would not budge. He wanted Gaillardet's name to be
the only one announced on the first night. Why? Modesty? That
would seem, to say the least, improbable. Perhaps he thought that
the critics who had come down heavily on *Charles VII chez ses grands
vassaux* would deal more gently with a beginner.

He wrote a generous letter to Gaillardet, in which he explained that
Harel had 'asked for some advice'; that he had been delighted at this
opportunity to help a young writer to get a hearing; that he felt it a
great pleasure to *give* rather than to sell his services — which seemed
true enough in view of the fact that Dumas's own remuneration, as
agreed with Harel, left Gaillardet's intact.

But the young man from Tonnerre replied with some bitterness that
he did not want to have a collaborator. Dumas hurried round to Harel,
who said: 'The fellow must be out of his mind: he didn't object to
Janin', and at once put Dumas's version into rehearsal. Gaillardet
arrived from Tonnerre, kicked up no end of a row and wanted to
challenge Dumas to a duel. At last a compromise was reached: the
play should be described on the posters as 'by Messieurs Gaillardet and
***'. Gaillardet's name alone should be given out after the first night,
and both authors should be entitled to include *La Tour de Nesle* in
their collected works. This seemed fair enough.

At rehearsal, with actors of the standing of Mademoiselle George and
Pierre Bocage, the play at once 'assumed vast proportions' (the phrase
is Dumas's own). He had, at first, thought of Frédérick Lemaître for
Buridan, but Frédérick, terrified at the thought of cholera, had run

away from Paris. Mademoiselle George had no wish to act opposite a man who would 'steal the play', and insisted on Bocage. As soon as this was known, Frédérick returned hot-foot to Paris. Harel refused to pay compensation to Bocage, and Frédérick's fury had to be seen to be believed.

Dumas would have liked to give his new protégé, Ida Ferrier, a chance: 'She's just the young woman, I am sure, that Harel needs: Juliette has no claim whatever to play an important part.'[7] Juliette was Juliette Drouet, who had once sat to Pradier, the sculptor. She was part demi-mondaine, part actress. Harel used neither Juliette nor Ida in *La Tour de Nesle*. The play opened on May 29th, 1832. Mademoiselle George was majestic and statuesque, Bocage, mephistophelian and star-crossed. Dumas in his *Mémoires* describes the evening's triumph with artless satisfaction:

The house was seething. Success was in the very air we breathed.

The end of the second scene was terrific — Buridan jumping out of the window, Marguerite tearing off her mask and revealing her blood-stained cheek ... the effect was staggering. And when, after the orgy, the flight, the murder, the laughs half-drowned in groans, the man flung into the river, the lover of a night dispatched without mercy by his royal mistress — when after all this, the voice of the watchman was heard calling: 'Three of the clock and all's well. Sleep quietly, people of Paris', the audience burst into a thunder of applause ... Then came the famous prison scene.

One day my son asked me (he had not, at that time tried his hand at playwriting):

'What are the first principles of dramatic composition?'

'Make your first act clear and explicit, your last act short, and, whatever you do, have no prison in the third!'

When I said that, I was guilty of ingratitude. I have never seen any stage effect comparable to that prison scene, superbly played by the two persons concerned, who have to bear the whole burden on their shoulders. ...

At last we reached the fifth act. It was divided into two scenes — the eighth, which was one of terrifying comedy, the ninth, which, for dramatic horror, was comparable to the second. There was something in it that recalled the classic fatality of Sophocles, combined with the scenic terror of Shakespeare. The success was immense, and the announcement of Monsieur Frédéric Gaillardet's name, as author, was received with applause.

On the next day, Harel had his posters out: LA TOUR DE NESLE by Messieurs * * * and Gaillardet. Dumas dashed round to see him.
'You're going to make fresh trouble for me with Gaillardet!' he said.
'My dear fellow,' said Harel: 'we've got a great success: a touch of scandal will turn it into an immense one . . . If Gaillardet makes a row, I get my touch of scandal . . . and, in that way at least, he'll have done something for the play . . . Don't run away with the idea, Dumas, that it's enough to turn out a masterpiece and then say "I had nothing to do with it". . Oh! dear me, no! Whether you like it or not, the whole of Paris is going to know that you most certainly had something to do with it. . . .'
At this moment there was a knock at the door. It was a court usher bringing a paper, sent by Gaillardet of Tonnerre (Yonne), demanding in legal form that 'Mr Three Stars' should appear, not first, but second on the bills. Harel refused to make the change. Gaillardet brought a case and won it, but the shrewd manager had got the free publicity he wanted. So great did the bitterness between Dumas and Gaillardet become that a duel with pistols was actually fought, though inconclusively. The three stars were down-graded. From the point of view of the law, the incident was closed.
It did, however, do harm to Dumas's reputation. The lesser newspapers, which had never been kindly disposed towards him, said that nothing in *La Tour de Nesle* was his, which was untrue. His enemies — and he had many, in spite of his kindness, because his boastfulness was irritating and his successes, both with women and in the theatre, a recurrent cause of resentment — did their best to prove that he never wrote a single word of his plays, but that his collaborators did everything. If that were so, one is entitled to ask how it came about that Gaillardet, left to his own unaided efforts, never again had anything but very minor successes, or downright failures.
The cross-grained Gustave Planche wrote: 'It looks as though M. Dumas, whose beginnings in the theatre go back no farther than 1829, will soon be forgotten.' He reproached him for having tried to substitute sordid realism for the idealism of the classic masters. 'M.

Dumas is not in the habit of thinking. With him, action follows on the heels of desire with childlike rapidity. Consequently, he has rushed into doing battle without having considered the value of the monument which he has wished to tear down.' It is indeed strange to find Dumas being accused of realism. What could well be less realistic than his dramatic output? It is more accurate to say, as Planche went on to do, that 'M. Dumas has all serious artists against him.' Round about 1830, Alexandre Dumas and Victor Hugo had been regarded by the younger generation as the joint creators of the modern drama. *Henri III et sa Cour* had opened the way for *Hernani*, and the general public would most certainly have set the two authors on the same level. But after 1832 refined taste was no longer of this opinion. Hugo was leading by several lengths. Sainte-Beuve, while not denying that Dumas had talent, added: 'But genuine though it is, there is something about that talent which one could almost describe as physical.' It was, he declared, more closely allied to high spirits than to art; more than anything else an overflow of temperamental vitality. But surely it is no bad thing for a temperament to *have* an overflow of vitality.

CHAPTER II

Peaceful Coexistence

IN 1832 and 1833 Dumas managed to divide his life between Belle and Ida. For the first of these two years he kept house with Belle Krelsamer, either in Paris (Square d'Orléans) or at Trouville, a Normandy fishing-port, where he took refuge at the inn to work. But, in 1833, Ida carried him off to an apartment which she had furnished in the rue Bleu (all lemon-wood and fur rugs), where she reigned supreme. Peaceful coexistence was made easier than it might have been because of the demands made upon him by the theatre. Both the ladies were actresses, and he made use of both. *Angèle*, which belongs to 1833, had both Mélanie (Serre) and Ida in its two chief roles. 'I want', he explained to the various managers, 'to have talents on which I can rely in any theatre to which I entrust a play of mine.' This was a tactful way of expressing it!

Ida Ferrier, who was more ambitious than Belle Krelsamer, demanded a degree of luxury which Dumas found far from displeasing. By this time he knew her serious defects. Ida made two or three scenes a day, plotted with the servants against him, and intercepted his letters. 'But she had', says the comtesse Dash[1] 'eyebrows painted with art, a skin like white satin, faintly flushed, coral lips, and hair curled into a thousand ringlets à la Mancini.' The threat of stoutness hung over her, and her pronunciation left much to be desired. She spoke as though she were suffering from a chronic cold in the head. But she was a gracious hostess, and Dumas soon came to attach more importance to her as the mistress of his house than of his heart. Though both Catherine and Belle had borne him children, it was Ida who occupied the position of favourite sultana, and even succeeded in making her mother, the widow Ferrand, a regular member of an irregular household.

The young Alexandre, Catherine's son, saw himself in the light of a sacrificial victim. He had left the Vauthier establishment for Goubaux's school. The headmaster, Prosper Goubaux, was, as has been already mentioned, one of his father's friends. In his spare time he wrote plays, and had collaborated, under the pseudonym of Dinaux, in a celebrated drama — *Trente ans ou la vie d'un joueur*. He had also supplied Dumas with the raw material for *Richard Darlington*. He was an intelligent man of considerable culture, with many of the qualities essential for a genuine educator of youth, and had founded the Saint-Victor boarding-school in the rue Blanche. This undertaking, which enjoyed the financial backing of Laffitte, turned out successfully. It was there that many of the sons of the nobility, of the world of high finance, and even of parents engaged in the luxury trades, were brought up. Dumas had chosen Goubaux because he had worked with him in the theatre. He had never for a moment foreseen what sort of a welcome would be extended to the needlewoman's natural son by a crowd of spoiled, corrupt and conceited urchins.

The mothers of several of the pupils were customers of Catherine Labay. It soon became known that she was not married, that her small son was a bastard. What happened then is barely credible. 'The boys', wrote Alexandre Dumas *fils* at a later date, 'insulted me from morning till night, and no doubt thoroughly enjoyed making use of this opportunity to bring into disrepute, through me, a name which my father had made famous, because my mother had the misfortune not to be legally entitled to it.'[2]

When the young Alexandre attempted to defend his mother's honour, he was sent to Coventry by his schoolfellows. 'One thought he had the right to point the finger of scorn at my poverty because he was rich; another to laugh at my hardworking mother because his own parents led a life of leisure; a third to mock at me as a working-class boy, because he had a noble father; yet another to despise me because I had no father, whereas he, perhaps, had two . . .'[3] When he was sleeping, they woke him up, and in the dining-hall passed him only empty dishes. In form, his tormentors played a regular game which consisted in asking the master: 'Please, sir, what was the nickname of the handsome Dunois?'

'The Bastard of Orléans.'

'What is a bastard, sir?'

The boy Dumas looked up 'bastard' in the dictionary. He found 'born out of wedlock'. The little bullies went so far as to fill his school-books with obscene drawings under which they wrote his mother's name. When his cup of humiliation was full, he cried in a corner. As a result of this persecution, both his character and his health suffered. He became suspicious, a prey to anxiety, and obsessed by a desire for vengeance.

The impressions left on him by 'this hell' went deep. All through his life he was haunted by the problem of seduced women and natural children. He confessed, later, that his mind had 'never wholly recovered its balance, that the bitterness which I had felt in those days has never been entirely set at rest, even in the happiest days of my life'. Once, when one of his former persecutors met him by chance on the boulevard and, with the generosity of a man who is quick to forgive a sin of which he has himself been guilty, came up to him with outstretched hand, the young Alexandre stopped him sharply. 'My fine friend,' he said, 'I am now taller than you by a head. If ever you speak to me again, I'll give you a thrashing.'⁴

As a result of these experiences he came to possess, in addition to many of his father's characteristics (great stature, sympathy with all who sought vengeance, and a desire to be one of them), qualities of a quite different kind. He loved solitude and meditation, whereas the elder Dumas needed to have round him always a crowd of mistresses and flatterers. He observed human beings instead of, like his father, inventing them. He was a reformer up in arms against established disorder and, once the hot passions of youth were over, curiously addicted to morality.

There was in General Dumas always a touch of insubordination and, in the author of *Antony*, something of the rebel. But, in the elder Dumas, anathema and imprecation were always a literary device. The hatreds of his son, however, being the products of his childhood's bitterness, were authentic and incurable. The father was bursting with health; the son frequently suffered from physical and mental crises which at times even threatened his reason. The father, in spite of his many disappointments, remained an optimist to the end; the son, in spite of much precocious success, died a pessimist. 'I start with the prophylactic assumption that all men are scoundrels, all women trollops. Then, if I find that I have been wrong about some of them, my surprise is pleasurable rather than painful.'⁵ We all of us judge shops by what we find in them. Dumas *fils*, on the threshold of life, had found the well-dressed young ruffians of the Pension Goubaux. He never forgot them.

★

In 1832, Dumas *père*'s career in the theatre was interrupted for some months by a prolonged tour of Switzerland upon which reasons of prudence had led him to embark. The July monarchy was still unpopular. There were hostile manifestations by students and workers. The funeral in June, of the Liberal general Lamarque had been the occasion of a serious outbreak. Dumas, recognized among those taking part, dressed in his artilleryman's uniform, had been denounced as a republican. A legitimist newspaper announced that he had been taken with arms in his hands, and shot. This was ridiculous, but the rumours about him were becoming a considerable source of danger. He had friends at court (first and foremost the young and charming duc d'Orléans, the heir to the throne) who advised him to go abroad for a month until the trouble should have blown over.

The trip was picturesque and dramatic, as were all those undertaken by Dumas. He saw Chateaubriand, Queen Hortense, and the guide Balmat.⁶ Two volumes of lively *Impressions de Voyage* appeared, first in the *Revue des Deux Mondes*, and subsequently in book form. He was persuaded, also, to write for the same periodical a number of historical stories which, though to a high degree romanticized, were treated with respect by historians. Sainte-Beuve, a scrupulously detailed portrait-painter, criticized Dumas for being superficial. Other readers were more indulgent.

His period in purgatory over, Dumas returned to Paris where Harel urged him to supply nourishment for the Porte-Saint-Martin. It was at this time that a quarrel developed between him and Hugo. The latter had spent his youth as a model husband and father. In 1833, the 'Holy Family' had been driven from its paradise. From then on, though Adèle and Victor agreed to maintain a respectable façade for the sake of the public and their four children, things were, in reality, very different. Adèle had allowed herself to be courted, and more than courted, by Sainte-Beuve, and Hugo had taken as mistress Juliette Drouet, an actress of striking beauty but mediocre talent. Up to that time, he and Dumas had got on reasonably well together. The self-confidence of each was sufficient to keep jealousy at bay, but actresses, among themselves, are a great deal fiercer than authors. No sooner had Hugo set himself up as Juliette's protector, and Dumas as Ida's, than conflict became inevitable, the more so since the two women were both 'after' the same roles in the theatre at which both appeared: the Porte-Saint-Martin.

Harel, its manager, and Mademoiselle George, its tutelary goddess, were more inclined to give support to Ida Ferrier than to Juliette Drouet, in the first place because Ida was the better actress, in the second because Juliette was the better-looking, but especially because Mademoiselle George bore a grudge against Hugo for never having attempted to make a conquest of her. Not that she wanted him as a lover, but that she resented so fine-looking a man being the lover of another, and a younger, woman. Harel did everything that his imperial and imperious companion wanted. He tried to give priority of treatment to Dumas, who had written a play for Ida (*Catherine Howard*), and to delay the production of Victor Hugo's *Marie Tudor*. This led to the first clash, which, however, Dumas's loyal and generous attitude managed to avert. He intervened with an attempt to make peace between Harel and Hugo.

But Hugo insisted that Juliette should be given the secondary part of Jane Talbot in his play, the first being entrusted to Mademoiselle George. Everyone in the theatre maintained that Juliette would kill the play, and that the part must be transferred to Ida. Those 'holy terrors', Pierre Bocage and Mademoiselle George, disliked the idea of having to play with Juliette, and were so insolent in their attitude to the poor girl that they entirely undermined her self-confidence and successfully destroyed what small talent she possessed. The first performance of *Marie Tudor* went very badly. Juliette was hissed. All the 'heroes of Hernani', with Sainte-Beuve at their head, pointed out that Ida, fortunately, knew the part, and that it was essential to have it played by her on the second night. Juliette, made ill by vexation, took to her bed, and Hugo, in order to save *Marie Tudor*, gave way.

Now, a few days previously, the *Journal des Débats* had published an article by Granier de Cassagnac accusing Dumas of having 'cribbed' from Schiller, Goethe and Racine, and of having, in *Christine*, sought inspiration from the fifth act of *Hernani*. Dumas could have afforded to laugh at this: after all, had not Vigny taunted Hugo with 'borrowing' from all and sundry? The real trouble was that Dumas knew that Hugo had been influential in getting this same Granier de Cassagnac taken on to the staff of the *Débats*. He flew into a temper and wrote to Hugo, saying: 'I am convinced that you knew all about the article.' Hugo protested his friendship for Dumas, and Granier de Cassagnac declared, in a letter to the *Journal des Débats*, that Hugo had had no sort of connection with the offending article. Contradictions of this kind are rarely believed, and still more rarely deserve to be. It seems pretty clear that this one suffered the usual fate of such things, for in one of Sainte-Beuve's letters there is the following passage: 'An article by one of Hugo's friends, directed against Dumas, has roused the latter. The two men have fallen out for ever, and, what makes matters worse, as the result of a scandal, a state of affairs which always casts discredit on poetry.'[7]

Thus spoke the beloved disciple! Sainte-Beuve was far too genuinely pleased by the sight of Dumas and Hugo at loggerheads to bother his head very much about poetry. But he reckoned without the natural amiability of Dumas, who disliked long-drawn-out quarrels. Shortly afterwards, having a duel on his hands, he applied to his old friend, Hugo:

> Whatever our relations, Victor, at the moment, I very much hope that you will not refuse the service I am going to ask of you. Some wretched cad has insulted me by name in a beggarly news-sheet, a four-footed abomination called *The Bear*. This morning he refused to meet me, on the ground, so he said, that he had not been informed of the names of my seconds. I have written to Vigny by this same post in order that the same excuse, should he try to use it again, may be clearly shown up as a bad joke. I shall expect you tomorrow, seven o'clock, at my house. Will you send me a line saying whether I may count on you? Perhaps, too, it may give us the opportunity of shaking hands. I badly want that.[8]

After this honourable advance, everything was amicably settled between them. In 1835, Dumas left France for a prolonged tour in Italy, from which he brought back 'three dramas, a translation of the *Divine Comedy*, and some new *Impressions de Voyage*'.

In the course of the following summer, at the invitation of Adèle, he lunched with the Hugos at Fourqueux, on the outskirts of Paris, where they were spending a holiday. He delighted the four children with his stories. He was too much in love with life to chew over a dead past, and quickly grew sick of quarrelling.

The year 1836 was marked for Dumas by another theatrical triumph: *Kean ou Désordre et Génie*, a play about the great English actor who had recently died as the result of his excesses. Like almost all Dumas's works, it was the outcome of a stroke of luck, and a meeting. Frédérick Lemaître had recently transferred his activities to the Théâtre des Variétés. 'Disorder and Genius' — the phrase was an adequate description of his own character. Dumas held him to be the leading actor of the day. He had given him the part of Napoleon to 'create', and considered that, as Buridan, when *La Tour de Nesle* was revived, he had been a great deal better than Bocage. But he was a difficult man to deal with. He came on to the stage half-drunk, made his exit by way of the prompter's box, and had suddenly put on a pair of green spectacles in which to play Buridan. He was madly vain, and never thought that his name was printed large enough on the bills.

Since he shared many of Kean's characteristics, he was anxious to make his début at the Variétés in that part. Two dramatists, Théaulon and Courcy, as prolific as they were careless, had submitted a draft to him. He was not altogether happy about their effort and asked Dumas for advice. This Dumas gave, with the result that what was, to all intents and purposes, a new play emerged. Dumas tightened up the plot, rewrote the dialogue, and appeared on the bills as the sole author. He had put much of Frédérick into the name-part — and of himself. The scene in which Kean abuses an English peer was suggested by an argument between Harel and Frédérick, at which Dumas had been present. The violent onslaught on the English critics which Kean delivers in the second act represented Dumas's own condemnation of their French colleagues.

The main outline of the plot was taken over direct from Théaulon. Kean is the rival of the Prince of Wales for the favours of the beautiful wife of the Danish ambassador, and interrupts a performance of *Romeo and Juliet* with an abusive tirade from the stage at the expense of the heir to the throne. As a result of this incident the great tragedian is 'invited' to make an extensive tour of America, leaves for the United States, and is accompanied into exile by a faithful young woman who has long been in love with him.

The picture presented of the world of the theatre, and the character of Kean, as played by Frédérick with 'disorder and genius', made a tremendous success of the play. Heinrich Heine who, as a rule, was no kindly critic, wrote: 'The truth to life of the whole production is staggering . . . Between the character and the actor there is an astonishing affinity . . . Frédérick is a sublime buffoon whose terrible clowning makes Thalia pale with fear and Melpomene radiant with happiness. . . .'[9]

The manager of the Variétés had promised a bonus of one thousand francs to Dumas should the first twenty-five performances of *Kean* bring in sixty thousand to the box-office. On the evening of the twenty-fifth, Dumas went to see him and demanded the sum arranged.

'You're out of luck,' said the manager, who had just totalled up the takings: 'the figure is 59.997 francs.'

Dumas promptly borrowed twenty francs from him, hurried round to the box-office, and bought a stall for five francs.

'Now it's 60.002', he said.

He got his bonus.

CHAPTER III

Two Marriages under Louis-Philippe

IN 1837 occurred the marriage of the duc d'Orléans. His father had tried to get one of the Austrian archduchesses for him, but the 'family of kings' cold-shouldered the 'usurper', who had to fall back on a German princess, Helena von Mecklenburg-Schwerin, a charming, romantic and cultivated woman. Louis-Philippe announced that the occasion would be marked by a great banquet at the Palace of Versailles, followed by a ball.

On the day before this scene of splendour, Dumas, in high dudgeon, went to see Hugo. There was to be a special Honours List. Dumas's name had appeared in the first draft, but had been struck out by the King, who had been animated by a feeling of resentment against a known republican, an artilleryman of the National Guard, and a former insubordinate junior clerk at the Palais-Royal. Dumas, deeply hurt, had returned the invitation sent him for the Versailles festivities. Hugo, very nobly, declared himself heart and soul with his friend and colleague. He wrote to the duc d'Orléans, explaining that he would not be present, and giving the reason for his abstention.

The royal prince, who was a great admirer of both writers, was heart-broken, and so, to an even greater extent, was his young duchess, who had been looking forward to meeting her favourite authors. The two of them made representations to the King and everything was satisfactorily settled: Dumas's name was restored to the Honours List, and the friends decided to go to Versailles together. Since uniform was obligatory, they agreed to appear as National Guardsmen, and so make the identity of dress another bond between them. They found Balzac — in full court get-up, which he had hired from a costumier — and Eugène Delacroix. The King and the princes were extremely gracious. Mademoiselle Mars played *Le Misanthrope* to an audience of disillusioned generals and high functionaries, who said: 'So that's *Le Misanthrope*, is it? I always thought it was funny . . .' At the end of the evening there was a scramble for carriages. Dumas and Hugo did not succeed in finding theirs until one o'clock in the morning, and got back to Paris at dawn.

From then on, the two authors were assured of the friendship of the royal couple. It brought Hugo the rosette of an officer of the Legion of Honour, and to Dumas the cross of a chevalier. Dumas, who had been notified of these awards by the prince, immediately informed Hugo:

> My Dear Victor: your cross and mine have been gazetted this morning. I have been instructed to tell you this *unofficially*. Madame la duchesse d'Orléans is very proud of your gift, and will write to you herself. This I am instructed to tell you *officially*. With love.[1]

Hugo accepted the honour with his customary haughty dignity. Dumas was as pleased as Punch with his, and walked the whole length of the boulevard wearing an enormous cross, together with the Order of Isabella the Catholic, a Belgian decoration, the Swedish Cross of Gustavus Wasa, and the Order of St John of Jerusalem. In every country he visited he solicited a decoration and bought any that were for sale. His coat, on high days and holidays, was a regular showpiece of medals and ribbons. A harmless weakness.

The general's widow had lived just not long enough to see her son receive an honour which had always been refused to her husband. She died, after a second stroke, on August 1st, 1836. Though he had never ceased to love her, Dumas had for some time been a rather neglectful son. She lived in the faubourg du Roule, not far from the rue de Rivoli, where the insatiable Ida had recently extracted from her lover an extremely sumptuous apartment. Dumas hastened to his mother and, while watching by her bed, wrote to the most faithful of his friends, the duc d'Orléans: 'Here, beside my dying mother, I pray God to preserve your parents . . .' An hour later, a footman arrived with the news that the prince was waiting for him below in his carriage. Dumas went downstairs, found the carriage door open, and burst into tears on the knees of the most human of Royal Highnesses.

After the death of his mother, Ida Ferrier became, more than ever before, the dominant influence in his life. He was perfectly willing to be ruled by an intelligent woman who, though he had not much love for her, did not interfere with his freedom of movement, who had proved once and for all that she was barren, and was a reasonably good actress. He had taken her to Nohant to see George Sand and the two women had got on extremely well together. Though each, in her own way, was involved in the romantic comedy, both were still solid realists at heart. In Sand's opinion, Ida, on the stage, was capable of 'sublime moments'. She was full of praise of her intelligence. Ida Ferrier had the wisdom not to complain of Dumas's passing fancies. She wanted to be, and was, the official sultana, the companion to whom the master could go back when disappointed in his other loves. In return, he kept her with him and maintained her in royal style, taking her with him on all his trips, and writing parts for her.

He spent much time with her in Italy, especially at Florence, where she had many noble admirers at her feet. She had put on a good deal of weight. 'It was not always so with her,' wrote Théophile Gautier, 'I remember the days when she was slim, almost thin.' But the good Théo almost immediately added: 'She has in almost luxuriant excess what half the women in Paris have not got at all — and so it comes about that the skinny find her fat and overpowering . . . I don't mind admitting, at the risk of being considered a Turk, that good health and an abundance of flesh are, in my eyes, very charming defects in women. *There is*, so Victor Hugo has said, *a skeleton in every woman*. Speaking for myself, I prefer that skeleton to be well covered and concealed.'[2]

Ida's supreme ambition was to appear at the Comédie-Française. In return for this favour, Dumas promised the theatre two plays. Ida was enrolled as a 'jeune première' on October 1st, 1837. For his mistress's first appearance there, and for his own glory, he had written a verse tragedy in six acts — *Caligula*, a subject drawn from the ancient world and presented in alexandrines. Here was Racine challenged on his own ground. The very artlessness of the attempt should disarm criticism. Two plots, one political, the other passionate, are here, as in *Marie Tudor*, intertwined. (Aquila, a young Gaul, agrees to kill the licentious emperor, because he has seduced the girl the hero is to marry.) For Ida, Dumas had provided the very insipid part of Stella, a Roman maiden turned Christian, who is desired and carried off by Caligula. In contrast with her, and in conformity with romantic tradition, is Messalina, a perverse and bloodthirsty character, 'for ever seeking strange nocturnal pleasures', and strongly reminiscent of Marguerite de Bourgogne.

Gautier, however, was loud in praise of this extravagant undertaking: '*Caligula* is the only poetic and conscientious piece of writing which the year 1837 has witnessed. In my opinion, none but a hero would have embarked on six long acts in verse at this period of the world's history ... I do not say that it is faultless, but it certainly deserves from the critics a more sympathetic welcome than it has received.'³ Good Théo was still as good as ever.

The Comédie-Française had spent money madly on the mounting of the play. The audience was treated to a number of elaborate stage-pictures: Street in Rome opening on to the Forum; a Villa, based on the House of the Faun at Pompeii (where Dumas had spent some time in absorbing 'local colour'); the Terrace of Caesar's Palace and, finally, the Imperial Triclinium. Dumas had even wanted to have Caesar's chariot drawn by real horses. The *sociétaires* were volubly indignant: 'What! Horses on the stage of the Comédie!' Dumas insisted. 'You ask us to provide horses?' said Samson, the doyen. 'Why, we're so poor that we can scarcely manage to play on foot!'

In the long run, the author had to climb down. The settings which had cost so much money merely provoked laughter. There was a plot afoot to hiss the piece off the stage. Most of the actors detested their parts. Ida's reception was far from warm. Her beauty was praised, but her stoutness and her chronic cold in the head were thought to be unfortunate. One paper went so far as to call her a 'callipygian martyr'. The sniping in the public press soon ceased, however, owing to lack of interest. Receipts fell off, and the play disappeared from the bills.

Not only Dumas, now, but Hugo, too, were in bad odour with the Comédie-Française. They, on their side, had some reason to complain of Harel. The two authors, now reconciled, sought permission to found a second Théâtre-Français. The duc d'Orléans, their good angel — to whom Dumas had complained that the new drama had no theatre of its own, and that what with the Comédie-Française on the one hand, dedicated to the cult of the dead, and the Porte-Saint-Martin, on the other, with its addiction to the stupid, modern art was left 'high and dry' — realized that they had a right to a playhouse of their own, and promised to have a word with Guizot.

'A theatre's all very well,' said Victor Hugo, 'but who's going to run it?' — and went on to suggest a dramatic critic who had done something to champion the younger school, Anténor Joly.

'Anténor Joly,' protested Dumas, 'why, he hasn't got a penny to bless himself with!'

'Once he's been granted the privilege, he'll find the money,' replied Hugo.

In September 1837 Joly was given the necessary grant of privilege and took a lease of the Salle Vantadour which, in due course, became the Théâtre de la Renaissance. Hugo was to write a play for the opening — *Ruy Blas*, news which was not altogether welcome to Dumas. Ida urged him to demand complete equality of opportunity with Hugo who, she maintained, had given secret backing to the anti-*Caligula* plot. Juliette lived in hope of being allowed to create the Queen of Spain in *Ruy Blas*. Adèle Hugo wrote to Anténor Joly to put him on his guard against permitting such a 'scandal'. The management yielded. Ida Ferrier once more intrigued, this time to get the part for herself. But this would have meant exposing poor Juliette to gross ill-treatment, and a third woman, Atala Beauchêne, was chosen. The presence of Frédérick Lemaître in the cast was a guarantee of success. Delighted to get away from his usual run of parts, he gave a masterly performance as Ruy Blas, and wisely advised Hugo to 'expand the comedy side of the play'.

In 1838 Dumas's turn came, with *L'Alchimiste*, a drama which, in spite of his diatribes against collaboration, he had written in association with a young and charming poet, Gérard de Nerval, who, in love with an actress called Jenny Colon and passionately eager to write something for her,[4] had already combined with Dumas in a comedy, *Piquillo*, to which only Dumas's name was appended, and in which Jenny created the principal role. It was after this that the two men collaborated in *L'Alchimiste* for Ida Ferrier, and *Léo Burckhart* which appeared with Nerval's name as author. It was based on the story of the student, Karl Sand, the murderer of Kotzebue, and its production was long delayed as a result of the intervention of the political censorship. This may have been why Dumas withdrew and left the whole credit of the play to Gérard, who, in any case (to judge from the style) had done most of the work.

At the time when *L'Alchimiste* was being written, Alexandre Dumas *fils* had turned fourteen. In 1838 he left the Goubaux establishment, and went to the Henon boarding-school at N° 16 rue de Courcelles, from which pupils were passed into the Collège Bourbon. The boy much preferred the swimming-baths in the Palais-Royal, and a gymnasium in the rue Saint-Lazare, to lessons in Latin and mathematics. Except for poaching and life in the forest, his too undisciplined youth was very much like what his father's had been, though the latter had not known the struggles of a deserted mother with a succession of tyrannical mistresses. Dumas *fils* was no more prepared to accept Ida Ferrier than he had been to recognize the claims of Belle Krelsamer.

One strange aspect of the situation was that the drama of the young Alexandre, Catherine Labay's son, closely resembled that of Marie, the daughter of Belle Krelsamer (alias Mélanie Serre). The tender-hearted Marceline Desbordes-Valmore was deeply perturbed: 'I found Madame Serre-Dumas more beautiful now than ever she was, still weeping over her sorrows and her daughter, *whom he won't let her see!* What an extraordinary despotism he does exercise!'⁵ This harsh attitude was imposed by Ida. According to Marceline, Dumas was 'doing himself a great deal of damage' by sacrificing Madame Serre who 'is much more beautiful, highly accomplished and as good as gold', to that egotistical woman.

In 1840, Dumas married Ida Ferrier. He had no illusions about her. Why then should he have changed into a permanent bond an attachment which was already weighing heavily on him? It was said that he had, one evening, committed the social blunder of taking her to a reception given by the duc d'Orléans and his duchess, hoping that she would pass unnoticed in the crowd of guests, and that the prince had said to him in a low voice: 'I am delighted to make the acquaintance of Madame Dumas, and hope that you will present your wife to us on some less formal occasion.' This, if the story be true, would have been not only a lesson in manners, but tantamount to an order. It seems, however, very unlikely that the interview ever took place. Viel-Castel maintains that Ida had bought back some bills which Dumas had backed, and had then offered him the choice between marrying her and going to prison for debt. The actor, René Luguet, said that Dumas, when the question was put to him, had replied: 'My dear fellow, I did it to get rid of her!'

When the banns were published, Mélanie Waldor's fury burst all bounds. Alexandre Dumas *fils*, who spent his holidays with his mother, had remained on affectionate terms with the first Mélanie. Under the influence of two abandoned mistresses, the young man wrote a letter to Dumas *père*. The reluctant fiancé was at that time in hiding at la Petite-Villette, in the house of Jacques Domange, the proprietor of a sewage-disposal concern, whom Ida called 'my dear benefactor', and who, in point of fact was about to provide the future bride with a dowry. It was there that Mélanie sent him, by the hand of Commandant Waldor's soldier-servant, the indignant missive in which a schoolboy expressed his opposition to the marriage of his natural father.

Dumas's plea in his own defence is an astonishing document:

It is not my fault, but yours, that the relationship between us is no longer that of father and son. You came to my house, where you were well received by everyone, and then, suddenly, acting on whose advice I do not know, decided no longer to recognize the lady whom I regarded as my wife, as should have been obvious from the fact that I was living with her. From that day, since I had no intention of taking advice (even indirectly) from you, the situation of which you complain, began and has lasted, much to my sorrow, for six years.

It can cease whenever you wish. You have only to write a letter to Madame Ida, asking her to be to you what she is to your sister:[6] you will then be always, and eternally, welcome. The happiest thing that could happen to you is that this liaison should continue, since, having had no child for six years, I am now certain that I never shall have any, so that you are now not only my eldest, but my only, son.

I have nothing else to tell you. All that I would have you consider is this, that, should I marry any woman other than Madame Ida, I might well have three or four more children, whereas with her, I shall have none.

I trust that in all this you will consult your heart rather than your interests, though this time — contrary to what usually happens — the two are in agreement. I embrace you with all my heart.[7]

The contract of marriage was signed in the presence of Maître Desmanèches (Jacques Domange's notary) at la Villette, on February 1st, 1840. Witnesses for the husband were the vicomte de Chateaubriand and François Villemain, Minister of Public Instruction in the Guizot cabinet. Those for the bride were the vicomte de Narbonne-Lara and the vicomte de la Bonardière, Councillor of State. The amount of the dowry was 120,000 francs 'in French gold and silver currency'.

Gustave Claudin attributes to Chateaubriand a saying which may

not be wholly apocryphal. Gazing at the corsage of the lady soon to
be Dumas's wife, the illustrious peer of France is said to have remarked with some bitterness, alluding at once to the French monarchy
and to Ida's somewhat sagging charms: 'I would have you note that
my destiny is always the same: no matter what I bless, it is sure to
fall!'⁸ The anecdote is racy, but whether it is true seems open to doubt.
Claudin's evidence is not altogether to be trusted, for his story contains
two major inaccuracies: (1) he mentions, among the witnesses, Roger
de Beauvoir who, in fact, was not present; and (2) he maintains that
the religious ceremony took place in the chapel of the Chamber of
Peers. Actually, it was in the church of Saint-Roch, the parish church
of the bridal couple who were, both of them, at that time living at
Nº 22 rue de Rivoli, that the nuptial benediction was pronounced
on February 5th, 1840.⁹

Chateaubriand, who was far from well on the appointed day, sent
a substitute to represent him at the church. The painter, Louis
Boulanger, the architect, Charles Robelin, and 'Jacques Domange,
householder', signed the register. Here is an amusing comment on the
marriage by Jules Lacroix (*le Bibliophile Jacob*):

Much has been said about the marriage of our friend Alexandre
Dumas. I have nothing to add except that the author of *Henri III*
and *Antony* was perfectly free to recognize the utility and sanctity
(if one may so call it) of article 165 of the Civil Code . . . How can
one bring oneself to blame or to criticize a *legitimate union*
(catechism style) witnessed by the Minister of Public Instruction
and Monsieur de Chateaubriand! Those two names are truly
worthy of any literary contract of marriage; those two names
may be said to have meant: 'Young man, you who have won and
have deserved the most outstanding dramatic successes of our
day; you, a poet and a novelist, you, a traveller, must of necessity
pass beneath the Caudine Forks of the classic Hymen if you are
to achieve ministerial employment and membership of the
Academy!'

On that basis, Alexandre Dumas is well-nigh sure of, one day,
becoming permanent secretary of the French Academy and
Minister of Public Instruction. Thanks to the sacrament of
marriage granted by Letters Patent of His Majesty the King of
the French, there is no position to which a man may not attain

in this Age of Gold and of the Civil List. Matrimoniomania of the Palace!

Messieurs Villemain, Chateaubriand and Charles Nodier (I think I left this bright representative of the French language in Techener's bookshop) accompanied the newly weds to the moderately solemn ceremony at the Mairie, but were replaced by fresher witnesses at the non-official ditto in the church. The said substitute witnesses were men of intelligence and talent, though drawn from elsewhere in the Academic sheepfold.

The curé of Saint-Roch who, in the King's name, solemnized the marriage of our friend Alexandre Dumas, had prepared a discourse suited to the occasion which he proposed to present to the court along with the first consecrated bread of his parish.

'Illustrious author of *La Génie du Christianisme*', (said he, turning towards one of the witnesses, a skilful painter of the colourist school) . . . 'and you, correct and polished writer who hold in your two hands the destinies of the French language and of Public Instruction' (he added, speaking to another of the witnesses who was nothing more than a good architect) . . . 'yours, gentlemen, is a noble and an honourable task, the task of vouching here for the young neophyte who comes to the foot of the altar to implore the holy baptism of marriage! etc. Young man, let me repeat to you the words spoken by the great bishop Remy to King Clovis: '*Bend your head, proud Sicambrian: adore what you have burned and burn what you have adored*' . . . May there henceforward come from your pen only works that are Christian, edifying and inspired by the Gospel! Put behind you the dangerous emotions of the theatre, the perfidious Sirens of the passions, the abominable pomps of Satan, etc. . . . I trust that you, Monsieur de Chateaubriand, and you, Monsieur Villemain (I regret that Monsieur Charles Nodier is not with us) will be responsible before God and before men for the literary conversion of this fiery and romantic heresiarch. May you be the godfathers of his books and of his children. That is what I hope for him, my very dear brethren. Amen.'

The curé of Saint-Roch did not realize his mistake until he read the signatures of the witnesses now preserved in the register in the sacristy. He had had, he said to his housekeeper, some doubts when he noticed that Monsieur de Chateaubriand was sporting a

Young France beard, and that Monsieur Villemain was wearing yellow gloves at two francs, fifty centimes the pair. Only when he had heard Alexandre Dumas's general confession did he cease from worrying.[10]

So far as Ida was concerned, the marriage was not very successful. Maybe it inspired her with too great a confidence in the indissolubility of the conjugal tie. There is an anecdote, probably apocryphal, to the effect that she almost at once deceived her husband, and, according to accepted standards, with the best friend of the family, Roger de Beauvoir, poet and dramatist, who was seven years younger than her husband. Beauvoir was a man of great charm.

> How madly smart and eccentric he was! [wrote the comtesse Dash] What pretty verses he wrote, and what nice suppers he gave. He combined the roles of Anacreon and Maecenas. He wrote novels and encouraged the arts. His ante-room was filled each morning with a crowd of authors lacking publishers, and of painters without studios, whom he received on rising and entertained to a cutlet and a glass of champagne. All of them, on leaving, made it generally known that he had an enchanting talent. . . .[11]

How could Ida possibly have resisted him?

Mélanie Waldor and Mélanie Serre both took the nuptials of their common friends on a note of high tragedy.

> *Marceline Desbordes-Valmore to her husband, February 7th, 1840:* You have, no doubt, learned of the marriage of M. Dumas and the fat lady? It is said that Messieurs de Chateaubriand, Nodier, Villemain and Lamartine signed the register! Madame Serre fainted dead away in the house. She had gone there to beg for the return of her daughter. Madame Waldor also hastened to the same spot, in an access of generous-minded joy, believing that he had married an honest woman. She had just written a letter in which she had said that she 'breathed freely on hearing that he had at last put an end to a most shameful liaison'. I leave you to judge of the effect produced by this missive. I myself have nothing to say. He is married, and that is all there is to it![12]

But marriage with a woman other than his mother was, for the young Alexandre, a fresh drama.

CHAPTER IV

Comedies

L'*ALCHIMISTE* was a failure. *Ruy Blas* had not been a success.
Genres grow old as quickly as men. Drama was at its last gasp.

Sorry though I am to say it [wrote Théophile Gautier] we
are in a condition of complete decadence. Manufacturing methods
have invaded every activity; a play is turned out like a suit of
clothes; one of the collaborators takes the actor's measurements,
another cuts the material, a third assembles the various pieces.
The study of the human heart, style, language, these are no longer
regarded as having any importance ... Collaboration, where a
work of intelligence is concerned, is something quite incomprehensible ... Just imagine Prometheus with a collaborator seated
in front of him, watching his struggles as the sharp-beaked vulture
skilfully probes his heart and liver, and not only watching, but
making notes in pencil on a small sheet of paper![1]

Dumas, who could feel instinctively the mood of the public, wanted
to see what a change of *tone* would do. It is surprising, all things
considered, that this man of exuberant vitality should have chosen to
write black and gloomy tragedies rather than rose-tinted comedies. If
he had the gift of inspiring terror, he had, still more, that of gaiety.
Now, within sight of his fortieth year, he made his bow with a new
type of theatrical composition — the play of wit. Gautier, with his
usual sharpness of intelligence, has explained this evolution of his talent.
'Comedy is not the favourite form of writers in their early youth,
because then they take everything seriously and with passionate intensity ... If M. Dumas were to rewrite *Antony*, Adèle d'Hervey would
not die, and her lover, after being introduced to the husband, would
sit down with him to a quiet game of cards ... As a man grows older,
he falls into a state of mortal gloom ... and takes to writing comedies.'[2]
In 1839, the Comédie-Française staged a comedy by Dumas,

Mademoiselle de Belle-Isle. Sainte-Beuve, who had always adopted an unsympathetic attitude towards Dumas, all of a sudden became curiously friendly:

> When a writer [he said] has to all appearances wandered off on the wrong track, and has tried in vain, with a pretentious show of 'poetry', to make himself bigger than he is, it is with pleasure that one welcomes from his pen a sudden brilliant and facile success which sets his feet firmly on the right road. M. Alexandre Dumas is much beloved of the public, and his lively, witty comedy has received its meed of sincere applause ... It is to be hoped that M. Dumas will strike roots in the new field lying somewhere midway between the Empyrean and the Boulevard — neither so high nor so low.[3]

The actors of the Comédie-Française were in full agreement with Sainte-Beuve.

'What a marvellous hand at comedy you are!' they told Dumas.

'Is it because I have always written dramas that you say that?'

The note struck in *Mademoiselle de Belle-Isle* resembled, with something less of grace, that of Marivaux and Beaumarchais, authors whom Dumas had studied with care, and now imitated with skill. After so many crimes, suicides and revolts, it was a pleasant contrast to find him moving among powdered wigs, elegantly insolent gallants, who knew how to take their pleasures without indulging in shouts and tears. Of the eighteenth century he retained little more than three characteristics: a pleasing freedom of manners; a mocking at wives who love their husbands (and vice versa); and the murky gloom of the Bastille following, for the vanquished, hard on the heels of a joyous indulgence in sword-play.

The subject of *Mademoiselle de Belle-Isle* is slight and tart. The duc de Richelieu, the greatest libertine of his age, takes a bet with a group of *roués*, that he will become the lover of the first woman, unmarried or widowed, who shall walk through the gallery where they are standing, and will be received at midnight in the lady's bedroom. At that very moment the marquise de Prie, mistress of the duc de Bourbon is announced.

'Ah! gentlemen,' says Richelieu, 'she doesn't count: the game would be too easy, and I should be robbing you of your money!'

Mademoiselle de Belle-Isle, who has come to beg the reigning favourite to exercise her influence on behalf of her father who is a prisoner in the Bastille, appears at the far end of the gallery. A young chevalier d'Aubigny at once steps forward and challenges Richelieu to make good his bet.

'I am to marry, in three days' time, the lady whom Monsieur de Richelieu has undertaken to dishonour this evening ... I answer for her.'

The swords are crossed.

In the second act, the marquise de Prie, who has taken the young girl under her wing, sends her off in a coach to see her father in the Bastille. The favourite then shuts herself into Mademoiselle de Belle-Isle's bedroom, and there, in darkness, awaits the coming of the over-confident Richelieu. 'In point of fact', says Sainte-Beuve, 'it is inconceivable that the duke, when he tiptoed into the presence of his tender prey, should not, almost at once, have realized the nature of the trick which has been played upon him ... I apologize for labouring the point, but the literary device conceals a physiological problem ... It is curious that, in discussing the truth to life of a stage play, one should have to go so deeply into a question of forensic medicine. The public has accepted the situation at its face value, and so will I.'⁴ A theatre audience will accept anything, especially the improbable, and in this case was only too willing to believe that Richelieu, when he creeps into the bed of Madame de Prie, really does think that he is violating a virgin. Consequently, the duke, in perfect good faith, sends a note to d'Aubigny announcing that he has won his wager.

Up to this point we have been moving in the world of Marivaux, or, rather, of Crébillon. But it must not be forgotten that we are dealing with Dumas, 'that churner-up of passions',⁵ who loved drama above all things and had a solid basis of popular morality. He had dis-honoured many young girls in his time, but as a playwright he frowned upon such villainy, and, from the third act onwards, mixed feeling with comedy. There is a scene of confrontation between d'Aubigny and his betrothed in which he, though still in love, accuses her, and she, having taken an oath not to reveal her visit to the Bastille, is unable to explain where she has spent the night. There follows a scene between Gabrielle de Belle-Isle and Richelieu who, convinced that he is speaking to a willing accomplice, complacently dwells upon the memory of their pleasurable adventure ... Despair of Gabrielle:

'My God! My God! have mercy upon me!'

'What has begun as a wager becomes an emotional torment.' From now, up to the final scene, we are in the full flood of Porte-Saint-Martin drama. All ends, however, on a note of comedy, and the gaiety of the denouement seems the sweeter for being unexpected. The duc de Richelieu, to whom Madame de Prie has revealed the truth, appears in the nick of time to reassure everybody. The solemn d'Aubigny has the last word. He contrives an introduction:

'Mademoiselle de Belle-Isle, my wife . . . Monsieur de Richelieu, my best friend.'

Sainte-Beuve cattily remarked that 'the duke ought surely to have smiled to hear himself addressed as "my best friend" on the occasion of a nuptial benediction. Perhaps a short and wholly comic act should have been added to the play, entitled *Two Years Later*'.⁸ Roger de Beauvoir would have been the perfect collaborator to undertake it. Such as it was, the play had a resounding success. It was the occasion of a final triumph for Mademoiselle Mars who, at the age of sixty, played the part of Gabrielle in a manner that was both touching and innocent. Youth, in the theatre, is merely a question of composition. Firmin, who had been Dumas's first friend at the Comédie-Française, carried through the role of the duc de Richelieu with an air of aristocratic insolence. In fact, the whole evening went off delightfully.

Dumas was so much encouraged by the reception, that he repeated himself. In 1841, he presented *Un Mariage sous Louis XV*. 'The subject', he admitted, 'is not a new one, but a judicious choice of detail may give it a fresh lease of life.' It is the old story of two people who, having entered on a marriage of convenience, separate by agreement. They come to see their mistake, and forget, the one his mistress, the other her gallant, both having realized, just in time, that they are not as much in love in these new circumstances as they have thought, and return to one another from inclination.

Les Demoiselles de Saint-Cyr (1843) met with less favour. 'It is like everything of Dumas's,' wrote Sainte-Beuve to Juste Olivier, 'lively, attractive, amusing up to a point, but spoiled by having been incompletely worked out, and marred by carelessness and vulgarity . . . With Dumas one always finds oneself saying — *what a pity!* I am beginning to think that this is a wrong judgment. He is one of those who would never really have got to the top as a serious and high-minded artist. When he turns to irresponsible entertainment he *seems* to have lost just those qualities which, in fact, he is utilizing, and gains from making people believe he could do better, whereas, actually, he never would . . .'[7] Jules Janin fell upon the play tooth and nail: 'If this sort of rubbish is to go on, they had better shut the Théâtre-Français for good and all . . . People say beforehand: "You're going to see *something!* You're going to hear *something.*" What an ado about *nothing!*'[8]

Dumas was cut to the quick. Naturally good-natured, he plunged into clumsy recriminations. Spitefulness was not his strong suit. He tried to be cruel, but succeeded only in being tedious, and in airing old grievances which had nothing to do with the matter in hand. He recalled the days when Janin was lodging in the rue Madame, under the same roof as Harel and Mademoiselle George, making a third, but in no way disturbing the harmony of the other two. This was merely a piece of sarcasm in the worst possible taste.

One of the reasons for Janin's excessive severity was that Dumas at that time was doing all he could to get himself elected to the Académie Française. Hugo's successful candidature had raised hopes in the breasts of all who belonged to the romantic generation. That was how Hugo himself saw it. 'Academies, like everything else, will belong to the new young. In the meantime, I am the living breach through which new ideas are entering today, and these men will enter tomorrow.'[9] What men? Hugo was thinking of Vigny, of Dumas, of Balzac, and even of his enemy, Sainte-Beuve, for he had greatness of mind. Dumas, for his part, was thinking only of Dumas. In 1839, after the success of *Mademoiselle de Belle-Isle*, he had written to François Buloz, the editor of the *Revue des Deux Mondes*: 'Do mention me in the *Revue*, in connection with the Academy, and express wonder that I am not up for election, seeing that Ancelot is . . .' *January 15th, 1841*: '. . . put a piece about me in your periodical with the Academy in view. I am not on the next list of candidates, but feel pretty sure that people are surprised that I am not. . . .'[10]

After Hugo's election, Dumas sent out a call to his old friend Nodier, who had been an academician for some time: 'Do you think I should stand a chance now? Here's Hugo in, and his friends are all, more or less, mine . . . If you think there is anything in my suggestion, do, please, climb into the academic rostrum, and say, in my name, to your honourable fellow-members how much I should like to take my seat among them . . . Mention your good opinion of me, if you have it, and even if you haven't . . .'[11] As matters turned out, he was never to force that particular door. Nor was Balzac. But Balzac died young. Dumas, though he lived to the age of sixty-eight, failed to achieve election.

Is being famous such an obstacle, then? — asked Delphine de Girardin, in angry mood. Why is it that the famous find it so difficult to get elected? Is it a crime to have a right to recognition? . . . Balzac and Alexandre Dumas write fifteen to eighteen volumes a year, and that, it seems, cannot be forgiven them. But these novels are excellent! That is no excuse; there are too many of them. But they are terrifically successful! That makes matters worse. Let a man write just one short, mediocre book which nobody reads, and then we'll think seriously about him. The same rule holds for the Academy as for the Tuileries Gardens. Those who are carrying big parcels are not allowed in. . . .[12]

It was not the immense bulk of Dumas's luggage that frightened the Academy. Hugo, who had been duly elected, was a no less prolific author. In the case of Dumas, however, there was fear of scandal. Difficult times might lie ahead for the king of bohemians. He had to reckon with two natural children, several stormy mistresses, and a considerable total of debts . . . He made a great deal of money, to be sure; but he always spent more than he made.

'I have never refused money to anybody,' he said, 'except my creditors.'

One day, when a subscription had been opened to provide a decent funeral for a process-server who had died in penury, he was asked for twenty francs.

'Here are forty,' he said, 'bury *two* of 'em.'

No doubt that was only a joke: but official bodies do not like jokes. 'Dumas is a charming fellow,' was the general view, 'but he is not serious-minded.' In France, if a man does not carry his head like the Blessed Sacrament, he may be regarded as an amusing character, but he is not respected. Bores enjoy priority.

CHAPTER V

The Prodigal Father

AFTER Dumas's marriage to Ida, relations between father and son remained difficult. The father's love for his son was steadfast, but of no great weight; the son's affection for his father alternated with fits of ill-humour. It seemed impossible not to love and admire so high-spirited a companion, but it took a long time for the son to grow used to his father's follies. Having completed his education — with no very great brilliance — Dumas *fils* tried, from time to time, to live under the domestic roof. What he saw there was not edifying. 'My boy,' said the father, solemnly, 'when one has the honour to bear the name of Dumas, one lives on a grand scale: one dines at the Café de Paris, and one never says no to pleasure. . . .'[1]

No matter how moral a young man may be by nature, and as the result of his early upbringing, he does not resist the lure of pleasure. Later, Dumas *fils* was to write: 'I led that kind of life more from irresponsibility, imitation and laziness, than because I had any positive taste for it.' And again: 'I did not enjoy those facile pleasures. I *observed*, rather than indulged in, that turbulent existence.'[2] The world smiled at the 'rather scabrous spectacle of father and son seeking their adventures in company . . . confiding each to each his love affairs, dipping into the same purse, and spending recklessly.'[3] There were those, however, who blamed the father for 'passing on to his son his worn-out shoes and his old mistresses'.

Disapprove though he might, the younger Dumas shared, for a while, in the luxurious and entertaining existence which was the rule in the paternal home. 'At the age of eighteen, I was plunged headlong into what I can only call the paganism of modern life . . . I did not, to be sure, live like a saint, unless it was in St Augustine's *first manner* . . .'[4] He frequented the ladies of the town who, at that time, were both numerous and superb. At eighteen, he had his 'first intrigue with a married woman, Madame Pradier'.

A set of bachelor chambers, elegant mistresses, the Café Anglais, these things cost a mint of money. He, too, ran into debt. When he began to grow uneasy: 'Work, and you'll be able to pay', said his father, who was very willing to make use of the budding talent of Alexandre II. 'Why not collaborate with me? You'll find it very easy, all you've got to do is to give me my head.'⁵ But Alexandre II had other ambitions. Merely to chug along after his father and skim through his phosphorescent wake was not enough for him. With the evidence before him of all that glittering fame, he longed for triumphs which should be more purely personal. He did not as yet know what he would write, nor even whether he would write at all — there were other possible ways of succeeding — but he was already a brilliant talker with a biting wit, and his father, proud of this new Dumas, took delight in quoting his epigrams. After hearing a reading of Ponsard's *Charlotte Corday*, Alexandre II had said:

> C'est ainsi qu'il périt. O Ciel! Quelle vengance!
> Pour un bain qu'il a pris, il n'a pas eu de chance.⁶

This piece of schoolboy doggerel delighted Alexandre I. But the son lacked his father's easy familiarity of address.

'Come, come, young man,' said an old friend of his father, 'I address the author of *Antony* as "tu", but speak to you as "vous". That really is too absurd: we must put it right.'

'Well then,' replied the young Dumas: 'you'd better start using "vous" to papa.'

From time to time there were quarrels between the two men about Ida who, though she had succeeded in making a conquest of her stepdaughter, Marie, tried in vain to win over her stepson. Dumas intervened with his wife:

> *Dumas père to Dumas fils*: You are quite wrong, my boy, for I have gained — or, rather, insisted upon — more. Madame Dumas *is going to write* asking you to come when we have guests. In that way you will have a footing in my real domestic interior, as well as company. This will bring me some compensation for your long absence, and will be a step towards settling everything for the future. Shall I see you this evening?⁷

He also advised him in the matter of a career:

My dear boy: your letter has somewhat relieved my mind so far as the money, and moral, aspects are concerned, though not at all on the question of your future. You have, yourself, chosen to devote it to intellectual labours. But I can see no likelihood of your finding any salaried position which would enable you to satisfy the *demands* you make on life, demands which have now become habits which, as much through my fault as yours, have grown upon you.

Fame finds its outward expression in money, but money only really comes as the result of fame. Do you think that the life you live, going to bed at daybreak, getting up at two or three, and being always preoccupied with the tiresome things that happened yesterday, or with the fear of what may happen tomorrow, leaves you enough time and leisure for reflection, without which you will never do anything well? It isn't the doing that matters, but the doing what you do well. Being paid doesn't matter but the earning of what you are paid. Work for a year, for two or three years. Then, on the solid foundation of your past efforts, you will be in a position to do as you like, and how you like. . . .[8]

In 1844, Alexandre II, finding it impossible any longer to put up with Madame Dumas, asked for a sum of money to enable him to travel. His father at first protested. He wanted to keep the handsome, brilliant young man with him, and did all he could to discourage the idea of his going away.

I am answering you, my boy, by letter, as you asked me to do, and at some length. You know that Madame Dumas is Madame Dumas only in name, whereas you are truly my son, and not only my son, but well-nigh the only happiness and distraction that I have.

You are entertaining the idea of going abroad, to Italy or Spain. I will say nothing of the ingratitude of which you are guilty in leaving me among people for whom I feel no affection, to whom I am bound only in a superficial and social way. But what future is there for you in Italy or in Africa? If it is merely a question of a trip, well and good, but even so I do think that you might wait until such time as we could make it together.

Your position in Paris is, you say, *silly* and *humiliating*. What exactly do you mean? You are the only friend I have. So invariably are we seen in company that people have got into the habit of never separating our two names. If there is *any* future for you, it is in Paris. If only you would work hard, would do some serious writing, you could make ten or so thousand francs a year. I see nothing either *silly* or *humiliating* in that. You must know perfectly well that I, for my part, accustomed as I am to impose upon myself, for the happiness of those around me, for whom I have assumed responsibility before God, every conceivable form of spiritual privation, will do as you want. If I did not, a day might come when, finding yourself unhappy, you might say that I had turned you from the way you wanted to follow, and believe that I had sacrificed you to the egotism of a father's love, the last and only love which my heart knows, which will be deceived by you, in your turn, as other loves have been in theirs.

What else is there you want? Some position, perhaps in a Paris library, which would make you more or less independent? But do you really think you have the courage, after having grown into the habit of being your own master, to face an existence which would mean having to sacrifice four hours of every day to working in an office?

One thing I would have you realize clearly: that any separation between me and Madame Dumas can be only a *virtual separation*. Actual disagreement between us as husband and wife would soon become public property, with unfortunate consequences for me. It is, therefore, *impossible*. What I do find very dishonest and very unjust is that you, who have all my heart and all my affection, should come to me and say: 'You must choose between me and the woman who, though she has nothing of *that*, does have your money.' You are wrong not to wish to talk about all this. I shall stay at home until three o'clock in the hope that you will come. It must be quite obvious that I belong wholly to you, whereas you only half belong to me. . . .'

Then, since Alexandre insisted on getting away from Paris, his father sent him to live for some time in Marseille, where he had made a number of good friends. There was a pleasant literary group established in that city: the poet, Joseph Autran, of an old Phocaean family; the eccentric and disconcerting Méry, librarian and author, and a certain Lady Susannah Greig, Maltese by origin, who presided over a salon in the rue Saint-Ferréol. At Marseille, the young Dumas made a number of flattering conquests.

The author of his being kept a watchful eye upon him from a distance, sent him money — which is the prime function of fathers, even of prodigal fathers — and put in his way opportunities of making more. He had been asked to write a small book about Versailles. Why should his son not relieve him of the task? He should have all the necessary reference books sent him, as well as the plan of the work. But so dismal and minor a commission was not likely to please a young and ambitious man who wrote verse, was working at a novel, and was giving all his attention to a beautiful actress just then appearing at Marseille. He followed her to Paris when she went back there, and informed Méry when the affaire was at an end. The letter is worth quoting, so full is it of the very essence of youth:

Alexandre Dumas fils *to Joseph Méry, October 18th, 1844*: My dear, good Méry: your window may be open, but mine is shut, though, to make up for that, I have a fire in my grate 'in the absence of the glow of Phoebus', as our friend Delille would say. I am deep in my Louis XV, as *you* would say, and, for the last fortnight, have been a prey to melancholy.

I expect you remember the day I left for Lyon, from which place I returned with a touch of the sun the more, and a pleasure the less. You said, when I told you what had happened, that I had acted wisely, that I had been stronger than you would have been. Well, dear friend, what I have just done drives all that home.

Recently, my father gave me the salutary advice to break free of the people I had come to Paris to be with again, but, in the absence of any valid pretext, it was difficult to do that. A day came, however, when the young and attractive female who had been so hospitable to me in your charming city spoke these memorable words: 'I am afraid that my relationship with you may have the effect of making things difficult for me with your father in the theatre. In spite of myself I have considerably more money to spend than you could ever give me, even if you pinched and scraped. Let us stay as we are. I swear that you have nothing with which to reproach me.'

I took this *au pied de la lettre*, and, for the last fortnight, have been giving her a wide birth. The day after I had made my decision she was running after me from dawn till dusk, going to my friends, sending them to me, making every imaginable concession—I answering nothing, and, when I was alone, shedding hot tears. At last our mutual despair calmed down. Last Sunday she paid me a visit and found me in. She gave me to understand that though she was living with another, whom she regarded in the light of a husband, serving him only for money, she would be only too delighted to continue going to bed with her Marseille friends.

Then I took her hands and, having first respectfully kissed them, told her that she had better not come too often to see me, because, should she do so, it would merely compromise her to no purpose. I accompanied her in brotherly fashion to the door, notwithstanding certain tears which stood like pearls in those wide blue eyes that have starred the firmanent of the Gymnase, and never have brother and sister been more chaste than we two were that day. Yesterday, Thursday, she came back, but I, mercifully, was absent at the races. There, dear friend, you have my news. I was under an obligation to send it, since it was under your wing that everything occurred.

Now I am no longer very sad. I am working, I am well, and, when I think of Marseille, which I do frequently, I see more often in imagination the house in the rue de Musée than N° 73 rue de la Palud. I must confess, however, that, from time to time, I still feel a tightness round my heart. The whole thing, as you will remember, began so oddly and so charmingly! Well, there it is! I can see you smiling as you read this. You are probably saying to yourself: 'I have been through it all myself! and always knew how it would end!' — and it is just because I, too, knew it, that I sometimes spoke to you of the beginning, and never of the future.

I have one piece of great news, dear friend. The house of Dumas is crashing to the ground. Husband and wife are on the point of separating, as did Abraham and Agar, though for a reason quite other than barrenness[10] — and I am quite convinced that it will not be long before you see passing through Marseille a fat woman on her way to live in Italy, there to remain for the rest of her life. All goes well in that direction. As to us, we are thinking of going to China next year, and we shall pick up Méry en route. So much for news and dreams. . . .[11]

There is something of cynicism in the attitude adopted by Dumas *fils* towards the woman with whom he had been briefly in love. The youth was still waxing sentimental and shedding a few tears, but already the tamer was cracking his whip.

It was true that the Dumas household was collapsing. Some years previously, when in Florence, Ida had achieved the conquest of a noble Italian, Edoardo Alliata, twelfth prince of Villafranca, Duke of Salaparuta, Grandee of Spain of the first class, Prince of Montereale, Duke of Saponara, Marquis of Santa Lucia, Baron of Mastra, Lord of Mirii, Mangiavacca, Viagrande and other places. The *Almanach de Gotha*, which does not take the authenticity of titles lightly, placed Edoardo de Villafranca (1818-98) among the serene highnesses. As Prince of the Holy Roman Empire, and Count Palatine, he had (in theory) the hereditary right of minting money.

As sole heir to so many fiefs, Villafranca had done his duty by marrying young and begetting a son to whom were given in baptism the names — Giuseppe-Francesco-Paolo-Gaspare-Baltassare. This accomplished, he had moved, leaving mother and son in Palermo, to the mainland where he lived, sometimes in Rome, sometimes in Florence, with Madame Alexandre Dumas. She was seven years older than her lover, and ten years older than the abandoned princess. But she was one of those women who, having succeeded in pleasing, also know how to dig their toes in. As a woman of the theatre, and glamorous with the prestige of Paris, she was not without intelligence. Her good sense enchanted the Sicilian. From 1840 onwards, she had spent several months of every year in Florence, where she was frequently joined by Dumas, who did not very much mind sharing her favours. Then, the Italian interval of the moment over, she returned to Paris where she ruled, with natural ease, over the house of the marquis de la Pailleterie.

Between Ida and Dumas *fils*, however, an active struggle continued for the control of Dumas *père*.

In 1844 husband and wife agreed to an amicable separation. Dumas found it very satisfactory to be completely detached from her. By a legal settlement, dated October 15th, 1844, he undertook to pay her an annual allowance of twelve thousand gold francs, with, in addition, three thousand francs for the 'upkeep of her carriage'. He even offered to buy back the furnishings (all in lemon-wood) of the nuptial bedroom for an outright payment of nine thousand francs.

On paper this munificence makes an impressive show, but the risks were not great. It cost him so little to distribute a non-existent allowance, and to undertake in writing to pay out sums of money in drafts on a bank account without funds! Ida knew, better than anyone, that her dowry (one hundred and twenty thousand gold francs) could never be recovered. Her future lay with Villafranca.

A total breach without legal proceedings. Dumas set great store by adopting a chivalrous attitude to the woman who bore his name. When Ida finally left for Italy, he gave her a letter to the French ambassador, a letter redolent of warmth, from which it was impossible to gather, even when reading between the lines, that the lady's journey indicated a final separation, or that a famous household had just been broken up. As much from indifference to anything that Ida might do, as from a passion for the nobility, the marquis de la Pailleterie considered that his marquise had taken a successor really worthy of him.

He was very well pleased to feel himself once more entirely free. Not that Ida had been jealous, but she had, as it was her right to do, occupied the conjugal domicile, and kept him from installing there the favourite of the moment. For Dumas, true happiness consisted of an isolated room; a table of unpainted wood; an enormous pile of lavender-blue paper; ten or twelve hours of work a day; a young and ardent woman for purposes of pleasure; a son and a daughter whom he could love with all his heart, could treat as companions, and never have to fear that they would preach at him; witty friends who would make themselves free of his purse, eat him out of hearth and home, drink his wine, and pay for what they had with epigrams; and all these things within the exciting atmosphere of the theatre, of ceaseless readings, and the surge of new and immense subjects to be written about. In short, he adored independence, power, gaiety; and dreaded nobody in the world except bores, complaining mistresses and creditors. This picture would be incomplete without the indication, against a magnificent and bohemian background, of a secret but conscious need to use all the latent powers of his mind in the service of the humble and the under-privileged, a need which his life did not satisfy; which he was free, from now on, to express in the pages of his novels.

PART FIVE

*

FROM *THE THREE MUSKETEERS* TO *THE LADY OF THE CAMELLIAS*

CHAPTER I

In which the Man of the Theatre turns Novelist

That no one could well be more theatrical is easy to see from his novels. ARSÈNE HOUSSAYE

ALL through the first part of his life, Dumas, in the eyes of public and critics alike, had been a 'theatre-man' par excellence. Nor were the public and the critics wrong. He had, it is true, written essays, like *Gaule et France*, travel sketches, and even novels, while he was busy with his plays; but he had brought to all those literary forms that instinct for action which is the distinguishing mark of the dramatist, and had not yet launched out on that immense enterprise which, more than his dramas, was to ensure his fame — the retelling of the history of France in fiction.

Literary forms are born of an encounter between genius and circumstance. Dumas had genius of a certain kind — the genius that comes of vigour and a sense of the dramatic. Circumstances did the rest. The first of these was the renaissance of the historical novel. Long before Walter Scott there had been novels in which the fictional characters had been interspersed with actual, and famous, people: 'La Princesse de Clèves', for instance. But Scott had been the first to recreate whole periods and whole worlds. It was he who had roused Balzac, Hugo, Vigny and Dumas to enthusiasm.

Why was this? The reason lay in the fact that he provided the necessary food for an epoch which had been deprived of the theatricalities of the Empire and was thirsting for the marvellous. It has been said that the imagination of the young men of 1820 was like an empty palace with the portraits of ancestors upon the walls. The palace had got to be furnished. If the present could not provide the wherewithal, then the writers must have recourse to the great storehouse of history. But history, badly told, can become a gloomy burial-ground. Walter Scott had made of it something living and picturesque. Even the historians had approved of him. 'I regard him as the greatest master there has ever been of the *instinctive* understanding of history', said Augustin Thierry.

And now the young French writers were following in Scott's footsteps. Alfred de Vigny had written *Cinq-Mars*; Hugo, *Notre-Dame de Paris*; Balzac, *Les Chouans*; Merimée, *la Chronique du temps de Charles IX*. These books had enjoyed a great success with an élite: Hugo, alone, had reached a wider public. That public, however, was as ready to read historical novels as it had been to sit through historical dramas, and for the same reason. A people which had *made* history, and witnessed vast changes, was longing to be taken behind the scenes of a past which was not so very far removed in time. But the only way of interesting the man in the street in kings and queens, in ministers and favourites, was to show the human being under the trappings, a task of which Dumas was to show himself a master.

He was neither a scholar nor a searcher of archives. He had a love of history but no respect for it. 'What is history?' he said. 'It is the nail on which I can hang my novels.' He rumpled the skirts of Clio, and considered that he had a perfect right to take liberties with her, provided he could get her with child. Conscious of his own virility, and quite sure that he could produce the infant, he was in no mood to listen to the detailed confidences, the dotting of the i's, the second thoughts, in which that slightly pedantic muse so fondly indulges. He knew that he would never be taken seriously as an historian. 'It is the unreadable histories that make a sensation. They are like the dinners one cannot digest. Those one can, are forgotten the next morning.'[1] He had not the necessary patience to acquire knowledge. He liked to reduce research to a minimum. What he needed was that somebody should present him with the raw material on which he could then exercise his vivifying art. Chance had equipped him not only with genius, but with the more modest, but precious, ability to devour Memoirs.

It will be remembered that the charming Gérard de Nerval had become one of Alexandre Dumas's most regular collaborators. Now Nerval had a friend, Auguste Maquet, who was the son of a rich industrialist, had a passion for letters, and an elegant appearance set off by a moustache *à la mousquetaire*. He had turned twenty in 1833, and from then on made one of a small, venturesome and anti-clerical group, where he rubbed shoulders with Nerval, Théophile Gautier, Petrus Borel, Arsène Houssaye, and the painter, Célestin Nanteuil. Thinking his name too unromantic, he adopted that of *Augustus MacKeat* within this select circle. He was a teacher of history at the

Lycée Charlemagne, but had no enthusiasm for schoolmastering, and longed to give it up. In 1836, he joined the staff of the *Figaro*, and set himself to cobbling plays. He submitted to Anténor Joly, the manager of the Renaissance, a drama entitled *Soir de Carnaval* which was rejected. 'Well written, but not suited to the stage', said Joly. The theologians of the theatre take a cruel delight in repulsing the profane.

Gérard de Nerval suggested that he should show this unwanted child to Dumas who was an orthopaedist renowned for his skill in straightening the limbs of plays born crooked. The verdict was: 'One and a half acts are good; one and a half need rewriting. Dumas has no time to give to it, because of *L'Alchimiste* which he has got to finish within the next fortnight.'[2] Nerval would have been more than willing to help his friend, but lacked the influence necessary to get the play accepted. *Gérard de Nerval to Auguste Maquet, November 29th, 1838*: 'My dear friend: Dumas has completely rewritten the play in accordance with your original idea. Your name will appear. It has been accepted, has delighted everybody, and will be put on. There! ... goodbye. I am arranging to introduce you to Dumas tomorrow. ...'

So it was that Auguste Maquet, at the age of twenty-five, had his three acts performed, and made the acquaintance of the great panjandrum. The play was given a new title, *Bathilde,* and was produced on January 4th, 1839. Delighted at such a beginning, young Maquet showed Dumas, in the course of the next year, the draft of a novel, *Le Bonhomme Buvat,* dealing with the conspiracy of Cellamare (the Spanish ambassador who had plotted against the Regent, and been escorted across the frontier). The story is seen through the eyes of an obscure copyist (Buvat), who becomes involved in the conspiratorial activities without really understanding what is happening. Dumas found the story attractive. The period was one which he had recently used as a setting for his comedies. He had the manners and 'atmosphere' at his finger-tips. He offered to refurbish and lengthen Maquet's text.

At this point a new influence began to make itself felt, which was to prepare the way for the 'serial' story. For some years, two newspapers, Émile de Girardin's *La Presse* and Ledru-Rollin's *Le Siècle*, had been making immense efforts to extend their readership. The subscription price was only forty francs a year, and this attracted a flood of readers and a large number of advertisers, but the problem was how to keep the circulation up. The best way was by publishing instalments of thrilling fiction. 'To Be Continued in Our Next' (a formula invented in 1829 by Dr Véron for use in the *Revue de Paris*) became the mainspring of journalistic enterprise.

In editorial eyes, the greatest novelist was the one who attracted the largest number of readers. Excellent writers might turn out to be bad 'serializers'. Balzac was in constant need of money, and nothing would have suited him better than to provide *all* the fiction needed. 'Whenever he nosed out a well-furnished cash-box,' said his enemies, 'he squatted down in front of it like a cat who has seen a mouse vanish into a hole and waits for it to come out again.' But editors were hesitant. They regarded Balzac as a difficult author. His long topographical descriptions, which occupied the first pages of his novels, failed to hold the reader's attention. According to them, the real masters of this particular technique were Eugène Sue, Alexandre Dumas and Frédéric Soulié. 'If I were King Louis-Philippe', said Méry, 'I would subsidize Dumas, Eugène Sue and Soulié, on condition that they kept the *Musketeers*, the *Mysteries of Paris* and the *Memoirs of the Devil* going indefinitely. Revolutions would be a thing of the past.'

> *La Presse* [said Sainte-Beuve] has indulged in a daring piece of speculation, and has recently bought up everything there is on the market in the way of writers. It doesn't mind what it pays, and has, one might say, made a 'corner' in them. It is behaving like those rich capitalists who, in order to remain masters of the situation, buy all they can lay their hands on in the way of oil and crops, in the certainty that they can re-sell everything retail at a later date. If, for example, a small paper proposes to dole out Alexandre Dumas to its subscribers, *La Presse* will at once sell him back to it, having bought everything that Dumas can produce, or contract for, over a period of twelve or fifteen years. It has more than it can possibly use itself, and can dictate its own terms ... *La Presse* has, furthermore, announced the forthcoming serialization of a *Mémorial de Sainte-Hélène*, newly edited by General Montholon, to which, it says, for greater vividness, Dumas has consented to devote his great gifts as a writer. *La Presse*, says the *Globe*, has recently waxed enthusiastic over that gentleman's literary style. What a joke! Could anyone succeed better in having the laugh of the public! In spite of these puny, but inevitable, middlemen, it would be true to say that Napoleon

has become one of the three chief contributors to *La Presse*.

The self-praise contained in this prospectus is supreme in its kind. Alexandre Dumas is put forward as the equal of Walter Scott and Raphael. . . .[3]

Dumas had given a great deal more thought than is generally supposed to his craft. He had studied with care the technique used by Walter Scott. The Scottish novelist established his characters from the very first page, by indulging in long descriptions of their peculiarities, so that the reader, meeting them again later, should recognize the persons with whom he has to deal. But in a serial, which must hold its readers' attention from the very first lines, the author cannot permit himself a long-drawn-out beginning, and Dumas, though strongly characterizing his people, jumped at once into dialogue and action. His dramatic gifts thus found full employment. The technique of the serial-writer consists in supplying a thrilling conclusion to each instalment, at the same time leaving the reader in suspense. Dumas had long been familiar with this trick, which was that of the 'curtain line'. In 1838, one of his novels, *Le Capitaine Paul* (an imitation of Fenimore Cooper's *Pirate*, and very skilfully handled) had brought *Le Siècle* five thousand additional subscribers in three weeks. Is it surprising that editors swore by Dumas, and by Dumas only?

Having remade Auguste Maquet's book, and given it the title of *Le Chevalier d'Harmental*, Dumas would have been only too glad to let the young man's name appear with his own. But this the paper would not allow. 'A serial signed *Alexandre Dumas* is worth three francs a line', said Émile de Girardin. 'Signed *Dumas and Maquet* it is worth only three sous.' Girardin humbly catered for the taste of his public. 'I have no time for reading', said he. 'If Dumas or Eugène Sue write, or get written for them, a lot of nonsense, the public, on the strength of the signboard, accept the result as a masterpiece. The stomach gets used to the food it is offered.' To Théophile Gautier, who complained at not being included among the 'elect', he made this cynical rejoinder: 'You're all of you great writers, that goes without saying, but you can't bring me ten subscribers. That's the long and the short of it.' Hungry for great names, the editors had a horror of the unknown. So Dumas's name appeared unaccompanied. Maquet received eight thousand francs, an enormous sum for the period, which he could never have earned without Dumas. This compensation he regarded as fair and equitable. Later he did complain, but at the outset of their collaboration he admitted that he was dazzled, grateful and delighted. The success of *Le Chevalier d'Harmental* made it clear to Dumas that there was a gold-mine waiting to be exploited in the field of fictionalized history. He therefore expressed the greatest enthusiasm when Maquet brought him the rough scenario of a book dealing with Louis XIII, Richelieu, Anne of Austria and Buckingham, which afterwards became *The Three Musketeers*. Which of the two authors it was, we do not know, who first discovered the *Mémoires de Monsieur d'Artagnan, capitaine-lieutenant de la première compagnie des Mousquetaires du Roi*, an apocryphal production the true author of which was Gatien de Courtilz (often known as Courtilz de Sandras, or Sandras de Courtilz), and published in 1700 at Cologne. A second edition was issued in 1704 at Amsterdam by Jean Elzevir. Maquet said that it was he; but a slip belonging to the Marseille library shows that the book was borrowed by Alexandre Dumas in 1843 and never returned. The librarian, who was no less a person than his old friend Méry, must have been very long-suffering.

What is certain is, in the first place, that many of the incidents of the novel and many of the names, including (slightly disguised) those of Athos, Porthos and Aramis, were taken over from Gatien de Courtilz; and, in the second, that, this scurrilous scribbler having but little talent, the best of the episodes (the stories of Madame Bonacieux and Milady de Winter) were entirely transformed, and largely invented, by Dumas and Maquet; finally, that if Maquet did the roughing-out, Dumas did the shaping. His methods of work, so far as his collaborators were concerned, never changed very much. The collaborator drew up a scenario. This Dumas quickly assimilated and then used as a draft on which to work. He rewrote, added thousands of vivid details, altered the dialogue (he was a master of dialogue), gave particular attention to the chapter endings, and lengthened the story so as to satisfy the demands made by a serial which had to last for several months without allowing the readers to draw breath.

In this case, he introduced several new characters — the servant, Grimaud, for instance, who always answered questions with a single word, an ingenious trick in view of the fact that the newspapers paid by the line. The resultant quick-moving dialogue had the double advantage of being easy to read and of increasing the author's remuneration. But a spoke was put in that wheel when *La Presse* and *Le Siècle* refused to recognize as a line anything that did not extend to over one half of the column. When that rule was announced, Villemessant, the editor of the *Figaro*, happened to be with Dumas, and noticed that he was busy reading the manuscript and deleting whole pages.

'What are you up to, Dumas?'

'I've just killed him.'

'Killed whom?'

'Grimaud . . . I only invented him as a fill-up . . . he's no good to me now.'

A contemporary writer, Vermersch, later wrote a parody of these Dumas dialogues:

'Have you seen him?'

'Whom?'

'Him.'

'Whom?'

'Dumas.'

'Father?'

'Yes.'

'What a man!'

'To be sure!'

'What fire!'

'I agree.'

'And how prolific!'

'Yes, indeed!'[4]

It cannot be denied that Maquet did a great deal of work on *The Three Musketeers*. Some of the anxious notes which Dumas sent him are still in existence: 'Copy, as soon as possible, and, especially, the first volume of d'Artagnan (the *Mémoires*) . . .' 'Don't fail to get hold of the volume of the History of Louis XIII which deals with the Chalais trial, and contains the relevant documents. Bring me, at the same time, what you have roughed out for Athos . . .' 'Here's an odd thing! I wrote this morning, asking you to bring the executioner on to the stage. Then I threw the letter into the fire, thinking that *I* would do it. Now the very first words I read show that our minds were working along the same lines. . . .'[5]

But there are other letters, too, which prove that Dumas was in the driving-seat.

Alexandre Dumas to Auguste Maquet: Something rather

charming might be made of a night at Marie Touchet's — the appealing creature who consoles a king for being all-powerful, and is the only person in the whole of his realm who truly loves him. The little duc d'Angoulême in his cradle. The king who forgets . . . Ponder, read, visualize.[6]

My dear friend: in your next chapter we have got to hear from the mouth of Aramis, who has promised to get the information for d'Artagnan, in what Convent Madame Bonacieux is, and what protection the queen is giving her.[7]

Dear friend: I don't think that our Gorenflot[8] has been made important enough. Since we're getting him out of the Monastery, it must be for some better and more serious reason. We really ought to meet tomorrow.

If we can't do much with the isolation and mutual ignorance of Dixmer and Maison-Rouge,[9] we must arrange for them to meet. It'll be difficult to show them operating in the same prison without recognizing each other.[10]

One more heave today at *Bragelonne* so that we can tackle it again together on Monday or Tuesday, and finish the second volume[11] . . . Then, this evening, tomorrow, the next day, and Monday heaps and heaps of *Balsamo*.[12]

At a later date, Maquet published the portion of the text covering the death of Milady as he had first written it. He wanted to prove that he was the real author of *The Three Musketeers*. Actually he proved just the reverse. All that is best in that particular scene, all that gives it life and colour, came from Dumas. It is not even true to say that Dumas never did any research. There were passages in Gatien de Courtilz in which that pamphleteer-author had been guilty of in-accuracies, and it was Dumas who corrected these by checking them against the treatment of the same subjects by Madame de la Fayette, Tallement des Réaux and others. His really important contribution, however, lies in his making of the Musketeers — in Gatien they are coarse adventurers with nothing to catch at the imagination — the legendary characters which they have since become. It was he who had inherited from his father a taste for those combats, seemingly incredible, but nevertheless true, in which a man single-handed, as on the Bridge of Brixen, disarmed a hundred; it was he who had that 'feeling' for French history which was his by right of being the son of a father who had played a part in the making of history.

A living *sense* of France — in that lies the secret charm of the four heroes: d'Artagnan, Athos, Porthos and Aramis. Fierce determination, aristocratic melancholy, a somewhat vainglorious strength, an elegance, at once delicate and gay — it is these qualities that make of them, as it were, an epitome of that gracious, courageous, light-hearted France which we still like to recover through the imagination. It contained, to be sure, in addition to the restless world in which amorous intrigue went hand in hand with political plotting, men like Descartes and Pascal, though even they were not without experience, in the course of their lives, of the ways of soldiers and men of the court. But what grace, elegance, decision, vigour and intelligence there is in those young men who meet as comrades in arms before being reunited in the garb of religion! There is no one, not even Madame Bonacieux, who does not rank courage above virtue.

D'Artagnan, the dexterous Gascon, twirling his moustache; the boisterous Porthos with the frame of a giant; Athos, the slightly romantic grand seigneur; Aramis, the discreet Aramis, the dashing pupil of the good fathers (*non inutile est desiderium in oblatione*), who conceals both his religion and his love-affairs: these four friends, and not, as Courtilz had imagined them, four brothers, stand for the four cardinal points of French civilization. What torrential perseverance and vigour they exhibit! How simply they carry through their deeds of prowess! They ride hell-for-leather, they overcome difficulties with those high spirits which, in France, raise courage to a higher level. The ride to Calais, merely indicated in the *Mémoires*, can rank in rapidity of execution with the campaigns of Italy: and when we see Athos sitting in judgment on his abominable wife, let us not forget the courts-martial and the tribunals of the Revolution. If Danton and Napoleon were exemplars of Gallic energy, Dumas, in *The Three Musketeers* is the national novelist who puts it into words.[13]

One generation may be deceived about the value of a work of art: four or five generations rarely are. The lasting and universal popularity of *The Three Musketeers* shows that Dumas, by artlessly expressing his own nature in the persons of his heroes, was responding to that craving for action, strength and generosity which is a fact in all periods and all places. So well adapted is his technique to this type of novel that it has remained a model for all who have since tried their hands at the same form of composition. Dumas, or Dumas-Maquet,[14] based many stories on sources already known, sometimes apocryphal like the *Mémoires* of d'Artagnan, sometimes authentic, like those of Madame de la Fayette, from which the *Vicomte de Bragelonne* was drawn. Madame de la Fayette narrates, without dialogue, the tale of the early loves of Louis XIV, the rupture with Marie Mancini, the meeting with Louise de la Vallière, the death of Mazarin and the disgrace of Fouquet. It is all told briefly, soberly, perfectly. The drama is implied rather than expressed. Madame de la Fayette carefully refrains from giving imaginative versions of scenes at which she was not present as an eye-witness.

Dumas, on the other hand, seizes hold of the characters, of the general framework, and uses everything as grist for his mill. Whenever he comes upon the hint of a scene, he writes it, treating it as he would do on the stage, with calculated effects of surprise, violence or comedy. Madame de la Fayette's delicate line-drawing becomes a collection of coloured, dressed-up figures, faintly caricatured, maybe, but creating the illusion of life. The personages of history are painted without any pretence of detachment. Dumas either loves or hates his people. *His* Mazarin is as antipathetic as the Mazarin presented by the Cardinal de Retz. Dumas takes up the cudgels for Fouquet against Colbert. History demands more subtle treatment. The reader of serials likes his characters to be either black or white.

Above all, and therein lies his secret, Dumas introduces secondary figures into his stories, who are entirely of his own imagining, and through the actions of these unknown persons explains the great events of the past. Sometimes they have actually existed. There is a vicomte de Bragelonne, a shadowy and barely glimpsed presence, in Madame de la Fayette: sometimes they are sheer inventions. The miracle is that the imagined heroes always happen to be on the spot at every crucial moment of genuine history. Athos, standing under the scaffold at the execution of Charles I, treasures his last words. It is to his ears that the famous 'Remember!' is addressed. Athos and d'Artagnan between them re-establish Charles II on the throne of England. Aramis tries to substitute for Louis XIV the twin brother who later becomes the Man in the Iron Mask. History is brought down to the level of loved and familiar characters and, at the same time, to that of the ordinary reader.

The method is infallible, always on condition that the author has as much temperament as Dumas had. No writer can create heroes who produce the illusion of reality without putting a great deal of himself into them. Molière found within himself both Alceste *and* Philinte; Musset both Octave *and* Coelio. So it was that Dumas divided himself in order to give birth to both Porthos *and* Aramis. Porthos is the incarnation of all that he had inherited from his father, while Aramis embodies the elegance which father and son owed to Davy de la Pailleterie. 'Strong muscles, and finely articulated joints' — there we have Dumas.

Nor must it be forgotten that his moral standards and his philosophy were those, not of the better educated and more thoughtful members of French society, but of the mass of his readers. Sir Walter, that sound and solid Scot, was kept supplied by a moral and artistic providence with virtuous epilogues. Dumas's moral code may be summed up as a love of glory combined with a considerable dose of 'good sense' not entirely free from cynicism. He combined in his own person the Frenchman of the *chansons de geste* and that other of the *fabliaux*, a mixture which, though it does not account for the whole of France, certainly represents a large part of it. Like Rabelais, Dumas loved eating, drinking and irresponsible love-making. If d'Artagnan were not a hero he would be singularly amoral. The Musketeers resembled their creator in this, that they saw no harm in changing mistresses, in having more than one at a time, or in asking them for money. This apart, Dumas's novels were neither indecent nor aggressively immoral. His work, taken as a whole, was in brilliant contrast to that storehouse of macabre accessories which furnished the stock-in-trade of his friends, the romantics. It gave pleasure.

'Wonder of wonders!' wrote Jules Janin, 'a novel which sweeps and spreads across all the greatest events of the European past!' This was true. Thanks to Dumas, Paris in 1845 was paying a great deal more attention to Anne of Austria than to Louis-Philippe; to the love-affairs of Buckingham than to the English threat.

CHAPTER II

Messrs Alexandre Dumas & Co.

NEVER in the whole course of French literature has there been anything comparable to Dumas's output between the years 1845 and 1855. Novels of from eight to ten volumes showered down without a break on the newspapers and bookshops. The whole history of France was passed in review. *The Three Musketeers* was followed by *Twenty Years After* (*Vingt Ans Après*) and that by the nostalgic *Vicomte de Bragelonne*. Another trilogy — *Chicot the Jester* (*La Reine Margot*), *La Dame de Monsoreau*, and *The Forty-Five Guardsmen* (*Les Quarante-Cinq*) — brought the Valois on to the stage. *Chicot* deals with the struggle between Catherine de Medicis and Henry of Navarre. *La Dame de Monsoreau* describes, in entertaining fashion, the reign of Henri III. In *The Forty-Five Guardsmen* Diane de Monsoreau takes her revenge on the duc d'Anjou for the death of her lover, Bussy d'Ambois.

Simultaneously with these, Dumas was busy narrating the decline and fall of the French monarchy — *The Diamond Necklace* (*Le Collier de la Reine*); *Le Chevalier de Maison-Rouge*, *Memoirs of a Physician* (*Joseph Balsamo*); *The Taking of the Bastille* (*Ange Pitou*), and *La Comtesse de Charny*. One is entitled to speak of Dumas's 'historic imperialism'. From very early on he had planned to annex the whole of history to his romantic domain. 'There is no end to what I want to do', he said. 'I long for the impossible. How am I to achieve what I have in mind? By working as no one has ever worked before; by pruning life of all its details; by doing without sleep ...' This programme accounts for the five or six hundred volumes which so astonish the reader.

In this vast production there were few failures. His novels have become the inexhaustible nourishment of the leisure moments of the whole world. No one has read *all* Dumas (that would be as impossible as for him to have written it); but the whole of the civilized world has read *some* Dumas. 'If', it was being said in 1850, 'there exists at this moment a Robinson Crusoe in some desert island, he will be found reading *The Three Musketeers*.' It should be added that the world at large — and France in particular — has learned French history in the pages of Dumas. It may not be entirely accurate history, but it is very far from being wholly false, and it is always remarkably dramatic. Does Dumas make us think? Not very often. Dream? Never. Go on turning the pages? Always.

Success begets a world of enemies. Dumas continued to infuriate a great many people with his fluency, his bragging, his decorations, his waistcoats, and he showed no respect for the conventions of the republic of letters. It was a scandal that a single writer should produce all the serials in all the papers; offensive that he should employ a team of anonymous collaborators — Félicien Mallefille (who was George Sand's property), Paul Meurice and Auguste Vacquerie (who were Hugo's), Gérard de Nerval, Henri Esquiros and, of course, Auguste Maquet. Making 'niggers' work for one has never been a glorious or sympathetic employment. If one has to have recourse to them, it must be within reasonable limits. Sainte-Beuve could never, without the aid of his secretaries, have got through the enormous amount of work he did. But, then, Sainte-Beuve respected the sacerdotal nature of his task. His assistants were regarded, not as slaves or as exploited wage-earners, but as acolytes assisting him in the performance of his priestly function.

It was the general, but quite erroneous, view that Dumas was in the habit of buying two hundred and fifty francs' worth of manuscript, and selling it again for ten thousand. People said that, having at the beginning of his career established a drama-factory, he had now added to it a novel-factory. At the time of *La Tour de Nesle*, the Gaillardet affair had had a lot of ugly publicity. This was followed by Granier de Cassagnac's article which had aroused a deal of suspicion. Round about 1843, a young scholar, Louis de Loménie, who had failed to achieve fame with his praiseworthy labours, had published the *Galerie des contemporains illustres par un homme de rien*. He complained of the 'formidable peal' which had drowned his own 'small bell'. He inveighed against 'this turning of literature into a *business*'. Sainte-Beuve had excommunicated 'commercial literature'. Loménie wrote: 'Attacked by this deplorable contagion of industrialism, which is the curse of the age, M. Dumas, one might, and should, say has given himself body and soul to the worship of the Golden Calf. On the bill of what theatre, however small, in what shop, what enterprise, dealing in the *grocery* of literature, is his name not displayed? It is a physical impossibility that M. Dumas should have written or dictated all that appears over his name.'

In 1845, a pamphleteer, Eugène de Mirecourt (his real name was Jean-Baptiste Jacquot) published a brochure entitled *Fabrique de Romans: Maison Alexandre Dumas & Cie*, which made a great sensation. It should be pointed out that Mirecourt, before attacking Dumas, had offered to work for him, and had actually suggested the subject for a novel which would be 'something pretty tremendous'. This Simon Pure, therefore, was not so very pure after all, but would have been glad to participate in the 'business', could he have done so. Having failed, he first of all approached the Société des Gens de Lettres with a complaint that certain 'methods' were making it impossible for other writers (so he said) to make a living. After being once again shown the door, he wrote to Émile de Girardin, the editor of *La Presse*, asking him to exclude from his paper the 'disgraceful commercialism of Alexandre Dumas' and to 'extend a welcome to young writers of talent', by whom he meant Eugène de Mirecourt. Girardin replied that his readers wanted Dumas and that he would see they got Dumas. It was then that Mirecourt decided to write and publish *Maison Alexandre Dumas & Cie*.

He had, it appeared, been fairly well briefed. Some of Dumas's collaborators, feeling that their services had been undervalued, and their genius cheated of its due share of glory, had been whispering in Mirecourt's ear. He went through all Dumas's work, play by play, novel by novel, and named those whom he dubbed 'the real authors': Adolphe de Leuven, Anicet Bourgeois, Gaillardet, Gérard de Nerval, Théophile Gautier, Paul Meurice, and, first and foremost, Auguste Maquet. This attack might have gone home had it been directed with moderation. But Mirecourt's bad faith was made very obvious by the insults which he levelled at Dumas.

'One has only to scratch the surface of M. Dumas's works', wrote the vitriolic author, 'to find the savage . . . He lunches off potatoes which he takes from the glowing embers of the fire, and devours in their jackets . . . He runs after honours . . . He recruits deserters from the ranks of the intelligentsia, paid adapters whom he reduces to the level of negro workers writhing under the lash of a mulatto!' He went so far as to attack Dumas's private life. He made fun of Ida Ferrier, marquise de la Pailleterie. In short, so gross was the pamphlet that even Dumas's enemies were nauseated. Balzac, who would have been only too pleased to see a rival, for whom he felt no love, touched on the raw, was severe in his comments on Mirecourt. 'Somebody has given me that Maison Dumas & C° pamphlet', he wrote; 'it is disgustingly stupid, though I am forced unwillingly to admit, that what it has to say is true ... And since, in France, people are far more ready to believe a piece of witty calumny than the truth coarsely presented, it won't do Dumas much harm. . . .'

Not only did it do him no harm with his readers, but he brought a successful action in the courts. Mirecourt was sentenced for slander to a fortnight's imprisonment, and an official announcement of the sentence was inserted in the public press. He lost all credit in the world of letters. The comic side to the whole business is that the defendant was, at a later date, in his turn accused, and rightly, of having employed collaborators and suppressing their names. In 1857 a certain Rochefort revealed, in a pamphlet entitled *Maison Eugène de Mirecourt & Cie, par un ex-associé*, that Mirecourt, having to write an historical novel at top speed, had farmed out the work to a scholar called William Duckett. He, having too much on his hands, had passed the whole thing over to Rochefort, who received for his pains the sum of one hundred francs. Dumas paid better than that.

In his attempt to drive Mirecourt from the field in disorder, Dumas called upon Auguste Maquet to vouch for him. Maquet wrote a letter to Dumas intended (he said) to cover him should any eventual heir of his own make a claim. In it he declared that in his dealings with Dumas he had received fair and honourable treatment. When some time later this letter was made public, Maquet, who had by that time quarrelled with Dumas, tried to make out that it had been got from him 'under pressure'. What that pressure was, he did not state. The document in question gives every sign of being sincere, and contains no qualification.

March 4th, 1845: Dear friend: our collaboration has always been conducted without any formal agreements or clearly defined terms. Friendship and loyalty were sufficient for our purpose; so much so, indeed, that we have written half a million lines about the affairs of other people without ever thinking it necessary to write one word about our own. But a day came when you saw fit to break this silence in order to clear us both of certain vulgar and stupid slanders which had been directed against us. In acting thus you did me the greatest honour I could have hoped ever to receive. You declared that I and you together had written a *number of works*. You went, my dear friend, almost too far. Not only have you not denied me thrice, but you have made me famous. You have already satisfied any claim I might have made in respect of the books which we have produced in close co-operation.

I have never had any contract with you, and you have never had a receipt from me. But suppose, dear friend, that after my death a grabbing heir should come to you, brandishing your declaration and claiming what you have already paid me? The written word must needs be supported by the written word, and I feel myself under some compulsion to blacken a deal of paper.

I here and now affirm that, from this date forward, I renounce any claim in respect of the reprint rights in the following books which we wrote in collaboration: *Le Chevalier d'Harmental*; *The Three Musketeers*; *Twenty Years After*; *The Count of Monte-Cristo*; *La Guerre des Femmes*; *La Reine Margot (Chicot)*; *Le Chevalier de Maison-Rouge*, and maintain that I have been duly, and once and for all, indemnified by you in accordance with our verbal agreement.

Keep this letter, dear friend, to show to the grabbing heir, and tell him to his face that during my lifetime I considered myself to be fortunate and honoured in having acted as collaborator to the most brilliant of all French novelists. May he follow my example!

MAQUET[1]

If we are to judge fairly of the matter, we must remember that in Dumas's day literary morality held that collective work was admissible. In this, no doubt, it was wrong, for the great artist is he who has set his mark on the whole of a work. All the same, many famous painters (Raphael, Veronese, David, Ingres) were in the habit of making use of their pupils on vast compositions. In the theatre, a play is almost inevitably the joint product of author, producer, actors, stage-designer and, sometimes, of the composer of the music. Dumas, in order to get his imagination working, needed someone to 'stimulate his ideas'. In this he was not alone. Balzac constructed more than one great novel on a subject given, or suggested, by somebody else (*Béatrix* — by George Sand; *Le Lys dans la Vallée* — by Sainte-Beuve; *La Muse du Département* — by Caroline Marbouty). Stendhal owed *Lucien Leuwen* to the manuscript of an unknown woman. Is that so very criminal?

Dumas was certainly no *roi fainéant* surrendering his power into the hands of astute mayors of the palace. Far from exploiting his collaborators, he attributed too much importance to them. The ease with which he transformed into stories bubbling with life any literary monstrosity which reached him in a half-dead condition induced him to believe in the genius of those who had none.

'I don't understand', he once said, 'what is lacking in Mallefille to make him a man of talent.'

'I'll tell you what it is,' replied his interlocutor, 'it's probably talent.'

'By Jove, that's true!' exclaimed Dumas. 'It had never occurred to me!'

When *Les Girondins* appeared, he wrote: 'Lamartine has raised history to the level of the novel.' It may be said of Dumas, not that he raised the novel to the level of history — which neither he nor his readers wanted — but that he brought history and the novel, embodied in unforgettable characters, on to the popular stage, before an audience consisting of the general public, which is *the* public, and that, as a result of *his* limelight, both history and the novel have taken on new life, to the great delight of the nations and the centuries.'

CHAPTER III

Marie Duplessis

Beneath the sumptuous camellias, I catch a glimpse of a small blue flower. ÉMILE HENRIOT

AFTER the departure of Ida for Florence, the relationship between father and son was marked by an increase of affection. Said Dumas *père* to Dumas *fils*: 'When you, too, have a son, love him as I love you, but do not bring him up as I have brought up you.' Dumas *fils* had come to accept Dumas *père* as nature had made him, powerful, excellent and irresponsible. The young Alexandre was determined to make a success on his own. He would write — oh! no doubt of that, but not like 'the author of *Antony*, and of his being'. Not that he wasn't fond of the latter, but his love was that of a father, not of a son. 'My father', he said, 'is a great big child whom I had when I was a little boy.' That was the picture of the man as presented to him by his mother, the wise Catherine Labay, who was now earning her living by keeping a lending-library in the rue Michodière. She had no sense of bitterness, and no illusions where her inconstant lover was concerned.

Sons frequently react against the failings of their fathers. Dumas *fils* could take pleasure in the intelligence and imagination of Dumas *père*, but felt humiliated by some of his more absurd aspects. He was distressed by his artless boasting. What he saw going on in a home where the paterfamilias was for ever wondering where he could lay his hands on a hundred francs, gave him a secret longing for security. Besides, Don Juanism in later life always gets on the nerves of the young. 'I am like', he said, 'the concierge charged with the duty of ringing the door-bell of your celebrity. No sooner do I give my arm to a woman than the first thing she does is to lift her skirt clear of the mud, and the second, to ask me to introduce her to you.'

People were already beginning to distinguish between the two men by referring to Alexandre Dumas *père* and Alexandre Dumas *fils*. This annoyed the elder:

Instead of signing yourself Alex[andre] Dumas, as I do — which may some day be a cause of embarrassment to both of us, because our two signatures are very much alike — you ought to take the name of Davy Dumas. My name is too well known, as I am sure you realize, for there to be any uncertainty about which of us is meant, and I really can't add '*père*' — I am still too young for that.[1]

At twenty, Dumas *fils* was a handsome, proud-looking young man, full of vigour and, apparently, of health. He was very tall, and his square shoulders were crowned by a fine head in which nothing, except perhaps a dreamy look in the eyes and a hint of fuzziness in the auburn hair, recalled the great-grandmother from San-Domingo. He dressed like a dandy or, as the phrase then was, a 'lion'. He wore a cloth coat with a broad collar, a white cravat, a piqué waistcoat of London make, and carried a cane with a gold knob. The tailor was not paid, but the general effect was superb, the air of vitality overwhelming. Somewhere behind the screen of elegant detachment there lurked a serious and sentimental temperament inherited from Catherine Labay, but he was at pains to conceal this side of his nature.

In September 1844 father and son were living together in the Villa Medicis at Saint-Germain-en-Laye. One day, on the road to that place, Dumas *fils* fell in with Eugène Déjazet, the son of the great actress. The young men hired a couple of horses and enjoyed a gallop in the forest, after which, back in Paris, they went to the Théâtre des Variétés. Autumn was only just beginning, and Paris still had an empty look. At the Comédie-Française, a company of 'young and as yet unknown players' were performing a series of old-fashioned and forgotten pieces to audiences of retired 'pros' . . . At the Palais-Royal and the Variétés there were several pretty and by no means standoffish young women in the auditorium.

Eugène Déjazet was as little concerned about conventional morals as Dumas *fils*. His mother spoiled him, and he had more money than his friend. The two men, on the look-out for a 'find', stared through their glasses at the charming members of the demi-monde occupying the boxes. They had the easy manners of good society, were adorned with beautiful jewellery, and might well have been mistaken for so-called women of fashion. Few in number, celebrated, and known everywhere in Paris, these 'high-class tarts' formed the aristocracy of their profession, and were quite distinct from the ordinary pick-ups and the shop-girls of easy virtue.

Though kept by rich protectors (a girl had got to live) they dreamed of pure love. Romanticism had left its mark on them. Victor Hugo had rehabilitated Marion de Lorme — and Juliette Drouet. Public opinion was indulgent to courtesans who had found justification in a guilty yielding to the lure of passion, or in excessive poverty. They themselves shared in this sentimental view. Most of them had started in life as work-girls, and had been unfortunate enough not to meet a good husband. Tivoli, a screened box at the Ambigu, the gift of a cashmere shawl, or a piece of jewellery, had sent them over the borderline into the world of kept women. Though turned mercenary, they still retained a longing for true love. George Sand had multiplied the misunderstood women who dreamed of 'eternal rapture'. All this explains how it was that our two youthful cynics at the Variétés concentrated their attention, not only on white, desirable flesh, but also on eyes which betrayed the presence of melancholy and tender thoughts.

On the evening in question, there was, seated in one of the front boxes, a woman widely known at the time for her beauty, her taste, and the amount of money she had got through. Her name was Alphonsine Plessis, though she called herself Marie Duplessis. 'She was', says Dumas *fils*, 'tall, very slender, with black hair and a pink and white complexion. She had a small head and elongated eyes which had that enamelled look to be found in the women of Japan. But there was in them something which indicated a proud and lively nature. Her lips were cherry-pink, her teeth the loveliest you could have hoped to see anywhere. She might well have been a Dresden figurine . . .'[2] Her small waist, her swan-like neck, her frank and virginal expression, her long ringlets, her low-cut dress of white satin, her river of diamonds and her golden bracelets all combined to make her royally beautiful. Dumas was dazzled, struck to the heart, conquered.

No woman in the whole of the theatre had a greater air of distinction; yet, with the single exception of Anne du Mesnil, a woman of sound Norman aristocratic stock who had married beneath her, all Marie's forebears had belonged to the farm-worker class. Her father, Marin Plessis, an unpleasant and vicious creature, was thought by the villagers to be a witch-doctor. He had married Marie Deshayes, the daughter of Anne du Mesnil, who bore him two girls before running away. Alphonsine had been born in 1824 and so was exactly the same age as the young Dumas. After being brought up in the country, she had, or so it was said, been sold to some gypsies, who took her to Paris where they placed her with a dressmaker.

As a work-girl with a head stuffed full of the novels of Paul de Kock, she had danced in Paris, here, there and everywhere, with students, and on Sundays, at Montmorency, let herself be inveigled into country strolls. A restaurant-proprietor in the Palais-Royal, who had taken her once to Saint-Cloud, furnished a small apartment for her in the rue de l'Arcade, but was almost at once supplanted by Agénor, duc de Guiche, an elegant student of the École Polytechnique, who in 1840 had left the army and become one of the leading dandies of the Boulevard des Italiens, and the 'Antinous' of the year. A week later, nobody at the Théâtre des Italiens, or at the Opéra, in the famous *loge infernale* which was, in some sort, an annexe of the Jockey Club, was talking about anything but the young duke's new mistress.[3]

This adorable girl was duly adored by all the most brilliant men in Paris: Fernand de Montguyon, Henri de Contades, Édouard Delessert and many others. These lovers, drawn from the ranks of the nobility and gentry, saw to it that she should acquire a grace of manner and a pleasing, if superficial, culture. In the hands of carefully chosen masters, being herself both gifted and sensitive, she blossomed and flowered. In 1844, when Dumas *fils* first knew her, she had in her library Rabelais, *Don Quixote*, Molière, Walter Scott, Dumas *père*, Hugo, Lamartine and Musset. She was well read in all these, and had a strong liking for poetry. She had also been taught the piano, and played barcarolles and waltzes with a good deal of feeling.

In short, she had, with quite remarkable speed, climbed the ladder of taste and fortune. In 1844 she was looked upon as the most elegant woman in Paris, the rival of Alice Ozy, Lola Montes and Atala Beauchêne. At her parties were to be met, not only the 'lions' of the Jockey Club, but Eugène Sue, Roger de Beauvoir, Alfred de Musset. The feeling she aroused in all was one of admiration mingled with respect and pity, for she was far superior to the profession she pursued. Why, then, did she continue in it? Because she had acquired the habit of spending a hundred thousand gold francs a year, and also because, feverish, sick and dissatisfied with herself, she needed the numbing effects of a life of pleasure.

On that evening at the Variétés, she had with her in her box a very old man, the comte de Stackelberg, who had once occupied the post of Russian ambassador. She told Dumas later that this old dotard was keeping her because she reminded him of a daughter whom he had lost. This was pure invention on her part. 'The count, in spite of his great age, was not concerned to find in Marie Duplessis an Antigone, like Oedipus, but rather a Bathsheba, like David.'⁴ He had set her up at Nº 11 Boulevard de la Madeleine, and given her a blue brougham and two thoroughbred horses. By him, and by other admirers, her apartment was kept constantly supplied, not only with camellias, but with all the flowers in season. But she had a dread of roses, which made her feel dizzy, and delighted in camellias, which are odourless. 'She was imprisoned', says Arsène Houssaye, 'in a fortress of camellias.'

From her box, Marie was making signs to a fat woman whom Dumas knew. Her name was Clémence Prat, whose real profession, though she did a little dressmaking, was that of a theatrical 'dresser'. Eugène Déjazet was on familiar terms with this individual, who also lived on the Boulevard de la Madeleine, next door to Marie Duplessis. The latter left the Variétés in her carriage before the end of the performance. Somewhat later, a cab set down Dumas, Eugène Déjazet and Clémence Prat at the 'dresser's' door, there to await events. In his novel, *La Dame aux Camélias*, Dumas *fils* has described the scene. Stackelberg appears in it as 'the old duke', and Clémence Prat as Prudence Duvernoy.

'Is the old duke with your neighbour?' I said to Prudence.

'No, she is almost certainly alone.'

'But she must be horribly bored!'

'We spend almost all our evenings together, or, if she goes out, she asks me to drop in on her when she gets back. She never goes to bed before two in the morning. She can't get to sleep earlier than that.'

'Why not?'

'Because she suffers with her lungs, and is scarcely ever without a temperature.'⁵

Very soon Marie called to Clémence from her window, begging her to come and save her from a tiresome visitor, the comte de N. . . , who was boring her to death.

'I can't,' said Clémence Prat. 'I've got two young men with me. One of them is Déjazet's son, the other Dumas's.'

'Bring them with you: anyone's better than the count. Only be quick.'

All three set off and, in the house next door, found the count leaning with his back to the drawing-room mantelpiece, and Marie seated at the piano. She received the two strangers with great charm of manner, and behaved so rudely to the count that he took his leave. As soon as he had gone, she became very gay. Supper was served, there was a great deal of laughter, but Dumas felt sad. He had admired the disinterested behaviour of this woman who had driven away a rich man who was prepared to ruin himself for her sake, but it caused him pain to see the sublime creature drinking to excess, 'talking like a bargee, and laughing louder and louder as the conversation became more and more outrageous'.⁶ With each glass of champagne she took, her cheeks assumed an increasingly feverish flush and, towards the end of supper, she was seized with a fit of coughing and hurried from the room.

'What is the matter with her?' asked Eugène Déjazet.

'She has been laughing too much, and is spitting blood,' said Clémence Prat.

Dumas went in search of the sufferer. He found her lying face downwards on a sofa. On a table beside her was a silver bowl and, in it, a few filaments of blood.

I went over to her, but she made no movement [wrote Dumas *fils*]. I sat down and took one of her hands which was lying on the sofa.

'Ah, so it's you, is it?' she said with a smile. 'Are you feeling sick, too?'

'No, but what about yourself? Are you still suffering?'

'Very little: I have become used to this sort of thing.'

'You are killing yourself,' I said, in a voice shaken with emotion. 'I wish I were a friend or a relation, so as to be able to prevent you from doing yourself so much harm.'

'Why this sudden devotion?'

'It springs from a feeling of sympathy with you against which I cannot fight.'

'In other words, you are in love with me? Why not say so straight out? It would make everything so much easier.'

'Perhaps I will say it some day, but not now.'

'It would be very much better for you if you never said it.'

'Why?'

'Because such an avowal could result in only two possible alternatives.'

'And what are they?'

'Either I shall refuse you, in which case you will harbour a grievance against me: or, I shall accept you, and you will find yourself with a gloomy mistress on your hands, a nerve-ridden, sick and melancholy woman, whose gaiety you will find sadder even than her grief: a woman who spits blood and spends a hundred thousand francs a year! That is all right for an old money-bag, but it's a poor look-out for a young man like you ... All the young lovers I have had have left me.'

I said nothing in reply, but only listened. I was so deeply moved at the thought of the miserable life from which the poor child was trying to escape through debauchery, drunkenness and insomnia, that I could find nothing to say.

'Come, we're talking a lot of childish nonsense,' she went on, 'give me your arm, and let us go back to the dining-room.'

How was it that she became his mistress? He was poor, and, for her, burning declarations of love were a daily occurrence; but he returned to the charge with passionate perseverance. 'This mixture of gaiety, melancholy, simplicity and prostitution, the very malady from which she was suffering, with its resultant nervousness and emotional instability — all these things merely increased my desire to possess her ...' There was about her a touching ingenuousness ... 'a recurrent longing for a quieter life ... a certain physical curiosity ... which moved me profoundly ... She had yielded to temptation and to the call of pleasure without ever losing a kind of pride which gave a certain air of decorum to her shame. ...'

The young Dumas was not without generous instincts. The love he felt for his mother had taught him to feel pity for all women unjustly outlawed by society. Artless and, at the same time, blasé, he was moved to compassion by their desperate situation, and persuaded them to confide in him. Behind their assumed mask of gaiety he could catch the glint of tears. There was no end to the indulgence he could feel for courtesans. He thought of them always as victimized rather than guilty. They were grateful to him for the respect he showed them in their degradation. No doubt that was what formed the strong bond between him and Marie Duplessis. One day she said to him: 'If you promise to grant all my wishes without saying a word, or making a comment, or questioning me, I may, perhaps, come to love you. . . .'⁸

Few young men of twenty would not have given that promise, impossible though it was to keep. For some time she almost completely abandoned her rich protectors in favour of this grave and charming 'squire'. She found pleasure in becoming once again a little *grisette*, in going for walks with him in the Bois or the Champs-Élysées. In her room, where 'on a dais stood a magnificent *boule* bed, with, at its four feet, caryatids in the form of fauns and bacchantes', she treated him to intoxicating 'orgies of the flesh'. Ah! how he loved those great, black-encircled eyes of hers, her air of innocence, her yielding waist, and the 'voluptuous fragrance which emanated from her!'

Dumas *père* has described how his son first told him of this conquest:

Come with me to the Théâtre-Français, where the play, I think, was *Les Demoiselles de Saint-Cyr*. As I was going down one of the passages, the door of a box opened. I felt someone catch hold of my coat-tails. I turned round. It was Alexandre.

'So it's you, is it? Good evening, dear boy.'

'Come in here for a moment, Father.'

'You're not alone.'

'All the more reason. Shut your eyes, put your head through the chink of the door. Don't be afraid, nothing unpleasant's going to happen to you.'

True enough. Scarcely had I shut my eyes, scarcely had I put my head through the door, than I felt upon my mouth the pressure of two trembling, feverish, burning lips. I opened my eyes. An adorable young woman of twenty, or twenty-two, was alone there with Alexandre, and had just bestowed upon me that far from daughterly greeting. I recognized her from having seen her more than once, 'in front'. She was Marie Duplessis, the lady of the camellias.

'So it's you, dear child?' said I, gently releasing myself from her arms.

'Yes, it seems one has got to take you by assault. Oh! I know that is not your reputation, but why are you being so cruel to me? I have twice written to you suggesting a meeting at the Opera Ball. . . .'

'I thought your letters were addressed to Alexandre.'

'To Alexandre Dumas; yes, they were.'

'To my son, I mean.'

'Oh, come! Alexandre is Dumas *fils*, but you most certainly are not Dumas *père*, and never will be.'

'Thank you for the compliment, my lovely lady.'

'But then, why didn't you come? I don't understand.'

'Let me explain. A beautiful young woman like you does not suggest lovers' meetings to men of my age unless she has need of them. What can I do for you? I offer you my protection without any question of love in return.'

'I told you so!' said Alexandre.

'On those conditions, then, I accept!' said Marie Duplessis with a charming smile, and letting the long black lashes veil her eyes.

'We shall meet again, shall we not, monsieur?'

'Whenever you wish, mademoiselle. . . .'

I bowed to her as I might have bowed to a duchess. The door closed behind me and I was back again in the passage. That was the only time I ever kissed Marie Duplessis; it was the last time I ever saw her. I waited for Alexandre and the lovely courtesan to visit me. A few days later, Alexandre came alone.

'Why haven't you brought her with you?'

'The fit has passed. She had an idea that she would like to go on the stage. They all dream of that! But actresses have got to study, rehearse, play: it's a stiff job to take on. It is far easier to get up at two in the afternoon, to dress, to drive round the Bois, to come back and dine at the *Café de Paris* or the *Frères Pro-vençaux*, to go on and spend the evening in a box at the Vaudeville or the Gymnase, to sup afterwards, and to go home at three in the morning, than to do what Mademoiselle Mars does! This particular aspirant has now forgotten all about her vocation . . . Besides, I think she is a very sick woman.'

'Poor girl!'

'You are right to pity her. She is so far superior to the trade she plies.'

'I hope what you feel for her is not serious?'

'No: what I feel for her is compassion,' answered Alexandre. I never spoke to him again about Marie Duplessis.'

The moral code of Dumas *fils* was stricter than that of Dumas *père*. Marie Duplessis was a reader of *Manon Lescaut*. She hoped to cast her handsome young man for the part of des Grieux. This he refused. What, then, did he hope? To reform her? To persuade her to change her way of life? It might have been within her capacity to do so, for there was more in her of sentimentality than of self-interest. Dumas himself said of Marie: 'She was one of the last of those rare courtesans who had a heart.'[10] But the costs of a single evening spent with her — theatre, camellias, sweets, supper, passing whims — were quite enough to ruin young Alexandre. He was making very little money and was reduced to begging endlessly from his father, who, himself in low water, gave him from time to time a voucher for a hundred francs on Madame Porcher to whom he entrusted the selling of such theatre tickets as were allotted to him.

Alexandre Dumas fils *to Madame Porcher*: Wait a few days, madam! I know that is like telling a man who is going to have his head cut off to dance the rigadoon or make a pun! But in a few days I shall be a millionaire! I shall be getting 500 francs. If I address myself to you now, if I plague you with my requests, it is because, just at the moment, I could give points to Job in the matter of poverty, and he, as you know, was the poorest man of all Antiquity. If you don't send me the hundred francs by the hand of my slave, I shall spend my last pennies on buying a clarinet and a poodle, and shall take up a pitch in front of your door, where I shall play the one and put the other through his tricks, wearing a placard on my front, saying: 'Please help a literary gent deserted by Madame Porcher!' Would you like me to give my head as security for these hundred francs? To shout 'Long Live the Republic'? Or to marry Mademoiselle Morales? Or would you rather I went to the Odéon in a crush-hat and wrote up Cachardy as an actor of talent? I will do anything you say, if only you will let me have a hundred francs, or more if you can:

Your very, very, very devoted

A. DUMAS

197

It doesn't matter to me whether I have the money in coin or notes, so don't put yourself out.[11]

Every morning Marie sent him the programme for her day: 'Dear *Adet*' — she had composed this name from her lover's initials, A. D. He fetched her in the evening. They dined together, after which they went to the theatre. Then they returned to Marie's boudoir where large china vases were filled with the scentless flowers. 'Some morning,' he said, 'I shan't go away until eight, and a day will come when I shan't leave you until noon.'

Sometimes she could not sleep, but 'sat naked under her white woollen dressing-gown on the rug in front of the fireplace, watching the flames in the grate with a sad look on her face'.[12] At those moments Dumas loved her passionately. At others, he feared he might be just a dupe. He knew that she often lied to him, perhaps from delicacy of feeling. Stackelberg still occupied a place in her life, as also did a younger man, Édouard Perregaux, the grandson, on his father's side, of the famous financier who had been Governor of the Bank of France, and, on his mother's, of the duc de Tarente. On a sheet of pink paper, folded into a cocked hat, Marie would write to him: 'It would give me great pleasure, dear Édouard, if you would come to see me this evening (Théâtre du Vaudeville, Box 29). I cannot possibly dine with you: I am far from well' and, on pale blue paper: 'My darling Ned, there is to be a very special performance tonight at the Variétés for Bouffé's benefit . . . I should be really delighted if you could manage to get me a box. Send me an answer, dearest of friends: I kiss your eyes a thousand million times. . . .'[13]

To Ned she explained: 'I am going out with Zélia' each time she went out with Dumas. To Dumas she played the part of the repentant Magdalene. Once, when somebody asked her why she had such a mania for lying, she burst out laughing, and answered: 'Lies keep the teeth white.' She tried in vain to 'reconcile love and business'. All this meant for Dumas was a few days of happiness followed by eleven months of anxiety, suspicions and scruples. He thought that he was set between Love and Honour. What a world of vanity those capitals disguise!

At the end of two months, reproaches were following hard on tenderness. He was seeing Marie less often. She guessed that he was keeping something from her. 'Dear Adet,' she wrote, 'why have you sent me no news of yourself, and why do you not write *frankly*? I hope to have a word from you, and to kiss you very tenderly — whether as a mistress or a friend, you must decide. Whichever it is, I shall always be your devoted — Marie.'[14] On August 30th, 1845, he decided to break with her.

Alexandre Dumas fils *to Marie Duplessis*: My Dear Marie — I am neither rich enough to love you as I would wish, nor poor enough to be loved by you as you would. Let us both, therefore, forget — you, a name which cannot mean very much to you, I, a happiness which is no longer possible for me. There is no point in my telling you how sad I am, since you already know how much I love you. Farewell, then. You have too much heart not to understand the reasons for this letter, and too much intelligence not to forgive me. A thousand memories.

A. D.

30th August, Midnight.[15]

In the artistic temperament love starts a new life when bodily satisfaction ceases. The vanished Marie haunted the broodings of *Adet*.

CHAPTER IV

An Unsentimental Journey

AFTER the father's breach with Ida Ferrier, and the son's with Marie Duplessis, the two Dumas lived together in conditions of disorder and mutual tolerance. The son had become the lover of an actress at the Vaudeville, Anaïs Liévenne. It was in the course of a supper-party given by her at the *Frères Provençaux*, that a duel, which was to give rise to much scandal, was arranged. It took place between a brilliant young journalist, Dujarrier, who was on the staff of *La Presse*, where he looked after the serials, and Rosemond de Beauvallon, a hired bully, who killed his opponent with a foul thrust, on the instructions, it was said, and for the benefit of, a number of rival papers. The war for subscribers had now gone to the length of murder.

At first acquitted, Beauvallon was ordered by the Cour de Cassation to appear before the Rouen Tribunal, by which he was sentenced to eight years' imprisonment. The two Dumas, who attended the trial as witnesses, accompanied by their mistresses, were severely censured by public opinion. In a letter written by Nestor Roqueplan to his brother, Camille, the following passage occurs:

As to Dumas [*père*], he has covered himself with ridicule for an answer he gave to the President of the Court. When asked: 'What is your profession?' he said: 'I should say dramatic author were I not in the land of Corneille.' Hyacinthe, the actor, parodied this piece of clowning. As a Sergeant in the National Guard, he was called upon to take the oath and to declare his titles and qualifications. He replied: 'I should say dramatic artist were I not in the company of Brindeau of the Comédie-Française.'

Dumas, in the whole of this affair in which he wished to be looked upon as an expert on points of honour, as a man of refinement, and a professed bravo, has discredited for ever the word 'gentleman', because of the way in which he has abused the term.

On the opening night of his play, *Une Fille du Régent*, the first character who used the word 'gentleman' was booed and hissed off the stage. During the whole of the Rouen trial, the Dumas, father and son, and their attendant females were openly living together.[1]

Dumas *fils* was much upset by this exhibition.

In 1846, father and son gladly took advantage of an opportunity to leave Paris for a while. Together they made a prolonged tour of Spain and Algeria. Why Algeria? Because the comte de Salvandy, Minister of Public Instruction, after a visit to that beautiful country, observed: 'What a pity it is that Algeria is so little known. We must find some way of popularizing it.' To this, his travelling-companion, the writer, Xavier Marmier, replied: 'Do you know, sir, what I should do in your place? I should arrange for Dumas to cover the same ground as we have done and turn out two or three volumes on the subject . . . He would have three million readers and might, perhaps, infect fifty or sixty thousand of them with a taste for Algeria.'

'That's an idea,' said the Minister, 'I'll think it over.'

After his return to Paris, Narcisse de Salvandy, himself a man of letters (he had received Victor Hugo, not without a certain acidity, into the Académie Française) invited Dumas to dinner.

'My dear poet,' he said, 'I have a service to ask of you.'

'A poet render a service to a Minister? I should be only too glad, were not the occurrence so rare. What have you in mind?'

Salvandy explained the project, and offered a travelling allowance of ten thousand francs.[2] With superb arrogance Dumas replied: 'I will add forty thousand out of my own pocket, and make the trip.'

Seeing that the Minister showed some surprise at so swollen a budget, the novelist explained that he would take with him, at his own expense, his son Alexandre, his collaborator Auguste Maquet, and the painter Louis Boulanger. All he asked was that a ship-of-war should be placed at his disposal for a journey down the Algerian coast.

'Do you realize,' said the Minister, 'that you are asking me to do for you what is done only for princes of the blood?'

'Certainly I do. If you are prepared to do for me no more than what anyone can do for himself, there would be no point in your putting me to a deal of inconvenience. I could perfectly well write to the Messageries Maritimes asking them to reserve the necessary accommodation.'

'Well, you shall have your warship. When would you like to start?'
'I have two or three novels to finish: shall we say in a fortnight?'
And why Spain? Because, on the morrow of this interview with the
Minister, Dumas had dined with His Royal Highness the duc de
Montpensier. In 1842, the duc d'Orléans, heir to the throne, patron of
letters, and the friend of Victor Hugo and Alexandre Dumas, had
suddenly and most unexpectedly died as the result of a carriage
accident. His loss was an irreparable disaster for France. It was the
cause of much sadness to Dumas, who kept, as a relic of the event, a
bloodstained towel which had been used to bandage the unfortunate
prince. Somewhat later, on the first night of *Les Mousquetaires*,[3] he
was presented to the fifth son of Louis-Philippe, the young duc de
Montpensier, who had treated him very affably, had spoken of the
friendship felt for him by his deceased brother, the duc d'Orléans, and
had extended to him the privilege of founding a new theatre which
would be called the *Théâtre Historique* or the *Théâtre Européen*, or,
perhaps, even, the *Théâtre Montpensier*. As author-director Dumas
should produce there, in addition to his own plays, those of Shakespeare, Calderon, Goethe and Schiller.

The granting of this privilege aroused much jealousy.

Nestor Roqueplan to his brother, the painter, Camille Roqueplan:
There is a deal of grabbing, here, there and everywhere, of votes,
patrons, deputies and princes. The prince has, as a rule, strong
views of his own in matters theatrical. It is the duc de Montpensier
who has just bestowed on Dumas a theatre of his own, a ridiculous
and outsize affair which I don't mind betting will be in the hands
of the Official Receiver within a year. Dumas's behaviour in all
this has been beyond belief! He says: 'In the last seventeen years,
the theatres have made ten million out of my plays. In the last
five, four newspapers have each made three hundred thousand out
of my novels. I want to own the theatre which brings in these
millions, the paper which alone nets these twelve-hundred thousand
francs.' And all this time the bailiffs are after him, and their runners
arrest him while he is standing a fine blow-out to the buskers who
have been playing the *Musketeers* at the Ambigu. His son keeps a
woman from the Vaudeville, Mademoiselle Liévenne, to the tune
of two thousand francs a month ... Dumas has announced that
he has already placed an order for the scenery of seven plays of

five acts each, which, so he says, he wrote a fortnight ago while supping with his mistress. The high spirits, the irresponsibility, the self-deception, the wit, the lack of method and the unreason of that fellow, his constitution and his ability to pour the stuff out, are phenomenal.[4]

The privilege was granted in the name of Hippolyte Hostein, a young man who combined medicine with criticism and writing for the stage. He had been secretary of the Comédie-Française, as well as director of several theatres. The capital was provided by the duc de Montpensier and the owner of the Passage Jouffroy, but Dumas took responsibility for running expenses. A site was bought at the corner of the boulevard and the Faubourg du Temple, and it was settled that an immense playhouse should be erected, to be ready as soon as the Algerian trip was over.

While dining with Montpensier, Dumas recounted to his host the conversation he had had with Salvandy.

'A first-rate idea!' said the young prince. 'Especially if you go by way of Spain and can be present at my wedding.'

The duc de Montpensier was to marry, on October 10th, 1846, an Infanta of fourteen, Louise-Fernande, the youngest sister and heir-presumptive of Queen Isabella II. The thought of this union (which might, one day, set a Frenchman on the throne of Spain) was already giving English Ministers sleepless nights. That very day, Dumas sent invitations for the journey to Auguste Maquet, Louis Boulanger and his own son. Victor Hugo noted down the following comment:

Alexandre Dumas has just been sent to Spain as historiographer in connection with the marriage of M. de Montpensier. The money is being found as follows: the Minister of Public Instruction has earmarked fifteen hundred francs from the funds devoted to the *Encouragements et secours aux gens de lettres*, plus a further fifteen hundred to be charged against the *Missions littéraires*. The Minister of the Interior has subscribed three thousand francs from the special fund. Monsieur de Montpensier has given twelve thousand francs. Total: eighteen thousand francs. On receiving this sum, Dumas said: 'Good: it'll just about pay for my guides!'[5]

It remained to discover a model servant. The caterer Chevet offered the services of an Abyssinian negro, who bore the fragrant name of

Eau-de-Benjoin. The party set off by rail, which at that time was a new method of transport, and Dumas began at once on his travel-notes. 'We could hear the acrid breathing of the locomotive. The immense piece of machinery was shaking and shuddering all over. The grinding jar of metal filled our ears. The lamps flitted by as rapidly as will-o'-the-wisps at a witches' sabbath, and on we went towards Orléans, leaving a train of sparks in our wake. . . .'[6]

A lot of noise about nothing. But, when brought to life by Dumas, a locomotive could become a character in a play. In his account of the journey, Maquet is presented as serious, brave and loyal, with a moral outlook and a physique both somewhat rigid. Louis Boulanger is the dreamy painter to whom everything seems grand and solemn (not for nothing was he Victor Hugo's best friend). As to Alexandre *fils*, 'he is all composed of light and shade . . . He is at once greedy and sober, open-handed and economical. He is blasé and ingenuous, witty at my expense, and loves me with all his heart. Last of all, he is equally capable of robbing me like Valère and doing battle for me like the Cid . . . madly impetuous, riding on horseback with the utmost resolution, always ready to draw his sword or shoot off his gun or his pistols . . . Now and again we quarrel, and then he leaves the paternal roof. When that happens, I buy a calf, and start fattening it. . . .'[7]

The Spanish journey of these four musketeers with their black Grimaud is as amusing as a novel. A hundred pages are devoted to a bull-fight. Maquet fainted at the sight of blood. Alexandre II did not fare much better and asked for a glass of water. It was brought. 'Take it to the Manzanares,' he said, 'it will do it good': for he had seen the river in its dried-up state. At night, at the inns, *posadas* or *paradors*, their fights with the landlords are worthy of Cervantes. A description of Spanish dances has all the grace of Gautier at his best. Father and son dreamed of balconies, guitars, duennas and bold young beauties. Alexandre *fils* had several adventures which he utilized as matter for poems addressed to Conchita or Anna-Maria. He rhymed in the Musset tradition, *Andalousie* with *jalousie*, and *Cordoue* with *joue*.

> Pouvez-vous croire, belle enfant,
> Que l'homme qui vous a connue
> Vierge, amoureuse, et demi-nue,
> Peut vous oublier un instant
> Quand, un instant, il vous a vue?[8]

Montpensier, in Madrid, extended a warm welcome to the little group of French writers and artists. The Spaniards, too, were eloquent in praise of Dumas. 'I am better known and, perhaps, more popular in Madrid than I am in France. The Spaniards find in my works a Castilian *something* which pleasantly warms their hearts. The truth of that can be seen from the fact that before ever I became a Chevalier of the Legion of Honour I was already a Commander of the Order of Isabella the Catholic, in Spain.'[9]

On Cuvillier-Fleury, the former tutor of the duc d'Aumale, who had accompanied the French princes to Madrid, he made a less good impression: 'Alexandre Dumas has just turned up on the nonsensical mission upon which Salvandy has sent him. He is fatter and uglier than he was, and quite terrifyingly vulgar . . .'[10] But, then, Cuvillier-Fleury was not a tolerant man, and he certainly had no sense of humour.

Two Spanish marriages were to be celebrated simultaneously; that of Queen Isabella II with the Infante don François-d'Assise (nicknamed 'Paquita'); and that of Montpensier with 'the sister, far prettier, with lovely eyes, superb hair, a noble carriage of the head, and a charming face'. The two weddings were solemnized at the Eastern Palace, in the *salon des ambassadeurs*, in the presence of the Spanish court, and again, on the following day, in the *Nuestra Señora de los Atocha* Cathedral, with the dazzled Dumas in attendance. A few days later (October 17th, 1846) he dined with the Catholic Queen in the Hall of Columns. The guests numbered a hundred. 'We felt completely at sea among people who did not know a single word of our language', wrote Cuvillier-Fleury. 'Alexandre Dumas had, as I did, a bishop on his right, and, on his left, a chamberlain with the key of office dangling at his back. This key, however, did not unlock the guests' tongues, and Dumas was reduced to eating in silence, like an ogre, and gathering some "travel-notes" from his tonsured neighbour: "the ugliest bishop imaginable", he remarked after dinner. . . .'[11]

The four young married people made the round of the rooms. Isabella II, barely sixteen years of age, glittered in the full panoply of her diamonds, 'but had a high colour and shiny cheeks'. The general view was that 'she is threatened with obesity, like her grandmother, who is now perfectly monstrous'. The King-Consort (for that was now 'Paquita's' official title) looked like a young girl dressed up as a general. He spoke in a piping voice. These two first cousins, now united in matrimony for political reasons, had been at daggers drawn since childhood. The infanta-duchesse de Montpensier, on the other hand, proud of her Prince Charming, was radiant with happiness. 'There is in her face a combination of grace and mischief.'[12]

From Madrid, on October 18th, 1846, Dumas *fils*, who, in spite of Conchita and Antonia, was haunted by the memory of Marie Duplessis, wrote imploring her forgiveness:

> Moutier has appeared in Madrid and tells me that when he left Paris, you were ill. Will you include me among those to whom the sight of your sufferings brings much melancholy?
>
> A week after this letter reaches you, I shall be in Algiers. If I find at the poste restante a note addressed to me, telling me that the fault I committed nearly a year ago has been forgiven, I shall return to France in a happier state of mind, knowing myself absolved — and wholly happy should I find you cured.
>
> Your friend
A. D.[13]

After the final display of fireworks, Alexandre I and his court crossed to Algeria. There he could enjoy himself to his heart's content: transferring to a ship-of-war, the *Véloce*; visiting Marshal Bugeaud; freeing some French prisoners in the hands of the Arabs (or, so he said, and, in the long run, came to believe); attending a banquet in his honour in the Algiers roadstead; taking part in an eagle shoot; buying a vulture which he named *Jugurtha*, and putting in at Tunis (to which place he had no right whatever to take a ship of the French navy).

On his return there was an uproar in the Chamber! How came it that a ship-of-war, with its officers and men, had been put at the service of a public 'entertainer'? On what grounds, asked the comte de Castellane, had a Minister entrusted a 'scientific mission' to a writer of newspaper serials? Was it true, inquired the deputy Maleville, from Périgord, that the Minister had said: 'Dumas will reveal Algeria to the deputies, who know nothing about it'? Salvandy faced his critics with courage. Dumas sent them his seconds. They claimed 'parliamentary privilege'. In all this the Musketeer played the 'sympathetic' part.

The Algerian episode marks the culminating point in the career of Dumas *père*. He was treated like a sovereign by the public authorities. The list of his successes lengthened, and so did that of his novels. Maquet-Dumas, or Dumas-Maquet, turned them into plays which drew enormous audiences. *The Musketeers*, at the Ambigu, started at half-past six and did not finish until one o'clock in the morning. Théophile Gautier wrote in his column: 'We are given time enough in which to get to know the characters, to grow used to the way they move, and to believe in their reality . . . The play', he added, 'will fill as many evenings at the Ambigu as the instalments of the novel filled issues of the paper in which it appeared — and that is saying a good deal. . . .'

This success [continued Gautier] is the more remarkable in that the drama does not contain any love-interest at all — there is not even an Aricie to satisfy the dandies, though the dandies, it is true, do not often visit the boulevard. All the interest of the piece is to be found in friendship and devotion, noble passions which deserve to have a drama to themselves. There is something moving in the spectacle of these four brave young fellows, at one in thought, in heart, in courage and in strength. These four who are brothers — not by birth but by choice — form a family which most of us would wish were our own. Which of us has not at some time tried to build such a relationship, only to find it break down at the first hint of danger or rivalry, by the fault of Orestes or of Pylades? In this lies the secret of the success of the novel, and now, of the play.[14]

There is wisdom, even profundity, in this judgment. It was Dumas's inexhaustible generosity of mind which brought him his enormous successes, and gave him the dominating influence which he came to exercise on serial-writing and the stage.

CHAPTER V

The Death of Marie Duplessis

The greatest praise one can give is to say that her spirit had so soon had enough of the life led by her body that she killed it, the more quickly to be free. PAUL DE SAINT-VICTOR

THE younger Dumas received no reply to his letter written from Madrid. Why, must now be explained.

Marie had never wanted to break with him. But, as a result of seeing her affections blighted, of having to obey the law which controls all ephemeral liaisons, of being compelled to go from lover to lover, she had become — says Jules Janin — 'so indifferent that she gave no more thought to the day's love than she did to the morrow's passion'.[1] Not, perhaps, so much indifferent as resigned. 'She was obsessed by a longing for peace, tranquillity and love. Her heart was the heart of a little shop-girl, and she had to make it come to terms, as best she could, with the body of a courtesan.' The courtesan had to keep a tight hold on her rich lovers, Stackelberg and Perregaux: the little shop-girl wanted a true love which might fill the gap left by 'Adet'.

Franz Liszt was introduced to her in 1845 by Dr Koreff — a strange figure out of Hoffmann, half charlatan, half genius, who attended on her in his medical capacity. Liszt, a great artist and 'as beautiful as a Greek god', had just ended his long liaison with Marie d'Agoult. Few men at that time enjoyed so great a prestige.

'Mademoiselle Duplessis wants you, and she'll get you,' said Jules Janin to the virtuoso.

She did, and he never forgot her. 'I have, as a rule, no great liking for the Marion de Lormes or the Manon Lescauts of this world, but she was an exception. She had a great deal of heart . . .'[2] He refused, however, to bind his life to that of the beautiful courtesan, and even to accompany her, as she wished, on a journey to the Orient.

Édouard Perregaux surprisingly suggested a trip of a very different kind. He took her to London, where on February 21st, 1846, he contracted a civil marriage with her before the Registrar of the County of Middlesex. She became the comtesse de Perregaux. It is doubtful whether the marriage was regular in law, since no banns were published.

It was certainly not valid in France, because the French Consul-General in London did not ratify the union of his two compatriots. Furthermore, husband and wife, on their return to Paris, resumed their liberty by mutual consent. What, then, is the explanation of the curious formality? Perhaps Perregaux wanted a close bond; perhaps he desired to satisfy the whim of a dying woman, for Marie, now afflicted with galloping consumption, knew that there was no hope for her. The 'death-bed' marriage in London gave her the right to have armorial bearings painted on the panels of her carriage. Only her most intimate friends, the most discreet of those who were in her confidence, knew this. Unpaid tradesmen took to addressing their bills to 'Madame la comtesse du Plessis'.

But by this time she was too ill to play any active part as either wife or mistress. In her cheeks the flush of exhaustion had banished her earlier and disturbing pallor. She tried to give herself something of a fictitious brilliance with the aid of her jewels. She made the round of the modish watering-places, dancing at Spa and at Ems, admired by all, and deservedly so. At each place she visited, her condition grew worse. Her hotel bills bear witness to her state . . . 'milk' . . . 'infusions'.

> *Marie Duplessis to Édouard Perregaux*: Pardon me, dear Édouard; I beg you on my knees to pardon me: if you love me enough, then send me just two words — friendship, forgiveness. Write to me poste restante, Ems, Duchy of Nassau. So, dear Édouard, tell me quickly that you forgive. Adieu.[3]

After her return to Paris, she was still for a while to be seen at parties, the pale ghost of her former self. But a day came when she could no longer leave her apartment on the Boulevard de la Madeleine. She was twenty-three and soon to die. 'A prie-dieu upholstered in velvet and two gilded Virgins' were now installed in her bedroom. Sometimes, when evening came, she leaned with her elbow on the window-sill, wrapped in her white dressing-gown, with a great red cashmere shawl round her head, to watch the fashionable world on its way to supper after the theatres emptied.

Because she could no longer make money with her emaciated body, she was driven to sell, one by one, the various items of her beloved jewellery. When she died, all that was left were two bracelets, a coral brooch, her riding-whips, and two small pistols. When Édouard Perregaux came to see her, she would not let him into the room. She died on February 3rd, 1847, at the very height of carnival, a few days before Mardi gras which, in those days, was a date of mad gaiety in Paris. The sound of revelry broke in waves against the windows of the small apartment where she lay in her last agony. One of the assistant priests of the Madeleine came to administer the Last Sacrament, and then departed, not without first partaking of a light meal: 'ham for the *praître*', her maid entered in the household accounts, 'two francs'.[4]

On February 5th, 1847, a crowd of curious sightseers followed the hearse, which was 'covered with white wreaths'. Of the friends of earlier days, only two walked bare-headed behind the bier: Édouard Perregaux and Édouard Delessert. In the Montmartre cemetery Marie was at first given only provisional burial. On Mardi gras, February 16th, the body was exhumed and laid permanently to rest in the plot of ground which Édouard Perregaux had just bought for 526 francs.[5] The ceremony 'took place under a dark and lowering sky which, during the afternoon, broke in a torrential cloud-burst, just as the procession of the Bœuf gras was on the move. That night, all over Paris, a hundred bands noisily celebrated the funeral pomps of Carnival with frenzied music'.[6]

Of this lingering death Dumas *fils*, then absent in Algeria and Tunisia, had known nothing. At the time of his return to France he was thinking a great deal about Marie Duplessis. He had never ceased to love a mistress who had been so completely unlike anybody else, and could move him so deeply. 'Thoughts of their nights were with him as he walked.' That, however, had not kept him, during his time abroad, from taking with open hands whatever fortune offered. After visiting Tunis, he had gone back to Algiers for Christmas. On January 3rd, 1847, the party, which had made the outward voyage on board the *Véloce*, embarked for the return journey on the steam-packet *Orénoque*. On the 4th they were at Toulon; next day, at Marseille. From there Dumas *père* set off post-haste for Paris, where his Théâtre Historique was clamouring for him. Dumas *fils* allowed himself to be tempted to stay on by the offers of hospitality which reached him from Autran and Méry. He hoped, far from Paris, to be able to complete a picaresque novel, *Aventures de Quatre Femmes et d'un Perroquet*, for which he was under contract with the publisher, Cadot.

It was while he was still at Marseille that the news of Marie's death reached him. He was overwhelmed with feelings of sadness and remorse. He had not behaved badly to her, but he had been severe, even unjust, at the expense of a young woman whose life had been less worthy of blame than difficult. Thoroughly dissatisfied with himself, he determined to set to work with a will in order to pay off all her debts — a promise more easily made than fulfilled. On his return to Paris, his eye was caught by a bill announcing the sale by auction of furniture, and other 'rich objects', at N° 11 Boulevard de la Madeleine. Intending bidders were invited to inspect the contents of the apartment. He went there at once and saw again the rosewood furniture which had witnessed his brief period of happiness; the fine linen which had once wrapped a smooth and precious body; the funeral clothes for which honest housewives were so soon to compete.

He bought, from a dealer, 'as a memento', Marie's gold chain. The sale produced 80,917 francs, a sum which far exceeded the liabilities of the estate. Any surplus there might be, Marie Duplessis had left to a niece in Normandy (the daughter of her sister Delphine by a weaver named Paquet) on condition that she should never go to Paris.

The life and death of Marie Duplessis played a leading part in the moral evolution of Dumas *fils*. His father, like all the romantics, had extolled the rights of passion, but this attitude had very soon, in his own case, ceased to be genuine. To mistresses of the type of Mélanie Waldor he had soon come to prefer the fickle and indulgent ladies of easy virtue. His son had, at the age of twenty, fallen into the routine of facile love affairs. But even then the example of his mother had shown him how painful their consequences could be, and Marie's had convinced him that the comedy of pleasure more often than not ends in tragedy.

In May 1847 he went to Saint-Germain and dreamed of the day when he had galloped there with Eugène Déjazet. It was after that ride together that the two friends had gone to the Variétés, and that everything had begun. He took a room at the Hôtel du Cheval Blanc, re-read Marie's letters, and wrote a novel about her, *La Dame aux Camélias*. It had been the fashion since the beginning of the century for writers to turn their love affairs into poetry. Hugo, Sand, Musset and even Balzac had thus romanticized their liaisons. Dumas's book was not an autobiography. It is true, of course, that the story was based on his adventure with Marie Duplessis, whose name he changed to Marguerite Gautier; but in real life Dumas had very soon given up any idea of redeeming the Magdalene, whereas, in the novel, Armand Duval tries to do precisely that:

Of one thing I am firmly convinced, that for a woman who has never been instructed in goodness, God almost always provides two paths which lead her back to it. One of these is that of grief, the other, of love. They are difficult, and those who walk them do so with bleeding feet and torn hands. But they leave their vice upon the briars at the wayside, and reach their goal naked, but unashamed, in the sight of the Lord.

The part played by Duval's father, his intervention with Marguerite Gautier, her decision to sell her hair and her jewels and to make atonement through love, the heroic renunciation of the courtesan who prefers to sacrifice herself rather than to injure the man she loves — these incidents were all invented by Dumas, as were the heartrending letters written by Marguerite when she is deserted, ruined and at the point of death. One cannot really believe that Dumas *père* would have treated Marguerite Gautier to a scene!

The novel had a very great success. Every kept or guilty woman found in it a pretext for growing maudlin over her own misdeeds. Consumption and pallor exercised their wonted and morbid attraction. A few days after the book's publication, the author met Siraudin, a writer of light comedies, who said to him: 'Why don't you turn your novel into a play? You've got fertile ground there, my friend, which shouldn't be allowed to lie fallow.'[7]

Dumas *fils* talked over the suggestion with his father who, at that time, was all-powerful at the Théâtre Historique, which had opened, on February 21st, 1847, with *La Reine Margot*. Dumas, when he established this playhouse, had, as usual, thought on a grand scale. It was his intention to put on the stage, as he had already put into his novels, a series of national dramas in the manner of Greek Tragedy and Shakespeare's 'Histories'.

The opening night had provided a scene of great brilliance, and a full money's worth! *La Reine Margot*, which began at six o'clock in the evening, did not end until three the next morning!

Alexandre Dumas [said Théophile Gautier, in his next day's article] worked the miracle of keeping in their seats a starving audience for nine consecutive hours. True, towards the end, in the brief intervals allowed them, people did begin to eye one another like the shipwrecked mariners on the raft of the *Medusa*, and those spectators who happened to be on the plump side were not

altogether easy in their minds. Thank God, no act of cannibalism
has been reported, but, in future, when dramas in fifteen scenes,
preceded by a prologue and finishing with an epilogue, are
presented, it should be clearly stated on the bills that a *succession
of meals will be provided.*[8]

Ten thousand idlers had gathered in the street to stare at the arrivals,
and gaze at the façade of the new theatre. The building shot up,
narrow but triumphant, on the Boulevard du Temple, between two
enormous blocks. Its appearance was original, for it resembled 'neither
the Stock Exchange, a temple, a guard-room, nor a museum'. The
architect or perhaps Dumas himself had hit on the idea of providing a
stylized version of the trestle stage on which the earliest dramas were
presented, substituting for the primitive barrels on which it had been
supported, two caryatids holding up a balcony. Théophile Gautier
was loud in praise of the architect, Séchan, who, he said, had avoided
the temptation to produce a Parthenon instead of a playhouse. It was,
he pointed out, by giving a significant character to buildings, and by
stressing the functional elements, that modern architecture would find
those new forms for which it had been looking in vain. In the frescoes
which adorned the interior were to be seen all Dumas's old friends:
Sophocles, Aristophanes, Aeschylus, Euripides, Corneille, Racine,
Molière, Marivaux — in addition to Talma and Mademoiselle Mars.
Like the ancients, he wished to have his gods about him.

The duc de Montpensier, and his young duchess of sixteen, were
present at this opening performance which cut so great a chasm in the
night. Béatrix Person, whom Dumas *père* was just then honouring
with his attentions, played the Queen-Mother, Catherine de Medicis.
Being no more than nineteen, she was young for the part, but the love
of great men has a way of placing laurels on the most unexpected heads.
At a later date, *Hamlet* replaced *La Reine Margot*: a very strange
Hamlet, for Dumas, who had made the adaptation, contrived a happy
ending, and, unlike Shakespeare, did not kill off the Prince of Denmark.

Dumas *fils* hoped that *La Dame aux Camélias* would follow his
father's dramas on the stage of the Théâtre Historique.

'No,' said Dumas *père*, '*La Dame aux Camélias* is not a suitable
subject for a play. I could never dream of putting it on.'

His son, however, was stimulated by this opposition, the more so
since several professional dramatists had offered to make the adaptation

for him. Why shouldn't I do it myself? he thought. He went into retirement at his little house in Neuilly, and, having had no time to buy paper, wrote on any scraps that came to hand. When he had finished, he hurried to his father who, though convinced that the project was quite mad, agreed, because of paternal affection, to hear the play read. After the first act, he said: 'Very good!' After the second act, Alexandre II was called from the room on urgent private business. When he returned, he found Alexandre I, who had finished reading the play for himself, in tears.

'My dear boy,' he said, embracing his son, 'I was entirely wrong! Your play shall be performed at the Théâtre Historique.'

But the days of the Théâtre Historique were numbered. France was slipping into a drama more actual than any written by Dumas-Maquet. A monarchy was on the verge of collapse: a literary school was growing old. In February 1847 Frédéric Soulié, author of the first *Christine*, died. The people of Paris flocked in great numbers to his funeral. He was much loved, and his *Closerie des Genêts* had recently enjoyed a resounding success. The masses, already in the ferment of approaching revolution, remained loyal to those who spoke to them of hope and pity: to Lamartine and Hugo, Michelet, Dumas, Sand and Soulié. At the graveside, Hugo delivered an oration. The soldiers of the line were just about to fire a parting salvo over the still open tomb, when shouts began to be heard: 'Alexandre Dumas! Alexandre Dumas!' Dumas stepped forward. He tried to speak, but tears choked him. They had an eloquence all their own. 'His thatch of grey hair', said Roqueplan, 'gave him the appearance of an old ram, his stomach, that of an ox.' Frédéric Soulié had been one of his first friends in the world of letters. It was he who, with his fifty saw-mill hands, had saved *Christine* from being booed by the pit. One of the faithful romantics, he died young and full of grief. 'Paris', he had said, 'is like the jar of the Danaïds. One casts into it the illusions of youth, the projects of maturity, the regrets of old age. It swallows them all, and gives nothing back.' Dumas *fils*, who was with his father, heard the following scrap of dialogue in the crowd:

'What a lot of people!'

'There'll be more still when Béranger's buried! They'll have to run excursion trains for that!'

A month later, on March 20th, it was the turn of Mademoiselle Mars to die. She was the only living person to be included in the decorative paintings of the Théâtre Historique. Somebody at the inauguration ceremony had said: 'Mademoiselle Mars has joined the company of the dead: she has not long to live.' The words were prophetic. Hugo went to the funeral service at the Madeleine. An immense crowd was waiting before the church on a day of perfect sunlight. Hugo, with Joseph Autran and Auguste Maquet, remained under the peristyle, leaning against one of the columns.

There were present a great many men in workers' smocks, who said much that was true and penetrating about the theatre, about art, and about poets. This people is hungry for glory. When it has neither a Marengo nor an Austerlitz it longs for and it loves men like Dumas and Lamartine . . . Alexandre Dumas and his son came up to us. The crowd recognized his shaggy head, and called to him by name . . . The hearse started off and we all followed it on foot. There must have been at least ten thousand people present. The crowd made a vast, dark flood which seemed to be pushing the hearse along, with its immense nodding plumes . . . Dumas and his son went as far as the cemetery . . . And the actresses of the Théâtre-Français, in deep mourning, carried enormous bouquets of violets which they threw upon the coffin.'

The largest bouquet of all was that of her rival, Rachel.

But though the Paris crowds recognized and honoured Dumas, his creditors were hard on his heels.

From then on, it was the son who had to look after his father with a devotion of which the elder man was soon to feel a painful need.

PART SIX

*

MONTE-CRISTO

The fictitious and the marvellous are more human than the men of flesh and blood. PAUL VALÉRY

CHAPTER I

'The Count of Monte-Cristo'

ONTE-CRISTO is the keyword to Dumas's work and to Dumas's life. It is the title of his best known novel after *The Three Musketeers*: it was the name of the crazy house which was his pride and his ruin. It conjures up, better than anything else could do, his dreams of magnificence and of justice.

The idea of the book had been working in his mind by fits and starts over a number of years. He tells, in his *Causeries*, how in 1824, happening to be in Florence, he was asked by Jérome Bonaparte, the ex-king of Westphalia, to accompany his son (the Prince Napoleon) as far as the isle of Elba, which was one of the spots sacred to the Imperial family. Dumas was then thirty-nine, the Prince, nineteen, but, of the two, the novelist was the younger. They reached Elba, explored it from end to end, and then went to join a shooting-party on the near-by island of Pianosa which abounded in rabbits and partridges. Their guide, pointing to a sugar-loaf rock rising straight out to the sea, said:

'That is where Your Excellencies ought to go, if you want good sport.'

'What's the name of the Fortunate Isle?'

'It's called the island of Monte-Cristo.'

The name enchanted Dumas.

'Monseigneur,' said he to the young prince, 'in memory of this trip, I shall call one of the novels I have still to write, Monte-Cristo.'[1]

In the following year, when he was back in France, he signed a contract with MM. Béthune and Plon, for eight volumes to be entitled: *Impressions de Voyage dans Paris*. He intended to make the book a long archaeological and historical ramble, but his publishers explained that that was not at all what they had in mind. They had been struck by the staggering success of *Les Mystères de Paris* which Eugène Sue had recently published. What they wanted was a book of romantic adventure set in Paris.

Dumas was an easy man to convince, and no literary project ever frightened him. He set about looking for a plot. It so happened that, some time before, he had put a marker in volume V of a work by Jacques Peuchet, called *Mémoires tirés des Archives de la Police de Paris*. He had been particularly interested in one chapter, headed *Le Diamant de la Vengeance*. 'What Peuchet made of it', he said in a somewhat ungrateful note, 'was nonsense ... but it was true, all the same, that deep in that oyster there lay concealed a pearl, a rough pearl, an un-shaped pearl, a pearl without any intrinsic value ... but a pearl awaiting the jeweller's art.'[2]

It was a fact that Peuchet had been the Keeper of the Archives at the Prefecture of Police. From his files he had compiled six volumes which, even today, would be a rich mine for the writers of serial novels. Here is the strange story which had so strongly appealed to Alexandre Dumas.

In 1807 there had been living in Paris a young shoemaker, François Picaud. This poor devil, who was a handsome chap, was engaged to be married. One day, dressed in his Sunday best, he went to the Place Sainte-Opportune to see a friend, the proprietor of a café, who, like himself, came from Nîmes. This man, Mathieu Loupian, had a flourish-ing business, but other people's successes made him extravagantly jealous. In the café Picaud found three of his compatriots from the Gard Department, who were also friends of the owner. They pulled his leg about his fine clothes, and he then announced his forthcoming marriage to an extremely beautiful orphan, Marguerite Vigoroux, with a fortune of a hundred thousand gold francs, whose affection he had been so fortunate as to engage. The four friends were dumbfounded by what they had heard, and dazzled by the shoemaker's good luck.

'When's the wedding to be?'

'Next Tuesday.'

When he had left, the envious and perfidious Loupian said: 'I'll put a spoke in *that* wheel!'

'How?' asked the others.

'A police inspector's looking in later. I shall tell him that I suspect Picaud of being an English agent ... He'll be questioned; he'll be very frightened, and the marriage will be postponed.'

Napoleon's police did not take political crimes lightly. One of the three men from Nîmes, Antoine Allut, said: 'I call that a dirty trick.'

But the others thought it a good joke: 'After all, one must have a bit of fun at carnival time!'

Loupian lost no time in putting his plan into action. The inspector turned out to be both imprudent and zealous. He jumped at this chance to distinguish himself and, without making any further investigation sent in a report to the police minister, Savary, duc de Rovigo, who at that time was much worried about certain insurrectionary movements in La Vendée. It's pretty obvious, he thought, that this Picaud is one of Louis XVIII's secret agents. The wretched young man was spirited away during the night, completely vanished, and not a word more was heard of him. His parents and his betrothed set inquiries on foot, but, failing to obtain any satisfaction, resigned themselves to the inevitable. The absent are always in the wrong.

Seven years passed. 1814 came, with the fall of the Empire. A man, prematurely aged by suffering, was released from the castle of Fene-strelle where he had all that time been imprisoned. It was François Picaud. His deeply lined face was barely recognizable, and his body was much weakened. While in captivity, he had, with great devotion, looked after an Italian prelate, who had been imprisoned on a political charge and had not long to live. The dying man had bequeathed to Picaud, by word of mouth, all his goods, and, in particular, a treasure hidden in Milan — diamonds, Lombard ducats, Venetian florins, English guineas, French gold francs and some Spanish currency. No sooner was he released than Picaud searched out this treasure, found it, and moved it to a place of safety. Then, under the name of Joseph Lucher, he went back to Paris, to the district in which he had formerly been living. There he asked what had become of a shoemaker called Pierre-François Picaud who, in 1807, had been going to marry the rich Mademoiselle Vigoroux. He was told that a carnival jest, played on him by four mischievous jokers, had resulted in the young man's disappearance. His betrothed had mourned him for two years, and then, believing him to be dead, had agreed to marry the café-owner Loupian, a widower with two children. Picaud asked the names of the other responsible parties, and was told: 'You can find out about them from a man called Antoine Allut, who lives in Nîmes.'

Picaud, disguised as an Italian priest, and with a quantity of gold and jewels sewn into his clothes, hastened to Nîmes, where he gave himself out to be the abbé Baldini. In return for a fine diamond, Antoine Allut gave him the names of the three other accomplices in the practical joke which had had so tragic a sequel. Some days later, a lemonade-hawker, Prosper by name, got himself a place as a waiter at the Café Loupian. This man, with a ravaged face and threadbare clothes, seemed to be about fifty years old. It was Picaud in yet another disguise. The two men from Nîmes, denounced by Allut, were still regular visitors to the establishment. A day came when one of them, Chambard, failed to turn up at his usual time. It was learned that, at five o'clock that morning, he had been found stabbed on the Pont des Arts. The knife had been left in the wound, and, on the handle, was written: *Number One*.

Loupian had had, by his first wife, a son and a daughter. The girl, then sixteen, was angelically beautiful. A dandy, claiming to be a marquis and a millionaire, seduced her. Finding herself pregnant, she was compelled to confess her fault to Loupian and his wife, and was kindly, even joyfully, forgiven, since the elegant gentleman was prepared to marry the future mother of his child. A civil and a religious ceremony took place, but, between the bestowal of the nuptial blessing and the wedding breakfast, it was discovered that the husband had fled. He turned out to be a liberated convict, and neither a marquis nor a millionaire.

Consternation in the bride's family. On the following Sunday, their house (which combined the functions of home and place of business) was mysteriously burned to the ground. Loupian was ruined. The only persons who stuck by him were his friend Solari (the last surviving member of the group of 'regulars') and Prosper, the former lemonade-hawker, who unknown to Loupian, was the author of all his misfortunes. As was only to be expected, Solari soon died, from poison. On the black drapery which covered his coffin, a piece of paper was found pinned, with, on it in block letters, the words — *Number Two*.

Young Eugène Loupian, the son of the proprietor of the café, a weak-charactered, harum-scarum lad, was led astray by a party of shady strangers from no one knew where. He became involved in an affair of 'breaking and entering' and was sentenced to twenty years imprisonment. The Loupians, husband and wife, penniless and dishonoured, fell lower and lower. They had lost everything — money, reputation, happiness, in this avalanche of disasters. The 'handsome Madame Loupian', the former Marguerite Vigoroux, died of grief, and, since she had borne her husband no children, what remained of her personal fortune went back to the members of her own family, who were her legal heirs.

Prosper, the lemonade-hawker, offered his savings to his destitute employer, but on condition that the haughty Thérèse, Loupian's daughter, should live with him. This the proud beauty agreed to do in order to save her father.

As a result of his misfortunes, Loupian was now half mad. One evening, in a dark alley of the Tuileries Gardens, a masked man appeared before him.

'Loupian, do you remember 1807?'

'Why should I?'

'Because it was the year of your crime.'

'What crime?'

'Have you forgotten that, through jealousy, you had your friend, Picaud, shut away?'

'Ah! God has punished me for it . . . punished me terribly!'

'There you are wrong. It was not God but Picaud who, to slake his vengeance, stabbed Chambard, poisoned Solari, burned your house, brought dishonour on your son, and gave your daughter a convict for husband . . . See now in Prosper that same Picaud, but in the very moment when he sets his mark upon his *Third Victim*!'

Loupian fell to the ground, murdered. But just as Picaud was about to leave the gardens, he felt himself held in a grip of steel, gagged, and, under cover of the darkness, carried off. In the cellar into which he was thrown, he found himself in the presence of a man whom he did not recognize.

'Well, Picaud, I suppose for you vengeance is no more than a joke, eh? But you are mistaken. It has become a raging mania . . . You have spent ten years of your life in hunting down three wretches whom you should have spared . . . You have committed a series of horrible crimes, and in them I have been your accomplice, since it is I who sold you the secret of your misery . . . I am Antoine Allut! I have followed you at a distance, and seen the way in which you have settled your accounts. Only at the last did I realize who you were. I came to Paris for the purpose of opening Loupian's eyes to your identity, but the Devil gave you a minute's start of me!'

'Where am I now?'

'What does that matter? You are in a place where you can expect neither help nor pity.'

Vengeance for vengeance. Picaud was put to death with the utmost savagery. His murderer escaped to England. In 1828, Allut, who had fallen desperately ill, sent for a Catholic priest to whom he confided a detailed account of these terrible events, and told him to communicate it, after his death, to the French judicial authorities.

Allut's last wishes were scrupulously observed by his confessor, and the precious document found a home in the police archives, where Peuchet must have come across it.

There, for Dumas, Balzac or Eugène Sue, was a novel ready-made: and not only for them, but for the general public as well. For thousands of years the unhappy human race has found release in cathartic myths. The most popular of their characters have ever been the Magician and the Dispenser of Justice. The humiliated and the injured live with the hope, which no ill-success can weaken, of witnessing the coming, sometimes of the god, sometimes of the hero, who will redress all wrongs, cast down the wicked, and, at long last, give the good man his deserts. For a time, this Dispenser of Justice was physically strong. Dumas, remembering his father, the general, had successfully incarnated in Porthos the myth of Hercules.

In the *Arabian Nights* the Dispenser of Justice is personified as a Magician. His power is no longer physical but occult. He can transport the innocent victim to a place where no persecutor can reach him, and can throw open to the poor great vaults filled with jewels. At the time when Dumas was writing, this enchanter had become confused with the 'nabob' whose wealth permitted him to indulge his every whim, no matter how wild. Dumas dreamed of becoming just such a distributor of earthly happiness. To the extent, now alas much reduced, to which his own financial difficulties allowed him to do so, he delighted in playing this part in the interest of his friends and mistresses. A cup would have held all the gold he had, but this he scattered with a nabob's open-handedness.

He delighted in the idea of creating a character possessed of a fabulous treasure, and scattering far and wide, through an inter-mediary, sapphires, diamonds, emeralds and rubies and, furthermore, of making that character the Avenger in some great cause. For Dumas, in spite of his happy exuberance, harboured deep within himself many grievances against society at large, and private enemies in particular. His father had been a victim: he himself was harassed by creditors, and slandered by those skilled in the art of blackmail. He shared with many human beings, who have been unjustly treated, that longing for vengeance which, since the *Oresteia*, has engendered so many master-pieces. He must have been sorely tempted to find compensation in fiction for the iniquities of the real world.

Peuchet gave him the plot for which he was looking. True stories provide an excellent framework, provided the artist can give them the necessary finishing touches. Dumas was already far advanced in his work when he sent out a call for help to Maquet.

I told him what had been already done, and what remained to do.

'It seems to me,' he said, 'that you have neglected the most interesting parts of your hero's life. I mean, his love affair with the Catalan woman, the treachery of Danglars and Fernand, and the ten years spent in prison with the abbé Faria.'

'I shall cover all that,' I replied.

'But you cannot *narrate* the matter of four or five volumes, and that is what the whole thing will amount to.'

'You may be right. Come and dine with me tomorrow, and we'll talk about it again.'

All that evening, all that night, and the next morning, I thought over what he had said, and so true did it seem, that I found my original idea completely changed. So, when Maquet next came, he found the work divided into three distinct parts: *Marseille — Rome — Paris*.

Together, that evening, we roughed out the first five volumes. Of these, one should be introductory, three should deal with the period of captivity, and the last should cover the escape and the rewarding of the Morel family. All the rest, though not completely finished, was more or less in draft.

Maquet considered that he had done no more than give me friendly advice. But I insisted on his playing the part of collaborator.'

It now remains to see how Dumas adapted Peuchet's material. His hero, Edmond Dantès is, like François Picaud, on the point of marrying the woman he loves, when a series of inexplicable misfortunes come upon him. His Mercédès is stolen from him by Fernand the fisherman as, in Peuchet's story, Marguerite, Picaud's betrothed, is lured into marrying Loupian. But Dumas splits Loupian into two, using him both for Fernand and for the traitor Danglars. The magistrate, Villefort, who sees in the ruin brought upon Dantès a chance of promotion for himself, is modelled on the real police inspector, who was overjoyed to believe Loupian's slanderous denunciation.

The abbé Faria (in the novel, Edmond Dantès's fellow prisoner in the Château d'If) plays the part of the rich Milanese prelate who left his treasure to François Picaud. Dantès, after his escape, assumes a variety of disguises, appearing successively as the abbé Busoni, Sinbad the sailor, Lord Wilmore and the Count of Monte-Cristo, just as Picaud had taken the aliases of Joseph Lucher, the abbé Baldini and the lemonade-hawker, Prosper.

It should not be forgotten that Loupian's daughter, inveigled by an impostor, believed that she was marrying into one of the noblest families in the land, by taking as husband a man who turned out to be a convicted prisoner masquerading as a marquis. This episode was too good to be ignored by the novelist. Dumas introduces under Danglars's roof a certain Benedetto, Villefort's bastard son, a swindler, a thief and a forger, who had once been imprisoned at Toulon and, after escaping, had passed himself off as an Italian prince. The charming Eugénie, Danglars's daughter, accepts his advances, but, on the very day which is to see the signing of the marriage contract in surroundings of the utmost splendour, the bridegroom to be, who is wanted for murder, is arrested.

But normal imagination had not been responsible for the stroke of genius which produced the name *Comte de Monte-Cristo*, which was to become so deeply imbedded in the memories of countless readers. The mysterious chemistry which assists at the birth of great works had been enriched with this precious reagent on the day when Dumas had gone shooting in the islands which lie about Elba.

The real Picaud had pursued his vengeance in too ruthless a manner to become a popular hero. Dantès must be an implacable avenger, but not a savage murderer. Picaud had assassinated his persecutors. He had taken vengeance into his own hands, whereas Dantès *is given* his vengeance. Fernand, after becoming the *général comte de Morceuf* and the husband of Mercédès, commits suicide. Danglars is ruined. Villefort goes mad. But to relieve the hideous darkness of the story, and to recreate the atmosphere of the *Arabian Nights*, Dumas presents Monte-Cristo with an oriental mistress, Haydée, the daughter of the

Pasha of Janina. She is the proud and noble slave whom Dumas would so much have liked to possess.

At the end of the book, Edmond Dantès, now sated with vengeance, goes so far as to provide a dowry for Mademoiselle de Villefort, his enemy's child, who marries Morel, his friend's son. But when the young couple wish to thank their benefactor, Monte-Cristo, and ask his sailor: 'Where is the count? Where is Haydée?' the man points towards the horizon:

> They looked in the direction indicated by the sailor and, on the stretch of dark blue water separating the Mediterranean from the sky, saw a white sail no bigger than a seagull's wing. . . .

And so the *Count of Monte-Cristo* finishes like a Charlie Chaplin film, with the back view of a man walking out of the picture.

CHAPTER II

In which a Novel becomes Real

In a note-book set apart
Dumas wrote what he had spent,
But into it there never went
All the sum of mind and heart.

ROGER DE BEAUVOIR

ONTE-CRISTO had a greater success than any book which
Dumas had so far published. The serial sent Paris into
ecstasies and, first and foremost, Dumas himself. He had
never established a sharp line of division between his fiction and his
life, and now, having found unceasing delight in leading, with Edmond
Dantès as his go-between, an entrancing existence, he was tempted to
turn the book into reality, with himself as hero. Was he not a nabob
of letters? Did he not make two hundred thousand gold francs a
year? Why, then, should he not build a Château de Monte-Cristo?

Ever since 1843, though still keeping an apartment in Paris, he had
taken a lease (at an annual rental of two thousand francs) of the Villa
Medicis at Saint-Germain-en-Laye, and an interest in the theatre of
that little town. Thither he brought the Comédie-Française company,
providing board and lodging for its members, and guaranteeing the
takings. This enterprise cost him a fortune. His court, his harem and
his menagerie swarmed delightedly about him, and the railway from
Paris to Saint-Germain found its receipts mounting rapidly. In order
to see the great man at close quarters, the curious flocked there. He,
the good prince, shook everybody's hand, made endless witticisms, and
was the first to laugh at them.

The King, in some surprise, one day asked Montalivet, the Minister:
'Why all this flutter at Saint-Germain?'

'Sire,' was the reply, 'is it Your Majesty's wish that Versailles should
become madly gay? Dumas has galvanized Saint-Germain in the space
of a fortnight. Order him to spend the same length of time at
Versailles.'

It was not, however, at Versailles, but on the main road from
Bougival to Saint-Germain, that Dumas bought a parcel of wooded
land on which to build the house of his dreams. To this hillside he
took the architect Durand, and said to him:

'This is where I want you to lay out an English park, and in the middle of it to make me a Renaissance château looking onto a Gothic pavilion surrounded by water. There are springs in the neighbourhood, and I wish to have a number of waterfalls.'

'But, Monsieur Dumas, the subsoil here is clay, and the structure will have no firm foundation.'

'Monsieur Durand, you will dig down to the rock ... There shall be two storeys of cellars and arcades.'

'That will cost several hundred thousand francs.'

'Indeed, I hope so!' said Dumas with a beaming smile.[1]

The remarkable thing is that the work was actually carried out. The extensive and beautiful English garden is still there, a rich profusion of romantic willows and clearings ringed with foliage. Two pavilions flank a lordly grille. On the other side of the road which leads to Marly-le-Roy stands a charming cluster of outbuildings (in the Walter Scott style) which, today, form a separate country house. The château itself is scarcely more than a villa, of so composite an architecture that the general effect is at once baroque and curiously pathetic. Balzac admired and envied it — quite wrongly. The windows, modelled on those of the Château d'Anet, call to mind Jean Goujon and Germain Pilon. The salamanders are part of the armorial bearings given by François I to the town of Villers-Cotterets where Alexandre Dumas was born. A frieze extends all round the house, of sculptured heads depicting men of genius from Homer to Sophocles, from Shakespeare to Goethe, from Byron to Victor Hugo, from Caspar Delavigne to Dumas *père*. Above the flight of steps leading to the front entrance is carved the owner's motto: *J'aime qui m'aime*. An Oriental minaret rises from the Henri II façade. The troubadour style rubs shoulders with Eastern fantasies belonging to the *Arabian Nights*. The roof is overloaded with vanes. The rooms, all small but all different, are distributed over three storeys, five to each, topped with mansard attics. The principal salon, all white and gold, is Louis XV. The Arab room is decorated with stucco arabesques, delicately carved. Several verses from the Koran, originally painted in gold and bright colours, are a prominent feature.

At a distance of about two hundred yards from the 'château' is an astonishing Gothic edifice: a miniature keep, a dolls' house fortress. A small bridge spans the moats which are filled with water. On each stone of it is carved the title of one of Alexandre Dumas's works.

The ground floor consists of a single room. The ceiling is sown with stars on an azure field. The hangings are blue, and the carved fireplace is surmounted by a panoply of weapons. There are chests in the medieval style, and a refectory table from some deconsecrated abbey. There Dumas could work in comparative peace. A spiral staircase led to a cell where, sometimes, he spent the night. There was a look-out platform from which he could watch his guests in the park below. The whole place was both Lilliputian and grandiose.

Léon Gozlan marvelled at what he saw: 'I can compare this precious jewel', he wrote, 'only with the Château of La Reine Blanche in the Forest of Chantilly, or to the house of Jean Goujon . . . It has bevelled corners, balconies of stone, stained-glass casement windows, turrets and vanes . . . It belongs to no especial period, neither to the art of Greece nor to that of the Middle Ages. Yet there is about it an atmosphere of the Renaissance which gives it a peculiar charm . . . Dumas, than whom none knows better the men of eminence in the contemporary world, has entrusted the execution of all the statues to Auguste Préault, James Pradier and Antonin Mime. He has set a frieze round the first floor, adorned with the busts of the great dramatists of every age . . . including himself. . . .'

Gozlan was lavish in his praise of the Tunisian craftsmen who had carried out a scheme of mouldings 'the like of which is to be seen only on the Moorish ceilings of the Alhambra, an interlocking pattern of incised lines, the general effect of which is to produce the illusion of lace . . . I was struck with admiration. No ceiling at the Trianon can compare with the one embroidered by Tunisian workmen for Monte-Cristo. From the principal balcony one looks out over a view more lovely than the one to be seen from the Terrace at Saint-Germain. . . .'²

Gozlan shows himself in this passage more Monte-Cristo than Monte-Cristo. The château is, in fact, little more than a bizarre, baroque and rather small house. But Dumas lived there like a great lord.

To the house-warming (July 25th, 1848) he invited *six hundred* of his friends to dine. The meal was provided by a famous restaurant (the Pavillon Henri IV at Saint-Germain) and the tables were laid on the lawn. Perfumes glowed in incense-burners. Everywhere there glittered the motto of the family of La Pailleterie: *Au vent la flamme! Au seigneur l'âme!* Dumas, in the seventh heaven, circulated among his guests. His coat shone resplendent with crosses and stars. A heavy gold chain spanned his magnificent waistcoat. He embraced the pretty women, and told marvellous stories all night long. He had never been happier.

Balzac to Eve Hanska, August 2nd, 1848: Monte-Cristo is one of the most delicious Follies ever built. It is the most royal chocolate-box in existence. Dumas has already spent 400,000 francs, and it will run him into another 100,000 before it is finished. But he will stick to it, if only to bring it to completion. It is I who discovered yesterday that it cannot be sold, for, would you believe it, he has no written agreement for the land on which the little château stands! It belongs to a peasant who gave only a verbal consent to sell it to Dumas, and it would be perfectly possible for him to serve a summons ordering him to remove the whole place, and to take back the ground for the purpose of growing vegetables! This gives you some idea of the way in which Dumas does things! Fancy constructing a marvel, for it is a marvel (unfinished), on somebody else's land without deed or contract! The owner might die, and his heirs, still minors, would be in no position to carry into effect the testator's verbal agreement!

If only you could see the place you would go mad about it. It is a charming villa, more lovely than the Villa Pamphili, for it looks on to the Terrace at Saint-Germain, *and there is water!* Dumas will finish it. It is as pretty, as delicate, as the portal of Anet which you saw at the École des Beaux-Arts. It is well planned and, in short, is a Louis XV *Folly* but executed in the style of Louis XIII, with the addition of Renaissance ornaments. They say that it has already cost 500,000 francs, and another 100,000 will be needed before work on it stops. He has been as surely robbed as he'd have been if he had been held up by highwaymen. The whole thing could have been done for 200,000.[3]

It is amusing to find Balzac scolding somebody else for prodigal spending, and giving a lesson in the art of how not to be robbed!

Life as organized at Monte-Cristo was unlike life as lived in any other place. The master of the house inhabited his study in the microscopic 'fortress', a room furnished with an iron bedstead, a table of unpainted wood, and two chairs. There he laboured from morning till night, and often from night till morning, dressed only in a shirt and a pair of duck trousers. He had grown much fatter, and his prominent stomach spilled over onto the table. His meals, for all that, were of exemplary frugality. It was for others that he provided feasts worthy of Pantagruel. At Monte-Cristo he kept open house. No matter who came was welcomed. He would hold out his left hand to the visitor, while continuing to write with his other, and ask him to stay to dinner. The cook was for ever being told to increase the number of *côtelettes béarnaise*. Sometimes Dumas, who was a very good cook, would turn out a dish of his own making, and stir the sauces with enthusiasm.

Every hard up writer or painter could come and settle down on Monte-Cristo. The house was permanently filled by a flock of parasites such as even Amphitryon had never known. They cost him 'several hundred thousand francs a year'. And then, there were the women. . . .

At the Château of Monte-Cristo the reigning sultanas succeeded one another with great rapidity: Louise Beaudoin, known as Atala Beauchêne; the young actresses of the Théâtre Historique; the women writers. The especial favourite of the year 1848 was Céleste Scrivaneck, a charming creature who, though still very young, understudied Déjazet, and sang musical-comedy airs delightfully. Mistress, friend and secretary, she would have liked also to play, in this unballasted home, the part of mother:

Céleste Scrivaneck to Dumas fils: My dear Alexandre — happiness could go no further; I shall not leave your father. He has agreed to let me help him with his work. I am to travel with you both, *as a boy*: the tailor has just been to take my measurements! I feel wildly gay! Forgive me, my good, my excellent friend, for not having told you all this before now. Day after day I made up my mind to have a few minutes' talk with you, but something always happened to prevent it. Your father keeps me hard at work: I write to his dictation. I am very proud and very happy to serve as secretary to *him*, the *universal* man. I hope to see you again a month from now, but meanwhile, do send me a few friendly words.

I have done what you asked of me. I am busy hemming your cravats. As soon as the tailor has finished your trousers everything shall be sent to you without delay. We are leaving this

evening for Versailles, and shall stay there for three whole days.
Adieu: send me news of yourself soon.

Your affectionate little mother
C. SCRIVANECK[4]

As to Lola Montes, though she may have stayed at Monte-Cristo,
it is highly improbable that she was ever Dumas's mistress, for having
become — by the grace of Ludwig I of Bavaria, her lover — comtesse
de Landsfeld, and all powerful, she wrote:

Munich: April 14th, 1847: My dear Monsieur Dumas: it was
with very great pleasure that a few days back I got your nice letter.
If you come here I can give you my word that you will be treated
in a way so talented and famous a man deserves. His Majesty the
King has told me to say thanks for the flattering things you said
about him when you wrote to me, and to tell you what a pleasure
it would be to him to see you in Bavaria. If you take my advice
you'll come quick. Everyone is bubbling over with your
wonderful works and I'm quite sure you'd be welcomed like
a king.

I'm telling you all this so that you don't fail to come and see
the king. I bet you'd both like each other.

I mustn't take up your precious time, knowing that a letter from
poor humble me can't interest you much. Let me, dear Monsieur
Dumas, sign myself one of your greatest admirers.

LOLA MONTES[5]

Lola Montes, though she might be a countess in Bavaria, was an
Irishwoman who passed for a Spaniard. Ill-written her letter may be,
but its tone is not that of a communication from a mistress, even
allowing that prudence may have kept it free of any hint of familiarity.

At Monte-Cristo an Italian majordomo, *il signor* Rasconi, ruled over
the household. The gardener, Michel, an odd job man, but a great
reader of the *Dictionnaire des Sciences naturelles*, was always careful to
give plants and animals their Latin names, much to Dumas's delight.
Another member of the staff was the little negro boy, Alexis, whom
Marie Dorval had one day brought to Dumas concealed in a basket of
flowers.

'I can no longer afford to feed him,' the charming but debt-ridden
actress had said, 'and so, *mon grand chien*, I am giving him to you.'

233

'Where is he from?'

'The Antilles.'

'What language do they talk in the Antilles, my boy?'

'They talk Creole.'

'And how do you say "*Bonjour, monsieur*" in Creole?'

'We say "*Bonjour, monsieur*".'

'Then it's all plain-sailing! We'll talk Creole . . . Michel! . . . Michel!'

The gardener came in:

'From now on, Michel, this young citizen will be one of the household staff.'

There was also a kennel man, and a man who looked after the aviary, for this jungle was peopled by animals about whom Dumas wrote a charming book, *Histoire de mes Bêtes*. There were five dogs, three monkeys (including one female), who were named after a famous novelist, a celebrated translator and a successful actress; two large parrots, a cat called *Mysouf*, a golden pheasant, *Lucullus*, a cock, *Caesar*, and the vulture, *Jugurtha*, which he had brought back from Tunisia. The bird's name was changed to *Diogenes* when he took up his residence in a barrel.

Agreeably entertained by the cheeping and squawking of this menagerie; surrounded by piles of paper—blue for his novels, pink for his articles and yellow for the poems which he addressed to his odalisques — all his energies absorbed by the demands of the Théâtre Historique, for which he had to adapt novel after novel in order to provide play after play, Monte-Cristo would have been divinely happy if only his son had been willing to become a partner in *Alexandre Dumas & Cᵒ*. Had the young man consented to play the part of Maquet, he could, said his father, easily have made forty or fifty thousand francs a year.

'Believe me, that wouldn't be difficult . . . I'll explain the whole business, and then you are at liberty to raise any objections you like. . . .'

Dumas *fils*, who was badly in want of money in spite of the success of his novel, finally consented, not without jibbing, to do some historical work for his father. *Dumas* père *to Dumas* fils: 'I am sending you five hundred francs. Try to get the third volume done for me by the end of the month. It'll mean two thousand for you. . . .'

Sometimes the son, under pressure from some light-o'-love, would apply to Hippolyte Hostein, the businesslike young man to whom Dumas *père* had entrusted the running of the Théâtre Historique:

> Dear Hostein, a church-mouse is richer than I,
> Who've not got so much as the price of a fly.
> Dulong's quite cleaned out — a broken-down screw,
> And Porcher is stony — his wife says it's true.
> Just three hundred, that's all, I'm depending on you.
> By lending me that, you would do me a service:
> Drop a note to say yes: I am yours — DUMAFICE

But even that thin trickle was soon to dry up.

CHAPTER III

In which Ruin comes to Monte-Cristo

A basket with holes in it? True enough, only it wasn't I who made the holes.
ALEXANDRE DUMAS

THE first season at the Théâtre Historique had been very profitable. The total takings amounted to 707,905 francs. The second opened with a Dumas-Maquet triumph, *Le Chevalier de Maison-Rouge*, a drama with a moving love story, played out against a background of the great events of the Revolution. It ended with the final banquet of the Girondins, and the singing of *Mourir pour la patrie*. On February 7th, 1848, a daring novelty was introduced — a play to be performed on two consecutive nights, *Monte-Cristo*.

The first, ending with the escape of Edmond Dantès, lasted from six o'clock until midnight:

> The audience dispersed [said Gautier] fully determined to return the next night. The ensuing twenty-four hours seemed no more than a somewhat prolonged 'interval'. On the second evening there were familiar greetings, friendships were formed, and an atmosphere of intimacy prevailed ... Those present made their own little arrangements and there was a deal of chit-chat. Spectators seemed more like permanent inhabitants. When the curtain fell for the last time, sighs of regret rose from all parts of the house. 'Must we really separate after only two days? Why should the great Alexandre Dumas and the indefatigable Maquet show so little confidence in us? We would gladly have given up a whole week to them.'[1]

But on February 24th, the revolution of '48 broke out. Rioting spelled the doom of the theatres. They played to empty benches. Only Rachel could still draw crowds to the Comédie-Française, where, between the fourth and fifth acts of Corneille or Racine, she sang the *Marseillaise* in a proud and ringing voice. Republican though he was, Dumas would have preferred less singing and larger audiences. Though he wasted no regrets over Louis-Philippe, whom he had never liked, he had lost valuable patrons in the young princes. Like Victor Hugo he would probably have been in favour of a regency administered by the duchesse d'Orléans. Since, however, this solution seemed impossible, he decided to rally to the new regime and get himself elected as a deputy.

'The revolutionary avalanche had swept away not only the crowned dotard, but the widowed mother and the sickly child as well', wrote Dumas. 'France, in her distress, turned to the best of her sons . . . I felt I had the right to consider myself one of the intelligent on whom she was calling for help . . .'[2] By this he meant that, like Lamartine and Hugo, he wished to play a part in public affairs.

The next thing was to choose the Department in which he should stand for election. Hugo had not hesitated for a moment. Paris was *his* city. The towers of Notre-Dame formed the H of his name. But Paris would never elect Dumas: he was too much the entertainer to command respect. How about the Aisne, where he had been born? He was afraid that there he might be looked upon as being more republican than the Republic. Seine-et-Oise, in which his estate of Monte-Cristo lay and where he had commanded the Saint-Germain battalion of the National Guard? Unfortunately, during the three days of the 1848 revolution, he had proposed marching his men on Paris, and they had not forgiven the 'irresponsible manner in which he had shown himself ready to risk their lives'. These National Guardsmen were perfectly willing to guard the nation, but only on their native heath, and they had demanded the dismissal of their over-bellicose commander.

A young man to whom Dumas had rendered certain services assured him that he was very popular in Yonne and could not fail to be elected. Certainly, he reflected, he was popular in Yonne, as he was everywhere, and no candidate would have any chance against him. What he forgot was that in the French countryside the local man always starts with a great advantage. 'Who is this fellow Dumas?' asked the people of Yonne. 'Is he one of *us*? Does he own vineyards here? Is he a wine merchant? No? Then he's just a political bastard, and a friend, too, of the Orléans princes, and a supporter of the Regency', said some: 'An aristocrat! A marquis!' said others. He had just started a paper, *Le Mois*, with the unassuming motto: *God dictates and I write*. He put forward in its pages a demand that the statue of the duc d'Orléans should be replaced on its pedestal in the

forecourt of the Louvre. The electors held this act of loyalty against
him. He replied eloquently, spoke of friendship and gratitude, recalled
the grief aroused by the death of the young prince, reduced half his
audience to tears and set the other half applauding. But he was not
elected.

Nevertheless, he had a Tree of Liberty planted in front of the
Théâtre Historique, saying to the manager, Hostein: 'We must be
popular at all costs. There will still be a great people in France when
princes have vanished from the earth.' In Yonne, at the conclusion
of one of his meetings, a working-class heckler shouted: 'Oho! the
marquis! Oho! the nigger!' His reply was worthy of the general — or
of Porthos. Seizing the man by the seat of his trousers, he held him
suspended over the parapet of the river. 'Apologize, or into the water
you go!' The fellow did as he was told. Dumas said: 'Good! I only
wanted to prove to you that the hands which, in the space of twenty
years, have written four hundred novels and thirty-six dramas, are the
hands of a workman . . .' For a moment he played with the idea of
standing for election in the Antilles. 'I will send them a lock of my
hair', he said, 'to show that I am one of them.' But, once again, he
had to abandon his project, and, since he could not *make* history,
resumed the writing of it.

But his output as novelist and dramatist was no longer sufficient to
hold back the mounting tide of debt. The takings of the Théâtre
Historique had fallen almost to nothing. A play by Balzac (May 25th,
1848), *La Marâtre,* was a complete failure. In spite of a revival of
La Tour de Nesle, the enterprise was virtually bankrupt. From the
very beginning, Dumas's prodigality had terrified Hostein who, wrote
Marceline Desbordes-Valmore, 'is not always as easy to handle as that
poor great child of a poet who has our interests so much at heart'.[3]
But the poor great child of a poet promised everything to everybody.
Engagements were showered right and left. 'Players fling themselves
at his head, and all are desperately afraid of his instability and of the
monstrous luxury in which he lives. He'll never, in the general view,
maintain his balance unless he becomes as mean as Bocage, and puts
his affairs in M. Hostein's hands . . .'[4] But a moment was coming when
even Hostein was to refuse to go on being 'Dumas's keeper'. In
December 1849 he resigned. His successors fared no better than he
had done. The insatiable Théâtre Historique made no more than a
mouthful of the new plays. From all sides Dumas's creditors fell upon

him. There was a distraint on Monte-Cristo, and the burden of mortgages soon amounted to a total of 232,469 francs and six centimes.

Ida Ferrier, or, as she called herself in Italy, the marquise Davy de la Pailleterie, was a creditor with claims to preferential treatment, for he owed her the hundred and twenty thousand francs of her dowry, plus interest, plus alimony. She now took steps to recover what was owing to her, though keeping herself in the background. Since August 1847 she had put her affairs in the hands of a lawyer, Maître Lacan,[5] to whom she wrote that she was averse to instituting proceedings against Dumas:

Naples, August 1st, 1847: What can a poor, lonely woman do whose only weapon is *the truth* which she has to use at a great distance against the perfidious suggestions and skilful lies of a man to whom his popularity as a writer must always give great influence? Whatever one's views of him as a man may be, as an author he exercises a power to fascinate which it is difficult to resist. That mind, so fertile in poetic and amusing invention, is no less so in resources against those he hates. He would not stop at the blackest of lies could they serve to crush me and to show him in a good light. No matter how well-established my rights may be, I have no choice but to succumb, or, at best, to rise from the ground so battered by the blows which disloyalty and lies have rained upon me, that my position would be no better. It is on that fact that M. Dumas has always counted to keep me from seeking justice . . . He knows *my horror* of scandal, and the sacrifices I have made to preserve a position in the eyes of the world, of which he has tried, by every means in his power, to deprive me.

We see things very differently. He maintains that the scandal of his life doubles the value of his books, and seeks it with as great a diligence as I employ to avoid it. I beg you, sir, most earnestly, to tell me what difficulties of this nature would be involved in a demand on my part for alimony? Utter destitution for me and mine would be a terrible thing to bear, but, on the other hand, it would be bitterly cruel to see myself exposed to public calumny which, being at a distance, I should be in no position to refute. Having lived, for several years, in the *very highest society of this country*, I must needs be very careful. You know, sir, the susceptibility of a world which M. Dumas can the more easily outface, being a complete stranger to it.

The marquise had on her side her step-daughter, Marie, whom she had completely won over, and who blamed her father's extravagance: also, naturally, her own mother, the widow Ferrand, to whom Dumas had promised, but never paid, an annuity. The dream of Madame Ferrand and of Marie Dumas was to join Ida, either in Naples or Florence, where 'friends' would maintain them.

Ida Dumas to Maître Lacan: My friends in Florence, judging, as I do, that I cannot stay on in a city in which I have not the means to maintain myself, and where my position, and the society in which I have lived for so many years, compel me to keep up appearances in a style which puts too heavy a strain on my resources, have been so kind as to make still further sacrifices on my behalf, by advancing a sum guaranteed by them which will enable me to come to Naples where I ought to have been for some time now, for reasons of health. Here, other persons have come to my assistance. Had they not done so, I should be in no position to await the result of the demand which we are to put forward, and on which I depend if I am to return to Florence and get my mother and my step-daughter to join me there.

I trust, sir, that the court will take into consideration the fact that I have to provide for *two* additional individuals, and that the allowance I am claiming is not for my use alone. Eighteen thousand francs, shared between his wife, his mother-in-law and his daughter, are, comparatively, a small amount when set against the literary earnings of M. Dumas — earnings which he himself, on more than one occasion, among others, in connection with a case which he brought against some newspaper, the name of which I forget (it occurred some time during the winter of 1845) declared to exceed two hundred thousand francs! These enormous profits are, if it comes to that, a matter of common knowledge.

Marie Dumas agreed to provide confirmation of these statements and to give evidence against her father. She called Ida 'dearest and beloved mamma', and complained of the effect produced upon a young girl of sixteen by the spectacle of so much money being extravagantly spent in the upkeep of Monte-Cristo.

Marie Dumas to her Step-Mother. Paris, August 28th, 1847:
Besides, my dear, good little mother, the life I am living here has
become intolerable. Add to that the grief I continually feel at being
separated from one whom I love better than anyone in the world.
Nor can I help feeling upset by the demands made upon me by
papa, who wants me to live with him ... Can you think of him,
darling, asking such a thing of me, his position being what it is?
It is impossible for me to consent. It has wounded me to the heart
to see that he quite unashamedly expects me to shake hands with
a woman of ill-fame. He has not hesitated to associate me with a
person whom his love as a father should have compelled to leave
Monte-Cristo as soon as I entered it. I should never have been
allowed to hear her so much as mentioned! Yes, darling, that is
what I can never get over, for not only have I been wounded in
my self-respect, but also hurt, deeply hurt, in my affection for you
... I beg you, therefore, on my bended knee, to let me come
back to you. I can no longer stay on in Paris where I am for
ever exposed to meeting with a woman whom papa was so shame-
less as to introduce to me. The mere sight of her revolts me!
I swear, *by you, my dearest friend in all the world*, that only physical
force will ever make me frequent such company.

Ida quite sincerely wished to undertake Marie's education.

Ida Dumas to Maître Lacan, Florence, February 1st, 1848: Let
me once again urge upon you with all the powers of persuasion
of which I am capable that my step-daughter should again be
entrusted to me. I am perfectly well aware that, for reasons of
self-interest, the mistress of her school will do all she can to oppose
such a plan. She has consulted M. Nogent de Saint-Laurent on the
subject. I beg you, sir, to explain to that gentleman the situation
in which a child whom I look upon as my daughter finds herself.
Everybody knows that the state of her father's affairs is such that
he will never give her a penny. What little she can hope for will
come from me. Is this young girl to stay on in Paris indefinitely
in boarding-school, having with her neither a mother nor a
family, and in surroundings which are altogether unsuitable?
What future can she look forward to? By coming back to me she
will rid her father of the burden of her school fees, and this, for

him, is by no means a minor consideration. I undertake to be responsible for the completion of her education.

Marie will live here in a society very much superior to any she could enjoy in Paris. She will be better placed in Florence than elsewhere to acquire a future establishment. By being kept on by force in Paris, not only will her heart be broken, but her future will be hopelessly compromised.[6]

Maître Lacan finally obtained a small allowance for the widow Ferrand, though Ida expressed it as her firm conviction that 'M. Dumas will never consent to any arrangement which he does not see a chance of one day repudiating'. The only security which the three women had was the Monte-Cristo property. The marquise de la Pailleterie was convinced that, sooner or later, by some clever piece of manipulation, Dumas would succeed in spiriting the house away. Still, it is only fair to Dumas to say that he could not feel much pity for a woman who, as he knew, was being kept by a rich Italian, and, further, that in his eyes the playing of the vanishing trick with assets was a legitimate occupation, since every creditor was to be regarded as an enemy. After all, had Porthos ever paid his debts?

On February 10th, 1848, the Tribunal of the Seine declared the Dumas couple to be legally separated and awarded damages against the husband. He was (1) to make restitution of the dowry of one hundred and twenty thousand francs which he had misappropriated: (2) to pay an alimony of six thousand francs a year on the security of a registered mortgage. Defeated in the French equivalent of our County Court, Dumas appealed. The revolution, in addition to ruining him, had still further complicated these family affairs. Monte-Cristo with all its contents was put up for sale, but Dumas saw to it that the sale should be a mere fiction.

Alexandre Dumas to Auguste Maquet: I want you to help me so far as your means will allow. In order to settle my business with Madame Dumas I have been compelled to sell the whole contents of my house, though it is my intention to buy back what I can. Can you disentangle your thousand francs from *Siècle*, and get a further thousand from your father or from Kopp; then use those two thousand to purchase certain objects which I will detail to you? Since the objects in question must be moved from the house, I want you to take them to Bougival (whence I will withdraw them) . . . I am not moving from the house. Come to me. I am anxious to see you not later than this evening.[7]

The 'château' of Monte-Cristo was sold, as the result of a court order, for the ridiculous sum of 30,100 francs, to Jacques-Antoine Doyen, who, no doubt, was a mere 'dummy', since he never took possession. On July 28th, 1848, the Court of Appeal confirmed the decision of the civil tribunal. Ida was accumulating legal successes, but of actual money she got nothing.

Ida Dumas to Maître Lacan, Florence, September 9th, 1848: All our efforts will, perhaps, turn out to have been quite useless, and come to nothing as a result of M. Dumas wriggling out of the legal decisions! But no matter what happens, no matter what results may ensue from the winning of our action, my gratitude to you remains unaltered . . . But for your energetic assistance, but for the kindness and devotion of my friends in Florence, I do not know how I should have found sufficient strength to face this time of waiting. My mother tells me that some time must, inevitably, elapse before we know whether we shall receive anything from the sale of Monte-Cristo. *She can no longer get her allowance paid*, and lives off loans and expedients of every sort, and that will continue until my fate is decided.

My step-daughter is with her father, alas! — and the fatal influence which I so much dreaded on so young a heart and head is already noticeable! I foresee that all the efforts I have made to save Marie from her evil destiny will be of no avail. But, as I have already said, monsieur, I still keep my hopes centred on Providence and on you.

My mother, who knows very little about business, has tried to explain to me the state of our affairs. She speaks of 'a necessary delay of three years', after which fresh proceedings will be instituted. I don't at all understand that . . . I am dreadfully afraid that the seizure of M. Dumas's property may have destroyed any hopes we might reasonably have entertained. No matter what our legal rights may be, so long as M. Dumas possesses no tangible assets, we are just where we were.[8]

Dumas who, truly enough, had no tangible assets, was a past master at making away with the impalpable. A bootmaker to whom he owed two hundred and fifty francs made the journey to Saint-Germain in the hope of being paid. The dispossessed master of the 'château' received him affably.

'Ah! my friend, you have come in the nick of time. I am badly in need of a pair of varnished pumps and some shooting-boots.'

'Monsieur Dumas, I have brought you my small bill.'

'And quite rightly . . . I'll have a look at it this afternoon . . . But first I would like you to take luncheon with me.'

After a succulent meal, the bootmaker again shyly produced his account.

'This is not the time . . . Digestion comes before business . . . I have had the carriage brought round to take you to the station . . . and that reminds me, here are twenty francs for your fare.'

This scene, worthy of Molière, was repeated each week. In the long run, the bootmaker had pocketed six hundred francs, and dined thirty times at Dumas's expense. Next, it was the turn of Michel, the odd-job man.

'I think I ought to tell you, sir, that there is no wine left for the staff. There's nothing in the cellar but Johannisberger and champagne.'

'I have no money. Drink the champagne, the lot of you: it'll do you good.'

Before long the bailiff's men went into action. They had the furniture taken away, the pictures, the carriages, the books, and even the animals! One of them left behind him the following acknowledgment: 'Received: one vulture: estimated value, fifteen francs.' This was the famous Jugurtha-Diogenes.

On the day when he had finally to leave the 'château', Dumas offered two small plums on a plate to a friend, who took one and swallowed it.

'You've just eaten a hundred thousand francs,' said Dumas.

'A hundred thousand francs?'

'Yes, those two small plums were all I had left of Monte-Cristo . . . and Monte-Cristo cost me two hundred thousand. . . .'

Balzac to Eve Hanska: I see in the papers that all Dumas's furniture from Monte-Cristo is to be sold on Sunday. The house has already gone, or will have gone soon. This news set me trembling, and I have made a resolve to work night and day so as not to have a similar fate. But I should never stay to meet it.

I should set off for the United States, there to live a pastoral existence, like M. de Bocarmé.[9]

One of Dumas's good qualities was that, even when utterly ruined, he could still be the most generous of men to those who were neither wife nor creditors. He did what he could to help the actors of the romantic generation who had sunk into a needy old age. Mademoiselle George, who had become monstrously fat with the passing of the years, was playing at the Batignolles, and had not twenty-five sous for a cab fare. Bocage, now manager of the Odéon, was absorbed in politics and administrative work. Frédérick Lemaître alone held the breach, and, like Kean, addressed the audience from the stage:

'Citizens! now more than ever is the time to cry, "Vive la République!" . . .'

'Get on with your part, busker!' retorted Musset. The part was that of *Tragaldabas,* in a play by Vacquerie, the last of the purely romantic dramas. Thirty years had been enough to kill stone dead a type of play which had to its credit *Christine, Hernani* and *Tragaldabas.*

Poor Marie Dorval, after losing her grandson, George, one of the last human beings she still loved, was compelled by circumstances, tired out though she was, prostrated with grief, with nothing to hope for, to resume the hard life of an actress on tour. But her troubles and difficulties had done their work. At Caen she had to take to her bed, suffering from an ulcerated liver. She was brought home in a dying condition, and sent for Jules Sandeau — her onetime lover, who did not answer her call, having turned into a mean-spirited bourgeois — and her *bon chien* Dumas, who hurried to her bedside. 'She, who in *Antony,* had so often choked out the words — "*oh, I am lost! am lost!*" knew that there was no hope. Her relations could not lay their hands on the sum necessary for the purchase of a burial site, and she was terror-struck at the idea of being thrown into the common grave reserved for paupers. Dumas swore that she should be spared this indignity . . .'[10] He would find the money.

As soon as Dorval was dead, he went to see the comte de Falloux, the Minister of Public Instruction, and asked him for his help. The Minister could take no official action, 'there being no funds available for helping actors and actresses'. All he could do was to make a personal contribution of one hundred francs. But Dumas was determined to keep his promise to the dead woman, and, his goodness of heart being as great as his financial improvidence, hurried round to the municipal pawnshop where he pledged his decorations, and thereby obtained the two hundred francs for the funeral. This was an act of heroism, for the kindly giant was passionately attached to his jewelled crosses and stars. Then he wrote a pamphlet: *La Dernière Année de Marie Dorval*, which was sold for '*fifty centimes to provide a grave*', and opened a subscription so that the actress's jewels (all in pawn) could be bought back and given to her grandchildren. This *Souscription artistique* brought in one hundred and ninety francs, fifty centimes. Ponsard gave twenty francs.[11]

Dumas's misfortunes in no way quenched his vitality. With Arsène Houssaye, at that time manager of the Comédie-Française, he embarked upon a curious experiment. It had occurred to him that 'a backstage comedy set in the days of Molière' was something that, so far, had never been attempted. Young actresses going over their lines, noblemen giving advice, coquettes flirting behind fans, the candle-lighter making jokes — from all this material it should be possible to concoct a charming entertainment for January 15th, Molière's birthday. He undertook to compose *Trois Entr'actes pour l'Amour médecin* in the course of a single night.

He won his bet, and the *Entractes* turned out to be longer than the comedy. Unfortunately, they were less good, and so obscure that the public did not understand a word. *Entracte*, for the audience, meant 'strolling about', and when the curtain fell on the first act of the real *Amour médecin*, everybody made for the corridors, saying: 'Not too bad, this comedy of Dumas's: he's imitated Molière.' Then, when the curtain rose again upon a scene by Dumas, they all, with the exception of a few quick minds, thought that this was the continuation of the play already begun. But somehow, the two texts seemed to have nothing to do with one another. Had the Comédie-Française turned into a Tower of Babel?

For a while the audience wavered. Was it Dumas or Molière? The Prince-Président sent for the manager to his box. Louis-Napoleon-Bonaparte understood no more than simpler mortals. Only a few actors and critics were amused, and even they were indignant at what they regarded as sacrilege: 'Fancy daring to lay hands on Molière! What profanation!' The second act of *L'Amour médecin* was booed, as though Molière were a 'prentice hand. The audience thought it was booing Dumas.

Madame Arsène Houssaye gave a dinner to 'make up for that boring evening', she said. 'Dear, good Alexandre, whom I love with all my heart, meant *so* well, and was *so* witty ... Mademoiselle Rachel is coming.' The dinner took place on the evening before Rachel's revival of *Mademoiselle de Belle-Isle*. Hermione temporarily 'on holiday', wanted to show that underneath the tragic actress there was a woman of flesh and blood. She succeeded beyond her wildest expectations.

At the end of the play, Alexandre Dumas lifted Mademoiselle Rachel off her feet, and embraced her, saying:

'You are a woman of every century, and all triumphs are within your grasp. You could play every one of my heroines, in drama as well as comedy.'

'Not all of them,' replied Rachel with a smile, 'for I do not wish to be murdered by Antony.'

'Oh! Antony would not murder *you!*'

'You mass of conceit!' said Rachel. 'Antony is you, and I suppose you think I could not resist Antony?'

'Not if we were still in 1831,' said Dumas, 'but those good days are gone!'[12]

The good days were, indeed, gone. The old singer, Béranger, moralized: 'Dumas has been as prodigal of his talent as certain women are of their beauty. But I very much fear that, like fidgety Phil, he will end in the gutter.' Béranger, under his air of affectionate humility, was not averse to showing his claws when a friend was under review. He could endure the misfortunes of others with a great show of joviality.

CHAPTER IV

The Lady of the Pearls

There is, for women, in every man on the prowl, an irritant quality which attracts them.
BALZAC

UNDER the watchful eyes of a pack of creditors, Dumas *père*, in 1850, was living in somewhat reduced circumstances. He was still carrying on his paper, *Le Mois*, in the columns of which he attacked the excesses both of demagogy and of repression. He put before the government a grandiose scheme for grouping, under his direction, a number of theatres which were more or less 'on the rocks' — the Porte-Saint-Martin, the Ambigu, the Théâtre Historique. What he had in mind was that he should be appointed Superintendant des Théâtres Littéraires. Scenery, company and administration would be common to all three. This, he maintained, would ensure great economy. He undertook to direct the policy of each of these theatres 'along the same line of historical, moral and religious activity, and the government need have no fear of a moment's uneasiness ...'[1] This plan for 'collective conformity' came to nothing.

Dumas *fils* was no longer living with his father. The two men were very fond of one another, frequently quarrelled, and then flung themselves into each other's arms. The son disapproved of the ever increasing youth of his father's mistresses. The latest favourite was an actress of twenty, a frail, pale, white-complexioned creature. Her name was Isabelle Constant, and she was the adopted daughter of a hairdresser whose name she had taken for stage purposes. Never, since the halcyon days of Mélanie Waldor, had Dumas been so sentimental.

Dumas père *to Isabelle Constant*: My sweet love ... you have restored to me the days of my youth, so don't be surprised that, since my heart has travelled back to what it was in my twenty-fifth year, my pen has done likewise. I love you, my angel! Alas! in every man's life there are but two genuine loves — the first, which dies: the last, of which *he* dies. That, unfortunately, is the love I feel for you.

You insist, dear child, that you are jealous of me. What! jealous of a man three times your age! Just think what my jealousy will be when I have to go a whole day — as has just been the case — without seeing you, half-mad, incapable of work, walking aimlessly up and down ... My angel, I cannot love like that; I cannot possess by halves. I am not referring now to physical possession. In my feeling for you there is both the passion of the lover and the affection of a father. But, for that very reason, I cannot do without you ... Think that over: I mean it very seriously, for in what I have just said lies the whole of our future, if, so be, you are willing to join some small part of your future with mine. Your presence is necessary to me, so that I may be yours, even if you are not mine.

There is one thing, angel, that in your pure chastity you will not be able to understand, and that is that there are in Paris hundreds of pretty young women who, simply because they want to better their condition, wait — not for me to go to them, but for me to allow them to come to me. So you see, my angel, that I am in your hands. Hold me tight and spread your white wings over my head. Make it impossible by your presence for me, in a moment of madness or depression, to commit one of those stupidities of which I have many times been guilty in the past, for they can well poison a man's life for years.

And now, if it be not entirely from love that you grant what I ask of you, let it be from ambition. You are in love with your art. Love it better than you love me, for it is the only rival I am prepared to tolerate. Where your career is concerned, never was the ambition of a queen so wholly satisfied as yours shall be. Never has any actress — not even Mademoiselle Mars — had, in all her life, such parts as I will give to you in the next three years.[2]

The effects of increasing age (though little visible in Dumas except for his greying hair), the uneasy combination of fatherly affection and virile desire, as well as the girl's fragility, go far to explain this emotional style of writing. A Géronte to another Isabelle, he enjoyed playing the domestic role, going to her and cooking dinner, taking her, like a husband, to see his friends. Not that all this prevented him from simultaneously conducting other love affairs with other passionate young females who made no difficulties over responding to his advances.

The son aimed higher. The success of *La Dame aux Camélias* had brought him an increased prestige. His very light blue eyes had the power to fascinate. Every 'artist' in those days presented an alluring, a frightening temptation to society women. Sometimes they tried, as did Henriette de Castries with Balzac, to enthral while giving nothing in return. Dumas *fils*, still young in years and in heart, observed these 'great ladies' in a rather simple-minded way. The fate of Marie Duplessis had saddened and disturbed him. 'The lost creatures with whom I rubbed shoulders at every minute of the day, who sold pleasure to some and gave it freely to others, who kept for themselves only shame inevitable, ignominy and a doubtful future, made me want rather to cry than laugh, and I began to ask myself why such things should be. . . .'³

One evening, after a dinner with a woman of easy virtue, the comte Guy de la Tour du Pin had said to him: 'Friendship and great age, for I am fifteen years your senior, entitle me to give you a bit of advice . . . We have just been dining with an extremely seductive and very intelligent woman. In her house one meets people of every sort, and there you will be able to make a great many valuable observations. Observe to your heart's content, but, by the time you have reached twenty-five, be careful not to be seen in those surroundings any more. . . .'⁴

His twenty-fifth birthday had fallen in 1849, and he was determined to bear these words in mind. He had, as mistress, a lady named Davin (or Dalvin) with a murky past. But he was received in a more brilliant, if not a more innocent, world. The Russian aristocracy constituted, in Paris, at that time, a sort of secret embassy of beauty. A number of young women: Marie Kalergis (Théophile Gautier's *Symphonie en blanc majeure*), her cousin, the Countess Lydia Nesselrode, and their friend, Nadejda Naryschkine, attracted statesmen, writers and artists to their drawing-rooms. While they had been living in Russia, the Czar, their husbands and their families, had compelled them to behave with a certain degree of prudence. In Paris, they 'let themselves go'.

At the house of Marie Kalergis, Dumas was introduced in 1850 to Lydia Zakrefsky, who had been married three years before to Count Dmitri Nesselrode. She was a ravishing creature, witty and extremely rich, and felt no love for her husband who was seventeen years older. Dmitri's father was the Chancellor, Count Charles Nesselrode, Russian Minister of Foreign Affairs, who, because of his intelligence and flexibility of mind, had wielded great influence over three Emperors.[5] In 1847, he had been recalled from Constantinople, where he was Secretary of Embassy, to marry this young heiress, whose marriage settlement amounted to three hundred thousand roubles, and whose father, General Count Zakrefsky, Governor of Moscow, enjoyed wide-spread respect.[6] Dmitri, who was a diplomat and a man of experience, thought that he would be able, without difficulty, to dominate the child-wife whom two powerful families had introduced into his bed.

But the marriage was a failure, both physically and emotionally. The young countess set out on a series of hydropathic cures which her deranged nervous system appeared to demand. She became a familiar figure at Baden, at Ems, at Spa, at Brighton, and, finally, in Paris which was for her the most efficacious and the most dangerous of all the 'treatments' in Europe. Her husband, having failed to dislodge her from the magic city, had to go back to Russia alone. Marie Kalergis, who was separated from her Greek husband, was having her daughter brought up at the Couvent des Oiseaux (which gave her a virtuous pretext for taking up residence at N° 8 rue d'Anjou). She promised Dmitri to keep a careful eye on Lydia. The two of them, together with Nadejda Naryschkine, formed a dazzling trio of Slav beauties. Lydia was for ever running backwards and forwards between Paris, Berlin, Dresden and St Petersburg. The Countess Charles Nesselrode observed the progress of her son's domestic life with an uneasy eye.

June 17th, 1847: Dmitri has written me only one letter from Berlin. As usual it contained very little. Since then, nothing. He is the one about whom I feel worried. Will he be able to conduct this long tête-à-tête with *tact*? The ideas of his companion have so little in common with his. He thought the responsibility would be a light one, but it has turned out to be very heavy. He has not realized how much patience will be needed before he can bring order into a pretty, but chaotic, head. If he does not give his refusals a coating of sugar, if he wearies her with proofs and arguments, a *coldness* may ensue. That is a very real danger. It worries me. I am writing to him in this sense, but I might as well speak to empty air.[7]

The antagonistic and lucid vision common to mothers-in-law is found, in a scarcely diluted form, in sisters-in-law. Hélène Chrepto-vitch and Marie von Seebach, both of them born Nesselrode, detested

Marie Kalergis, whom they accused (not without reason) of playing, in her dealings with the chancellor — whom she called 'my adorable uncle' — the same role as that which the duchesse de Dino, another badly behaved niece, had so long filled in old Talleyrand's house. Marie Kalergis, the 'snow-fairy', had too great a liking for poets and pianists. Her cousins were suspicious of her, and put Dmitri on his guard against her evil influence.

In February 1850 Lydia Nesselrode gave birth to a son, Anatole, nicknamed *Tolly*, much to the satisfaction of the all-powerful grand-fathers. But in a very short while the attractions of French life proved too strong for the flighty but delightful countess. The way in which she spent money was enough to set brains reeling. On the occasion of one single party at the house she had leased in Paris, the cost of the flowers alone was eighty thousand francs. Her dresses, all of them signed *Palmyre*, cost fifteen hundred francs each, and she ordered them by the dozen whenever she visited her dressmaker. She had bought herself a necklace of fine pearls, seven yards in length. To go with a red ensemble she invested in a set of rubies (tiara, necklace, bracelet and earrings), and with one of blue velvet a corresponding panoply of sapphires. In this way she built up a pyramid of debt.

Lydia had wanted to make the acquaintance of the author of *La Dame aux Camélias*. The fancy took her to become his mistress. Vanquished rather than vanquishing, Dumas *fils* was intoxicated. What young man would not have been? A beauty of twenty, the daughter-in-law of the Russian First Minister, an irresistible coquette, and a woman of the highest culture, she flung herself at the head of a penniless writer who had only just started on his career. How could Alexandre have doubted that the most wonderful love affair had fallen into his lap?

Dumas *père* has described in his *Causeries* how his son took him, one night, to 'an elegant Paris house of the kind that are let furnished to foreigners', and there introduced him to a young woman 'wearing a dressing-gown of embroidered muslin with pink silk stockings on her legs, and slippers from Kazan on her feet'. Her wonderful black hair hung loose to her knees. She was 'lying on a settee upholstered in straw-coloured damask . . . It was easy to see from her sinuous movements that she was innocent of stays . . . Round her neck was a triple row of pearls. There were pearls on her arms and in her hair'.

'Do you know my name for her?' said Alexandre.

'No, what is it?'

'The Lady of the Pearls.'

The Countess Nesselrode asked the son to recite to his father some verses he had written for her on the previous day.

'I don't like reciting poetry to my father: it makes me feel shy.'

'Your father is drinking his tea, and not looking at you.'

In a slightly shaky voice, Alexandre began:

> Hier, nous sommes partis au fond d'une voiture,
> Enlacés l'un à l'autre ainsi que deux frileux,
> Emportant, à travers une sombre nature,
> Le printemps éternel qui suit les amoureux.

The poem went on to describe a walk in the Park at Saint-Cloud, a young woman holding up her silk skirt, long avenues, marble goddesses, a swan, a date and a name carved on the pedestal of a statue:

> A la saison des fleurs enfin, j'irai, madame,
> Revoir le piédestal portant le nom tracé,
> Ce doux nom dans lequel j'emprisonne mon âme
> Et que le vent d'hier a peut-être effacé.

> Qui sait où vous serez alors, ma voyageuse?
> Je serai seul, peut-être, et vous m'aurez quitté.
> Aurez-vous donc repris votre route joyeuse,
> En me laissant l'hiver au milieu de l'été?

> Car l'hiver, ce n'est point la bise et la froidure
> Et les chemins déserts qu'hier nous avons vus;
> C'est le cœur sans rayons, c'est l'âme sans verdure,
> C'est ce que je serai quand vous n'y serez plus. [8]

The indulgent father ends his account as follows: 'I left the two handsome, carefree young people at two o'clock in the morning, with a prayer to the god of lovers to watch over them.' The god of lovers watched to no very good purpose. Viel-Castel makes mention in his Diary, under the date, March 29th, 1851, of a scandal which, he says, was being talked about at that time with bated breath. Three great foreign ladies, two of whom were Marie Kalergis and the Countess Nesselrode, 'had conceived the idea of a small circle the members of which would indulge in amorous orgies, the partners being interchangeable. The young men were recruited from among the more free and easy writers . . . The Nesselrode put herself under the tutelage of Dumas *fils*: the Kalergis chose Alfred de Musset . . . and the end of the whole business was that an order came from Petersburg recalling the countess to Russia. . . .'[9]

Viel-Castel enjoyed exaggerating scandals, but the story of the steps taken by the husband, and of the Czar's order, is authentic. In March 1851 Dmitri Nesselrode 'abducted' his wife in order to make sure of her leaving Paris, and to put an end to her irresponsible behaviour. All the same, the *marito* refused to believe that the worst had happened. He defended Lydia — 'an inexperienced child with more beauty than is good for her' — against slander. 'Some pert French fellow has had the effrontery to compromise her, but that has all been put right now.'

In the Dumas camp the drama was, very naturally, seen from a different angle. Dumas describes how, one morning in March, his son came to him and asked:

'Have you any money?'

'Three or four hundred francs, maybe: you'd better look in the drawer for yourself. . . .'

The young Alexandre did so.

'Three hundred and twenty francs . . . with what I've got on me that makes six hundred — more than I need to get away. Can you give me a letter of credit on some German town?'

'A thousand francs — if that'll help — on Meline and Cans of Brussels. They're friends of mine and will see to it that you don't go short.'

'Good! In case of urgent need, you can always send money to me in Germany. I'll let you know my address as soon as I've settled down anywhere.'

'And you're going . . . ?'

'I'll tell you that when I get back.'[10]

Alexandre Dumas *fils* was away for nearly a year. He pursued his mistress across Belgium and Germany. He wrote to a confidante whose maiden name was Élisa Bottée. She lived at Corcy, a village near Villers-Cotterets, and called herself Éliza de Corcy. The letter was intercepted by the secret police:

Alexandre Dumas fils *to Éliza Bottée de Corcy, March 21st, 1851*:
Dear friend: *we* have reached Brussels. Heaven knows where she'll take me next. I saw her two or three times tonight, looking pale,

sad and red-eyed. The sight of her would have shocked you. The long and the short of it is, I'm in love!

His pursuit took him from Belgium into Germany. From Dresden, from Breslau, he wrote to his father asking for money, and Dumas, always an enthusiastic promoter of adventures, sent what he could.

Dumas père *to Dumas* fils: My dear friend, Vieillot has done everything I asked him to, but no one has been prepared to supply a penny-piece. You must count, therefore, only on me, but of me you may be sure. Matters have reached a point where they must be pushed to a conclusion. Only *do* be careful of the Russian police. They are devilish tough customers, and, in spite of the protection of our three Polish ladies, perhaps even because of it, they are perfectly capable of putting you across the frontier in double quick time ... Yesterday I sent your mother twenty francs ... Look after yourself ... I am letting you have all I can manage at the moment. It will be another fortnight before I shall be able to make up the five hundred francs you need ... My love to you. You have added cubits to your stature in Isabelle's estimation.[11]

From railway station to railway station, from hotel to hotel, young Dumas trailed the Nesselrode couple. But when he reached the Russian-Polish frontier, at Myslowitz, he found it 'locked and bolted' against him. The customs officials had orders not to let him enter Russia. The two Nesselrodes, father and son, had given instructions that the 'pert French fellow' should be turned back. Dumas *fils* spent a fortnight (May 1851) at a village inn over a thousand miles from his own country, with nothing to distract him but the reading of a number of holograph letters from George Sand to Frédéric Chopin.

Dumas fils *to Dumas* père: While you, my dear father, were dining with Madame Sand, I too, was occupied with her ... Just fancy! I have here, in my hands, the whole of her correspondence with Chopin, covering a period of ten years! ... Unfortunately, these letters have only been lent to me. How comes it, you will ask, that here, at Myslowitz, in the depths of Silesia, I should have found a collection of letters which had their origin in Berry? The explanation is quite simple. Chopin was a

Pole, as you may or may not know. After his death, his sister found them among his papers, kept, docketed and put away in their envelopes, with the most loving care. She took them away with her, and, when about to enter Poland, where the police, without showing her the slightest consideration, read every thing readable which she had with her, left them with one of her friends who lived in Myslowitz. This, however, did not save them from profanation, as is proved by the fact that I have had access to them. Nothing could well be sadder, more touching, believe me, than these letters, with the ink already faded, which once were handled and rapturously received by one now dead! For a moment I was tempted to wish that the man who held these letters in trust, who is a friend of mine, might die suddenly, and I, being left with them, might offer them to Madame Sand, who, perhaps, would find some pleasure in reliving one small part of her dead yesterdays. The wretch (my friend), however, is terribly hale and hearty. Thinking that I should be off on the 15th, I returned to him all the papers — which he has not had the curiosity even to read. This indifference may not seem so incredible when I tell you that he is junior partner in an export business.[12]

When George Sand was informed by Dumas *père* of this find, she put in a strong claim for the return of the letters to her.

Dumas fils *to George Sand, Myslowitz, June 3rd, 1851*: Madame, I am still in Silesia, and very happy to be so, since my presence here may enable me to be of some service to you. In a few days time I shall be back in France, and shall bring you, in person, with or without the consent of Madame Jedrzeiewicz[13] the letters you so much want to have back. Some actions are so obviously just that they require no authorization ... Of all these indiscretions nothing now remains but the happy result that they did, in fact, take place. Please believe me, madame, when I say that there has been no profanation. The heart, so indiscreetly and after so long a lapse of time, made the recipient of your confidences, was long your own, and its admiration has the stature and the age given to it by a great and long-standing devotion. Please believe this, and forgive me.[14]

It was in this manner that Madame Sand recovered her love letters to Chopin. She burned them. Between Dumas *fils* and the Lady of Nohant, a friendship began which, at first finding expression only in an epistolary exchange, was to become closer.

One day, in the June of 1851, Dumas *père* received a visit from a young man with a beard, who said to him:

'What! Don't you recognize me? ... I was so bored at Myslowitz, that I amused myself by letting my beard and moustache grow. Good morning, papa!'

On December 30th, he made a pilgrimage to the Park of Saint-Cloud and, on returning, handed his father a sheet of paper.

'This is the pendent piece to the poem I read to you a year ago.'

Here is what Dumas *père* read:

Un an s'est accompli depuis cette journée
Où nous fûmes, au bois, nous promener tous deux.
Hélas! j'avais prévu la triste destinée
Qui devait succéder à quelques jours heureux.

Notre amour ne vit pas la saison près de naître.
A peine un doux rayon de soleil luisait-il,
Que l'on nous séparait — et, pour toujours, peut-être,
A commencé le double et douloureux exil.

Moi, j'ai vu ce printemps sur la terre lointaine,
Sans parents, sans amis, sans espoir, sans amour,
Les yeux toujours fixés sur la route prochaine
Par où tu m'avais dit que tu viendrais un jour....

Et le jour s'enfuyait comme avait fui la veille.
Rien! — Pas un mot de vous! — L'horizon, bien fermé,
Ne laissait même pas venir à mon oreille
L'écho doux et lointain de votre nom aimé ...

Un morceau de papier, c'est pourtant peu de chose;
Quatre lignes dessus, ce n'est pourtant pas long!
Si l'on ne veut écrire, on peut prendre une rose
Éclose le matin, dans un pli du vallon;

On la peut effeuiller au fond d'une enveloppe,
La jeter à la poste et l'exilé, venu

Du fond de son pays presque au bout de l'Europe,
Peut sourire en voyant que l'on s'est souvenu! . . .

Nous voici revenus à la fin de l'année
Et le temps patient, qui ne s'arrête à rien,
Nous rend le même mois et la même journée
Où vous parliez d'amour, votre front près du mien.[15]

Alexandre had wished to write his *Tristesse d'Olympio.* He was not
Victor Hugo, but, all the same, his feelings lacked neither strength nor
truth. He had loved his beautiful foreigner with mingled passion and
pride; and that, at twenty-five, can be overwhelming. It is easy to
understand that he should have been surprised and distressed at receiving from her no sign of life, not even an unsigned note, not even a few
dried petals, nor a pearl.

Sophisticated though he might seem, he was still a sentimentalist,
and could not imagine what depths of cold cynicism the heart of a
coquette of twenty might conceal. While he gloomily brooded in
Poland, strange things were happening in Russia within the Nesselrode
family. Dmitri, wounded mysteriously in the arm (a duel? an attempted
suicide?) found himself threatened with an amputation which was only
just avoided. Lydia had left her husband, and the ever indulgent
Zakrefsky parents were sheltering the cruel and temperamental fugitive
in Moscow.

*The Chancellor Nesselrode to his daughter, Hélène Chreptovitch,
June 1st-13th, 1851:* Dmitri has been in the hands of the four best
surgeons of the city. Three of them insisted on amputation, but
the fourth was opposed to it, and, thanks to him, your brother will
keep his arm. He was resigned to the worst, and asked only for
a respite of 48 hours, so that he might receive Communion and
make his Will. His courage was wholly admirable. In the midst
of this time of cruel tribulation, I was disagreeably surprised by
the arrival here of Lydia and her mother who, at the first news of
the *accident*, turned up to make a scene and bring about a reconciliation. But their attempt entirely missed fire, and they left without even seeing your brother . . . The only satisfaction which I felt
I ought not to refuse them was to see the child, and I had it taken
round to them every day.[16]

The Chancellor, 'an easy-going fatalist, and endlessly tolerant', never breathed a word about the scandal. He detested family scenes. Besides, a statesman in power does not quarrel with the enormously rich Governor of Moscow, especially when his own grandson is heir to that Governor's wealth. He advised some form of friendly agreement, though not reconciliation, since the charming Lydia was going from lover to lover, from Woronzoff to Bariatinsky, from Rybkine to Droutskoï-Sokolnikoff. Dumas *fils* never saw her again. In vain did he send Éliza de Corcy to Dresden, at great expense, when he heard that Lydia, having broken with her husband, was travelling in Saxony.

Dumas fils *to Éliza de Corcy, Brussels, December 12th, 1851:* Dear Eliza, I am writing from Brussels where I am, with my father. He has just lost a lawsuit which may result in his having to pay two hundred thousand francs, and it is well that he should be away from Paris while the affair is being settled . . . I have just written to the countess. I told her that I am in Belgium . . . May I remind you of the promise you made to write to me, telling me the truth, the *whole truth?* Red wax for you; wax of a different colour for her.

December 26th, 1851: Get in touch with the countess, that is all that really matters.[17]

But to have got in touch with the countess would have been useless. So far as she was concerned, the adventure was a thing of the past. Dumas must have brooded long and painfully on the corruption and the lies of so young a woman, who once had seemed to him all sweetness and tenderness. His meeting with her marked him for life. It was his destiny always to form attachments for women who would make him suffer, never for sincere adorers who might have given him a sense of emotional security. The thought of adultery, too, and its consequences, ever after filled him with feelings of disgust. It was only in 1852 that a verbal message, breaking off their relationship, was delivered to him by the Princess Nadejda Naryschkine, Lydia Nesselrode's confidante and accomplice, and another beautiful Slav. How the messenger took the place of the woman who had sent her will be seen in due time.

The adventure with Marie Duplessis had deeply moved Dumas *fils:* that with Lydia Nesselrode had the effect of hardening him. A single word may turn a youth into a mature human being. Love betrayed withers the heart of a grown man.

PART SEVEN

★

FATHER AND SON

CHAPTER I

The Magnificent Exile

Thoughts of the Quai d'Anvers, dear friend, still in my memory dwell,
And of that band of brothers whose firmness nought could quell.
VICTOR HUGO, *To Alexandre Dumas*

THE year 1851 was no less bitter for Dumas *père* than for Dumas *fils*. The men of law were pressing hard on the genial giant. His joviality was a thing of the past. The coup d'état came just at the right moment to enable him to escape from his creditors and his lawsuit without loss of face. Like Victor Hugo, he took refuge in Belgium: but Hugo, it was said, was in flight from the excesses and rigours of tyranny: Alexandre Dumas from the activities and executions of the bailiff's men. But, if it be true that Dumas had left Paris for personal reasons, it is no less true that he was by no means on good terms with the new master. Early in the regime of the Prince-President, he, like Victor Hugo and George Sand, had had hopes of the former *carbonaro*. Later, however, he came out strongly in opposition to the coup d'état. In Brussels he was the courageous and loyal friend of the refugees. Not being, himself, technically an exile, he could, when he wished, run a shuttle-service between Brussels and Paris, where he had left his young protégée of the moment, Isabelle Constant, nicknamed 'Zirzabelle'. But, when he made these journeys, he spent only a very short time in France, that his creditors might be given as little opportunity as possible to have him arrested.

On January 5th, 1852, the furniture of the apartment which he occupied in Paris (the lease of which he had, in vain, tried to transfer to his daughter, Marie, still a minor) was sold, 'as the result of a distraint made by his landlord in respect of arrears of rent'. The sum fetched by the auction exceeded the amount due by no more than one thousand eight hundred and seventy francs, seventy-five centimes. This, at the time, was the only liquid capital available to Dumas & Co.

On January 20th, 1852, 'Alexandre Dumas, man of letters, recognized as carrying on a business by a decree in the Paris Court of Appeal, dated December 11th, 1851', filed a petition, in absentia, through his authorized agent, 'le sieur Chéramy', and was declared bankrupt.

The documents relating to this drama — worthy of Balzac — are to be found today in the archives of the Seine. Neither the creditors of the Théâtre Historique, nor the publishers' claims in respect of loans, appear in the petition. Many debts of long standing are merely summarized in a memorandum, without any statement of precise amounts, as is the case, for instance in regard to a claim made by 'the woman Krelsamer, 42 bis, rue de Clichy'.[1] Though the 'failure' of the Théâtre Historique, as a corporate body, had been treated separately from that of Alexandre Dumas, as a physical entity, the certified liabilities amounted to 107,215 francs, though after the words 'Memorandum of the total assets', the acting Receiver made no entry in the appropriate column. He did, however, put in a request to the Civil Tribunal to 'annul an alleged sale, subject to the right of repurchase by the vendor, which Monsieur Alexandre Dumas had carried out in 1847, of his published works and copyrights'. The Receiver regarded this transaction as a disguised attempt to provide collateral security, and added: 'Since the formalities prescribed by law for the ratification of such contracts were not complied with, this security is declared null and void. Consequently, the copyrights over which the assignees of Monsieur Alexandre Dumas have exercised their alleged privilege must be included as assets in the action for bankruptcy.' It is further added that 'the amounts in question are considerable, it being well known that Monsieur Alexandre Dumas has at his disposal a large theatrical repertory, and has, in addition, entered into a number of agreements with newspapers and publishers for the printing and sale of his literary productions'. This could not be denied.

The procedure known as 'proof of liabilities', which began on June 12th, 1852, was not completed until April 18th, 1853, on which date the official registration of liabilities was completed. It is not surprising that the heavy work involved of verifying the complicated details should have lasted for ten months, since one hundred and thirty-three creditors had put in claims against the physical entity known as Dumas. The list of these 'Furies' goes far to explain what happened to the sums earned by *The Three Musketeers* and *The Count of Monte-Cristo*.

The French outlaws in Brussels — Hugo, Hetzel, Deschanel, Colonel Charras, Arago, Schoelcher — formed, at the beginning of 1852, a small and aggressive company, the members of which prided themselves on their poverty and austere manner of life. Hugo, to whom his wife had recently sent three hundred thousand francs in French government bonds, slept on a pallet and took his meals at a cookshop. Dumas, who possessed neither bonds nor capital, leased two houses on the Boulevard de Waterloo, had an opening made in the party wall, and several inside partitions taken down, thereby procuring a charming residence with a balcony and a carriage entrance. There was a thick carpet on the staircase, the bathroom was lined with marble, the drawing-room had a dark blue ceiling studded with golden stars, and curtains made from cashmere shawls — all on credit. 'In Brussels,' said Charles Hugo, 'Dumas, for the time being, is riding pretty in that chariot of Fortune which has so often given him a spill.'

He had taken as his secretary a good republican who had been expelled from France: Noël Parfait. 'Never was a man so suitably baptized: christian name — gaiety: surname — wisdom.' This decent young fellow with the untidy chin-tuft, always dressed in black though without giving the impression that he was in mourning, had brought with him his wife and children. Dumas offered hospitality to the whole family, in exchange for which Parfait undertook to superintend his business affairs, and spent his time from morning till evening copying the novels, memoirs and plays which the author turned out so quickly that the professional copyists could not cope with them.

Four copies each — for Brussels, Germany, England and America — of eleven works, comprising thirty-two volumes! 'No one but Dumas could have written, no one but Parfait have copied, them.'[2] In order to save time, Dumas omitted all punctuation. Parfait inserted the commas and verified the dates. In addition, he acted as Minister of Finance, and did all he could in that prodigal household to make ends meet. 'He sent in demands for payment of arrears of royalties, arranged for a revival of *La Tour de Nesle*, published what still remained in manuscript of *Impressions de Voyage*, and kept a watchful eye on the last incomings from the sales of *Monte-Cristo*.'[3] With savage devotion he defended Dumas's money against Dumas. Monte-Cristo hunted in his drawer for money, and never found any. As a result of this new arrangement, his affairs were in rather better shape than they had been. But he felt that he was being controlled, and this irked him. With his warm and kindly smile, he would exclaim: 'It's odd, but since I've had a *perfect* man about the place, things have never been so bad!'

In spite of this severe stewardship (and thanks to it) Dumas lived in great style at Brussels. Many of the exiles, including Victor Hugo took their meals with him. He would gladly have treated them as guests, but, in order to retain their self-respect, they offered to pay him what they would have been charged at the cookshop: 1.50 francs. But the food provided was too rich, and the 'open house' policy resulted in a deficit of forty thousand francs. Dumas gave a number of parties on the true Monte-Cristo scale. One of them he called *A Dream of the Arabian Nights*. The setting was devised and constructed by Séchan, the artistic director of the Théâtre de la Monnaie. A lavish buffet was set up in the Winter Garden. Pietro Camera conducted a performance of Spanish dances. After the show was over, Dumas distributed among his guests the Indian cashmeres which had been used to drape the platform. Hugo did not come: as a serious-minded exile he could not participate in a 'Dumas carnival', but his health was drunk.[4]

This continual hurly-burly did not stop Amphitryon from working. All day long, from morning till night, he sat writing at a table of unpainted wood on the top floor of the house. Innumerable adventures with women, some of them simultaneous, kept him in a confusion of intrigues. In addition to all this, his eagerness to be of help and his naturally courageous disposition led him to do what he could to serve his political friends, such as undertaking to carry Victor Hugo's letter to his wife, who had stayed on in Paris, and bringing back her replies. It is a matter for amazement that this harassed and overworked man should have conceived literary projects on a vaster scale than ever. To satisfy his gargantuan appetite, the history of the whole planet had to be drawn upon. Here is an astonishing letter which he wrote to the publisher, Marchant:

What would you say to an immense novel beginning with Jesus Christ and ending with the last man of creation, divided into five separate episodes: one under *Nero*, one under *Charlemagne*, one under *Charles IX*, one under *Napoleon*, and one set in the future? ... The principal characters are to be: The Wandering Jew, Jesus Christ, Cleopatra, the Fates, Prometheus, Nero, Poppaea, Narcissus, Octavia, Charlemagne, Rolland, Vittikind, Velleda, Pope Gregory VII, King Charles IX, Catherine de Medicis, the Cardinal of Lorraine, Napoleon, Marie-Louise, Talleyrand, the Messiah, and the Angel of the Cup. I suppose this sounds mad to you, but ask Alexandre, who knows the work from end to end, what he thinks.[5]

What his son thought, we do not know; but the father was perfectly sure of himself. Had he not, since his earliest years as an author, dreamed of writing the whole history of the Mediterranean? Why, if it comes to that, should we smile at these superhuman plans? Balzac, another giant, also found pleasure in setting himself gigantic tasks. 'I surveyed my future and furnished it with work to be done', he said; and again: 'Astride upon my thoughts, I galloped across the world, ordering everything in accordance with my wishes.' Dumas, even in the years of his maturity, retained this divine fire. The difference between the two men lies in this: Balzac felt no need to turn his dreams into reality. He could imagine mistresses, and was a great deal happier when, like Eveline Hanska, his 'polar star', they stayed at the other end of Europe. Dumas wanted to have them with him, and very much in the flesh. Balzac *dreamed* grandiose speculations: Dumas speculated, constructed, fascinated — and so amassed an accumulation of burdens. He was compelled to choose. No man can live, at one and the same time, in the real and the imagined. Those who want both succumb.

During his time of retreat in Brussels, Porthos still supported without flinching the enormous burden he had laid upon himself. His creditors had driven him deep within a cave: the rock of debt weighed heavily on his back. A cluster of women dragged at his shoulders. The contracts which he had made with his publishers exceeded not only one man's power to work, but that of ten men, of a hundred men, and the undaunted giant had but one desire — to take on more and more. He got his *Mémoires* ready for publication: he wrote plays for the theatre: he thought of starting a paper: he courted and conquered a fresh succession of women, while, at the same time, keeping his hold on the conquests of the past. It was as though the Dumas of the Brussels period were saying: 'I am burdened with debt: I am bound hand and foot with contracts: I create.' There is, in the spectacle of this confident strength and of this ageing man who still clung to the illusions and recklessness of youth, something both generous-minded and charming. Monte-Cristo had been forced to capitulate, but Dumas, his double, had taken to the woods where he put up a heroic resistance.

He had made his daughter, Marie (twenty-one years old) come to him in Belgium, where he wanted her help in the paternal love affairs which were both multiple and simultaneous. When he was incognito in Paris, and had a few moments to spare while waiting between trains, he wrote to her in Brussels, asking her to undertake strange missions.

Dumas père *to Marie Dumas*: I am coming back with Madame Guidi. If the portrait of Isabelle has been put back in my room, have it taken down.

It is true that he also said: 'I love you beyond everything — even love.' But the young girl received her father's favourites with an ill grace, and ingeniously contrived, with feigned lack of tact, to provoke warfare among his women. This was easy. To Anna she said that he must certainly be with Madame Guidi: to Madame Guidi that he was alone in Paris at the Hotel Louvois (in fact, Isabelle Constant, far from well, was there with him). There were occasions on which Marie Dumas committed deliberate mistakes, which led her father to indulge in violent but fleeting bursts of rage. Reconciliation was rarely long delayed.

Dumas père *to his daughter Marie*: My dear love: ever since I got here I have been both worker and sick-nurse, and have performed the two functions so conscientiously that I have had no time in which to write to you, not wishing to do so in a tearing hurry, nor to send you a mere ten words or so.

When I left you, my darling, I was somewhat flustered. I had been working badly for three or four days, and didn't quite see where I was to get any money. But it has all been for the best, and now, far from being penniless, I am in hopes that, tomorrow, I may be in a position to send you a thousand francs, and to bring back with me as much again, without breathing a word of it to anyone. Out of the money I am sending you tomorrow, you must give a little something to the cabinet-maker and the ironmonger (to the cabinet-maker so as to have the right to get him to make a cupboard for the little mirror-drawing-room; to the ironmonger, in order to get from him an iron bedstead wide enough to take the mattress which is in the wood-shed).

I hope to come back on the night of Saturday/Sunday. Our affairs are going splendidly. Madame Dumas and Madame Ferrand are now far away, so we can count on reaching an agreement. We shall have some money, perhaps, even, lots of money — and then, first and foremost, everything my darling wants shall be hers.

My overcoat has just about reached you, I expect, much to your surprise. The explanation is that *I pretended to be leaving this evening*, and that Isabelle (who can't get out) sent me the overcoat which I had left by mistake with her. It was handed to a gentleman who is just setting off (he would have hunted for me all over the train without success!) and he will return the object to you.[6]

In Paris, it was Dumas *fils* who, now back from his own sentimental journeys, was organizing the 'lines of communication'.

Dumas père *to Dumas* fils: Isabelle thanks you a thousand times. She tells me that you have been charming to her. *Every now and again* I find her very necessary to me. I shall be back home on Monday. The house has been furnished without involving me in a pennyworth of debt. All the receipts are in your name, and the lease as well.[7]

When the father went to Paris, the two men dined with Prince Napoleon (who was pretty critical of his Imperial cousin, and in bad odour with him), in a party consisting of Rachel, Bixio and Maurice Sand. On one of these evenings they all went on to the Odéon to see a play by Méry, their friend from Marseille: *Don Guzman le Brave*. It was a failure, and during the interval Alexandre II said: 'Are we going to keep on as far as the cemetery?' which delighted Alexandre I, who was always very proud of his son's witticisms. He wrote to Marie: 'Alexandre is a scoundrel who hasn't a penny to bless himself with', but he was pleased to know that he could always count on this staunch, shrewd friend to keep the last-but-one favourite, Béatrix Person, out of the way, for the benefit of Isabelle Constant.

Dumas père *to Dumas* fils: Mademoiselle Person is not going to play *Ascanio* ... because I'm not handing out parts to the people who were responsible for putting me in the bankruptcy-court. Isabelle, who seems made for the part of Colombe, will play Colombe. If they don't want to have her on a year's contract, then they must make an ad hoc arrangement with her, which is what I should prefer. Fifteen francs a day is not ruinous ... I beg you to make no change in these terms, and also to ask Meurice to let his name *only* appear on the bills. He will receive my share of the royalties together with his own, and will send it on to you, *without anything in writing*.[8]

By suppressing his own name as part author, and receiving his share of the proceeds from his collaborator, Paul Meurice, Dumas avoided having to share any part of it with the creditors in his bankruptcy. There is a limit to everything — even to honesty.

Dumas père *to Dumas* fils: My dear boy: Isabelle is more and more taken with you. I enclose a letter to Madame Porcher. She may sell tickets for *Ascanio* on condition that everything over and above the twelve hundred francs she will be sending me shall be credited to our account. I am sending you the end of *Conscience*. It has been settled that Anténor is to let you have five hundred francs. Of the thousand still outstanding, 200 are for Marie — 300 for Chéramy — 300 for Madame Guidi, and two hundred more, if possible, for me.

March 14th, 1852: Dear boy: since we are on the subject of figures, this is what you must reckon:

Room	6 francs
Alexis	4 francs
Light and fuel ..	3 francs
Breakfast ..	3 francs
Service	1 franc
Letters	2 francs
	18 [*sic*] francs a day

say, with incidental expenses, twenty francs. You left on January 9th, which makes, until March 9th, two months.

Twenty francs a day amounts to six hundred francs a month. Add to this hotel expenses for Madame Guidi's two journeys, Chéramy's two, and Isabelle's two — so there you are with your seventeen hundred francs well and truly accounted for. The little house is now ready — and wholly unencumbered.⁹

Ascanio, which was produced on April 1st, 1852, had its title changed during rehearsals to *Benvenuto Cellini*. It was a dramatization by Dumas and Meurice of one of Dumas's novels, published in 1843. Isabelle Constant played the principal role, and served as model for a statue of Hebe, which Mélingue as Benvenuto Cellini worked at on the stage in one scene. To this actress, his father's maîtresse en titre, Dumas *fils* was instructed to pay a number of more than modest subsidies.

Dumas père *to Dumas* fils: First, herewith enclosed my letter for Morny. Second, have you given, or can you give, those hundred francs to Isabelle? She is impatient for her wretched hundred francs! As soon as you get this, do your best to let her have them ... Isabelle is to come and see me here. Look in on her this morning and give her some advice about the journey. She's completely at sea. If she comes on Tuesday, as I hope she may, you might make sure that the vases travel with her, marked *Freight* and *Very Fragile*.[10]

How would Marie Dumas, who hated Isabelle Constant, behave to the intruder? The incorrigible Don Juan was far from easy in his mind. At the Boulevard de Waterloo, when she lay fast asleep upstairs, he wrote to his daughter, and put the letter in her room during the hours of darkness.

Dumas père *to his daughter Marie*: Dear love, so fearful am I of annoying you that I have come upstairs to tell you something which I *had not* dared to mention before: that, in spite of my every effort to prevent her from making the journey, Isabelle will be here this evening!

What's to be done, my child? I have been rather miserable for the last four or five days, because, for the last four or five days I have had a feeling that as soon as she was better she would come at top speed. The last thing in the world I want is that, as happened on the occasion of her last trip, you should be cross with me. I love you so well, my darling child, that in your face lies all my happiness or grief. Do you be brave enough, therefore, to spare me pain during the three or four days which she will spend here. Still, what are we to do about luncheons and dinners? Not to have you with me, as always, would make me very unhappy. Could we not have meals in your studio, and so be better hidden from any chance visitor?

In any case, the front door shall be kept shut during mealtimes ... Later, if you prefer it so, I will use the excuse of her not being well to have dinner served to her and me in Alexandre's room.

Do exactly as you wish, but do it in such a way as to cause me as little grief as possible. I love you far more and far better than I love myself, but even now I have not really said what I wanted to say to you.[11]

It remained for Dumas *fils* to get such sums as were due from the Paris newspapers, to stir up the theatrical managers, and from time to time, to lull the suspicions of Isabelle who was jealous of Madame Guidi, Anna Bauër, Berthe, Emma, Madame Galateri — actresses playing in the Brussels theatres — and of all the women of Brabant. Sometimes he protested against his father's 'schemings', or the demands made by Madame Guidi. 'Let us get this straight,' his father replied, 'I have had a number of mistresses. You have known all of them. With each one you have started off by being on good terms, and have ended by being on bad. I have still got the letter in which you told me that Madame Guidi is a charming woman!'[12]

Dumas père *to Dumas* fils: Isabelle is going to see you tomorrow, and I shall join her. At what time shall I come? I have no idea . . . Not a word to her about the journey I made the day before yesterday. Please ask your friends not to mention it to her.[13]

Marie Dumas, a somewhat restive confidante, was kept informed of yet another, but more effectively concealed, liaison. Between 1850 and 1851 Dumas had confessed to her that a young married woman, Anna Bauër, was with child by him. She had taken up an attitude which was scarcely pleasing to her father.

Dumas père *to his daughter Marie*: Dear Marie, I have one or two rather serious things to say in reply to your letter. I don't see the matter in the same light as you. You consider it from the sentimental point of view: I propose to examine it from the social, and especially, from the human, one.

Each one of us is responsible for his faults, and even for his infirmities. No one has the right to lay the weight of them upon the shoulders of others. If an accident, or some physical malformation has resulted in this, that or the other man being impotent, it is for him to bear the consequences of that infirmity, and face them fairly and squarely, whatever form they may take.

If a woman has been guilty of a fault; if she has allowed herself to forget what she looked upon as a duty, then it is for her to atone for her weakness with strength, as a crime may be atoned for with repentance. But no woman who has been guilty of a fault, no man afflicted with impotence, has the right to shift on to the back of a third person the burden of her personal fault, or the consequences of his misfortune.

Before ever the child was conceived, I had been aware of these objections. They were carefully weighed, and my conclusions may be stated thus: *for the sake of my child I shall have the strength to acknowledge everything, and to see that everything turns out for the best.* It was as a result of this determination of mine that the being who does not yet exist, who has been condemned in advance, was set in train.

Nothing would have been easier than *not* to have forced birth on a being who, now that he is on the way, though not yet born, is already in the position of being refused social recognition. Children of adultery can be acknowledged neither by the father nor the mother. This one, therefore, will be doubly branded by the fact of adultery.

What will be his position with a mother in the state of health we all know — her own opinion is that she may die at any moment — and a father already old who, by asking for another fifteen years of life, might seem to be making an excessive request? By the time it is fourteen, the child may find itself stranded without resources in a hostile world.

If it turns out to be a girl, and a pretty one, she will at least be able to register with the police and go on the streets at ten francs a time. If it is a boy, he will play the part of an Antony until such time as he may, perhaps, play that of a Lacenaire.[14]

In that case it would be better to destroy a life, and better still not to create it. But it would anger me should such a decision be taken as a result of sentimental mawkishness. It would do violence to all my ideas on the subject of justice and injustice. It would deprive you of some part of my esteem, and, with that part of my esteem, I very much fear, of all my love.

Monsieur is impotent — so much the worse for him. Madame has been weak — so much the worse for her. But let no one dare say 'so much the worse for the being that owes its life to that impotence and that weakness'. Each of us risked something in the action in which we both of us were involved. Madame X ... risked an action for divorce, and so determined was she to face the possibility that it was arranged that she should send me a copy of her marriage contract — which, in point of fact, she has not done. I, for my part, risked a sword-thrust or a pistol-shot, and that is a risk I am still perfectly prepared to run.[15]

Matters, however, did not turn out so tragically. Henry Bauër was born in 1851. All through his life he bore the name of his mother's husband, but his physical appearance, and the generous nature of his character, provided striking and indisputable proof of the paternity of Dumas *père*.

While Dumas was living in Belgium, he began writing his *Mémoires*, and for this purpose set about collecting the relevant documents. Everything was grist to his mill, even the details of dead and gone love affairs.

> *Dumas* père *to Dumas* fils: Dear boy, if you can dig up the verses I wrote in the long ago to the Waldor girl, send them to me. I want to include them in my *Mémoires*. If you can get hold of her *Épitaphe*, I should like to have that, too.[16]

It will be remembered that the romantic Mélanie, at the time of the breach with Dumas, had composed her own epitaph, and then neglected to die. Her cry of despair had now become 'copy'.

In such short periods of leisure as he had, Dumas continued to see something of the 'outlaws'. In the house of the Belgian, Collard, he met Hugo, Deschanel, Quinet and Arago. Often, too, he sat with them on the terrace of the Café des Mille Colonnes. The passers by recognized Hugo and Dumas and saluted them with respect. The group had hesitated about patronizing the Café de l'Aigle, which seemed somewhat too evocative of the Empire, but Arago having argued 'the Eagle is the emblem of all great men', Hugo, a lifelong intimate of eagles, had expressed his approval, and, from then on, the Café de l'Aigle became one of the meeting-places of the exiles.[17]

But gradually the bonds between them were loosening. In July 1852, Hugo set off for Jersey, accompanied to Antwerp, to the boat in which he was to sail, by Dumas *père*, who was beginning to feel nostalgic cravings for Paris. 'How much of our century will remain?' he asked. 'Almost nothing. The elect are in exile. Livy is in Brussels, Tacitus in Jersey.'[18] He was anxious to be granted his discharge as a bankrupt, so that Livy might return with head held high. He proposed to surrender to his creditors one-half share in the literary property of all his works, present and to come. A former secretary of the Théâtre Historique, Hirschler, a clever and devoted accountant, got him slightly better terms: 55 per cent for himself, 45 per cent for the creditors. The Receiver wrote: 'M. Alexandre Dumas has shown the greatest loyalty and zeal in carrying out his undertakings.' That was almost true.

At the beginning of 1853, the agreement was signed, and Dumas gave a superb farewell dinner to his friends in Brussels. The house in the Boulevard de Waterloo had been leased to him until 1855. He offered it to Noël Parfait. The 'Minister of Finance' asked for his final discharge as auditor. This his sovereign gave him by pitching all the accounts into the kitchen stove. Monte-Cristo had carried the burden of bankruptcy without becoming bankrupt.

CHAPTER II

New Incarnation of 'La Dame aux Camélias'

WHEN he returned to Paris, Dumas found his son aureoled with brand-new fame. During the whole of the year 1851, Alexandre had been hard up. Not that for the last few years he had failed to do a great deal of work. He had published a volume of poems (*Péchés de Jeunesse*). 'They were neither good nor bad: they were just young', he said later. That is not true: they were, almost without exception, frankly bad. Among his other productions of this period were a story, intended to be funny, *Aventures de Quatre Femmes et d'un Perroquet*; an historical novel, *Tristan le Roux*; and a queer book, *Le Régent Mustel*. None of them had taken the public fancy. Only *La Dame aux Camélias* had a success. But it was not until February 1852 that the dramatized version was performed.

It will be remembered that it had been accepted by Dumas *père* for the Théâtre Historique. The manager, Hostein, had protested. 'It is,' he said, '*La Vie de Bohème* minus the wit.' In 1849 the Théâtre Historique had closed down. The young Alexandre had then offered his manuscript to the Gaieté, the Ambigu, the Vaudeville and the Gymnase. All had returned it. 'It is not actable,' said the men of the theatre. 'It is not moral,' said those of conventional outlook.

By stressing the beauty of the role, he had tried to tempt Virginie Déjazet, a famous actress and intelligent light of love adored by the public. She admitted that the part was excellent, but said that she could play it only with twenty years subtracted from her age, a great many more 'tirades', and a happy ending. She predicted success for the play, but, 'if you are to have it, three things are essential,' she said, 'a revolution which will do away with the censorship; Fechter in the part of Armand; and me *not* playing Marguerite, because I should just make a fool of myself'.

Charles Fechter, a young and extremely attractive actor with a gentle, melancholy face, had completely won Déjazet's heart one evening when he was appearing in the part of Captain Phoebus de

276

Châteaupers in *Notre-Dame de Paris*. All through the play until the fall of the curtain, he had kept his eyes fixed on her ripening charms. She returned on the next night, and then, on every night for the rest of the week. They became lovers. Fechter had not long been married: Déjazet was twice his age. But she was still a powerful influence in the theatre, still charming, and the young Fechter was wildly ambitious.

Virginie Déjazet to Charles Fechter: You didn't take more than ninety-six francs at Dieppe! That really is appalling, although I know what a dead and alive hole it is. The women there prefer parties to plays. Still, 96 francs is little enough in all conscience! Besides, why trot your wife about with you? It doubles your expenses, and detracts from your poetic appeal. The public doesn't like displays of domesticity . . . You would do much better if you were alone, and in a position to gratify the stale romantic imaginations of the female members of your audience. That may all be very shocking, but, unfortunately, it is true.

By suggesting to Dumas that he should cast Fechter for the part of Armand Duval, Déjazet was giving good advice. But a theatre had still to be found. Up till 1850 he had still not solved this problem, and, since his father could no longer help him, was more financially embarrassed than ever. He gloomily made up his mind that he had better put the play in a drawer and forget about it. He did, however, give one final reading of it on January 1st, 1850. Early that morning he had paid a visit to the grave of Marie Duplessis. His future seemed blank and hopeless. He was wasting his mind and his heart on trivial productions and trivial love affairs. All this he confided to the poor dead girl. On returning home, he closed the shutters, lit the candles, and had another look at his manuscript. Then, since one of his friends, Mirault, had just looked in, he read him *La Dame aux Camélias*. They both of them cried. So it *was* good, after all! But who would see that, or, if anyone did, say so?

Somewhat later, in the spring of the same year, walking one day past the Café Cardinal on the Boulevard des Italiens, Alexandre caught site of the actor Hippolyte Worms seated at a table with the fat Bouffé, the Lucullus of Bohemia, one of those theatrial managers whom no one is ever surprised to find a millionaire one week and a beggar the next. Bouffé called to the young Dumas to come across to his table.

'Worms tells me you've made a first-rate play out of *La Dame aux Camélias*. I'm taking over the Vaudeville shortly: give me a six months' option, and I promise to put it on.'

Time passed. The year 1851 was that of his love affair with the Countess Nesselrode and of his journey to Germany. When he got back, Bouffé was, as he had predicted, manager of the Vaudeville, and put the play into rehearsal. Fechter agreed to play Armand. The part of Marguerite Gautier was given to Anaïs Fargueil. She had the right type of good looks but was so stupid that she got on Dumas's nerves.

'Oo!' she said. 'Is this girl supposed to cough up her lungs in every act?'

'If you will forgive me, mademoiselle, I would point out that it is only in the fifth act that she finds herself reduced to that painful extremity.'

'All right: but since you've lived in that world, I'd like you to give me a few hints on how girls of that sort behave. You see, I don't know anything about them.'

'Heavens, mademoiselle! If you don't know anything about them at your age, you never will!'

So intolerable did she become that both author and manager agreed that another Marguerite would have to be found. Fechter suggested Madame Doche. 'That's an idea,' said Bouffé, 'Doche is extremely attractive; it's the very part for her. But how the devil can we lay hands on her? I've no idea where she is.' 'I know,' said Fechter: 'she's in England. I'll hop across and get hold of her.'

Madame Doche had had a by no means ordinary career. Her real name was Marie-Charlotte-Eugénie de Plunkett. She belonged to an aristocratic Irish family which had settled in Belgium, where she was born. Her father died when she was fourteen, and she decided to go on the stage. She did so with considerable success. At the age of seventeen, she married the composer Alexandre Doche,[1] at that time conductor of the theatre orchestra at the Vaudeville. He was a widower in his forties, and the marriage was disastrous. At the end of two years, Doche emigrated to Russia, abandoning his child-wife who had deceived him in the grand style. The public continued to shower praises on 'the little Doche' with her swanlike neck and willowy figure. She was the aristocratic type of actress, dressed superbly, collected a fine library, bought pictures by the great masters, and was always generous in helping her less fortunate comrades.

Dissatisfied with the parts she had been offered in Paris, she went to London, resolved, so it was said, never again to appear on the stage. Fechter talked to her about *La Dame aux Camélias*. 'Every actress in Paris has refused the part. Will you take it on?' She listened to a reading of the play, applauded, wept, packed her trunks and started rehearsing on the very next day after her arrival in Paris. 'Nothing was lacking,' said Dumas later, 'neither youth, brilliance, beauty nor talent ... When one saw her in the part, one really had the feeling that she had written it ...'² Bouffé, the manager, was not encouraging. 'You'll play the *Dame* alternating with *Ouistiti*, that's to say, every second night, perhaps twelve or thirteen times in all.'³ The other members of the company were uneasy. The subject, they thought, was too daring to go down well with the public. The censorship, unfortunately, agreed with them. The Minister in 1851, Léon Faucher, an austere and pompous individual, banned the play. This happened before the coup d'état, and Dumas *père* was still on good terms with the Prince-President. The son, in despair, asked his father to put in a good word for him. But the censor, Monsieur de Beaufort, maintained that, if only to protect the reputations of the two Dumas, he could not permit such a scandal.

'If we licensed a play like that,' he said, 'the audience would be flinging the benches on to the stage before the end of the second act.'

'One day,' said Dumas *fils*, 'there will be a Minister of sufficient intelligence to allow my play to be performed. I invite you to come and see it when that day arrives. It will be an enormous success.'

'I hope you are right, monsieur, but I doubt it.'

Madame Doche had known Louis-Napoleon and his new Minister of the Interior, Persigny, very well, in London. She pleaded the cause of *her* play.

'Let's give the child her part,' said Persigny.

The duc de Morny attended one of the rehearsals. He was not a man to be easily frightened. All he asked was a certificate of moral soundness — 'just to cover himself' — signed by three competent writers. Dumas *fils* went to see Jules Janin, Léon Gozlan and Émile Augier. In spite of this threefold authority, Léon Faucher dug his toes in. December 2nd dawned. The regime changed overnight to a Life-Presidency, soon to become an Empire. Morny replaced Faucher. Three days after his appointment, the prince's half brother gave the required permission.

The success was tremendous, and the author was acclaimed to the accompaniment of a shower of bouquets 'which the ladies', said Théophile Gautier, 'tore from their bosoms, drenched in tears'.

At last Marie Duplessis has the statue which we asked for her. The poet has taken over the task of the sculptor, and instead of the body, we have the soul, to which Madame Doche has lent her own charming envelope of flesh ... What does the poet the greatest honour is that there is not the least hint of plot, surprise, or complication in the whole of these five acts ... As to the 'idea' of the play, it is as old as love, and as eternally young. Strictly speaking, it is not an idea at all, but a feeling. The clever must be prodigiously surprised by this success, which they will completely fail to explain, since it gives the lie to all their theories. The immortal story of the courtesan in love will always tempt the poets ... But much ability has been needed to put upon the stage, in the teeth of that Anglo-Genevese cant which is de rigueur nowadays, scenes of modern life as it really is, without any hypocritical disguise ... The dialogue is rich in vivid touches which drive home by reason of their very unexpectedness; thrusts and parries which flash and clash with the impact of crossed swords. One is conscious, throughout, of a new and fresh mind at work, of a wit which does not hoard up its best sallies in a notebook for use when the right moment comes.[4]

Madame Doche fainted in good earnest, and Fechter was so carried away that he tore six thousand francs' worth of lace. When the play was over, several friends gathered to celebrate the success. The author begged to be excused. 'I am supping with a lady,' he told them. The lady was his mother, Catherine Labay. 'That night there was a true Venetian feast, a wonderful meal: ham, lentils cooked in oil, Gruyère and plums. In all my life I have never supped so well!' To his father, who would not leave Brussels until he had been granted his discharge as a bankrupt, he sent a telegram: 'Great, great success, so great I felt I was witnessing first night of one of your plays.'[5] Some time later, Déjazet, who, while paying a visit to Brussels, attended the first night of *La Dame aux Camélias* in that city, met Dumas *père* beaming all over.

Dumas père *to Dumas* fils: My dear friend: I spent all yesterday evening with Madame Pasca, talking of you, of your success, of your laurels, of your curtain-calls, of Madame Doche's talent, of Fechter's genius. That is all splendid. Madame Pasca tells me that you have been twice to see Morny. Get him to give you the cross: once you've got it no one can take it away from you. The practical advantage I see in all this is that a certain quantity of pennies will come your way which will enable you to get washed such small quantities of dirty linen as you may have. If the amount turns out to be considerable, give the hundred francs I sent you (by way of the rue d'Enghien) to the rue de Laval.[6]

Gautier was not the only critic who praised *La Dame aux Camélias*. Jules Janin spoke of 'the clarity of tone, the purity of truth, which have turned this drama of facile love into a literary event'. Monsieur Prudhomme was shocked and accused the author of having 'beatified the trade of courtesan'. The Vaudeville itself put on, in the course of the following year, a counterblast, *Les Filles de Marbre* by Théodore Barrière and Lambert-Thiboust, in which 'those women' were pitched into. 'Hang it all! This sort of thing has been going on for quite long enough! Hide away in the shadows, my fine ladies: draw your carriages to one side, and make way for the decent women who walk on foot!'

In point of fact, when Dumas wrote *La Dame aux Camélias* he made no pretence of either attacking or defending courtesans as such. He was at the time suffering from the death of a weak and charming creature whom he had loved. He had painted a picture of life and of his own heart. Had that death been immoral? Should that attempt at redemption be blamed, and, if so, why? 'The author, here, has assumed the functions neither of an advocate nor of a public preacher. He has been content to remain an artist pure and simple — and so much the better . . .'[7] He vibrated with sympathy for his model. He did not judge his heroine, but treated her with friendship and with pity. It was only later that the play was transformed in the author's mind; that the romantic youth became, as he grew older, a relentless moralist.

CHAPTER III

'The Musketeer'

You will return now to the very heart of those glittering, varied, dazzling, happy and innumerable works, where all is daylight. VICTOR HUGO

THE shocks administered by history have a way of opening deep fissures in the substance of society. Those with sufficient strength of character cross them, though it does not always follow that they feel at home upon the other side. The revolution of 1848 marks a clean cut in the life of France. *Change of scene*: the divine machinist had whisked the court of Louis-Philippe up into the flies. *Change of cast*: new men sat in the seats of the mighty: public taste altered. Victor Hugo, as a result of exile and a new upsurge in his productive powers, extricated himself, with head held high, from the frustration of political opposition. Balzac escaped by dying at fifty-one. Dumas *père* returned from Brussels quite unchanged, and chock-full of confidence and plans.

He was in a hurry to renew acquaintance with old friends, with the life and agitation of the streets, with all that he most loved. But how was he to live? His first idea was to found an evening paper, *The Musketeer*: subscription, 36 francs in Paris, 40 francs in the country. Offices at the Maison d'Or at Nº 1 rue Laffitte. The Maison d'Or was better known under the name of the Maison dorée, a famous restaurant, opposite which the offices of the paper with, above them, an apartment for Alexandre Dumas, occupied a square, tower-like edifice. The title had been well chosen. It immediately brought to the mind of the public Dumas *père* and his most famous novel. The top of the front page carried a design representing a seated musketeer. The first issue announced, as forthcoming, fifty volumes of the *Mémoires* of Alexandre Dumas. 'Fifty volumes!' said Méry. 'Say, rather, twenty-five bottles of water which he hopes to induce the public to swallow . . .' No doubt about it, there would be a deal of 'padding', and the strong wine of the Dumas vintage would be much diluted. But the public loved Dumas's padding, and the list of contributors to the paper was brilliant: Alexandre Dumas *fils*, Gérard de

282

Nerval, Octave Feuillet, Roger de Beauvoir, Maurice Sand, Henri Rochefort, Alfred Asseline, Aurélien Scholl and Théodore de Banville. The first few issues made it clear that success had been achieved. 'Start a paper *now?* Impossible!' had been the verdict of the augurs.

'If it hadn't been impossible,' replied Dumas, 'should I have got myself mixed up in it?'

On the street level of the Maison d'Or the inquiring visitor was confronted by a small square of white paper pinned to the door, and on it, written in the proprietor's own hand, *Le Mousquetaire: please turn the handle.* Having done this, he found himself in a small front office containing a deal table and two or three chairs. At what appeared to be a cash desk, Michel, formerly the odd-job man at Monte-Cristo, sat enthroned upon a straw-seated stool. Why Michel? What Dumas needed was a man who was good at figures, what he got was a gardener. 'Just suits me,' he had said. 'Michel knows nothing about figures: I'll make him our cashier.' It was well that he did know nothing about figures, for the till was always empty. Dumas had started *The Musketeer* with a capital of three thousand francs, and no one on the staff was paid.

Nevertheless, the paper appeared punctually every day. How was the miracle achieved? There might be no money in the editorial office, but there was no shortage of paper and pens. The members of the staff drew no wages, but they stuck loyally to their employer. Dumas had only to promise them fame, and address them familiarly, to set them all working with a will. In the early days, Martinet, the business manager, bewildered by what was going on, would go to see Dumas, and would say to him:

'Monsieur Dumas, I have no money.'

'But what about the subscriptions? What about the single-copy sales?'

'*Cher maître*, only ten minutes ago you took from me the three hundred francs which came in this morning.'

'Naturally, I've provided a thousand francs' worth of copy.'

And that was no more than the truth, for Dumas, up on his third floor, seated at a deal table, dressed only in a pair of strapped trousers and a pink shirt, was churning out mile after mile of *Mémoires*. It amused him to make his father and his mother live again, Villers-Cotterets, childhood days in the forest, poachers, and his own beginnings in the theatre. As he wrote, he drew a number of portraits in words:

Leuven, Oudard, Louis-Philippe, Marie Dorval. He indulged in long digressions, narrating the whole of Byron's life, of Victor Hugo's youth. What he wrote was completely devoid of any planned construction, but it was alive, amusing, exciting stuff and certain passages (those, for instance, about Dorval) were delightful. Simultaneously with his recollections, he published *Les Mohicans de Paris* (with Bocage), *Les Compagnons de Jéhu*, and a series of *Great Men at Home*, for which, armed with a blank notebook, he went to interview Delacroix, who complained: 'That terrible fellow Dumas! Once he's got his claws into you, he won't let you go. He came to see me notebook in hand. God knows what he's going to do with all the details I was so foolish as to give him! I'm very fond of him, but we're as different as chalk from cheese. . . .'¹

His public followed where he led, and *The Musketeer* reached a circulation of ten thousand copies, which in those difficult times was a great deal. Even the most serious-minded read it. Lamartine wrote to him: 'You ask for my opinion of your paper. I have views about human matters, but not about miracles. You are superhuman: my opinion can be expressed by an exclamation mark! Men have long sought the secret of perpetual motion; you have gone one better, you have sought and *found* the secret of *perpetual astonishment*! Goodbye. Long life to you, which means, long writing. I am all agog to read . . .'² From Jersey, Victor Hugo sent his pontifical blessing: 'Dear Dumas: I am a constant reader of your paper. You are a reincarnation of Voltaire. Supreme consolation for a humiliated and downtrodden France. *Vale et me ama.*'³

At first, the paper sold so well that a number of influential editors, among them Millaud and Villemessant, offered to buy *The Musketeer*, keeping Dumas on as a contributor at a very high rate of pay. This offer he refused. The letter in which he did so was not marked by excessive modesty. 'My dear comrade,' he wrote to Villemessant, 'what you suggest, and that good and excellent Millaud, with the heart of gold, is unexceptionable . . . But I have dreamed all my life of having a paper of my own, my very own. I am, therefore, sticking to it, and the least it can bring me is a million a year. I have not yet received a penny for my articles: at forty sous a line, I have already earned, since the first issue, something like two hundred thousand francs. This sum I am leaving untouched until such time — say, a month from now — as I can draw five hundred thousand in a lump. In these circumstances

I need neither money nor a managing-director. *The Musketeer* is a gold-mine which I intend to exploit entirely on my own. . . .'⁴

But no miracles can go on for ever. If they do, they cease to be miracles. In the long run even the most loyal of contributors grew tired of being paid only with familiar forms of address. One after the other, they disappeared. So, too, did the subscribers. They were getting nothing *but* Alexandre Dumas *père*. They liked this well enough, but could not make of it their sole intellectual nourishment. Ultimately, the members of the staff and even the clerks resigned in a bunch. Dumas complained bitterly of their 'ingratitude'. *The Musketeer* foundered in 1857.

Dumas sought consolation in dining out a great deal, and derived much satisfaction from his own fluency. He 'talked' the articles which he no longer wrote. He frequented the Princesse Mathilde who, though she was a first-cousin of Napoleon III, had no objection to her guests criticizing the Second Empire. In her house, Dumas posed as a politician. He said that by reason of his popularity he was as powerful as the Emperor. 'Just call me Dumas,' he told the Princesse, 'that's what I've been working for for the last twenty-five years.'

He wrote political epigrams:

> Dans leurs fastes impériales
> L'Oncle et le Neveu sont égaux;
> L'Oncle prenait des capitales,
> Le Neveu prend nos capitaux.⁵

This sort of thing pleased neither the Princess nor the contemptuous Viel-Castel, who noted angrily in his Diary: 'It is a mistake to receive Dumas and let him play the great man.' But in the eyes of the Princess, and those of the general public, Dumas was still Dumas the immense. He spoke of Napoleon III with scorn. 'Hugo', he said, 'has published some magnificent things about Napoleon. I am storing up for him things even more vigorous in the pages of my *Mémoires* . . . That play-actor has not even the courage of his position. In the days when he was no more than a Pretender, he stupidly let himself be arrested. He should have done as I did, and armed himself with a pistol. In 1830, I took the town of Soissons single-handed, simply by threatening to blow out the Commandant's brains. . . .'⁶

He had come to believe that this was literally true.

He blamed the Emperor for not treating artists with sufficient respect.

After one of his more than usually violent outbursts against the regime, somebody asked the Princesse Mathilde whether she had broken with him. 'Certainly, I have broken with him for good and all', she replied '. . . He is dining with me this evening.'⁷ After 1857, she took the son under her wing. She wanted to present him to the Emperor and get a decoration for him. Dumas *fils* refused the offer, giving as his excuse his pride and his shyness. Nevertheless, he was decorated on August 14th, 1857, and chose his father as sponsor.

> *Dumas* père *to Dumas* fils: My dear boy: three days ago, I received your cross, and, with it, authority to bestow on you the title of chevalier. When you get back I shall embrace you even more lovingly than usual, if that be possible, and the ceremony shall be gone through.⁸

In the case of Dumas *père*, occasions for pride were not lacking. When the Queen of England paid a State visit to France, and was asked what play should be performed in her honour at St-Cloud, Victoria chose *Les Demoiselles de Saint-Cyr*. This was duly given at the official reception, and the sovereign expressed herself enchanted. 'I know,' said Dumas (whom the Emperor had not invited), 'I know what would have entertained the Queen even more than seeing my play, and that would have been seeing me in person. Indeed, that would have entertained me as well . . . So remarkable a woman, who will probably go down in history as the most celebrated woman of the century, ought to have met the most famous man in France. It is a pity that she should have gone home without setting eyes on the best our country has to offer.'

Dumas *père* was well aware that Dumas *fils* paid frequent visits to Catherine Labay. The former needlewoman of the Place des Italiens was entering on a dignified old age in complete retirement. The great success of *La Dame aux Camélias* had enabled the young dramatist to instal his mother in Neuilly, at Nº 1 rue d'Orléans. The apartment was on a corner, with plenty of sunlight and a view onto the Bois de Boulogne. For some time she had been keeping a small lending-library in the rue de la Michodière. The virtuous Alexandre, an exemplary son to Catherine Labay, had also remained the deferential and devoted friend of Mélanie Waldor. She had published book after book and had achieved a respectable success with her novels and plays. François-Joseph Waldor, fated to spend his life, thanks to the efforts of his wife, in distant garrison-towns had ended his military career as Commandant of the Island of Aix.

The noisy and much publicized appearance of the *Mémoires* of Alexandre *père* was regarded as highly offensive by the only two women who had ever really loved him. Their author had made a clean sweep of Catherine Labay. When it came to introducing their son into the narrative, he had done so in an indirect manner: 'On July 29th, 1824, while the duc de Montpensier was making his entry into the world at the Palais-Royal, a duc de Chartres was being born to me at the Place des Italiens . . .'⁹ no mention being made of the mother. As to Mélanie Waldor, she found herself treated with contempt: 'At the time when I was writing Antony, I was in love with a woman who was far from being a beauty, though I was horribly jealous of her . . . because she happened to be in the same position as Adèle, that is to say, her husband was an officer in the army . . .'¹⁰ It seemed to give the author pleasure to create a wounding confusion between his two mistresses of the period 1830-31. It will be remembered that Belle Krelsamer had taken the stage name of Mélanie Serre. In Dumas's *Mémoires* the mother of his natural daughter is always referred to as Mélanie S***. 'My travelling companion was proposing to take a lease of three, six or nine years . . . Maybe she was right, poor Mélanie! . . .'¹¹ When this passage appeared, Madame Waldor, a respectable grandmother, was close on sixty. She was deeply hurt.

The legitimate wife had long been engaged in a lawsuit against 'le sieur Dumas, Alexandre'. She was still living in Italy where she was richly maintained by the Prince of Villafranca, who was more in love and more generous than ever. It has already been told how Dumas, at the beginning of his liaison with Ida Ferrier, had taken her to Nohant, where the young actress had managed to get herself into the good graces of George Sand. When, in 1855, the famous woman-novelist was travelling in Italy, with her son (Maurice Sand) and her private secretary (Alexandre Manceau), and passed through Rome, she found her 'dear Ida' in that city. Dear Ida hastened to pay her respects and gave George Sand a bouquet of flowers. From the latter's Diary for the year 1855, we learn that she returned her friend's visit on Friday, March 30th.¹² The two women 'got along like a house on fire', spent an hour chatting about the misdeeds of husbands (Dudevant and Dumas), then went to dine at Frascati with Maurice, Manceau and the Prince of Villafranca. On April 19th,

George was invited to a dinner party by Madame Dumas, which she summed up in four words: 'Romantic tales; Music; Autographs.'

Manceau's Journal, April 22nd, 1855: Party at Madame Dumas's. Dinner. Music by Alexandro. Among the guests were le baron de Gassiod, the prince Don Pietro, a sculptor and two priests, one of them a monstrous trimmer ... We left at 11 o'clock, taking with us a ham and some cakes. Charming evening.

On Monday, April 23rd, George Sand left Rome. She made the following entry in her diary. 'Goodbyes took a long time. Ida, the Prince and the Baron all came. Much kissing and hugging. They are delightful.'[13]
In 1857, the Prince of Villafranca, who wanted to spend a few months in Paris, leased a handsome colonnaded mansion, which still exists, at N° 38 Avenue Gabriel. Ida was in great pain. She was supposed to be suffering from dropsy. In fact, she was soon to die from a cancer of the uterus. Her 'prince charming' (the phrase is George Sand's) tended her devotedly, and insisted on her seeing the most renowned doctors in Paris. During this, her last, stay in France, Ida's relationship with Dumas was that of creditor and debtor. She left again for Italy, where the progress of her ailment became terribly accelerated. It was at Genoa, in the Casa Picasso, Acqua Sola, that she received the last Sacraments, and died on March 11th, 1859.

George Sand to the Prince of Villafranca, March 14th, 1859: My poor dear friend: we are in despair ... Dear God! what a blow for you, and what pain, what immense regret for all who knew her. A great spirit and a high intelligence! Such a terrible loss for you. What are you going to do? You *cannot* remain in a country where everything, at every moment of your life, will bring the memory of her back. You must return to France, to Paris ... It is to us that you will find it easiest to speak of her ... If only we could press your hands, that might help to soften the terrible grief which now oppresses all three of us.[14]

Dumas *père* was now a widower, though for the time being he scarcely noticed it, since he was staying at Châteauroux with his daughter. Marie Dumas had married, on May 4th, 1856, a man of Berry, Pierre-Olinde Petel, her two witnesses being Lamartine and (by proxy) Victor Hugo.

Dumas père *to Victor Hugo*: My very dear and very great friend: my daughter is getting married on the 28th of this month. She is writing, my dear Victor, to ask you to be one of her witnesses (by proxy), the other being Lamartine. We see one another frequently, and, when we do, never fail to talk of you. But then, you see, you have become part of the essential furniture of my heart, dear Victor. I speak of you, old friend that I am, as an indiscreet lover might talk of his mistress. It is one of the great mysteries of nature, one of the sweetest evidences of God's mercy, that men, though they may separate us in the body, can have no power over the heart.

As I have said already, as I have already written, and will say again and write again unceasingly, my dear and great friend, my body may be in Paris, but my heart is in Brussels and in Guernsey — wherever you have been, wherever you are.

I *should* so much like it, my dear, great man, if you would write out on one side of a large sheet of paper the beautiful verses which you addressed to me. Then I could have it framed and hung between your two portraits. There you would be, the whole of you, ever before my eyes.

Au revoir dear friend. Marie is waiting for a letter from you agreeing to be her witness (acting through Boulanger). That will be for her a title of nobility. Tell Madame Hugo that I kneel at her feet. Her letter was that of a poet, of a wife, of a mother. I am keeping it, not with the idea of having it framed, but so as to be able to re-read it, in the manner of a sleeper with wide-open eyes, by wearing it against my heart ... *Au revoir*, my good Victor. May God re-unite us, whether in France, in exile, or in Heaven.[15]

It was from Alphonse Karr, then living at Nice, which is not far from Genoa, that Dumas heard of Ida's death. *Dumas to Karr*: 'My dear friend: I was at Châteauroux when your letter arrived, and found it here on my return ... Thank you! ... Madame Dumas was here a year ago, and managed to get her dowry out of me: 120,000 francs! I hold her receipt. I am just starting for Greece, Turkey, Asia Minor, Syria and Egypt....'[16]

Dumas had married Ida under pressure in the distant past. He had been long separated from her. Who can say whether he felt relieved to know that he was once again wholly free? Meanwhile, Villafranca, the inconsolable lover, was weeping for the woman who lay buried in the cemetery at Staglieno. He wrote George Sand a letter in which he begged her to compose the epitaph to be carved upon the grave of his lost adored one:

> *George Sand to the Prince of Villafranca*: Dear friend, the fewer the words the better, and what you have written to me of her would suffice. If you wish to add a few more, summing up her life, put: — not 'Here Lies' nor 'Here Rests' — for souls do not rest in the earth — but 'To the Memory of' — and, after her name: ... 'whose high intelligence and noble spirit have left a profound mark in the lives of all who knew her. She was a Great Artist and a Generous-Minded woman. She went from us while still young and beautiful, still lovable, still devoted.
> 'The heart of a man lies buried in this grave.'[17]

The good Théo who, twenty years before, had so much admired the fair Ida Ferrier, mourned her, too: 'Since the deaths of Madame Émile de Girardin and of her friend, Madame Alexandre Dumas, the world holds no more women of intelligence.'[18]

But that only goes to show that Théophile Gautier was growing old.

CHAPTER IV

'Diane de Lys'

'Not suffering from your stomach?'
'No.'
'Just you wait until you've been working a bit longer in the theatre.'
LABICHE TO DUMAS *fils*

IN spite of the success of *La Dame aux Camélias*, for he had been honest enough (mad enough, his father would have said) to use his good fortune to pay off his debts, riches had not come the way of Dumas *fils*. In 1853, being once more short of money, he had gone to live in the villa Monte-Cristo, on the Saint-Germain road, over which the bailiffs were still quarrelling. The house was empty. He hired a few pieces of furniture and settled down in it with three friends, one of whom was the fat painter, Marchal. 'We shared expenses, we ate off tin plates; the gardener cooked for us. It was there that I wrote *Diane de Lys*.'[1]

The son possessed neither the facility nor the high spirits of his father. Writing, for him, was an 'exhausting physical labour which brought on fits of dizziness, and gave him cramps in the stomach'. His unhappy affair with Madame Nesselrode, coming on top of his precocious experience of courtesans, had left him disenchanted. Lacking the powerful imagination which enabled his father to be radiantly happy in a squalid world, he observed mankind with a bitter and appraising eye. His ideal, like his mother's, was comprised in the words honesty and decency. He would have dearly loved to found a family, the very opposite of his own.

Dumas *fils* would have liked to find in every woman the 'lady fair' of high romantic chivalry. But women of flesh and blood no more resemble the 'ladies' of chivalry, than real men resemble 'knights errant'. Even the best of them has her moments of madness. Shakespeare and Musset took those moments and turned them into poetry, using them to paint a picture of poetry and charm. Chateaubriand loved the 'mingling of weakness and fal-lals'. Dumas *fils* had less wisdom and less tolerance. The Countess Nesselrode had revealed to him the female animal in her most seductive and most formidable aspect. 'He had learned in the school of immorality.' He had observed

the world of the Second Empire with its ravening libertines, like the
duc de Morny; its husbands who were stupid men about town; its
shrewd and depraved women. Imbecile men of the world, who, in
youth, got dressmakers' assistants with child, and, when married,
deceived their wives; women unhappily married and poor girls seduced;
poor girls seduced and women unhappily married — he could not
escape from the vicious circle.

What would he have liked to be? A decent fellow with a happy home.
Failing that, the righter of wrongs, the friend of women, but also their
judge. The characters he created should put their swords, like the
Musketeers, at the service of what he believed to be sentimental justice.
They should fight with words, brutal though those words might sometimes be. To what end? To save simple-minded young men from
dangerous mistresses, laundry girls from rakes, pure young women
from corrupt husbands. He must combine the tactician with the tamer
of wild beasts. Dumas *fils* was making ready to enter the cage of
lionesses, whip in hand. But, before adopting this noble though
unpleasing role, he must first liquidate the Nesselrode episode, and
free himself from it through the medium of his writing.

This he did, for the first time, in 1852, in a novel, *La Dame aux
Perles*, in which he narrated something of what had happened to him,
scarcely, if at all, disguised. Its heroine, a foreign duchess, had been
married at eighteen to a man who, like Dmitri Nesselrode, bore a great
name, and occupied one of the highest positions in his country.
Everything is there; the hostile sister-in-law; 'Lydia's charming,
indecipherable handwriting'; the lovers' confidante who, in the novel
was called Élizabeth de Norcy, and, in real life, Éliza de Corcy. The
author obviously intended to identify himself with the hero, Jacques de
Feuil, for the duchess says to him: 'If ever you write my story, you
must call it *The Lady of the Pearls*: it will be a pendant to the book on
which you are now engaged, the heroine of which is a courtesan . . .'
The only difference between real life and fiction was that the outcome
of the novel was more flattering to Dumas *fils* than actuality had been,
since Annette, the duchess, after being separated from her lover, dies
of grief, whereas the real Lydia lived and forgot.

Diane de Lys, which began life as a short story and ended as a
drama in five acts, deals once again with an unhappy patrician lady who
falls in love with an artist, Paul Aubry. Deserted by her husband, she
wantonly compromises herself. Paul Aubry, yet another portrait of

the author, saves her from these 'shameful frivolities' with a noble delicacy. The husband, however, intervenes. He does not love his wife, but that doesn't matter. He *is* her husband, and as such he has 'his rights'. He is determined to separate Diane from Paul 'by every means the law allows', as Nesselrode had once abducted his wife. When Paul and Diane seek freedom in flight, the comte de Lys gives them, very coldly, some legal advice:

THE COUNT It may be, sir, that society is badly constituted, that you wish to redress its evils, that Madame and I should never have been married. All that is possible, but one thing is certain, and that is that I am Madame's husband, that I am going to keep her, that nothing can prevent me from doing so, simply and solely because she *is* my wife . . . If I ever again find you with Madame in these circumstances, I swear to you that I shall make use of the right which the law gives me, and shall kill you.[2]

How should he end the play? Quite simply, with a pistol shot? This solution tempted him, because it would balance the conclusion of *Antony*. In *Antony* the lover kills the wife: in *Diane*, the husband should kill the lover. Partly, too, because the moralist, though he detested the insufferable husband, felt in his heart of hearts that he would be justified. But he knew that the public would prefer a victory for the sympathetic lover.

He hesitated for a long while over the problem. After the triumph of *La Dame aux Camélias* he would have no difficulty in getting a second play accepted by a theatrical manager. Once again the censorship stood in his way, not because the subject was immoral, but because Persigny, once the young man's patron, bore him a grudge for refusing to write words for a cantata to be sung at a special performance, in honour of the regime, at the Opéra. The reasons given by Dumas *fils* for his decision were perfectly sound. France at that time had a number of great poets: Lamartine, Vigny, Hugo, Musset. If these refused, or were thought to be unsuitable, it would ill become a young beginner, who was very little of a poet and set great store on remaining independent, to be a substitute for them. The Director of the Opera, Nestor Roqueplan, asked for a straight answer: 'yes' or 'no'. 'No.' 'So be it,' said the other with a laugh, 'and you are perfectly right.'[3]

Montigny, the manager of the Gymnase, intervened in favour of

Diane de Lys. He was a thoroughly good fellow, muscular, with a square head, short hair, whiskers and a clipped moustache. He looked like a faithful watch-dog. His theatre was called the 'Gymnase' because, at the time it was founded, it appeared that it was entitled by charter to serve as a theatre school to be used by the pupils of the Conservatoire for practice. At a later date it became the home of light musical pieces. Montigny had been fighting hard since 1844 to recapture a public which was sick to death of comic colonels, peasant girls, and the stars of operetta. In 1847 he had married the most charming of his actresses, Marie-Rose Cizos, a bred-in-the-bone professional though still very young, who rejoiced in the stage name of Rose Chéri. Scribe, a dramatist much in favour at the Gymnase, had been asked to serve as the mouthpiece for Montigny's proposal. 'I've got a most delightful and original part for you,' he said to the youthful Rose. 'Has it plenty of dramatic situations?' 'I sincerely hope not.' 'Does it end with a wedding?' 'On the contrary, it begins with one.'

Manager and actress made an exemplary pair. Rose Chéri, gentle and reserved by nature, turned out to be a perfect housewife. Her not very exciting, but conscientious and distinguished playing was popular with the audiences at the Gymnase, which she now completely transformed. The presence of the manager's wife behind the scenes imposed a standard of decent behaviour on everybody, while the somewhat chaotic conditions reassured the unconventional. The green room (with its single chair for the use of the lady of the house) resembled nothing so much as a neglected bus station. In Montigny's office, piles of manuscript stood heaped on the American-cloth-covered sofa, on the table, and in every corner. He realized that Diane would be a perfect part for his wife, asked for the ban to be lifted, and succeeded in his efforts.

During rehearsals, a strong bond of friendship was knit between Montigny, Rose Chéri and Dumas *fils*. The author found both of them so intelligent, so loyal and so kindly, that the Gymnase became *his* theatre. It was largely through him that Rose Chéri was established as an almost legendary figure, the patron saint of the actors' guild. Montigny begged Dumas to give *Diane de Lys* a happy ending. But the author clung passionately to his idea of a pistol shot, and refused to make any change. Both audience and critics were baffled, and the success of the play, though considerable, was nothing like that of *La Dame aux Camélias*. It was all very well for the comte de Lys to say: 'This man was my wife's lover: I took the law into my own hands, and killed him.' The 'savage legalism' of this attitude was thought to be shocking.

The author defended himself against the charge of 'preaching'. 'Is it the purpose of art, and of dramatic art in particular, to refine the manners of the working-class? ... The emotion aroused by the depicting of genuine passion, be that passion what it may, expressed in fine acting, is worth any number of declamatory passages ... It produces on the spectator an entirely different kind of moral effect, by making him look into his own heart, and by stirring human nature to the depths . . .'⁴ So far, in his first two plays, he had built upon a foundation of autobiography. In *Le Demi-Monde*, which followed *Diane de Lys,* he gave a picture of conditions which he had carefully studied.

They were those in which women, occupying a position midway between the woman of the world and the courtesan, lived. The demi-monde, according to Dumas *fils*, 'is not just a swarm of courtesans: it is, rather, the class of the déclassées'. Those who, later, applied the term 'demi-mondaines' to women carrying on the trade of 'love', were guilty of a misuse of words. Dumas's 'half-world' is still, to some extent, the 'world'. It contains mistresses who do not present a bill the next morning, love, in their case, being a voluntary gift. Free and for nothing? In theory, yes. But, after all, the wives 'put away' for infidelity, the young girls with a stain on their characters still have to live. It is these who make up the half-world. They seek salvation in a husband, or, if the worst comes to the worst, in a permanent 'protector'. 'This society begins where the reign of the legal consort ends: it finishes where the venal consort begins. It is separated from that of honest women by public scandal: from that of the courtesan, by money.'⁵

Towards the unfortunate creatures who make up the demi-monde, who, after all, differ from the so-called femmes du monde only by accident, Dumas *fils* displayed a savagery which we cannot but find revolting. In his eyes the first of all duties is to prevent a man from marrying an adventuress. So insistent is that duty that, in order to fulfil it, the righter of wrongs is prepared to go to all lengths in caddishness. To extricate his friend, Raymond de Nanjac, a simple-minded and trusting lover, from the wiles of the baronne d'Ange, Olivier de Jalin (who here stands for the author) does not hesitate to fight with any weapon he can find. He looks on a woman of that type as a poisonous snake which must be trodden underfoot without pity.

Olivier de Jalin is the first of a long line of argumentative characters put upon the stage by Dumas *fils*. They are the clear-sighted men who can penetrate the secrets of the human heart. They are aggressive and irritating by reason of their complacency, of their conviction that they are always infallible, of the privilege which they arrogate to themselves of fulfilling the function of directors of conscience. They seem, at first sight, to be disillusioned sceptics; actually, they are the champions of a conventional morality. Already, in Paul Aubry, some of their characteristics had been visible, but Paul Aubry was himself emotionally involved. Olivier de Jalin, on the other hand, wants to remain detached and to dominate the action. In the earliest version of the play, he is even more dogmatic and tiresome. 'There are many things which, as a rule, a man of my age does not know. But I have already explored them deeply, and see them for what they are. I have told you once, and I tell you again, that one of those things is love as it is understood in the world we live in. That kind of love which lays siege to another man's wife and forces her to adopt the low shifts of adultery and condemns her to an existence of daily lies . . . that kind of love I could never feel, not even for you, especially not for you . . . It is from seeing you so pure, so loyal, so trusting that I have come to realize the terrible harm that such a love can do to a woman . . .' That was what Dumas *fils* himself was like at thirty; sickened of the facile episodes of passion, exhausted by love hedged round with difficulties, his mind entirely taken up with women, seeking to adopt towards them an attitude of which he could approve, and demonstrating in the theatre the character he would wish to be — a d'Artagnan to whom every adventuress is a 'Milady'.

The 'outspokenness' of *Le Demi-Monde* frightened Montigny, but delighted Rose Chéri, who saw in the baronne d'Ange a 'golden opportunity', a part entirely different from any she had been accustomed to play. For some weeks the Minister, Achille Fould, did his best to get the play for the Théâtre-Français, into which he was anxious to inject new life. But Dumas, who was determined to remain loyal to the Gymnase, had recourse to a trick. He submitted to Fould a manuscript into which he had introduced certain crudities of expression, innocent in themselves, but which it would have been held impossible to utter on the stage. The Emperor and the Empress had the play read to them and loudly expressed their horror. The Gymnase was saved.

At rehearsal, Dumas was filled with admiration of the remarkable intuition which enabled the fundamentally 'good' Rose Chéri, with the face of an angelic but naughty child, to guess at, and express, feelings which, seemingly, were wholly at variance with her own. Olivier de Jalin would no doubt have said that every virtuous woman carries within her a potential adventuress. As to poor Montigny, he found it completely impossible to dissociate the idea of 'Madame Montigny' from that of the character which, according to him, stained her honour. Dumas was all for her giving as much vividness to the character as she could. Montigny, on the other hand, tried to restrain her. Behind her husband's back, Rose would make signs to Dumas to dig his toes in. By common consent, author and actress reserved for the first night certain particularly daring effects which, had they been rehearsed, would have shocked her husband. 'She was as excited as a schoolboy planning a prank, and said: "The boss mustn't suspect anything!" . . .'⁶ The surprise-denouement assured for the play a tremendous success. Even Dumas *père* was swept off his feet. He had just returned to Paris, and thoroughly enjoyed his son's triumph, with a father's pride.

The moralist may propose, but chance and passion dispose. While Dumas *fils* in his plays was pronouncing sentence of death on adultery, he himself had formed an attachment for a married woman and snatched her from her husband. Once again, she was a Russian and a princess. Of Baltic origin, the daughter of a councillor of state, Nadejda Knorring, 'a green-eyed siren', was twenty-six years old when she took Dumas as her lover. After a brief and unruly period of adolescence, she had become the child-wife of the elderly Prince Alexander Naryschkine. This ill-assorted match had turned her into an unsatisfied and unmanageable creature. She had been the friend, the confidante and the accomplice of Lydia Nesselrode. Bored in a life dominated by icons, she did not hesitate to throw everything to the winds and live in France with Dumas as his wife. When she fled from Moscow, however, she was careful to leave behind her neither her little daughter, Olga Naryschkine, nor her husband's hereditary jewels.

'What I love in her', wrote Dumas *fils* to George Sand, 'is that she is so completely a woman from the toes of her feet to the depths of her Slav soul ... I find her physically very attractive. She has great purity of line and beauty of modelling. With her warm colouring, her tigress's claws, her long, fox-coloured hair and her sea-green eyes, she *suits me down to the ground!*[7] There was something intoxicating for him in the thought that he had in his power this 'great lady' who was ready to sacrifice everything in order to belong to him. If it be true that Eveline Hanska was, for Balzac, the visible embodiment of his revenge upon the disdainful marquise de Castries, it is no less true that in Nadejda Naryschkine Dumas *fils* found compensation for his desertion by the fickle Nesselrode. The better to assert his victory over the Czarist nobility, he affected a certain contempt for aristocrats, vast estates in the steppe and golden roubles. All the same he was tenderly attached to his 'Great Russia' (Nadejda) and his 'Little Russia' (Olga), as he called them in his letters to George Sand. 'I delight', he wrote to the lady of Nohant, 'in re-making this lovely creature who has been flawed by her country, her upbringing, the company she has kept, by coquetry, and, above all, by idleness ...'[8] Pygmalion believed that he was modelling his mistress, but the statue took its revenge upon the sculptor.

I have known her only for a short while, but the tussle (for between two such temperaments as hers and mine that is the only word), the tussle, I say, began seven or eight years ago, and it was not until two years ago that I succeeded in *throwing* her ... I have rolled in the dust with her a good deal, but now I am on my feet, and she, I think, is finally down. Her last journey gave her the coup de grâce. ...[9]

The princess's visits to Russia were unavoidable. In order to collect her personal income, and to renew her permit to live abroad, she had to go once a year to St Petersburg. There, an accommodating doctor prescribed a cure at Plombières, on the ground that the climate of Russia 'was harmful to her in her pulmonary condition', and advised a prolonged period of residence in the South of France. Dumas *fils* was hoping to marry his 'foreigner', in order to adjust his behaviour to his theories. But Prince Naryschkine refused to divorce her. The Czar, who was rigidly opposed to any public rupture of the conjugal relationship, insisted that, in the ranks of the aristocracy, marriages should be indissoluble. Disobedience to the autocrat would mean exposure to immediate reprisals. Divorce, said Naryschkine, would result in stripping his daughter, Olga, of some part of the property to which she was the sole heir.

A mistress who was both a married woman and a mother! ... Nothing could well have been less 'Dumas' than the private life of Dumas *fils*. The lovers suffered greatly from this situation. They concealed their love. In 1853, a handsome villa in the English Georgian style (Ionic pilasters, triangular pediment) was bought at Luchon by the princess's mother, Olga de Beckleschoff, 'domiciled in Moscow, with the authority of her husband, Jean de Knorring, Russian State Councillor'.[10] This house, at that time called Santa-Maria, is known today under the name of the Villa Naryschkine. Between 1853 and 1859, a handsome young man, a pretty little girl, and a lady with sea-green eyes might have been seen any day, playing with a balloon on the grass and the sanded paths.

CHAPTER V

Russian Journey

THE *Musketeer* episode being now liquidated, and the paper
dead, Dumas *père* was longing for a change of scene. He had
always loved travelling, and could make abundant copy out of
his journeys. This time, he was tempted by Russia.

His connection with that country dated from the early days of his
career. In 1829, *Henri III et sa cour* had been acted there with success.
The great actor, Karatiguine, played the duc de Guise, and his wife,
the duchesse Catherine. Karatiguine later translated *Antony, Richard
Darlington, Teresa* and *Kean*, plays which brought about what
amounted to a literary revolution in Russia, where members of the
aristocracy swelled the crowded audiences. But Gogol, for aesthetic
reasons, and the critics for political ones, commented upon them with
some reserve. All these discontented heroes (Antony, Kean) who
declared open war upon society and were opposed to marriage, caused
grave concern in Government circles. But the liberals, Bielinski and
Herzen, took Dumas seriously and gave him unstinted praise.

In 1839, Dumas had thought of presenting the manuscript of one of
his plays, *L'Alchimiste*, ornately bound, to Nicholas I, Emperor of all
the Russias. The reason was this: the painter, Horace Vernet, had just
made a triumphal tour in Russia, where he had received from the Czar
the Order of Saint-Stanislas (second class): Dumas, who was an ardent
collector of decorations, hankered after this one; a secret agent of the
Russian Government in Paris communicated this wish to his Minister,
Count Ouvarov, adding that he thought it might be good policy to
grant it since Dumas, being the most popular writer in France, wielded
great influence on public opinion which, at that time, was anti-Russian,
because of a sentimental attachment to Poland. 'This Order, conferred
by His Majesty, would be more visible on Dumas's breast than on that
of any other French author.' In saying this he showed a very precise
knowledge of Dumas and of the breadth of his chest.

The Minister sent a favourable reply, and the manuscript, illuminated

300

and beribboned, was forwarded to Russia with a letter signed *Alexandre Dumas, chevalier du Lion de Belgique, de la Légion d'honneur et d'Isabelle la Catholique*. This was a decided hint, but, before anything could be done, an Imperial decision would be necessary. The Minister applied for it: 'Should Your Majesty consider it advisable to take this occasion of bringing a section of French opinion to a better understanding of Russia and of her Sovereign, Your Majesty might, perhaps, be willing to give Alexandre Dumas the Order of Saint-Stanislas of the third class . . .' In the margin of this document there is a pencilled note by the Emperor Nicholas: 'A ring with a monogram will be sufficient.'

Sufficient? For whom? Certainly not for Dumas, but the Czar, from instinct and from taste, had a horror of romantic drama. He once said to the actor, Karatiguine: 'I would come to see you more often if only you didn't play these extravagant melodramas. How many times this year have you stabbed or strangled your wife on the stage?' Dumas was advised of the dispatch of a diamond ring with the monogram of his Imperial Majesty. As time went on and the ring did not appear, he lodged a complaint and, eventually, received it. He expressed his thanks in very cold terms, dedicated *L'Alchimiste*, not to the Czar, but to Ida Ferrier (then in high favour) and shortly afterwards published, in the *Revue de Paris*, a novel entitled: *Mémoires d'un Maître d'Armes*, which must have caused much offence to the Czar, since it was (under cover of fictitious names) the story of two members of the Decembrist conspiracy, Annenkov, an officer in the Guards, and his wife, a young French dressmaker, who shared with her husband his exile in Siberia. The narrative is put into the mouth of the maître d'armes, Grisier, whose pupil Annenkov had been. The novel was banned in Russia where, naturally enough, all who could get hold of a copy, read it secretly — including the Empress.

Dumas, therefore, so long as Nicholas lived, was persona non grata in Russia. This he completely failed to realize and when, in 1845, his friends, the Karatiguines, came to Paris, reiterated his wish to see their country and to have an audience of the Emperor. The Karatiguines lost no time in dissuading him and, for some years, he thought no more about the matter. Then, in 1851, he began once more to take an interest in Russia because of the love affairs of his son who had, twice in succession, been smitten with two great Russian ladies, the Countess Dmitri Nesselrode and the Princesse Naryschkine.

These two 'unions' served to increase Dumas *père*'s lively and natural liking for the Russians. They were people after his own heart. The men were giants who took their spirits neat; the women had the reputation of being the most beautiful in Europe. The history of the country abounded in bloody and passionate dramas unknown in France (where nobody but Prosper Mérimée, who appealed only to a limited public, had made literary use of them). This combination of attractions constituted a powerful temptation alike to man and author.

And so it was that when, in 1858, he made the acquaintance, in Paris, at the Hôtel des Trois-Empereurs, Place du Louvre, of a certain Count Koucheleff-Besborodka and his family, who were touring Europe with two million in bills of exchange on all the Rothschilds of Vienna, Naples and Paris, he dogged their footsteps. The Koucheleff-Besborodkas already numbered in their suite an *illustrissimo maestro* from Italy, and a Scottish spiritualist, Daniel Douglas Home (the medium so dear to Elizabeth Barrett Browning), who from childhood had had the gift of second sight and the power to raise spirits. They were only too anxious to adopt so famous and amusing a Frenchman.

'Monsieur Dumas,' said the countess, 'you must come back with us to St Petersburg.'

'But that is impossible, Madame . . . the more so since, if I went to Russia, it would be not only to visit St Petersburg. I should like to see Moscow, also, and Nijni-Novgorod, Astrachan, Sebastopol, and to return by way of the Danube.'

'But that would work out wonderfully,' said the countess. 'I have an estate close to Moscow, my husband has one at Nijni, as well as at Kazan in the steppes, fishing on the Caspian Sea and a country house at Isatcha. . . .'[1]

This was enough to go to the head of a traveller who was held in Paris only by a hair — and that hair, a woman's. Alexander II having by this time succeeded Nicholas I, there was no longer any difficulty about obtaining a visa. Dumas *père* accepted the invitation. A few days later he went by train to Cologne, Berlin, Stettin, from which latter place he continued his journey to St Petersburg by boat. He occupied the time by learning, from books and from the conversation of his companions, all he could about the history of the Romanovs, which had more than its fair share of tragedy and scandal.

At last the steamer entered the Neva. Dumas landed, and looked wonderingly at the droshkis with their drivers in long-skirted coats, caps — 'for all the world like pots of pâté de foie gras' — and brass licence-plates hanging on their backs. He made acquaintance with the St Petersburg cobblestones which at that time could be relied upon to ruin any carriage, no matter how strongly built, in less than three years. With the count and countess he was present, in their great drawing-room at the 'Mass of welcome' said by the domestic 'pope'. His hosts were more Monte-Cristo than Monte-Cristo itself. The park had a circumference of over thirty miles. Two thousand persons lived on the estate.

From St Petersburg he went to Moscow, where he was entertained by Count Naryschkine, who was living with a Frenchwoman, Jenny Falcon, a 'graceful fairy' and sister to the famous singer, Cornélie Falcon. He pressed his attentions on his hostess: 'I can kiss only your hand, though envying the man who may kiss all that I may not.'[2] Fifty years later, Jenny Falcon, then in her eighties, allowed it to be understood that she had not been able to withstand the ardent assaults delivered upon her by the Musketeer.

He had been promised that he should be taken to the Nijni-Novgorod Fair. The promise was kept. Suddenly, at a bend in the Volga, he saw the river vanish into a forest of flower-decked masts. On the quays he heard the murmuring of two hundred thousand human voices. 'The only way I can describe the swarm of people moving along the banks is to compare the scene to the rue de Rivoli after a firework display, when the good householders of Paris start moving homewards. . . .'[3]

He found himself at once the lion of Nijni. The Governor, General Alexander Mouravieff, introduced him to the Count and Countess Annenkov, whom, without ever having seen them, he had made the central figures of *Le Maître d'Armes*, published in 1840. Husband and wife had been pardoned by Alexander II. They extended a warm welcome to the man who had turned them into characters in his novel.

The greatest happiness in the whole course of his journey was the realization that among educated Russians Lamartine, Victor Hugo, Balzac, Musset, George Sand and he were as well known as they were in Paris. In Finland he had come across the mother superior of a convent who had read *Monte-Cristo* with gusto. Everywhere the grand dukes, the provincial governors, the marshals of the nobility and the Boyars gave him a warm welcome. The officials addressed him as 'General', because he always wore at least one cross round his

neck. He offered to give them cooking lessons, and was taught, in
return, the art of dressing sterlets and sturgeon, and shown how to
make rose jam with honey and cinnamon. He acquired a liking for
shachlik (roast lamb cooked over a coal fire after being marinaded for
twenty-four hours in a mixture of vinegar and chopped onion, and
served on a skewer), but hated vodka.

Dumas père *to Dumas* fils: My dearest boy, your letter reached
me at Astrachan. Lockroy has said: 'No one ever returns from
Astrachan.' For a moment I thought that Lockroy would turn
out to be the prophet of prophets. For a moment I feared that I
was blockaded in Astrachan for the whole winter. But don't
worry: I shall be on the road again tomorrow.

Would you like me to give you some idea of my journey to
date? Take a map of Russia; it'll be well worth the trouble. You
know all about my itinerary as far as Moscow, so I won't say
anything more about that. Between Moscow and Borodino you
will notice two crossed swords: that is where the famous drubbing
of 1812 took place. From Borodino I went to Moscow and from
Moscow to Troïtza. You will find Troïtza by moving northwards
up the map. It is close to a lake chock-full of herrings. You know
how fond I am of them, and so will not be surprised that I made a
trip to Pereslaff just in order to eat them.

From Pereslaff to Apatino (don't bother to look, you won't find
it). It is a stretch of country of thirty thousand acres, but not
worth marking on a map of Russia. From Apatino to Kalaisine
(you will find Kalaisine on what the Russians call 'la Volga',
since, not speaking French very well, they don't know that Volga
is masculine). From Kalaisine to Kastrama (take a look at
Mérimée's *Le Faux Démétrius* as you follow me along the river as
far as Kastrama). From Kastrama to Nijni-Novgorod: the Fair of
Fairs in which there is a complete town composed of six thousand
booths *and one brothel containing four thousand girls*. Everything,
as you see, is done on the grand scale.

From Nijni, where I met Annenkov and Louise, the hero and
heroine of *Le Maître d'Armes*, now back in Russia after thirty
years of Siberia ... To Kazan, travelling the whole way down
le or *la* Volga. Then to Kameschin. We will pause a while at
Kameschin, for I am approaching the Kirghis ... Look on your

map for a lake, or rather, three lakes: Lake Elston. There I camped in the middle of the steppe, and took my meals with a charming man, M. Beklemicheff, ataman of the Astrachan Cossacks. Astrachan mutton compared with that of Normandy is nothing. The tail was served separately: it weighed fourteen pounds. At dessert my host presented me with his cap which, in Paris, would make a very smart muff: you shall see it and judge.

Now follow me from Lake Elston to Lake Barkonchatt, a very pretty lake, twenty-five miles round. When we had made the circuit, I was asked whether I would like to see the third lake. For the moment I had had enough of steppes and water. I started off again down the Volga, and reached Tzaritzine. You will find Tzaritzine at the spot where the Don approaches the Volga. There I transferred to a boat which took me to Astrachan.

At Astrachan I did a little shooting along the Caspian, where wild geese, duck, pelicans and seals abound. They are as plentiful as wheatears and bull-frogs are on the Seine. When I got back, I found an invitation from Prince Tumaine. He is a kind of Kalmuck king, having fifty thousand horses, thirty thousand camels, ten million sheep, and a charming wife of eighteen with slanting eyes and teeth like pearls. She speaks only Kalmuck. She brought to her husband as dowry fifteen hundred tents with those who live in them (he has already ten thousand of his own). This dear prince has, in addition to his fifty thousand horses, thirty thousand camels, ten million sheep and eleven thousand five hundred tents, two hundred and seventy priests, some playing on the cymbals, others on the clarinet, some on seashells, others on trumpets twelve feet long. He treated us, first of all, in his pagoda, to a *Te Deum* which had the tremendous merit of being short. Five more minutes and I should have come home minus one of my five senses.

After the *Te Deum*, bless me, if he didn't give me a very good luncheon, the pièce de résistance of which was fillet of horse. If you see Geoffroy Saint-Hilaire, tell him I agree with him that, compared with horse, mutton is no better than veal. I say 'veal' because I believe it to be the meat you most hold in contempt. After the feast there was a race of one hundred and fifty horses, ridden by young Kalmucks of both sexes, at which four of the

Princess's ladies-in-waiting were present ... The prize was won by an urchin of thirteen: it consisted of a young horse and a calico dressing-gown.

After this we had a race of sixty camels, ridden bareback by Kalmucks of twenty-five, each uglier than the last. Had the prize been awarded for Ugliness and not for Racing, the Prince would have had to crown all of them.

We then crossed the Volga which, opposite the palace of Prince Tumaine, is only a mile and a quarter wide, and went to see a herd of four thousand wild horses. The Prince apologized for not being able to show me a larger number. Since he had been warned of my impending visit only on the previous evening, that was all he could get rounded up during the night.

Then began a really thrilling display: hunting wild horses with the lassoo. Ridden barebacked by Kalmucks, they dashed with their riders right into the Volga. They fought in the water, rolled on the sand, lashed out with their hooves, whinnied, bit — and all that in tens, twenties and fifties. The whole scene became a hurricane of riders which you must have seen to believe.

We went back to the other side of the Volga and watched a display of hawking, falcons against swans. That, together with the dresses of the Prince, the Princess, and the ladies-in-waiting had a medieval look which would have delighted you, champion of the modern though you are. Then we sat down to table again. We started with foal soup which needed only a raven to be as good as our suppers of Sainte-Assise. The rest, apart from brawn made from horse's head, was just a variant of ordinary bourgeois cooking. Meanwhile, out in the courtyard, three hundred Kalmucks were being regaled with raw horseflesh minced with onions, and two cows and ten sheep roasted. . . .

Would you believe it, I have eaten raw horseflesh with little onions, and found it excellent? I can't say the same of mare's-milk brandy. Ugh! We went to bed late, after taking tea in the Princess's tent. We'll have tea in my garden under one just like it. Since I was the guest of honour I was draped in a black sheepskin cloak. Two Kalmucks, by sheer force, fastened round me a silver belt which gave me a waist like Anna's. Then they put a whip in my hand. With one of these whips Prince Tumaine can kill a wolf at a single blow by striking it on the nose. You shall see it. I'll lend it to you to finish off Rusconi, if Rusconi isn't already dead.

Then, we turned in (that's a terrific affair!). You should know that, since being in Russia, I've not had so much as a whiff of a mattress. Beds are completely unknown articles of furniture, and I met with them only on the days, or, rather, the nights when I slept in the houses of French people. But there were bedrooms with beautiful parquet floors, and, after a while, one finds that certain varieties of parquet are more yielding than others. I prefer them of deal, in spite of the fact that they do not encourage frolicsome thoughts.

Next morning, we were each of us brought, *in bed*, a great bowl of camel's milk. I drank mine with a prayer for protection to the Buddha . . . I don't mind telling you, in confidence, that Buddha is a false god, and that if he'd had an altar in the open air I'd have paid him back in his own coin. At last, luncheon over, I took my leave of Prince Tumaine by rubbing noses with him, which is the Kalmuck way of saying 'Yours for life'.

As King Dagobert said to his dog, there's no company so good that one doesn't have to leave it some time. I had to leave the Kalmuck prince, the Kalmuck princess, the Kalmuck sister, the Kalmuck ladies-in-waiting. I tried to rub noses with the princess, but was told that that form of politeness is for use only between men. I left with a sad heart.[4]

Accuracy had never been his strong point, but the stories he told after his return from Russia beat anything in *Monte-Cristo*. Still, travellers are expected to draw the long-bow and, anyhow, what did it matter? His listeners were enchanted. He was so good, so vivid a raconteur, what he said, he said with such a show of conviction that everyone believed him — he most of all.

But the joy of getting home soon faded. Paris was a disappointment to him. A woman who went to see him at that time, Céleste Mogador,[5] a former haunter of the Bal Mabille, and ex-equestrienne of the Cirque Franconi, who had become, as the result of a moment's madness on the part of a young man of good family, comtesse de Chabrillan, found him in low spirits. 'The master's money-troubles', she wrote, 'were only too easily deduced from the broken window-panes, the warped and dusty floorboards, the melancholy perches bereft of their multi-coloured birds. . . .'[6]

'So, it's you, is it, perfidious woman?'

She held out her hand: he took her in his arms.

'I shake hands only with men,' he said.

Alexandre Dumas *fils* was present. He was not very popular with the visitor, who thought that he was too much given to irony, and was only too plainly anxious to keep his father free of any new entanglement. Later, however, the cunning Céleste succeeded in becoming a friend of both the Dumas. She preferred the father, finding him 'altogether nicer and more forthcoming'. Dumas *père* informed her that it was better for the good of his soul to be indulgent and generous than to confess that he had been a fool, to beat his breast and say: *mea culpa* — 'I'm a swine'. The purpose of her visit was to show him a novel (*Émigrantes et Déportées*), and to ask him to revise it, put his name on the title-page, and share the proceeds with her.

'No,' he said, 'I do that sort of thing only in the case of beginners ... Besides, you'd do a great deal better to turn dramatist. Novels involve digressions: they are indispensable, but tedious to write ... Plays are far easier ... No descriptions of places, no portraits, no details of dress to work up ... that's what the stage-designers are for.'

Then, all of a sudden, he suggested that she should enter her name for a course at the Association des Auteurs Dramatiques, and even said that he would go there with her and help her with the formalities. This, coming from him, was a great favour, for he hated having to put on a tie. As they walked along the rue d'Amsterdam (Dumas had taken a lease of a small house in that street, which is still standing, N° 77) Céleste noticed that many of the passers by, recognizing the shock of grey, crinkly hair, took off their hats respectfully to father Dumas.

'How pleased people are to recognize you by sight!' she said.

'They salute me,' he replied, 'but they admire you.'

At the corner of the rue Saint-Lazare, he decided to take a cab. The driver looked at the pot-bellied colossus, obviously calculated his weight, and refused to take him aboard for fear of breaking the springs of his 'growler'.

One of Dumas's friends, happening to pass at that moment, stopped and said:

'Hullo, Dumas, how are you? ... I was just on my way to your place.'

At the sound of the famous name, the driver's face brightened: 'Are you Monsieur Dumas? Monsieur *Alexandre* Dumas? . . . Hop in, I'll drive you anywhere you like.'

Céleste Mogador could see that 'the great man was susceptible to such little popular demonstrations'. They touched, even more than they heartened, him. The world of the Second Empire was treating him less well than that of Louis-Philippe had done. The Princesse Mathilde was in the habit, now, of saying that he had 'become quite impossible', adding that 'she had invited him in the old days merely because he was an amusing piece of nonsense'. The duc d'Orléans and the duc de Montpensier had shown more delicacy in their speech and in their thoughts.

CHAPTER VI

His Father's Father

There is one dramatist whose defects and whose merits Dumas *fils* almost exactly repeated:
— Dumas *père*. LÉON BLUM

IT was about 1859 that father and son began to enjoy an equal celebrity. They were alike in features, in their burliness, and in their love of swagger. In some ways, however, they were very different, and indulged in mutual criticism. 'I find my subjects in my dreams,' said Dumas *père*, 'my son takes his from real life. I work with my eyes shut, he with his open. I draw, he photographs.' And, again: 'What Alexandre produces is not so much literature as music. One notices only bars, and, now and again, a few words.'[1] The father had created a number of superb righters of wrongs, but he thought nothing of behaving badly himself. His son, in his own life, was for ever playing the part of Athos the magnanimous.

They often quarrelled. The son reproached his father for having brought him up badly. 'I naturally did what I saw you do, and lived as you had taught me to live.'[2] He was censorious about the debts and the numerous love affairs of a man who was now well past middle age. Sometimes Alexandre II would treat Alexandre I with almost paternal severity. Then the head of the old grizzled goat would droop in contrition, and that evening he would come home with a gift of fine apples for his son, as once, to win forgiveness, he had brought a melon to Catherine Labay.

Dumas *fils* found in his relations with his father the subject matter of some of his plays. *Le Fils naturel* (1858) and *Un Père prodigue* (1859) were autobiographical, in so far as any work of art can be auto-biographical, that is to say with distortions that went deep. Dumas *père* applauded. He knew that his son loved him; besides, the latter had once said:

> You have become *Dumas père* to the respectful, *le père Dumas* to the insolent, and amidst all the chatter, you must sometimes have heard these words: 'No doubt about it, the son has the greater talent.' How you must have laughed!

The answer to that is 'No'. You have been proud, you have been happy, just like any other father. You have always wanted to believe, and you have, perhaps, believed what people say. Dear simple-minded great man, you have given me your fame as once, when I was young and idle, you gave me your money. It is a matter of great happiness to me that now, at last, I can make my bow to you, can publicly express my homage, can embrace you as I love you, bring the future what it may.[3]

All anger, all bitterness forgotten, Dumas *fils* saw in his father his best friend, his master, and even his disciple, for the older writer, living marvel that he was, had taken on a new lease of life. Just as the son had made a profound study of the structure of his father's plays, so now, under his son's influence, the father was becoming more of a realist. He abandoned his kings and his duchesses in favour of the middle class, and of even humbler folk. *Le Marbrier* is a simple piece of domestic theatre. *Le Comte Hermann* is a *Monte-Cristo* stripped of all vengeance and all declamation. Both father and son had that 'family toughness' which could grapple with dramas and comedies alike. Both of them, too, the son in particular, held that a writer may, and, indeed, should, deal with 'problems'. This made Gustave Flaubert indignant: 'I would have you note that people now rank me with young Alex. My *Bovary* is now a *Dame aux Camélias*! Boum! ...'[4]

After the death of Dumas *père*, Hugo compared the two men. 'It was the father who was the genius,' he said, 'indeed, he had more genius than talent. His imagination could conceive any number of facts which he would then shovel pell-mell into his furnace. Whether the resultant matter would turn out to be bronze or gold was something he never asked himself. Not even his vast output could exhaust the fervour of his tropical temperament. He felt the need to love, to expend his devotion with lavish prodigality, and he ever regarded his friends' successes as his own.' 'And the son?' somebody asked. 'Just the reverse. Father and son were poles apart. Dumas *fils* is the embodiment of talent, of as much talent as a man can have, but it is *nothing more* than talent.'[5]

That, too, was the opinion of the comtesse Dash, who wrote, in 1859:

One can be angry with Dumas only when he is not there. One may come into his presence with a perfectly rational grudge rankling in one's mind, even with feelings of hostility. But at the sight of that friendly, intelligent smile, of those flashing eyes, at the feel of that hand so frankly extended in welcome, one first of all forgets all about one's grievance, then remembers it in order to express what one feels in words, but, somehow, one can't let oneself go. Shame overcomes one: one feels that to speak as one had intended to speak would be too much like trying to dominate him. One comes to terms with oneself, though later, when he has finished talking, the old grumble re-emerges.

He is, at one and the same time, *frank* and *dissembling*. There is no falsity in him. He very often lies, but he does not know that he is lying. He begins (as we all do) by telling some necessary, some careless, untruth. He retails some apocryphal story. A week later, both story and untruth have become, for him, the truth. He is no longer lying, but believes implicitly in the accuracy of what he has been saying. He persuades himself, and so persuades other people.

What *is* true, though most will refuse to believe it, is the fabulous constancy of the great novelist in affairs of the heart. I don't say *fidelity*, mark you. He himself considers those two words to have a completely different meaning. According to him they are no more alike than are two things. *He has never deserted a woman.* If women had not the decency to desert him, he would still have all his mistresses, from the first to the last. No one is more faithful to his habits. He is very gentle, very easy to lead: he asks for nothing better than to be led.

Dumas is sincere in his admiration of others. When Victor Hugo is the subject of conversation, his face lights up; he enjoys praising him, and would quarrel violently with anyone who contradicted him. That is not just an assumed attitude, but perfectly real. He ranks himself just as highly, but likes to feel that he and Hugo stand together. He feels the need to share with him the incense which is burned to both of them. Hugo, and a few others, are part of *his* glory: without them it would seem incomplete.[6]

Of Dumas *fils*, the same woman of letters writes:

The children of confectioners and pastry-cooks are not greedy. The son of Alexandre Dumas, the paymaster of those who never pay back, is incapable of making free with either his money or his friendship. His extreme reticence is the result of his upbringing, and of the example given him by others. His father's life is, for him, a warning lighthouse on the edge of an abyss.

Dumas *fils* is, primarily, *a man with a sense of his responsibilities.* He is scrupulous about fulfilling them. You will not find in him that warm expansiveness which is characteristic of his father. There is something cold in his expression, and, maybe, he has really grown cold now that the first fire of his passions has been damped down. His childhood — I would go so far as to say his adolescence, too — was tempestuous . . . He began to settle down when he started to be successful and to make money. *He matured in twenty-four hours,* under the warmth of a theatre chandelier, and to the sound of applause. He is now a sensible and rational being, with his whole future carefully planned. He does nothing without due consideration. He analyses people and things, avoids surprises, never lets himself be carried away, or fall into habits, no matter how pleasing nor how harmless.

He is a man of honour. He keeps his promises. He is serious-minded and practical. He saves, he worries about Stock Exchange prices, and works out a planned career for himself. His dream is to live in the country. He is already looking forward to rest and retirement.

He lacks self-assurance, and has a poor opinion of the human race. He tries to find a reason for everything . . . His irony goes deep. It does not laugh, but bites. He has a number of friends who are very fond of him, fonder than he is of them. His great defect is *disenchantment,* which is in him, the bitter fruit of experience.

Passion, in the sense in which it was understood twenty-five years ago, is the perpetual target of his witticisms. Misunderstood or disorderly women will go to him in vain for sympathy. If they wept, he would take pleasure in saying: 'What does that prove?'[7]

Both were brilliant talkers, but in a different style. Dumas *père* improvised while talking, and would rough out in speech a whole chapter of a novel.

I have heard Alexandre Dumas describe the whole series of movements which went to make up the battle of Waterloo [says

Doctor Menière] to an audience of generals who took part in that action. On he went, shifting the troops here, there and everywhere, quoting heroic utterances. At last, one of the generals managed to get a word in edgeways:

'But it wasn't like that at all, my dear sir: we were there, we . . .'

'All I can say, general, is that you didn't see what was going on.'[8]

Dumas *fils*, though much more briefly, produced just as great an effect with his callous, often brilliant, epigrams.

Goncourt Journals, May 20th, 1868: This evening, at the Princess's, we were treated, for the first time, to a taste of young Dumas's wit. There is a zest in it, somewhat on the coarse side, which, nevertheless, always strikes home: ripostes which cut everybody to ribbons without any consideration for good manners: self-assurance which amounts to insolence and gives to all he says a sort of success: most noticeable of all a cruel bitterness . . . but, beyond any doubt, a wit stamped with his own personal mark, mordant, cutting, with plenty of 'punch' — a great deal better to my mind than what he puts into his plays, because of its economy and its sharpness of improvisation.

He had been propounding a theory that, in every case without exception, all feelings and all impressions depend upon the good or bad state of the digestion, and told, in support of his contention, the story of a friend of his, a married man who had dined with him on the very day his wife had died, a wife, mark you, whom he adored. He had just given his guest a slice of beef, when the latter held out his plate and, in a voice broken with sobs, said: 'A little more fat, please.'

'All a question of digestion, you see,' added Dumas. '*His* digestion was excellent, with the result that grief could make no deep impression upon him . . . Just like Marchal. With a stomach like his no man could ever be overcome with grief.'[9]

The private life of Dumas *fils* with his green-eyed princess was far from easy. But he continued to admire 'these Russian ladies whom Prometheus must have fashioned from one of the blocks of ice he had found on the Caucasus, and one of the rays of sunlight he had stolen from Jupiter . . . these ladies endowed with a fineness of sensibility and an intuition far above the average, which they owe to their double inheritance as Asiatics and Europeans, to their cosmopolitan curiosity, and their indolent habits . . . these strange creatures who speak every language, hunt the bear, live off sweets, and laugh in the face of every man who cannot master them . . . these females with voices at once musical and hoarse, superstitious and sceptical, fawning and fierce, who bear the indelible mark of the country of their origin, who defy all analysis, and every attempt to imitate them. . . .'[10]

Periods shape temperaments. Dumas *père* came upon the scene in the days when strokes of luck were a commonplace. The Paris of 1828, sunk in boredom, was waiting to be taken by storm. Only just past was the time when a private soldier could become a general in the space of four years. People were eager to see everything and have everything. They were willing to accept extravagance because life itself was extravagant. Dumas *père* had the gift of being spontaneously dramatic, wittily emphatic, unconventional without scruple. The son entertained a quite different ambition: to make the world go back on its earlier view that a Dumas could not be serious, and to show that a writer of plays could still be an honest man, in the classic meaning of the word. He made himself the champion of all that had most been lacking in his own case, the family; and the pitiless enemy of what had most wounded him to the quick, the rake, the courtesan and the adulteress.

He came to suffer increasingly from the more squalid aspects of his father's life. In 1858 a painful lawsuit developed between Dumas and his ex-collaborator, Maquet. Ten years earlier, the latter had given Dumas a sort of general 'discharge', in exchange for certain under-takings for the future which had not been honoured. Dumas *père*, who kept a harem and had on his payroll ten mistresses, past and present, spent not only his own share of royalties, but that of Maquet, a careful bourgeois who made do with one mistress (a married woman with whom he had run away) to whom he was faithful, and whom he hid away in the country so that she should not be compromised. Provoked beyond bearing, he finally sued Dumas, claiming part paternity of *The Three Musketeers, La Dame de Monsoreau, The Count of Monte-Cristo* and all the other novels.

Many took his part. The former editor-in-chief of *Le Siècle*, Charles Matharel de Fiennes, wrote to him as follows:

January 22nd, 1858: My Dear Monsieur Maquet: just a line to tell you that I have read the official report of your case, and think that my evidence might serve to rectify a mistake. In 1849, *Le Siècle* was publishing *Le Vicomte de Bragelonne* . . . I was told at six one evening that the next instalment (which we had sent a messenger to fetch from Alexandre Dumas's house at Saint-Germain) had been lost! *Le Siècle* had got to have it . . . Both the authors were known to me: one lived at Saint-Germain, the other in Paris. I went off to see the one I could most easily reach. You were just sitting down to your dinner, but were so very kind as to leave your meal and come back with me to the office. I can see you, even now, working away there. You worked with nothing but a bowl of soup and a glass of Bordeaux supplied to you by the munificence of *Le Siècle*. Page after page flowed from you between seven o'clock and midnight. I passed them, at intervals of a quarter of an hour, to the composing-room. At one o'clock in the morning, *Le Siècle* went to press with its *Bragelonne*. Next day, the instalment was sent to me from Saint-Germain. It had been found on the road. Between the Maquet and the Dumas versions *a bare thirty words* out of the five hundred lines which formed the instalment were not the same!

That is the truth. Do what you like with this statement. Since it might be said that my memory is inaccurate, I have had the facts checked by the editor of the paper, the compositor and the reader.[11]

This was not conclusive evidence, and Maquet lost his case. But negotiations continued. The two men needed one another. The perfect Noël Parfait tried to intervene.

Noël Parfait to Dumas père, *October 6th, 1860*: I firmly and sincerely believe that in suggesting you should make it up with Maquet, I am giving you good advice — and that no one who loves you will say differently . . . Just one word from you will, I hope, settle the whole affair. Who, if not you, should yield to a good impulse? I have always been surprised, knowing you as I do, that you should have persisted in these suits against Maquet, and can only account for your action by assuming that you have been *badly advised*. Free yourself from the claws of men of business, and be, once again, yourself, that is to say, the good, the excellent Dumas, ready to open your heart once again to those who may seem, for a moment, to have failed to appreciate it.[12]

Dumas *père* seemed to be on the point of yielding, but then changed his mind:

> *Dumas* père *to Dumas* fils, *Naples, December 29th, 1860*: Maquet is a man with whom I can have no further dealings. I trusted him, and what did he do? He got himself paid *directly*, and not through me, for one-third of *Hamlet*,[13] on which he had done no work, and for two-thirds of *The Musketeers*,[14] and kept every penny for himself. In my eyes he is no better than a thief.
>
> My works belong to me, and have cost me dear, in all conscience. They are the property of you and your sister, and, to make sure that there shall be no doubt about their ownership, *I intend to make them over to you by deed of sale* in which no money will be involved except the registration fee. But so long as I live, friend Maquet shall have no further contact with me or with my books.[15]

To Noël Parfait he had just written in precisely opposite terms. 'Show Maquet your letter, and tell him, with a handshake, that nothing will give me greater pleasure than to follow your advice. . . .'

All this squalid litigation sickened Dumas *fils*. The dowry promised to his sister (120,000 francs) had never been paid, and this was the more embarrassing to Marie because she was living at Châteauroux with Madame Petel, her husband's mother, who was for ever taunting her with her poverty. Since Dumas *père* was always on the move, or else living in sentimental privacy with one or other of his female comforters, it was Dumas *fils* who had to follow the court proceedings and satisfy the demands of the journalists. Sometimes he complained to Sand, who did her best to calm him.

> *George Sand to Dumas* fils, *Nohant, March 10th, 1862*: Believe me when I say that your father owes the abundance of his gifts to the prodigal manner in which he squanders them. I, myself, have simple tastes, and, consequently, do only things that are as simple as shelling peas. But don't you realize that simple tastes for a man who, like him, carries within himself a world of incidents, heroes, traitors, magicians and adventures, who is drama incarnate, would mean the extinction of his fire? He needs a life of excesses if he is to keep the enormous blaze going. You will never change him, and you will always have to carry a double weight of

glory, yours and his: yours, with all its fruits, his with all its thorns. What do you expect? He has engendered your great gifts, and feels that he has discharged his duty to you ... It is not a little hard and difficult, at times, to be one's father's father.[16]

Hard it certainly was, but it was impossible not to have feelings of loyalty and affection for the man who, with an enormous gold chain stretched across a white piqué waistcoat distended by a vast stomach, loudly applauded *Un Père prodigue*, rose to his feet when the audience shouted 'Author!' and looked so happy and so proud that it was as though he were saying: 'It's *my* boy, you know, who wrote this play!'

The boy, for his part, admired his father. 'He is what he is without realizing it. That is the sign by which one recognizes men of real, natural genius.' That his father was prodigal and lecherous could not, alas! be denied. But that he was the best of men and the most generous of writers, in the fullest meaning of that fine word, the son never ceased to be acutely aware, and, in his better moments, happy in that awareness.

PART EIGHT

★

LA PEAU DE CHAGRIN

All richness of living shortens life. ALAIN

CHAPTER I

In which Dumas père conquers both Émilie and Italy

IN 1860, Dumas *père* was longing, not for the first time, to get away from Paris and from France. Whenever he travelled, he brought back an enormous sheaf of *Impressions* which easily yielded from four to six volumes. He found amusement and money in his adventures; a double profit at which the wits laughed:

> Alexandre Dumas erre pour nous donner
> Ses impressions de voyage,
> Et le public est si content de son message
> Que toujours il voudrait, je gage,
> Envoyer l'auteur promener.[1]

The prodigal, by some miracle, had money in the bank. He had just signed a contract with the publisher, Michel Lévy, for his collected works, with an advance of one hundred and twenty thousand gold francs.[2] To anyone else this would have meant wealth for the rest of his life. But, in his eyes, to be so 'flush' was little less than a scandal. How should he get rid of all that cash? The problem was a simple one. Why should he not follow the example of Lamartine and Chateaubriand, and make a trip to the Orient? By doing so he could satisfy a curiosity of long standing, and also remove from Paris the woman with whom he was at present in love.

Once again, the favourite was a fair and fragile actress, Émilie Cordier. Her father was a maker of wooden buckets for water-carriers.[3] She had been delicate when young, and had read much in Victor Hugo, Balzac and, above all, Dumas, whom she adored. When she had grown a little bit stronger, her parents apprenticed her, first to a sewing-woman, and then to an establishment in the Central Markets. But her private dream was to go on the stage. In 1858, one of her mother's women friends took her to see Dumas, hoping that he might give her a small part. He was just on the point of starting for Russia; but he did not forget the pretty girl and, when he got back in 1859, wrote to her suggesting that she should come to see him in his ramshackle little house at N° 77 rue d'Amsterdam. Émilie went there, and there she stayed. At that time she was nineteen; Dumas, fifty-seven. It was not long before she revealed the passionate temperament of a bacchante, and soon enslaved the insatiable lover. Unfortunately, her gifts as an actress were less marked than her satisfying skill as a mistress.

Dumas, with his usual simple-mindedness, entertained the hope that his daughter (whose marriage had turned out a failure) might form a friendship with her; but Marie Petel, true to her usual method, committed a number of what she led him to believe were mistakes, sent telegrams to forbidden addresses, left the most compromising letters lying about in the most dangerous places, and created a general atmosphere of discord. It was essential that he should get away.

In the spring of 1860, having had a small schooner, *Emma*, built for him at Marseille (it was really no more than a decked-in fishing-smack), he embarked with Édouard Lockroy, Noël Parfait, and a pretty young creature dressed as a musical-comedy sailor, who was known on board as 'The Admiral'. This was no other than Émilie Cordier. Dumas passed her off sometimes as his son, sometimes as his nephew.

The trip was, at first, all gaiety. The single cabin was so low that the giant was continually banging his head. He cooked, talked and made love. When they put in at Genoa, he learned that Garibaldi, the champion of Italian independence, was on the point of starting on an adventure with the object of recovering Sicily and Naples from the Bourbons, and giving them to Italy (which, he hoped, would achieve unification). Dumas knew Garibaldi of the proud air, the red beard, and the poncho which he had brought back from his campaigning days in South America. He had once been to see him in Turin, and had had the idea of writing a book about him. From General Dumas he had inherited a legitimate grievance against the Bourbons of Naples, and at once made up his mind to join Garibaldi in his spirited expedition.

What business was it of his? None: but, according to Charles Hugo, Dumas insisted on never being absent from the stage when sounding deeds were the order of the day. Whenever he came across a provisional government, he charged in like a bull, or an old friend. Forward he went, embracing all and sundry, and said: 'Hullo, what's up? Here

I am!' So well known a man, he thought, must always be expected to turn up at the critical moment.

> Revolutions are his concern [Charles Hugo wrote], all nationalist parties are his party. In Paris, in Rome, in Warsaw, in Athens, in Palermo he has given more or less assistance to the patriots when their fortunes were at the lowest ebb. He offers, en passant, the advice of a much preoccupied man, implying that it had better be taken without delay, because he has twenty-five volumes to deliver before the end of the week. There you have Dumas in the world of politics. He approaches great events with the easy self-confidence of his celebrity; and History, that stickler for ceremony, taps him affectionately on the shoulder, in her more unbuttoned moments, with a 'dear old Dumas!'[4]

A plan of campaign was immediately drawn up. Two ships, and *Emma*, transported the troops to the coasts of Sicily. The English, who had some warships there, observed a more than benevolent neutrality. Less than a month after leaving Marseille, Dumas was in Palermo. Garibaldi's 'Thousand' were welcomed by the Sicilians with delirious joy. One of them has described Dumas's arrival:

> On our way back to the Palazzo Pretorio, we were about to clamber over a barricade when we caught sight of a remarkably handsome man coming to meet us. He addressed the General [Garibaldi] in French. This great strapping fellow was dressed completely in white, and wore on his head an immense straw hat with three plumes in it, one blue, one white, and the third red.
> 'Who on earth can that be?' Garibaldi asked me.
> 'Who, indeed!' I replied: 'Louis Blanc? Ledru-Rollin?'
> 'No, dammit!' said the General with a laugh: 'it's Alexandre Dumas!'
> 'What? The author of *The Count of Monte-Cristo* and *The Three Musketeers?*'
> 'The very same!'
> The great Alexandre embraced Garibaldi, lavished marks of affection on him, and then walked beside him to the Palazzo, talking and laughing in a loud voice as though he wanted to fill the building with his bursts of mirth and his thunderous tones.
> A meal was announced. Alexandre Dumas was accompanied

by a *grisette* dressed like a man and, what is more, like an Admiral. She was tiny, all smiles and pouts, a stuck-up little piece if ever there was one, who took her place, quite unaffectedly, at the General's right.

'For what does this famous writer take us?' said I to my neighbours. 'It is true that a certain amount of licence is granted to poets, but the authority he arrogates to himself in seating this diminutive daughter-of-sin beside the General can be given by neither men nor gods!'

The great Alexandre ate like a poet, and was so talkative that no one else could get a word in. I must confess that he talked as well as he writes, and that I listened to him open-mouthed.[5]

'The Admiral' was expecting a child. A few weeks previously, Dumas had written to his friend, Robelin:

My dear Robelin: I address myself to a man who has had fourteen children; who, therefore, having known misfortune, can sympathize. The charming little creature whom you met at my house, though a boy by day, is in the habit of becoming a woman at night. On one of the occasions when he was a woman, an accident occurred the results of which showed only too clearly in the course of the following month. Monsieur Émile has vanished, and Mademoiselle Émilie is pregnant. Consequently, in a couple of months' time she will have to leave me to continue my journeying alone. Some time between July 15th and 20th, she will be in Paris. Can you find her some furnished lodgings in the country, near you? ... Write, addressing the letter to Malta, dear friend ... Tomorrow, or the next day, we leave for Palermo ... I need not tell you that Mademoiselle Émilie, once again transformed into Monsieur Émile, will rejoin me at the earliest possible moment.[6]

Dumas liked to conduct his life on the 'to be continued in our next' principle. After the Sicilian expedition, Garibaldi had planned to cross the Strait of Messina and march on Naples. But he was short of guns, ammunition and the money to buy them with. With his customary and princely generosity, Dumas offered the schooner and fifty thousand francs to the cause of *Italia unita*. Garibaldi accepted. On September 7th, 1860, dressed in a red shirt, Dumas made his entry into Naples.

The royal family who once had tortured and imprisoned his father he now chased from their capital. A magnificent revenge in the Dumas-Edmond Dantès style.

At Naples, Garibaldi appointed him Director of Antiquities, with headquarters in the Palazzo Chiatamone, once the summer residence of King Francis II. Dumas was in his glory. He carried out excavations at Pompeii. He founded a paper *l'Independente*. The Neapolitans at first laughed at this fat, exuberant and light-hearted man. A new life had begun which consoled him for the ingratitude of the French.

On December 24th, 1860, 'Admiral Émilie' was brought to bed in Paris of a little girl, 'no bigger than a thumb' — Micaëlla-Clélie-Josepha-Élisabeth. Céleste Mogador, comtesse de Chabrillan, acted as godmother; Giuseppe Garibaldi (by proxy) as godfather.

> *Dumas* père *to Émilie Cordier*: Happiness and good fortune be yours, my dear love ... You know that I wanted it to be a girl, and I'll tell you why. I love Alexandre a great deal better than I do Marie. I don't see Marie as often as once a year, and I can see Alexandre as often as I like. All the love I might have had for Marie will now, therefore, be given to my dear little Micaëlla.[7]

In February 1861 Émilie was able to join Dumas in Naples. The nurse and the baby followed later. Émilie acted as hostess at the Palazzo.

The amount of work that Dumas got through at that time for his paper well-nigh beggars belief. Political editorials, news items, a 'Roman Letter', long historical articles on the wonderful island of Ischia, on Dandolo, with, needless to say, the current serial, were all provided by him. The large-size sheets of lavender blue paper which he covered with his sergeant-major's handwriting during those months would fill fifteen or twenty volumes. Among his contributions are to be found proclamations, controversy, plans for military campaigns.

> Two hundred pupils from the School of Painting came recently to express their thanks to us for having made it our business to defend them against certain professors who appear to have forgotten the duties incumbent upon them ... If the municipality will provide me with a site, I, Dumas, will find the necessary hundred thousand ducats for the building of a theatre. ...

At this same time, Dumas was writing with his own hand a history of the Bourbons of Naples in eleven volumes, a novel (*La San Felice*), and *Mémoires de Garibaldi*. Benedetto Croce⁸ quotes with unstinted praise a pamphlet written by Dumas and dated 1862, dealing with 'The origin of brigandage, the reasons for its continuance, and the means of getting rid of it'. It makes abundantly clear that this man, so often charged with being superficial, had analysed far better than the experts the solid basis on which agrarian reform in Southern Italy must be built.

The fecundity of the writer remained inexhaustible. The ceaseless battle waged by him against mistrust and suspicion was still showing only discouraging results. Even Porthos found the weight of the rock heavy on his shoulders.

Dumas fils *to George Sand, August 22nd, 1861*: Even father Dumas is becoming discouraged. I have had a letter from him in which he says: 'Give a thousand loving messages from me to our friend who never grows old, and makes such good use of the paper, pens and ink which will be the death of me.' If papa is going to unload all his gloomy thoughts on me, it's a pleasant look-out, I must say! Do write to this father of mine giving him all the advice you are so eminently entitled to give, but which I can't . . . Make it clear to him what sort of a life it is that keeps your youth and your talent fresh — and perhaps he will grab hold of the pole you hold out to him. He is so strong, and his first impulses are always so good.⁹

But what serves it to be strong, if others are not? Cavour, a faithful servant of the House of Savoy, thought it his bounden duty to oppose Garibaldi, though the latter wanted, no less ardently than he did, the unification of Italy, but surrounded himself with republicans. Garibaldi hesitated. Dumas, 'more garibaldian than Garibaldi', was anti-Cavour. To the French Consul at Leghorn (who reported the conversation in a dispatch to his Minister) he declared that he wanted to drive from Naples, not only the Bourbons, but the new King, Victor-Emmanuel:

In writing a play [said Dumas to the Consul], when one has got the last ounce out of a character, when all the possibilities of the part have been exhausted, one neatly gets rid of him: one suppresses him. That is what we are going to do.

'But once the Piedmontese are driven out, whom are you going to put in their place?'

'Us, my dear fellow, us!'

'Meaning . . .?'

'Garibaldi. . . .'

'But what are you going to make of Italy?'

'We shall organize Italy as a Federal Republic.'[10]

George Sand, feeling that he was unhappy, invited him to go to Nohant for a rest. This suggestion father Dumas refused in a gloomy and pessimistic letter:

Dumas fils *to George Sand, September 12th, 1862*: What a capricious creature my father is, to be sure! What has brought about this change in him? You, dear Mamma, have done more than anyone had a right to expect of you, and perhaps it is best that things should have gone as they have done. God knows what trouble this wild bird would have caused in your nest of young warblers! Leave him to himself. He'll come back to us once he's got a charge of pellets in his wing.

As to our friend Garibaldi, here is what I wrote to Didier last year: 'I very much fear that my hero's dye may be of the wrong tint.' He's not of the stuff of which really great men are made. Those who have set out to regenerate society by the sword don't talk so much. 'God is pushing me forward', said Attila; and forward he went. This chap, on the contrary, no sooner sees a balcony than he starts to sermonize, and every stray scrap of paper is a pretext for him to issue proclamations. He is a poem by Dante to which Viennet has given a conclusion. I hope, for the sake of his reputation [Garibaldi's] that this denouement has been settled with Victor-Emmanuel, and that he has said to the King: 'I've talked too much: I'm committed too far. I've got to go on. Have me arrested sword in hand: make it impossible for me to go further.' Then they'll give one another their words of honour. Garibaldi will be offered some little fief somewhere: he'll be made an Italian Abd-el-Kader, and in some such way the whole business will be concluded. I only hope to God he doesn't publish his *Mémoires* with a Preface by Jules Lecomte! But I wouldn't put it beyond him![11]

Ingratitude, alas, is a universal failing. The people of Naples, oblivious of all that Dumas had so generously done for them, very soon began demonstrating in front of his Palazzo, shouting: 'Out with the foreigner! throw him into the sea!' The good-hearted giant dissolved in tears: 'I did not think that Italy would be ungrateful!' Then, five minutes later, once more philosophical: 'to expect human nature not to be ungrateful is like asking wolves to be vegetarians'. When Garibaldi handed over Naples and Sicily to Victor-Emmanuel II, Dumas noticed that not a soul in the King's entourage was wearing a red shirt. Those who had borne the brunt were not given the glory. That is what always happens.

In October 1862 another grandiose and visionary project tempted him. A certain Prince Scanderbeg, president of the 'Graeco-Albanian Junta' wrote to him from London, asking him to do for Athens and Constantinople what he had done for Palermo and Naples. It was a question, quite simply, of driving the Turks out of Europe. Dumas offered his schooner, *Emma*, and such money as he had left, to this 'New Crusade'. In return for this he was made 'Superintendent of the Military Establishments of the Christian Army of the Orient'. The title was as ephemeral as it was flattering, for Prince Scanderbeg turned out to be a common crook.

Maxime du Camp, who was staying with Dumas at the Palazzo Chiatamone, was filled with admiration for the simplicity and patience of the kind-hearted Hercules with his perpetual smile and his crinkly, grizzled hair. Dumas was going on with his excavations at Pompeii. 'Just you wait and see what we turn up,' he said to Maxime du Camp, 'if we work long enough with our pickaxes, we shall uncover the whole of antiquity.' But, in the long run, even he grew weary of this occupation. Garibaldi had left Naples. Those holding high office could not forgive Dumas for the services he had rendered. He decided to go back to Paris. France, for all its diabolical side, had some things in its favour. When he got out of the train, at ten o'clock at night, after a journey of eight days, he asked his son to drive him to Neuilly, to the house of their friend, the poet, Théophile Gautier.

'But it's late, Papa: and you've had a long journey. You must be tired.'

'I tired? — why, I'm as fresh as a daisy!'

When they reached the house, Gautier was asleep. Dumas shouted. The good Théo appeared at a window, protesting loudly: 'Everyone's gone to bed!'

'Lazy devils!' said Dumas; 'you don't find *me* going to bed!'

They sat up gossiping until four o'clock in the morning, when, at last, Dumas *fils*, completely worn out, persuaded his father to walk home with him to his house in the Champs-Élysées. All the way down the Avenue de Neuilly and the Avenue de la Grande Armée, Dumas talked unceasingly. It was six o'clock by the time they reached home. He at once asked for a lamp.

'What d'you want a lamp for?'

'To light: I'm going to settle down to work.'

Next day he installed himself temporarily at N° 112 rue de Richelieu, and resumed the rhythm of his fantastic symphony. He finished two novels almost simultaneously — *Les Garibaldiens* and *La San Felice*. Émilie Cordier slipped out of his life. She had spoken a little too often of marriage, and Dumas had no wish to start on *that* experience again. He expressed a wish to acknowledge officially as his child the little Micaëlla, whom he called 'Bébé' and loved devotedly. In this way he could have given her equal standing with Alexandre Dumas *fils* and Marie Petel.

But Émilie wanted marriage or nothing. Vexed at not being made an honest woman by the 'seducer' to whom, she said, she had sacrificed the flower of her innocence, and jealous for her rights over a child whom she had already acknowledged as her own, she was strongly antagonistic to Dumas's proposal, thus depriving poor little Micaëlla of her share in the family inheritance.[12] The prodigal once dead, and his debts paid by the estate, his literary property would be of considerable value during the posthumous period of copyright.

Having broken with 'The Admiral on half-pay', Dumas learned, a few months later, that the young woman had borne twins to a rich protector, named Edwards, who lived in Le Havre.

Dumas père *to Émilie Cordier*: I forgive you ... An accident has occurred in our life, and that's all there is to be said. That accident has not killed my love. I love you just as much, only in a different way, as I might love a lost object, a dead object, a shadow.[13]

This incident did not alter his feeling of affection for Micaëlla, his 'cher Bébé' whom he loaded with dolls, dedications to books, and, later, gifts of money. Now that the faithless lover had reached the age of a grandfather, he made an excellent father.

CHAPTER II

Dumas fils *and George Sand*

This great shining son of mine. GEORGE SAND

WHEN, in 1851, Dumas *fils* had come across George Sand's letters to Chopin on the Polish frontier and restored them to her, she made a great effort to get him to Nohant. It is even conceivable that she hoped to establish a more intimate relationship with the magnificent young man. But since the Princess Naryschkine, a woman of thirty, had broken into, and filled, the life of Dumas *fils*, George Sand, then in her fifties, had resigned herself, thenceforward, to treating him as a very dear son. In his first letters he had addressed her as 'Madame and dear master', but, when she wrote: 'I herewith adopt you as my own son', he replied with 'Dearest Mamma . . .' Their two roles were now clearly defined. She occasionally met him in Paris, but the fierce little princess kept herself at a distance from the great world. In 1859, she sold the Luchon villa and took a lease of the Château de Villeroy, near Cléry (Seine-et-Marne). Though 'this vast building' contained forty-four bedrooms, the princess shared her own with her daughter, Olga, so fearful was she that Prince Naryschkine (who had turned up at Sciez, on the Lake of Geneva, 'for reasons of health') might have her abducted.

Did Alexandre Dumas and Nadejda Naryschkine ever think of that Lydia Nesselrode who, once the mistress of the one and the close friend of the other, had bound the two of them together by the fact that she had laid upon her confidante the duty of telling a betrayed husband that the breach between him and his wife was now complete and final? Whether or no, an astonishing piece of news, which reached them in 1859, suddenly brought Lydia vividly back into their thoughts. The ex-Countess Nesselrode had become, as the result of a second marriage, Princess Droutskoï-Sokolnikoff. She had braved the interdict of the Czar (who had formally expressed his disapproval of this double divorce in two of the highest placed families of the Russian aristocracy), and in the church of a tiny village, every soul in which belonged to the Zakrefsky owners, induced an ignorant 'pope' to pronounce an illicit blessing on their union.

Chancellor Nesselrode to his son Dmitri, April 18th/30th, 1859: Lydia's marriage is an accomplished fact, attested by no less a person than Zakrefsky, who has, all along, been in favour of it. He has blessed the new couple and given them a passport. The Emperor is beside himself. Zakrefsky is no longer Governor of Moscow, but has been superseded by Serge Stroganoff. That is all I know at the moment ... Being in no fit state to appear at Court yesterday, I have seen nobody who can give me any authentic details about the effect of this bombshell. I must have them before I can advise you what steps you should take. Will the Government take action, or must you make representations to the Consistory in order to apply for, and obtain, a divorce?

The wild and headstrong Lydia, by daring to disobey the Emperor of all the Russias, had completely ruined her father's career. The harsh dismissal of General Zakrefsky helps us to understand why Prince Naryschkine had opposed divorce. Nadejda, for her part, believed that she could reconcile her free union by submission to the Czar — in other words, that she could live in France with her Frenchman without having to sever her connections with Russia. The moment of decision came in 1860, when the Princess Naryschkine found herself with child by Alexandre Dumas *fils*. She discreetly concealed her pregnancy in the country, though she was anxious, in order to profit by the skill of an eminent gynaecologist, Dr Charles Devilliers, to be brought to bed in Paris. Under the assumed name of 'Nathalie Lefébure, of independent means' she leased an apartment in the rue Neuve-des-Mathurins, and it was there that, on November 20th, 1860, a little girl was born, father unknown. She was given the three christian names which the law imposed on bastards, and the surname of Colette.

It was a painful experience for the author of *Le Fils naturel* to have a natural daughter. But what could he do about it, how legitimize the child, so long as the husband-in-name, and, therefore, the presumed father, was alive?

Very soon George Sand, a strong-minded woman, became the confidante of, and dispenser of consolation to, Dumas *fils*, who had taken refuge in hypochondria.

Dumas fils *to George Sand, February 1861*: I am completely worn out in body and in mind, heart and spirit, and moulder a bit more with each day that passes. I have reached the point where I no longer open my lips, and there are moments when I truly believe that I could not, if I would ... Try to imagine a man at a ball, waltzing away at top speed without bothering about anybody else, and then suddenly making a false step and finding it impossible to recover the rhythm. There he stands, one leg in the air, incapable of getting back into the movement, though he has the beat in his ears as he had it a moment before. The other dancers push and jostle him and try to get him out of the way, and, in the end, he can only stammer excuses to his partner and creep alone into a corner. That is the condition I am in. I leave it to you to judge whether or no I feel, not only the wish, but the need, to be with you ... I have never really put into words what I think of you, because, by raising yourself so high, you have put yourself far above all comment, whether good or bad, but you're a dam' good fellow, and your equal has never been born.[1]

In 1861, Dumas *fils* was engaged in the wholly disinterested labour of making a play from one of Madame Sand's novels, *Le Marquis de Villemer*. She had begged him to help her, for he had his father's gift of literary bone-setting. They saw a great deal of one another. She begged him to bring 'Great Russia' and 'Little Russia' to Nohant, there to see a performance by a company of amateurs, as well as the famous marionettes. George Sand who, in the old days, had had an infatuation for the comtesse d'Agoult for no better reason than that she had been courageous enough to run away with Liszt, could scarcely fail to be curious about a princess with green eyes and heavy coils of copper-coloured hair, who had been capable of leaving behind her in Russia an all-powerful lord, owning thousands of 'souls', in order to live as his wife with a young French dramatist at Neuilly-sur-Seine. But the woman novelist terrified the foreign princess. *Dumas* fils *to George Sand*: 'The Princess insists that I should draft her letter to you ... But I don't want to ... Princesses are rather foolish creatures, when one comes to think of it! ...'

The princess found an excuse to stay behind in her Château of Villeroy, and Dumas went alone on a visit which lasted from July 9th to August 10th. He was passing through a period of utter despondency. In the evenings, on the terrace, he and Madame Sand exchanged confidences. George had heard much ill of Nadejda. He protested:

Dumas fils *to George Sand*: As to the Person in question, she is not a bit like what you have been told, but, unfortunately, she has never sufficiently *regulated* her life ... I am equally prepared to adore her as an angel and to kill her as a wild animal, and I won't go so far as to say that there is not something of each in her, so that she is now one, now the other, though (I must admit) much oftener the first than the second. She has given me proofs of a *disinterested* devotion for which she does not even expect me to be grateful. In fact, she thinks it perfectly natural in me to have forgotten all about them. I speak to you about her, in short, if not with the passion of first discovery, at least with that of *renewal*, for it is my pleasure to remodel this lovely creature ... So accustomed have I become to moulding and forming her, at every hour of the day, according to my whim, to think aloud before her about everything under the sun, and to dominate, though not enslave her, that I could not bear to be without her.[2]

He told Sand that it was his great wish to marry 'the Person'. She responded by telling him about the failure of her own marriage. As he listened to her, a number of 'subjects' came to birth in the dramatist's mind. At first the gay and childish pastimes of Nohant left him cold. George Sand found it difficult to 'rid him of his boredom'. She tried to inject into this 'great shining son of hers' something of her own belief in life, and succeeded, for a while, in bringing him peace of mind. When he left, he had recovered a certain degree of mental calm, and she continued, by letter, her cure of cheerfulness:

George Sand to Dumas fils: I send you my love. Go on with your reaping. It's a devilish good cure for iron in the soul. Showerbaths are good too, so is work, so is the country. Everything helps so long as the mind is healthy, and the heart sincere. With youth and genuine talent, one can get over anything ... I am an optimist in spite of all that has torn me to pieces: it is probably my only good quality. You'll see, it'll come to you. When I was your age I was just as tormented as you, and far more sick in body and mind. I grew tired of digging down into other people and myself, and a day came when I said: 'To hell with all that!' The world is wide, the world is beautiful. The things we believe to be important are so ephemeral that it's not worth while thinking about them. In life there are only two or three really genuine and important things, and they, so obvious and so easy, are precisely those which I have ignored and despised. *Mea culpa!* But I have suffered as much as it is possible to suffer. I deserve to be forgiven. I'd better set about making my peace with the Good God.[3]

He had grown so deeply attached to Nohant that he longed to go back there with the princess, and did, finally, overcome her shyness. He was then at Villeroy, and referred, with delicacy, to his 'hostess'.

Dumas fils *to George Sand, September 20th, 1861*: I thank you, as Monsieur Prudhomme would say, for yours of the 15th ult. and take my pen in hand to express my lively sense of gratitude. I understand that my hostess has written to you ... I won't conceal the fact that to be received by you at Nohant, and to see you face to face, will, in her opinion, be a great occasion. If you are a good woman, she is a very good child: so, you see, there will be no awkwardness ... The one outstanding problem is the little girl whom she does not want to leave all alone among the forty-four rooms of this great barrack of a place, and would like, with your permission, to introduce to you. She can sleep in her mother's room on a sofa. She, as a young Muscovite traveller, will love that! So don't think our bringing her with us will in any way embarrass you.

But now, be prepared to tremble! Here is the bitter pill! I have a friend, a very great friend, who is very much like one of your Newfoundland dogs. He is known as Marchal the Gigantic, weighs thirteen stone, and has a brain to match. He can sleep anywhere, under a tree, under the well. May I bring him?[4]

Naturally, Sand replied that the young Slav and the bulky painter would be welcome. Charles Marchal was an intimate friend of Dumas, an artist from Alsace with no very great talent, but an agreeable companion who made witticisms and was attractive to women. This chubby giant was known to his friends under the nickname of 'Brimborion I', or, alternatively, 'The Mastodon'. His unconventionality bordered on tactlessness. An inveterate sponger, and a not very discreet

Don Juan, he made no bones about telling everybody of his successes. The indulgence shown him by Dumas *fils* was worthy of Dumas *père*. It is amusing to picture the arrival at Nohant of the Villeroy caravan, and the astonishment of the Naryschkine princesses on being introduced into the high-spirited and well-found bohemianism of life in that famous house. Dumas was the bearer of a sad item of news. Rose Chéri, of whom he and Sand were both so fond, had died of diphtheria caught while nursing her sick children. 'You mustn't cry,' the charming actress had said to her husband a short while before her death, 'because our children are safe.' Rose left behind her an unsullied memory of perfection and self-sacrifice.

George Sand's Diary, September 25th, 1861: After dinner, at ten o'clock, Madame and Mademoiselle Naryschkine arrived, with Dumas and his friend Marchal, who has a nice face. We talked for a while in the drawing-room ... then gradually dispersed. We were gay, but sadness was lurking round the corner, and we could not keep from speaking about poor Rose.

October 1st, 1861: Dumas read aloud the beginning of *Villemer*. It is quite charming. Went upstairs to do some work. In the evening, Dumas recited and read some poetry.

October 9th, 1861: Dumas left at seven in the morning. Marchal is staying on.

October 10th, 1861: Long visit to Marchal. Spent the evening with him in sensible talk while they were rehearsing downstairs.

October 16th, 1861: Marchal and Maurice gave us a marionette performance.

October 19th, 1861: Marchal is becoming my big baby.[5]

And so it was that, having arrived at Nohant as odd-man-out with Dumas and his Russian females, Marchal prolonged his stay in Berry long after his friends had departed. He had gone for two days; he remained for several months. His passion for the marionettes had won him Maurice's devoted friendship. George's feelings, of a quite different nature, were extremely displeasing to Manceau (who had been prince-consort for more than ten years). On the pretext of painting his hostess's portrait, Marchal shut himself away with her in the studio. Dumas *fils* sent them his blessing.

Dumas fils *to George Sand, November 23rd, 1861*: I told you how good an influence you could have on him with the high authority of your talent, your example, and your advice. That is a thing I could not have, being too near in age, character and sex to the overgrown urchin. It gives me great pleasure to know that you appreciate him at his true worth, and also that he has discovered a new talent in himself. I have often told him that he ought to try his hand at *portraits*, but painters have a curious way, which I don't understand, of looking down on that department of their craft.[6]

At last, in December, Marchal left Nohant. No letter, no word of affection, nor even of thanks, came from him. In vain did Sand write over and over again. No reply reached her. Mad with anxiety, she turned to her 'dear son' Alexandre, in the hope of finding out what had happened to her big baby, her painter-in-ordinary:

Dumas fils *to George Sand, February 21st, 1862*: I shall always be terrified of introducing anyone into that house of yours where everything functions so smoothly between friends that the least bit of grit in the machinery may easily throw it out of gear! Our friend Marchal has already shown himself ungrateful, has he? It's rather soon, I must say! He might at least have thanked you for the six thousand francs commission which he has received from the Prince, because it was only thanks to you that he got it. Alas! alas! I very much fear that humanity is not the noblest work of God![7]

February 26th, 1862: I am in a furious temper today, largely as a result of my mastodon's silence! I know no more than you do where he is. Lack of education prolonged into maturity looks a great deal too much like lack of heart. The poor fellow does not realize even yet that when one has enjoyed the hospitality of somebody like you for so long a period, hospitality so sincere and so profitable, one ought at least to answer the letters one so frequently receives ... The rascal is as egotistical as Nature herself, and shows an artlessness, a seeming innocence which goes far beyond anything I have ever known.[8]

Throughout the year 1862, an active correspondence went on between the 'dear son' and the 'dear mamma'. Dumas finished *Le*

Marquis de Villemer, and generously surrendered all his rights in it to George Sand. He moaned a good deal about life:

> I have just spent a week in that state of despair which is the product of an utter inability to work. I have found it impossible to write a single line of either the novel or the play. I have taken a solemn vow that, if I can complete them as I have planned, I will send pens and ink to the devil! I have been splashing about in that particular pond ever since I was born, and I've had about enough of it. Unless one can completely transform oneself three times in one's life, as Raphael did, and as others have done whom I need not name, art is a wretched calling. Besides, I am *not* an artist — neither in form nor in content. I use my eyes adequately: I see reasonably well, and express what I see to some purpose — but I bring nothing to my work of enthusiasm, poetry or exaltation. What I produce is all dry and ironic. That kind of writing may amuse and startle the public, but, in the long run, they grow sick of it, and it most certainly kills the author. Once I've got this double job off my hands, I shall try to live *for myself*, and if something new emerges from this second life, a new sensation, a new faith, even an illusion, then I will communicate it to others. If not — I won't.
>
> I wonder whether the person of whom you and I have so often spoken will be united *in name* or *in fact* with this second life? Not that it very much matters. I don't take the life of her world so seriously as to split hairs. All I want is simple happiness, like that hero of one of Méry's plays who asked no more
>
> > . . . pour prix de ses services
> > Que de passer ses jours dans le sein des délices.
>
> Well, we shall see, and none of all those good and true generalizations which you have made to me will be lost in the great argument which I shall conduct with myself.⁹

On the whole, he inclined to marriage with the Person:

> And now, about the little girl. On that point you are absolutely right. We must wait until she is married, or, anyhow, until she is old enough to decide, of her own volition, that she does not want to marry. About her character I will say nothing. You would have to watch it in action for some considerable time before you

could draw any conclusions. She loves her mother, intelligently. She is never really happy except when she is in the country. She loves food and never wearies of talking about her digestion — a favourite pleasantry with women of breeding. She pushes economy so far as to have her mother's old dresses remade for her own use, and to darn her own stockings! She will gladly give her money to the first needy person who comes her way. Very dignified and haughty with her equals, she is gentle and sympathetic with simple folk of no matter what social class. *Names* do not matter in the least to her, and she would be perfectly willing to be called Madame Benoît. Study delights her, especially study of the exact sciences, not for any reason of pride, but because she is as economical of her small stock of learning as she is of her pocket-money. It is for herself that Olga wants to *know*. She is, as a rule, silent, and speaks only when speaking is necessary. She suffers from her liver, and that throws a sort of melancholy over all I have told you of her. She has no imagination. That is as I see her. It is for you, dear Mamma, in your woman's wisdom, to draw your own conclusions.

For the time being, mother and daughter are going to settle down in the Bois de Boulogne, where they have found a charming house with a lovely garden, which communicates with your son's without too indiscreetly seeming to do so. We shall be able to see as much of one another as we want, but each will have his, or her, own home, and so appearances will be maintained. Now that the back of the job has been broken, it remains for God and Czar to do the rest. It is their turn.[10]

CHAPTER III

In which George Sand presents Dumas fils *with Two Children*

SAND'S strength and wisdom always exercised a profound influence on weak men. She had torn masterpieces out of
Musset; she had bolstered up Chopin; she had consoled Flaubert.
Dumas *fils* had confessed to her the nature of his own private distress.
'Life was never presented to me in its true colours. Those whose duty
it was to see to my upbringing had other things to do, and it would
ill become me to blame them for not having, when dealing with me,
the wisdom they never had when dealing with themselves.' George
had described to him, with that masculine outspokenness which was
so peculiarly her own, the physical breakdown of her marriage, and
had made him understand what a horrible ordeal the first experience
of sex may be for a young girl, if her husband is lacking in delicacy.
'We bring them up like little saints,' said George, 'and we hand them
over to their husbands like young fillies.'

Out of this idea, Dumas, after a long period of reflection, made a
play, *L'Ami des Femmes*. Madame de Simerose, terrified by the
memory of her own wedding night, has separated from the clumsy and
unimaginative husband whom, without realizing it, she still loves. She
finds herself alone in the world, exposed to the assaults of those who
promise her a 'different kind of love'. She would be utterly lost were
she not watched over by the 'friend of women', Monsieur de Ryons,
who, like Olivier de Jalin in an earlier play, is a projection of the
author's own temperament. Monsieur de Ryons knows everything,
understands everything, foresees everything. Women's hearts and
men's desires hold no secrets for him. He contrives meetings, or
prevents them. He guesses intentions, and denounces faults. In short,
he plays, in the universe of Dumas *fils*, the same part as does Monte-
Cristo in that of Dumas *père*. He imposes missions on himself; he lays
traps; he conducts interrogations. Pitiless to evil-doers, he is the
author of cruel sayings:

From the way in which Monsieur de Ryons hides behind a mask of irony [says Paul Bourget], from the mordant way in which he darts his bitter words to right and left, always on his guard, always armed; from the attitude of moral bravado which he assumes at every meeting, whether it be with a woman or a man, with a young girl or an old fogy, it is clear that, for this misanthrope, life has been too hard. He never admits that it has dealt him wounding blows, nor does he complain. For that, he is too proud. But the tone in which he speaks, bantering and deliberately ferocious, the way in which he strives to master his interlocutor from the very first exchange of words, and to impose his own superiority, his evident mistrust of every phrase and every gesture — all these things are, as it were, a sort of avowal and a sort of indictment.[1]

It was the complaint of Dumas *fils*, himself.

Jane de Simerose astonished and shocked the Paris public. For forty days *L'Ami des Femmes* struggled against astonishment, silence, embarrassment and, at times, noisy interruptions. A man in the stalls, after Jane's description of her wedding night, jumped up and shouted: 'This is disgusting!' A courtesan, famous for her innumerable and openly acknowledged love affairs, said: 'It outrages every woman's most intimate feelings of modesty.' Nevertheless, every woman, or almost every woman, knew in her heart that the play contained a deal of truth. But Dumas had 'betrayed the sex, and divulged the mysteries of the Bona Dea'. At that time, nobody spoke openly of such things, especially not in the theatre, where women reigned supreme. If a play hoped to succeed, it must deify woman and sacrifice man.

Monsieur de Ryons irritated the female members of the audience. Admittedly, he *is* irritating. But what they could not forgive him was not the fact that he was their master (women never feel hatred for the men who master them) but that he never allowed himself to be enslaved by any of them. In the first version of the play, a beautiful, rich and intelligent young woman flings herself at his head, and is repulsed. So great was the hostility of the public to this incident that, as the result of a protest made by Montigny when the play was revived, Monsieur de Ryons was made to marry Mademoiselle Hackendorff. Taine and, later, Bourget, protested. They preferred Monsieur de Ryons to be uncompromising in his attitude. Dumas, in his preface to the play when it appeared in print, dared, at a safe distance from the gold and scarlet auditorium, to reaffirm his thesis that 'women must be kept in a condition of slavery'.

> Woman is a limited being, passive, functional, there for the asking, living in a perpetual attitude of expectation. She is the only uncompleted work which God has left to man to take and finish. She is an angel on the scrap-heap. Nature and society are in agreement, and always will be, no matter what claims women may advance, that they should be subjected to the Male. Man is God's instrument, Woman is Man's. *Illa sub, ille super.* There is no getting away from that.[2]

In real life, Monsieur de Ryons did get married. Prince Naryschkine having died at Sciez on May 26th, 1864, Dumas was able to wed the princess, now a widow. On Saturday, December 31st, 1864, Maître Ancelle, Baudelaire's guardian, and mayor of Neuilly-sur-Seine, declared Alexandre Dumas *fils* and Nadejda Knorring, widow of Alexandre de Naryschkine, to be man and wife (in the presence of Alexandre Dumas *père* and Catherine Labay, both consenting parties).

The bride had chosen as witnesses her lawyer, Henri Mirault, and her gynaecologist, Charles Devilliers. Dumas was accompanied by two friends: the painter, Chandellier, and the Assistant-Keeper of the Bibliothèque Nationale, Henri Lavoix. There were no other guests. The ceremony had been kept secret because every Act of Marriage has to be read aloud, and this one contained a very unusual clause:

> The future husband and wife have made a declaration in my presence acknowledging as their own a female child, registered at birth at the Mairie of the Ninth Arrondissement of Paris, on November 22nd, 1860, under the names of Marie-Alexandrine-Henriette, born on the 20th of the same month, to Nathalie Lefébure, explaining that the name of the mother was supposititious. . . .

For four years, the 'little Lefébure' had been accounted for as an orphan whom the Princess Naryschkine had found and brought up.

Dumas fils *to George Sand, December 15th, 1864*: Dear Mamma: I am getting married in a few days from now. That irrevocable decision was reached only an hour ago. I inform you of it without the loss of a moment. I do not ask for your consent, because I know that I have it already. But, as an obedient and respectful son, I am giving you the news before it becomes common property. I embrace you with all my heart, and Manceau, too.[3]

Sand's wedding present was a vase in the shape of an urn. Was it, perhaps, designed to receive the ashes of liberty?

Dumas fils *to George Sand, January 1st, 1865*: When I received that beautiful bowl, and everyone round me was saying: 'Where can that lovely thing have come from?' I said: 'I bet it's from Mamma.'

Free at last to acknowledge his paternity, Dumas did so with delight. His letters to George Sand are filled with allusions to Colette, a ravishing and highly gifted child. At five she knew French, Russian and German, and said her evening prayer in all three languages.

March 28th, 1865: Colette is wonderfully well. She is not yet in a fit state to appreciate her grandmamma but that will come.

On August 21st, 1865, Sand lost Manceau, her lover-secretary, who had for some time been suffering from lung trouble. It only remained for Marchal to take his place. George clung to him and heaped upon him the most flattering attentions.

George Sand to Charles Marchal: *Cher petit*, I have never seen *Orphée aux Enfers* which, I hear, is pretty and amusing. I daren't ask Offenbach [for seats] though he has always treated me with great kindness. Since you must know it by heart, I won't condemn you to seeing it again with me ... Reserve for me some part of your time and good-will for us to go together to see something you may find amusing, or something, at least, you have not seen before. I send you a hug. I suppose you know that Madame Dumas is now *over her trouble*? I am going to see her tomorrow.[4] I was at Palaiseau today. Madame Plessy told me yesterday that she would try to get us two good seats for *Le Lion amoureux*.[5]

But the Mastodon clung to his independence. He worked away in his studio with charming, nude and unreluctant models. Whenever Sand paid him surprise visits she found the door locked. He was more than willing, however, to attend the Magny dinners with her, Dumas *fils* and Olga Naryschkine, who, at eighteen, was growing into a beautiful, a very beautiful, young woman. Nadejda (whom her husband had rechristened 'Nadine') had made a slow recovery from her miscarriage, and was convalescing at Marly in preparation for the ordeal of a renewed pregnancy, the couple being set on producing a 'Dumas grandson'.

> *Letter from Dumas* fils: Madame Dumas has been sentenced to seven months in bed if she really wants to produce a new Alexandre — the need for whom is markedly felt, in spite of the good health, intelligence and splendour of the other two ... I certainly did a good job there! ... That damned sea-bathing always has the same result![6]

By reason of her years and her looks, the young Olga found herself in a somewhat difficult position where her mother was concerned. It is never very easy for a newly married mistress to have a daughter of marriageable age. Dr Devilliers having prescribed rest and country air, Dumas had persuaded his old friend Leuven to lend him his house at Marly. There he installed his ailing wife, while Olga, for educational reasons, remained at Neuilly. Several compatriots, freshly arrived from Moscow, took it upon themselves to enlighten 'Little Russia', now a grown woman, on her legal position. She was beginning to wonder whether her mother's romantic adventure might not seriously have prejudiced her future, by compelling her to live far from a fairy court where she would have occupied a distinguished position as a cousin of the Romanovs.

> *George Sand's Diary, February 3rd, 1866*: Fetched Marchal and went with him to dine at half-past six with the Jauberts. The parents of both husband and wife were present, Lehmann, the Dumas, father and son, and three or four friends of the family. Dumas *père* had cooked the whole meal, from soup to salad! Eight or ten wonderful courses. After dinner we chatted ... he really is charming ... Marchal took me home.

> *February 4th, 1866*: Alexandre came at two. I read *Jean*[7] to him. Delighted to find that he likes it. I didn't read too badly. He gave me some excellent advice. He has such a quick, lucid way of seeing the problems, and knows exactly how to get over them. I feel happy in my mind now about Bouli,[8] and am writing to him

at once ... Alexandre is going to find out whether the rue de Richelieu would like it.[9] If not, then it'll be the Gymnase. Dined alone at Magny's. Weather perfectly frightful ... not a very gay evening ... Odéon: *La Vie de Bohème*: what a delightful play — all charm and heartbreak!

February 6th, 1866: Demarquay just looked in to tell me that Madame Dumas has had a miscarriage, and that Thursday's dinner has been put off. Took me to Magny's where I dined, after which I hired a fly and, in spite of a blinding headache, drove to the Avenue de Neuilly. The driver was drunk, so was the horse. But the three of us were on excellent terms and managed to find the house. Madame Dumas is calm and very brave. No pain for the moment — but will there be tomorrow? The child is *alive* and waiting to be born. It's all very odd. Alexandre was sweet to his wife. Went home in the same fly. The horse stumbled and the driver slept. But my headache had gone.

February 9th, 1866: Snatched an hour from work to pay a few visits and write some letters. Madame Dumas has had a miscarriage. A good deal of pain, but everything all right now. Walked to Magny's for dinner.

February 11th, 1866: Went to Neuilly — such a business in the dark, and cost me ten francs. Madame Dumas has been through a very bad time. Will have to keep her bed for a month. Alexandre and Olga never leave her side.

In August 1866 George Sand went to see Alexandre *fils* at Puys, a small fishing village near Dieppe, where he had bought a rather ugly and not very comfortable house, but in a beautiful position.

George Sand's Diary, With Alex at Puy [sic], Sunday, August 26th, 1866: Perfectly lovely country. Marvellous weather. Charming company. Lavoix, on the point of leaving: Amédée Achard, staying on: Madame de Belleyme, just arrived. The children delightful. The lady of the house *most* friendly, but not a good manager. Servants, impossible! A sort of ingrained grubbiness everywhere. Nothing but a jug and a bowl for washing, and then one has to fetch the water for oneself! Windows that don't shut, and the bed icy . . . But everything wonderful in daytime. Went to look at the woods and the sea . . . These wooded slopes are a

real garden of Eden. The sea pearly-grey with blue lights ...
white sand and quartz pebbles shaped like starfish. The cliff
white and chalky. General effect pale and soft. A children's dance
at the casino. A lot of overdressed and ugly women. Excellent
dinner at the house, but at eight o'clock the lady was taken ill.
Alexandre went to bed. Impossible to read with only a candle!
Storm in the night. Torrents of rain and very cold. I coughed
and coughed until I thought I should tear myself to pieces.

With Alex at Puy [sic], *August 27th*: Weather damp but
quite pleasant. Stayed on to hear the Preface and two acts. All
very fine and good. Excellent dinner after which everyone drifted
away and I was left alone with Madame de Belleyme! This sort
of life which ends at eight, leaving one with an overfed feeling,
doesn't suit me at all! And what a business washing, dressing, and
all the rest is, to be sure! *How* uncomfortable everything is, but
charming, all the same.[10]

From Puys, George Sand went on to Croisset, to see Flaubert.
There she found 'efficient servants, cleanliness, plenty of water, all one's
needs anticipated — in fact, everything perfect'. Flaubert's mother, a
charming old lady, was a very much better housewife than 'la Grande
Russie'.

The failure of *L'Ami des Femmes* kept Dumas *fils*, for some time,
out of the theatre. The difficulties of marriage with a complaining
wife 'who oscillated between apathy and violence' served to confirm
his misogyny. Nadine, when pregnant, was sunk in a state of sluggish
lethargy. When convalescent, she had outbursts of jealousy. When she
saw Alexandre the centre of a group of women admirers, she compared
him to Orpheus among the bacchantes. Now that Madame Dumas
was in her forties, she suspected every young woman, even her own
daughter, of flirtatious intentions. The nervous instability of 'la
Grande Russie' made of her an intolerable companion. Dumas *fils*, at
that time, was carrying on a lively correspondence with a naval officer
who was also a talented writer, Commandant Rivière. On him he
poured out all his gloom.

Dumas fils *to Henri Rivière*: Dear friend ... I am delighted to
hear that you have returned to your sailor's life. It was high

time you broke free from those inferior varieties of excitement which are unworthy of a man like you. The high seas with all their tempests are infinitely preferable to those storms in a teacup by which women now try to persuade us that we ought to allow ourselves to be victimized. Take the word of a man who has frequently made his escape by swimming, and now feels the solid ground under his feet, that the truth lies in work, and in that solidarity with humankind on which men of intelligence, like you and I, do exercise, and should exercise, an influence. It is far better worth while to command a good crew, or to write a good play, than to be loved, no matter how sincerely, by the most alluring of women. *Amen.*

You are the kind of man who ought to keep the watch from midnight till four a.m., on the bridge of a ship, and not cheek by jowl with Madame Canrobert. Woman is an element to which one must needs be inured, as I have been, from childhood, if one is to be able to do battle with it and remain unwearied and unendangered. All these lovely goddesses have worn you out, and not enriched you with any new experience, because they are as hollow as bells. The sea saddens me, I don't like it, except when I am on it, and, to that extent, it is rather like women. This rather boisterous jollity on my part will prove to you that my body is in a somewhat better state, though it has not been so often afloat on the female element as I would seem to imply . . . Meanwhile, I am working, from habit or impulsion, with all the discouragements inherent in that strange occupation which turns the brain into the semblance of a threshing machine.

One woman, one only, and she an optimist, still found favour in the eyes of this resentful individual — George Sand. Her rapid recovery after Manceau's death astonished Dumas:

Dumas fils *to Henri Rivière*: I would have answered your letter before now had it not been for the fact that I had to give all my attention to Madame Sand who has just suffered a great grief. She has lost Manceau who, for the last fifteen years, has been her companion, and the managing-director of her life. He died after four months of terrible suffering, in the small hours, at Palaiseau where they lived together . . . We buried him three days ago, and have been trying, since then, to provide distraction for the survivor. She has enormous vitality and great strength of will. A brain like hers makes us men feel humbled, because few of us would be capable of starting a new life, as she has done, after enduring such a succession of shocks as have come her way. Since life is nothing but pain and a weariness of the spirit, we must come to terms with it once and for all, and try to watch the passage of events like the cows which chew the cud by the roadside, and look at the carriages going by. Let us be like Minerva, the cow-eyed goddess. This epithet, which most people find incomprehensible, was, no doubt, intended to express the impassivity of supreme wisdom, which, I suggest, is only another name for supreme indifference. Friendship seems to me to be the only sentiment worth living for.[11]

Since a vague feeling of apprehension kept him, at that time, from writing for the theatre, he was working at a novel, *L'Affaire Clemenceau*. In this he found release for his frustrated resentment against women. It is the confession of a murderer who has killed his wife, after having long adored her, not only because she has deceived him, but because she has been the very essence of lying and falsity wrapped in an outer covering of perfect beauty. Pierre Clemenceau, a sculptor, and (of course) a natural son, has had (no less of course) a needle-woman for mother. The whole of the first part of the book has every appearance of being autobiographical. The woman whom the hero marries, Iza Dobronowska, is a Pole (a fact which permits the author to take an indirect revenge upon the whole race of perfidious Slavs). We know from Dumas that this Iza had much in common with his first mistress, Madame James Pradier.

Dumas fils to George Sand, May 26th, 1866: This wretched *Affaire Clemenceau* is rapidly getting on my nerves, and the sooner I can be rid of it, and back in my own small world of the theatre, where a man cannot talk French even if he wants to, the better. I am floundering about within sight of the end, but the knock-out blow won't somehow come ... Life isn't always fun. Until one is twenty, it's all right, but after that, all one can hope for is a quick end. Meanwhile, until the happy consummation comes, I'd better go on churning out copy, since that seems to be the only thing I am fit for.

June 5th, 1866: Dear Mamma, last Thursday, at twenty minutes past six in the evening, Iza finally passed away, thus justly expiating the abominations of which she had been guilty. Until that moment, her murderer, who has the honour to be your son, had been working like one of the negroes from whom he is descended on his father's side. Ouf! I have no feelings of remorse, though I am as much torn in pieces as I would be if I had, and am more than usually conscious of my admiration for you who can turn out so many masterpieces so quickly.[12]

L'Affaire Clemenceau became the talk of the town. Dumas was pleased by its success though he was exhausted by all the work he had put into it.

Dumas fils *to Commandant Rivière*: You will see from my handwriting that you have to do with somebody who has gone flabby. I can no longer hold a pen in my fingers, so hard have I driven it for the last two months. But now the creature is dead, dead as a doornail, I have just had two hours' rest. Last night I slept for eleven. I'm no longer good for anything else. It is the same with Madame Dumas. As a result of having to get some rest for the two of us, and that just for the sake of a book which only I was concerned in the making of, I hope that in a month I may be in a fit state to begin all over again.[13]

He was, and started to write again for the theatre. The strange thing is that this giant of a man should have been reduced to such a state of exhaustion by what had been, after all, a very short novel. The only explanation is that the passions aroused in him by so much brooding on immodesty and lust had been excessively violent. In order to achieve some degree of calmness, he now set himself the task of putting a good woman on the stage, and decided to go into the country while doing so. He had leased — in the hope of finding peace and quiet in which to work — a small châlet at Etennemare, high above Saint-Valéry-en-Caux. It reminded him of the happy days of his youth.

There he wrote a new play, once again inspired by George Sand, *Les Idées de Madame Aubray*. His central character, a woman of the Sand type, professes the most high-minded ideas on marriage, on social problems and illegitimate children. Suddenly she finds herself on the horns of a most painful dilemma. Either she must be false to the ideas of a lifetime, or she must allow her own son to marry Jeannine, a young woman whom he loves. This girl has previously had a lover, and now works in order to bring up her fatherless child. Madame Aubray hesitates, momentarily breaks down, and finally chooses the heroic solution. In the name of faith and humanity she blesses the union of her only son and the unmarried mother.

Dumas first read the play to Madame Sand. Edmond About and Henri Lavoix were also present. Its success was not for a moment in doubt. Sand, the idealist, and About, the sceptic, mingled their tears. Not content with this first test, Dumas went to Provence where he read it to another friend, Joseph Autran. The same success, the same tears, greeted it. Autran, who suffered with his heart, even had a slight seizure. What author could ask for more? Montigny accepted the play with enthusiasm for the Gymnase. All the same, Dumas was apprehensive. How would the hypocritical public receive this affront to their prejudices? He was soon reassured.

George Sand's Diary, Nohant, March 17th, 1867: Good news: according to a telegram from Alexandre, *Madame Aubray* has been a 'colossal success' ... *March 18th*: An article by Sarcey on *Madame Aubray*. Letters about Dumas. I *must* go to Paris! ... *Paris, March 23rd*: Dinner with Dumas, then home. Received and wrote a number of letters. To the Gymnase with Esther. *Madame Aubray* wonderful. I cried. Superbly acted.[14]

The doctors had kept Nadine Dumas in bed since October, so that she might, in due time, be delivered of the hoped-for son and heir.

Dumas fils *to George Sand, February 26th, 1867*: The infant is knocking as hard as *he* can at the door of the world. Obviously, he does not know what sort of a place it is. Madame Dumas is swelling as hard as *she* can.

April 20th, 1867: The little Dumas looks like arriving at about the same time as this letter will arrive at Nohant.

But, alas! Nadine's child turned out to be a girl. She was called Jeannine, after the heroine of *Les Idées de Madame Aubray*.

CHAPTER IV

Twilight of a God

How will the end come? White hairs are sounding a respectful summons. BALZAC

DUMAS *père* had brought back with him to Paris, on his return from Italy, a singer named Fanny Gordosa, 'black as a prune', but appetizing, and, in the matter of love, of so extreme an ardour that her Italian husband, completely worn out by her demands, had insisted on her wearing damp towels round her middle parts. Dumas freed her from her wrappings, and satisfied her needs, with the result that she became passionately attached to him. They lived, at first, in the rue de Richelieu, opposite the famous photographer, Reutlinger and, later, at Enghien, where Dumas rented the Villa Catinat for the summer months of 1864. There, the old Monte-Cristo racket began over again. The Gordosa filled the house with trombone-players, fiddlers and lutanists. She practised her singing all day long, snuffing up the fulsome flattery of all the spongers who settled down on the premises, rifled the sideboard and made hay of the food. Dumas, godlike as ever, worked on the second floor, and went down to the billiard-room in the evenings, where he met old friends: Noël Parfait, Nestor Roqueplan, Roger de Beauvoir and a host of anonymous parasites. When the larder appeared to be exhausted, he would discover in odd corners, rice, tomatoes and ham with which he concocted wonderful risottos.

Many women put in an appearance at Enghien: Eugénie Doche, who was still playing in the son's *La Dame aux Camélias*, but by no means turned up her nose at the father; the charming Aimée Desclée of the velvety eyes, to whom Dumas *père* had paid court in Naples when she was appearing there in the plays of Dumas *fils*; the pretty young beginner, Blanche Pierson; the superb tragedienne, Agar, who, though christened Léonide Charvin, had taken a biblical name in the hope of bringing Rachel to the public mind; Esther Guimont, with the hoarse roar of a lioness; and Olympe Audouard, who had a way of fainting at the most inopportune moments. In vain did the Signora Gordosa mount guard. 'An woman!' she would cry when some female intruder turned up. 'Say her that Dumas him ill!' Dumas put up with the tantrums of this spitfire of a Fury, who went about swathed in a transparent dressing-gown which revealed all the delights in store.

To Mathilde Schoebel, the daughter of a French orientalist, whom he had known as a child, and always called 'my little briar-rose', he said: 'Fanny's a bit eccentric, but she's got a heart of gold.' Then he added, not without a smirk of self-satisfaction: 'It's sheer humanity that makes me have mistres*ses*: if I had only one, she would be dead in a week! . . . I don't want to exaggerate, but I really believe that, up and down the world, I have got more than five hundred children!'[1]

When he went back to Paris in the autumn, he installed The Gordosa at his new address, N° 70 rue Saint-Lazare. For some time he gave a big dinner-party every Thursday, after which the diva sang, while the master of the house hid away out of earshot of the 'screeching', and worked. It was not long before a storm burst. The hot-blooded exponent of coloratura caught Dumas, one night at the theatre, *en flagrant délit*, in one of the boxes, and roused the audience with her screams. Finally, he got rid of her. She left, announcing that she was going back to her husband, taking with her what little money remained in the drawers.

Dumas went to live at N° 107 Boulevard Malesherbes, with his daughter, who had parted company with her Berrichon husband, Olinde Petel, now suffering from mental derangement. After making a retreat at the Convent of the Assumption, she took to illuminating old missals. She, too, seemed to be not quite right in the head. She dressed as a Druidess, wore a garland of mistletoe round her forehead, and carried a sickle attached to her girdle. Dumas was proud of her, as he was of everything that had to do with him: less than he was of Alexandre, to be sure, but then, Alexandre rather frightened him. 'He loves moral problems,' he confided to Mathilde Schoebel, 'look at this last book of his; see what he's written on the fly-leaf: "To my dear papa, from his big son and colleague." ' There was a note of bitterness in Dumas's voice, as he added: 'He's put the adjective the wrong way round, just to please me, but he doesn't believe a word of it.'[2]

In this he was wrong, but he feared the reproaches of the 'young 'un', and took infinite care that he should never meet at his father's house the lightly clad nymphs with whom the old man surrounded himself. Dumas *fils* had bought, at N° 98 Avenue de Villiers, a house with a small garden, which drew a gibe from his father. 'It's all very nice, Alexandre,' he said, 'all very nice, but you really ought to leave your drawing-room window open just to give your garden a breath of air.' The son, who was saddened by the sight of so libidinous an old age, seldom went to see his father, and this was the cause of much complaint. 'I never see him now, except at funerals,' he said, 'perhaps I shan't see him again until my own.'

The 'Cordelia of this King Lear'[3] was the little Micaëlla, Émilie Cordier's daughter, a sickly child, with waxen-yellow cheeks, a large, lipless mouth, but inexpressibly charming eyes. He gave her dolls dressed by Marie Petel. 'I *do* hope my little pet will come,' he would say when he had a Madame de Pompadour or a Louis XV ready for her. The little pet came, and he smothered her with kisses. He was always afflicted with feelings of regret that the 'stupid admiral' had prevented him from officially recognizing her as his daughter.

Dumas père *to Micaëlla Cordier, January 1st, 1864*: My dear little Bébé, I shall give you a great hug, I hope, in three or four days' time. I long to see you again, but you must not tell anyone that I am coming, because I want to have plenty of time for kissing you. Marie and I are bringing you two lovely dolls and some toys. Expect me any day after the third.

Your father: A. D.[4]

Dumas *fils* disapproved of the presence of Micaëlla under his father's roof, referring to her as 'that trollop's daughter'. He refused to regard her as his half-sister.

'I saw your father at the Odéon. Heavens! what an amazing man he is!' wrote George Sand, in 1865. At sixty-three he was still a 'force of nature'. His powers of work had in no way diminished. He had just had two plays performed, each excellent in its kind: *Les Mohicans de Paris* and *Les Prisonriers de la Bastille*. *Les Mohicans de Paris* had long been censored on the grounds that the play, set in 1829, contained too many liberal allusions. A letter from the author to the Emperor had routed the censor. Napoleon III raised the embargo.

In the meantime, he had published one of the best of his novels, *La San Felice*, the action of which takes place in the Naples of Marie-Caroline, Lady Hamilton and Nelson. It was the period in which the generals of the French Revolution were making and unmaking kingdoms; the period of young heroes girt with the tricolour sash; the period of General Dumas. The background is provided by the highly individual city in which the author had just spent four years, and the book is filled with memories of Neapolitan friendships. An Italian hero, worthy of the Musketeers, fells six men single-handed. The seascapes of the Bay of Naples, the descriptions of fishing-smacks in a storm, glow with natural colour. If his intention had been to show that, in order to be Dumas, he had no need of Maquet or of anybody else, he succeeded admirably. *La San Felice* appeared as a serial in *La Presse,* and Girardin paid Dumas at the rate of a centime a line — 'as much as Madame Sand gets', he said with pride. It was his swan-song — 'by no means wet with tears, but touched with an unaccustomed gentleness'.

The Goncourts have sketched two remarkable portraits of Dumas *père* in his sixties:

February 1st, 1865: Dined yesterday with the Princess — a company of literary men, among them, Dumas. A kind of a giant with a negro's hair now turning 'pepper and salt', the small eye of a hippopotamus, bright, shrewd and for ever on the watch even when the lids are half closed, and all this in an enormous face the features of which are vaguely hemispherical, like those the caricaturists give when they portray the moon with human characteristics. There is something about him very hard to define, something of a 'barker' at a fair, something of a merchant from the *Arabian Nights.* He is never at a loss for words, though what he says is neither very brilliant nor very mordant, and quite lacking in verbal colour. What he talks about is facts, curious facts, *staggering* facts which he drags up in a hoarse voice from the recesses of a tremendous memory. And always, always, always, he talks about himself, with the vanity of a great child which never gets on one's nerves. He will inform you, for instance, that an article of his on the subject of Mount Carmel has produced 700,000 francs for the Order ... He drinks no wine, takes no coffee, and does not smoke. He is an abstemious athlete of the world of the newspaper serial and of literary 'copy' in general.[5]

February 14th, 1866: Just as we were conversing, in came Dumas *père*, white tie, white waistcoat, enormous, sweating, puffing, shouting with laughter. He is just back from Austria, Hungary and Bohemia. He talked about Pesth, where he is being played in

Hungarian; about Vienna, where the Emperor lent him a room in the Palace for a lecture; about his novels, his theatre, the plays of his which they won't put on at the Comédie-Française; about his *Chevalier de Maison-Rouge*, which has been banned; then, about some piece of theatrical privilege which he cannot get, then, again, about a restaurant which he wants to start in the Champs-Élysées.

A prodigious 'I', an 'I' on the scale of the man, but brimming over with a sort of boyish good nature, and always sparkling with humour. 'What can you expect', he said, 'when the only way the theatres can make money is to have plenty of tights — which split? . . . That's what's happened to Hostein. He told his dancers never to wear anything but tights which would be sure to split . . . and always in the same place. That pleases the opera-glass addicts. But the censor stepped in at last, and the opera-glass sellers are now on their beam ends.'[6]

But, though his talent was as great as it had ever been, he was finding it difficult to get his plays produced. He was becoming like one of those old actors who, in order to make ends meet, will accept any engagement in no matter what theatre. A Grand Théâtre Parisien had been built under the arches of the Vincennes railway line. It was as oddly constructed as it was situated. Dumas had one of his best dramas revived there, *Les Gardes Forestiers*, which had first been seen at the Grand Theatre, Marseille, in 1858. The trains set the whole place shaking, the whistles of the locomotives drowned the voices of the actors. The play went so badly that it had to be taken off almost at once.

To help his company, he organized a tour, and promised to go round with it whenever he could. In the suburbs and in the provinces his prestige was still high, and he was loudly acclaimed. In his native Department, the Aisne, the enthusiasm passed all bounds. At Villers-Cotterets, two performances had to be given. Then all the inhabitants of the little town crowded in front of the hotel where he was staying. Through the windows he could be seen in an apron and a cook's cap 'stirring the gravy, and generally turning out a dinner for his people'. The ovation redoubled. This reception consoled him for the well-intentioned but slightly mocking condescension which Parisians now showed towards their old entertainer. Once more he dreamed of having a theatre *of his own*, and tried to start a Nouveau Théâtre

Historique by opening a subscription. He sent out thousands of prospectuses, but the only replies he got were from a few young admirers of *The Three Musketeers*. His ancient magic no longer worked. Had he been practical-minded and sensible, he could still have lived in ease. In 1865, Michel Lévy paid him forty thousand gold francs; in 1866, he signed a contract, on terms very advantageous to himself, for an illustrated edition of his works.[7] But money ran through his fingers. Ten times he had made a fortune, and eleven times he had been ruined. 'I have earned millions', he said. 'I ought to have a regular income of two hundred thousand francs, and all I've got is two hundred thousand francs' worth of debts.' He could no longer even pay the allowance he had been making to his sister, Madame Le Tellier.

In 1866 he left Paris, which had become, for him, an inhospitable dwelling-place. He visited Naples, Florence, then Germany and Austria. From this journey he brought back a novel, *La Terreur Prussienne*, well written and shrewdly observed. He had sensed the threat of impending danger. 'Nobody who has not travelled in Prussia can have any idea of the hatred felt for us by the Prussians. It amounts to a monomania which clouds even calm and untroubled minds. No minister in Berlin can hope to be popular unless he makes it pretty plain that, sooner or later, war with France is inevitable.' Under the name of the Count of Boeseweck, he had painted a premonitory portrait of Bismarck. As was fitting, the hero of the novel, a young Frenchman, Benedict Turpin, challenges the German nationalists to tests of skill in pistol-shooting, fencing and boxing, and beats them all. (The Bridge of Brixen. Porthos *Unter den Linden*.) He was writing at the top of his form, and the book, at any other time, would have made the reputation of a young author. But the public now had other needs and other gods. His warnings on the subject of Prussia were laughed at. 'How that fellow Dumas does love a leg-pull!' It was not possible to take seriously an old sultan who dropped on his outlandish odalisques 'his last half-dozen handkerchiefs'.

CHAPTER V

The Death of Porthos

Alexandre Dumas had no fear of death. 'She will be kind to me', he said, 'because I will tell her a story.' ARSÈNE HOUSSAYE

By 1867 his debts were still mounting. In spite of the loyalty of his readers, the Dumas account with Michel Lévy showed a debit balance. The rent of his apartment on the Boulevard Malesherbes was unpaid. Much of the furniture had already been sold. The only precious mementoes from which he refused to be separated were the sketch which Delacroix had made on the occasion of the famous ball in the days of his youth, and the towel spotted with the blood of the young duc d'Orléans. The servants gave notice. To his 'little briar-rose', Mathilde Schoebel, he complained that some of his 'lady friends' showed rather too much greediness in the way they searched the drawers of his desk. 'They haven't left me so much as a twenty-franc piece!' he said with comic despair.

Mathilde had found him ill, lying in his study which served him also as a bedroom. On the walls were collections of old-fashioned weapons, a portrait of General Dumas, and another of Alexandre *fils* by Horace Vernet.

'What a good thing you came!' he said. 'I'm not well. I want some herb tea . . . I've called, but nobody answers . . . I think I've been left alone . . . and I've got to go out tonight . . . Do be a dear and see whether there are any shirts in the chest of drawers, and a white tie.'

But all she could find were two night-gowns — unironed.

'Have you any money on you? If so, can you lend me enough to buy an evening shirt?'

The young girl hurried to the shops, but it was late, and, in the few which she found still open, there was nothing large enough for that gigantic body. At last, at *'la Chemise d'Hercule'*, she discovered a starched dicky dotted with red devils. An evening shirt embroidered in red! Dumas took his courage in both hands, and put it on. It was a great success. 'People thought it was a souvenir of my friendship with Garibaldi!'[1]

Don Juan's last effort was the conquest of a young American equestrienne and actress, Adah Isaacs Menken[2] who, on the stage of the Gaîté, clad in the minimum of clothes, rode a fiery thoroughbred. She looked charming in pink tights, and had just taken London by storm in *Mazeppa*, a drama inspired by Byron's poem. Breathlessly, the audiences watched her stretched and bound on her horse's back, being carried up a practicable mountainside at the gallop. The final leap had, more than once, nearly cost her her life. Crowded houses applauded such daring allied with so much beauty.

A Jewess, born in Louisiana (though she claimed obscure Spanish origin, and signed her name '*Dolores Adios los Fuertos*'), Adah Menken had turned horsewoman after hesitating for some time on a choice of vocation. Turn and turn about, she had been a stage 'extra', an actress, a dancer, and had posed, naked, for a number of sculptors. She had worked for a while on a paper (*The Cincinnati Israelite*), and had toured the country lecturing on Edgar Allan Poe. This extraordinary young woman knew English, French, German and Hebrew. After a conversation on the immortality of the soul, she had once swallowed three glasses of brandy. She was mad about poetry, and wrote melancholy verses on the subject of her short-lived and unhappy love affairs. Walt Whitman, Mark Twain and Bret Harte had all been her friends.

Three times divorced,[3] she had married her last husband, James P. Barkley, only because she wished to legitimize the child with which she was already pregnant. Her fourth marriage took place in New York, on August 19th, 1866. Two days later, the bride embarked on the steam-packet *Java*. She was never again to see either America or her husband.

She felt drawn to Paris. She made her first appearance there, on December 31st, 1866, at the Théâtre de la Gaîté. Somewhat later, early in 1867, Dumas went to her dressing-room to congratulate her. She flung her arms round his neck. Both hungry for publicity, the two of them thought it fun to make a public spectacle of their mutual and memorable 'love at first sight'. Dumas proudly annexed his conquest. She made a point of being seen everywhere hanging on his arm. He showed her old Paris, and explained to her the living Paris of their own day. She found it pleasing to her vanity to have her name linked with that of a 'giant of the literary world'. She could not love him, but he amused and flattered her. For some weeks he recaptured

357

something of his youth, and took the horsewoman to Bougival, to the very same inns where, forty years earlier, he had taken Catherine Labay, the young needlewoman. Along the river bank the oarsmen were singing.

In those days, when photography was still a marvel, Adah Menken enjoyed posing before the camera with all the great men in her life. It was a 'rite' to which the eccentric traveller clung passionately. Dumas committed the imprudence of allowing himself to be thus perpetuated, in his shirtsleeves, with his mistress, wearing a close-fitting jersey, perched on his knee. Yet another 'picture' shows her snuggling in his arms with her head pressed to his enormous chest. He looks as though he were choking, but his bright eyes are softened by a veil of infinite kindliness. It is as though he were saying: 'Yes, I know it's all very absurd, but she wanted to be taken like this, and I love her dearly!' The photographer, Liebert, to whom Dumas owed a small sum of money, thought that the loudly publicized sale of this group would compensate him for the unpaid bills. He had the prints exhibited in a great many shop windows. The young Paul Verlaine composed a triolet on the subject:

L'Oncle Tom avec Miss Ada,
C'est un spectacle dont on rêve.
Quel photographe fou souda
L'Oncle Tom avec Miss Ada?
Ada peut rester à dada,
Mais Tom chevauche-t-il sans trêve?
L'Oncle Tom avec Miss Ada,
C'est un spectacle dont on rêve.[4]

George Sand to Dumas fils, *May 30th 1867*: How this business of the photograph must have annoyed you! But there you are! The consequences of a bohemian life make a sad spectacle in old age. What a pity it all is.[5]

When lectured by his son, Dumas *père* replied: 'My dear Alexandre, in spite of my burden of years, I have found a Marguerite with whom to play the role of your Armand Duval.'[6]

He was mad about the wonderful young woman, with her misty blue eyes, long black hair and magnificent body, whose stories enchanted him. She was an inexhaustible Scheherazade, and had constructed for herself an imaginary past, the fantastic episodes of which she loved to talk about. It was untrue that she had hunted buffalo with cowboys in the Far West, but she could discuss theology with as much knowledge as horsemanship. She had never been a dancer at the opera, nor a tragedienne in California (for seven years Adah Menken had had only one part, 'Mazeppa'). On the other hand, it was true that she could read both Greek and Latin. Her story of being captured by redskins whom she had 'hypnotized' by dancing the movements of a serpent was but an epic fable. At Dayton (Ohio) she had *not* performed the duties of captain of the Guard, dressed as a man. But Charles Dickens and Dante Gabriel Rossetti did write her friendly letters which she proudly displayed to her French admirers.

From Dumas *père*, her lover of sixty-five, she received ardent declarations: 'If it be true that I have talent, how much truer it is that I have love — and both are for you.'[7] The departure of Adah for Austria, where she had to fulfil an engagement at the Theater an der Wien, as 'Mazeppa', put an end to a liaison the scandal of which had helped further to destroy such prestige as the old man still had.

As a result of his follies, he was passing through a period of acute financial distress. His son would gladly have helped him, but he disliked having to admit that he was in 'embarrassed circumstances'. He started a new paper, *Le d'Artagnan*, which was to appear thrice weekly. He asked his friends to spread the news of its forthcoming publication. 'I needn't tell you who the fellow is. Thank heavens, he's been talked about quite enough already. What *is* important is that people should know that he has been resuscitated, and is once again drawing his sword in defence of his old principles.'[8]

But *Le d'Artagnan* was a failure. Dumas wrote to the Emperor, asking him once again to subsidize a theatre. The Emperor refused. The days of miracles had gone. Old age is hard on magicians.

In 1868 a maritime exhibition was organized at Le Havre, and Dumas was invited to lecture. He spoke also at Dieppe, Rouen and Caen. At Le Havre he made renewed contact with his daughter Micaëlla whose mother was living there in married bliss with Edwards (after bearing five children, *'the Admiral'* had at last succeeded in becoming a wife). In Le Havre, too, he again met Adah Menken who, having only just recovered from a fall, and finding Fate against her in England, was on her way back to Paris, where she had succeeded in getting an engagement at the Châtelet. At first there had been some idea of Dumas writing a play for her, but Hostein, the manager, thought it more economical to revive *Les Pirates de la Savane*, for which scenery and costumes already existed. During rehearsal, she was taken seriously ill, and died on August 10th, 1868. Her maid, her grooms, a handful of actors (fifteen persons in all) and her favourite horse, followed the hearse from the rue Caumartin to Père-Lachaise.

The news of her death reached Dumas at Le Havre. When he returned to the Boulevard Malesherbes, feeling far from well, he engaged a small, timid creature as secretary. He stuffed her with sweets, and poured into her ears, from morning till night, plans for new plays and new novels. But a day came when his ideas seemed confused, and his stories all mixed up. He shut himself away and started to re-read his earlier books.

'Each page reminds me of a day gone by,' he said. 'I am like one of those trees with bushy foliage filled with birds. They are silent at noon, but wake towards the end of the day. When evening comes they people my old age with song and the beating of wings.'

His son came to see him, and found him deep in a book.

'What's that you're reading?'

'The *Musketeers* . . . I always promised myself that when I was old, I would find out for myself what it's worth.'

'How far have you got?'

'I've finished it.'

'And what's your considered view?'

'It's good.'

But, when he re-read *Monte-Cristo*, he said: 'It's not a patch on the *Musketeers*.'

Ever since Dumas senior had deserted Catherine Labay, she had lived a model life. The idea of bringing the two old people together, and, perhaps, of marrying his parents at long last, must frequently have occurred to Dumas junior, the moral preacher and the moral man. Dumas *père*, when sounded, seemed to be tempted. At Neuilly he would have found a solid home and a thoroughly domesticated woman, who could have run the house and received his friends. No doubt he also hoped that an aged companion, long disillusioned, would have put up with his final flings.

The refusal came from Catherine Labay. 'I am over seventy', she wrote to a woman friend; 'I am always ailing, and live very simply with one servant. Monsieur Dumas would blow my small flat to smithereens . . . It is forty years too late.'[9] The story of Adah Menken made her smile. 'Ah!' she said, 'he's still the same; age has taught him nothing.' She died on October 22nd, 1868. She was seventy-four.

Dumas fils *to George Sand, October 23rd, 1868*: Dear Mamma, my mother died yesterday evening, very peacefully. She did not recognize me, and did not know that she was leaving me. Does one, if it comes to that, ever really 'leave'?[10]

Dumas *fils*, accompanied by his friend, Henri Lavoix, Keeper of the Bibliothèque Impériale, went to the Mairie at Neuilly to register her death. He made a declaration that the dead woman was 'a spinster without profession', and gave his own name, adding — 'her only son, Alexandre Dumas Davy de la Pailleterie'. But in the space headed DAUGHTER OF . . . the following words are written on the official register: 'The names of the father and mother (of the deceased) have not been supplied'; which seems to indicate that Catherine was the natural child of parents unknown.

Dumas fils *to George Sand, Seignelay, near Auxerre, Yonne* (*end of October, 1868*): We are in Burgundy, with friends. It was there that I heard the tragic news, and there that I returned after the sad duties had been completed. I have done a deal of crying, and still do. It was an outlet which I needed, not having cried at all for more than twenty years. It has been said that a mother should do good to her son, even in dying . . . Maurice's book was lying on my table all through the night which followed the agonizing event. The most I could do was to cut the pages. I have it with me, and will read it as soon as I am once more capable of taking in what I read.[11]

Dumas *père* spent the summer of 1869 at Roscoff in Brittany. He was looking for a quiet spot in which to write a *Dictionary of Cooking* which had been commissioned by the publisher, Lemerre. He had brought a cook with him, Marie by name, who did not at all like Roscoff. 'Ah! monsieur,' she said, 'we can't stay in this place.' 'It is possible that *you* won't stay, Marie, but I shall.' 'But monsieur will find nothing to eat!'[12] That evening, the good people of Roscoff, proud of having the great Alexandre Dumas in their midst, brought him a gift of two mackerel, a lobster, a sole and a skate as big as an umbrella. But though there was an abundance of fish, the artichokes were as hard as nails, the beans full of water and the butter far from fresh. 'Curious items on which to have to depend while writing a book on cookery.' But this did not prevent Dumas from writing with his usual zest. Marie, however, was furious, and gave a week's notice. Then Roscoff collectively adopted Dumas. He dined now in one house, now in another, and his hosts went out of their way to provide him with delicacies. 'In this eagerness to make much of me,' he wrote, 'there was something which brought tears to my eyes.' In March 1870 the manuscript (unfinished) of the *Grand Dictionnaire de Cuisine* was delivered to Alphonse Lemerre. This monumental work was not published until after the war, with the unexpected collaboration of one of Lemerre's 'young men', Anatole France.

In the spring of 1870, Dumas left for the south. He felt that he was at the end of his strength, and hoped that the sun would give him new life. It was at Marseille that he heard of the declaration of war. The news of the first disasters brought about a complete collapse. Partly paralysed as the result of a stroke, he dragged himself as far as Puys, and rang at his son's door. 'I have come to you to die,' he said. He was given an affectionate welcome. 'My father was brought to me in a completely paralysed condition. It was a painful sight, though not wholly unexpected. Beware of women, that is the lesson to be drawn.' It was the return of the prodigal father. He was put to bed at once in the best room in the house, and fell asleep.

He was still uneasy about the value of his works. One morning he told his son that he had had a dream, and in that dream he was on the top of a mountain each stone of which was one of his books. But the mountain had collapsed beneath him like a sand-dune.

'Sleep soundly on your block of granite,' Alexandre said to him. 'It is high enough to make one giddy, but very solid; as lasting as our language, as immortal as our country.'

At that the old man's face brightened. He pressed his son's hand and embraced him. Close to his bed, on a table, were two golden louis, all that remained of the millions he had made. One day, he took them between his fingers, gazed at them for a long while, then said: 'Alexandre, everybody says that I have been prodigal. You yourself wrote a play on the subject. Well, see how wrong people can be. When I arrived in Paris for the first time, I had two golden louis in my pocket . . . Look, I have them still.'

The little Micaëlla, who was in a *pension de famille* at Marseille, wrote, asking for news. It was Dumas *fils* who answered her letter.

Dumas fils *to Micaëlla Cordier*: Mademoiselle — the three letters which you wrote to my father were delivered to me. I was unable to communicate their contents to him, because you spoke in them of his illness, and we are doing our best to hide from him the fact that he is ill at all. The affectionate name you give him is proof that you love him as much as one can love anybody at your age, and that he has a deep affection for you. I believe that I once saw you in his house, when you were very small.

I have decided to send you news of him, since he cannot do so himself. He has been extremely ill but is now a little better ... Should he be well enough to read the letters addressed to him, I will let you know ... I will send you his answer. It is natural, Mademoiselle, that, since you love my father, I should do everything in my power to render you a service.[13]

It was not long before the sick man relapsed into almost complete silence. When the weather was fine, his chair was wheeled down to the beach, where he sat gazing at the waves. Now and again, a sentence, a word, showed that he was thinking of death, God and immortality. 'Alas!' he murmured, 'I am one of those beyond all hope, who say *adieu*.' Of what was he dreaming while the green swell rolled in almost to his feet? Perhaps of his many heroes, of the *Musketeers*, of the *Forty-Five*, of Buridan and Antony; of those who had given life to his plays, Dorval and Bocage, Frédérick Lemaître and Mademoiselle George, of Mademoiselle Mars and Firmin; perhaps of a dusty office in the Palais-Royal where, in a book left open at random, he had found the subject of his first drama; of the little room where he had made love to Catherine Labay; of the first bird he had shot; of a slated, pointed steeple; of General Dumas, a persecuted hero, a giant unarmed; perhaps of the day when he had bestridden Murat's sabre.

Alexandre Dumas fils *to Charles Marchal*: Dear friend: just as your letter reached me I had it in mind to write to you of the unhappiness which has fallen upon us, though we had seen it coming for some days. My father died on Monday evening, at ten o'clock, or rather, he fell asleep, for he suffered no pain. On the preceding Monday he had expressed a desire to go to bed at midday; since then he did not wish, and, after Thursday, was unable, to get up. He slept almost continuously. Nevertheless, when we spoke to him, he replied perfectly distinctly, and always with a smile. His unbroken silence, and his apparent indifference to all around him, did not begin until Saturday. He woke only once more, but then with the old familiar smile which you have so often seen. It had not changed. It needed death to wipe it from his lips. As soon as he was dead, his face underwent an immediate alteration, and the severe and solemn lineaments asserted themselves.

His reason, even his wit, showed no deterioration. He told us many interesting things which I shall confide to you because you will make only good use of them. To give you some idea of the gaiety which animated him, he said, on one occasion, after a game of dominoes with the children: 'You must give them something when they play with me, because it must be very tedious for them.' A Russian maid whom we have, developed a great fondness for the huge invalid, who was always so smiling and so gentle, and at times had to be helped like a small child. My sister one day said to my father: 'Anouschka thinks you are very handsome.' 'Encourage her in that view!' he replied.

He said one of the loveliest and most poetical things imaginable about Olga. She came often to see him, and, as you know, looks a little bit like the Virgin of Perugia, with her long dresses, her slender hands, and our baby whom she leads or carries with her wherever she goes. Her air of a great lady, of Our Lady, had always much impressed my father, and he was ceremonious, even respectful in his manner towards her. The other day, when he was dozing, she went into his room, and, seeing him sleeping, withdrew. He opened his eyes, and said: 'Who's there?' 'It is Olga,' said my sister. 'Let her come in.' 'So you're fond of Olga, are you?' 'I scarcely know her, but young girls are the very essence of light.'

Every day he said something either gay or touching, of the kind I have described. Latterly, I asked him: 'Do you feel you'd like to work?' 'Oh, no!' he answered, and in the tone of his voice I seemed to catch the memory of all the work he had done in forty years.

These, dear friend, are a few details of which you can make use should you have occasion to speak of him. They will serve as a denial of the rumours which have become current, that there had been a softening of that powerful brain, whereas what it asked was only the right to enjoy a little rest. He found that rest among the elements of nature, and in the bosom of his family, with, before his eyes, the wide expanse of sea and sky, and his children round him. He had a genuine passion for Colette. He felt so happy and so comfortable in a peace which had been so rarely his in the course of his wandering, prodigal and restless life, that he drew in contentment with every breath he took. They say that the Prussians will be in Dieppe today! So, you see, he will have lived and died in the atmosphere of an historical novel.

I write in haste, before the ceremony which is to take place in the little church of Neuville, close to Dieppe, today, December 8th, at eleven o'clock. I am having him temporarily buried there.[14]

Micaëlla learned of the death of her papa from something said at the table-d'hôte in her pension at Marseille. She burst into tears. Her mother dressed her in mourning black. George Sand was at Nohant, cut off from Normandy by the German army. All the same, her 'last little one' tried to write to her:

Dumas fils *to George Sand, Puys, December 6th, 1870*: My father died yesterday, December 5th, at ten o'clock in the evening, without pain. You would not be to me what you are if I did not send this news, first of all, to you. He loved and admired you more than he did any other woman.[15]

Only later, after the conclusion of hostilities, could she send him her sympathy:

George Sand to Dumas fils, *Nohant, April 16th, 1871*: You are reported to have said about your father; '*He died, as he had lived, without noticing.*' I don't know whether you did actually use those words, or whether they have merely been attributed to you, but here is what I wrote in the *Revue des Deux Mondes*: '*His was the genius of life, and he was not aware of the coming of death*' — which means the same, doesn't it?[16]

Dumas fils *to George Sand, April 19th, 1871*: The remark you quote is true. I wrote it to Harrisse, and lay claim to it now only because you and I were of one mind, though using different terms. I am trying to find here (and will have it sent from London if it is not available in Dieppe) your article on my father. You will realize how eager I am to read it. Why did you not have the happy thought of sending it to me, or, at least, of telling me in advance on what date it was to appear? I care very little what views Monsieur de Saint-Victor, or any other wag, may have expressed about my father (whom he has probably never read), but yours are precious to me. One day, perhaps, I too shall put into words (now that father and son are separated) what I think of that extraordinary and exceptional man. He towered over his contemporaries, and was a sort of childlike Prometheus who, in the long run, overcame Jupiter, and spitted his vulture. There is a most interesting and curious study to be made on the question of how much the racial mixture influenced him. But am I the right person to embark on that kind of physiological inquiry? That remains to be seen when I have done it. If it turns out to be good, true and useful, then I *shall* have been the right man to undertake it. Meanwhile, I am reading and re-reading him, and am over-whelmed by his vitality, erudition and fecundity: by his good humour, his wit, his charm, his power, his passion, his temperament, and by that gift he had of assimilating things, and even people, without either imitating or plagiarizing. He is always lucid, precise, luminous, healthy, simple-minded and good.

He never dug deep into the human heart, but he had an instinct which took the place in him of observation, and into the mouths of some of his characters he put utterances which were truly Shakespearian. He may not have sounded the depths, but he very often rose to the highest point of the ideal. What a sure and firm hand he had when it was a matter of getting the right lines into the right places; and how admirable was his feeling for composition and perspective! There is a gusty richness of fresh air in every-thing he wrote, and what a variety of tone! Just consider for a moment some of the characters — the duchesse de Guise, Adèle d'Hervey, Madame de Prie, Richelieu, Antony, Yacoub, Buridan, Porthos, Aramis — to say nothing of his *Impressions de Voyage*. He was so amusing, too! Somebody once said to me: 'How is it that your father never wrote a boring line?' 'Because,' I answered, 'it would have bored him to do so.' The whole man is in his *sayings.* He had the good fortune to have been able to write *more* than anybody else, and of always having *had* to write in order to support himself and God knows how many other people. Yet he never wrote anything it didn't amuse him to write. Get somebody to read to you some evening, what you probably never have read — the travel book about Russia and the Caucasus. It is amazing. You travel through the country, and through his experiences, more than seven thousand miles, without once drawing breath or feeling tired. You, Balzac and he are the three great ones of this century. But now, farewell to all that. There is no one else, and there won't be![17]

Another woman, when the war was over, wrote generously: Mélanie Waldor, who had survived for forty years so many broken geraniums:

Mélanie Waldor to Dumas fils, *Fontainebleau, April 20th, 1871:* I think of you, my dear Alexandre, in thinking of your father whom I shall never forget. I have brought with me your two letters, which moved me deeply and touched my heart, especially that of October 18th, which is so beautiful in its simplicity and its truth that I re-read it often because it makes me feel that I am back again with your father and with you, whom I shall never cease to love.

I know you feel convinced that there is another life, and have studied much in the Sacred Books. In them alone can one find strength and lasting consolation. If ever there was a man who was always good and charitable, that man was most certainly your father. Only his genius equalled his great kindliness and his unceasing desire to serve others. God was kind in giving to him, at a time of frightful disasters for France, a painless death surrounded by his children. He never knew the immense, the eternal grief of seeing those die to whom he had given life.

Goodbye, my dear child. I am still very weak and dare not surrender to my memories. When shall we be able to go back to Paris, safely? While we wait for that more or less distant time, I want you to know that I shall feel an almost maternal happiness in seeing you, and talking with you, again.

Your old and very sincere friend

M. Waldor[18]

Dumas *fils* had written to Maquet, both to announce his father's death, and to ask what had happened to the records relating to the financial arrangements which had been made between the two collaborators. Dumas *père*, in the course of his last talks with his son, had muttered something about 'secret accounts'. The son, while expressing doubts on the subject, had asked whether any concealed transactions had, in fact, taken place.

Auguste Maquet to Dumas fils, *September 26th, 1871*: My dear Alexandre, the sad news you send has deeply pained me. As to 'secret accounts', that was pure imagination on your father's part. He never ventured to speak to me on the matter, but, had he done so, five minutes explanation would have settled everything.

Actually, my dear Alexandre, you know better than anyone how much work, talent and devotion I gave to your father in those tremendous collaborations which, so far as I was concerned, swallowed up both fortune and renown. But I should like you to know, too, that my share of his generosity and delicacy was even greater. Please believe that between me and your father there was never any misunderstanding about money, and that no 'account' could ever have been settled between us for the very good reason that even if *half a million* were in question, I should still be the debtor.

With a sense of the greatest delicacy you have asked me to tell you the truth. Here it is, straight from my heart. My affection for you is of long date, and still remains constant.

A. MAQUET.

Please do not believe a word of what your father may have told you about these mysterious accounts. He, I am sure, never can have.[19]

Dumas *père* was buried in December 1871 at Neuville-lès-Pollet, less than a mile distant from Dieppe. The manager of the Gymnase, Montigny, who also was living at Puys, spoke in the name of the friends of the dead man. As soon as the war was over, Dumas *fils* had the body exhumed and taken to Villers-Cotterets. Baron Taylor, Edmond About, Meissonier, the Brohan sisters, Got and Maquet were all present on this occasion. The grave had been dug next to those of General Dumas and Marie-Louise Labouret.[20] After the speeches,

Dumas *fils* said a few words: 'My father had always wished to be buried here, where he had left so many memories and friendships. Those memories and friendships welcomed me yesterday evening, when so many arms were offered to assist the bearers in carrying the body of their great friend to the church ... It was my wish that this ceremony should be not so much one of mourning as of festival, less a burying than a resurrection.'[21]

What a strange mixture of persons and events: a Norman marquis, a black slave, an hotel-keeper of the Valois, a Swede with a passion for the theatre, a well-read civil servant, a professor interested in history, a romantic period, a popular press — all these had combined to give birth to the greatest story-teller of all time and of all lands.

PART NINE

GOD THE SON

Have you converted Dumas *fils* to the religion of art? If you have, then you are, indeed, a great magician. GUSTAVE FLAUBERT, *Letter to Feydeau*

T HE old Pan had left the world 'all but empty'. In his place, the public found a noble figure, no less powerful than he had been, who had inherited his glory. Popular feeling made scarcely any distinction between *The Three Musketeers* and *The Lady of the Camellias*. The apotheosis of the father had become that of the son, who already wore the halo of an immense prestige. The war of 1870, and its fatal after-effects, had fanned and justified his moral fervour. Like Renan, he saw the root cause of defeat in the decadence of manners. From now on, he set himself in his plays to pillory the faults of the age, and, in his essays, to suggest remedies for what he condemned. He wanted to be a lay-preacher.

On June 15th, 1871, he wrote in a newspaper, *La Sarthe*: 'The time has come for France to make a collective effort, to set its shoulder to the wheel, to show energy and determination, to be animated with one only, unceasing, fanatical idea — to discharge its obligations abroad, to work for national regeneration at home. France must live austerely and think intensely, must be patient and unassuming. Fathers must work, mothers must work, children must work, and servants, too, until such time as the honour of the house has been regained. When, throughout the world, the regular and continuous beat of all this labour shall be heard, and someone asks: "What is that noise?" each one of us should be in a position to say: "It is France in the process of transformation, France striving to liberate herself." '

The most difficult thing of all for the moralist is to live in accordance with his own principles. Dumas's private life was far from being what he wanted it to be. No doubt he loved his daughters, no doubt he drew the bonds of faithful friendships tight. But Nadine Dumas, nerve-racked, irritable, jealous and violent, could scarcely be considered the ideal companion for a writer. A great many women, often charming women, were only too ready to play, in the life of a man who was generally held to have outstripped all his contemporaries in the knowledge of the human heart, a role which was inadequately filled by the official mistress of his home. These queens of the jungle caressed the tamer. Dumas resisted their advances, or, when at times he yielded, did so with such discretion that his moments of weakness left few traces. Nevertheless, temptations were not lacking, and some of them were sweet. One of the most interesting of these incidents concerns his relations with Aimée Desclée.

CHAPTER I

Aimée Desclée and 'Une Visite de Noces

THERE are some actresses who make a brilliant start in their careers but never develop into geniuses; others who, after a flat beginning, flower in the hothouse atmosphere of passion, and astonish their fellow professionals. To this latter group Aimée Desclée belonged. She was the daughter of a lawyer; her background was that of the upper bourgeoisie, and she had been brought up with the aim in view of making a rich marriage. Her father, who knew nothing of business, was ruined, and she found herself faced with the necessity of earning a living. She was lovely to look at, an excellent musician, and might have become a singer. She thought, however, that success might come more easily to her as a comedy actress. She trained at the Conservatoire, but showed no real enthusiasm for her work, and received no award when she took part in a competition as the countess in the *Marriage of Figaro*. Her elegant figure was pleasing, her fine eyes looked with nonchalance at the jury, but her performance lacked power. Her beauty, nevertheless, brought her an engagement from Montigny who tried her out, at the Gymnase, as Rose Chéri's understudy in *Le Demi-Monde*. The experiment was a failure. She seemed to be saying all the time: 'I really don't know what I'm doing here.' The lack of enthusiasm in the audience, the author, and the other members of the company, soured the spoiled child in her. She left the Gymnase for the Vaudeville where, out of sheer perversity, she soon found herself on the slippery slope which leads to employment as a figurante in tights.

She was twenty-three, a ravishing creature, and much courted. She decided to leave the stage and to live off her admirers. Why should she work hard without any tangible result, when, merely by pleasing, she could make a fortune from accepting what so many men were eager to give? She passed from lover to lover. Her epigrams were quoted. She became one of the wittiest women in Paris. In 1861, the death of Rose Chéri gave her the chance of returning to the theatre in big and important parts. But she no longer felt any interest in acting. She wandered from country to country, from Baden to Florence, from Spa to St Petersburg. Many light women were envious of her, but, after each ephemeral adventure, her lovely, disillusioned eyes seemed to be saying: 'No, I've not yet found what I want.' At a fancy-dress ball given by the Gymnase company, at which she appeared as a vivandière, she met Alexandre Dumas *fils* in pierrot costume. It was a melancholy occasion which neither seemed to find amusing. He thought her brilliant and aloof, and felt that she was moving in a dream. 'She seemed,' he said, 'like the princess in the fairy-tale, bewitched, and waiting for the prince who should awaken her.'

'I have had,' she told him, 'a few pleasures, a few moments of joy, but never happiness.'

At twenty-five she passed through a religious crisis, and thought of entering a convent. But 'a priest who had, apparently, never read the parable of the lost sheep, repulsed me, saying that I was not worthy to enter into the House of the Lord'.[1]

Sickened (like Juliette Drouet and Marie Duplessis before her) by the freakish whims of her rich 'protectors', she decided to resume her career as an actress, and make herself independent. She returned to the stage in a mood of humility, resigned, patient, prepared to take small parts and to do as she was told. But a professional past of successive failures dogs an actress. No one took her seriously, and no friendly hand was extended to her. What should she do? Go on tour? A theatrical manager, Meynadier, took her to Italy and gave her the leading female parts in the plays of Dumas *fils*. 'The Meynadier company has brought us the charming Desclée,' wrote Berton's mother to her son, 'you would scarcely believe how she has come on ...' She was now giving good performances because she had learned through suffering. In Italy she had an immense success, social as well as professional, due to her charm, her distinction, her wit and her talent. At Naples, Dumas *père*, then in the full glory of his Garibaldi adventure, threw his 'arms, his heart, and his house, open to her'.

Aimée Desclée to Dumas fils: I have played for the people of Naples all the adorable women you have created. My success has been terrific. We have often talked about you, and from my heart I thank you for all this happiness.[2]

While ceaselessly working she continued, in Italy, from 1864-7, to live a rather wild life, always looking for 'the prince', for the man who should bring her salvation. But the abyss grew ever deeper between her true wishes and her way of life. In 1867, her manager took her to Brussels where she played in a revival of *Diane de Lys* at the Théâtre des Galeries-Saint-Hubert. To Dumas *fils*, who happened to be in Brussels at that time, rehearsing *L'Ami des Femmes* at the Théâtre du Parc, she wrote, asking him to come to see her: 'Everybody tells me that I have made progress, but I shall not believe it until *you* tell me so.' He went, more out of politeness than curiosity, and not at all hopefully, but she had not been on the stage for five minutes before he was amazed to discover that she had become a great actress. 'An odd sort of drawling, nasal voice reminiscent of Arab singers' seemed, at first, monotonous, then gripped the attention. Her figure was elegant, her waist supple (she wore no stays). Her eyes were large and black, and her expressive face could pass in a moment from tenderness to violence. Her cheeks, 'even under the make-up, showed, as it were, a perpetual pallor, eloquent of some secret suffering. Her shoulders were thin, and her breast almost flat. Taken all in all, she was one of those women whom other women call ugly, though, compared with her, all the pretty women seem to be utterly insignificant. . . .'[3]

He went round to congratulate her and, when he got back to Paris, told Montigny that he must at once offer Desclée an engagement at the Gymnase. Montigny did not say much. Dumas was talking of the woman who had made so poor an impression on him, as though she were a second Dorval! But he did offer her a contract, though on pretty poor terms. Dumas begged Desclée to accept, and promised to write a new play for her. She replied that she found Paris frightening, that in other countries she had had the feeling that the audiences loved her, and had been able to play as she knew she ought to play without any sense of being inhibited, and without constantly watching herself; that she loved a bohemian way of life, and that, apart from all that, the Parisians thought her ugly, stupid, etc. etc.

Dumas fils *to Aimée Desclée*: You are neither old, ugly, nor stupid: you are just a highly strung, unstable and irresolute woman. No sooner have you done something than you begin to wonder whether that was what you really ought to have done, and you are once again in the grip of curiosity about some totally different sensation which will have precisely the same effect on you as its predecessors. You are now in the mood to wonder whether you should appear at the Gymnase, and you would not be displeased should something arise which would give you an excuse for wanting to do something quite different from what you wanted at first. You will get no such pretext from me. Since we are exchanging philosophic confidences, it is well that we should pursue the argument to the end, and both of us realize clearly why it is that I take an interest in your person and your talent. Not only are you neither too old nor too ugly for the part I have written for you, nor for any other part, but you have reached just that point in your career at which a woman who has been on the stage for ten years, can, and ought to, become a great artist. What, occasionally, makes you sad is that you are going through a phase, which comes to everybody, when they already tend to look back to the past, and dare not look forward to the future. You are beginning to ask yourself whether your instincts, your tastes, your intelligence, your whole temperament, in short, do not call on you to do something other than what you have done so far. To be a pretty woman, to act here, there and everywhere, to have a lover, or several lovers, to be called before the curtain after the fourth act, to exhibit your beauty while, all the time, keeping your heart under lock and key until you find a man worthy of opening the box — whom no woman ever does find — all that may, for a while, create an illusion by letting external activities become substitutes for real life; but it cannot last for ever. A moment comes (it has come to you now) when one takes a backward look, when one says to oneself: 'What's the use?' — when one can already count more than one funeral on the road one has trodden, when one's armour weighs too heavy, when one regrets all the things for which one has been able only to hope, when, under the compulsion of discouragement, one cries out: 'Too late!' Well, it is precisely at such a moment that really well-tempered natures remake themselves, transform themselves, achieve a new birth. It is the moment of metamorphosis.

Then it is that, instead of remaining a strolling-player making the round of shabby provincial theatres, and living on the crumbs which fall from the theatrical tables of Paris, one takes one's stand on solid ground and becomes an intelligent and convinced artist. If one comes on a play in which one can find one's own personal impressions, one's own secret feelings, one can take from its box the heart which has served no purpose, offer it for the public to eat, and have it given back, still intact and ready for another creation. This may not be the happiness of which you have dreamed; it may not be the absolute good, but neither is it absolutely bad. It is possible to work upon the intelligence, the sensibility, the enthusiasm and the noble aspirations of the human spirit, to serve the purpose of something temporary, something elusive, something which, all the same, has its long-range effect, like a ray of sunshine on a drop of water, which comes just when it is needed. If one loves, one knows what one wants: if one is loved one knows that it is for some reason quite different from the more or less of pleasure which one animated corpse can give to another corpse in the grip of a desire to reproduce itself. I don't suppose you expected this little lecture. I send it to you because I believe you capable of understanding it, and worthy of receiving it. Now is your moment. Take advantage of it. You are in a station where many lines of rails converge. Be sure you are on the right one, and the right one is that which I have indicated. You will live to thank me when you are really old.⁴

There is something of the arrogant self-assurance of Monsieur de Ryons or of Olivier de Jalin in this tirade, but it had a substratum of truth. Desclée obeyed, returned from Florence, and went to see Montigny. He was disappointed. 'What sort of a woman is this,' he asked Dumas, 'whom you've made me take on? She came to see me at the theatre in a green and grey-checked woollen dress, and a creased hooded cloak such as Norman peasant-girls wear ... What's it all about? I'm beginning to feel frightened! No *Diane de Lys*, no *Froufrou* will ever emerge from that!' 'Be patient,' replied Dumas, 'you'll soon change your mind.' He was right. Desclée's new appearance on the Paris stage was a triumph. Dumas *fils*, after seeing a few rehearsals, went back to Puys. Desclée wrote him a charming letter in which she begged him to be present at her first night, on September 1st, 1869, but in vain.

Aimée Desclée to Dumas fils: Next Wednesday, a charming little play is to be put on at the Gymnase. The sky is overcast: it is real theatre weather. But mark this: it has been announced that a little actress will be making her first appearance. The newspapers all agree that she is really very pretty. It seems that there is some sort of music in her gullet, that those who have heard once come back to hear again. Is that true? The gentleman who is going to see you at Puys, bearing this letter, has promised to bring you back with him, but can his promises be taken seriously? Monsieur Alexandre Dumas *fils*, I love you. Your little servant —

AIMÉE DESCLÉE[5]

He did not go. She gave him an account of the occasion:

It's all over. Ouf! I had lovely dresses of every colour, and an aigrette in my hair which made me look like a little performing dog. The house was packed to bursting ... I spent the whole evening feeling my pulse to see whether it was beating more quickly than usual: nothing, a flat calm; no uneasiness, no fear, no joy, absolutely nothing. This, therefore, a first try-out, will be the end. Poor me! When it was all over, the manager said to me: 'You were as good as Rose,' and that's saying a lot. He wanted me to sign an extension of my contract on the spot. I only hope that Monsieur Montigny will write to you, because I don't really know what to say, except that I take infinite pleasure in chatting with you, my dear confessor.[6]

A revival of *Diane de Lys* set the seal on her success. 'What a transfiguration!' said the critics: 'she is now a living spirit'. They praised the sureness of her inflexions, the charm of the unexpected, the impeccable technique. The truth is that she had worked hard, that she had been through terrible storms, that her knowledge of the theatre made it possible for her to 'express her raw experience of life'. Dumas, proud of his find, became her director of conscience. She would have liked to have had more from him. 'I love you very much, and have done so for a long time ...' But he was suspicious of love that is born of gratitude, and ends in misunderstanding. He kept their relations on the level of affectionate friendship. She was not annoyed by this. Indeed, she actually thanked him for having refused to have her as a mistress, and, instead, keeping her as a friend. 'How fortunate that it has all turned out in this way! It would be no pleasure for me to give you an old woman's draggled remains, and I do find immense happiness in loving you with all my heart . . .'⁷ The old woman was thirty years of age.

She was not happy:

> Except during those years of sorrow . . . when I was a daughter of joy who looked as though she was the well-looked-after child of a respectable family, and since I have escaped from all that, I have had nothing and nobody to complain of. Most women in my position would bless their lucky stars! I am well; the house is crammed every night; I have enough flowers and triumphs to sate all the minotaurs of the theatre — but it means nothing to me . . . Well, no matter: the fact remains that it is to you that I owe all this relative happiness, this complete absence of anxiety, this independence . . . also, whether you like it or not, it seems to me that you are the person I love more and better than anybody in the world.⁸

But, even had he wished to be her 'prince', he would still have remained mistrustful of all love, and especially of love between dramatist and actress. 'I shall have gone through the whole of my career without once having levied that only too commonplace tax.' In the theatre, he thought, there are a number of honest women. The others may 'fall for' a soldier, a financier, an athlete, and actor, but between author and actress there is a professional incompatibility. The actress needs the author far too much ever to believe in the sincerity of any love between them. He, for his part, having so often seen actresses playing love scenes while all the while carrying on a whispered conversation with their fellow performers, with the audience dissolved in tears, cannot take seriously, at moments of intimacy, the expansive outpourings such as he has so often rehearsed from the prompter's box. What raises the actress to great heights is intelligence: it has nothing to do with the activities of the heart. Off the stage, all he can get back from the woman is innocence and a genuine friendship.

It pleased Desclée to construct a novel on what might have been her relationship with Dumas *fils*. He, on the other hand, saw her only as an actress of genius whom he might develop by utilizing as much as he could find in her of the genuine woman. He had recommended her to his friends Meilhac and Halévy for one of their light, but moving plays, *Froufrou*. In this she had a tremendous success, and wrote to thank him:

Have you any idea, I wonder, how much I owe to you, my dear Providence? First of all, you found me; then, through all my times of discouragement, you were my stay. You gave me back dignity and self-esteem. Having paid bitterly for my experience, I, a poor Magdalene, was fumbling in uncertainty, striving to find the right road. You showed it me, you indicated the goal, and, thanks to you, I have now reached it. Many people, you among them, have spoken to me about the 'fortune' I have amassed. How and where that fable originated I have no idea. I rich, indeed! That would be highly illogical. How should a woman of my sort acquire wealth? There is no such thing as men who give, but only women who know how to make them give. I am poor, and proud of it. But Monsieur Montigny has just sent me a third contract on the most wonderful terms! So, no more fits of the blues, no more talk of convents! I am earning my living! Also, I love you, so, please, let yourself be loved, for, if it be true that my daily bread is assured, and that I can sleep with a full stomach, its neighbour, my poor heart, is passing through a terrible crisis! All this work, all this expenditure of self each evening, far from wearying, on the contrary, over-stimulates, it. Gusts of love mount to my brain, make me feel drunk, and sometimes are brought up short at my lips. I feel a need for tenderness and caresses so violent that it terrifies me. This skinny little body hides within it a great store of riches, and they stifle me. To whom shall I give them? Who wants them? They would not be appreciated. That they 'are not worthy of you' you have yourself told me more than once. I believed what you said, then, accusing myself of pride and presumption, forced myself to descend to the level of *so-and-so*, only to climb back again almost at once, having remembered in time what you had said to me. I must see you often: you will be my support, because I am, and want to remain, worthy of what you *do* give me.'

Between performances, this famous, solitary woman lived in the country with her birds, her spaniel and her old maid, Césarine. She felt sad and useless. She was filled with a burning desire to give herself. She asked of Dumas the gift of strength and will-power:

You are suffering at the moment [he replied] from the fatal and logical consequences of your position as an independent woman, the most wretched of all the conditions a woman can know. Women are born to be subordinate and obedient, first, to their parents, then to their husbands, last of all, to their children. They are always slaves to duty. When, as a result of their own impulses, or of the bad influence of those who surround them, they find themselves divorced from their natural functions; when, if they are born vicious, they have made a gesture of defiance and claimed their freedom, then they fall lower and lower and finally succumb because they lack the organs necessary to support the demands of dissolute living. If they have merely been led into evil ways, if they have just been weak, a moment comes when they feel that they have a different mission to fulfil, when they are frightened by the glimpse they get of the bottomless pit in the course of their progressive descent and cry aloud for help. . . .

Thus do those women think and speak who have reached the point at which you are now, and they have only to see within reach or sight some man who is not just like everybody else, to set their imaginations working, and blow him up to twice his natural size, for the simple reason that they are in a mood of feverish excitement. Then they exclaim: 'At last he has come! the saviour, the Messiah! Save me! oh, save me!' . . . I am neither an imbecile nor a god; consequently I can be neither your lover nor your redeemer. You would like a child. Fortunately, you cannot have one, for it would be for you but a brief distraction, while its own life would be a prolonged misery. Children grow into men and women — that is something that never occurs to women when they long for them, and even when they have them . . . You are barren, and so much the better. You will give birth neither to a depraved nor to an unhappy being. . . .

What is there left for you to do? This: to take advantage of the life you have made for yourself. You are still young: you are pretty; you have a great source of vitality on which to draw. . . . You have a most attractive voice and a deal of intelligence. Be a coquette, if you wish; that will be at once for you a distraction, a safeguard, a means of vengeance; and, since you have genuine talents, throw yourself heart and soul into your work . . . Profit from your independence, never sell yourself, and do your best never again to make a free gift of yourself. . . .

In conclusion, dear child, we can none of us change ourselves, but we can make use of what we have got. Keep all your qualities and all your defects in full employment ... Be a great artist, in other words, somebody who has put her heart into her head, her soul into her voice, and can play on human nature as on an instrument. Remain what you call a *femme de luxe* by giving yourself an ever higher polish, the better to deal with people of intelligence, for only with them you can live. In short, do not try to become either Lucrece or Mary Magdalene. Be content to be Ninon by day and Rachel by night. Not too bad a fate![10]

This was not good advice; but, then, no advice is good. We can none of us be sure what the needs of other people are, and can do no more than impose on them our own pattern of life. Sometimes example will change a character, but no elderly writer can be an example to a young woman who is bored to death. Aimée Desclée took refuge with her daemon, which had assumed the form of a man 'in a high social position', tall, fair-haired, with a slight beard, strong and vigorous.

Desclée to Dumas fils: At last, my sweet confessor, I have ceased to be an angel ... I am now convinced that chastity is incompatible with my profession. Besides, I really was getting too thin.

The sweet confessor reacted, as Victor Hugo would have done, with a display of kindliness which, though sententious, was not lacking in eloquence:

Dumas fils *to Aimée Desclée*: Alas! poor soul, how you are floundering! You are so much readier to cry than to laugh, and you know perfectly well how false the whole situation is. You will lose from your wings those young feathers which had just begun to sprout again: and when it is all over, you will want, quite seriously this time, to go into a convent. But to what purpose? You would most certainly not stay there. Besides, there is a convent everywhere for those who will use their eyes. The true convent is self-respect, and it has no need of bars or bolts, of confessional or priest. You do not love the man to whom you have given yourself, and you seek to find an excuse for what you have done by laughing at him! Do, at least, love him, other-wise the odours of your bed, perfumed when one loves, miasmic when one does not, will turn you giddy, and then, one fine morning you will wake up, you will write a beautiful letter into which you will put all your unsatisfied ideals, and then you will kill yourself. That will be an end — or, perhaps, a beginning.[11]

Juliette Drouet had already heard somebody talking of 'my angel whose wings are sprouting again'.

The wings remained irremediably atrophied, and he ceased to bother himself about Desclée. Besides, the war and his father's death had cut him off from Paris for several months. But, in October 1871 he made her play a part in what she called 'a little marvel of a piece', which even today retains its power to hold an audience: *Une Visite de Noces*. It expresses one of Dumas's deepest convictions which may be summed up in the phrase: 'All that adultery amounts to is, for the woman, hatred, and for the man, contempt: so what's the point of it?' At a later date, Henry Becque said much the same thing in *La Parisienne*. It needed no little courage to champion that view in an extremely corrupt society which regarded a single love — in Dumas's eyes the only true form of love — as both improbable and absurd. 'What does it all amount to, indeed!' protested Francisque Sarcey, an influential critic: 'Why, to happiness for six months, for a year, or, for all we can tell, longer!' He admired the author's sureness of touch and solid mastery of technique, but blamed his cynicism. 'The matter with him is that he does not like women, or, if you prefer, woman. She is, for him, no more than the raw material of dissection. The whole thing is as harsh and rasping as the hangman's noose.'

There was a deal of truth in this diagnosis. Dumas *fils* had no liking for women: some he pitied, on others he sat in judgment. As to actresses, he entertained the curious idea that they were as wax in his hands, waiting to be given shape. What he really cared about was knowing enough of women to let him draw from an actress the tones and inflexions which he needed. Drama is a strange art, an orchestra in which living creatures are the instruments, a palette on which the colours are not dead matter, but quivering reality. In *Une Visite de Noces*, the heroine, Lydia, nauseated by the cowardice of her former lover, who has deserted her in order to get married but is perfectly ready to betray his wife with her, flicks her handkerchief, as though to get rid of a bad smell, wipes her lips, drops the handkerchief on a table, and exclaims: 'Faugh! I must rid myself of this fine gentleman.

I pray that I may never hear of him again, that I may think of him as someone who is dead, that I may never know whether he is still alive. I must go and get a breath of fresh air — I need it . . . I could never have believed that one could so despise a man whom one had loved so much . . .'[12] That 'Faugh!' Desclée had spoken, at rehearsal, only 'from the lips'. Dumas insisted on her dragging up from her innermost being the cry he needed. She stood out against him, because she felt that to do as he wanted would mean tearing herself to pieces.

One day, when only *the actress* was performing, and the *woman* was wholly absent, we had a regular battle. She dreaded the state of nerves in which she would be for the rest of the day if she gave that cry as I meant her to. She tried every sort of trick to avoid doing so. But I did not yield an inch, and at last she wrenched out of herself, from where I knew it could be found, the ejaculation precisely as I knew it had to be. 'There! that's what you want, isn't it?' she said in an exhausted voice. 'You know where it comes from, don't you? — but you'll kill me!' 'What does that matter,' I replied, 'so long as the play is a success?' Then she sat down in an almost fainting condition, with both hands pressed to her heart. 'He is right,' she said a few moments later, 'that's how I've got to be treated if I'm to be any good at all. . . .'[13]

The cry forced from her by the author brought the actress three salvoes of applause, and she was recalled when she made her exit, in the middle of the act. They both of them knew where that agonizing 'Faugh!' had come from — from her disgust with a past which she held in abhorrence; from the horror occasioned in her by men unworthy of love; from the pain of a wounded heart struggling with torments which she could not smother. Desclée had been, partly through her own fault, 'dirtied, defiled, humiliated and insulted'. Now, out of her past, she had made a work of art. But her own sufferings alone had not sufficed. Unceasing work had been necessary. The cry had come, and it was work that had given it its final form. The art of the theatre exacts from its practitioners the creation of that cruel chemical amalgam from which the heart draws nourishment for the actor's craft.

Edmond About to Dumas fils, *November 10th, 1871*: Ah! my friend, what a superb artist you are! I had read, and re-read, the play, but I did not really get to the heart of it, so true is it that genuinely dramatic works can come to life only behind the foot-lights. The manuscript had dazzled me, the performance knocked me sideways. This Desclée of yours, whom I was seeing for the first time, struck me at first as ugly, skinny, vulgar; a woman with a hoarse voice. But at the end of a few minutes, it was not her I was looking at, but something a thousand times more than her, a thousand times better. It was your play in a grey dress.

My wife and I had taken a box just for our two selves, so egotistically determined were we not to have to share the emotions produced by such a performance with others who might be indifferent to what they were seeing. We left the theatre scared. Alex said: 'Your friend has just provided a spectacle of fifteen hundred people dancing on a tightrope. I wonder we didn't all break our necks: but no matter: I'm glad I went.' To speak for myself, I am as yet in no fit state to use my reason on the ex-perience. I feel as though I had had a douche of intelligence flung over my head, or, rather, a waterspout, and that only later shall I fully understand. Meanwhile, I am revelling in that disinterested delight which all decent men must feel when they come up against something stronger than themselves, stronger than anything else in all the world — an exhibition of sheer brainwork such as Nature does not produce more than once in fifty years.[14]

This letter expresses the general tone at the time. In 1871, Dumas *fils* was held to be infallible. He, himself, felt that he was the holder of some priestly office. To Madeleine Lemaire, a painter then much admired, who was making a mess of her emotional life, he wrote severely:

Dumas fils *to Madeleine Lemaire*: You most certainly are one of the most completely to be pitied creatures — using the word in its moral sense — whom I know. The letter I have just had from you is but another proof of that. You have too much virile intelligence to amuse yourself with what suffices the majority of women, and are too much of a woman to ignore it altogether. Consequently, you bear a grudge against those women who you feel — or think — are happier than yourself, and against men for not knowing how to give you the happiness to which you believe yourself to be entitled.

Thence arises that inner bitterness which sounds in your loud, indifferent laughter, and betrays itself in irony, and, occasionally, in backbiting, which is unworthy of so distinguished a mind. For, as compensation, nature has endowed you with one great gift — a wide sweep of intelligence coupled with great keenness of perception. There is nothing about which one cannot talk to you, nothing which you cannot fully understand, even if you cannot always make use of that understanding. You are an artist to the tips of your lovely fingers, and you cling to your work so as not to fall into despair or profligacy — which is the despair of the body. You must have tried many things which have disgusted and bored you, without ever, for a moment, grasping what they seemed, at first, to promise. In short, you are at the crossroads, at what, in woods and forests, are known as *étoiles*. Ten paths diverge from your feet in different directions, like the spokes of a wheel which splay out from the hub to the rim, and, no matter how fast the wheel turns, never meet again.

You have too much talent, and the habit of work is too deeply ingrained in you, for love now to take the foremost place in your life. Love, being a way of life, is also a master, and, like Caesar, would rather occupy the first place in a small town than the second in Rome. Love which is only a distraction is not love. It is galanterie, and you have enough experience of *that* to know what disgust and emptiness it brings in its train. You can no longer give all of yourself wholly and freely as those who truly love want to do, and ought to do. The social commitments with which you have saddled yourself would compel you to love piecemeal, at certain hours, in certain places, and with certain reservations. Your intelligence, and, at times, your sense of dignity, tells you that love of that kind is insufficient and grubby. If you had sensual needs you would be content with scraps of satisfaction here and there, provided they were frequently repeated. But you have no such needs. You are suffering from that peculiar frustration which is the fate of women who are without them.

What solid basis, then, have you got left? Great intelligence and a small amount of heart. With what can you feed those two things? First, with work; secondly, with a child. That is why I have advised you to find occupation in your painting and in your daughter. If you do what I say, your life will soon acquire a solidity such as you have never known. It won't stop you from

laughing, but it will make your laughter more sincere and gayer
... You will take your place among the truly valuable persons of
your period. But there is something else still more honourable.
You will quite certainly find one of those strong male friendships
which round off the destiny of women like you, and set them on
the heights to which neither the silliness nor the vulgarity with
which you are surrounded, and which are still a cause of
embarrassment to you, can ever attain.

That, my lovely friend, is how I see the matter. My views
may seem to you slightly solemn, but, where you are concerned,
they are drawn from one of the many thousand lessons which
life has taught me, and which, from time to time, I put at the
service of those I love, of whom you are one.[15]

Such tough but affectionate arrogance was not unpleasing to his
penitents.

CHAPTER II

From 'La Princesse Georges' to 'La Femme de Claude'

THE miseries of France had strengthened the apocalyptic prophet in him. He leaned over the rim of that 'crucible in which human souls are in fusion' — Paris — and from the seething of the city had seen issuing a beast with seven heads and ten horns. And the Beast 'held in his hands, which were as white as milk, a golden bowl filled with all the abominations of Babylon and Sodom and Lesbos ... and over the ten diadems, in the midst of many words of blasphemy, was one word larger than all the others — *Prostitution*'.[1] Most men are obsessed by fixed ideas. The doctor sees, in no matter what illness, the one in which he has specialized. Dumas attributed the defeat, the Commune, the loss of two French provinces, to the Beast Prostitution which, by gradually undermining morality, faith and the family, had opened the way to disaster.

In 1870, he had been pondering a play which should have as its subject a patriotic and pure-minded man of science betrayed by a vicious wife who would steal from him, not only his honour, but also a secret of national importance. Since this woman was to be a resuscitation of Messalina, the husband must be called Claude, the wife, Césarine. The title of the play was to be *La Femme de Claude*. The denouement seemed, to the Lover of Justice, inevitable. The man must destroy the Beast; the husband must kill his wife. But just when Dumas had written at the top of the still blank page: Act I; Scene i, he suddenly envisaged his play in reverse. A woman of irreproachable morals is married to a weak man who has fallen victim to an adventuress. The husband of the adventuress discovers that his wife has a lover, and swears to kill him. The princesse Georges de Birac (such is the heroine's name) knows that the comte de Terremonde (the injured husband) is lying in wait for the man who is to visit his wife in her room. If she says nothing and lets Birac keep his rendezvous with death, she will be avenged with no danger to herself. The perfect crime. But she chooses instead to save her guilty husband, and to forgive him.

It was this second play, centring round an adulterous male, that Dumas wrote first, and finished in three weeks. It contained two fine women's parts — the princesse Georges, Sévérine, which was designed for Desclée, and Sylvanie de Terremonde, to be played by Blanche Pierson, a ravishing creole, born on the island of Bourbon (Réunion), whose beauty had just then turned all heads. The members of the Jockey Club came in a body to applaud her. Until the production of *La Princesse Georges*, Dumas had known her only as a clever comedy actress, remarkably pretty, but quite devoid of genius: but now, here she was, 'the smiling, audacious, cool-headed, implacable embodiment of *woman*, the eternal feminine', as Dumas had painted her, as women would never admit her to be.

> Those who saw Mademoiselle Pierson will never forget her entrance — the opulent coils of hair which looked like sunbeams inextricably braided and twisted; the blue eyes, china-blue with a metallic glitter, under the regular line of the brow, points of light on the frozen surface of a pool; the straight, delicately chiselled nose of a Tanagra figurine ... the bare shoulders starred with diamonds. Neither rubies nor sapphires nor emeralds broke the white surface of that mysterious being who seemed as though moulded from the transparencies of the waning moon and the first colours of the waxing dawn ... Add to all this a smooth and rhythmic gait, a musical voice, always kept to one level tone so as to give the same impression of impenetrability as the face; unfocused, restless, shifting eyes, moving from one to another of the four points of the horizon, as though on the look-out to see from which direction the enemy would come. But once the enemy was seen, or sensed, they became fixed and piercing as though trying to *bore into* the spot on which they rested. Never have I seen a character and its interpreter so completely one.[2]

To what was this miracle due? Dumas let it be understood that Blanche Pierson, under the mask of her perfect beauty, concealed the same frigidity which was the fundamental characteristic of Sylvanie de Terremonde.

> Let us [he says] take a look into Mademoiselle Pierson's dressing-room. She takes off her glove before offering her hand to those who have come to congratulate her ... Raise that hand to your

lips ... press it, and you will be astonished. What is there so strange about it? That child's hand, the hand of that lovely creature, so white-skinned, so fair, so gay, is as resistant, as hard to the pressure, as it is soft and silky to the touch. But that is not all. She is as cold as crystal. Has not Madame de Terremonde just said that her hands are *always icy*? But Madame de Terremonde and the actress who plays her are two different women. Are they? I am not so sure. The first time I touched that hand, I had precisely the same impression as you. Then I looked her straight in the eyes. She understood the meaning of that look, and began to laugh. 'Yes,' she said: 'that is just what I am like!' So you see that when I wrote the part of Madame de Terremonde, I knew at once where I should find the woman to play it, and, as I later told her, play it to perfection.[3]

Between Aimée Desclée and Blanche Pierson there developed, in real life, a rivalry of quite a different kind, but scarcely less violent than that between Séverine and Sylvanie. What was at issue was the conquest, not of a man, but of the public. Once, when Pierson played one of Dumas's parts which had originally been 'created' by Desclée, the latter wrote to her: 'Dear Blanche, tomorrow you are going to play my part. Try not to make the audience altogether forget your friend — DESCLÉE.' On the day after the performance in question, there was another letter: 'My dear little Blanche, you most certainly are the most charming of colleagues. Yours DESCLÉE.' It was spiteful, but not altogether lacking in wit.

Dumas had written *La Princesse Georges* for Desclée. A letter written to his friend, Lavoix, keeper of the Bibliothèque Nationale and a reader for the Comédie-Française, proves this, and, in addition, shows that the author, though still a young man, felt himself, at that time, to be ailing.

Dumas fils *to Henri Lavoix*: I think, dear sir, that you will be pleased with the three acts which I have completed and that Madame Desclée will be so, too. She will have something to get her teeth into. The whole thing will, I think, be original, full of life, with an odd denouement. I should have finished it by now if only the trouble in my wretched noddle didn't start into life now and again, and all the rachidian, sympathetic and other nerves, with it. The weather is fine and very cold, but I demanded too much of my carcass in the old days, and it is now in a state of revolt. Very soon now I shall feel a little spasm of pain above my eyebrow, pitch forward on my nose, and all will be over. Sarcey will write a lot of nonsense about me, *l'Illustration* will publish my picture — and then, what?

I have only one act left to write, a matter of no more than twenty-four hours. But the twenty-four hours I need strike only on certain days. While I wait I am going to put myself into a sweat so as to loosen up the brain a bit, and take a cold bath to stimulate the internal organs. You must really begin to show me some respect, for I would have you know that Monsignor Dupanloup recently wrote a letter (which I have seen) to a lady, his sister in Christ, in which he declares that he has read the *Idées de Madame Aubray* and finds in it a number of sublime passages!

When next you see Arago give him my compliments.[4] What times we live in! always the same old thing — showing politeness to our enemies and refusing the cross to [Paul] Chabas who produced a masterpiece last year, and, with his three medals, has some right to ask for it, and giving it instead to the painter of Ornans, who treats us like mud, and throws it in our teeth . . . Great painting should be encouraged . . . Pull his leg a bit, for my sake.

Everyone here is very well, and Colette, who'll grow up into a sturdy little person, made a very characteristic remark the other day. I said to her: 'I am going to make my Will. Should we all of us die, except you, to whom shall I leave you?' She thought for a few moments, and then replied: 'To the Princess.'[5]

Dumas always preferred Chabas to Courbet. It was one of his weak points.

La Princesse Georges was a success; *La Femme de Claude*, a failure. According to Dumas, the feminine elements in the audience — always the most important — refused to be reconciled to the fact that the chief woman's role was that of a monster, and was still less prepared to agree that Claude Ruper should arrogate to himself the right to kill her. 'The public doesn't like a woman to be killed. They continue to think of her as a weak little creature who must be loved in the first act, and married in the last. If she falls by the way, she must be pardoned, and, if she is killed, then the murderer must die with her.'[6]

Desclée dreaded the part of Césarine, and said as much to the author. The fact of the matter is that the play is worthless. The theft of military secrets, in the most improbable circumstances, has all the defects of a bad 'thriller'. Claude is too perfect; Césarine, too evil. At the beginning of his career, because he was making use of personal memories and emotions, Dumas could combine into an acceptable mixture private bias and reality. Now, obsessed by a number of abstract ideas, he was producing problem-plays which had nothing to do with real life.

Into *La Femme de Claude* he had introduced the character of a Jew, Daniel, who dreamed of the unification of his people in a Palestinian state. The part of Daniel was sympathetic, but several Jews who saw the play protested. Their burning French patriotism, made more than usually sensitive by the recent disaster (many of them were from Alsace), refused to accept the idea of a second national home.

> *Dumas* fils *to Baron Edmond de Rothschild*: When a People has established a whole moral code for humanity on ten short biblical verses, then it can truly regard itself as the Chosen People of the Lord ... To what purpose, I ask myself, should I devote the whole of my existence were I a member of that Race ... and my answer is that I should have but one idea, to enter again into the possession of the land to which I owed my origins and my traditions, there to rebuild the Temple in Jerusalem ... To that idea I have given living and bodily form in the person of Daniel.[7]

On the strength of this letter we may perhaps be allowed to say that Dumas *fils* was one of the earliest Zionists, and was, perhaps, influenced in this attitude by Baron Edmond who, when he died in Paris in 1934, expressed a wish to be buried in Israel.

No more than the general public did the critics like the 'complicated symbolism' of *La Femme de Claude*. Cuvillier-Fleury, an academic critic, though not without talent, gave the author a rough handling in the *Journal des Débats*, taking his stand on those laws, both human and divine, which say: 'Thou shalt not kill.' What then, thought Dumas, should I do?

> When I forgave *La Dame aux .Camélias* I was accused of rehabilitating a loose woman, and now, because I do *not* forgive *La Femme de Claude* I am told that I am preaching murder ...

There seems to be a general agreement that I present on the stage, and glorify, only worthless females and abominable exceptions; that I have thus forfeited all right to speak of virtue and honour; that it is I who have corrupted modern society which, before my coming, was but a herd of snow-white sheep to be led, from birth to death, by a shepherd's crook festooned with pink ribbons; that I advance untenable propositions, and, more particularly, that I do so in a place the sole purpose of which is to provide honest folk with recreation ... finally, that I have become a public danger by attacking the laws of my country to the point of advising husbands to kill their wives. ... [8]

'By what right', Cuvillier-Fleury had asked, 'does Monsieur Dumas pose as a moralist? Does he practise what he preaches? Does he deserve the respect we give to the legislator, the preacher and the magistrate?' Then, providing the answers to his own questions — a favourite polemical trick — Cuvillier-Fleury said 'No'. Dumas protested vigorously. Why not? Because he was neither a judge, a priest, nor a member of the Academy? But judges and priests had condemned Calas, and Voltaire, a mere man of letters, had avenged the victim. For the same reasons, a mere man of letters like himself had a perfect right to speak the truth to a theatre audience. Molière had performed his function as a man of genius without asking permission of anybody. He, Dumas, was the more justified in passing judgment on French law, because he himself had suffered from it. Whereupon he embarked, for Cuvillier-Fleury's information, upon a long recital of his difficult life, of the humiliations to which he had been exposed as a natural child, of the cruelty of his schoolfellows. 'Having been born of a blunder, I am more than usually qualified to fight against blunders.'[9]

Then he dealt with the period during which he had been living with his father:

You, sir, knew my father. You remember his kindliness, his unchanging and powerful gaiety of spirit, the prodigal way in which he spent money, talent, strength and life itself. By affection he made up for what was legally lacking to his paternity, and I grew up to be his best friend ... When I was eighteen his exuberance made up for the difference in our ages, and a mutual curiosity formed a strong bond between us. Together, the two of us tasted the pleasures of the world, of many different worlds.

No doubt that was all very *shocking*, but, Heavens above! observation and experience are learned in many and various schools, and more efficaciously, perhaps, in the places we went to than in fat books of philosophy.[10]

In 'those places' he had met many 'lost women'.

Since I had no patrimony to squander, to such spending as I could permit myself, I added a little pity. I was the spectator of much despair, and the recipient of a great many confidences. For all the superficial show of pleasure, I witnessed many tears that were both sincere and bitter ... The novel of *La Dame aux Camélias* was the first-fruit of those impressions. I was twenty-one when I wrote it....[11]

He had chosen with care the point on which, throughout his career, his gift of observation was to be directed, because it was the one about which he had most to say. That point was love. In the fields of scientific and political truth he felt himself to be incompetent; but where moral truth was concerned, so far as it bore on the relations between men and women, he regarded himself as a master. In the theatre, however, he had found himself up against an undisputed fact — that it was impossible to display man as superior to woman. In the theatre the woman always revenged herself upon the stronger sex which invariably supplied the oppressors in real life. *She,* always *she.* Everything for love and by way of love.

Dumas had found himself imprisoned in this convention. He had struggled in vain to break free of it. In a pamphlet which made a considerable sensation — *L'Homme-Femme* — he went over to the attack.

Women never yield to reason; not even to proof. When they do surrender it is always to feelings or to force. They must be either in love or cowed; either Juliet or Martine! Nothing else is of the slightest interest to them. I am writing, therefore, for the instruction of the male. If, after this revelation of the truth, men still persist in making mistakes about women, it will no longer be my fault, and I shall do as Pilate did....[12]

Men are of two kinds: those who know what women are, and those who do not. The first are rare, and it is their duty to enlighten the others. To a son (a hypothetical son, the little Dumas boy whom Nadine had failed to produce) he explained that the perfect Man-Woman couple could exist only if two irreproachable beings became united, took an oath of absolute fidelity, and kept it. His advice was — and he had known many women who were depraved, untruthful or half mad — that a man should choose for wife someone who was religious-minded, modest, hard-working, healthy, gay, *but not ironical.*

And now if, in spite of all your precautions, your investigations, your knowledge of persons and things, your virtue, your patience and your kindness, you have been deceived by appearances and duplicities, and have linked your life to someone who is unworthy of you; . . . if, refusing to listen to you as husband, father, or even as friend, she not only abandons your children, but proposes to bring others into the world with the first chance-comer; if nothing can be done to stop her from prostituting not only *her* body but *your* name; if she obstructs you in carrying out your divinely inspired activities; if the Law, which has taken upon itself to bind, has refused to shoulder the responsibility of unbinding, and has declared itself to be powerless in such matters, then you must yourself be both judge and executioner. She is not just *any* woman, nor even a *particular* woman. She plays no part in the divine intention. She is purely animal, a monkey from the land of Nod, a female version of Cain — and so, you must kill her. . . .[13]

Such was the moral teaching of Dumas *fils.* The women sided with Cuvillier-Fleury in disliking what he taught. The men, entirely occupied with politics, paid little or no attention to him. He realized that he was losing touch with his public. He came down from his oracular tripod, and wrote *Monsieur Alphonse.* He wanted Desclée to play the principal role, but she was seriously ill. She complained of a pain in her side, and it was discovered, sometime later, that she was suffering from a malignant tumour. The poor woman, tired of her successes and already marked with the pallor of approaching death, wanted only to be allowed to rest.

Aimée Desclée to Dumas fils: I shall not sign the contract unless you definitely order me to, and even then you will have to hold my hand. I shall end my life in a convent: that is absolutely certain: it is my *idée fixe.* What am I doing here? Why all this endless agitation, all these arrangements, all this useless study, this mountebank trade?'[14]

After the failure of *La Femme de Claude*, Desclée, who was urgently in need of money, had gone to London where she made thirty appearances. She returned in a state of complete exhaustion. 'I am foundering within sight of land.' She was told that she ought to go to Salies-de-Béarn for the waters. What mockery for a dying woman! She spent her last days in the apartment she had on the Boulevard Magenta. She could not eat. Her face expressed nothing but the most atrocious suffering. 'Let me rest!' she begged: 'kill me!' Péan was of the opinion that an operation would be useless. Desclée was doomed. The priest who confessed her said: 'She has a beautiful soul.' She died on March 8th, 1874. So great a crowd had not been seen since Rachel's funeral, nor such a display of emotion. Thousands were unable to get into the church of Saint-Laurent. At Père-Lachaise, Dumas delivered an oration. 'She knew how to move our hearts, and she has died of it: that is the sum total of her story. . . .'

She had left her precious fan to Blanche Pierson; to Dumas an example of what art is at its greatest — something that feeds on true emotions.

CHAPTER III

Quai Conti

When Dumas *fils* was asked to whose chair he would succeed at the Academy, he replied:
'To my father's.'

IN France in 1873-9 it was 'the time of the Notables'. The Third
Republic, from its very start, had the appearance of being more solid
than the Second Empire which, even in the years of prosperity, had
always had about it a whiff of haphazard adventure. Under the
presidency of Adolphe Thiers, power lay partly with the aristocracy
of birth, partly with the oligarchy of money. Only with the coming
of Gambetta to a position of influence did the middle classes begin
to conquer the Republic. Fashionable life was still as brilliant as ever,
and the great clubs — the Jockey, the Union — retained their prestige.
Not yet were the characters of Dumas's plays outmoded.

Dumas *fils* himself became one of the characters of Dumas *fils*. The
journalists who went to interview him in his house at N° 98 Avenue de
Villiers, were struck by its 'air of authority'. The austere vestibule
seemed designed to give admittance to a temple rather than a dwelling.
Set symmetrically round it were pot-bellied jars filled with exotic plants.
From the ceiling hung a wrought-iron lantern. On one wall was
displayed a picture by Bonington — *The Rue Royale in 1825*. There
was also a bust of Molière. In the dining-room, which was hung with
Cordova leather, was a boule clock. The walls of the salon were
panelled with red-striped satin framed in wood. The work-room was
lit by two windows looking on to the garden. An enormous Louis XIV
writing-table occupied the middle of the floor. 'It is snowed under
with papers. Much order in apparent disorder ... Close to the great
book-case is a *full-size* model, in terra-cotta, of the tomb of Henri
Regnault. The most important room in the house is the great gallery,
a vast apartment divided into two parts, on one side a billiard-room,
on the other a cosy corner where guests converse in a circle about
Madame Dumas.'[1] In this gallery were two busts of Alexandre and
Nadine Dumas by Carpeaux. They are now in the Petit-Palais.

The house contained over four hundred pictures, good and bad:

Diaz, Corot, Déubigny, Théodore Rousseau, Vollon, were all represented. There were Dévéria's portrait of Victor Hugo in youth, a
study of cats by Eugène Lambert, a flower-piece by Madeleine Lemaire,
Lefébvre's *Jeune Fille couchée,* Lehmann's *La Merveilleuse,* and an
Intérieur d'Atelier by Meissonier, showing the immodest Louise Pradier
posing, naked, for her husband. Between Houdon statuettes hung
sketches by Prud'hon. On the writing-table was a cast of the hand
of Dumas *père* in bronze. On every available piece of furniture there
were other hands in plaster and marble; the hands of murderers, of
actresses and duchesses: a grotesque collection.

Dumas rose early and went to bed early. He lit his fire himself,
and heated the soup which he preferred for his breakfast to coffee or
tea. Then he sat down at his table, on which was a quantity of blue
hot-pressed paper, and a bundle of goose-quills. He worked until
noon, at which hour he joined his wife for luncheon, and his two
daughters, Colette, fourteen in 1875, and Jeannine, who was eight.[2]
He proudly retailed their sayings, which had the true literary flavour.
Once, when a lady had asked the elder of the two what kind of a
man she would like to marry: 'I?' replied Colette: 'I should like to
marry an imbecile, and if I ever found anyone even more foolish I
should have but one regret — that I had not chosen him instead.'

'Don't worry!' exclaimed Jeannine. 'You could never find anyone
more foolish than the man who would marry you!'

When, after a domestic scene, Dumas said to Colette: 'If your father
and mother were to separate, with which of them would you live?'

'With the one who would not go away.'

'Why?'

'So's I shouldn't have to be inconvenienced.'

At table he drank ordinary water, but always had it served in a
mineral-water bottle, so as to 'cheat the stomach'. He never worked in
the afternoon. He attended auctions, made the round of the picture-
dealers, or busied himself with hanging the canvases he had bought.
When he was asked what present would please him most, he said:
'A set of carpenter's tools.' But what use were presents to him? He
was rich, very rich. His copyrights brought him in a lot of money,
and those of his father, now that the old faun was not there to squander
the proceeds, were building up a large reserve in the publishing house
of Michel Lévy, where the Dumas *père* account now, for the first time,
showed a big credit balance.

Though he held disdainfully aloof from the regime, some of the new legislation caused him considerable uneasiness. His obsessive ideas had not changed their nature: the protection of decent women against rakes, and, consequently, the necessity of establishing paternity, and giving to natural children the right to inherit: the protection of decent men from loose women, and, consequently, the necessity of waging war against prostitution by married women, and to set on foot an agitation in favour of divorce. He was very little interested in purely economic or political reforms. They involved problems in which he was barely versed. What formed his constant subject was love: love between men and women; love between parents and children. How could he be expected to show familiarity with the worlds of manual labourers, land-workers and tradesmen? He lived in the most up to date of the 'smart' quarters (the Plaine Monceau), surrounded by thickly upholstered furniture, statues, and green, growing things. That was his universe, his setting: that was the direct cause of his limitations.

He was now at the height of his powers as a dramatist. *Monsieur Alphonse*, which was produced at the Gymnase in 1873, with Blanche Pierson playing (very well) the part which he had written for Aimée Desclée, is a solid piece of theatrical construction. It was to give him the distinction of having added a word to the French language. An *Alphonse* became the synonym for a venal man, and, later, for a pimp. What is the play about? A young profligate, Octave, has got a girl, Raymonde, with child. This child he has boarded out with a peasant family, and goes to see it under the name of 'Monsieur Alphonse'. Raymonde has succeeded in marrying a naval officer, older than herself, Commandant de Montaiglin, who knows nothing of her past. Octave, in pressing need of money, is on the point of wedding a woman who was formerly maid at an inn and whom a deathbed marriage with the landlord has enriched. He must at all costs conceal from his future wife the fact that he already has a natural daughter. He therefore entrusts her to Montaiglin who, needless to say, has no idea that the little Adrienne is his wife's child. It needs no great effort of imagination to guess that Victoire Guichard and Marc de Montaiglin forgive the past; that the child stays with its mother; that Octave, or 'Monsieur Alphonse', is dismissed with contumely. The play had a happy ending, and the public was pleased.

The important preface contains a new piece of special pleading on behalf of the woman seduced against the seducer and, in particular, against the legislator who acquiesces in the irresponsible attitude of the father, and says, in effect: 'You want to remain unknown? All right, you shall, and you shall be legally entitled to bring into the world other children (legitimate), without anyone having the right to call you to account. Yet, the man who avoids the consequences of fatherhood is a far worse criminal than the man who slips out of doing his duty in the service of his country.'[3] In what, then, does the remedy consist? In giving equal civic, and even political, rights to men and women. 'Why not? Is not a woman a living creature who thinks, works and suffers, who possesses that of which we are all so proud — a soul — and pays her taxes just as you and I do?'[4] Was not this equality already a commonplace of American social life? Was not the same idea gaining ground in England?

Dumas's opponents accused him of contradicting himself, because he wanted women to be the equals of men in the political field, while remaining subject to men in the world of the family. To this he replied that the submission of the wife to the husband-protector ought to be voluntary, and that what he was doing was to break a lance on behalf of the numberless women who had *no* domestic haven. To women he said: 'Man has made two moral codes: one which permits him to make love to any woman who takes his fancy; one which allows you to love only one man in exchange for the permanent loss of your freedom. Why?' Then, yielding to his passion for apocalyptic utterances, he prophesied the coming conflict of East and West, involving millions of men, compared with which the war of 1870 would look like a village squabble. He foresaw battles under the sea and in the air; 'thunderbolts which will burn whole cities to the ground, mines which will blow sky-high whole sections of the globe'.[5] There would be fatherless children beyond counting in the immense overthrow of the nations yet to come! Should not the governments make one huge family of all those who would never have a family of their own?

These pages lack neither eloquence nor wisdom. Among the first to praise them was one of his oddly faithful readers, Monsignor Dupanloup, Bishop of Orléans, and a Deputy in the National Assembly. The irregularity of the bishop's own birth goes far to explain the indulgence shown by the prelate to the unbeliever. Monsignor Dupanloup was the natural son of a poor girl of Chambéry who had been deserted by her seducer. This heroic mother had not only brought

up her son unaided, but had given him an excellent education. Entering
Saint-Sulpice at twenty, he had become a priest, the director of a
seminary, religious instructor to the sons of Louis-Philippe, and a
member of the Académie Française. In the Assembly he enjoyed the
respect of Right and Left alike for the proud attitude he had adopted
during the war. In his violet soutane, with his rugged face which
looked as though it had been hewn from a block of wood, he made a
fine impression when he mounted the tribune to address the House.
A man of independent views, he followed with sympathy all Dumas's
projects for social reform. He discussed with him the possibility of
making the establishment of paternity part of the Civil Code. Goncourt
records something that the Bishop of Orléans once said to Dumas:
'What do you think of *Madame Bovary*?'

'I think it's a delightful book.'

'It's a masterpiece, sir! . . . Yes, a masterpiece certainly in the
eyes of all those who have listened to confessions in country
parishes.'[6]

Monsignor Dupanloup strongly urged Dumas to stand for election
to the Académie Française. His candidature was received with remarkable favour. The name was doubly illustrious, the man's nobility
of mind beyond criticism. Women, who had so often felt the sting
of his lash, conducted a campaign on his behalf. 'This Alexandre
Dumas is truly fortunate,' wrote Goncourt in a mood of vague regret,
'the sympathy felt for him by everybody is prodigious.'[7] Victor Hugo
returned to the Academy for the first time since his exile in order to
cast his vote for the son of his old friend, though there was no love
lost between the two men. Dumas *fils* maintained that Victor Hugo
had behaved badly to Dumas *père*, and that *Marie Tudor* had been a
plagiarism of *Christine*. Hugo who had thought the father vulgar,
though a man of genius, would concede no more than talent to the
work of the son. The votes were taken. Dumas *fils* was elected with
a total of twenty-two in his favour, of which one was Hugo's. That
evening he called on Hugo to express his thanks, and, not finding him
at home, left a card: 'Mon cher maître, I wanted my first call as an
academician to be paid to you. To a noble spirit all honour. I embrace
you. . . .'[8] The kiss of peace — but chilly.

Dumas *fils* was received 'sous la Coupole' on February 11th, 1875,
by the comte d'Haussonville. Goncourt, who had never been present
at one of these occasions, wanted to 'see with my own eyes, and hear

with my own ears all these ridiculous monkey-tricks'. It was an intensely cold day, but Dumas drew a full house, and great ladies in their splendour had to make their way through crowds of gentlemen wearing rosettes in their buttonholes. The Princesse Mathilde, who had brought Goncourt with her, occupied a small box from which he could look down on the assembly.

The hall is of no great size, and the world of Paris, eager for a glimpse of this ceremony, was so thick on the ground that it was impossible to see so much as a scrap of the faded upholstery on the benches below, so much as an inch of the wooden staircase cutting through the tiered arena seats, to the great rostrums on the first landing, so crowded and so packed were the learned, rich and martial bottoms. Through a crack of the door of our box, I caught sight, in the corridor, of a woman of the highest elegance, seated on one of the treads of the stairs, and prepared to remain there all through the two 'addresses'.

A group consisting of those intimately connected with the Institution, a few men, together with the wives of academicians, sat packed tightly in a species of small enclosure protected by a balustrade. To right and left of them, in two rostrums draped in black, projecting from the walls, were the members of all the academies. The sun, which had decided to shine for the occasion, picked out the many faces sloping steeply upwards, their features set in the expression which is conventionally supposed to express beatitude. One was conscious, in all the men, of admiration held in leash, and eager to break loose. In the smiles of the women there was a hint of moisture. The voice of Alexandre Dumas became suddenly audible, and at once a sort of religious concentration fell upon the spectators, soon to be followed by little bursts of kindly laughter, affectionate applause, punctuated by ecstatic exclamations.[9]

Dumas began by saying that, if the great doors had been flung wide open to receive him, this was not because of any merit of his own, but because of the name he bore, 'which for so long you have sought an occasion to honour, and can honour only in my person ... By permitting this fond memory to receive, on this day, so great a tribute of glory through me, you have extended to me the highest honour for which I could ever hope, the only honour to which I truly have a right'.

After this tribute to his father, he spoke of his predecessor, Pierre Lebrun, a poet in the taste of the Empire, pompous and precocious, who, in 1797, at the age of twelve, had written a tragedy on the subject of Coriolanus, and had died in 1873, at the age of eighty-eight. The great Napoleon had once been his patron. 'That Achilles', said Dumas, 'had dreamed of having a Homer in his lifetime. He was to have one only after his death.' Homage to Victor Hugo. Lebrun had flung down his literary challenge in a drama entitled *Le Cid d'Andalousie*, but triumph had been drowned in boredom. In spite of Talma, in spite of Mademoiselle Mars, the play had been performed only four times. Mention of this work gave Dumas the opportunity to speak of the other *Cid*, Corneille's, on which Richelieu had instructed the Academy to express an opinion:

> The situation was an embarrassing one. You owed everything to your founder, and you did not wish to displease him. You knew that he was extremely anxious to have the play condemned, but you were unwilling to slam the door, as the result of a biased judgment, on the career of a man whose first production had revealed a master.

Why, asked Dumas, had Richelieu persecuted Corneille? Jealousy of a brother writer? To accept such an explanation was to diminish the stature of two great men.

> My own explanation is that the great Cardinal sent for Corneille and said to him: 'At the very moment when I am trying to drive back and exterminate the Spaniards who are harassing France on every side, you must needs hold up for admiration on the French stage the literature and the heroism of Spain ... Look fairly and squarely at this *Cid* of yours. From the point of view of drama it is, admittedly, a masterpiece. From the moral and social one, it is a monstrosity. What sort of a society would you have me establish with women who are willing to marry their father's murderer, with military leaders who are prepared to sacrifice their country because their mistresses fail to love them? ... Do you intend seriously to maintain that the courage of a great captain and the destiny of a great country depend, more or less, on the movement of a young woman's heart? ... Off with you, poet, and create heroes whom men may imitate.' And then, Corneille

engendered *Horace*, the very antithesis of the *Cid*, and dedicated
it to Richelieu. . . .

But, unfortunately, Dumas continued, it was the theme of *Le Cid*,
not that of *Horace* which triumphed.

> In point of fact, all the battles waged by the heroes of our literary
> works have as cause, and should have as reward, the possession of
> a Chimène.[10] When they win her and marry her and are happy
> ever after, that is Comedy. When they fail to win her, fall into
> despair and die of it, that is Tragedy or Drama . . . The theatre
> has become a temple dedicated to the glory of women. It is there
> that we adore them, pity them, excuse them. It is there that
> woman takes her revenge on man; there that, in spite of man-
> made laws, she is queen and mistress of her tyrant . . . Everything
> by her! Everything for her!
>
> Yes, gentlemen, there lies our inferiority . . . Between the
> theatre audience and ourselves it has been tacitly agreed that we
> shall treat of love . . . Life or Death as the result of love, that is
> our theme, and it is always the same. That is why certain
> serious-minded men think of us, the authors of plays, as less than
> serious. But though the majority of men may not be on our side,
> we have one natural and powerful ally — the bulk of womankind
> . . . Girl, mistress, mother, wife — all have but one single impulse,
> one thought, one glory — love . . . That is why women have an
> insatiable appetite for the theatre: that is why, when we have won
> women to our side, we may be sure of success; that is why, in the
> last analysis, Corneille, qua dramatist, was right when he wrote
> *Le Cid*, and Richelieu, qua statesman, was right when he fought
> against it. . . .

When Greuze painted the portrait of Bonaparte, he gave him the
features of Mademoiselle Babuti. Dumas *fils*, faced by the necessity
of saying something about Lebrun, harked back to the favourite ideas
of Dumas *fils*. He reminded his audience that when Lebrun received Émile Augier in 1858 'under this same Coupole', he had said:
'He has made popular on the stage, to the benefit of certain females
outlawed from society, a taste for rehabilitation which, I must admit,
I can as little understand as share. It is the fashion nowadays to
present to the public the spectacle of defiled and fallen women are who

purified and made whole again by passion. These women are set upon a pedestal, and our wives and daughters are told: "Look upon them, for they are better than you"....'

This, clearly, was a condemnation of *La Dame aux Camélias*, and Dumas proceeded to defend the work of his youth.

> The theatre [he said] is not intended for young girls. Not Juliet, nor Agnès, nor Desdemona, nor Rosine, are examples to be offered to the young ... Yet it would be a great misfortune if we were to be deprived of Agnès, Rosine, Desdemona and Juliet, simply because parents insist on taking their daughters to the play. I speak to you, gentlemen, as a man of the theatre. Young girls should never be allowed near us ... I feel for them too great a respect ever to let them hear all I wish to say, and too great a respect for my art to reduce it to the level of matters suited to their ears. ...

Here he treated himself to a small revenge upon his predecessor. All said and done, Lebrun had not been a conspicuous success in the theatre. Was not the reason for his relative failure to be found in his insistence upon acquiescing too wholeheartedly in the conventional attitude to morality? 'To be quite frank, gentlemen, let me say, though in a very low voice, that all we dramatists are revolutionaries.' Lebrun had had too little confidence in his art, in his public and in himself. That was the basic reason for his failure and for his premature withdrawal from the stage. 'Yes, gentlemen, we are gathered here today to do honour to the memory to a writer who was not, strictly speaking, a writer of genius. I hope that I may not be found lacking in respect if I do not place him on a height which was not within his reach, even in a burst of academic enthusiasm. ...'[11]

Panegyric? — far from it: this was the execution of a capital sentence. But it was received with applause and the stamping of feet by an audience drunk with the heady fumes of eloquence. After a short interval, 'there rose to the princess's box', says Goncourt, 'the acid tones of old d'Haussonville's voice'.

> Then began the dispatch of the new member. It was conducted with the salutations, the kow-towings, the ironical grimaces and ferocious implications which are the common currency of academic good manners ... Monsieur d'Haussonville made it quite clear to Dumas that he was, to all intents, a nobody; that

his youth had been spent in the company of hetaerae; that he had
no right to speak of Corneille. In all this head-chopping there
was a mingling of contempt of a man of letters for his literary
achievement, and a great noble for a mere clodhopper. After the
bitter violence with which each phrase began, uttered in a loud
voice, with the speaker's face raised towards the cupola in the roof,
the cruel orator would drop suddenly to a deep chest-note when it
came to paying the commonplace compliment with which the
period ended — and which nobody heard. I felt as though I were
watching a Punch and Judy show, and seeing the respectful bow in
which Punch indulges after he has hit his victim over the head
with his stick.[12]

It must have been the tone in which the words were delivered that
produced this impression, for the speech, when read, does not convey
any effect of deliberate cruelty. The comte d'Haussonville began by
denying that the choice made by the Academy was in any way an act
of reparation to Dumas *père*. 'We are conscious of no injustice done
to the author of *Antony* . . . It is not we who are guilty of forgetfulness
. . . Your illustrious father would, no doubt, have gained our votes
had he solicited them. . . .' As to Monsieur Lebrun: his criticism had
certainly not been aimed at *La Dame aux Camélias*, seeing that, in
1856, it had been he who, as a member of an imperial commission, had
suggested that a prize should be awarded to Dumas *fils* 'as the most
moral dramatist of the day'. Speaking for himself, d'Haussonville
declared that he feared neither boldness in the theatre nor revolutionaries among the dramatists.

It would be very unfair to condemn your plays for lacking
moral fervour. I would say, on the contrary, that they overflow
with it! . . . At all events, sir, you may claim with justice that you
have neglected nothing that might awaken in women a sense of
their duties, or exhibited to them the consequences of their faults
. . . You have employed to this end, not only the arts of persuasion
and sweet reasonableness, but also the weapons of fire and steel . . .
You must, however, admit that there is some reason why they
should feel embarrassed. In the last act of *Antony*, the lover, in
order to save Adèle's honour, cries, as he stabs her: 'She resisted
me, and so I killed her.' *You*, on the other hand, say to the husband
of an unworthy wife: 'Do not hesitate, but kill her.' Well then,

if wives deserve to die, some because they have resisted, others because they have not, then, being a woman looks like presenting rather too many difficulties. . . .

Henry Becque, who had no especial liking for Dumas *fils*, said of this session of the Academy that it was Clavaroche being received by the duc de Richelieu: 'For there is in Dumas something of the Clavaroche, something of the soldier and the conqueror, of the man who was charming, brilliant, coarse and boastful.' As the company was leaving the hall, Méry of Marseille remarked: 'Strange, isn't it? Two men exchange pistol shots, and one is left dead on the ground: they exchange speeches, and lo! one of them becomes Immortal!' And Marest: 'D'Haussonville thinks he is a wit because he married Mademoiselle de Broglie in the days when husband and wife held everything in common.' True Parisian witticisms, both of them.

CHAPTER IV

Place du Théâtre-Français

FOR many years Dumas remained faithful to the Gymnase. After
the Académie-Française, the Comédie-Française sought his
adherence. When this proposal was made to him, he felt both
'desire and fear': 'fear' because the wide, carpeted staircase, the ushers
with chains round their necks, the monastic-looking attendants, the
vestibule adorned with marble busts, had something of a sacerdotal air.
It was the foremost theatre in the world, the home of Molière, Corneille,
Racine and Beaumarchais. Dumas thought it might be wiser to wait
until he was dead before being admitted there: 'desire' because it was
a great institution. The classics were a superb training-ground for actors
and actresses, keeping taste and talent at a high level. Elsewhere, a
performer of genius, a Frédérick Lemaître, a Marie Dorval, a Rose
Chéri, an Aimée Desclée, could achieve perfection. Only at the
Comédie-Française was there a *community*, an incomparable *ensemble*,
which could give to a modern play, for a few evenings, the magic of
the classic masters.

In the old days it had been Baron Taylor (now eighty-five) who had
opened the doors of this temple to Dumas *père*, now it was another
Administrateur-Général, Émile Perrin, who was to extend the welcome
of the Théâtre-Français to Dumas *fils*. Perrin was a tall, thin man,
who always wore a short black jacket. He was to be found at the
theatre from one o'clock till six, and from nine till midnight. The
manner in which he received visitors was polite but glacial. He had
a squint which made it impossible to be sure at whom, or at what,
he was looking. A very young actor, feeling that he was being stared
at, nervously fingered his tie. 'What's the matter?' asked Perrin. 'It's
your shoes I'm worrying about.' His harshness sometimes hurt, but
he had brought new life into his theatre, had started a most successful
system of 'subscription evenings', and, by engaging Mounet-Sully, had
resurrected tragedy. Part of his plan was to attract contemporary
authors to the Comédie-Française. He suggested to Dumas a revival of

Le Demi-Monde; then, after the dazzling success of this venture, asked him for a new play. Dumas gave him *L'Étrangère*, yet another incarnation of the Beast of Revelations.

The 'Stranger' of the title is an American, a Mrs Clarkson who, as mistress of the duc de Septmonts, wants to arrange a rich marriage for this broken-down aristocrat, and has discovered a business man, a millionaire ten times over, Mauriceau, who is prepared to offer his daughter, Catherine, with a considerable dowry. In the first act, Catherine organizes a charity fête at which Mrs Clarkson has the effrontery to be present. The duke is bad-mannered enough to force his mistress on his wife. In the eyes of Dumas, Mrs Clarkson and the duc de Septmonts are typical examples of those who have brought about the 'death of a society'. The duke, a useless and noxious individual, deserves to be killed — as a measure of public safety. Mrs Clarkson's husband, an American who is as 'quick on the draw' as only those bred in the Far West can be, undertakes the duty of executioner, so that Catherine may be free to marry the engineer, Gérard, her governess's son, whom she has loved since she was a girl. Everything turns out for the best, through the medium of the best of crimes.

The play is no less strange than the 'Stranger'. In what way can Mauriceau, who has sacrificed his daughter out of snobbery, and Catherine, who has accepted the bargain, be considered more interesting than the duc de Septmonts? Did the latter really deserve to be killed? 'He could have escaped', was Dumas's reply to his critics, 'in a society where divorce is permitted.' What condemns the unworthy husband is indissoluble marriage.

Let the Chambers put divorce on the Statute-Book, and one of the immediate results ... will be a sudden and complete transformation of the French theatre. Molière's cuckolded husbands, and the unhappy wives of our modern drama, will vanish from the stage, since it is only the indissolubility of marriage which justifies revenge taken in secret, and the public lamentations of adulterous wives ... Once the wife of Sganarelle has been proved false, he will put her away. No longer will it be necessary for Antony to kill Adèle: Colonel d'Hervey will register the fact that she is an adulteress, and with child by another, and so recover his freedom and clear his good name. Claude will no longer be reduced to the

necessity of shooting Césarine like a wolf-bitch, and we shall no
longer have to bring Clarkson all the way from America in order
to free poor Catherine from her abominable husband. There will
be an entirely new aesthetic of the theatre, and that will be not
the least happy consequence of my proposed modification of the
law. . . .[1]

The press was indignant. Sarcey choked with rage. The *Revue des
Deux Mondes* thundered. But all these violent attacks awakened the
curiosity of the public. Crowds went to see a play which contained
such brilliant dialogue and was so admirably acted. The part of the
duchesse de Septmonts was taken by Sophie Croizette, a woman of
rare and noble beauty, with tawny hair, long, narrow eyes, and a curt,
harsh voice. 'The way in which she carries her head, and the inflexions of her voice, are enough to charm a crocodile', said Sarcey.
Her motto was 'Give everything!' She had been trained at the
Conservatoire, where her teacher, Jean-Baptiste Bressant, had from the
first neglected all the other students in the class, and given his attention
wholly to her. Engaged by the Comédie-Française, she had drawn
full houses when she appeared in the *Sphinx* by Octave Feuillet, because
of the appallingly realistic death-scene. While rehearsing, she had gone
so far as to observe the effects of strychnine on a dog.

Sophie Croizette seemed designed by Providence to play the part
of Mrs Clarkson, but Perrin had given it to Sarah Bernhardt, and
persuaded Dumas to let Croizette appear as Catherine. Before the
first night, author and interpreter had become fast friends.

> *Sophie Croizette to Dumas* fils: I find that my position has become
> quite horribly exhausting. I suddenly feel as though I were in a
> waiting-room watching the train through a window. I want to get
> into it, because that is why I am there, and I don't like being kept
> waiting. At the same time, my heart is heavy because I am about to
> start into the unknown. For me, the unknown is the duchess.
> What if I run off the rails? O! Heavens above! . . . I know that it
> doesn't matter to you. You just let your puppets wriggle and
> squirm while you laugh yourself sick! I think a great deal more
> about you than you think about poor Croizette.[2]

The actresses thought Dumas very strong-minded because, in his
dealings with them, he kept his distance.

In 1879 Paul Bourget, then a young critic of twenty-seven, whose precocious authority was increasing daily, paid a visit to Dumas *fils*, about whom he was writing an article. He found a man 'in the full flower of vigorous middle age', with the build of an athlete, the piercing gaze of a surgeon, and something about him of the soldier. His blue, slightly protuberant eyes seemed to bore into his interlocutor. To Bourget, who was immensely interested in psychology, he said: 'I can't help feeling that you are like a man of whom I have asked the time, who takes out his watch and smashes it in order to show me how it works.' Then he burst into a loud laugh. In this way did the famous dramatist and the young novelist become friends. The Bourget family was invited to Marly:

> *Dumas* fils *to Paul Bourget*: My very dear friend, as soon as I got your yesterday's letter I sent you a telegram with the time of the train, 10.5, without stopping to think that that might mean a rather early start for Madame Bourget, and that perhaps you had better take the 11.15. My eagerness to see you led me into this psychological error. A young woman, living in the rue Monsieur, wants to accept an invitation to lunch in the country. She has a choice of two trains, one an hour later than the other. It is impossible to believe that she would take the earlier. Forgive me. If you really can come, I shall expect you by the train leaving Paris at 11.15.
>
> Your letter touched me deeply. I am very, very fond of you, because of your talent, because of your character, and everything I have written to you recently should be proof of that. I was afraid lest I might have compromised your dignity, as I very nearly did, both as a writer and as a man. As to quarrelling, we shall never do that. When people of our sort are fond of one another, they don't quarrel. Yours affectionately....[3]

He enjoyed, no less, lunching with the young Maupassant, and regretted that he had not had the moulding of him. 'Ah! if I could have given a direction to such gifts, what a moralist I might have made of him!' Flaubert had tried to make an artist of him. 'Flaubert?' said Dumas. 'A giant who cuts down a whole forest in order to make a box ... The box is perfect, but the cost is too high.' Flaubert, on his side, grumbled:

> ... m'lord Dumas has parliamentary ambitions ... Alexandre

sprinkles the newspapers with his philosophic reflections. It's the same with him in the theatre. He doesn't worry about the play *as* a play, but the idea about which he wants to pontificate. Our friend Dumas's fondest dream is to achieve fame à la Lamartine, or, rather, à la Ravignan. Preventing petticoats from being lifted has become a perfect mania with him. . . .[4]

It was clear that Dumas's moralizing ardour got on Flaubert's nerves. 'What's his purpose? Does he want to change human nature, write good plays, or become a Deputy?' Flaubert spoke with disgust of 'the great-man pose, the public preaching, all of which stinks of Dumas'. Bourget saw more truly. Behind the façade of stern authority there lurked, he guessed, much doubt and a profound lassitude. In spite of his stage successes, Dumas was not a happy man. The faithful friend saw his friends disappear one after the other. The poor 'Brimborion', Marchal the Giant, having lost the support of George Sand, and feeling himself to be threatened with blindness, committed suicide in 1877. The moralist who preached against adultery had a mistress, the beautiful Ottilie Flahault, to whose house, the Château de Salneuve, not far from Châtillon-sur-Loing in the Loiret department, he frequently went for the purpose of working. 'I do believe', he wrote to Commandant Rivière, 'that if there is any seeming happiness in life, it is in love that we find it — but who is there who loves? . . . Nowadays, all women have the same handwriting, the same coloured hair, the same fashion in boots, and the same telegraphic manner of making love.'[5]

His enemies said that he was the 'most immoral of moralists', and called him the 'Tartuffe of the Danube', which was completely unjust. Life was tearing him in pieces, as it does all men. His princess was becoming more and more subject to gloomy moods and fits of despair, periods of jealousy which were not far removed from insanity. Nevertheless, he went to her room every morning, sat on her bed, and had long, patient talks with her. Every Tuesday, they had friends to dinner.

The miseries of his step-daughter Olga saddened him. He had foreseen, but could do nothing about, them. In spite of his warnings and her mother's, 'Little Russia', when barely of age, had married a spendthrift libertine, who had courted her for her dowry, the marquis de Falletans. Of this ill-starred marriage two little girls were born at the time when the head of the family was squandering the Naryschkine inheritance. Olga, in real life, played very much the same part as a 'Princesse Georges' or a 'Catherine de Septmonts'. It may be that she had, to some extent, served as a model for the creator of those two characters.

When Dumas went into the great world, it was without his wife. He was the chief ornament of the salon of Madame Aubernon, the lion-hunter, who used to wear a miniature bust of him in her hair. Madame Arman de Caillavet (whose brother married Colette in 1880) was determined that he should be the centre of that young woman's circle, which she was already busily planning. 'He also', said Léon Daudet, 'went regularly to imbibe poison at the house of the Princesse Mathilde, in the company of Taine, Goncourt and Renan. At dinner, he would fire off cruel epigrams which were received with "Ohs!" and "Ahs!" by the ladies of the party.'⁶

He talked like the characters in his own plays. On one occasion, when the conversation turned on one of his pieces in which he had depicted women of fashion, a pert young thing said: 'I wonder where you learned about *them?*' 'At home, dear lady,' he replied. A certain bore, whom he had nicknamed 'The India Mail', because he never stopped, started to tell a story, broke down in the middle, asked the company's pardon, and explained that he had forgotten the end of it. Dumas heaved a sigh of relief: 'How fortunate!' he said. Somebody began talking of Durantin, whose play, *Héloïse Paranquet*, Dumas had revised and rewritten. 'Who *is* this Monsieur Durantin?' asked one of those present. 'A distinguished lawyer,' was the reply, 'and a dramatist in *my* spare time.' Once he described meeting Mademoiselle Duverger, whom he had known thirty years earlier. 'Alas!' he remarked. 'She reminded me of my youth — but not of hers.'

Whistler, having listened to one of these firework displays, said with his diabolical chuckle: 'He goes about collecting squibs, hee! hee! — and some of them are damp, ha! ha!' Léon Daudet, irritated by the great man's diatribes against adultery, decided that there was in him something of the 'protestant manqué', but had to admit that he showed a courageous independence. 'He never toadied to those in high places ... in his own way he was true to himself ... a man who collected compliments with an air of aloofness... All in all, he was, with certain reservations, a person of considerable charm.'⁷

This charm had a powerful effect on women, but he remained unmoved by their advances. To Léopold Lacour, a young professor from Nevers, who had written a book about him as a dramatist, he made a number of confidences. He asked him to come and have a talk. Lacour, much thrilled at meeting 'this king of the French theatre', accepted the invitation.

I took advantage of the Easter holidays of 1879 to visit him in the Avenue de Villiers, where he had a medium-sized and very unostentatious-looking house, a typical middle-class dwelling of the kind one sees in country towns. The only thing in it which one could call in any way sumptuous was a fairly important collection of pictures which was housed in a gallery on the first floor, but this I did not see on the first occasion when I went there. I must admit that when subsequently he showed it to me with pride, I only partially admired it. Certainly, it contained a number of canvases — landscapes and portraits — of undeniable value (in particular, if I can trust my memory after so long a lapse of time, a Théodore Rousseau, a Dupré and a Bonnard) but there were too many which owed their importance only to signatures, which were highly prized in the days of the Second Empire, and not to any intrinsic value they might possess. These, for the most part, were no more than *amusing*. Him, as soon as I found myself in his presence, I admired without reservation. He received me in his work-room where the only object of luxury was a fine Daubigny hanging above a large, black and very ordinary writing-table. I had never before set eyes on him. He was tall, broad-shouldered, very upright, and truly imposing. Curly hair, only just beginning to go grey — he was no more than fifty-five — crowned a head which gave a strong impression of authority (I have spoken of it before) and seemed to justify his reputation for pride. I could detect no resemblance to his father. It was in his brother (on the wrong side of the blanket), Colonel Henry Bauër, that I was later to see the living image of the author of *Monte-Cristo* ... After again thanking me, without the slightest hint of flattery, he questioned me about my work as a teacher, about the books I most liked, and then to my astonishment, said:

'Do you know why Jesus has conquered the world?'

'In the first place,' I was brave enough to reply, 'He has conquered only part of it.'

'I grant you that, but the part He *has* conquered is by far the most interesting so far as modern civilization is concerned. Therefore, I repeat my question.'

'Well then, my answer is this — because He died on the cross for preaching a doctrine of universal charity and love.'

'No doubt, but chiefly because the preacher of love died a virgin.'

(Dumas was obsessed — though I did not know it — by the idea of writing a play to be called *L'Homme vierge*.)[8]

The best and most devoted of wives will, sooner or later, do you terrible injury. Madame Littré, who was a saint, had to wait forty years for her chance. Then to the bedside of the atheist whom she venerated she brought a priest who would have dishonoured his memory by delivering him to the Church, had he managed to impose upon him in his dying condition. There are Delilahs of the sacristy as there are of the bedroom or the divan. Only the virgin man is invincible . . . and that is why I say again that, if Jesus had not died a virgin, He would never have conquered the world.[9]

He brooded long over *L'Homme vierge*. 'I shall put the whole of myself into it,' he said to Léopold Lacour. The whole, thought the latter, in the character of an exorcist? Dumas desired and adored what he said he execrated, and that was why so many women loved him. It is a strange and, when all is said, a moving spectacle, this, of a dramatist who had turned himself into a preacher to actresses, but had first to preach to himself, that he might not succumb. The theme of 'The Man in Flight from Temptation' occurs again and again during the middle years of Dumas *fils*. There exists a collection of very strange letters which he wrote to an anonymous woman who had sinned. It begins with an answer to a request that he would get her an engagement: 'My dear child: . . . I can do nothing for you at the Théâtre-Français. For the last two years I have been plaguing Perrin to take on a certain person. I thought there would be no difficulty about getting him to agree, but even now I am still unsuccessful. I neither can, nor will, ask anything more of him. . . .'

This is followed by a fine letter about Mademoiselle Delaporte, a charming and modest young actress, who was one of Dumas's dearest women friends, and had been generally supposed, quite wrongly, to be his mistress:

Mademoiselle Delaporte has good reason to speak of me as she does. There is certainly no woman for whom I feel a greater esteem. I have never met one who is more deserving of praise, who is more worthy of succeeding, or more courageous. We have had for one another great affection and great respect ... All manner of things have been supposed to exist between us which, in fact, never did, and I am delighted that, in this, people should have been wrong ... The great mistake of men in general is to imagine that physical possession is the indispensable way of really possessing a woman. On the contrary, material possession, unless it is consecrated and sanctified by marriage, by reciprocal duties, and the rearing of a family, contains the germ, and is the cause, of mutual *dis*possession. There is, it is true, in such friendship no intoxication, but there is also no satiety; and the sentiments which spring from such a commerce of the spirit are so pure and so fresh that they, so to speak, keep the two individuals who have experienced them, from growing physically older.[10]

This portrait ought, so Dumas decided, to serve as a model for the 'Sinner'. But what woman has ever shown willingness to copy another? This one gave him to understand that she was bored, and that a lover, especially an illustrious lover, would bring a note of romance into her life. She was snubbed for her pains:

I have made a profound study of life, and I know it as well as, if not better than, most. My observations have at last convinced me that the best chance for happiness lies in goodness. You are, materially speaking, independent, and should take advantage of that happy situation. You have confidence in me, and confidence is the only word I want to hear from you at my time of life. You talk about love because you are a woman, young, enthusiastic, and, being enthusiastic, young and a woman, can understand nothing except in terms of love. All that is good in you, all that nobody has thought to make use of, has come to me in response to the first sincere and loyal appeal which I have made to you. For that you are so grateful that you really do believe that I am the only person you have ever loved. It is for me to take advantage of that in an attempt to make you happier in the future than you have been in the past. If I succeed, then, surely, all the

means I have used will turn out to have been good — won't they?
Good night, Mademoiselle, and sleep soundly.[11]

She reproached him with having made her fall in love. He justified
himself on technical grounds:

> It was first of all necessary to attract a human soul, to give it
> confidence, and the only way of doing that, with someone in
> your particular situation, of getting possession of it, was through
> love. Women are more susceptible to feeling than to reason, and
> the best tactic to employ with them is to make oneself beloved.
> Once they love they can understand, since the man they love is
> endowed, in their eyes, with every charm and every variety of
> genius. . . .[12]

The adventure ended with her as a very similar one with poor
Desclée had done. The Sinner, disappointed at the resistance put up
by the Great Man, gave herself to a worthless fop, though still continuing, so she said, to love Dumas. The Moralist preached a harsh
sermon over the grave of love:

> No man, says an old proverb, can find flour in a sack of coal,
> which means, in this case, that one cannot find, all at once, love,
> virtue, fidelity, platonism and candour in a woman who has lived
> for fifteen years as you have lived. Certain delicacies of feeling
> are bound to get lost in that kind of life. You are the victim of
> your family (if it can be called a family), of your birth, of your
> unhealthy upbringing, of the corrupt society which you have kept,
> of an unfortunate first love affair, and of other venal loves, since.
> Because you are worth a great deal more than most of the women
> with whom you consort, because you still have a particle of the
> spiritual in your make-up, you have made a number of definite
> efforts to free yourself from the mud and slime in which you are
> floundering. High over the mountain there is a patch of blue
> sky . . . but you are not strong enough to climb the mountain
> unaided. No woman can do anything so long as she is not two.
> You found a saviour and a companion in one of our colleagues.
> He would certainly have married you, or kept you close by his
> side. Then you needs must compromise yourself with a busker,
> with a dandy of the fairground, with the result that the saviour
> let everything go, and back you fell into the mud . . . Your heart,

which is not wholly corrupted, and your self-respect which still sometimes shows a spark of life, have both suffered grievously in this business, and your poor body, which is the battle-field of all these agitations, has suffered, too. You cry aloud for help, but all in vain. There is no longer anyone else on the road with you. Make a great effort, save yourself single-handed, because, if you lose control this time, you will sink straight to the bottom where the slime oozes. . . .

If you lack the courage to divide yourself between your work and a child which will not be your own, and if you truly have religious cravings, then, throw everything to the winds, and boldly enter a convent. Be the La Vallière of actresses. It is a position well worth occupying. . . .[13]

The last item in this correspondence is a note of condolence addressed by Dumas to the Sinner on the occasion of a sad loss:

I never believed in your love, but I never doubted your heart. So now, in this time of your unhappiness, I embrace you tenderly.[14]

Fundamentally, he had changed very little since the days of *La Dame aux Camélias*. But does one ever change?

PART TEN

★

CURTAIN

God has considered the beginning, and most certainly He will consider the end. I find it hard to believe that the end will be like that of one of Anicet Bourgeois's dramas.

DUMAS *fils, Letter to Henri Rivière*

CHAPTER I

Towards Retirement

UNTIL the very last year of his life, Dumas *père* had never, either as writer or as lover, felt that he was growing old. Dumas *fils* was already talking of retirement even before he had reached his sixtieth birthday. In his Preface to *L'Étrangère* (1879) he gave voice to disillusioned and melancholy reflections:

> As a dramatist grows older [he said] he loses in clarity and suppleness, in the power to bring his stage alive, what he gains in his knowledge of the human heart . . . A moment comes when he finds himself pushing the study of character and the analysis of feeling too far. He frequently becomes heavy, obscure, solemn, portentous, and, not to beat about the bush, a bore. When he reaches a certain age, and I, alas, have just about got to that point, there is nothing for the playwright to do but to die, like Molière, or withdraw from the battle like Racine and Shakespeare. In that way, at least, he can resemble them. One may compare the theatre with love. It demands full possession of the faculties, health, potency and youth. The man who wishes always to be loved by women or made much of by the mob will find himself exposed to painful disappointment. . . .[1]

A hard counsel of perfection. Retirement is a painful business, and rarely beneficial. Dumas stopped writing prefaces, and turned, instead, to open letters: to Alfred Naquet (on divorce); to Gustave Rivet (on the registration of paternity); and, in spite of his declared intention, returned to the stage with *La Princesse de Bagdad*, in 1881. The play was dedicated to 'My Dear Daughter, Madame Colette Lippmann; Always be a Good Woman, for That is the Foundation on Which Everything Else is Built'[2] — admirable in sentiment, but commonplace in style.

The first night was stormy, and the press notices were execrable.

421

Dumas attributed this failure to political animosity. His *Lettre sur le Divorce*, he said, had never been forgiven. This may, to some extent, explain the antagonism of the fashionable and bourgeois worlds, but the real reason for the play's bad reception is to be found in the fact that *La Princesse de Bagdad* suffers from precisely that unreality which Dumas himself had denounced in the work of elderly authors. Could there ever, anywhere, have been a nabob like Nourvady? This millionaire Antony seemed 'older and more out-dated' than the Antony of 1831. No woman has ever talked like Lionnette de Hun, the daughter of the king of Bagdad and of Mademoiselle Duranton. He seemed to have lost contact with the real world.

All Dumas's best plays are autobiographical. *La Dame aux Camélias*, *Diane de Lys*, *Le Demi-Monde*, *Le Fils naturel*, *Le Père prodigue*, had been based on personal memories. No doubt Marguerite Gautier and la baronne d'Ange, like all stage characters which come alive and remain alive, were not just portraits, but simplified creations sharply defined. Nevertheless, they were the outcome of first-hand observation. Lionnette de Hun (like Mrs Clarkson in *L'Étrangère*) had ceased to be a type, and was, instead, a symbol, a figure of allegory. How came it that he, who had seen the danger so clearly, should have fallen into this particular mistake? 'Many people, after reaching a certain age, and, in particular, a certain degree of success,' wrote Ferdinand Brunetière, 'find themselves shut off from the world around them, cease to observe, and have eyes only for what goes on inside themselves. Gone for them are what Goethe called the "prentice years", and they fall back on imagination.'[3] The author of *La Princesse de Bagdad* was imagining, but imagination in a vacuum has no solid foundation. It needs, like Kant's dove, if it is to fly at all, the resistance of a medium — in this case, a social medium. What did this king of the theatre really know about in his ripe middle age? — the literary world and the worldly world: one tiny corner of Paris, a 'fine-drawn society of vice and fashion'. The literary output of writers swimming in such waters is never more than a collection of pathological cases. It contains nothing perfectly healthy nor perfectly simple.

In *La Princesse de Bagdad* Dumas's two fixed ideas, which had already produced the stillborn *L'Étrangère*, are again in evidence: admiration, mixed with terror, for the corrupting influence of money; adoration, mixed with fear, for the power of women. But these ideas were incapable of engendering human beings.

Barbey d'Aurevilly was severe in his judgment of *La Princesse de Bagdad*:

> The play fell to the ground as though it were not by Monsieur Dumas at all — an event no less astonishing than would have been the collapse of the great theatre chandelier on to the heads of those below . . . On the next evening — the subscription performance — the fallen play found no crutches on which to struggle to its feet. Is this the end of a reign? Rightly or wrongly, the public has decided that Monsieur Dumas is the Napoleon-the-Little of the theatre, at a time when there is no Napoleon-the-Great. I don't say that *La Princesse de Bagdad* is his Waterloo, but it most certainly is his Farewell at Fontainebleau.[4]

After this catastrophe Dumas remained silent for a long while. In four years he produced neither a new play nor a new novel. He lived like a lord in the Avenue de Villiers during the winter, and at Marly in summer, on a property, 'Champflour', lent, and ultimately left, to him by his father's oldest friend. He bought pictures, gave dinners at which, like Victor Hugo, he brought together 'the most distinguished persons of the day', and wrote innumerable letters in that 'copper-plate' hand which he had inherited from his father. The letters are interesting by reason of their frankness and of the loftiness of their tone. In them we hear Jupiter thundering from the summit of Olympus:

> *To an unknown writer*: My dear colleague: I should find it difficult to explain your letter, were it not that I know how sensitive poverty can make a man. You are poor; you are hardworking; you are worth a great deal more than certain persons who have achieved success. You have, therefore, every reason to be astonished and hurt, even to indulge in self-pity, when one of your fellow-writers who happens to be happy, rich and acclaimed seems to be avoiding you, and failing to do for you what you think he ought to do, what it would be only natural in him to do. That is the trouble, is it not?
>
> Please consider, for a moment, my own position. I think I can say, without exaggerating, that I get anything from forty to fifty letters like yours every month. You are not the only man alive who works, waits and finds his talents unrewarded. Others, besides yourself, approach me. When I manage to snatch two

days' shooting, I have, believe me, fully earned them. What is it you want me to do? To ask the Théâtre-Français, or some other theatre, to produce one of your plays? Do you know what the answer would be? — 'In your opinion it's good — eh? Fine: put your name to it, and we'll start rehearsing right away.' Now, neither I nor you want it to appear with my name to it. You want to have a chat with me? I should like nothing better: fix a day and a time when I may expect you. And then? Tell me what you want me to do, and I will do it or, rather, I would do it if you and I were the only two men in the world, and the world belonged to me. I would gladly give you half, or even three-quarters of it. But, as it is, there are others to be considered, and those others have interests of their own, passions, mistakes and habits of their own. Them I cannot influence. All I *can* do, I do: but I cannot, nor do I want to, have anything refused me, even on behalf of another. . . .⁵

That is not lacking in style, and is a great deal better written than *La Princesse de Bagdad*. The next letter is to a royalist journalist who had been shocked by a play which Dumas *fils* had constructed from his father's *Joseph Balsamo*:

Puys, September 24th, 1878: We live at a time when one cannot speak the truth without running the risk of outraging some group or other. Since we now have a republic, the royalists are momentarily in agreement that all monarchs were angels, including even Louis XV. I have even been told that Madame Dubarry was really a very well-brought-up person, and that, in attributing certain scabrous witticisms to the woman who said to the King: 'That's a bit steep, that is!' and to Monsieur de la Vallière when, on the occasion of Louis XVI's accession, he brought her the royal order to go into exile: 'That's a bloody fine beginning to a reign!' I am calumniating the one-time tart whom Lamartine summed up in an admirable sentence: 'So died a woman who brought dishonour upon throne and scaffold alike.'

What am I to say to that? There are those who maintain that in painting the character of Gilbert as I have done, I am insulting the People, that glorious People who were soon to chop off Madame de Lamballe's head, first bludgeoning her to death and then desecrating what remained of her body at a street corner. For the

moment it is generally agreed that all the men of the People —
being electors — are angels. What a universal paradise! Others
there are who say that, by representing Marat as I have done, and
putting into his mouth words which, as a matter of fact, I took
straight from the novel — for don't forget that the play was an
adaptation of a book which *I* did not write — I encouraged the
Commune. We are, all of us, just now, walking on our heads
with our feet in the air. What do you want me to do about it?
We have got to get through this moment of history somehow.
The next revolution will manage matters by cutting off feet
instead of heads. Universal Suffrage, Gambetta's speeches, and
Les Cloches de Corneville are enough to ensure the happiness of
my country. I've nothing to say against that, and do not claim
that I can take people's minds off them with my plays, my novels
or my ideas. . . .[6]

When Naquet succeeded in getting the Chamber to vote the law
on divorce which had for so long been awaited and longed for by
Dumas *fils*, the senator from Vaucluse called upon the dramatist, in
a letter published in *Le Voltaire*, to rally to the support of a republic
which had given to France so important a measure of reform. But
Dumas clung to his independence:

In nothing, and to nobody, have I committed myself. I belong
to no party, to no school of thought, to no sect, to no ambition,
hate or even hope . . . You, sir, who are one of those who have
demanded freedom for all, should be happy and proud. I *have*
that freedom, complete, unconditional, unassailable; and everyone
can have it, too, without proclamation, without noise, without
riots and without violence. All it needs by way of encouragement
is work, patience, respect for oneself and for others.[7]

He had no belief in political labels, and refused to wear any one
of them.

As to what sort of government shall rule our country, I care
not at all what its name or its nature may be. It can be what it
wishes, or can manage, to be so long as it makes France great,
respected, free, unified, tranquil and just. If the Republic
produces this result, then I shall range myself behind the Republic,

and, if that happens, I think that I can promise you the adhesion of all honest folk who are not yet ready to support it.⁸

In saying this he was sincere, though, in his heart of hearts, he regretted the world of the Second Empire, which had been the world of his youth.

CHAPTER II

'Denise'

HIS athletic build, his uncompromising attitude, his fame, the
memory of *La Dame aux Camélias*, his romantic marriage with
a Russian princess — all these things still combined to attract
to Dumas feminine characters in search of an author. One of the most
interesting of the women who gravitated to him was Adèle Cassin.
She was very rich and a collector, who lived at N° 1 rue de Tilsitt,
in a house detached on all four sides, with a hundred windows and a
view on to the Arc de Triomphe. It was filled with works of art.
She it was who was to provide him with the material for his
'come-back'.

Adèle Caussin, known as 'Cassin', the daughter of a dyer, was born
at Commercy in 1831. While still quite young she had taken a post
as reader to a great Sicilian lady. Like a true Dumas heroine, the
'companion' had allowed herself to be got with child by the eldest of
the four sons of the House of Monforte (descended from the Montfort
whom Charles of Anjou had taken with him from France in the
thirteenth century). She had fled for refuge to her native country of
the Meuse, and had there been brought to bed of a girl: Gabrielle.

That was the starting-point of the life of 'Madame Cassin', an
intelligent and very beautiful woman who was determined to rise in
the world. The banker, Édouard Delessert, one or two of the Rothschild barons, and the founder of the Georges Petit Gallery had made it
possible for her to buy one of the fine 'houses of the Marshals' between
the Champs-Élysées and the Étoile. There she had assembled her
famous collection of pictures which, in addition to examples of the
Italian and Spanish masters, contained Théodore Rousseau's *L'Allée
des Châtaigniers* and Henri Regnault's *Salome*. The portrait of herself
in an ivory satin dress, and another of her daughter with dishevelled
hair, bore the signature: Gustave Ricard.[1]

Madame Cassin was not a 'baronne d'Ange'. The life she led was, to all appearances, beyond reproach. The men who came to her dinner-parties belonged to the highest circles of society, but they never took their wives to the rue de Tilsitt. She counted among her friends Ministers of the Republic like Gambetta and Ribot, and painters like Gustave Doré and Léon Bonnat. She had persuaded a benevolent gentleman from Bordeaux, with a vaguely aristocratic name, to acknowledge her daughter, whom she had married off, in 1869, to the Count Ruggiero Monforte, the youngest brother of her own former lover, now the Duke of Laurito. In this way did Gabrielle assume by marriage the name which should have been hers by birth. Richly provided for, she now lived in Florence, and had more or less broken with her mother who invented for herself the nickname of 'la mère Goriot'.

It was in 1880 that Madame Cassin first met Dumas. She had long admired his plays. The two of them talked painting together. She showed him her collection, and he, in return, took her to see his Meissoniers, his Marchals and his Tassaerts. He set a high value on the work of the last of these three, who had committed suicide in 1874, after having been, all his life, a painter of tears, a sort of a Greuze á la Dumas. Three of his pictures were called: *La Famille malheureuse*; *Le Vieux Musicien*; and *Les Deux Mères*. During his second period he had specialized in nudes: *Suzanne au bain*: *Diane au Bain*. Suicide had increased his prestige. Dumas *fils*, who bought a plot of ground for his tomb in the cemetery of Montparnasse, liked to say with pride: 'I have got forty Tassaerts, including the self-portrait which is finer than anything by Géricault.' One large room in the Avenue de Villiers had every wall covered with Tassaerts — a source of great pride.

After this visit, Adèle Cassin sent Dumas a Tassaert and with it her first letter: 'You must let me lay it at your feet . . . It belongs to you by right . . . Everything of Tassaert's ought to be yours.' She added that she had not dared to bring it in person: 'My lawyer would have denounced you to my heirs, and the ducs de Montfort have a great love for what is mine. . . .'[2]

Dumas wished, in return, to give her a picture, but she protested: 'Please do not send me pictures! I wish you to remain the man who owes me nothing: to whom, on the contrary, I owe great emotions. How sad it all is! You want nothing from me. What have I done to deserve such hardness of heart? Be my friend to the hundred-thousandth degree, and you will have filled me to overflowing.'[3] A few days later

428

she wrote: 'I know no one in the whole world, Monsieur, who is more fair-minded or better-balanced than you ... Above all, you are someone whom, already, I love deeply.'

Then she began to confide in him:

I should regard it as a gift of the gods if you would grant a scrap of *friendship* to me, who have, so far, inspired only what men are pleased to call *love*! What is, I think, peculiar to myself, is that I have never had the experience, unlike other women, of finding friendship treading on the heels of love. What I do know is that *hatred* almost always follows the most exaggerated and most false of sentiments. Few people realize what fantastic feelings a rich woman can inspire! The years have gone by, and I am now a grandmother, but I do not notice any marked change in all the nonsensical play-acting which has made my life sadder and emptier, because the sort of talk I hear has no sincerity behind it. It would only remain for me to believe that I am happy, if I listened to those who assure me that money can give one everything. The good God, when he created me, must have said: 'You shall be blest with good fortune: everything you touch shall succeed without you even having to express a wish — but that shall be my only gift to you ...' You, sir, must be familiar with letters like this. Madame Cassin asks your pardon. The truth of the matter is that she resembles one of those cold plants which yearn for a little warmth. ...⁴

It was her misfortune that she had happened on a man who, though not lacking in warmth, took a sort of pride in never communicating it to others. In vain did she enumerate the sufferings of 'mère Goriot', and complain of Gabrielle's hard heart. Dumas merely fixed her with those 'steely eyes' of his which, she said, 'could plumb the very depths of the soul', and then told her that she alone was responsible for the way in which her daughter had been brought up. 'You can hit hard when you have a mind to it!' she replied, but, like all the others, humbly submitted.

Adèle Cassin to Dumas fils: In a few days' time I am leaving for Biarritz. It would be an act of grace on your part to tell me how you are, and also that you have not forgotten me. I need not say *how great a need I have of you*: you know that already. You are the solid tree-trunk on which I have grown accustomed to lean. You must not fail me; that would be too sad. In the great emptiness of my life, you are everything. I know that in our relationship sex plays no part; all the same, I am a woman and feel the need of your protection — but only in a moral sense.[5]

She described to him her numerous suitors. At fifty she had enough of wealth and beauty to bring men to her feet. Lord Poulett, the sixth earl, took her into Somerset, to Hinton St. George where he owned a house and an estate of 22,129 acres, the annual revenue from which amounted to 21,998 pounds sterling. This noble lord introduced Adèle to his mother, as well as to all the gentry of the neighbourhood, and (though already twice a widower, the first two countesses having died young) begged the charming Frenchwoman to marry him.[6] Madame Cassin told Dumas of her successes. Though thanking him for not paying court to her, she declared that she was wildly jealous of Madame Flahault.[7] He snubbed her for her sentimentality. She professed to be indignant at the cynicism he so much liked to display.

September 20th, 1881: How can you say anything so infamous as that 'there is no such thing as a broken heart'? That is news to me, and you must take the trouble to explain your meaning. I believed you, more or less, when you wrote to me that there are no such things as ailments of the spirit. That may seem to be true, because you added: 'but only organs which lack the necessary strength to endure pain, etc.' But to say there is no such thing as a broken heart! 'Oh how barbarous!' as the duc d'Ossuna would say.[8] And to think that it is you who tell me so, and dare to do so to me! Either you must have been enjoying a hearty laugh when you wrote such words, or, you have always been, till now, the happiest of men. What — have you never known heartbreak? . . .[9]

Oh yes, he had known it, but had let his pride prevail; had thrown out his chest as an alternative to breaking down. Their friendship lasted for a long while. Adèle was kept informed of Dumas's domestic difficulties; of the 'princess's' moods — she, like George Sand referred to her as 'The Person' — of the unbalanced Nadine's recurrent threats of suicide. Perhaps she hoped that in a few years' time she might take the place of 'The Person' in Dumas's life. But he left her with no illusions on that score. Then she played with the idea of marrying the duc de Montfort, as her daughter, Gabrielle, was always urging her to do:

Commercy, May 6th, 1886: I keep wondering how I am ever to emerge from this state of melancholy. I can see no remedy, unless it be to make a new life for myself by marrying the duke, if he still wants me to — for I have handled him very roughly over a number of years. As his wife I should, perhaps, find peace for my poor tormented heart.[10]

Dumas's disapproval was churlishly expressed. 'You will find,' said he (and it might have been Olivier de Jalin speaking), 'that the bronze doors of the great world will be slammed in your face!'

To this she sent an immediate answer:

Hotel Kaiserhof, Kissingen. It seems to me that you are deliberately trying to lessen me in my own eyes. How hard you are! I do most certainly believe that I possess the spirit of humility (in its proper place): nevertheless, you go too far. I shall be, you say, 'a duchess only to the tradespeople and the servants'. You might leave *me* to say that instead of saying it *to* me so cruelly.

One thing is certain, that I shall be la duchesse de Montfort to my grand-daughters,[11] and that is as much as I can reasonably hope for in this world. If the uncle of my darlings were called Jacques or Jean, it would be all the same to me! He would still be the root of the tree under which I must shelter. As such, he is Plantagenet. You think it stupid of me to marry him, don't you? My grand-daughters, I hope, will not be of that opinion. They will never come to see mademoiselle their grandmother; but they will come running to the wife of their uncle, the duke!

It is possible that, placed as I am, I may, to some extent, be blinded: but it is also possible that your feeling of friendship for me makes you exaggerate the sadness of the future on which I am about to enter. If I am guilty of self-deception it is for a very good reason, and, should all the misfortunes which you prophesy fall upon me, no one else will suffer because of them, and I shall console myself with the memory of the last few years through which I have lived, and so find that all is for the best.

Mademoiselle de Vallière once said: 'If I am unhappy with the

Carmelites, I shall only have to remember what all *these* people have made me suffer.' Why cannot you understand that, and help me with your friendship, since you do feel friendly towards me, don't you? What sort of a friendship is it that refuses me all consolation?'[12]

Ultimately, Dumas's authority prevailed. Madame Cassin did not marry the duke. Inspired, however, to some extent, by the memory of his friend, Dumas, though, after *La Princesse de Bagdad*, he had sworn to have no more to do with the theatre, did, in the long run, write another play, *Denise*, which he gave to the Comédie-Française. The promises of dramatists are as much to be relied on as those of drunkards. What is the play about? It is a variation on *Les Idées de Madame Aubray*. A young girl who has been seduced by the son of the family for which she works has had a child by him. The child has died, and the carefully preserved secret is known only to the parents of Denise Brissot. A few years later she falls in love with a decent man, André de Bardannes, and is loved by him. From a sense of loyalty, she reveals her guilty past to him. He marries her. Such an ending in 1885, seemed to be 'terribly daring'.

The Comédie-Française did all it could for the play. Julia Bartet, one of its young sociétaires, acted with a grave and touching distinction; Worms used his beautiful voice to advantage in the part of Bardannes; Coquelin and Got were — Coquelin and Got; Blanche Pierson, brought from the Gymnase, proved herself worthy of her new colleagues. The public reacted very much more favourably than it had done to *La Princesse de Bagdad*, because there was more of humanity in the play and because, as Dumas would have said, the moralist, on this occasion, came down heavily on the side of the woman.

Count Primoli, one of the author's old friends, wrote a notice for an Italian magazine: '*La Dame aux Camélias* is the work of a young man: *Denise* is the work of the same man in his maturity. There is no connection between the two, but perhaps only those who have loved Marguerite can properly understand Denise ...' To have that understanding it was especially necessary to realize that Dumas was the son of a defeated Denise who had been deprived of a chance to make a new life, and the confidential friend of another Denise who, though victorious, had known the meaning of despair.

The success of the play was tremendous: 'without precedent at the

Comédie-Française in the last thirty years', said Perrin. The audience was reduced to sobs in the last act. After each curtain Dumas was dragged on to the stage, and given an ovation. The President of the Republic, Jules Grévy, sent for him to his box and congratulated him. After the performance, the author had supper at Brebant's with his daughter Colette, his son-in-law Maurice Lippmann and his friend Henri Cain who, as he stepped into the cab, cried to the driver: 'To the Panthéon!'

Nadine Dumas, whom ill-health had kept at Marly, received twenty-eight telegrams describing the effect of each scene on the audience. The Minister, Cochery, had given instructions that the post-office was to be kept open. A Dumas *fils* first night had become an event of national importance.

CHAPTER III

'Bonjour, Papa'

IN 1880, a Committee had been formed, under the presidency of
Adolphe de Leuven, now an old man, for the purpose of arranging
for a statue to Dumas *père* to be erected in the Place Malesherbes.
But the public showed ingratitude to the memory of a writer who had
provided it with so many thrills over so long a period. The subscription produced only a mediocre sum. Gustave Doré very generously
offered to give his work free, and designed the monument which, alas,
he never saw in its completed state, because he died shortly before the
inaugural ceremony which took place on November 3rd, 1883.

Doré had drawn his inspiration from the dream once described by
Dumas *père* to Dumas *fils*: 'I was on the top of a mountain, each stone
of which was one of my books.' On the summit of a gigantic stone
pedestal, the very one of which he had dreamed, was set a bronze
statue of Dumas with a smile on his lips. At his feet was a group of
three figures — a student, a workman and a young girl — his eternal
readers. On the other side, a seated d'Artagnan kept watch.

Dumas *fils*, with his wife and his two daughters beside him, listened
to the speeches with brimming eyes. Jules Claretie spoke first: 'It has
been said that Dumas gave entertainment to three or four generations.
He did something even better; he brought them consolation. If he
showed humanity as more generous than, perhaps, it is, we must not
hold that against him. The reason was that he painted it in his own
image . . .' Then came Edmond About:

This statue, which could have been made of solid gold if all
Dumas's readers had each subscribed one centime, this statue,
gentlemen, is that of a great madman in whose kindly humour
and dazzling gaiety is to be found more wisdom and good sense
than we here, taken all together, could possibly provide. It is the
image of a man of disorderly life who won his case against order;

434

of a man of pleasure who might well serve as a model to all hard-working men; of one who sought out adventures in love, politics and war and, in his own person, accomplished more in the way of study than three Benedictine monasteries. It is the portrait of a prodigal who, after squandering millions in liberalities of every kind, left, without knowing it, a King's inheritance. This beaming face is that of an egotist who devoted himself, all through his life, to his mother, his children, his friends and his country; of a weak and easy-going father who rode his son on a loose rein, but had the rare good fortune to see himself continued, in live flesh and blood, by one of the best and most illustrious men whom France has ever applauded.

Dumas *père* once said to me: 'You have good reason to be fond of Alexandre: he is a profoundly human person, and his heart is as sound as his head. Let him be; and, if all goes well, the boy will turn into God the Son.' Did that splendid fellow realize that, in speaking thus, he was arrogating to himself the title of God the Father? Perhaps he did, but with Dumas the 'I' was never hateful because it was always simple-minded and good. Kindliness was at least three-quarters of the rich, strange and heady compound of his genius... This passionate writer, as powerful and as irresistible as a torrent in spate, never acted from motives of hatred or vengeance. He was merciful and generous to his worst enemies, and has, therefore, left behind him only friends... That, gentlemen, is the moral significance of this ceremony.[1]

It was a wonderful day for Dumas fils. After the death of Dumas *père* the newspapers had lost no time in suppressing the word *fils*, but he had at once corrected their mistake: 'That word is part of my name: it is like a second surname which has taken precedence of that of my family.'

Between his own house and the house in which Alexandre I had lived, Alexandre II saw his father's monument set, admired, loved and acclaimed. All the orators had associated the two men in their tributes. The son, for a passing moment, accepted his good fortune, and shook hands on this occasion with men whom, twenty-four hours earlier, he would have refused to recognize. The gathered assembly had been reminded that his father had called him 'my best work'; that, almost alone in this, among the sons of great artists, far from feeling as a burden the weight of a great name, he had added to its glory. From now on, each day as he went home, he would pass the image of that fat, good man, and say to a statue: 'Bonjour, Papa.' That evening, at the Comédie-Française, the company placed a wreath on the bust of Dumas *père*, and *Mademoiselle de Belle-Isle* was played. The only false note came from Gaillardet, of the *Tour de Nesle* imbroglio, who protested against the inscription of that title, among so many others, on the pedestal of the monument. Dumas replied to the effect that he there and then authorized, in anticipation, the use of that same title by the future Committee which should be entrusted with the duty of erecting a statue to Gaillardet.

It is difficult for us today to realize the precise nature of the position occupied by Dumas *fils* in the Paris of the 'eighties. Not only was he all-powerful in the theatre; he also dominated the Academy, where he behaved as a true Musketeer. When Pasteur put his name forward for election, Dumas wrote to Legouvé: 'I positively forbid him to call upon me: it is I who should go to thank him for wanting to be one of us. . . .'

> *Louis Pasteur to Dumas* fils: Monsieur: I am more deeply touched than I can say by your support, and by the gracious and spontaneous manner in which you have offered it to me. Your letter to Monsieur Legouvé has taken its place in our family archives. Copies of it have been made with happy eagerness for those of my domestic circle who are far from home . . . Therefore, I thank you, my dear sir, in the hope that, God willing, I may be in the position to speak of myself, and sign myself, your very devoted colleague.[2]

On Thursdays, at the Academy, the two men, drawn together by a mutual attraction, occupied adjoining seats. Pasteur appreciated 'the delicate sensitiveness of a heart, the offer of which is the more welcome for being made deliberately . . .'[3] On one occasion Dumas, while listening to a discussion, made a bird from a piece of paper. Pasteur asked for it, that he might give it to his little daughter. Dumas handed it to him, after writing on one of its wings: 'One of my heroines, as yet unknown.'

Pasteur knew that if Dumas were told of any case of genuine distress, he always responded generously. There was a popular legend that he was 'close-fisted'. His enemies called him the 'far-from-prodigal son', and attributed the witticism to George Sand. There was no truth in this. Madame Sand knew better than anyone the disinterested kindness of the man who had helped her with the dramatization of more than one novel, and had always refused to take a penny for doing so. Warned by his father's example, Dumas *fils* was careful with money, but prudence is not the same thing as avarice.

He never lacked for enemies. His epigrams, some of them brutal, had left many scars. To his friend, Baron Edmond de Rothschild, he once said: 'Is it because I wrote *Le Demi-Monde* that you invite me to dine with my heroines?' To Madame Edmond Adam (Juliette Lamber) who wanted him to meet Henri Rochefort, he wrote:

My dear friend, let me say, without beating about the bush . . . that this man, who is everlastingly in revolt against things and people for the simple reason that the people and things in question are beyond his reach; who insults everybody because he envies everybody; who makes innuendoes about his former friends when he cannot bite them; who owes his life to those he would like to kill; whose gratitude to those who saved him finds expression only in insults and calumny; who conducts a filthy paper, knowing it to be filthy, for the sake of making money and procuring for himself pleasures which he blames in others — is contemptible and justly contemned. You are able to breathe in that atmosphere: you have a very special organic constitution. I, on the other hand, should break a window in order to get a breath of fresh air.

You find it amusing to entertain at the same table former friends of the Empire and this monster of yours with whom, at the same time, you would like to reconcile your friend Dumas, because you feel pained and annoyed that the one should be so frequently insulted by the other. There are those by whom it is a good thing to be insulted because, in the last analysis, there are some honest folk and others less than honest. Your friend Rochefort falls into the second category, and nothing you can do will ever get him out of it. . . .

Why should a creature of light and radiance like yourself consort with this being of chaos and the refuse bin? Is it that you think you can illuminate this drain, and cleanse this bog? . . .'

If indignation can inspire poetry, polemics can give a sharp edge to prose. On the other hand, many of Dumas's sayings which enjoyed an increasing celebrity in his own day often seem but mediocre stuff to us. He sprinkled his Tuesday dinners (Detaille, Meissonier, Lavoix, Mirault, Meilhac), and those given by Madame Aubernon, with them.

'I am deaf though a senator,' Marshal Canrobert once said to him.

'I can imagine no happier fate for a senator.'

To a young actress who, on making her exit, said to him: 'Feel how my heart's beating. Well, how do you find it?' 'I find it round,' he replied. When he was told that his friend, Narrey, who was putting on a paunch, had just lost a little weight; 'Yes,' said he, 'annoyance at growing fat has thinned him.' To Prince Napoleon, who had disparaged one of his plays in company, and then, on meeting the author, had congratulated him, he said: 'Monseigneur, it would be better if you spoke well of my play to others, and ill of it to me.'

The Comédie-Française had become, after the Gymnase, the theatre most closely associated with Dumas. The death of the Administrator-General, Émile Perrin, was a cause of much grief to him. There had been a strong bond of friendship between the two men, both of them, by temperament, cold and distant. When Perrin fell a victim to an incurable and painful malady, Dumas went frequently to comfort him. One day, in June 1885, Perrin sent word that he would like to see him as soon as possible. Dumas went. 'I may die at any moment now,' said Perrin, 'and I wanted to shake you by the hand, to say goodbye, and to thank you for giving me the last great happiness of my life — the success of *Denise*.' On returning home, Dumas said to his daughter: 'It would be impossible for anyone to die more stoically.'

Another grief was the death of Adolphe de Leuven, the oldest friend of both the Dumas. Afflicted by a cancer of the stomach, Leuven let himself starve to death surrounded by four dogs who licked his hands, and a cageful of singing birds. Dumas went to see him three times a day.

'How are you feeling?' he asked him. 'Like a man who is about to leave this world. I am glad to be going. I have lived long enough, and nothing any longer interests me.'

Dumas tried to persuade him to take some nourishment. 'Why should I?' said the sick man: 'I am lucky enough to be dying without pain. If I rallied now, who knows in what sort of a state I should pass out later?'

Leuven, at eighty-two, was tall and thin, with an elongated, reddish face. He wore a very high hat tilted jauntily over one ear, very stiff collars, and a long cravat wound several times round his neck. He had not changed in appearance since the days of Louis-Philippe. In spite of his great age, his dress and his beard remained obstinately black. Though naturally nervous and irritable, he had always got on well with Dumas *père*, and did so now with Dumas *fils*, to whom he had left everything, including his Marly estate in memory of the happy summers they had spent there together. He particularly asked that his horses should be kept until they died of old age. He did not like to think of them drawing cabs or farm-waggons. He had set aside a small sum of money to be used for the maintenance of his dogs. The funeral service took place at Marly, and he was buried in the Pecq cemetery. Dumas *fils* delivered an oration, and read a passage from the *Mémoires* of Dumas *père*, in which the author of *Antony* describes his first meeting with the Swede who was to turn him into a French dramatist:

All who ever knew Leuven [said Dumas *fils*] even those who saw him only in his last years, will recognize the whole man in that portrait of him as he was in youth. He was like one of the pine trees of his wild northern land, which stand straight and green, even when covered with snow. Until his eighty-second year, our friend never ceased to be tall and thin, with an elegant appearance and a careless, aristocratic carriage. His eyes expressed both pride and gentleness. As to those qualities of mind and heart of which my father speaks so often in the latter part of his *Mémoires*, time only developed and strengthened them. Though there was a certain coldness in his manner — as there always is in those who like to know precisely what they are doing when they give their friendship, because they wish a feeling of esteem to go with it, and are fearful of having to withdraw either — Leuven was the most dependable and devoted man you could hope to find anywhere, and the most lavish of tenderness to those who had managed to break through the top surface of ice. . . .

On the morning of April 14th, I saw, from a number of unmistakable signs, that Death had decided to bring to him, sharply and suddenly, the rest he so longed for. From then on I did not leave him. 'I only hope it will be a fine day.' Those were the last words he was able to whisper, and it is the only one of his wishes which it has not been in my power to fulfil. From that moment, the gentle pressure of his hands, an increasingly raucous sound in his breathing, certain movements of his head and eyes, made it plain that the time for the last farewell had come ... The room began to grow dark; the birds fell silent; night came. His calm old face, set in rigid lines, was illuminated only by a small night-light. His breathing became more regular, slower, weaker, and I had to lean over him in order to make sure that this was indeed the sleep of death. He died without the least shock, or show of struggle. I closed his eyes, I pressed one final kiss upon his cheek, and did not leave him until his servants, all praying and weeping, had dressed him as he had wished to be dressed for that night which would bring him no awakening.

That is how this good man took his leave of the world. A gentler, simpler death could not be imagined, nor one nobler or more worthy to serve as an example to human improvidence and terror. I have carried out his wishes. He rests next to his wife, and with piety I have laid the friend whom my father found more than sixty years ago, on a lovely stretch of road when the daisies and the hawthorns were in flower, within the grave he longed for, surrounded by his best friends, and covered with flowers. . . .[5]

Now that Taylor and Leuven were dead, there remained but one other who had known his father as a young man, and he, the greatest of them all, Victor Hugo. He, too, disappeared in 1885. Dumas *fils* did not greatly mourn him. First, unhappy memories, and, later, politics, had separated the two men. Hugo believed in progress and the Republic: Dumas in decadence and the vanity of all things. The final procession from the Arc de Triomphe to the Panthéon, irritated Dumas. 'Had Hugo's writings', he said, 'been hostile to the Republic instead of to the Empire, his poems would not have been a whit the less beautiful, but he, himself, would not have been given a public funeral ... Had he lived behind the Place du Trône instead of near the Place de l'Étoile, his talents would have been no less great, but he would not have been borne beneath the Arc de Triomphe. Musset, who was also a great poet, had less than thirty persons at his funeral.'[6]

These obsequies had been the subject of much discussion at the Academy. Should Maxime du Camp, at that time its Director, speak in its name? Several academicians argued that, in view of Maxime de Camp's political opinions, it would be better not to risk a hostile demonstration.

'The Academy', was Dumas's stern comment, 'should be above public prejudices. It has its rules and regulations, and it is for us to see they are observed.'

The whole man is in that arrogant and military phrase.

CHAPTER IV

'Francillon'

JULES CLARETIE succeeded Perrin at the Comédie-Française. He
was a clever young man with a snub nose, who had invented the
weekly gossip-column. His *Semaine à Paris*, published in *Le
Temps*, amused the public by reason of its unexpected and flimsy transi-
tions. At the Comédie-Française after the severe Perrin, he gave the impression that he lacked backbone. He promised everything to everyone.
He was nicknamed '*Guimauve le Conquérant*';[1] 'Yes-No-If'; 'The
Master-Hedger'. The caricaturists showed him running down the
passages to escape importunate actresses. But he held his post for
twenty-eight years.

One of his first actions as Administrator had been to ask Dumas for
a new play. 'Bring up the Guard!' he exclaimed. Dumas, 'our crown-
ing hope, our finest brain', began a play for him, *La Route de Thèbes*,
but made only slow progress. He was *too* determined that it should
be really good. 'When one is so soon to leave the world, one should
say only what is worth saying . . .' Old age begins on the day when
daring dies.

When the date of his promised delivery of *La Route de Thèbes*
drew near, he realized that it would not be ready in time. But Claretie
was counting on him. What was to be done? He remembered a first
act, written some time before, built round a daring but light-hearted
theme. A wife says to her husband: 'If ever you deceive me, I shall
take a lover.' The husband does deceive her. She goes to a ball,
picks up the first young man she comes across, has supper with him,
and returns home, saying: 'I have taken my revenge!' That, in fact, is
not true, but her husband believes her. She is determined to play out the
comedy to its bitter end, even if it means the break-up of her marriage.
But the young man turns up suddenly in the guise of a lawyer's clerk
sent to collect evidence for divorce proceedings. He, better than
anyone, knows that nothing serious has taken place. He says as much,

442

and succeeds in convincing the husband. Exit Drama. The Comedy ends in comedy.

Dumas sent *Francillon* to Claretie with this note:

> Finished
> Very dangerous
> Too long
> Very tired.
> A. D.

The idea was not new. Louis Ganderax had already submitted to Dumas a play, *Miss Fanfare*, on the same subject, and Dumas had rewritten the first act. Ganderax, preferring his own version, had willingly given Dumas permission to use his own revision of the act, which thus became the starting-point of *Francillon*. It is far from being a masterpiece, but it is a gay piece of writing, and one of its author's more charming productions. Ganderax lavished generous praise on the old virtuoso's skill:

> Alexandre Dumas, third of that name, is now more than sixty-two years of age: but the vitality of the line shows in him as still unexhausted. What a man! What an admirable Negro! He treats us like so many poor whites. He makes us feel the weight and, sometimes, the brutality of his strength. But we are well pleased to be his victims. Whether he leads the public, or drives it, the hand is the hand of a master. He controls and guides it as well as his grandfather ever did his horse. If there is any real difference between him in his young days and him now, it is not that he is less strong today than he was then. It is that he is fonder now, having derived much enjoyment from his natural gifts and from his art, of indulging in exercises which are, at once, simpler and more violent. . . .[2]

The world portrayed in *Francillon* is, as always with Dumas, the world in which men in white ties go from their wives' drawing-rooms to the club, and thence to the bedrooms of 'those women'. Nothing of the *dumafiste* faun was lacking. The irresponsible husband; the wife wounded to the quick; the man-friend — impenitent and philosophic haunter of the clubs; the sympathetic confidante; the conventional young person, half sweet simplicity, half knowingness, of 1887

— all were there. But the dialogue was sparkling and the action lively. The public acclaimed its conqueror.

Francillon was applauded to the skies. When the curtain rose on the first act, it got 'a round' on its own account. 'A strange implement, made of wood and nickel, drew every eye. Never, before this memorable evening, had a telephone been seen on the stage of the Théâtre-Français. 'What a daring fellow this Claretie is!' murmured the audience.

'I was no less charmed, carried away and staggered than the public', wrote Sarcey. 'The first act is dazzling ... the dialogue brilliant, relevant to the action and true to character — genuine wit. So rich is the texture of the whole performance that nothing I can say will give any idea of it!' Julia Bartet made of Francine de Riverolles 'a little prancing mare, pawing the ground, quivering in every limb'.[3]

'Oh this Dumas!' said the salons: 'he wants to make us believe that a woman of the world, just because her husband has been false to her, will go off with the first man she meets, and boast the next day that she has let herself become this unknown's mistress. What a fantastic piece of rigmarole!' Others saw in the play a serious argument: '"An eye for an eye, a tooth for a tooth": that is your heroine's motto, and you back her up in it. "Kill her!" was what you used to say, and the revolvers went off obediently to an accompaniment of applause from the members of the jury. *"Deceive him!"* you say now, and the supper-restaurants are falling over themselves to reopen, and seeing that the locks on the doors of their private rooms are working properly.'

Dumas had *not* said: 'Deceive him!' Quite the contrary. But he had maintained that a man's adultery, though it may not have the same consequences as a woman's, is not just an amusing trifle.

What does astonish the readers of our day, who have become hardened to this sort of thing, is that the play should have been thought 'coarse'. It was not lacking in truth. The world of *Francillon* was not the world of the Faubourg Saint-Germain, still less that of the Marais. It was the world of the Champs-Élysées and the Plaine Monceau. 'In this district of Paris virtue is less rare than modesty. Women of honest life are to be found in it, but the jargon they speak, often mixed with slang, does something to outface honesty. The occasion at which M. Dumas invites us to be present, resembles, more than anything else, an evening spent in the drawing-room — or rather, in the *hall* — of a young couple, with only intimates as guests.'[4]

Ganderax concluded by stressing Dumas's origins, which he knew would not displease his friend:

What delights us even more than the work itself is the author. His virtuosity makes us conscious of his strength. The play springs from his gaiety and good humour. We all of us admire M. Dumas: we love him, and if there are things we have to forgive in him, we do so with pleasure because the grandson of the hero of Brixen, forty years — or nearly — after his first entry into the world of letters, exhibits, together with the temperament of a Negro, the highest degree of sharp-edged reasoning, the most brilliant, the most clearly defined, the toughest form of wit of which a Parisian is capable.

CHAPTER V

Love and Old Age

Talent cannot give back what time has effaced. Glory rejuvenates only our name.
CHATEAUBRIAND

IT was true that Dumas could still, by fits and starts, produce a surprising impression of gaiety. This scorner of love had at length to admit that he had been vanquished by it, as only a man in his sixties can be vanquished when he falls a victim to a young woman, and loves love with the despairing passion which the last flickering flames of hope warm into life.

He had long cultivated the friendship of an old actor, now in retirement, doyen honoraire of the Comédie-Française — Regnier de la Brière, known more generally as 'Regnier'. Nothing could well be more pleasing than the Regnier family circle. The husband, once an actor of the first rank, then archivist of the Théâtre-Français, professor at the Conservatoire, general-manager, and, later, stage-director at the Opéra, had been educated by the Oratorians. He was a small, pleasant and sarcastic man, whose spontaneous and subtle art could both stir and amuse an audience. 'He did not deliberately study his effects; they came to him of their own accord.' He had written a number of excellent books, among them *Le Tartuffe des Comédiens*. His wife, a woman of quite unusual beauty, was the daughter of the 'lovely Madame Grévedon', for long the adored mistress of Scribe. His daughter, no less marvellous in her own way, had been married at seventeen to an architect, Félix Escalier. Dumas had known this ravishing Henriette as a small child. He had watched her grow in charm and grace. He admired her.

Her marriage with the architect had turned out to be a lamentable failure. It appeared that this man of stone was the only person who did not idolize the woman — his own wife — to whom so many others paid court in vain. After much suffering she separated from him, and went to live with her parents, disappointed and discouraged. Henriette had long admired Dumas, though he intimidated her. She 'felt like a small girl in his presence'. She sought from him advice about her

446

reading, and showed gratitude for his pity. 'It is not *pity* that I feel
for you,' he replied, 'but an infinite tenderness.' She complained of
her loneliness, and asked the author, crowned with laurel, whom she
thought 'as handsome as a god', to be her support and her distraction.

Dumas fils *to Henriette Escalier, November 1887*: My charming
young friend: here is the gold piece you were so good as to ask of
me for one of your charities. But why did you ask so little?
Can it be that you believe the legend of my miserliness? Even if
it were true, I should never be a miser with you. Make full use
of my purse which will always be larger than your little hands.
I shall be endlessly happy to do good with you, since you could
never wish to do ill. My charming little friend, I kneel at your
feet, which cannot be larger than your hands.

If you have a photograph which is really like you, please give
me a copy. It shall be returned to you in a book which tells the
story of a goddess whom I think you resemble. You will find that
all your friends will be of the same opinion, though I was first in
the field. My respectful greetings to your mother.[1]

The portrait was duly returned to the giver with a copy of *Psyché*,
by La Fontaine. Dumas had had the two volumes bound in turquoise-
blue morocco, and had stuck Henriette's picture on the inside of the
front cover. A letter accompanied the gift:

My dear little friend, summon the seven sages of Greece;
assemble the judges of the Areopagus; join with them Phidias,
Leonardo, Correggio, Clodion, and say to them: 'My friend Dumas
says that I am like Psyche.' They will all reply, each in his own
tongue: 'And he is right!'

That is why I am giving you the story of the king's daughter
whom Cupid turned into a goddess, together with a portrait of
yourself (which you will, I hope, replace) that those into whose
hands this book may come when you and I have left this world
may realize that not the sages, nor the judges, nor the artists, nor
I were wrong, and see in you the divine features of her who made
Venus jealous and Cupid faithful.

My young friend, I kiss your hands in gratitude for your New
Year's gifts. . . .[2]

Astonished by the degree of interest so obviously shown in him by this young and desirable creature, he dared not pluck the happiness of which it seemed to give him the promise. He had long ceased to believe in the possibility of sincere love. Whenever he set himself to analyse a woman's feelings, he found pride, ambition, the longing for protection, but never the absolute, the rare, fidelity which had been the dream of the boy and was still the grey-haired man's ideal. Therefore, he pitilessly cast out from his life all those who laid siege to him — actresses, women of the world, sinners and penitents, alike. It was about this time that he replied as follows to a young woman who had written to him from Cette, offering herself to him, without reservation:

> My dear child, I understand, though I wish I did not, because I ought not . . . God save me from risking the whole of your life on a first impulsive outpouring from you, and on my one last illusion! I have done with the world of the feelings, and you are young enough to be my daughter. You are possessed of the charm and the value which I most respect — virginity. It is not for me to make you like other women, and to lay up for you a store of every kind of pain and misery, of the regrets and remorse which follow on the heels of a first fall. I know them too well, and whither they lead.
>
> I do not wish that you should ever have occasion to complain of me, nor that I should have to blush for you. I have set you on a high pedestal in my heart, the only one which you can worthily occupy.
>
> Do not tempt me to go beyond the limits of friendship. You already have all that is best in me.
>
> I embrace you.[3]

Henriette Escalier, who was genuinely in love with, or, at least, dazzled by, the eminence, fame and charm of Dumas *fils*, did not despair of overcoming his resistance. Emboldened by what she knew of his broken home life, of the nerve-ridden 'princess', of the mere friendship into which his liaison with Ottilie Flahault (now a grandmother) had dwindled, she deliberately set herself the task of conquering the great man. Regnier had died in 1885, and Dumas saw a great deal of the two bereaved women. He advised and helped them. There was soon no possible doubt that victory might be within reach. The light of it already gleamed in Henriette's eyes.

Victory? Would it not rather be for him defeat? He was tempted by her radiant face, her wonderful body, her appealing freshness. The memory of the young girl whom, such a long while ago, he had seen shivering in the sea, innocent and ignorant of herself, was now disturbingly mingled with the fleshly allurements of flowering womanhood. But how, he thought, could Henriette find satisfaction in a liaison with an old lover who was too experienced not to be madly jealous? How could she be expected to put up with his melancholy, his misanthropy, with those crises of despair induced by the unhappy temperament of an artist who was convinced that he had come to the end of his tether?

One day, in particular, he was always to remember, that April 13th, 1887, when, with their first kiss, she had given herself to him spontaneously. *April 13th, 1887*: 'My destiny found its goal upon your lips.' She might have replied, like Juliet:

> 'I am too fond,
> And therefore thou mayst think my 'haviour light.'

'Did I sufficiently ask myself, that day, whether your agitation was genuine, assumed, or something that had become a habit, whether I had but to take you . . . Ah! if it be true that I wakened your senses then for the first time, it is no less true that you can boast of having made me doubt my knowledge of psychology, and that you are the only woman I have never succeeded in explaining satisfactorily to myself.'

Then he tried to feel convinced that the astonishing rapidity with which Henriette had yielded was a favourable omen. 'When doubts return to plague me, it is the *immediate* gift of yourself that most persuades me of your innocence. A woman who had already belonged to another man would never have bestowed the gift so quickly. She would have been too frightened of being suspected, even of being denounced, by reason of that facile surrender.'

Dumas fils *to Henriette Regnier, October 1887*: Whither are we heading — to what conclusion, what catastrophe? I do not know. It is now six months since you flung yourself into my arms with the secret presentiment that all your happiness and all your misery are bound up with me. All such strength and intelligence as I may have during the time that still remains to me to live shall be devoted to making you happy. Do not argue, do not question, do not torment yourself. Just let yourself live and be adored as woman, angel, goddess, child, according as you may wish. You have ceased to belong to yourself. You wanted to find a master, and could not have hit upon a better than the one you have. Do you know that you are the best loved creature in all the world?'

It was true that he loved her as he had never loved any woman since Marie Duplessis and Lydia Nesselrode. Perhaps he loved her even more intensely, because Henriette Regnier was more like the ideal which, like so many men, he had sought in vain. 'You have appeared suddenly in my life, giving to my ideal the most brilliant form and substance ... Not only are you the girl whom I adored at first sight, you are her whom I have always adored in secret, in spite of all the shapes which the feminine animal has assumed in the years between. ...'

It was a great physical passion. Thanks to her he now knew, in the evening of his days, the joy of coming, trembling with desire, to trysts which she punctually kept. In 1890 Henriette obtained her divorce. She had been separated from Escalier for several years, and hoped, no doubt, to make a new life with Dumas. But how could he marry her? Could he repudiate Madame Dumas, now in her sixties and seriously ailing? Could he compromise the future of their daughter who had not yet found a husband? The sworn foe of adultery saw himself condemned to a long and clandestine 'affair'. Deeply concerned for the good name of his beloved, he wrapped the whole adventure in artless precautions, signing 'Denise' the telegrams he sent to Henriette when he was parted from her at holiday time.

With his happiness was mingled, as always through the whole length of his ill-adjusted existence, a vague feeling of dissatisfaction. This love, for which he was no longer suited, had undermined the very foundations of what he had always wanted to be an exemplary life.

For seven years [he wrote in 1893] not an hour has passed without my thinking of you. A star falling into the sea could not produce more disturbance than you have done by suddenly flinging yourself, as you have done, into my life. All that I had ever dreamed of love, convinced that I should never find it, I have found in you: physical perfection and the possibility of moral perfection as well, if I am to believe all you say ... 'Ah! Suzon, Suzon, how you make me suffer!'

The man of the theatre quoted Beaumarchais; the man of the beating heart suffered. Why? Because he could not believe in his own happiness. 'I spend the whole of my life in rebuilding yours. I look for you; I follow you through the years, saying to myself: "What was Henriette doing *then*? Why was she at such and such a place at such and such a time?" and when I come upon obscurity, when, like Phoebe, whose pearly whiteness you have, you pass behind a cloud, I doubt, I worry, I suffer.'

Madame Regnier had rented for the summer a chalet at Lion-sur-Mer, and took her daughter with her. On that shore, where Gyp reigned supreme, Henriette was bored. Dumas was obsessed with terror of the young men, of the games played upon the sands and in the sea, of the traps into which idleness might lead her. For re-assurance she sent him her girlish diaries in which, already, she had written so much about him.

Dumas fils *to Henriette Regnier, September 22nd, 1893*: You are wrong not to like the seaside, for it was there that you first appeared to me (in 1864) riding on a donkey ... There are English novels that begin in that way.... Why did not God put himself out to the extent of whispering in my ear: 'One day you will be loved by that child. Keep yourself for her.' Some angel, also, might have said to you: 'One day you will be eternally adored by this man. Keep yourself for him.' God did not do what he should have done: the angel passed close to you without uttering a word; but you had a vision, and the sense of it has stayed with you. When I plunge down into your past with the help of the diaries you have given me to read, of the letters of which you have made me free, I find there, from time to time, my own name, which seems to draw you like a magnet ... until the moment came when you fell into my arms, never again to leave them. ...

But, in spite of these touching premonitions, he continued to torture himself. In the course of his life he had found so many reasons for jealousy that her solemn promises brought him no comfort. 'Actually, your letters do really have the accent of *the first time*, but, then, Mercury is so mischievous, and you are so wholly woman from the toes of your feet to the hair on your head....'

Jealous of whom? Of her husband? Not the least little bit. 'The man to whom you were given at seventeen, without you having the

faintest idea of what lay behind the gift, matters nothing to me ...'
No, just jealous of the men she *might* have chosen freely; of the
composer, Paladilhe, who had made her work at her singing, of the
drawing-room tenors. He was as jealous of the past as of the present,
suffering atrociously at the idea of 'the least profanation'. She complained of his lack of trust which, she said, was especially unjust at
a time when she was forcing herself to avoid all 'approaches and
temptations'. He pleaded not guilty. How could he be other than
he was?

> I have never seen around me anything but vice, lying and
> corruption, in their every manifestation. I have had, by making
> an unconscious but irresistible effort, to free myself from them,
> single-handed, without the help of anybody else ... I have
> remained very suspicious. When I met you at a period of my life
> when I should have said goodbye to all illusions, you so com-
> pletely realized the dreams of my earliest youth that I let myself
> be drawn by desire. What the women who had crossed my life,
> *including her who shares it*, had done, and could still do, brought
> me no suffering, because I did not love them. I was not happy,
> but, thanks to my work, I was at peace. Had I not met you, I
> should soon have forgotten that such beings as women existed.
> I had never given them anything of my inner self, and my body
> had reached a point at which disgust and nausea were paramount...
> I was born chaste... I had never known a woman who did not lie.
> Why, then, should you not lie like the rest of them?

When Madame Regnier felt that she was dying, she sent for Dumas,
and said to him with every sign of concern: 'Henriette will be all
alone.' He promised to marry her, should he ever be free to do so.
The hypothesis seemed reasonably probable, for, in 1891, Nadine
Dumas, mad with jealousy, had left the Avenue de Villiers and gone
to live with her daughter Colette. Dumas, however, could not seek
divorce from a woman of unbalanced mind who, according to the
doctors, was suffering from an incurable mental condition. Besides,
was he sure that he really wanted it? Once again, Olivier de Jalin
hesitated over what form of ending to adopt:

> *Dumas* fils *to Henriette Regnier*: And now there has come this
> complicated business of the possibility of freedom for me. You

have no illusions about the thoughts which this eventuality has awakened in my mind. I have come to dread as a misfortune a fact which I had had every right to hope for as a revenge ... Twenty-eight years ago, when I so mistakenly did my duty, I did it at the imminent risk of losing my life, and, still more probably, my reason. But, in the long run, I did come to feel that I was devoting myself to something, and I grew to believe in work and fame.

This proud man must, indeed, have been 'knocked sideways', if he could confess what he had always kept hidden from his friends, and even from George Sand: the tragic failure of his marriage.

CHAPTER VI

'La Route de Thèbes'

AFTER *Francillon* no new play by Dumas was produced. Eight years of silence — that is a long time for a famous author, in full possession of his faculties, and unceasingly canvassed by the senior theatre of France. But the giant had always been easily discouraged. His sudden lassitude recalled the moods of dejection which had come upon his grandfather in Italy and Egypt. 'I have been at grips with life ever since I was seven years old,' he told the young Paul Bourget, 'my attitude is due not to melancholy but fatigue. There are moments when I feel, really feel, that I have had enough, when I should like to lie down with my nose to the wall, so as no longer to hear anyone speak of anything, and, especially, to hear no one speak of me.'

His private life accounted for much of his gloom, but he was beginning to have doubts, too, of his art. Certain younger men were dogging his footsteps with demonstrations of sarcastic hatred, which concealed a deal of envy. In the corridors of the Théâtre-Français which had just accepted *La Parisienne* for production, Henry Becque, 'broad of back and hard of eye under the thick thatch of his brows, with his clipped moustache and ill-tempered mouth', went about reciting epigrams punctuated with 'how d'you like that?' spoken in a loud voice:

> Ainsi que deux Corneille, on connaît deux Dumas;
> Mais aucun d'eux n'est Pierre et tous deux sont Thomas.[1]

To which Dumas replied:

> Si ce coup de bec de Becque t'éveille,
> O Thomas Corneille! en l'obscur tombeau,
> Pardonne à l'auteur qui bâille aux Corneille
> Et songe au public qui bâille aux *Corbeaux*.[2]

But if Becque took bitter pleasure in these pleasantries, Dumas, now sick of everything, thought them despicable and pointless. He knew, well enough, that the stars of Becque and Ibsen were in the ascendant. He knew that the younger critics now spoke with contempt of the 'well-made' — too well-made — 'play'. The success of his own revivals — *Une Visite de Noces*, in which Bartet had taken over the part originally played by Desclée, and spat out the famous 'Faugh!' with genius: *L'Ami des Femmes*, in which she interpreted the role of Jane de Simerose with an admirable mixture of modesty and boldness — did nothing to restore his self-confidence. Revival is not creation. He had written one act of *Les Nouvelles Couches* which, he said, was to be his *Figaro*, and four acts of *La Route de Thèbes*, which was to consist of five. But he never finished either of them.

> *Dumas* fils *to Paul Bourget*: I have taken up *La Route de Thèbes* again, but cannot see my way to an ending, and fear now that I never shall. Enthusiasm and excitement have become, for me, things of the past. I know what I want to say, but I keep on asking myself 'what's the point of saying anything?' The truth of the matter is that I know too much about human nature.

Actually, what he was doing was to project his own dissatisfaction. He took a gloomy view of the world because, in spite of his success both as man and author, he had suffered much. He could have turned against himself the words of one of his characters:
'No doubt about it, you are very strong.'
'Maybe, but I am not happy.'
Was he even very strong? To Léopold Lacour who, in 1894, questioned him on the subject of *La Route de Thèbes* which was being impatiently awaited by the Comédie-Française, he replied:

> I am coming to doubt more and more whether I shall ever finish it. There are so many things to pack into it, too many things. For a dramatist who has wanted to be more than a mere entertainer, to set the minds of his audience working, because that is what his has been doing, the experience of life, with all the nourishment it provides for meditation, becomes, little by little, a temptation to indulge in over-great ambitions, because, as a craftsman, he no longer has that fearlessness, that self-confidence, which, twenty years ago, might have made it possible for him to

realize them. And then, you see — and you can take my word for
this — I have never had the gift of arrogance, in spite of a legend
to the contrary which gratifies too many people to be easily let
die. All the same, it may be that, without absurdly flattering
myself, I have formed too high an idea of the value of my work,
may have hoped that when death comes, I shall not take all
of it into the grave with me. God knows, I may have had reason
to do so because of the success I have enjoyed, especially of that
kind of esteem which men of clear-headed intelligence, men like
Taine, for instance, have felt for me. But I realize that public
taste is changing. Part of the younger generation is moving
towards Becque and his disciples, while part acclaims the plays of
Ibsen. I am watching the decline of *my* type of art. All my plays
are destined to perish.[3]

His father had said much the same in the last months of his life, but,
then, Dumas *père* had with him, as a source of reassurance, a son whom
he admired. Léopold Lacour was deeply moved by the pale, bleak and
solemn smile with which these admissions had been made. He told
the old master that *La Dame aux Camélias* and *Le Demi-Monde* would
go on being played indefinitely. Had not Sarah Bernhardt recently
revived *La Femme de Claude* with success? Had not a critic written:
'Dumas did what Ibsen has done long before Ibsen was ever heard of.'
Again the bleak smile showed:

You are sincere [said Dumas] and for that I thank you. The
trouble is that I have lived too long, and have seen too often those
returns of popularity which are always followed by a fresh, and
final, neglect. This turning back of the wheel of time, which it
would be foolish to regard as decisive, I probably owe entirely
to Sarah Bernhardt who is very much better in the part than
Desclée ever was. The triumph of a great artist which suddenly
breathes new life into a play which has fallen into disrepute brings
sweet solace to an author. But he must not, because of it, deceive
himself. What he needs to know is whether the future, a far
distant future, will ratify the verdict. What has happened to
Voltaire's plays? No one reads them nowadays. Yet, what
dramatic poet was more admired at one time, more flattered, than
the author of *Zaïre* and *Mérope*? Does having readers, and here
and there his bust in prose in that necropolis which is what, more

often than not, literary histories amount to, mean continued life for a man whose productions were meant to be acted? Artistic survival for that kind of writer can take the form only of having at least two or three genuine masterpieces to his credit which can still hold their own on the stage. I can point to scarce three or four such masterpieces in the records of the French theatre in the nineteenth century — not the great dramas of Victor Hugo — their verbal magnificence will not for ever save them from oblivion — but a few of Musset's comedies. I say nothing about my father. His genius was as natural to him as the trunk is to an elephant. . . .⁴

On returning home, Léopold Lacour noted down that, in spite of the inherent melancholy of the words, there was still power in the high carriage of Dumas's head. 'The icy and metallic gleam of that bright blue eye has not been dulled. A swinging movement of the shoulders, which is definitely "dated" and evokes an ideal of elegance prevalent in the days of Napoleon III, imparts to him an air of something like military abruptness. The suppleness of the cavalry officer is less marked now; the speech is slower than it used to be.' A cloak of melancholy hung about the last years of a life which had once appeared so splendid. Late love had failed to achieve rejuvenation.

Another journalist, Philippe Gille, had much the same impression. 'Are we', he had asked, 'ever to see *La Route de Thèbes?*'

Dumas answered with another question: 'How am I to risk a campaign at my age, when all I can expect is to be a target for blows? No; I had far better leave *La Route de Thèbes* in a drawer. I really do think that it is one of the best of my plays: but I think, too, that it will never see the light.'

Then he spoke of his distress: 'Faced by the nothingness of life, by the uselessness of all effort, by the despairing cries which we send up to a so-called Providence which shows no concern for us, seeking help, I have sometimes seriously thought of entering a monastery . . . There, at least, one is shut away from life . . . Oh! don't worry: I should never have the courage to do it . . . People would say that I had tumbled into religion under the influence of priests and women . . . Besides, I should be bored to death!'⁵

Émile Bergerat, Théophile Gautier's son-in-law, found Dumas obsessed, nevertheless, by thoughts of Christianity:

'My dear friend,' he said, 'you have two grave defects: you smoke and you are a pantheist . . . We can look only to Calvary for light.'

'Yes,' said Bergerat: 'the Magdalene . . . *la Dame aux Camélias* of the desert.'

'Leave *la Dame aux Camélias* out of it . . . The woman you mean is in the Gospel.'

A footman came into the room to say that X . . . had come, asking for a louis.

'Better give the poor devil five,' said Dumas, 'in that way he'll be saved four more journeys.'

It was Dumas *père* speaking from the grave, with this difference, that the five louis really did exist.[6]

To Jules Claretie he read the four acts already completed of *La Route de Thèbes*, and outlined the fifth. What was the play to be about? As once, on the road to Thebes, Oedipus encountered the Sphinx, so the learned Dr Didier, on the last stretch of life's road, meets a mysterious and disturbing beauty, Miliane Dubreuil, own sister to the female monsters who are the central figures in the plays of Dumas *fils*. Didier, a famous medical man, here stands for the author. A writer, anxious not to portray writers, turns them into painters or scientists, but the masks are transparent.

The Doctor, an atheist and materialist, has a wife and a daughter, both of them believers, and a non-believing disciple, Mathias. Didier's daughter, Geneviève, is in love with Mathias, but he, a confirmed bachelor, rebuffs her, and sneers at her faith.

'Your soul,' he tells her, 'is nothing but the sum total of the functions of the grey matter of the brain . . . If I struck you on the temple, what would your soul say?'

'It would forgive you,' Geneviève replies.

The first act takes place in the doctor's house. Didier is temporarily absent. Mathias is engaged in giving a consultation to a young man from the country, Dominique de Juniac, who is passing through a terrible crisis. His father has, from interested motives, opposed his marriage. The young man, who is desperately in love, is prepared to take matters into his own hands, but his fiancée has made it plain that she will not marry without his father's consent. Having said this, she has gone away with her mother, leaving no address. Dominique is searching for the fugitives in Paris where, he suspects, they are hiding. He has but one idea, either to possess the woman he adores, or to kill her. Mathias gives the excitable young man some good advice, but sends him away unconvinced. Dr Didier comes home and, almost at once, several shots sound from the street. Mathias rushes to the window and recognizes the murderer, who takes to his heels.

The victim, a ravishing young woman, is brought in, and Didier examines her. The wound is not serious. He proposes to shelter the girl in his house until she is convalescent. It appears that her name is Miliane Dubreuil. She is twenty years old. The mother, when questioned, gives evasive answers. The assailant, she says, is unknown to her, and she proceeds to supply an entirely false description of the bungling young criminal.

The second act is set, three weeks later, in Dr Didier's country house. Miliane, now cured, is there with her mother. Nothing is said about her going away. Didier employs her as his secretary, and Mathias embarks on long philosophic discussions with her. Geneviève confesses to her mother that she is jealous of the stranger. Madame Didier begs her husband not to keep the two women under the same roof. He consults Mathias, who says: 'You are in love with Miliane, though you don't know it.' Instead of begging her to leave, the doctor says to her: 'I need to feel that you are part of my life.' The disturbing young person agrees to postpone her departure.

Meanwhile, Didier has been called upon by a deputation of Scandinavian students who have come to pay him homage. Their spokesman, who is called Stephen, makes an excellent impression on the master, who cannot help thinking that so likeable a young fellow would make an excellent husband for his daughter Geneviève.

Two days pass. In the third act, Dominique de Juniac reappears. His father is dead, and there is no longer any obstacle to his marriage. Mathias hurriedly sends word to Miliane who, disagreeably surprised, refuses to marry the man who has tried to kill her. Dominique proceeds to brandish, not a revolver, but his fiancée's letters, all of them, it appears, couched in the most tender terms, and revealing the fact that intimacy has occurred. The 'Disturbing young Person' boldly confronts Mathias.

'You take me for a Sphinx, and are trying to solve my riddle.

You are convinced that I am stuffed full of deep and criminal schemes. You are wrong.'

Nevertheless, Didier's assistant asks her what she would do if she were offered a hundred thousand francs to make herself scarce. She replies coldy:

'I should ask for a million.'

Fourth act. Geneviève bares her heart to her father, and tells him of her state of moral perplexity. Doubt has crept into her mind. She questions the Wise Man:

'What is there beyond this life?'

'The Unknown.'

'Does not your science provide justification for any of the hopes given us by religion?'

'No.'

'But that is a counsel of despair.'

'Sometimes.'

Didier, however, succeeds in calming his daughter. Then he turns to the ever enigmatic Miliane. She makes no bones about the admiration she feels for him, and goes so far as to declare that she is prepared to do all he may want of her: *all.* He answers:

'I love you. For three weeks now, thanks to you, I have been living through that twentieth year of mine through which I passed without so much as being aware of it ... You are young. I am young no longer. You are free. I am not. You cannot love me. Leave me then, leave me, and find the young man, the darling of the gods, who shall be worthy to become your husband, and whom I shall love as a son.'7

There the manuscript ends. On April 2nd, 1895, Madame Dumas died at the age of sixty-eight, at the house of her daughter Colette, N° 17 Avenue Niel. A few days later, Madame Regnier passed away in the little house in the rue de Rome, built by Escalier, which she shared with her daughter, Henriette. Dumas had the 'princess' buried at Neuilly-sur-Seine, in the same tomb as Catherine Labay and, on June 26th, less than three months after he had become a widower, married Henriette at Marly-le-Roi. He loved her with a desperate passion. We know, however, from what Dumas told Victorien Sardou, his neighbour, that, when making this grave decision, he was torn with doubts. Was it not sheer madness for a man who had for so long been haunted by the apocalyptic vision of the husband-wife relationship, to tie himself, at over seventy, to a young woman of such superlative beauty? He thought it was, but kept his promise.

On July 27th, 1895, he made his Will:

Today I enter on my seventy-second year. It is time I made a Will, the more so that, from certain symptoms, it appears more than probable that I shall not see the end of the year which I am now beginning ... That does not alter the fact that, precisely one month ago, I married somebody who is very much younger than me, and am determined to give her this proof of my esteem and affection, which she has truly deserved in every way. I am certain that she will worthily bear my name for so long as she may choose to do so after I am dead. Furthermore, she is both energetic and brave, and will see that my wishes, here expressed, are faithfully carried out.

I hereby express, in the strongest possible terms, my wish to be buried without any religious ceremony. I desire that no oration shall be delivered over my grave, and that no military honours shall be paid me. In this way my death will intrude on nobody who does not want to be intruded upon.

I wish to be buried at Père Lachaise,[8] in a vault containing two compartments, in one of which Madame Dumas shall be laid beside me after what, I hope, will be a long interval. I wish to be dressed in one of my red-bordered linen shirts and in one of my working-suits, made in one piece; my feet to be left bare.

I leave all my papers, correspondence and manuscripts to Madame Henriette Alexandre Dumas who will put them in order, and knows what is to be done with them.[9]

In the month of August he wrote from Puys to Jules Claretie:

Your letter reached me just as I was revising the last scene of the fourth act, the key-scene for the play, and for Mounet-Sully. If we are to fall to the ground, that is where the fall will come. If, on the other hand, we pull that scene off we shall be well set for a big success, even though the finishing off of the play is not going to be easy. . . .

In another letter, speaking of *La Route de Thèbes*, he said: 'Either you will have it in a year, or I shall be dead.' Georges Claretie, the son of Jules, has described in an article[10] a fifth act which Dumas read, in his presence, in its 'finished version', to the Administrator-General of the Théâtre-Français:

Very suddenly, Miliane falls head over heels in love with Stephen, the elegant and handsome Swede, who had headed the deputation of foreign students. On the day when she was to have fled with Didier, she leaves Paris with the young Scandinavian. The woman of Paris follows the example of Ibsen's heroine. Love is for youth. That is the moral of the play. The crisis is resolved. The Sphinx has gone. Didier, looking at his daughter, Geneviève, shakes his head, and murmurs:

'Maybe there is a soul — who can tell?'

Seated in a corner, Mathias, in an interval between two experiments, is playing on his flute, like Frederick II between two battles. He answers Didier's words with a few high-pitched notes of ironic fiddlededee.

It is not impossible that Dumas, in the state of profound melancholy into which his ill-health had plunged him, may have hit on some such ending. But on October 1st, he took a turn for the worse, and realized that his last play would never be finished.

'Assume that I am already dead,' he said to Claretie, 'and don't count on me.'

To his daughter Colette, he confessed: 'I don't know what's the matter with me; it's as though a grasshopper were scraping away all day long in my ears.' The blood was pulsing in his hardened arteries. Soon he began to feel pains in his head, and was afflicted with strange fits of absent-mindedness which terrified his wife. The specialists refused to commit themselves. Some talked of congestion, others expressed a fear that there might be a tumour on the brain. Towards the end of November, the great doctors assembled round his bed at Marly gave it as their opinion that there was no hope. Like his father, just before his death, on the beach at Puys, he spent whole days in a confused state of dreaming.

Some months earlier, having promised to write a preface for an edition de luxe of *The Three Musketeers*, he had addressed with tenderness the father who had been both his pride and his despair:

Does one still remember, in the world where now you are, the things of this world of ours, or does eternal life live only in the human imagination made childlike by its fear of no longer existing? That is something we never discussed in the days when we lived together, nor do I think that you ever worried your head with metaphysical speculations.

Then he evoked the memory of those months which they had spent in each other's company — fifty years before, after Ida had gone — in brotherly intimacy:

Ah! what a good time that was! We were the same age, you forty-two, I twenty. What happy talks we had, what sweet unburdenings we made! To me it seems like yesterday . . . For close on a quarter of a century you have been sleeping under the great trees of Villers-Cotterets, between your mother who served you as a model for all the good women you portrayed, and your father, who inspired all those heroes to whom you gave the gift of life. And I, whom you always regarded — and so did I — as a child at your side, have hair more white than any you could show. The world moves fast. Soon we shall meet again. . . .[11]

Those words sound a premonitory nostalgia. It was to be not long before the son rejoined his father. On November 28th he seemed to be slightly better. An autumn sun was shining on the fine trees in the garden. He had recovered consciousness and smiled at his daughters.
'Go and have your lunch,' he said to them, 'and leave me to get some rest.'
The doctor had just left the room when Colette called him back. 'Come quickly! Papa is having convulsions. . . .'
A final spasm shook him. He was dead.
Next morning the papers were full of him. Henry Bauër wrote a fine article:

In himself he had that imperious force which is known as will . . . He was the equal, though with a difference, of the first genius of his line . . . Before *La Dame aux Camélias* our daughters of joy were social outcasts, marked for damnation. Nobody has ever exercised a greater influence, so far as pity and redemption is concerned. In a hundred years from now, poor young folk, their hearts pulsating with love, will still be shedding tears over Marguerite Gautier. . . .[12]

Because at the beginning of his life he had been a victim, because his mother had suffered, he had pleaded in defence of the innocent, often with talent. If, later, he had assumed the airs of a tamer, it was because he had found himself surrounded by wild beasts. He had either to subdue the lionesses or be eaten. Arrogance had covered with a thin crust the most vulnerable of hearts. Now, at this fag-end of November 1895, the battle was over. The late autumn warmth hung about the garden at Marly. Friends, colleagues, journalists, men of politics, women of fashion and a great crowd of common folk, moved past the body. The trains from Paris unloaded on the platform of the little station hundreds of admirers and of the merely curious, who walked in procession to Champflour.

There they were shown into the room where, on the Empire bed with its bronze adornments and its full weight apparently supported on two great swans carved in lemon-wood, Alexandre Dumas *fils* lay at rest, wearing, in obedience to his final wishes, his working clothes. His feet were bare. Like General Dumas he had been always proud of their fine, arched insteps. Looking down from the wall was a large portrait of his father, and a small sketch of Catherine Labay on her death-bed. For a whole century the three Dumas had played out, against a backcloth of France, the finest of all dramas — their life. Here, now, the last of them was left alone 'before the lowered curtain, with night and silence'. The young widow and his daughters, already draped in deepest black, stood thinking of the dead man, and of the difficult future. The epic melodrama had come to its end as a middle-class comedy . . . and, perhaps, as tragedy.

Notes
(pp. 17-57)

PART ONE, CHAPTER I (pp. 17-23)

[1] See Ernest Roch, in *Le Château de Villers-Cotterets*, p. 248. This work appeared in the *Bulletin de la Société Historique Régionale de Villers-Cotterets* for the year 1909, pp. 22-346 (Villers-Cotterets, Imprimerie Naten, 1910).

[2] This letter is printed by Ernest Roch in *Le Général Alexandre Dumas*, pp. 91-2 (*Bulletin de la Société Historique Régionale de Villers-Cotterets* for the year 1906).

[3] Archives of the City of Soissons.

[4] Letter printed by Ernest Roch in *Le Général Alexandre Dumas*, p. 95.

PART ONE, CHAPTER II (pp. 24-37)

[1] On February 13th, 1796, General Dumas had had a second daughter, Louise-Alexandrine, who lived for only a year.

[2] H. Taine, *Les origines de la France contemporaine, Le Régime moderne*, vol. I, p. 88.

[3] Hitherto unpublished. Spœlberch de Lovenjoul Collection, G. 1191, Box 38, the Pilastre dossier, folio 6.

The *Souvenirs* of Nicolas-René Dufriche des Genettes, known as Desgenettes (1762-1837) were edited in 1893 by E. Pilastre, legal adviser to the publishing house of Calmann-Lévy. So as to avoid giving pain to his friend Alexandre Dumas *fils* he omitted the above passage.

[4] Alexandre Dumas, *Mes Mémoires*, vol. I, p. 135 of the Josserand edition.

[5] Ibid., pp. 146-9 of the Josserand edition.

[6] Hitherto unpublished. Spœlberch de Lovenjoul Collection, G. 1191, Box 38, the Pilastre dossier, folio 6.

[7] Alexandre Dumas, *Mes Mémoires*, vol. I, p. 158 of the Josserand edition.

[8] Ibid., vol. I, p. 160.

[9] Ibid., vol. I, p. 161.

[10] Ibid., vol. I, p. 177.

PART ONE, CHAPTER III (pp. 38-42)

[1] Alexandre Dumas, *Mes Mémoires*, vol. I, p. 185.

[2] Henri Clouard, *Alexandre Dumas*, p. 20.

[3] Jacques Collard (1758-1833), Deputy in the Corps Législatif from 1807-11.

[4] François-Antoine Lallemand (1774-1839), general of cavalry, and Henri-Dominique Lallemand (1777-1823), general of artillery. Both of them, after the Hundred Days, were sentenced to death in their absence. The younger of the two died in the United States, where he had taken refuge. The elder returned to France when Charles X was driven from the throne.

PART ONE, CHAPTER IV (pp. 43-51)

[1] Alexandre Dumas, *Mes Mémoires*, vol. I, p. 390.

[2] Ibid., vol. I, p. 392.

[3] Jean-François Ducis (1733-1815) was a French tragic poet who had made adaptations of Shakespeare, using Letourneur's insipid translations.

[4] Poumerol, *La jeunesse d'Alexandre Dumas*, p. 38. This article was published in the *Bulletin de la Société Historique Régionale de Villers-Cotterets* for the year 1905, pp. 34-44 (Soissons, Imprimerie Centrale, 1905).

[5] Maurice Descotes, *Le Drame romantique et ses grands createurs*, p. 26 (Paris, Presses Universitaires de France (undated)).

[6] Alexandre Dumas, *Mes Mémoires*, vol. III, pp. 61-2 in the ten-volume Calmann-Lévy edition.

PART TWO, CHAPTER I (pp. 55-60)

[1] Alexandre Dumas, *Mes Mémoires*, vol. III, pp. 124-7.

[2] Now Place Boïeldieu.

[3] All the biographers have maintained the contrary, but, in order to get at the truth, one has only to read the legal document, and also the registration of Catherine Labay's death.

[4] Alexandre Dumas, *Mes Mémoires*, vol. III, p. 251.

PART TWO, CHAPTER II (pp. 61-70)

[1] Eugène Delacroix, *Correspondance générale*, p. 197.

[2] Alexandre Dumas, *Souvenirs dramatiques*, vol. II, p. 93.

[3] Alexandre Dumas, *Mes Mémoires*, vol. IV, p. 280.

[4] Ibid., vol. V, p. 24.

[5] I am here following Dumas's own account. The *Mémoires* of Samson, at that time doyen of the Comédie-Française, give a different version. It will be found in *Le Drame romantique et ses grands créateurs*, by Maurice Descotes, p. 95.

[6] Alexandre Dumas, *Mes Mémoires*, vol. V, pp. 24-37.

[7] Alexandre Dumas, *Souvenirs dramatiques*, p. 225.

[8] After first attributing to the duchesse de Guise, in his *Henri III et sa Cour*, the adventure which belonged by right to Madame de Montsoreau, Dumas later used the same episode in a novel (published in 1846), and in a second play (produced in 1860), both with the same title: *La Dame de Monsoreau*. In each of these, Françoise de Montsoreau is called Diane de Monsoreau. Her true story has been written, more recently, by Monsieur Maurice Rat in *Dames et Bourgeoises du XVIème siècle* (Paris, Plon, 1955).

PART TWO, CHAPTER III (pp. 71-6)

[1] Parigot, passim.

[2] Mathieu-Guillaume Villenave (1762-1846).

[3] Descotes, *Le Drame romantique*.

[4] Alexandre Dumas, *Mes Mémoires*, vol. V, pp. 100-5.

[5] *Courrier des théâtres*, February 13th, 1829.

[6] Alexandre Dumas, *Mes Mémoires*, vol. V, p. 111.

PART THREE, CHAPTER I (pp. 79-86)

[1] François-Joseph Waldor, born at Namur on March 30th, 1789, naturalized by Royal Decree on March 12th, 1817, had married Mélanie Villenave in 1822. Drafted as a private to the 94th Infantry Regiment in 1809, he was commissioned (in 1816) as a second lieutenant in the departmental Legion of the Dordogne, and confirmed in his rank when the Legion became the 13th Regiment of Infantry. He was promoted lieutenant in 1822, captain in 1827. He died at the age of sixty-seven in 1856.

[2] Bib. Nat., Département des manuscrits, N.A.F. 24,641, folio 280.

[3] Ibid., N.A.F. 24,641, folio 293.

[4] Ibid., N.A.F. 24,641, folio 297.

[5] Quoted by Charles Glinel in his *Alexandre Dumas*, p. 256.

[6] Alexandre Dumas, *Souvenirs dramatiques*, vol. II, p. 329. See, too, Descotes, *Le Drame romantique*, passim.

[7] Clément-Janin, *Drames et comédies romantiques*, p. 109.

[8] Alexandre Dumas, *Mes Mémoires*, vol. VIII, p. 278.

[9] *Courrier des théâtres*, January 17th and March 16th, 1830.

[10] Théodore de Banville, *Mes souvenirs*, p. 199.

[11] Théophile Gautier, *Histoire de l'art dramatique en France*, vol. I, p. 50.

[12] Descotes, *Le Drame romantique*, p. 174.

[13] Charles Glinel, *Alexandre Dumas*, p. 262.

PART THREE, CHAPTER II (pp. 87-91)

[1] A property in La Vendée belonging to the Villenave family.

[2] Bib. Nat., Département des manuscrits, N.A.F. 24,641, folio 301.

[3] Ibid., N.A.F. 24,641, folio 297.

[4] Ibid., N.A.F. 24,641, folio 280.

[5] Ibid., N.A.F. 24,641, folio 313.
[6] Hippolyte Parigot, *Alexandre Dumas père* (Hachette, 1902).
[7] Alexandre Dumas, *Théâtre complet*, vol. II, pp. 225-6.
[8] Alexandre Dumas, *Antony*, Act IV, Scene 6. *Théâtre complet*, vol. II, p. 53.

PART THREE, CHAPTER III (pp. 92-7)

[1] Alexandre Dumas, *Mes Mémoires*, vol. VI, p. 73.
[2] Ibid., vol. VI, p. 102.
[3] Bib. Nat., Département des manuscrits, N.A.F. 24,641, folio 329.
[4] Ibid., N.A.F. 24,641, folio 330.
[5] Ibid., N.A.F. 24,641, folio 332.
[6] Ibid., N.A.F. 24,641, folio 336.
[7] Simone André-Maurois Collection.
[8] Alexandre Dumas, *Mes Mémoires*, vol. VII, pp. 157-8.

PART THREE, CHAPTER IV (pp. 98-106)

[1] Alexandre Dumas, *Souvenirs dramatiques*, p. 245.
[2] Ibid., pp. 247-8.
[3] George Sand, *Histoire de ma Vie*, vol. IX, p. 130.
[4] Théodore de Banville, *Camées Parisiens*, 2nd Series, p. 67.
[⁵]George Sand, *Histoire de ma Vie*, vol. IX, p. 121.
[6] Belle Krelsamer had presented Dumas with a child on March 5th, 1831.
[7] Alexandre Dumas, *Mes Mémoires*, vol. VII, pp. 182-90.
[8] Théodore Gautier, *Histoire du Romantisme*, p. 167.
[9] *Le Figaro*, May 4th, 1831.
[10] Théophile Gautier, *Histoire du Romantisme*, pp. 167-70.

PART THREE, CHAPTER V (pp. 107-15)

[1] Bib. Nat., Balachowsky-Petit Bequest of August 9th, 1954.
[2] Ibid, Balachowsky-Petit Bequest.
[3] The contents of this letter (hitherto unpublished) were communicated to me by Monsieur Raoul Simonson. (Author.)
[4] Bib. Nat., Balachowsky-Petit Bequest.
[5] Ibid., Balachowsky-Petit Bequest.
[6] Woe! woe to me, whom Heaven in this world
Has set, a stranger, alien to its laws. . . .
[7] H. Blaze de Bury, *Mes études et mes souvenirs: Alexandre Dumas*, p. 8.
[8] Ibid., p. 12.
[9] Maurice Spronck, *Alexandre Dumas fils, ses origines et ses débuts, Revue des Deux Mondes*, March 15th, 1898, p. 406.
[10] Archives de la Seine.
[11] H. Blaze de Bury, *Mes études et mes souvenirs: Alexandre Dumas*, p. 9.
[12] Letter published by Marcel Thomas in *La Table Ronde*, May 1951, pp. 84-6.
[13] Alexandre Dumas *fils, L'Affaire Clemenceau, mémoire de l'accusé*, p. 8.

PART THREE, CHAPTER VI (pp. 116-24)

[1] Adèle Hugo, *Victor Hugo raconté par un témoin de sa vie*, vol. II, pp. 357-8.
[2] Antoine Fontaney, *Journal intime*, edited by René Jasinski, p. 22.
[3] Ibid., p. 57.
[4] Ibid., pp. 93-4.
[5] Maurice Descotes, *Le Drame romantique et ses grands créateurs*, pp. 234-5.
[6] Antoine Fontaney, *Journal intime*, pp. 115-18.
[7] *L'Artiste* for the year 1833, vol. I, p. 119.
[8] A character from the Italian *Commedia dell Arte*. (Translator.)
[9] *L'Artiste* for the year 1833, vol. I, pp. 120-1.

PART FOUR, CHAPTER I (pp. 127-36)

¹ Alexandre Dumas, *Mes Mémoires*, vol. IX, pp. 165-8.

² Louis X, the Headstrong (1289-1316). The details of the play are imaginary. The only historically accurate fact is that Marguerite and her sisters-in-law, Blanche de la Marche and Jeanne de Poitiers, were accused of adultery. Louis X, who was being urged, for political reasons, to make a new marriage with Clémence of Hungary, had his wife suffocated between two mattresses, at Château-Gaillard, where she was a prisoner. The dead queen was barely twenty-five years of age.

³ It is impossible that Marguerite de Bourgogne should have had a lover, and a son, *in 1293*. She was born in 1290, and, at the time in question, was three years old! (Author.)

⁴ Alexandre Dumas, *La Tour de Nesle*, Act I, Scene 4, *Théâtre complet*, vol. III, p. 14.

⁵ Ibid., Act I, Scene 6, *Théâtre complet*, vol. III, p. 24.

⁶ Ibid., Act I, Scene 5, *Théâtre complet*, vol. III, p. 21.

⁷ Letter from Dumas *père* to the actor, Ferville (March 22nd, 1832). Bib. Nat., Département des manuscrits. N.A.F. 24,261, folio 231

PART FOUR, CHAPTER II (pp. 137-44)

¹ The pen-name of Gabrielle-Anne de Cisterne, vicomtesse de Saint-Mars, author of *Mémoires des autres*; novelist and journalist.

² See Maurice Spronck, *Alexandre Dumas fils, Revue des Deux Mondes*, March 15th, 1898, pp. 408 et seq.

³ Alexandre Dumas *fils*, *L'Affaire Clemenceau*, p. 31.

⁴ Alexandre Dumas *fils*, *Lettre à Cuvillier-Fleury* (Preface to *La Femme de Claude*).

⁵ Quoted by Victorien Sardou in a speech delivered at the unveiling of a monument to Dumas *fils*, on the Place Malesherbes (1906).

⁶ Jacques Balmat, a native of the Chamonix valley was the first man to reach the summit of Mont-Blanc. This he had done in 1786. (Translator.)

⁷ Sainte-Beuve, *Correspondance générale*, vol. I, p. 398.

⁸ Hitherto unpublished letter. Francis Ambrière Collection.

⁹ Heinrich Heine writing in the *Gazette d'Augsbourg*.

PART FOUR, CHAPTER III (pp. 145-54)

¹ Hitherto unpublished letter. Francis Ambrière Collection.

² Théophile Gautier, *Portraits contemporains*, p. 406.

³ Théophile Gautier, *Histoire de l'Art Dramatique*, vol. I, p. 86.

⁴ Marguerite-Jenny Colon (1808-42) had, during a tour in England, married the actor, Pierre Lafont, at Gretna Green. After the birth of a son she had regained her freedom, and was for a long time 'kept' by Hoppe, the Dutch banker. Nerval, who made use of her in his *Aurélia*, remained devotedly in love with her from 1834-8, in which latter year she married the flautist, Louis-Gabriel Leplus, and died in childbed.

⁵ *Lettres de Marceline Desbordes à Prosper Valmore*, edited by Boyer d'Agen, Vol. I, pp., 140 and 149.

⁶ Marie Dumas, at that time nine years of age, was bought up under her father's roof by Ida Ferrier, for whom she felt a very genuine affection. She never saw her mother, Belle Krelsamer.

⁷ Letter published by Marcel Thomas in *La Table Ronde*, May 1951, pp. 86-7.

⁸ Gustave Claudin, *Mes Souvenirs* (Paris, Calmann-Lévy, 1884), p. 29.

⁹ The biographers of Alexandre Dumas assert (in agreement with Claudin) that the marriage took place on February 1st. The official documents say the 5th.

¹⁰ Hitherto unpublished. Simone André-Maurois Collection.

¹¹ Jacques Reynaud (Comtesse Dash), *Portraits contemporains*, pp. 111-13 (Paris, Amyot, 1859).

¹² *Lettres de Marceline Desbordes à Prosper Valmore*, vol. I, p. 280.

PART FOUR, CHAPTER IV (pp. 155-60)

¹ Théophile Gautier, *Histoire de l'Art Dramatique*, vol. I, pp. 82-3.

² Ibid., vol. II, p. 117.

[3] Sainte-Beuve, *Premiers lundis*, vol. II, pp. 390-2.

[4] Ibid., vol. II, pp. 396-7.

[5] Hippolyte Parigot, *Alexandre Dumas père*, p. 103.

[6] Sainte-Beuve, *Premiers lundis*, vol. II, p. 401.

[7] Sainte-Beuve, *Correspondance générale*, vol. V, p. 207.

[8] *Journal des Débats*, July 27th, 1843. When Jules Janin collected his articles into a volume with the title of *Histoire de la Littérature Dramatique*, he omitted his violent attack on *Les Demoiselles de Saint-Cyr*.

[9] Letter from Victor Hugo to Alphonse Karr, printed by the latter in *Le Livre de Bord; Souvenirs*, vol. III, p. 129 (Paris, Calmann-Lévy, 1879).

[10] Spœlberch de Lovenjoul, Marie-Louise Bourget-Pailleron Bequest.

[11] Letter quoted in Étienne Charavay's Catalogue of *Autographes composant la collection Alfred Bovet*, No 872, p. 318 (Paris, 1887).

[12] Vicomte de Launay, *Lettres Parisiennes*, May 5th, 1845, vol. IV, p. 192 of the Calmann-Lévy edition (Paris, 1882).

PART FOUR, CHAPTER V (pp. 161-8)

[1] Noël C. Arvin, *Dumas fils*.

[2] Alexandre Dumas *fils*, *Lettre à Cuvillier-Fleury*, Preface to *La Femme de Claude*, *Théâtre complet*, acting edition, vol. V, p. 236.

[3] Maurice Spronck, *Alexandre Dumas fils*, *Revue des Deux Mondes*, March 15th, 1898, p. 411.

[4] Alexandre Dumas *fils*, *Lettre à Cuvillier-Fleury*, op. cit., p. 235.

[5] See *Le Gaulois*, July 20th, 1924.

[6] Thus did he die. O! what a price to pay
For taking just one bath. He had no luck that day.

[7] Bib. Nat., Département des manuscrits, N.A.F. 24,641, folio 45.

[8] Ibid., N.A.F. 24,641, folio 48.

[9] Hitherto unpublished letter. Bib. Nat., Département des manuscrits, Balachowsky-Petit Bequest, 10,586.

[10] The young Dumas is here confusing Sarah, Abraham's barren wife, with Hagar, the young slave by whom the patriarch had a son, Ishmael.

[11] Hitherto unpublished letter. Simone André-Maurois Collection.

PART FIVE, CHAPTER I (pp. 171-81)

[1] H. Blaze de Bury, *Mes études et mes souvenirs: Alexandre Dumas*, p. 45 (Paris, Calmann-Lévy, 1885).

[2] Gérard de Nerval, *Correspondance générale*, pp. 779-81 in the Pléiade edition.

[3] Sainte-Beuve, *Correspondance générale*, vol. V, pp. 734-5.

[4] Quoted by Henri d'Alméras in *Alexandre Dumas et les Trois Mousquetaires*, p. 75.

[5] Ibid., p. 80.

[6] Bib. Nat., Département des manuscrits, N.A.F. 11,917, folio 162.

[7] Ibid., N.A.F. 11,917, folio 164.

[8] A character in *La Dame de Monsoreau*.

[9] Characters in *Le Chevalier de Maison-Rouge*.

[10] Bib. Nat., Département des manuscrits, N.A.F. 11,917, folio 195.

[11] *Le Vicomte de Bragelonne* and *Joseph Balsamo* (*Mémoires d'un médecin*) were published in the same year (1848).

[12] Bib. Nat., Département des manuscrits, N.A.F. 11,917, folio 195.

[13] Hippolyte Parigot, *Alexandre Dumas père*, pp. 140-1.

[14] This formula was suggested by Albert Thibaudet who hoped that it would become as familiar as Erckmann-Chatrian.

PART FIVE, CHAPTER II (pp. 182-7)

[1] See Henri d'Alméras, *Alexandre Dumas et les Trois Mousquetaires*, pp. 65-6 (Paris, Edgar Malfère, 1929).

PART FIVE, CHAPTER III (pp. 188-99)

[1] Letter published by Marcel Thomas in *La Table Ronde*, May 1951, p. 87.

[2] Alexandre Dumas *fils*, Preface to *La Dame aux Camélias, Théâtre complet*, vol. I, p. 1.

[3] Antoine-Alfred-Anténor de Gramont, duc de Guiche (afterwards tenth duc de Gramont, 1819-80) had, in 1840, only just attained his majority.

[4] Johannes Gros, *Alexandre Dumas et Marie Duplessis*, p. 172 (Paris, Louis Conard, 1923).

[5] Alexandre Dumas *fils*, *La Dame aux Camélias*, p. 96 of the third edition (Paris, Michel Lévy, 1852).

[6] Ibid., p. 115.

[7] Ibid., p. 123.

[8] Ibid., p. 131.

[9] Alexandre Dumas *père*, *Causeries*, pp. 8-12 of the new edition published by Calmann-Lévy in 1885.

[10] Alexandre Dumas *fils*, Preface to *La Dame aux Camélias* (the play), *Théâtre complet*, vol. I, p. 1.

[11] Hitherto unpublished letter in the Collection of M. Alphandéry.

[12] Alexandre Dumas *fils*, *La Dame aux Camélias* (the novel), p. 173.

[13] Henry Lyonnet, *La Dame aux Camélias de Dumas*, pp. 33-4 (Paris, Edgar Malfère, 1930).

[14] This note was included by Adolphe Brisson in his *Portraits intimes*, vol. III, p. 193. Johannes Gros does not quote it in *Alexandre Dumas et Marie Duplessis* (Conard, 1923), but does so in *Une Courtisane romantique: Marie Duplessis*, p. 191 (Paris, Au Cabinet du Livre, 1929).

[15] See Henry Lyonnet, *La Dame aux Camélias de Dumas*, p. 32.

PART FIVE, CHAPTER IV (pp. 200-7)

[1] A hitherto unpublished letter in the Collection of M. Daniel Thirault.

[2] The equivalent to two million in 1957.

[3] In defiance of chronological order, *Les Mousquetaires*, a play in five acts, bearing the names of Dumas and Maquet, was produced four years before *La Jeunesse des Mousquetaires*, to which it is the sequel. This did not appear until February 17th, 1849.

[4] This hitherto unpublished letter comes from the Collection of M. Daniel Thirault.

[5] Victor Hugo, *Choses vues*, vol. I, p. 199, in the Imprimerie Nationale edition.

[6] Alexandre Dumas, *Impressions de Voyage, de Paris à Cadix*.

[7] Ibid., p. 20 of the new Michel Lévy edition (Paris, 1861).

[8] Alexandre Dumas *fils*, *Péchés de Jeunesse, A Conchita*, p. 371.

> Think you, my dear, the man who stood,
> And watched you, young and semi-nude
> And passionate, might for a moment's time forget
> When for a moment he had seen you once — or could?

[9] Alexandre Dumas *père*, *Impressions de Voyage, de Paris à Cadix*, p. 174.

[10] Cuvillier-Fleury, *Journal intime*, vol. II, p. 432.

[11] Ibid., vol. II, p. 445.

[12] Ibid., vol. II, p. 448.

[13] This hitherto unpublished, and very important, letter was communicated to me by Madame Privat. (Author.)

[14] Théophile Gautier, *Histoire de l'Art Dramatique*, vol. IV, pp. 134-6.

PART FIVE, CHAPTER V (pp. 208-15)

[1] Jules Janin, Preface to *La Dame aux Camélias* (the novel), p. ix.

[2] Janka Wohl: *Franz Liszt, souvenirs d'une compatriote* (Paris, Ollendorff, 1887).

[3] Note quoted by Johannes Gros in *Alexandre Dumas et Marie Duplessis*, pp. 304-5 (Paris, Louis Conard, 1923).

[4] Johannes Gros, *Une Courtisane romantique: Marie Duplessis*, p. 256 (Paris, Au Cabinet du Livre, 1929). This is an édition de luxe, illustrated by Viset, of the book by Johannes Gros, published by Conard in 1923. The text is, however, extensively revised, certain passages being deleted and others added.

[5] See Henry Lyonnet, *La 'Dame aux Camélias' de Dumas fils*, p. 46.

[6] Johannes Gros, *Alexandre Dumas et Marie Duplessis*, p. 350.

[7] Henri de Lapommeraye, *Histoire du début d'Alexandre Dumas fils*, ou les *Tribulations de la Dame aux Camélias* (Paris, Michel Lévy, 1873), p. 5.

[8] Théophile Gautier, *Histoire de l'Art Dramatique*, vol. V, p. 41.

[9] Victor Hugo, *Choses vues*, vol. I, pp. 235-6.

PART SIX, CHAPTER I (pp. 219-27)

[1] Alexandre Dumas, *Causeries*, pp. 273-4.

[2] Hitherto unpublished. British Museum, 39,672, *Dumas manuscripts*, folios 68-72.

[3] See Jacques Peuchet, *Mémoires tirés des archives de la police de Paris*, vol. V, pp. 197-228 (Paris, Levavaseur-Bourmancé, 1838).

[4] British Museum, 39,672, *Dumas manuscripts*, folios 68-72 (hitherto unpublished).

PART SIX, CHAPTER II (pp. 228-35)

[1] L. Henry Lecomte, *Alexandre Dumas*, p. 51 (Paris, Tallandier, 1902).

[2] Léon Gozlan, *Le Château de Monte-Cristo*, published in the *Almanach comique* (Pagnerre, 1848). It is quoted by Charles Glinel in *Alexandre Dumas et son œuvre*, pp. 407-12 (Rheims, F. Michaud, 1884).

[3] Honoré de Balzac, *Lettres à l'Étrangère*, vol. V (still unpublished in 1956). Spœlberch de Lovenjoul Collection, A. 303, folios 529-30.

[4] Simone André-Maurois Collection.

[5] Ibid.

PART SIX, CHAPTER III (pp. 236-47)

[1] Théophile Gautier, *Histoire de l'Art dramatique*, vol. V, pp. 219-20.

[2] Alexandre Dumas, *Histoire de mes Bêtes*, p. 284 (Paris, Calmann-Lévy, undated).

[3] Marceline Desbordes-Valmore, *Lettres à Prosper Valmore*, vol. II, p. 144.

[4] Ibid., vol. II, p. 97.

[5] Adolphe-Jean-Baptiste Lacan (1810-80), member of the Bar Council for thirty-four years, and twice its president.

[6] These hitherto unpublished letters are from the Pierre Lhoste Collection.

[7] Dumas — the grasshopper; Maquet — the ant. At the time when the prodigal's house was being put up to auction, Maquet had just bought a villa at Bougival. He ended his days as a rich landowner in his Château of Sainte-Mesme, near Dourdan.

[8] Unpublished letters in the Pierre Lhoste Collection.

[9] Honoré de Balzac, *Lettres à l'Étrangère*, vol. V (still unpublished in 1956). Spœlberch de Lovenjoul Collection, A. 303, folio 444.

[10] Simone André-Maurois, *Introduction à la Correspondance inédite entre George Sand et Marie Dorval*, p. 138.

[11] See Alexandre Dumas, *La dernière année de Marie Dorval*, pp. 81-4.

[12] Arsène Houssaye, *Les Confessions*, vol. III, pp. 101-4.

PART SIX, CHAPTER IV (pp. 248-59)

[1] Henri Clouard, *Alexandre Dumas*, p. 337.

[2] Bib. Nat., Département des manuscrits, N.A.F. 24,641, folios 16 and 17.

[3] Alexandre Dumas *fils*, Preface to *La Femme de Claude* (lettre à Cuvillier-Fleury), *Théâtre Complet*, vol. V, p. 236.

[4] Alexandre Dumas *fils*, Notes on *Francillon*, *Théâtre Complet*, vol. VII, p. 432.

[5] Charles, Count Nesselrode (1780-1862), had married in 1812, Marie Gouriew, daughter of the Minister of Apanages, by whom he had three children. He was Minister of Foreign Affairs for forty years (1816-62).

[6] Arsène Andreievitch, Count Zakrefsky (1785-1856), had been promoted general during the campaigns of 1813-14. He was Governor-General of Finland in 1823; Minister of the Interior in 1828; Military Governor of Moscow (1848-58). He was retired for having given his consent to the second marriage of his daughter, Lydia.

[7] Hitherto unpublished: file No. 10 of the *Nesselrode Archives* bequeathed in 1910 to the French Ministry of Foreign Affairs by Count Anatole de Nesselrode, the chancellor's grandson, who was married to a Frenchwoman and lived at N° 15 rue Jean-Baptiste Dumas.

[8] Alexandre Dumas *père*, *Causeries*, vol. I, pp. 23-40. Dumas *fils* later antedated the poem when he printed it in 1882.

> We set out yesterday upon a winter drive,
> Pressed each to each to keep the cold away,
> And through a dark'ning world did strive
> To bear love's deathless spring upon the way.
>
> .   .   .
>
> And when the time of flowers is come, I'll walk apart
> To muse upon the name carved in that stone,
> The sweet name which imprisons all my heart,
> Effaced, perhaps, by winds that round it have made moan.
>
> Dear sharer of that day, ah! where will you be then?
> I, perhaps, uncompanioned, hearing not your feet;
> Will you be treading happy ways again?
> And I be left, Winter in Summer's heat?
>
> For Winter's not the roads we looked upon,
> Now empty; not the angry blast and frore:
> It is the sunless heart, the spirit dark and dun;
> It is what I shall be when you are there no more.

[9] *Mémoires du Comte Horace de Viel-Castel*, vol. I, pp. 107-9.

[10] Alexandre Dumas, *Causeries*, vol. I, p. 31.

[11] Hitherto unpublished. Bib. Nat., Département des manuscrits, the third of the Balachowsky-Petit bequests.

[12] This letter was printed by Wladimir Karénine in her *George Sand*, vol. III, pp. 627-8.

[13] Louise Chopin, sister and heiress of the composer, had married Joseph Jedrzeiewicz.

[14] Letter printed by Wladimir Karénine in her *George Sand*, vol. III, p. 629.

[15] Alexandre Dumas, *Causeries*, vol. I, pp. 32-6.

> A year has passed since we two all alone
> Walked side by side along the woodland ways,
> And I, alas! foresaw what Fate has done
> To bring sad sequel to those happy days.
>
> Our love was not to see the coming Spring.
> Scarce a mild ray of sun then shone on us,
> A final separation heralding,
> Fraught with an exile shared and dolorous.
>
> I saw that season in a distant land,
> Friendless and loveless, hopeless of what might be;
> My eyes fixed on the road so close at hand
> By which you once had said you'd come to me.
>
> One day took wing — and others came and went:
> Nothing! . . . a lowering sky . . . and no word came;
> No distant echo reached the ear I bent
> To catch the murmur of a much-loved name.
>
> No scrap of paper, only that to enclose;
> Four lines which could have brought me some delight;
> Or, if you would not trace them, just a rose
> New-born that morning in some valley bright.

Just a few petals in an envelope,
Dropped in the post, that an exile to a spot
Far from his home, at the limits of Europe,
Might smile to know that he was not forgot! ...

We now have reached the ending of the year,
And that importunate enemy, old Time,
Has brought the same month and the same day here
When once you spoke of love, your cheek pressed close to mine.

[16] Hitherto unpublished. *Archives Nesselrode*, File X, Ministry of Foreign Affairs.
[17] Letters printed by Charles Nauroy in *Le Curieux* for January 1887.

PART SEVEN, CHAPTER I (pp. 263-75)

[1] She can be none other than the mother of Marie Dumas. (Author.)
[2] Charles Hugo, *Les Hommes de l'Exil*, p. 79.
[3] Ibid., p. 83.
[4] I owe this information to Monsieur José Camby. (Author.)
[5] Letter printed by Marcel Thomas in *La Table Ronde* for May 1951, p. 95.
[6] Hitherto unpublished letter. Bib. Nat., Département des manuscrits, Balachowsky-Petit second bequest, August 9th, 1954.
[7] Ibid.
[8] Bib. Nat., Département des manuscrits, N.A.F. 24,461, folio 69.
[9] Hitherto unpublished letter. Bib. Nat., Département des manuscrits, Balachowsky-Petit third bequest (1956).
[10] Bib. Nat., Département des manuscrits, N.A.F. 24,461, folio 71.
[11] Hitherto unpublished letter. Bib. Nat., Département des manuscrits, Balachowsky-Petit second bequest (1954).
[12] Hitherto unpublished letter. Bib. Nat., Département des manuscrits, Balachowsky-Petit third bequest (1956).
[13] Bib. Nat., Département des manuscrits, N.A.F. 24,461, folio 63.
[14] A notorious criminal and murderer, posing as an 'enemy of society', who was executed at Paris in 1836. (Translator.)
[15] Hitherto unpublished letter. Bib. Nat., Département des manuscrits, Balachoswky-Petit second bequest (1954).
[16] Bib. Nat., Département des manuscrits, N.A.F. 24,461, folio 81.
[17] I owe this information to Monsieur José Camby. (Author.)
[18] *Mémoires du Comte Horace de Viel-Castel*, vol. II, p. 223.

PART SEVEN, CHAPTER II (pp. 276-81)

[1] Alexandre-Pierre-Joseph Doche (1799-1849). His wife, who all through her life managed to look two years younger than she was, was born in Brussels in 1821 and died in Paris in 1900.
[2] Catalogue d'autographes Emmanuel Fabius, June 1939.
[3] Adolphe Brisson, *Portraits intimes*, p. 198.
[4] Théophile Gautier, *Histoire de l'Art Dramatique*, vol. VI, pp. 304-8.
[5] Henry Lyonnet, *La 'Dame aux Camélias' de Dumas fils*, pp. 100-1.
[6] Hitherto unpublished letter. Bib. Nat., Département des manuscrits, Balachowsky-Petit third bequest (1956).
[7] Louis Ganderax, *La Passion dans le théâtre de Dumas fils*, Revue des Deux Mondes, May 15th, 1884, p. 456.

PART SEVEN, CHAPTER III (pp. 282-90)

[1] Eugène Delacroix, *Journal*, vol. II, p. 120.
[2] Quoted by John Charpentier in *Alexandre Dumas*, p. 176 (Paris, Tallandier, 1947).
[3] Quoted (inaccurately) by John Charpentier in *Alexandre Dumas*, p. 177.
[4] Letter quoted by Henri d'Alméras in *Alexandre Dumas et les Trois Mousquetaires*, pp. 131-3 (Paris, Edgar Malfère, 1929).

[5] *Mémoires du Comte Horace de Viel-Castel*, vol. II, p. 185.

> In all the Imperial fun and games
> Nephew with Uncle equal status claims:
> Uncle took capitals as toys to play with;
> Nephew our *Capital* has made away with.

[6] Ibid., vol. III, p. 209.

[7] Joachim Kuhn, *La Princesse Mathilde*, p. 206 (Paris, Plon, 1935).

[8] Part of a hitherto unpublished letter. Balachowsky-Petit second bequest (August 9th, 1954).

[9] Alexandre Dumas, *Mes Mémoires*, vol. IV, p. 127.

[10] Ibid., vol. VIII, p. 117.

[11] Ibid., vol. VIII, p. 185.

[12] Bib. Nat., Département des manuscrits, N.A.F. 24,816, folios 35-41.

[13] Ibid., N.A.F. 24,816, folio 42.

[14] Spœlberch de Lovenjoul Collection, E. 915, folio 56.

[15] Hitherto unpublished letter. Simone André-Maurois Collection.

[16] Alphonse Karr, *Le Livre de Bord*, vol. III (Paris, Calmann-Lévy, 1880).

[17] Spœlberch de Lovenjoul Collection, E. 915, folio 531.

[18] See Jacques Reynaud, *Portraits contemporains*, p. 280 (Paris, Amyot, 1864).
'Jacques Reynaud' was one of the pen-names used by the vicomtesse de Poilloüe de Saint-Mars, who before her marriage was Gabrielle-Anne de Cisterne de Courtiras (1804-72). She also wrote as 'comtesse Dash'.

PART SEVEN, CHAPTER IV (pp. 291-9)

[1] Marie-Louise Pailleron, *Les écrivains du Second Empire*, p. 86 (Paris, Perrin, 1924).

[2] Alexandre Dumas *fils*, *Diane de Lys*, Act IV, Scene xiii, *Théâtre Complet*, vol. I, pp. 409-10.

[3] Alexandre Dumas *fils*, Notes to *Diane de Lys*, *Théâtre Complet*, vol. I, p. 440.

[4] Alexandre Dumas *fils*, Preface to *Le Demi-Monde*, *Théâtre Complet*, vol. II, pp. 18-19.

[5] Ibid., vol. II, p. 10.

[6] Alexandre Dumas *fils*, Notes to *Le Demi-Monde*, *Théâtre Complet*, vol. II, p. 241.

[7] Hitherto unpublished letter. Bib. Nat., Département des manuscrits, Aurora Sand bequest, N.A.F. 24,812.

[8] Ibid., N.A.F. 24,812.

[9] Ibid., N.A.F. 24,812.

[10] See Robert Mesuret, *Alexandre Dumas chez la Princesse Narischkine*, an article in *Le Petit Commingeois*, September 19th, 1948.

PART SEVEN, CHAPTER V (pp. 300-9)

[1] Alexandre Dumas, *Impressions de Voyage: En Russie*, vol. I, p. 73, of the new Calmann-Lévy edition (Paris, 1876).

[2] Spœlberch de Lovenjoul Collection. Quoted by Clouard.

[3] Alexandre Dumas, *Impressions de Voyage: En Russie*, vol. III, p. 247, of the new Calmann-Lévy edition (Paris, 1878).

[4] Hitherto unpublished letter. Bib. Nat., Département des manuscrits, third Balachowsky-Petit bequest.

[5] Élisabeth-Céleste Vénard, known as Céleste Mogador, comtesse Lionel Chabrillan (1824-1909).

[6] Françoise Moser, *Vie et aventures de Céleste Mogador*, p. 181 (Paris, Albin Michel, 1935).

PART SEVEN, CHAPTER VI (pp. 310-18)

[1] P. Lamy, *Le Théâtre de Dumas fils*.

[2] Alexandre Dumas *fils*, *Un père prodigue*, Act I, Scene xii, *Théâtre Complet*, vol. III, p. 318.

[3] Alexandre Dumas *fils*, Preface to *Le Fils naturel*, *Théâtre Complet*, vol. III, p. 20.

[4] Gustave Flaubert, *Correspondance*, vol. IV, p. 190.

[5] Quoted in *L'Opinion*, August 1st, 1924.

[6] Jacques Reynaud (comtesse Dash): *Portraits contemporains*, pp. 17-21 (Paris, Amyot, 1859).

[7] Ibid., pp. 31-3.

[8] *Journal du docteur Prosper Menière*, p. 7 (Paris, Plon, 1903).

[9] *Journal des Goncourts*, vol. III, pp. 207-8 of the original edition (Paris, Charpentier, 1888).

[10] Alexandre Dumas *fils*, Notes to *Le Fils naturel, Théâtre Complet*, vol. III, pp. 248-9.

[11] Bib. Nat., Département des manuscrits, N.A.F. 11,917, folio 145.

[12] Ibid., N.A.F. 11,917, folio 363.

[13] A drama in five Acts and eight Scenes, produced at the Théâtre Historique, on December 15th, 1847.

[14] *Les Mousquetaires*, with the names of Dumas and Maquet as joint authors, was first played at the Ambigu on October 27th, 1845.

[15] Bib. Nat., Département des manuscrits, N.A.F. 24,641, folio 108.

[16] George Sand, *Correspondance*, vol. IV, pp. 322-3.

PART EIGHT, CHAPTER I (pp. 321-9)

[1] Alexandre Dumas goes a'tracking
     Just to give us what comes to his net,
     And so keen is the public on what it'll get
     That it never grows weary, I bet
     Of sending the author a'packing

[2] Files of the publishing house of Calmann-Lévy.

[3] Émilie Cordier (1840-1906) was the child of Pierre-François Cordier (1796-?) and Arsène Françoise Guimoussin (1810-71).

[4] Charles Hugo, *Les Hommes de l'exil*, pp. 94-5.

[5] Giuseppe Bandi, *Les Mille: expédition de Garibaldi en Sicilie*, pp. 201-2 (Florence, A. Salani, 1906).

[6] Hitherto unpublished letter. Simone André-Maurois Collection.

[7] See L.-Henry Lecomte in *Alexandre Dumas, sa vie intime, ses œuvres*, p. 249 (Paris, Tallandier, undated).

[8] Benedetto Croce, *Uomini e Cosa della Vecchia Italia*.

[9] Spœlberch de Lovenjoul Collection, E. 882, folios 67-8.

[10] Georges Bourgin, *Alexandre Dumas père et l'Italie*, an article in *Rendiconti della Classe di Scienze morali, storiche, e filologiche* published by *l'Accademia Nazionale dei Lincei*, Series VIII, vol. IX, fasc. 1-2, January/February 1954.

[11] Bib. Nat., Département des manuscrits, Aurore Sand bequest, N.A.F. 24,812. Hitherto unpublished.

[12] Émilie's attitude becomes easier to understand if we remember that it was because Dumas admitted paternity of his son that he had been able, in 1831, to snatch the little Alexandre from the defenceless Catherine Labay. 'The Admiral' referred to this precedent in a letter to Pierre-François Cordier. She did not want, she said, to see herself 'stripped of a mother's authority' by a natural father who, as such, would have priority over the child's unmarried mother.

[13] See L.-Henry Lecomte, *Alexandre Dumas père*, p. 251.

PART EIGHT, CHAPTER II (pp. 330-8)

[1] Hitherto unpublished letter shown me by Madame Balachowsky-Petit. (Author.)

[2] Hitherto unpublished letter. Bib. Nat., Département des manuscrits, Aurore Sand bequest, N.A.F. 24,812.

[3] See Wladimir Karénine in *George Sand, sa vie et ses œuvres*, vol. V, pp. 407-9.

[4] Hitherto unpublished letter. Bib. Nat., Département des manuscrits, Aurore Sand bequest, N.A.F. 24,812.

[5] Bib. Nat., Département des manuscrits, N.A.F. 24,823.

[6] Hitherto unpublished letter, Bib. Nat., Département des manuscrits, Aurore Sand bequest, N.A.F. 24,812.

[7] Ibid., N.A.F. 24,812.

[8] Ibid., N.A.F. 24,812.

[9] Ibid., N.A.F. 24,812.

[10] Ibid., N.A.F. 24,812.

PART EIGHT, CHAPTER III (pp. 339-49)

[1] Alexandre Dumas *fils*, Notes to *L'Ami des Femmes, Théâtre Complet,* vol. IV, p. 278.

[2] Ibid., vol. IV, p. 9.

[3] Bib. Nat., Département des manuscrits, Aurore Sand bequest, N.A.F. 24,812.

[4] Nadejda had just had a miscarriage in the fifth month of her pregnancy. See George Sand's *Diary,* under the date February 9th, 1866.

[5] Hitherto unpublished letter. Simone André-Maurois Collection.

[6] Amaury Duval Collection, Autun, communicated by Francis Ambrière.

[7] This play was eventually called *Le Don Juan de Village.*

[8] Maurice Sand's nickname.

[9] In other words, the Théâtre-Français.

[10] Bib. Nat., Département des manuscrits, N.A.F. 24,828.

[11] These hitherto unpublished letters to Rivière are from the Collection of Madame H. Dumesnil.

[12] Hitherto unpublished letter. Bib. Nat., Département des manuscrits, Aurore Sand bequest, N.A.F. 24,812.

[13] Hitherto unpublished letter in the Collection of Madame H. Dumesnil.

[14] Bib. Nat., Département des manuscrits, N.A.F. 24,829.

PART EIGHT, CHAPTER IV (pp. 350-5)

[1] Mathilde Shaw, *Illustrés et Inconnus, souvenirs de ma vie,* pp. 184-91 (Paris, Fasquelle, 1906).

[2] Ibid., pp. 183-5.

[3] John Charpentier, *Alexandre Dumas,* p. 201.

[4] Bib. Nat., Département des manuscrits, N.A.F. 24,642, folio 64.

[5] Edmond and Jules De Goncourt, *Journal,* vol. II, pp. 194-5.

[6] Ibid., vol. III, pp. 19-20.

[7] Records of the publishing house of Calmann-Lévy.

PART EIGHT, CHAPTER V (pp. 356-69)

[1] Mathilde Shaw, *Illustrés et Inconnus, souvenirs de ma vie,* pp. 213-18.

[2] Her birth certificate has never been found, fires during the Civil War having destroyed all the records in New Orleans. Her biographer, Bernard Falk, thinks that she was born in 1835. Other writers say 1832. She herself maintained that it was 1841, but her numerous photographs seem to disprove this, since the latest in date certainly do not show a young woman. It seems a great deal more probable that she was thirty-three or thirty-four when she died.

[3] In 1856, she married Alexander I. Menken; in 1859, a boxer, John Carmel Heenan; in 1862, an impresario, Robert H. Newell. Her two children did not survive her. In an ecstasy of symbolism she had wanted to make the first (who was born in 1866 and died in the following year) the godson of George Sand, that is to say, to give him as his second name, in the American manner, the surname of his godmother. She knew, as did everybody, that Aurore Dudevant had made her bow to the literary world under the pseudonym of George Sand. When, therefore, she registered a male child as Louis Dudevant Barkley, it was actually Casimir Dudevant, the woman writer's official husband, whom Adah Menken gave, as putative godfather, to her baby son.

[4] Quoted by Bernard Falk in *The Naked Lady,* p. 182 (London, Hutchinson & Co, 1952).

It is impossible to translate this triolet. With the knowledge that *souda* means welded, and that *dada* is the French equivalent of 'gee-gee' the reader may make out the sense easily for himself. (Translator.)

[5] Spœlberch de Lovenjoul Collection, E. 882, folio 462.

[6] Bernard Falk, *The Naked Lady,* p. 175.

[7] Ibid., p. 168.

[8] Hitherto unpublished letter. Simone André-Maurois Collection.

[9] Ibid.

[10] Bib. Nat., Département des manuscrits, Aurore Sand bequest, N.A.F. 24,812.

[11] Ibid., N.A.F. 24,812.

[12] Alexandre Dumas *père, Dictionnaire de Cuisine,* p. 89.

[13] Bib. Nat., Département des manuscrits, N.A.F. 24,642, folio 66.

[14] Hitherto unpublished letter. Simone André-Maurois Collection.
[15] Spœlberch de Lovenjoul Collection, E. 882, folio 527.
[16] Ibid., E. 882, folio 527
[17] Ibid., E. 882, folios 532-4.
[18] Hitherto unpublished letter. Simone André-Maurois Collection.
[19] Bib. Nat., Département des manuscrits, N.A.F. 11,917, folio 342.
[20] On a fourth tombstone can be read today the words, *Jeannine d'Hauterive, born Alexandre Dumas (1867-1943)*.
[21] See the *Figaro* of November 5th, 1883, and the *Journal de l'Aisne* of April 18th, 1872.

PART NINE, CHAPTER I (pp. 373-87)

[1] Alexandre Dumas *fils*, *Théâtre Complet*, vol. V, p. 82.
[2] Ibid., vol. V, p. 82.
[3] Alexandre Dumas *fils*, Notes to *Une Visite de Noces*, *Théâtre Complet*, vol. V, p. 77.
[4] Ibid., vol. V, pp. 78-80.
[5] Ibid., vol. V, p. 81.
[6] Ibid., vol. V, p. 81.
[7] Ibid., vol. V, p. 82.
[8] Ibid., vol V, p. 82
[9] Ibid., vol. V, pp. 88-9.
[10] Ibid., vol. V, pp. 90-3.
[11] Ibid., vol. V, p. 95.
[12] Ibid., vol. V, p. 63.
[13] Ibid., vol. V, pp. 96-7.
[14] Bib. Nat., Département des manuscrits, N.A.F. 24,636, folios 1-3 (hitherto unpublished).
[15] Hitherto unpublished letter. Simone André-Maurois Collection.

PART NINE, CHAPTER II (pp. 388-97)

[1] Alexandre Dumas *fils*, *Lettre à Cuvillier-Fleury*, *Théâtre Complet*, vol. V, pp. 248-9.
[2] Alexandre Dumas *fils*, Notes to *La Princesse Georges*, *Théâtre Complet*, vol. V, pp. 213-14.
[3] Ibid., vol. V, pp. 214-15.
[4] Arago had just been made a minister.
[5] The Princesse Mathilde Bonaparte. Hitherto unpublished letter.
[6] Alexandre Dumas *fils*, Notes to *La Princesse Georges*, *Théâtre Complet*, vol. V, p. 212.
[7] Letter quoted by Dr Israël Margulitis.
[8] Alexandre Dumas *fils*, *Lettre à Cuvillier-Fleury*, *Théâtre Complet*, vol. V, pp. 228-9.
[9] Ibid., vol. V, p. 234.
[10] Ibid., vol. V, pp. 234-5.
[11] Ibid., p. 236.
[12] Alexandre Dumas *fils*, *L'Homme-Femme*, p. 6 of the twenty-ninth edition (Paris, Michel Lévy, 1872).
[13] Ibid., pp. 175-6.
[14] From the Collection of Madame Balachowsky-Petit.

PART NINE, CHAPTER III (pp. 397-407)

[1] Un Passant, *Alexandre Dumas fils chez lui*, an article published in the *Moniteur Universel*, December 3rd, 1879. See also the *Figaro* of February 7th, 1875, and also Georges Ripp, *l'Hotel de M. Alexandre Dumas fils*, in the *Figaro* of November 5th, 1892.
[2] Olga Naryschkine had married Thierry, marquis de Falletans, in 1871.
[3] Alexandre Dumas *fils*, Preface to *Monsieur Alphonse*, *Théâtre Complet*, vol. VI, p. 15.
[4] Ibid., vol. VI, p. 28.
[5] Ibid., vol. VI, p. 35.
[6] Edmond de Goncourt, *Journal*, vol. V, p. 176 of the Flammarion edition.
[7] Ibid., vol. V, p. 86.
[8] Victor Hugo, *Choses vues*, vol. II, pp. 218-19.
[9] Edmond de Goncourt, *Journal*, vol. V, pp. 140-1.
[10] Wife of *Le Cid*. (Translator.)

[11] Alexandre Dumas *fils*, *Discours de réception à l'Académie Française*.
[12] Edmond de Goncourt, *Journal*, vol. V, p. 143.

PART NINE, CHAPTER IV (pp. 408-18)

[1] Alexandre Dumas *fils*, Preface to *L'Étrangère, Théâtre Complet*, vol. VI, pp. 228-9.
[2] Hitherto unpublished letter. Bibliothèque de l'Arsenal, R t 6691.
[3] Hitherto unpublished letter. Simone André-Maurois Collection.
[4] Gustave Flaubert, *Correspondance*, vol. VI, p. 252.
[5] Hitherto unpublished letter in the Collection of Madame H. Dumesnil.
[6] Léon Daudet, *Écrivains et Artistes*, vol. V, pp. 161-2.
[7] Ibid., vol. V, pp. 162-5.
[8] Léopold Lacour, *Une longue vie: Mémoires*, vol. II, which has never been published. The manuscript was shown to me by Mademoiselle Harlor, the executrix of the writer's Will.
[9] Léopold Lacour, *Alexandre Dumas fils, Notes sur l'homme*, an article published in *Les Nouvelles Littéraires*, April 3rd, 1926.
[10] Alexandre Dumas *fils*, *Lettres à une Pécheresse*, *Revue de France*, March 15th, 1924, pp. 245-8.
[11] Ibid., pp. 251-2.
[12] Ibid., p. 257.
[13] Ibid., pp. 260-3.
[14] Ibid., p. 263.

PART TEN, CHAPTER I (pp. 421-6)

[1] Alexandre Dumas *fils*, Preface to *L'Étrangère, Théâtre Complet*, vol. VI, pp. 241-2.
[2] On June 2nd, 1880, Colette Dumas had married Maurice Lippmann (1847-1923), the brother of Madame Arman de Caillavet, whose maiden name had been Léontine Lippmann (1844-1910). Two sons, both of them still living, were born of this marriage: Alexandre and Serge Lippmann. She obtained a divorce on May 25th, 1892, and, on October 2nd, 1897, married a Rumanian doctor, Achille Matza (1872-1937).
[3] Ferdinand Brunetière in the *Revue des Deux Mondes*, February 15th, 1881.
[4] Barbey d'Aurevilly, Theatre Notice in *Triboulet* of February 7th, 1881.
[5] Hitherto unpublished letter in the Collection of Monsieur Alphandéry.
[6] Hitherto unpublished letter. Simone André-Maurois Collection.
[7] Alexandre Dumas *fils*, *Lettre à Monsieur Naquet*, pp. 14-16 (Paris, Calmann-Lévy, 1882).
[8] Ibid., p. 47.

PART TEN, CHAPTER II (pp. 427-33)

[1] These two canvases were bequeathed to the Petit-Palais by La Marquise Landolfo Carncano.
[2] Bib. Nat., Département des manuscrits, Balachowsky-Petit bequest, 8,944.
[3] Ibid.
[4] Ibid., Balachowsky-Petit bequest, 8,944.
[5] Ibid., Balachowsky-Petit bequest, 8,944.
[6] William Henry, sixth Earl Poulett, and Viscount Hinton (1827-99), married in 1849 Elizabeth Lavinia Newman and, in 1871, Emma Sophia Johnson, whom he lost in 1879. After Adèle Cassin's refusal of his offer, he took as his third wife Rosa Melville who survived him. His mother (Catherine, Countess Poulett) was the daughter of Sir George Dallas, Bart.
[7] Ottilie Hendley had married the painter Léon Flahault. Though possessed of a statuesque and undeniable beauty, Madame Flahault had a long nose, which led to her being called 'the daughter of Venus and Punch'.
[8] Pedro de Alcantara, thirteenth duc d'Ossuna (1812-93), was one of the frequent visitors to the rue de Tilsitt.
[9] Bib. Nat., Département des manuscrits, Balachowsky-Petit bequest, 8,944.
[10] Ibid., Balachowsky-Petit bequest, 8,944.
[11] Madame Cassin had three granddaughters (Giovanna, Carolina and Margherita). The eldest was sixteen in 1886.
[12] Bib. Nat., Département des manuscrits, Balachowsky-Petit bequest, 8,944.

PART TEN, CHAPTER III (pp. 434-41)

[1] See the *Figaro*, November 4th, 1885.
[2] This letter has been communicated to me by Professor Pasteur Vallery-Radot. (Author.)
[3] René Vallery-Radot, *Vie de Pasteur*.
[4] Maurice Lippmann, *Journal intime*, March 16th, 1885. A hitherto unpublished letter.
[5] *Figaro*, April 18th, 1884.
[6] Maurice Lippmann, *Journal intime*, June 10th, 1885.

PART TEN, CHAPTER IV (pp. 442-5)

[1] There being no word for 'marshmallow' in English which gives the syllable GUI in Guimauve and Guillaume, this sally must be left in its native French. It might, perhaps, be atrociously rendered as — 'Jellyam the Conqueror'. (Translator.)
[2] Louis Ganderax, *Revue dramatique: Francillon de M. Alexandre Dumas fils*, *Revue des Deux Mondes*, February 1st, 1887.
[3] Albert Dubeux, *Julia Bartet*, pp. 117-21.
[4] Louis Ganderax, *Revue dramatique: Francillon de M. Alexandre Dumas fils*, *Revue des Deux Mondes*, February 1st, 1887.

PART TEN, CHAPTER V (pp. 446-53)

[1] Hitherto unpublished letter in the possession of Madame Alexandre Sienkiewicz, the daughter of Madame Hetzel, and the god-daughter of Madame Escalier.
[2] Ibid.
[3] Hitherto unpublished letter. Simone André-Maurois Collection.
[4] From the private collection of Madame Balachowsky-Petit.

PART TEN, CHAPTER VI (pp. 454-64)

[1] Just as two Corneilles, we have the two Dumas
But neither is a Peter and both are a Thomas.

[2] If the pecking beak of Becque makes quail
You, poor Tom Corneille in your forgotten haven,
Forgive the author yawning through Corneille,
And think of the folk who yawning hear *The Raven*.

[3] Léopold Lacour, *Alexandre Dumas fils: Notes sur l'homme*, *Les Nouvelles Littéraires*, April 3rd, 1926.
[4] Ibid.
[5] Philippe Gille, *Alexandre Dumas fils*, an article published in the *Figaro*, November 28th, 1895.
[6] Émile Bergerat, *Souvenirs d'un enfant de Paris*, p. 119.
[7] Jacques Suffel, *La dernière pièce d'Alexandre Dumas fils*, an article published in *Aesculape*, September/October 1954, pp. 188-91.
[8] It is not at Père Lachaise but in the cemetery of Montmartre that Alexandre Dumas *fils* and his second wife (d. 1934) lie under the flat stone base of a monument designed by the sculptor, Saint-Marceaux. By a strange coincidence, the grave of Marie Duplessis is only a few paces from this imposing mausoleum.
[9] Will deposited with Maître Delapalme, Notary.
[10] Georges Claretie, *Du Demi-Monde à La Route de Thèbes*, *Le Figaro*, October 1st, 1904.
[11] Alexandre Dumas *fils*, Prefatory Letter to the edition de luxe of *Les Trois Mousquetaires* illustrated by Maurice Leloir, with engravings on wood by J. Huyot (Paris, Calmann-Lévy, 1894).
[12] Henry Bauër, *Alexandre Dumas*, an article published in *l'Écho de Paris*, November 29th, 1895.

BIBLIOGRAPHY

Bibliography

THE most important of the manuscript and unpublished sources are the Balachowsky-Petit bequests and the Aurore Sand bequests in the Bibliothèque Nationale; the Auguste Rondel bequests at the Bibliothèque de l'Arsenal; the Spœlberch de Lovenjoul Collection; the Archives of Soissons and Laon, and the holographs now in the Alexandre Dumas Museum at Villers-Cotterets. I have been given access to a great number of private collections, and these I have named in the Preface. My wife owns the valuable unpublished correspondence between Dumas *père* and Dumas *fils*, from which I have printed extensive extracts. In dealing with the childhood and youth of Dumas *père* it is extremely difficult to check the accuracy of the *Mémoires*; I have taken full advantage of the excellent edition established and annotated by Pierre Josserand (only the first volume of which, unfortunately, has so far appeared) and of the exact information supplied by Charles Glinel. The few authentic letters belonging to this period which I have been able to find confirm to a far greater extent than I had expected the narrative of Dumas *père*.   ANDRÉ MAUROIS

BIBLIOTHÈQUE NATIONALE, DÉPARTEMENT DES MANUSCRITS

Balachowsky-Petit bequests: 8,944; 10,586. Unpublished letters from Mélanie Waldor to Dumas *père*; unpublished letters from Dumas *père* to Dumas *fils*; unpublished letters from Mélanie Waldor to Dr Valerand; unpublished correspondence between Dumas *père* and his daughter Marie; unpublished letters from Adèle Cassin to Dumas *fils*; unpublished letters from the Princess Aurélie Ghika to Dumas *fils*.

Aurore Sand bequests: N.A.F. 24,812. Unpublished letters from Alexandre Dumas *fils* to George Sand.

George Sand's Diaries: N.A.F. 24,816 (for the year 1855); N.A.F. 24,823 (for the year 1861); N.A.F. 24,828 (for the year 1866); N.A.F. 24,829 (for the year 1867).

N.A.F. 24,641: Letters from Dumas *père* to Mélanie Waldor; letters, in part unpublished, from Dumas *père* to Dumas *fils*; letters from Dumas *père* to Isabelle Constant; unpublished letters from Dumas *père* to Adolphe de Leuven, to Catherine Labay, to Mademoiselle Mars, to Collin, to Louis Ferville, etc.

N.A.F. 24,642: Unfinished and unpublished *Mémoires* of Micaëlla, the natural daughter of Dumas *père* and Émilie Cordier; unpublished letters from Dumas *père* to Micaëlla; an unpublished letter from Dumas *fils* to Micaëlla Cordier.

Auguste Maquet bequest: N.A.F. 11,917. Letters from Dumas *père* to Auguste Maquet; unpublished letters from Auguste Maquet to Dumas *fils* and to Peregallo;

a letter from Charles Matharel de Fiennes to Auguste Maquet; unpublished letters from Noël Parfait to Maquet. N.A.F. 11,918; Will of Auguste Maquet, etc.

N.A.F. 24,636: Unpublished letter from Edmond About to Dumas *fils*.

SPŒLBERCH DE LOVENJOUL COLLECTION

A. 303: Unpublished letters from Honoré de Balzac to Madame Hanska (to appear in the future vol. V of *Lettres à L'Ètrangère*).

E. 882: Unpublished letters from George Sand to Dumas *fils*.

E. 915: Unpublished letters from George Sand to the prince de Villafranca.

G. 1191: box 38, The Pilastre Dossier.

C. 493: An unpublished letter from Ida Ferrier to Théophile Gautier.

Marie-Louise Bourget-Pailleron bequest: Letters from Dumas *père* to François Buloz.

Archives of Soissons: Documents relating to the military career of General Dumas. Letters from General Berthier to General Dumas, etc.

Rolin Museum, Autun: Amaury-Duval bequest. K⁸, 33: Unpublished letters from Dumas *père* to Amaury-Duval.

Archives of the Seine: Documents relating to the bankruptcy of the Théâtre Historique and to the personal bankruptcy of Dumas *père* 'déclaré commerçant par arrêt de la Cour d'Appel'.

Greffe de l'état-civil: Extraits des registres des actes, IIème arrondissement, IXème arrondissement, Neuilly-sur-Seine.

Bibliothèque de l'Arsenal: R^t 6,691.

British Museum, Dumas manuscripts: 39,672.

Nesselrode Archives, bequeathed in 1922 to the French Ministry of Foreign Affairs by the Count Anatole de Nesselrode: Files X and XI.

Alexandre Dumas Museum, Villers-Cotterets: Unpublished letters from General Alexandre Dumas to la citoyenne Dumas.

Records of the publishing house of Calmann-Lévy: Contracts of Alexandre Dumas *père*. Abstract of author's royalties.

PRIVATE COLLECTIONS

M. Serge Lippmann-Dumas Collection: The unpublished private Journal of Maurice Lippmann; unpublished letters from Alexandre Dumas *fils* to his daughter Colette (Madame Maurice Lippmann).

Madame Alexandre Sienkiewicz Collection: Unpublished letters from Alexandre Dumas *fils* to Henriette Regnier de la Brière; verbally communicated information and personal recollections.

M. Pierre Lhoste Collection: Unpublished letters from Ida Ferrier (Madame Alexandre Dumas *père*) to her advocate, Lacan; unpublished letters from Marie Dumas to her stepmother; unpublished letters from Dumas *père* to Henri Lafontaine.

BIBLIOGRAPHY

Maître Daniel Thirault Collection: Unpublished letters from Nestor Roqueplan to his brother Camille.

Madame Henri Dumesnil Collection: Unpublished letters from Dumas *fils* to Commandant Henri Rivière.

Mademoiselle Harlor's Collection: Unpublished MS. of vol. II of Léopold Lacour's *Mémoires: Une Longue Vie*.

M. Francis Ambrière Collection: Unpublished letters from Dumas *père* to Victor Hugo.

Professor Pasteur Vallery-Radot's Collection: An unpublished letter from Louis Pasteur to Dumas *fils*.

M. Alfred Dupont's Collection: An unpublished letter from Dumas *père* to Roussin. Unpublished correspondence of Mademoiselle Mars.

M. Georges Alphandéry's Collection: An unpublished letter from Gérard de Nerval; an unpublished letter from Dumas *fils* to Madame Porcher; an unpublished letter from Dumas *fils* to a young writer.

Madame Privat's Collection: An unpublished letter from Dumas *fils* to Marie Duplessis.

M. Raoul Simonson's Collection: An unpublished letter from Dumas *père* to the notary Jean-Baptiste Moreau. Documents relating to Catherine Labay, mother of Dumas *fils*.

Madame Sonia Eugène-Petit (née *Balachowsky*) *Collection*: Letters from Aimée Desclée to Dumas *fils*; letters from Dumas *fils* to Henriette Regnier de la Brière.

M. Jacques Suffel's Collection: Unpublished letter from Dumas *père* to Armand Durantin.

Madame Théodore Rousseau (née *Xantho*) *Collection*: Unpublished letters from the Princess Aurélie Ghika to Madame Nicolas Xantho.

Personal recollections of M. José Camby.

Simone André-Maurois's Collection: Holograph report on La Vendée by Alexandre Dumas *père*. This report has marginal notes by King Louis-Philippe. Unpublished letters from Dumas *père* to Victor Hugo, to Delestre-Poirson, to Robelin, to Achille Devéria, to Hostein, to Millaud, to Buloz, to Bonnaire, to Anténor Joly, to Emmanuel Menessier-Nodier, to Léontine Fay, to Bernard Léon, to Zimmermann, to Laferrière, and other correspondents. MSS of articles, and various fragments. Unpublished letters from Lola Montès and from Francis Magnard to Dumas *père*. Letters from Auguste Maquet to Victorien Sardou, to Deslandes, etc. Unpublished note by Paul Lacroix (le bibliophile Jacob) relating to the marriage of Dumas *père* and Ida Ferrier. Unpublished letter from Catherine Labay. Unpublished letters from Marie Dumas to various correspondents. Copy of the *Légende des Siècles* given by Dumas *père*: 'A mon cher petit Bébé, que Dieu préserve de tout malheur. Son père, A. Dumas.' — verified by Émilie Cordier, mother of Micaëlla, as having been given to the child at the Palazzo Chiatamone, Naples, on May 20th, 1863.

Unpublished letters from Mélanie Waldor to Dumas *fils*; unpublished letters from Dumas *fils* to his father, to his daughter Colette, to Madeleine Lemaire, to la comtesse Hallez-Claparède, to Paul Bourget, to Joseph Méry, to Charles Marchal, to Madame J. Paton, to Alfred Tattet, to Thérèse Berton, to Jules Claretie, to

BIBLIOGRAPHY

Émilie Schiller, to Daniel Bernard, to Mademoiselle Foixart, to Émile Bergerat, to Léopold Lacour, to Frédéric Febvre, to Édouard Fournier, to Georges Petit, to Jean Aicard, etc. Unpublished letters written to Dumas *fils* by Céleste Scrivaneck, Alice Ozy, Réjane, Laurent Pichat. Unpublished letters from George Sand to Charles Marchal. A copy of *Péchés de Jeunesse* given by Dumas *fils* to Henri Meilhac, with holograph poems on the fly-leaves (hitherto unpublished) (No. 537 in the catalogue of the Meilhac sale, April 28th, 1922).

PRINTED SOURCES

ABOUT (Edmond): *Discours lu à l'inauguration du monument par Gustave Doré, élevé à la mémoire d'Alexandre Dumas père*. Published in *Le Figaro* of November 4th, 1883.

ALMÉRAS (Henri d'): *Alexandre Dumas et les 'Trois Mousquetaires'* (Paris, Edgar Malfère, 1929).

AMBRIÈRE (Francis): *Marie Dorval ou la femme romantique* (*La Revue de France*, January 1st and January 15th, 1937). *Marie Dorval et Jules Sandeau* (*La Revue de France*, December 15th, 1937).

L'Artiste for the year 1833, vol. I, pp. 119 et seq.

ARVIN (Noël C.): *Dumas fils*.

AUDEBRAND (Philibert): *Alexandre Dumas à la Maison d'Or* (Paris, Calmann-Lévy, 1888).

BANDI (Giuseppe): *Les Mille, expédition de Garibaldi en Sicile* (Florence, A. Salani, 1906).

BANVILLE (Théodore de): *Camées parisiens* (Paris, Pincebourde, 1866). *Mes souvenirs* (Paris, G. Charpentier, 1882).

BARBEY D'AUREVILLY (Jules): *Le Théâtre contemporain*. Vol. I: *La Reine Margot; Les Idées de Madame Aubray* (Paris, Frinzine, 1887). Vol. II: *Les préfaces d'Alexandre Dumas* (Paris, Quantin, 1888). Vol. III: *Le Filleul de Pompignac* (Paris, Quantin, 1889). *Dernières Polémiques* (Paris, A. Savine, 1890). *Le Théâtre contemporain*, vol. IV: *La Princesse de Bagdad; La Princesse Georges; Une Visite de noces* (Paris, Tresse & Stock, 1892). *Portraits politiques et littéraires* (Paris, A. Lemerre, 1898). *Romanciers d'hier et d'avant-hier, L'abbé Prévost et Dumas fils* (Paris, A. Lemerre, 1904). *Femmes et Moralistes* (Paris, A. Lemerre, 1906). *L'Affaire Clemenceau* (*Le Nain Jaune*, July 4th, 1866). *Les Madeleines repenties* (*Le Nain Jaune*, March 28th, 1869). *La préface de 'L'Ami des Femmes'* (*Le Constitutionnel*, May 10th, 1870). *'Manon Lescaut' avec une préface d'Alexandre Dumas fils* (*Le Constitutionnel*, March 2nd, 1875). See also his *Feuilleton dramatique* in *Triboulet* for February 7th, 1881.

BAUËR (Gérard): *L'esprit d'Alexandre Dumas* (*L'Écho de Paris*, April 1st, 1926). *Un grand Auteur dramatique: Alexandre Dumas fils* (*L'Écho de Paris*, July 28th, 1924).

BAUËR (Henry): *Alexandre Dumas* (*L'Écho de Paris*, November 29th, 1895).

BECQUE (Henry): *Œuvres Complètes*, vol. VII: *Conférences, Notes d'album; Poésies, Correspondance* (Paris, G. Crès, 1926).

BIBLIOGRAPHY

Les Belles Femmes de Paris et de la Province, a Symposium with contributions by Honoré de Balzac, Roger de Beauvoir, Théophile Gautier, Gérard de Nerval, Victor Hugo and Jules Sandeau, 2 vols. (Paris, Au bureau, rue Christine, 10, and at all bookshops, 1840).

BELLESSORT (Andrê): *Alexandre Dumas* (*Journal des Debats*), April 4th, 1928). *Les Voyages d'Alexandre Dumas* (*Revue des Deux Mondes*, December 1st, 1932).

BERGERAT (Émile): *Souvenirs d'un Enfant de Paris*, vol. II: *L'Homme moderne, Alexandre Dumas* (Paris, Fasquelle, 1912). *Les trois Dumas* (*Les Annales*, May 19th, 1912).

BERSAUCOURT (A. de): *Dumas père et Dumas fils* (*L'Opinion*, August 1st, 1924).

BERTAUT (Jules): *Alexandre Dumas, directeur de journal* (*Le Gaulois*, December 4th, 1920). *Les Publics de Dumas fils* (*Le Figaro*, July 26th, 1924).

BIDOU (Henry): *Alexandre Dumas fils, La vengeance de Francillon* (*Revue hebdomadaire*, April 13th, 1918). *La Société imaginée par Dumas fils* (*Revue hebdomadaire*, April 20th, 1918). See also *Revue hebdomadaire* for the year 1918: vol. II, pp. 170-94, 346-67, 472-516; vol. III, pp. 26-46, 172-88, 304-28, 457-70, 611-29; vol. IV, pp. 186-203, 323-41.

BLAZE DE BURY (Henri): *Mes Études et mes Souvenirs: Alexandre Dumas* (Paris, Calmann-Lévy, 1885).

BOURGET (Paul): *Essais de Psychologie contemporaine*, vol. II: *Alexandre Dumas fils: Le moraliste; L'analyste d'amour; L'impuissance d'aimer; Sources de mysticisme; A propos de 'Francillon'. Souvenirs personnels sur Alexandre Dumas fils* (Paris, Plon, 1901). *Pages de critique et de Doctrine*, vol. I (Paris, Plon, 1912). *Discour prononcé à l'inauguration de la statue d'Alexandre Dumas fils* (*Gazette de France* June 13th, 1906). *Centenaire d'Alexandre Dumas fils, La morale de la souffrance* (*Revue Française*, July 6th, 1924). *Le Maître* (*Le Gaulois*, July 26th, 1924).

BOURGIN (Georges): *Alexandre Dumas père et l'Italie* (*Rendiconti della Classe di Scienze morali, storiche e filologiche*, ACCADEMIA NAZIONALE DEI LINCEI, Series VIII, vol. IX, fasc. 1-2, January-February 1954).

BRISSON (Adolphe): *Portraits intimes*, 5th series (Paris, A. Colin, 1901). *Le Théâtre*, vol. VII (Paris, Librairie des Annales, 1912). *Le Théâtre pendant la guerre; 'La jeunesse des Mousquetaires'; La collaboration Dumas-Maquet* (Paris, Hachette, 1918). *Le Théâtre et les Mœurs*, vol. II (Paris, Flammarion, 1907) and vol. IV (Flammarion, 1909). *Le Théâtre*, vol. VI (Librairie des Annales, 1912). *Alexandre Dumas cuisinier* (*Le Salut publique*, Lyon, May 4th, 1902). *Alexandre Dumas père inconnu; Le labeur de Dumas* (*Les Annales*, October 30th, 1904). *Reprise de 'Charles II et Buckingham'* (*Le Temps*, February 14th, 1916). *Auguste Maquet et Alexandre Dumas* (*Conferencia*, January 1st, 1918). *Remarques sur le théâtre d'Alexandre Dumas fils* (*Le Temps*, June 21st, 1915). *Réflexions sur 'Le Demi-Monde'* (*Le Temps*, July 31st, 1916). *Réflexions sur 'L'Ami des Femmes'* (*Le Temps*, September 11th, 1916). *Remarques sur 'Monsieur Alphonse'* (*Le Temps*, March 25th, 1918).

BRISSON (Pierre): *Les deux Dumas* (*Le Temps*, May 30th, 1932).

BRUNETIÈRE (Ferdinand): *Les Époques du Théâtre français* (Paris, Hachette, 1892). *Manuel de l'Histoire de la Littérature française* (Paris, Delagrave, 1897). *Alexandre Dumas père* (*Revue des Deux Mondes*, August 1st, 1885). *A propos de la*

'*Princesse de Bagdad*' (*Revue des Deux Mondes*, February 15th, 1881). *La Recherche de la Paternité* (*Revue des Deux Mondes*, September 15th, 1883).

CHARPENTIER (John): *Alexandre Dumas* (Paris, Tallandier, 1947).

CLARETIE (Georges): *Du Demi-Monde à la Route de Thèbes* (*Le Figaro*, October 1st, 1904). *La Dernière Pièce de Dumas le jeune* (*Deutsche Revue*, January 1902).

CLARETIE (Jules): *La Vie moderne au théâtre*, 2 vols. (Paris, G. Barba, 1869-75). *Alexandre Dumas fils* (Paris, A. Quantin, 1882). *La Vie à Paris, 1880-1914*, 21 vols. (Paris, Havard et Fasquelle, 1881-1914). *Alexandre Dumas père et le Théâtre* (*Le Soir*, January 12th, 1874). *Alexandre Dumas homme politique* (*Le Gaulois du Dimanche*, May 13th, 1906). *A propos d' 'Antony'* (*Le Temps*, March 22nd, 1912). *Portraits contemporains*, vol. I (Paris, Librairie illustrée, 1875). *Un livre unique: 'L'Affaire Clémenceau'* (*Gazette des Beaux-Arts*, 1880). *Célébrités contemporaines*, vol. VI: *Alexandre Dumas fils* (Paris, A. Quantin, 1883). '*La Femme de Claude*' (*Le Soir*, January 20th, 1873). *Alexandre Dumas fils, La Dernière Page* (*Le Temps*, November 30th, 1895). *Dumas fils et le Sifflet* (*Les Annales*, June 9th, 1912).

CLAUDIN (Gustave): *Mes souvenirs* (Paris, Calmann-Lévy, 1884).

CLÉMENT-JANIN: *Drames et Comédies romantiques* (Paris, Le Goupy, 1927).

CLOUARD (Henri): *Alexandre Dumas* (Paris, Albin-Michel, 1955).

CONSTANTIN-WEYER (Maurice): *L'Aventure vécue d'Alexandre Dumas père* (Geneva, Éditions du Milieu du Monde, 1944).

COUPY (Émile): *Marie Dorval*. Unpublished critical and biographical documents (Paris, Librairie Internationale, 1868).

Courrier des Théâtres, February 13th, 1829.

CROCE (Benedetto): *Uomini e Cose della Vecchia Italia*.

CUVILLIER-FLEURY: *Journal Intime*, 2 vols. (Paris, Plon, 1900-3). *Nouvelles Études historiques et littéraires* (Paris, Michel Lévy, 1855).

DASH (Comtesse), pseudonym of la vicomtesse de Saint-Mars: *Mémoires des autres; Souvenirs anecdotiques sur mes contemporains*, 6 vols. (Paris, Montgrédien, Librairie illustrée, 1896-7). Under the pseudonym of Jacques Reynard: *Portraits contemporains* (Paris, Amyot, 1859).

DAUDET (Alphonse): *Pages inédites de Critique dramatique* (Paris, Flammarion, 1923).

DAUDET (Julia Allard, Madame Alphonse): *Souvenirs autour d'un groupe littéraire* (Paris, Fasquelle, 1909).

DAUDET (Léon): *Écrivains et Artistes*, vol. V (Editions du Capitole, 1925). *Fantômes et Vivants* (Paris, Nouvelle Librairie Nationale, 1914). *Le Centenaire de Dumas fils* (*L'Action Française*, July 30th, 1924).

DELACROIX (Eugène): *Correspondance générale*, edited by André Joubin, 5 vols. (Paris, Plon, 1936-45). *Journal*, 3 vols. (Paris, Plon, 1950).

DESCOTTES (Maurice): *Le drame romantique et ses grands créateurs* (Paris, Presses Universitaires de France, undated).

DOUMIC (René): *Essais sur le théâtre contemporain* (Paris, Perron, 1897). *Hommes et Idées du XIXème siècle* (Paris, Perrin, 1903). *Sur une édition des 'Trois Mousquetaires'* (*Revue Bleue*, December 30th, 1893). *Alexandre Dumas père* (*Revue des Deux Mondes*, January 15th, 1902). *Portraits d'écrivains: Alexandre Dumas fils*,

Émile Augier, Victorien Sardou (Paris, Delaplane, 1892). '*L'Ami des Femmes*'; '*La Princesse de Bagdad*' (*Revue des Deux Mondes*, April 15th, 1895). '*Diane de Lys*' (*Revue des Deux Mondes*, March 15th, 1900). *Alexandre Dumas fils et la Guerre de 1870* (*Revue des Deux Mondes*, August 15th, 1915). *Alexandre Dumas fils* (*Le Gaulois*, January 16th, 1918). *De Scribe à Ibsen* (Paris, Delaplane, 1893).

DUBEUX (Albert): *Julia Bartet* (Paris, Plon, 1938).

DU CAMP (Maxime): *Souvenirs littéraires*, 2 vols. (Paris, Hachette, 1882-3).

The Collected Edition of the *Complete Works* of Alexandre Dumas *père*, in the 'Collection Michel Lévy', runs to 301 volumes. I have thought it unnecessary to enumerate here all these titles. The works most frequently mentioned in *Three Musketeers* are the following:

La Chasse et l'Amour (Paris, chez Duvernois, cour des Fontaines, 1825). *La Noce et l'Enterrement* (chez Bezou, au magasin des pièces de théâtre, 1826). *Henri III et sa Cour* (Paris, Vezard et Cie, 1829). *Christine, ou Stockholm et Fontainebleau* (Paris, Barba, au Palais-Royal, 1830). *Napoléon Bonaparte* (Paris, chez Tournachon-Molin, 1831). *Antony* (Paris, Auguste Auffray, 1831). *Charles VII chez ses grands vassaux* (Paris, Publications de Charles Lemesle, 1831). *Richard Darlington* (Paris, Barba, 1832). *Teresa* (Paris, Publications de Charles Lemesle, 1832). *La Tour de Nesle* (Paris, J.-N. Barba, 1832). *Impressions de Voyage*, 5 vols. (Paris, Adolphe Guyot, Charpentier et Dumont, 1834-7). *Angèle, Catherine Howard* (Paris, Charpentier, 1834). *Kean* (Paris, J.-N. Barba, 1836). *Piquillo* (Paris, Marchant, 1837). *Caligula* (Paris, Marchant, 1838). *Mademoiselle de Belle-Isle* (Paris, Dumont, 1839). *L'Alchimiste* (Paris, Dumont, 1839). *Le Maître d'armes*, 3 vols. (Paris, Dumont, 1840-1). *Un Mariage sous Louis XV* (Paris, Marchant, 1841). *Le Chevalier d'Harmental*, 4 vols. (Paris, Dumont, 1842). *Les Demoiselles de Saint-Cyr* (Paris, Marchant, 1843). *Ascanio*, 5 vols. (Paris, Pétion, 1844). *Les Trois Mousquetaires*, 8 vols. (Paris, chez Baudry, 1844). *Le Comte de Monte-Cristo*, 2 vols. in-8vo (Paris, Au bureau de l'Écho des Feuilletons, 1846). *Monte-Cristo* (dramatic version), 2 vols. (Paris, N. Tresse, 1848). *La Reine Margot*, 6 vols. (Paris, Plon, 1845). *Vingt Ans après*, 10 vols. (Paris, Baudry, 1845). *Le Chevalier de Maison-Rouge*, 6 vols. (Paris, Alexandre Cadot, 1845-6). *La Dame de Monsoreau*, 8 vols. (Paris, Pétion, 1846). *Les Quarante-Cinq*, 10 vols. (Paris, Cadot, 1847-8). *Impressions de Voyage. De Paris à Cadix*, 5 vols. (Paris, Garnier frères, 1847-8). *Le Vicomte de Bragelonne*, 26 vols. (Paris, Michel Lévy, 1848-50). *Le Comte Hermann* (Paris, Marchant, 1849). *Le Collier de la Reine*, 11 vols. (Paris, Cadot, 1849-50). *La Barrière de Clichy* (Paris, Librairie Théâtrale, 1851). *Ange Pitou*, 8 vols. (Paris, Cadot, 1851). *Mes Mémoires*, 10 vols. (Paris, nouvelle edition Calmann-Lévy, 1865-9). *Mes Mémoires*, edited and annotated by Pierre Josserand, vol. I (Paris, Gallimard, collection 'Au temps présent', 1954), only one volume, containing the first two volumes of the Calmann-Lévy edition, has so far been published. *La Comtesse de Charny*, 19 vols. (Paris, Cadot, 1852-5). *Le Marbrier* (Paris, Michel Lévy, 1860). *La dernière Année de Marie Dorval* (Paris, Librairie Nouvelle, 1855). *Causeries*, 4 vols. (Bruxelles, Hetzel, 1857). *Histoire de mes Bêtes*, 2 vols. (Bruxelles, Hetzel, 1858). *De Paris à Astrakan, nouvelles impressions de voyage*, 5 vols. (Bruxelles,

Hetzel, 1858). *Les Garibaldiens: Révolution de Sicile et de Naples* (Paris, Michel Lévy, 1861). *La San Felice*, 9 vols. (Paris, Michel Lévy, 1864-5). *Les Gardes forestiers* (Paris, Michel Lévy, 1865). *La Terreur prussienne*, 2 vols. (Paris, Michel Lévy, 1868). *Souvenirs dramatiques*, 2 vols. (Paris, Michel Lévy, 1868). *Grand Dictionnaire de Cuisine* (Paris, Alphonse Lemerre, 1873).

The titles mentioned in connection with Alexandre Dumas *fils* in the present work, are:

Péchés de Jeunesse (Paris, Fellens et Dufour, 1847). *Aventures de quatre femmes et d'un perroquet*, 6 vols. (Paris, Cadot, 1846-7). *La Dame aux Camélias*, A Novel with a Preface by Jules Janin. Revised and corrected edition (Paris, Michel Lévy, 1852). *Diane de Lys*, A Novel (Paris, Baudry, 1851). *Le Régent Mustel*, 2 vols. (Paris, Hippolyte Souverain, 1852). *La Dame aux Perles*, A Novel (Paris, Librairie Nouvelle, 1853). *L'Affaire Clémenceau* (Paris, Michel Lévy, 1866). *L'Homme-Femme* (Paris, Michel Lévy, 1872). *Discours prononcés dans la séance publique tenue par l'Académie Française pour la réception de M. Alexandre Dumas fils* (Paris, Firmin Didot, 1875). *Entr'actes*, 3 vols. (Paris, Calmann-Lévy, 1878-9). *Les femmes qui tuent et les femmes qui votent* (Paris, Calmann-Lévy, 1880). *La Question du Divorce* (Paris, Calmann-Lévy, 1880). *Lettre à M. Naquet* (Paris, Calmann-Lévy, 1882). *La Recherche de la Paternité. Lettre à M. Rivet, député* (Paris, Calmann-Lévy, 1883). *Théâtre complet*, édition des Comédiens, 7 vols. (Paris, Calmann-Lévy, 1882-93). *Lettre-préface à l'édition de luxe des Trois Mousquetaires*, illustrated by Maurice Leloir and J. Huyot (Paris, Calmann-Lévy, 1894). *Preface de Miremonde d'Henry Roujon* (Paris, Ollendorff, 1896). *Lettres à une Pécheresse*, correspondence published in the *Revue de France*, March 15th, 1924.

DUPLAN (Paul): *Lettres d'Aimée Desclée à Fanfan* (Paris, Calmann-Lévy, 1895).

DUQUESNEL (Félix): *Souvenirs littéraires: George Sand, Alexandre Dumas, figures intimes* (Paris, Plon, 1922). *Alexandre Dumas intime. Le cottage de Puys* (*Le Temps*, September 20th, 1913).

ENDORE (Guy): *King of Paris: Lives of Alexandre Dumas père et fils* (New York, Simon and Schuster, 1956).

FALK (Bernard): *The Naked Lady: a biography of Adah Isaacs Menken* (London, Hutchinson, 1952).

FERRY (Gabriel): *Les Dernières Années d'Alexandre Dumas: 1864-1870* (Paris, Calmann-Lévy, 1883). *Souvenirs sur la mère d'un auteur dramatique* (*Revue d'Art dramatique*, March 15th, 1887). *Une Évolution nouvelle de M. Alexandre Dumas fils* (*Revue d'Art dramatique*, July 1st, 1887). *Les Derniers Drames d'Alexandre Dumas* (*Revue d'Art dramatique*, for the year 1888, vol. XI, pp. 139 and 158). *Alexandre Dumas et le Parti républicain* (*Revue Politique et parlementaire*, 1903). *Les Derniers Jours d'Alexandre Dumas* (*Revue des Revues*, June 5th, 1903).

FLAUBERT (Gustave): *Correspondance*. New and enlarged edition, 13 vols. (Paris, Louis Conard, 1926-54).

FLEISCHMANN (Hector): *Rachel intime* (Paris, Charpentier et Fasquelle, 1910).

FONTANEY (Antoine): *Journal intime*, with an Introduction and Notes by René Jasinski (Paris, Les Presses Françaises, 1925).

FRANCE (Anatole): *La Vie littéraire*, vol. I, pp. 25-35; *Alexandre Dumas moraliste* (Paris, Calmann-Lévy, 1888). *Ibid.*, pp. 107-16: *Sur le quai Malaquais. M. Alexandre*

BIBLIOGRAPHY

Dumas et son discours. Vol. II, pp. 1-9: *Le châtiment d'Iza et le pardon de Marie* (Paris, Calmann-Lévy, 1890). *Alexandre Dumas* (*Le Temps*, January 16th, 1887). *M. Alexandre Dumas fils* (*Le Temps*, December 20th, 1887). *Le Théâtre complet d'Alexandre Dumas fils, avec notes inédites* (*Le Temps*, October 23rd, 1892). *Pages d'hier. Alexandre Dumas moraliste* (*Le Figaro*, July 26th, 1924).

GAILLARD (Robert): *Alexandre Dumas. Avec un frontispice de Jean Cocteau* (Paris, Calmann-Lévy, 1953).

GALDEMAR (Ange): *Un matin chez Dumas fils* (*Le Gaulois*, July 24th, 1924).

GALIPAUX (Félix): *Les Luguet* (Paris, Librairie Félix Alcan, collection 'Acteurs et actrices d'autrefois', 1929).

GANDERAX (Louis): *Le Drame populaire:* '*Monte-Cristo*', '*Les Premières Armes de Richelieu*' (*Revue des Deux Mondes*, November 1st, 1881). *A propos d'un procès de théâtre* (*Revue des Deux Mondes*, March 15th, 1884). *Reprise d'* '*Antony*' (*Revue des Deux Mondes*, May 1st, 1884). *La passion dans le théâtre de Dumas fils* (*Revue des Deux Mondes*, May 15th, 1884). '*Denise*' (*Revue des Deux Mondes*, February 1st, 1885). '*Francillon*' (*Revue des Deux Mondes*, February 1st, 1887). '*L'Affaire Clémenceau*' (*Revue des Deux Mondes*, January 15th, 1888). '*La Femme de Claude*' (*La Revue hebdomadaire*, vol. XXIX, pp. 298-312).

GAUTIER (Théophile): *Histoire de l'Art dramatique en France depuis vingt-cinq ans*, 6 vols. (Paris, Hetzel, 1858-9). *Histoire du Romantisme* (Paris, Charpentier, 1874). *Portraits contemporains* (Paris, Charpentier, 1874).

GILLE (Philippe): *Alexandre Dumas fils* (*Le Figaro*, November 28th, 1895).

GINISTY (Paul): *Bocage* (Paris, Librairie Félix Alcan, collection 'Acteurs et actrices d'autrefois', 1932).

GLINEL (Charles): *Alexandre Dumas et son œuvre* (Reims, F. Michaud, 1884).

GONCOURT (Edmond et Jules de): *Journal; Mémoires de la vie littéraire*, 9 vols. (Paris, G. Charpentier, 1887-96).

GOZLAN (Léon): *Le Château de Monte-Cristo* (*L'Almanach comique*, Paris, Pagnerre, 1848).

GROS (Johannès): *Alexandre Dumas et Marie Duplessis* (Paris, Louis Conard, 1923). *Une Courtisane romantique: Marie Duplessis* (Paris, Au Cabinet du Livre, 1929).

HAUSSONVILLE (Comte d'): *Réponse au discours de M. Alexandre Dumas, prononcé dans la séance du 11 février, 1875* (Paris, Didier, 1875).

HEINE (Heinrich): Chronicle published in the *Gazette d'Augsbourg*.

HENRIOT (Émile): *Portraits de Femmes; Factures et reliques de la Dame aux Camélias*, pp. 376-82 (Paris, Albin Michel, 1950). *D'Artagnan et son romancier* (*Le Temps*, November 1st, 1927).

HOUSSAYE (Arsène): *Les Confessions; souvenirs d'un demi-siècle*, 6 vols. (Paris, Dentu, 1885-91). *Souvenirs de Jeunesse*, 2 vols. (Paris, Flammarion, 1896).

HOUVILLE (Gérard d'), pseudonym of Madame Henri de Regnier, *née* Heredia: *La Dame aux Camélias* (*Le Figaro*, November 17th, 1928). *Le Théâtre de Dumas fils et la Société contemporaine* (*Le Figaro*, April 4th, 1932).

HUGO (Adèle): *Victor Hugo raconté par un témoin de sa vie*, 2 vols. (Bruxelles, A. Lacroix, Verboeckhoven et Cie, 1863).

HUGO (Charles): *Les Hommes de l'Exil* (Paris, A. Lemerre, 1874).

BIBLIOGRAPHY

HUGO (Victor): *Choses vues* (Geneva, La Palatine, 1944).

JANIN (Jules): *Les Demoiselles de Saint-Cyr* (*Journal des Débats*, July 27th, 1843). (Dumas *père* replied to this article in *La Presse*, July 30th. Jules Janin struck back in the *Journal des Débats*, August 7th, 1843). *Critique dramatique*, 4 vols. (Paris, Librairie des Bibliophiles, 1877).

KARÉNINE (Wladimir), pseudonym of Varvara Komarow: *George Sand, sa vie et ses œuvres*, 4 vols. Vol. I: 1804-33, and vol. II: 1833-8 (Paris, Ollendorff, 1899); vol. III: 1838-48 (Paris, Plon-Nourrit, 1912) and vol. IV: 1848-76 (Paris, Plon, 1926).

KARR (Alphonse): *Les Guêpes* (Paris, V. Lecou, Blond, M. Lévy, 1839-59). *Le Livre de Bord, Souvenirs* (Paris, Calmann-Lévy, 1879).

KUHN (Joachim): *La Princesse Mathilde* (Paris, Plon, 1935).

LACOUR (Léopold): *Trois théâtres: Émile Augier, Alexandre Dumas fils, Victorien Sardou* (Paris, Calmann-Lévy, 1880). *Une Longue Vie, Histoire d'un homme*, vol. I (Paris, Edgar Malfère, 1938). *Une Longue Vie*, vol. II (still unpublished). *Alexandre Dumas fils, Notes sur l'homme* (*Les Nouvelles littéraires*, April 3rd, 1926). *Alexandre Dumas* (*La Revue illustrée*, August 1st, 1888).

LAMY (Pierre): *Le Théâtre de Dumas fils* (Paris, Presses Universitaires de France, 1928).

LARROUMET (Gustave): *Alexandre Dumas père* (*Revue des Cours et Conférences*, August 5th, 1893). *Le Drame d'Alexandre Dumas* (*Le Temps*, September 25th, 1899). *Le Centenaire d'Alexandre Dumas* (*Le Temps*, July 21st, 1902). *Études de Littérature et d'Art*, vol. III (Paris, Stock, 1895). *Petits Portraits et Notes d'Art* (Paris, Hachette, 1897). *Le Théâtre en 1887* (*Revue bleue*, July 16th, 1887). *Dumas père et Dumas fils* (*Le Temps*, July 21st, 1902).

LAUNAY (Vicomte de), pseudonym of Delphine Gay, Madame Émile de Girardin: *Lettres parisiennes* (Paris, Calmann-Lévy, 1882).

LE BRETON (André): *Le Théâtre romantique. De Dumas père à Dumas fils* (Revue des Cours et Conférences, December 30th, 1921, January 15th, 1922, March 15th and 31st, 1922, May 15th, 1922, July 15th and 30th, and December 15th, 1922).

LECOMTE (L.-Henry): *Alexandre Dumas* (Paris, Tallandier, 1902).

LEMAÎTRE (Frédérick): *Le Figaro*, May 4th, 1831.

LENOTRE (G.): *Le Vrai Chevalier de Maison-Rouge* (Paris, Perrin, 1894). *Le Centenaire d'Alexandre Dumas* (*Le Monde illustré*, July 5th, 1902). *Alexandre Dumas père; La conquête et le règne* (*Revue des Deux Mondes*, February 1st, 1919). *Les Mousquetaires et autres Fantômes* (*Revue des Deux Mondes*, February 15th, 1919). *Femmes, Amours évanouies. Le secret de la Dame aux Camélias* (Paris, Bernard Grasset, 1933).

LIPPMANN (Maurice): *Alexandre Dumas fils intime, Deux années de sa vie* (*Revue des Deux Mondes*, August 1st, 1924).

LOMÉNIE (Louis de): *Galerie des Contemporains illustres, par un homme de rien*, vol. V (Paris, A. René, 1842).

LUCAS-DUBRETON (J.), pseudonym of Hervé de Peslouan: *La Vie d'Alexandre Dumas père* (Paris, Gallimard, 1928). See also under PESLOUAN.

LYONNET (Henry): *La 'Dame aux Camélias' de Dumas fils* (Paris, Edgar

Malfère, 1930). *Dictionnaire des Comédiens Francais*, 2 vols. in-4to (Geneva, Bibliothèque de la Revue Internationale, undated).

MARX (Adrien): *Alexandre Dumas chez lui (Supplement Littéraire du Figaro*, February 7th, 1875).

MAUREL (André): *Les trois Dumas. Le Général; Alexandre Dumas père et fils* (Paris, Librairie illustrée, 1896).

MAURETTE (Marcelle): *La Vraie Dame aux Camélias ou l'Amoureuse sans amour* (Paris, Albin Michel, collection 'Les grandes pécheresses', 1939).

MAUROIS (Simone-André): *Introduction à la Correspondance inédite entre George Sand et Marie Dorval* (Paris, Gallimard, 1953).

MÉNIÈRE (*Journal du Docteur Prosper*), edited by his son, le docteur E. Ménière (Paris, Plon, 1903).

MESURET (Robert): *Alexandre Dumas chez la princesse Naryschkine (Le Petit Commingeois*, September 19th, 1948).

MIRECOURT (Eugène de), pseudonym of Jean-Baptiste Jacquot: *Fabrique de Romans, Maison Alexandre Dumas & Cie* (Chez tous les marchands de nouveautés, 1845).

MOGADOR (Céleste, comtesse Lionel de Chabrillan): *Mémoires*, 2 vols. (Paris, Michel Lévy, 1858).

MOREAU (Pierre): *Le Romantisme* (Paris, J. de Gigord, 1932). *De Dumas père à Dumas fils (Revue des Deux Mondes*, June 1st, 1923).

MOSER (Françoise): *Vie et Aventures de Céleste Mogador* (Paris, Albin Michel, 1935). *Marie Dorval* (Paris, Plon, 1947).

NAUROY (Charles): Correspondance published in *Le Curieux*, January 1887.

NERVAL (Gérard de): *Œuvres*, edited with notes by Albert Béguin and Jean Richer. *Correspondance*, pp. 707 to 1114 (Paris, Gallimard, Bibliothèque de la Pléiade, 1952).

NOZIÈRE (Fernand): *Marie Dorval* (Paris, Librairie Félix Alcan, collection 'Acteurs et actrices d'autrefois', 1926).

PAILLERON (Marie-Louise): *François Buloz et ses amis. La vie littéraire sous Louis-Philippe* (Paris, Firmin-Didot, 1930). *La Revue des Deux Mondes et la Comédie-Française* (Paris, Firmin-Didot, 1930). *Les Derniers Romantiques* (Paris, Perrin, 1923). *Les Écrivains du Second Empire* (Paris, Perrin, 1924).

PARIGOT (Hippolyte): *Alexandre Dumas père* (Paris, Hachette, 1902).

PARIS-SOIR: *Supplique en vers de Dumas fils à Hippolyte Hostein*, July 27th, 1924.

PASSANT (UN): *Alexandre Dumas chez lui (Le Moniteur Universel*, December 3rd, 1879).

PESLOUAN (Hervé de): *Mesdames Dumas père* (Paris, Éditions des Portiques, 1933). See also LUCAS-DUBRETON.

PEUCHET (Jacques): *Mémoires tirés des Archives de la Police de Paris*, 6 vols. (Paris, Levavasseur-Bourmancé, 1838).

PLANCHE (Gustave): *Portraits littéraires*, 2 vols. (Paris, Werdet, 1836). '*Teresa*' (*Revue des Deux Mondes*, February 15th, 1832). '*La Question d'Argent*' (*Revue des Deux Mondes*, February 15th, 1857).

POUMEROL (Alfred): *La Jeunesse d'Alexandre Dumas père (Bulletin de la Société Historique de Villers-Cotterets* for the year 1905, pp. 34-44).

RAT (Maurice): *Dames et Bourgeoises du XVIème siècle* (Paris, Plon, 1955).

REYNAUD (Jacques): *Portraits contemporains* (Paris, Amyot, 1859). See also COMTESSE DASH.

RIPP (Georges): *L'Hôtel de M. Alexandre Dumas fils* (*Le Figaro*, November 5th, 1892).

ROCH (Ernest): *Le Château de Villers-Cotterets* (*Bulletin de la Société historique de Villers-Cotterets* for the year 1909, pp. 22-346. Villers-Cotterets, imprimerie A. Naten, 1910). *Le Général Alexandre Dumas* (*Bulletin de la Société historique de Villers-Cotterets* for the year 1906, pp. 87-109. Soissons, 1907).

SAINTE-BEUVE: *Premiers Lundis*, new edition by Maurice Allem (Paris, Garnier frères, 1934). *Correspondance général*, edited with notes by Jean Bonnerot (Paris, editions Stock, Delamain et Boutelleau, 1935-49).

SAMSON (Isidore): *Mémoires de Samson, de la Comédie-Française* (Évreux, imprimerie Charles Hérissey, 1882).

SAND (George): *Histoire de ma Vie*, 10 vols. (Paris, Michel Lévy, 1856). *Correspondance*, 6 vols. (Paris, Calmann-Lévy, 1882-4). *Correspondance inédite entre George Sand et Marie Dorval*, edited with notes by Simone André-Maurois (Paris, Gallimard).

SARCEY (Francisque): *Quarante Ans de Théâtre*, vols. I, IV and V (Paris, J. Strauss, 1900-2). '*La Jeunesse de Louis XIV*' (*Le Temps*, May 23rd, 1874). '*Mademoiselle de Belle-Isle*' (*Le Temps*, April 12th, 1875). '*Henri III et sa Cour*' (*Le Temps*, June 4th, 1883). *Les Jeunes Filles dans le théâtre de Dumas fils* (*Revue politique et littéraire* for the year 1867, vol. IV, pp. 188-91). *Réponse à Dumas* (Paris, E. Lachaud, 1871). '*La Princesse Georges*' (*Le Temps*, December 19th, 1874). '*La Dame aux Camélias*' (*Le Temps*, September 27th, 1875). '*Les Danicheff*' (*Le Temps*, January 17th, 1876). '*Le Fils naturel*' (*Le Temps*, December 9th, 1878). *L'œuvre d'Alexandre Dumas fils* (*Le Temps*, November 29th, 1895). *Chronique théâtrale* (*Le Temps*, December 2nd, 1895). *Alexandre Dumas fils* (*Cosmopolis*, January 1st, 1896).

SARDOU (Victorien): *La Pièce à thèse* (*Le Gaulois*, July 26th, 1924). *Discours prononcé à l'inauguration du monument d'Alexandre Dumas fils* (Paris, Firmin-Didot, 1906).

SAUNDERS (Edith): *La Dame aux Camélias et les Dumas*, translated from the English by Lola Tranec (Paris, Corrêa, 1954).

SÉCHÉ (Alphonse): *Alexandre Dumas, Sa dernière pièce: 'Francillon'* (*Revue d'Art dramatique*, for the year 1903, vol. XIII, pp. 297-8). *Les Grandes Interprètes du Théâtre d'Alexandre Dumas fils* (*Le Monde illustré*, June 16th, 1906).

SÉCHÉ (Alphonse) and BERTAUT (Jules): *La Passion romantique: 'Antony', 'Marion de Lorme', 'Chatterton'* (Paris, Fasquelle, 1927). *L'Évolution du Théâtre contemporain* (Éditions du Mercure de France, 1908).

SEILLIÈRE (Baron Ernest): *L'Évolution passionnelle dans le théâtre contemporain. Le morale de Dumas fils* (Paris, Félix Alcan, 1921).

SHAW (Mathilde): *Illustres et Inconnus. Souvenirs de ma vie* (Paris, Fasquelle, 1906).

SILVAIN: *Frédérick Lemaître* (Paris, Librairie Félix Alcan, collection 'Acteurs et actrices d'autrefois', 1927).

BIBLIOGRAPHY

SIMON (Gustave): *Histoire d'une Collaboration, Alexandre Dumas et Auguste Maquet*, unpublished documents (Paris, G. Crès, 1919).

SPRONCK (Maurice): *Alexandre Dumas fils, ses origines et ses débuts* (*Revue des Deux Mondes*, March 15th, 1898).

SUFFEL (Jacques): *La Dernière Pièce d'Alexandre Dumas fils* (*Aesculape*, September/October 1954, pp. 188-91).

TAINE (Hippolyte): *Les Origines de la France contemporaine. Le Régime moderne*, vol. I (Paris, Hachette, 1891).

TALVART (Hector) and PLACE (Joseph): *Bibliographie des Auteurs modernes de langue française*, vol. V (Paris, Éditions de la Chronique des Lettres Françaises, aux Horizons de France, 1935).

THOMAS (Marcel): *Lettres inédites d'Alexandre Dumas à son fils* (*La Table Ronde*, May 1951).

TRAHARD (Pierre): *Alexandre Dumas et les 'Trois Mousquetaires'* (*Revue d'Histoire littéraire de la France*, January/March 1932).

TREICH (Léon): *Almanach des Lettres françaises et étrangères*, 2 vols. (Paris, G. Crès, 1924). *L'Esprit d'Alexandre Dumas* (Paris, Gallimard, 1926).

VALLERY-RADOT (René): *La Vie de Pasteur* (Paris, Hachette, 1900).

VIEL-CASTEL (Comte Horace de): *Mémoires sur le règne de Napoléon III, 1851-1864*, 6 vols. (Berne, imprimerie Haller, et chez tous les libraires, 1883-84).

VIGNY (Alfred de): *Lettre sur le théâtre, à propos d' 'Antony'* (*Revue des Deux Mondes*, June 1831).

VILLEMESSANT (Hippolyte de): *Mémoires d'un Journaliste*, 6 vols. (Paris, E. Dentu, 1867-78).

WOHL (Janka): *Franz Liszt, Souvenirs d'une compatriote* (Paris, Ollendorff, 1887).

INDEX

INDEX

INDEX

INDEX

INDEX

INDEX

GRANIER DE CASSAGNAC (Bernard-Adolphe), 140-1, 183

GRÉGOIRE (L'abbé), 39-40, 42, 43-4

GREIG (Lady Suzannah), 164-5

GREUZE (Jean-Baptiste), 404, 428

GRÉVEDON (Henriette-Louise-Laure), 446-53

GRÉVEDON (Madame), 446, 447

GRÉVY (Jules), 433

GROS (Johannes), 470, 471

GUICHE (Antoine-Alfred-Agénor, duc de), 191, 470

GUIDI (Madame), 268, 270, 272

GUIMONT (Esther), 350

GUISE (Catherine de Clèves, duchesse de), 69, 171, 466

GUISE (Henri, duc de), 69, 71

GUIZOT (François), 148, 151

GUSTAVUS III, King of Sweden, 46

GUSTAVUS WASA, King of Sweden, 146

GYP (Sybille de Mirabeau, comtesse Martel de Janville), 451

HALÉVY (Ludovic), 379

HAMILTON (Emma Lyon, known as Emma Hart, Lady), 352

HANSKA (Éveline, comtesse Rzewuska), 231, 244-5, 267, 298

HAREL (Félix), 83-5, 98-9, 118, 127-8, 131, 132, 133, 135, 140, 141, 143, 148, 159

HARLOR (Mlle), 478

HARTE (Francis Bret), 357

HAUSSONVILLE (Othenin-Bernard de Cléron, comte d'), 402, 405-7

HAUSSONVILLE (Princesse Louise de Broglie, comtesse d'), 407

HEENAN (John Carmel), 476

HEINE (Heinrich), 143, 468

HENRI III, King of France, 69, 70, 71, 182

HENRI IV, King of France, 69

HENRIOT (Émile), 12

HERZEN (Alexandre), 300

HETZEL (Pierre-Jules), 264

HIPPOLYTE, 35

HIRSCHLER, 275

HOCHE (Lazare, General), 26

HOME (Daniel Douglas), 302

HOPPE, 468

HORTENSE (DE BEAUHARNAIS), Queen of Holland, 140

HOSTEIN (Hippolyte), 203, 235, 238, 276, 354, 359-60

HOUDON (Jean-Antoine), 398

HOUSSAYE (Arsène), 171, 172, 192, 246, 356, 471

HOUVILLE (Gérard), pseudonym of Madame Henri de Regnier.

HUGO (Adèle Foucher, Madame Victor), 64, 87, 140, 142, 149, 265-6, 289, 467

HUGO (Charles), 265, 322-3, 473, 475

HUGO (Joseph-Léopold-Sigisbert, General), 32

HUGO (Sophie Trébuchet, Madame Léopold), 32

HUGO (Victor), 11, 50, 58, 64, 66-7, 72, 74, 79, 80, 83, 85, 105, 111, 116, 117, 130, 136, 140, 141-2, 145, 146, 147, 148-9, 159-60, 171, 172, 191, 202, 211, 214, 229, 237, 258, 263, 264-6, 274, 282, 284, 285, 288-9, 293, 303, 311, 312, 382, 398, 401, 403, 423, 440, 457, 469, 470, 471

HYACINTHE (Louis Duflost), 200

IBSEN (Henrik), 455, 456

INGRES (Dominique), 186

ISABELLA II, Queen of Spain, 203, 205-6

ISABELLA THE CATHOLIC, Queen of Castile, 146, 205

JANIN (Jules), 98, 128, 132, 133, 159, 181, 208, 279, 281, 469, 470

JASINSKI (René), 490

JEANNE DE BOURGOGNE, comtesse de Poitiers, 468

JOANNY (Jean-Bernard Brissebarre), 62, 73, 122

JOHANNOT (Alfred), 121

JOHANNOT (Tony), 109, 121

JOLY (Anténor), 148-9, 173

JOSÉPHINE (Marie-Josèphe Tascher de la Pagerie, vicomtesse de Beauharnais, later Madame Bonaparte, and later still, Empress), 24, 27-8

JOSSERAND (Pierre), 465, 483

JOUBERT (Barthélemy, General), 26

JOUBIN (André), 488

JOURDAN (Jean-Baptiste), Marshal of France, 55, 56

KALERGIS (Marie Nesselrode, Madame Jean), 250-4

KANT (Emmanuel), 422

KARATIGUINE, 300, 301

KARÉNINE (Varvara Dmitrievna Stassow, Madame Komarow, who wrote under the name of Wladimir Karénine), 472, 475

KARR (Alphonse), 289, 469, 474

KEAN (Edmund), 61, 62, 142-3, 245

KEMBLE (John Philip), 61, 62

KLÉBER (Jean-Baptiste, General), 28

KNORRING (Jean), 299

KNORRING (Olga de Beckleschoff, Madame Jean), 299

KOCK (Paul de), 191

503

INDEX

INDEX

LOUPIAN (Eugène), 222
LOUPIAN (Mathieu), 220-3
LOUPIAN (Thérèse), 222-3, 226
LUCAS-DUBRETON, 492. *See also* PESLOUAN (Hervé de)
LUDWIG I, King of Bavaria, 233
LUGUET (Dominique-Esprit-Bénéfand, known as René Luguet), 150
LYONNET (Henry), 470, 471, 473

MACK (Karl, General), 31
MACREADY (William Charles), 62
MALEVILLE (Léon de), 206
MALLEFILLE (Félicien), 183, 187
MANCEAU (Alexandre), 287, 335, 342, 346
MANCINI (Marie), 137, 180
MAQUET (Auguste), 172, 173, 175-80, 183, 184, 185-6, 201, 203, 204, 206, 214, 215, 225, 234, 236, 242-3, 315-17, 353, 368
MARAT (Jean-Paul), 425
MARBOUTY (Caroline Pétiniaud, Madame Jacques), wrote under the name of Claire Brunne, 187
MARCEAU (François-Séverin, General), 26
MARCHAL (Charles), 291, 314, 334-6, 342-3, 363-4, 412, 428
MARCHANT, 266
MARGUERITE DE BOURGOGNE, Queen of France, 128, 131-2, 147, 468
MARGULITIS (Dr Israel), 477
MARIE, Dumas *père*'s cook, 361-2
MARIE-CAROLINE, Queen of Naples and the Two Sicilies, 352
MARIVAUX (Pierre de), 67, 99, 156, 157, 213
MARMIER (Xavier), 201
MARS (Anne Boutet, known in the theatre as 'Mademoiselle Mars'), 60, 61, 67-8, 72, 73, 79, 80, 99-102, 111, 122, 130, 145, 158, 196, 213, 214-15, 363, 403
MARTINET, 283
MASSÉNA (André), later duc de Rivoli et prince d'Essling, Marshal of France, 25
MATHAREL DE FIENNES (Charles), 315-16
MATHILDE BONAPARTE (La Princesse), 285-6, 309, 353, 402, 413, 477
MATZA (Dr Achille), 478
MAUPASSANT (Guy de), 411
MAUREL (André), 493
MAURETTE (Marcelle), 493
MAUROIS (Simone André-), 467, 468, 469, 471, 474, 475, 476, 477, 478, 479, 494
MAZARIN (Giulio Mazarini), 180
MEILHAC (Henri), 379, 438
MEISSONIER (Ernest), 398, 428, 438
MENKEN (Adah Isaacs), 357-61
MENKEN (Alexander I.), 476

MENNESSON (Maître), 42, 48
MÉRIMÉE (Prosper), 302, 304
MÉRY (Joseph), 164, 165-6, 174, 176, 210, 269, 282, 407
MESNIL D'ARGENTELLE (Anne du), 190-1
MESURET (Robert), 474
MEURICE (Paul), 183, 184, 269-70
MICHEL, gardener at 'Monte-Cristo', 233-4, 244, 283
MICHELET (Jules), 214
MICHELOT (Pierre-Marie-Nicolas, known as 'Théodore', 122
MILLAUD (Alphonse), 284
MIRAULT (Henri), 277, 438
MIRECOURT (Jean-Baptiste Jacquot, known as Eugène de), 184-5
MOGADOR (Elisabeth-Céleste Venard, known as 'Céleste Mogador'), comtesse Lionel de Chabrillan, 307-9, 325, 474
MOLIÈRE (Jean-Baptiste Poquelin), 11, 57, 67, 181, 191, 213, 244, 246, 393, 397, 408, 409
MONALDESCHI (Giovanni, marquis de), 62-3, 83
MONFORTE (Carolina and Margherita), 478
MONFORTE (comte Ruggiero) 428, 451-2
MONFORTE (comtesse Ruggiero), *see* ALBOURQUERQUE
MONFORTE (Filippo), 427-8, 431
MONFORTE (Giovanna), in French, Jeanne de Montfort, 478
MONFORTE (Guido), 427-8
MONTALIVET (Camille Bachasson, comte de), 228
MONTES (Maria-Dolores Porris y Montes, known as Lola Montes), 191, 233
MONTGUYON (Fernand de), 191
MONTHOLON (Charles-Tristan, General comte de), 174
MONTIGNY (Adolphe Lemoine), 293-4, 296-7, 340, 349, 368, 373, 375, 377, 378, 380
MONTPENSIER (Antoine de Bourbon-Orléans, duc de), 202, 203, 205, 206, 213, 287, 309
MONTSOREAU (Charles de Chambes, comte de), 70
MONTSOREAU (Françoise de Maridor, comtesse de), 69-70, 466
MORALES (Léontine), 197
MOREAU (Maître Jean-Baptiste), 110
MOREAU (Pierre), 493
MORNY (Charles-Auguste, duc de), 271, 279, 281, 292
MOSER (Françoise), 474, 493
MOUNET-SULLY (Jean-Sully Monnet, known in the theatre as 'Mounet-Sully'), 408, 461
MOURAVIEFF (Alexandre Nicolaievitch, General), 303

INDEX

INDEX

INDEX